Barbara.
070.454293

The Prentice-Hall Series in Marketing
PHILIP KOTLER, *Series Editor*

GLOBAL
MARKETING
MANAGEMENT

Fourth Edition

Warren J. Keegan

Professor, International Business and Marketing
Executive Director, Institute for Global Business Strategy
Pace University, New York City and Westchester

Prentice Hall, Englewood Cliffs, New Jersey 07632

Library of Congress Cataloging-in-Publication Data

KEEGAN, WARREN J.
    Global marketing management

    (The Prentice-Hall series in marketing)
    Rev. ed. of: Multinational marketing management.
3rd ed. c1984.
    Includes bibliographies and indexes.
    1. Export marketing—Management. 2. Export
marketing—Management—Case studies. I. Keegan,
Warren J. Multinational marketing management.
II. Title. III. Series.
HF1009.5.K39 1989   658.8′48   88–15137
ISBN 0-13-357260-9

Editorial/production supervision and interior design: Alison D. Gnerre
Cover design: Wanda Lubelska
Manufacturing buyer: Magaret Rizzi

Previously published under the title of Multinational Marketing Management

 © 1989, 1984, 1980, 1974 by Prentice-Hall, Inc.
A Division of Simon & Schuster
Englewood Cliffs, New Jersey 07632

Printed in the United States of America
10 9 8 7 6 5 4 3 2 1

ISBN 0-13-357260-9

Prentice-Hall International (UK) Limited, *London*
Prentice-Hall of Australia Pty. Limited, *Sydney*
Prentice-Hall Canada Inc., *Toronto*
Prentice-Hall Hispanoamericana, S.A., *Mexico*
Prentice-Hall of India Private Limited, *New Delhi*
Prentice-Hall of Japan, Inc., *Tokyo*
Simon & Schuster Asia Pte. Ltd., *Singapore*
Editora Prentice-Hall do Brasil, Ltda., *Rio de Janeiro*

To
my wife
Carolyn

ABOUT THE AUTHOR

Dr. Warren J. Keegan is professor of International Business and Marketing and executive director of the Institute for Global Business Strategy at Pace University, New York City and Westchester; adjunct professor, Columbia Business School; and president of Warren Keegan Associates, Incorporated.

He has an M.B.A. and doctorate from the Harvard Business School and is a former M.I.T. Fellow in Africa, where he served as assistant secretary, Ministry of Development Planning. He has been a visiting professor at INSEAD, Fontainebleau, France; The Stockholm School of Economics; Emmanuel College, Cambridge University; and the University of Hawaii. He was previously on the faculty of Columbia Business School, Baruch College, The George Washington University, and New York University Graduate School of Business.

Dr. Keegan specializes in assisting clients in global business and marketing strategy formulation and implementation, and design and delivery of executive educational development programs. In addition to the corporate strategy practice for selected clients, Dr. Keegan works closely with Cambridge Capital Holdings, Inc. of New York in venture capital and special situation equity investing and in providing investment banking services for selected clients.

He is the author of *Global Marketing Management, Fourth Edition* (Prentice Hall), *Multinational Marketing Management, Third Edition* (Prentice-Hall), and *Judgments, Choices, and Decisions: Effective Management Through Self-Knowledge* (John Wiley & Sons). He has published numerous articles in many journals, including *Harvard Business Review, Administrative Science Quarterly, Journal of Marketing,* and *Journal of International Business Studies.*

Keegan is a Life Fellow of the Academy of International Business and is director of American Thermal Corporation, Inc., Nashua, New Hampshire; Douglas A. Edwards, Inc., New York (corporate real estate); Inter-Ad, Inc., Rochester, New York; Samaritan Counseling Center, Rye, New York; Halfway Houses of Westchester, Inc.; and Wainwright House, Rye, New York.

CONTENTS

16   Exporting and Importing   524

IV   MARKETING THE MULTINATIONAL MARKETING PROGRAM

17   Global Marketing Planning   594

18   Organization for Global Marketing   627

PREFACE

This book introduces the student and the practitioner of international marketing to a systematic treatment of marketing on a global scale.[1] The practice of marketing around the world has evolved from focus on a single domestic market to focus on global markets. This development has resulted in the exploitation of major opportunities that have yielded increasingly significant rewards for venturesome firms. At the same time, it has exposed companies to risks and problems that have resulted in an appalling number of failures and blunders. A recent study of international business blunders reveals that 53 percent were associated with marketing, 35 percent with management, and only 12 percent with legal, production, and finance functions.[2] The goal of this book is to provide students and marketing managers with the conceptual and analytic tools and a solid data base that will enable them to seize opportunities and avoid the pitfalls of global marketing.

The fourth edition has been written to achieve three objectives:

1. To update each section of the book. Since the third edition was published in 1984, there have been major changes in both the market environment and in the field of international marketing itself. These include a major drop in commodity prices; a decline in world inflation rates; the growing perception of the reality of global markets and an accelerating trend toward mergers and global strategic partnerships to create enterprises that are capable of competing and operating on a global scale; the continuing evolution of countries as both markets and competitors; and the continuing evolution of companies as global competitors. This revision reflects these changes.

[1]The terms international, multinational, and global marketing are not well-defined words in general usage, even among business practitioners. They are used as synonyms but they may also be used in a specific differentiated sense as well. In this book, we define each term. *International marketing* is the extension of the home country marketing strategy and plan to the world; *multinational marketing* is the development of a strategy for each country that responds to the unique differences and conditions in each country; and *global marketing* is the integration of the international and multinational approach where the objective is to create the greatest value for customers and the greatest competitive advantage for the company.

[2]For a fun report of this study, see David A. Ricks, *Big Business Blunders: Mistakes in Multinational Marketing* (Homewood, Ill.: Dow Jones-Irwin, 1983).

2. To add a new chapter, "Global Competitive Strategy," which presents the major conceptual developments and company approaches that have expanded our understanding of this vital topic.

3. To revise and update completely the case selection with cases of proven classroom effectiveness.

Part I presents a conceptual overview of the world market environment. Part II describes the major characteristics of world markets: their complexity and diversity and also the unifying elements that reward integration of global marketing programs. It also provides a design for a global information system and directions on how to conduct marketing research on a global scale.

Part III focuses on the formulation of global marketing strategy. It opens with a chapter on the tools available for international growth and expansion, and continues with a chapter on global competitive strategy. The section then shifts to each element of the marketing mix and concludes with a chapter on exporting and importing. The integrating processes of planning, organizing, and controlling a global marketing program are examined in Part IV, which concludes with a look at the future. The appendices identify sources of information and some basic data on global markets.

The book develops three basic dimensions, each of which is fundamental to the successful practice of global marketing. The first is the focus on the market environments of the world to develop a perspective and an overview on the types of market environments that exist in the world. The second dimension is the crossing of national boundaries with elements of the marketing mix, marketing strategies, and programs. What happens to a product, price, promotion, and place when you go global? What happens to positioning and strategy for products? A third dimension of the text is the management of marketing on a global scale. The simultaneous conduct of marketing programs presents major opportunities for leverage and is the basis for much of the success and advantage of the global company. This book focuses on how to create leverage and competitive advantage by formulating and implementing a global marketing strategy.

Warren J. Keegan
Rye, New York

ACKNOWLEDGEMENTS

This edition, like the previous three, reflects the contributions, insights, and labor of many persons. My colleagues and associates at the Lubin Graduate School of Business, Pace University, Columbia Business School, and at many other universities around the world have stimulated my thinking and provided encouragement and support for this work. Although many colleagues have contributed, I especially want to thank Derek Abell, Vern Atwater, Steve Blank, Jean Boddewyn, William Brandt, Chris Combe, Susan Douglas, John Eger, John Farley, George Fields, Bill Freund, Fariborz Ghadar, Donald Gibson, Tom Griffin, Gary Hamel, David Heenan, Donald Henley, Hermann Kopp, Eric Langeard, Peter Lauter, Theodore Levitt, Myron Miller, Ed Mccarthy, Taylor Ostrander, Howard Perlmutter, Chip Parks, Donald Sexton, Ken Simmonds, Julian Sobin, Brian Squires, William Stolze, Jim Stoner, Robert Vambery, Yoshi Tsurumi, Ann Tweedy, Dean Van Nest, Len Vickers, Ulrich Weichmann, David Zenoff, and Jack Zwick.

I have also been constantly stimulated by my students at Pace and Columbia University and by participants in various executive programs, especially the International Business Fellows of Atlanta, Dallas, and Minneapolis.

I am grateful to the U.S. Department of Education and to Susanna Easton of that department for the generous grant and encouragement to develop leading edge case studies in global marketing strategy. Many of the new cases in this edition were developed with the support of this grant. My case writer and project research associate, Charles Anderer, prepared most of the cases developed under this grant. The exceptional quality of these cases is an acknowledgement of his effort and his achievement.

I am indebted to the following colleagues at other universities who have provided insightful suggestions that have led to significant improvements in this edition: Sayeste Daser, Wake Forrest University; R.W. Oliver, Vanderbilt University; and Jerry P. Gallo, Long Island University.

My faculty assistants Robert Chwasky, Jati Bannerji, Rajiv Desai, and Rona Martin provided valuable and tireless research assistance. My secretaries, Betsy Vickers and Robin Gellis, provided indefatigable and expert secretarial assistance.

The talented and creative staff at Prentice Hall have as always been a pleasure to work with. My editor, Whitney Blake, provided wise counsel and advice, and my production editor, Alison Gnerre, did an excellent job of supervising the manuscript through editing and layout and design to publication.

Finally, my greatest debt is to my customers: the faculty who adopt this text, and the students and executives who purchase the book to study and learn about how to be a player in the exciting and profitable world of global marketing. To all of you I say, thank you for your support and inspiration and best wishes for successful global marketing.

1

AN INTRODUCTION TO GLOBAL MARKETING MANAGEMENT

I am not an Athenian or a Greek, but a citizen of the world.

Socrates, 469–399 B.C., from
Plutarch, Of Banishment

INTRODUCTION

Global marketing management is the process of focusing the resources and objectives of an organization on global market opportunities. The post–World War II decades have been a period of unparalleled expansion of national enterprises into global markets. Two decades ago, the term *global marketing* did not even exist. Indeed, the first edition of this book, published in 1974 with the innovative title *Multinational Marketing Management,* departed dramatically from the approach of the existing texts of that period that were entitled *Export Management* and *International Marketing.* These titles reflected the *marginal* and peripheral approach to marketing outside the home country at that time. Today, global marketing is essential not only for the realization of the full success potential of a business, but even more critically, for the survival of a business. A company that fails to go global is in danger of losing its domestic business to competitors with lower costs, greater experience, better products, and, in a nutshell, more value for the customer.

This book concentrates on the major dimensions of global marketing: the environment of global marketing, the identification of global opportunities and threats, the formulation of global marketing plans, and the organization and control of global marketing. The major environmental dimensions of world markets are described and a set of concepts and tools specifically tailored for global marketing is presented. It is assumed that the reader is familiar with marketing as a discipline and with marketing practice in at least one national market environment.

The largest national market in the world, the United States, is today less than 25 percent of the total world market for all products and services. For U.S. companies that wish to reach more than 25 percent of the potential market for their products (the U.S. share of gross *world* product), it is essential to go global.[1] For non-U.S. companies, the opportunities are even more dramatic, for they include the supergiant U.S. market. For example, even though the home market for Japanese companies is the second largest in the free world (after the United States), the market outside Japan is 90 percent of the world potential for Japanese companies. For these companies, 25 percent of world potential is in the United States alone.

The importance of going global to ensure company survival is a more powerful motive for many companies than the attraction of opportunity abroad. Industries that were entirely national in scope only a few years ago are dominated today by a handful of global companies. The rise of the global corporation closely parallels the rise of the national corporation, which emerged from the local and regional corporation in the 1880s and the 1890s in the United States. The plow company that remained in Illinois in the nineteenth century has disappeared, and only national companies such as Deere remain. The auto industry provides an even more dramatic example. In the first quarter of this century, there were thousands of auto companies in the world, and over 500 in the United States alone. Today, fewer than twenty companies remain worldwide, and in the United States, there are only three.

In most industries it is clear that the companies that will remain at the end of this century will be global enterprises. Companies that do not face the challenges and opportunities of going global will be absorbed by more dynamic enterprises if they are lucky; the others will simply disappear in the wake of the more dynamic competitors.

MARKETING

The first and most fundamental fact about marketing is that it is a universal discipline. The marketing discipline is as applicable in Aden as it is in Zanzibar. It is as applicable in the United States as it is in Japan. Marketing is a set of concepts, tools, theories, practices and procedures, and experience. Together these elements constitute a teachable and learnable body of knowledge. Although marketing is universal, the

---

[1]Going global does not mean going to every country in the world. It does mean expanding horizons in the world to scan for opportunity and threat. The decision to enter overseas markets or engage in overseas sourcing depends on the company's resources and the nature of opportunity and threat. Coke and IBM operate in over 100 countries because they began their international expansion over 50 years ago. Medical Diagnostics, Inc., operates in the United States only because it began operations in 1984 and is still establishing itself in the U.S. market. Each of these companies should be a global corporation. See more on this in Chapter 10.

experience of marketing of course varies from country to country. Each person is unique, and each country is unique. This reality of differences means that we cannot necessarily apply experience from one country to another. If the customers are different, if the competitors are different, if the channels of distribution are different, if the available media are different, it *may* be necessary to change our marketing plan. Notice that *may* is italicized: It *may* be necessary to change the entire marketing plan, or it *may* be possible to extend the entire plan or major elements of the plan. The decision about what to extend, what to adapt, and what to create is the task of the global marketing manager.

The Marketing Concept: From Old to New

The foundation for a successful global marketing program is a sound understanding of the marketing discipline. Marketing is the process of focusing the resources and objectives of an organization on environmental opportunities and needs. During the past three decades the concept of marketing has changed dramatically. The old concept of marketing focused on the product, and companies concentrated their efforts on making a "better" product. The definition of "better" was based on internal standards and values. The objective was profit, and the means to achieving the objective was selling, or persuading, the potential customer to exchange his or her money for the company's product. The "new" concept of marketing, which appeared about 1960, shifted the focus of marketing from the product to the customer. The objective was still profit, but the means of achieving the objective expanded to include the entire "marketing mix" or the "four P's" as they became known: product, price, promotion, and place (channels of distribution).

The Strategic Concept of Marketing

By 1980 it was clear that the "new" concept of marketing was outdated and that the times demanded a strategic concept. The strategic concept of marketing, a major evolution in the history of marketing thought, shifted the focus of marketing from the customer or the product to the firm's external environment. Knowing everything there is to know about the customer is not enough. To succeed, marketers must know the customer in a context which includes the competition, government policy and regulation, and the broader economic, social, and political macro forces that shape the evolution of markets.[2] In global marketing this may mean working closely with home country government officials and industry competitors to gain access to a target market.

Another revolutionary change in the shift to the strategic concept of marketing is in the marketing objective—from profit to stakeholder benefits. Stakeholders are

---

[2]For an excellent outline of the importance of political forces in shaping marketing strategy and action, see Philip Kotler, "Megamarketing," *Harvard Business Review,* March–April 1986, pp. 117–124.

individuals or groups who have an interest in the activity of a company.[3] They include the employees and management, customers, society, and government, to mention only the most prominent. There is a growing recognition that profits are a reward for performance (defined as satisfying customers in a socially responsible or acceptable way). To compete in today's market, it is necessary to have an employee team committed to continuing innovation and to producing quality products. In other words, marketing must focus on the customer in context and deliver value by creating stakeholder benefits for both customers and employees.

Profitability is not forgotten in the strategic concept. Indeed, it is a critical means to the end of creating stakeholder benefits. The means of the strategic marketing concept is strategic management, which integrates marketing with the other management functions. One of the tasks of strategic management is to make a profit which can be a source of funds for investing in the business and for rewarding shareholders and management. Thus profit is still a critical objective and measure of marketing success, but it is *not* an end in itself. The aim of marketing is to create value for stakeholders, and the key stakeholder is the customer. If your customer can get greater value from your competitor because your competitor is willing to accept a lower level of profit reward for investors and management, the customer will choose your competitor, and you will soon be out of business. The spectacular inroads of the "clones" into IBM's PC market illustrate that even the largest and most powerful companies can be challenged by competitors who are more efficient or who are willing to accept lower profit returns.

Marketing, in addition to being a concept and a philosophy, is a set of activities and a business process. The marketing activities are the four P's plus research,[4] and the marketing management process is the task of focusing the resources and objectives of the organization upon opportunities in the environment. Three basic principles underlie marketing:

The Three Principles of Marketing

1. Customer value
2. Competitive or differential advantage
3. Focus

The essence of marketing is creating customer value that is greater than the value created by competitors. This can be accomplished only by focusing or con-

---

[3] Any individual or group with an interest in the activities of a corporation is known as a stakeholder, as opposed to a stockholder who has an equity interest in the corporation and a claim on dividends paid by the corporation. A stockholder is a stakeholder, as are employees, managers, lenders, customers, residents of communities, cities, states, and countries impacted by the companies' operations, and so on.

[4] Or, the five P's: Product, Price, Promotion, Place, and Probe (research).

TABLE 1–1 Marketing Defined

1. THE EVOLVING MARKETING CONCEPT

Concept	Focus	Means	End
Old	Product/service	Selling	Profit via sales
New	Customers	Integrated marketing	Profits via customer satisfaction
Strategic	Environment	Strategic management	Stakeholder benefits

II. MARKETING ACTIVITIES (the Marketing Decision "Mix")

Product decisions (design, durability, size, service, etc.)
Pricing decisions
Place decisions (physical distribution and channel structure)
Promotion decisions (advertising, promotion, personal selling)
Research

III. THE MARKETING MANAGEMENT PROCESS

Marketing is the process of focusing the resources and objectives of an organization upon
    opportunities in the environment.

IV. THE PRINCIPLES OF MARKETING

1. Create customer value
2. Achieve competitive or differential advantage
3. Focus and concentrate objectives, resources, and efforts.

centrating resources and efforts on well-defined needs and wants. The definitions of
marketing are summarized in Table 1–1.

GLOBAL MARKETING ACTIVITIES

As companies become involved in marketing in two or more countries, the question
arises, "Are there differences between domestic and global marketing?"[5]
    There are important differences, and at the same time there are basic similar-
ities. First, as we have already pointed out, the basic concepts, activities, and
processes of marketing, summarized in Table 1–1, apply as fully to global as they
do to domestic marketing. When a company expands its operation to a foreign
market, the basic requirements for market success are not relaxed. This seemingly
obvious point is overlooked with surprising frequency. Companies enter foreign
markets without analyzing both customers and competition, although they would

[5] See Robert Bartels, "Are Domestic and International Marketing Dissimilar?" *Journal of Marketing,* July 1968, pp. 55–61.

not think of doing this at home. They fail to integrate their total marketing program, although careful attention to integration and fit is standard operating procedure in their home market. They embark upon marketing programs without a clear idea of their ultimate objective or any appraisal of the obstacles that lie in the path of sales and profits.

The differences between domestic and global marketing derive entirely from the differences in national environments within which global marketing is conducted and the differences in the organization and programs of a company operating simultaneously in different national markets. Global marketing can be divided into two basic activities—foreign and international-multinational-global—which are described in the following section.

Foreign Marketing

Foreign marketing is marketing in an environment different from that of the home or base environment. The very concept of foreignness presumes that there is a familiar or home base. Foreign marketing requires the managing of the same activities that are involved in domestic marketing but in an unfamiliar national environment.

The interesting aspect of "foreign" marketing is that one individual's or company's foreign market is also another individual's or company's home or base environment. France is a foreign market to a U.S. manufacturer who has never operated there, but it is the home market to all French-based manufacturers. To the U.S. company with operations in France, the country may be simultaneously a "foreign" market to the U.S. headquarters and a "domestic" market to the company's French subsidiary.

As time passes, however, the U.S. company with operations in France may cease to think of France as a foreign market and may consider it no more "foreign" than any other area, including the United States. This occurs when French operations become truly integrated into the corporate operating structure. Thus the company has shifted its orientation from the binary foreign-domestic market concept set for operating markets to a unitary definition of operating markets by which they are all considered basic "operating" markets. In such a company, nonoperating markets might still be considered as "foreign" markets, but more likely they would simply be considered markets in which the company has not yet established operations.

Foreign marketing as a dimension of global marketing still exists in most organizations, but in an increasing number of companies the concept of "foreign" is breaking down because of the growing involvement of the corporate headquarters in the company's marketing programs, regardless of location. For example, IBM operates worldwide, with product and functional specialists at headquarters taking responsibility for its products and functions on a global basis. To these specialists and to the president of IBM there is no such thing as a "foreign" market in the psychological sense—there are markets in different parts of the world, at different stages of development, with different characteristics. Company operating units are expected to understand their own markets in depth. IBM knows as much about the French market for data processing equipment as it knows about the U.S. market.

International - Multinational - Global Marketing:
A Typology

The multinational corporation is obsolete. The company, which J. J. Servan-Schreiber predicted (in his best-selling 1967 book *The American Challenge*) would in 15 years become the world's third greatest industrial power after the United States and Russia, has been defeated and overtaken by its successor, the global corporation. The global corporation, unlike the multinational, is not an exclusive American creation. Global corporations operate with bases in the United States, Japan, and Europe, and are beginning to emerge in the developing countries of the Second World and even in the less developed countries of the Third World.

The death of the multinational is not just a change in terminology. The global corporation is a distinctly different company: It has a different focus, vision, orientation, strategy, structure, R&D policy, human resource policy, operating style, communications pattern, financial policy, sourcing policy, new product development policy, and investment policy.

Paradoxically, even though the global corporation is the most advanced company type, every company, regardless of size and geographic scope, must become a global corporation in order to achieve its full potential or, in many industries, in order to survive.

The practice of global business has so outdistanced language and established meaning that we must live today with a literal, semantic jungle of terminology. There is no established, standardized usage of terms describing companies which are in different stages of evolution in their approach to identifying and serving world markets. Table 1–2 outlines a typology of terms that describe the characteristics of companies at different stages in the process of evolving from domestic to global enterprises.

STAGE ONE.   Stage one companies are domestic in their focus, vision, and orientation, and their strategy is focused on domestic markets, domestic suppliers, and domestic competitors. Their scanning is limited to the geographic scope of the domestic market. The unconscious motto of these companies is that if it's not happening in the home country, it's not happening. The world's graveyard of defunct companies is littered with stage one companies who did not realize what had hit them until it was too late to do anything about it. They were sunk by the Titanic syndrome: the belief, often unconscious, that they were, on their own turf, invincible.

STAGE TWO.   Stage two in the evolution of the global corporation begins with the domestic company focused on domestic market objectives, oriented toward opera-

TABLE 1-2 Stages of Corporate Development: A Typology

Stage	Company Type	Focus	Vision	Orientation	Strategy	Structure	Marketing Strategy	R&D Location Focus	Human Resources Policy	Operating Style
One	Domestic	Domestic market	Domestic horizons	Domestic	Domestic	Domestic	Domestic	Domestic	Domestic	Domestic
Two	International	Similarities in foreign markets	Self-Reference Criterion (SRC)	Ethnocentric/home country	International	International division	Extension	Home Country	People of home country developed for key positions everywhere in world	Centralized—Top down management
Three	Multinational	Differences in foreign markets	Sees each country as unique (UN model)	Polycentric	Multi-domestic	Area/worldwide product division	Adaptation	Home and Host Not integrated	Nationals of each country developed for key positions in their own country	Decentralized—Bottom up management
Four	Global	Reality—similarities/unifying influences and differences in world markets	Sees world complexity	Geocentric	Global	Mixed/matrix structure	Extension Adaptation Creation	Integrated	Best person regardless of nationality developed for key positions everywhere in world	Integrated—Interactive management

Stage	Communications	Behavior	New Product Development Policy	Financial Policy	Manufacturing Sourcing	Investment Policy	Preferred Form of Partnership	Score Keeping
One								
Two	Top down	Predictable	New products developed to satisfy market needs in home country	Relies on home country financial markets for financial resources	Relies primarily on home country for sourcing	Home country resources are used worldwide	Seeks licensees to "exploit" technology and know-how	Home country score is the name of the game. Home country share of market is the key measure of success.
Three	Limited—High country autonomy	Predictable	New products developed to satisfy market needs in each country	Relies on each operating country for financial resources for country financing	Relies on manufacturing in host country to supply country markets	Investment funds for each country are raised in each country	Forms joint ventures which are focused on serving the partners home country	Separate score kept for each country. Share of market is measured on a country-by-country basis.
Four	Intensive—Top down, bottom up, and lateral exchange of directions, information, reports, and experience	Situational, reality driven	New products developed to satisfy national and global market needs based on perception of relative opportunity	Obtains financial resources from lowest cost source in world for use where needed	Sources product from lowest cost source worldwide to supply world markets	Cross subsidization of projects is the norm. Funds are routinely transferred from one country to another to support global strategic objectives.	Forms Global Strategic Partnerships (GSPs)—two or more companies with a common long-term strategy aimed at world leadership	Performance is measured on a global basis. Share of market measured on a world basis.

tions in the home country market with a structure and product strategy that reflect the strategic objectives and missions of the firm.

When such a company decides to pursue international opportunities, it evolves into a stage two category. The classic stage two international company is still focused on the home market, which it considers the primary area of opportunity, and its orientation is ethnocentric or home country-oriented. The ethnocentric company unconsciously, if not explicitly and consciously, operates on the assumption that home country methods, approaches, people, practices, and values are superior to those found elsewhere in the world.

Because there are few, if any, people in the stage two company with international experience, it typically relies on an international division structure where people with international interest and experience can be concentrated to focus on international opportunity. The product strategy of the stage two company is extension (i.e., products that have been designed for the home country market are "extended" into markets around the world).

An example of stage two companies is the entire British motorcycle industry, which first lost its position and share of market in major export markets in the 1960s and early 1970s and then lost its position and market in the home market. The British assumed that the markets which they had created and dominated for over fifty years were secure. They were unprepared for the challenge of the stage four Japanese companies who innovated in marketing, engineering and design, and manufacturing. The efforts of the Japanese companies resulted in the creation of new markets, greater value for customers in old markets, and a clear, decisive competitive advantage. They were the result of a drive and discipline that focused efforts on creating value for customers and creating a differential advantage over their competitors.

Today, the British industry is defunct—it no longer exists. The fate of the British companies is a dramatic example of what can happen to stage two companies when faced with competition from stage four companies.

STAGE THREE. After a certain period of time, the stage two company discovers that the difference in markets around the world demands adaptation of the marketing mix in order to succeed. The company decides to respond to market differences and evolves into a stage three multinational which pursues a multidomestic strategy that responds to national competitive and market dynamics. The focus of this company is multinational (as opposed to home country) and its orientation is polycentric. The polycentric orientation is based on the assumption that markets around the world are so different and unique that the only way to succeed internationally is to adapt to the unique and different aspects of each national market. The polycentric company manages each country as if it were an independent city-state. The stage three company relies upon an area structure where each country is part of a region which is part of a world organization. The product strategy, called adaptation, is to change or adapt products to meet local preferences and practices.

STAGE FOUR. Stage four is the global corporation that continues to create value for customers by extending products and programs (the stage two company approach) and by adapting products (the stage three company approach). In addition to these programs, the global *also* focuses on serving emerging global markets. A global market is one that can be reached with the same basic appeal and message and with the same basic product. Both the product and the advertising and promotion may require adaptation to local customs and practices. For example, cars sold in the United States must be equipped to drive on the right side of the road. Cars sold in Britain, Sweden, Australia, Japan, and Bermuda—to mention only a few countries—must be equipped to drive on the left side of the road. Electrical products sold in North America must be capable of operating on 120V (60 cycles), whereas electrical appliances sold in other markets must be capable of operating on different voltages and cycles. The essential difference between the global corporation and the multinational corporation is that the global corporation seeks to serve a basically identical market appearing in many countries around the world. The focus of the global corporation is on serving global markets for basic needs, and on developing global strategies to compete with other global competitors.

The geocentric orientation of the global corporation is based on the assumption that markets around the world consist of similarities and differences *and* that it is possible to create a global strategy that recognizes similarities and takes advantage of opportunities to leverage experience, products, R&D, and appeals *and* which also recognizes differences and responds to differences whenever this response is cost effective.

The structure of the global company is mixed or matrix in which there is overlapping product area and functional responsibility. A mixed structure combines two or more of the structural alternatives.

The product strategy of the stage four global enterprise is a combination of extension, adaptation, *and* creation. In addition to creating value in the same way as the international and multinational companies do, the global company serves global market needs by creating from scratch products which are specifically developed to meet the identical needs of customers in market segments that exist in many countries. The global company is on the alert to identify global markets. For example, the market for most drugs today is global. The world market for cardiovascular medication alone is more than $10 billion dollars. As a result, the global market for cardiovascular medication is fiercely competitive among global companies.

The stage two international, ethnocentric company is predictable. It will always extend its home country marketing mix. The stage three multinational, polycentric company is also predictable and will always adapt its home country marketing mix to meet unique requirements and customs.

The stage four global corporation is distinguished from each of its predecessors because it is not predictable. It is reality driven. It sees similarities and differences in markets and is fully open to the possibility of global markets. The stage four corporation will extend products where appropriate, adapt to local needs where appropriate, and in addition, will always be alert to opportunities to create products that are specifically developed for a global market.

The stage four global corporation develops product strategy on a case-by-case basis and will, if there is an opportunity, create greater value for its customers by eliminating product duplication. It does this by focusing its marketing, research, and manufacturing resources on creating global products for global markets.

OUTLINE OF THIS BOOK

This book, designed for the student and practitioner of global marketing management, is divided into four parts.

Part I presents a conceptual overview of the global marketing management process and the basic theory of global marketing.

Part II identifies the major dimensions of the environment of global marketing: economic, including the location of income and markets, patterns of trade and investment, stages of market development; social and cultural elements; regional market characteristics; legal and political dimensions; and the financial framework. It concludes with a chapter on marketing information systems and research.

Part III, the core of the book, discusses sourcing decisions, global production strategy, strategy alternatives for entry and expansion, and competitive strategy. It also focuses on the key decision elements of a marketing program: product, price, channel, and promotion decisions. Exporting and importing are addressed in a separate chapter.

Part IV examines the integrating and managerial dimensions of global marketing: planning, organization, control and the marketing audit, strategy implementation, and the future of global marketing.

SUMMARY

Global marketing is the process of focusing the resources and objectives of a company on global market opportunities. The driving motives for this are twofold: One is to take advantage of opportunities for growth and expansion and the other is survival. Companies that fail to pursue global opportunities will eventually lose their domestic markets because they will be pushed aside by stronger and more competitive global competitors. This book presents the theory and practice of applying the universal discipline of marketing to the global opportunities of world markets.

DISCUSSION QUESTIONS

1. What are the differences among domestic, international, multinational, and global marketing?
2. What is a stakeholder?

3. Who are the stakeholders of a national company? Of a U.S.-headquartered multinational company?

4. Assume that two companies operate in the same 50 countries. The only difference between the companies in their operating strategy is that one is headquartered in the United States and the other is headquartered in Switzerland. What, if any, is the difference between the stakeholders of these two companies?

5. At a recent meeting of the American Marketing Association, two marketing scholars presented a paper entitled "The Japanese: The World's Champion Marketers." Do you agree? Why? Why not?

BIBLIOGRAPHY

Books

CAVUSGIL, S. TAMER, AND JOHN R. NEVIN. *International Marketing—An Annotated Bibliography*. Chicago: American Marketing Association, 1983.

CHANNON, DEREK F., AND MICHAEL JALLAND. *Multinational Strategic Planning*. New York: AMACOM, 1979.

DANIELS, JOHN D., AND LEE H. RADEBAUGH. *International Business,* 4th Ed. Reading, Mass.: Addison-Wesley, 1986.

DAVIDSON, WILLIAM H. *Global Strategic Management* (Marketing Management Series). New York: Wiley, 1982.

HEENAN, DAVID A., AND HOWARD V. PERLMUTTER. *Multinational Organization Development*. Reading, Mass.: Addison-Wesley, 1978.

KINDLEBERGER, CHARLES P., AND DAVID B. AUDRETSCH, eds. *The Multinational Corporation in the 1980's*. Cambridge, Mass.: MIT Press, 1983.

KIRPALANI, V. H., ed. *International Marketing: Managerial Issues, Research and Opportunities*. Chicago: American Marketing Association, 1983.

MAJARO, SIMON. *International Marketing: A Strategic Approach to World Markets,* 2nd Ed. London: Allen & Unwin, 1982.

———. *International Marketing,* 3rd Ed. Hinsdale, Ill.: Dryden Press, 1982.

VERNON, RAYMOND, AND LOUIS T. WELLS, JR. *Manager in the International Economy,* 4th Ed. Englewood Cliffs, N.J.: Prentice Hall, 1981.

Articles

The following list includes all of the articles on global marketing that appeared in the various journals between 1975 and 1985.

Journal of Marketing
1985

BELLO, DANIEL C., AND NICHOLAS C. WILLIAMSON. "The American Export Trading Company: Designing a New International Marketing Institution," (Fall), pp. 60–69.

GREEN, ROBERT T., AND ARTHUR W. ALLAWAY. "Identification of Export Opportunities: A Shift-share Approach," (Winter), pp. 83–88.

LAZER, WILLIAM, SHOJI MURATA, AND HIROSHI KOSAKA. "Japanese Marketing: Towards a Better Understanding," (Spring), pp. 69–81.

SCHANINGER, CHARLES M., JACQUES C. BOURGEOIS, AND CHRISTIAN BUSS. "French-English Canadian Subcultural Consumption Differences," (Spring), pp. 82–92.

1984

LILIEN, GARY L., AND DAVID WEINSTEIN. "An International Comparison of the Determinants of Industrial Marketing Expenditures," (Winter), pp. 46–53.

1982

AYAL, IGAL. "Industry Export Performance: Assessment and Prediction," (Summer), pp. 54–61.

BODDEWYN, J. J. "Advertising Regulation in the 1980's: The Underlying Global Forces," (Winter), pp. 27–35.

1981

AYAL, IGAL. "International Product Life Cycle: A Reassessment and Product Implications," (Fall), pp. 91–96.

DAVIS, HARRY L., SUSAN P. DOUGLAS, AND ALVIN J. SILK. "Measure Unreliability: Hidden Threat to Cross-National Marketing Research," (Spring), pp. 98–109.

McGUINNESS, NORMAN W., AND BLAIR LITTLE. "The Influence of Product Characteristics on the Export Performance of New Industrial Products," (Spring), pp. 110–122.

1980

COLVIN, MICHAEL, ROGER HEELER, AND JIM THORPE. "Developing International Advertising Strategy," (Fall), pp. 73–79.

DOWLING, GRAHAME R. "Information Content of U.S. and Australian Television Advertising," (Fall), pp. 34–37.

FARLEY, JOHN U., JAMES M. HULBERT, AND DAVID WEINSTEIN. "Price Setting and Volume Planning by Two European Industrial Companies: A Study and Comparison of Decision Processes," (Winter), pp. 46–54.

HULBERT, JAMES M., WILLIAM K. BRANDT, AND RAIMAR RICHERS. "Marketing Planning in the Multinational Subsidiary: Practices and Problems," (Summer), pp. 7–15.

KAIKATI, JACK G., AND WAYNE A. LABEL. "American Bribery Legislation: An Obstacle to International Marketing," (Fall), pp. 38–43.

1979

AYAL, IGAL, AND JEHIEL ZIF. "Market Expansion Strategies in Multinational Marketing," (Spring), pp. 84–94.

1978

CARR, RICHARD P., JR. "Identifying Trade Areas for Consumer Goods in Foreign Markets," (October), pp. 76–80.

HOOVER, ROBERT J., ROBERT T. GREEN, AND JOEL SAEGERT. "A Cross-National Study of Perceived Risk," (July), pp. 102–108.

PEEBLES, DEAN M., JOHN K. RYANS, JR., AND IVAN R. VERNON. "Coordinating International Advertising," (January), pp. 28–34.

1977

DOUGLAS, SUSAN P., AND CHRISTINE D. URBAN. "Life-style Analysis to Profile Women in International Markets," (July), pp. 46–54.

MCINTYRE, DONALD R. "Your Overseas Distributor Action Plan," (April), pp. 88–90.

NAGASHIMA, AKIRA. "A Comparative 'Made In' Product Image Survey Among Japanese Businessmen," (July), pp. 95–100.

VAN DAM, ANDRÉ. "Marketing in the New International Economic Order," (January), pp. 19–23.

1976

DUNN, S. WATSON. "Effect of National Identity on Multinational Promotional Strategy in Europe," (October), pp. 50–57.

KAIKAT, JACK G. "The Reincarnation of Barter Trade as a Marketing Tool," (April), pp. 17–24.

1975

GREEN, ROBERT T., AND ERIC LANGEARD. "A Cross-National Comparison of Consumer Habits and Innovator Characteristics," (July), pp. 34–41.

LAUTER, G. PETER, AND PAUL M. DICKIE. "Multinational Corporations in Eastern European Socialist Economies," (October), pp. 40–46.

WALTERS, J. HART, JR. "Marketing in Poland in the 70's: Significant Progress," (October), pp. 47–51.

Journal of Marketing Research
1985

JOHANSSON, JOHNY K., SUSAN P. DOUGLAS, AND IKUJIRO NONAKA. "Assessing the Impact of Country of Origin on Product Evaluations: A New Methodological Perspective," (November), pp. 388–396.

1982

LINDBERG, BERTIL C. "International Comparison of Growth in Demand for a New Durable Consumer Product," (August), pp. 364–371.

1981

CAVUSGIL, S. TAMER, AND JOHN R. NEVIN. "Internal Determinants of Export Marketing Behavior: An Empirical Investigation," (February), p. 114.

1979

MUNSON, J. MICHAEL, AND SHELBY H. MCINTYRE. "Developing Practical Procedures for the Measurement of Personal Values in Cross-Cultural Marketing," (February), pp. 48–52.

1976

GRONHAUG, KJELL. "Exploring Environmental Influences in Organizational Buying," (August), pp. 226–229 (a Norwegian study).

1975

ARNDT, JOHAN, AND EDGAR CRANE. "Response Bias, Yea-Saying and the Double Negative," (May), p. 218 (a Norwegian study).

HUEGES, MICHEL. "An Empirical Study of Media Comparison," (May), p. 221 (a French study).

The Columbia Journal of World Business
1985

CHAKRAVARTHY, BALAJI S., AND HOWARD V. PERLMUTTER. "Strategic Planning for a Global Business," (Summer).

CZINKOTA, MICHAEL R. "Distribution in Japan: Problems and Changes," (Fall).

HARVEY, MICHAEL G., AND ILKKA A. RONKAINEN. "International Counterfeiters: Marketing Success Without the Cost or Risk," (Fall).

KOTLER, PHILIP, SOMKID JATUSRIPITAK, AND LIAM FAHEY. "Strategic Global Marketing: Lessons from the Japanese," (Spring).

1984

CZINKOTA, MICHAEL R. "The Business Response to the Export Trading Act of 1982," (Fall).

HARRIGAN, KATHRYN RUDIE. "Joint Ventures and Global Strategies," (Summer).

PITTS, ROBERT A., AND JOHN C. DANIELS. "Aftermath of the Matrix Mania," (Summer).

STARR, MARTIN K. "Global Production and Operations Strategy," (Winter).

1983

DORDICK, HERBERT S. "The Emerging World Information Business," (Spring).

GRAHAM, JOHN L. "Foreign Corrupt Practices: A Manager's Guide," (Fall).

ONKVISIT, SAK, AND JOHN J. SHAW. "An Examination of the International Product Life Cycle and Its Application within Marketing," (Fall).

1982

BERGSTROM, GARY L., AND MARK ENGLAND-MARKUM. "International Country Selection Strategies," (Summer).

DOUGLAS, SUSAN P., C. SAMUEL CRAIG, AND WARREN J. KEEGAN. "Approaches to Assessing International Marketing Opportunities for Small and Medium-sized Companies," (Fall).

Harvard Business Review
1986

GORBACHEV, MIKHAIL S. "Remarks on US-USSR Trade," (May-June), pp. 55–58.

QUELCH, J. A., AND E. J. HOFF. "Customizing Global Marketing," (May-June), pp. 59–68.

1985

ENCARNATION, D. J., AND SUSHIL VACHANI. "Foreign Ownership: When Hosts Change the Rules," (September-October), pp. 152–160.

HAMEL, GARY, AND C. K. PRAHALAD. "Do You Really Have a Global Strategy?" (July-August), pp. 139–148.

WEBBER, ALAN M. "Globalization and Its Discontents," (May-June), pp. 38–44.

1984

SCOTT, BRUCE R. "National Strategy for Stronger U.S. Competitiveness," (March-April), pp. 77–91.

YANG, CHARLES Y. "Demystifying Japanese Management Practices," (November-December), pp. 172–182.

1983

BANKER, PRAVIN. "You're the Best Judge of Foreign Risks," (March-April), pp. 157–165.

BARTLETT, CHRISTOPHER A. "MNCs: Get Off the Reorganization Merry-Go-Round," (March-April), pp. 138–146.

CLAUSEN, A. W. "Let's Not Panic About Third World Debts," (November-December), pp. 106–114.

DICKSON, DOUGLAS N. "Case of the Reluctant Multinational," (January-February), pp. 6–18.

JEFFCOAT, A. E., AND A. D. SOUTHERN. "Why and How to Court Foreign Shareholders," (July-August), pp. 30–38.

LEVITT, THEODORE. "The Globalization of Markets," (May-June), pp. 92–102.

WEIGAND, ROBERT. "International Investments: Weighing the Incentives," (July-August), pp. 146–152.

1982

BUSS, MARTIN D. J. "Managing International Information Systems," (September-October), pp. 89–90.

CRANE, DWIGHT B., AND SAMUEL L. HAYES, III. "The New Competition in World Banking," (July-August), pp. 88–94.

DAVIDSON, WILLIAM H., AND PHILLIPE HASPESLAGH. "Shaping a Global Product Organization," (July-August), pp. 125–132.

HOUT, THOMAS, MICHAEL E. PORTER, AND EILEEN RUDDEN. "How Global Companies Win Out," (September-October), pp. 98–108.

KILLING, J. PETER. "How to Make a Joint Venture Work," (May-June), pp. 120–127.

LIMPRECHT, JOSEPH A., AND ROBERT H. HAYES. "Germany's World-class Manufacturers," (November-December), pp. 137–145.

RUMER, BORIS, AND STEPHEN STERNHEIMER. "The Soviet Economy: Going to Siberia?" (January-February), pp. 16–38.

STERN, RICHARD. "Insurance for Third World Currency Inconvertibility Protection," (May-June), pp. 62–64.

WATSON, CRAIG M. "Counter-competition Abroad to Protect Home Markets," (January-February), pp. 40–42.

1981

BRINK, JOHN W., AND SETH W. MORTON. "Invisible Exports That Service Companies Generate," (November), p. 36.

DRUCKER, PETER F. "Behind Japan's Success," (January), p. 83.

HAYES, ROBERT H. "Why Japanese Factories Work," (July), p. 56.

HEENAN, DAVID A. "Moscow Goes Multinational," (May), p. 48.

LUMSDEN, ARTHUR J. "New Interest of U.S. Industry in the Caribbean," (July), p. 140.

WHEELWRIGHT, STEVEN C. "Japan—Where Operations Really Are Strategic," (July), p. 67.

WRIGHT, PETER. "Doing Business in Islamic Markets," (January), p. 34.

1980

DOZ, YVES L., AND C. K. PRAHALAD. "How MNCs Cope with Host Government Intervention," (March), p. 149.

GLUCK, FREDERICK W., STEPHEN P. KAUFMAN, AND A. STEVEN WALLECK. "Strategic Management for Competitive Advantage," (July), p. 154.

KAIKATI, JACK G., AND RAYMOND LaGARACE. "Beware of International Brand Piracy," (March), p. 52.

ROBY, JERRY L. "Is the China Market for You?" (January), p. 150.

VERNON, RAYMOND. "Gone Are the Cash Cows of Yesteryear," (November), p. 150.

1979

HEENAN, DAVID A., AND WARREN J. KEEGAN. "Rise of Third World Multinationals," (January), p. 101.

WALTERS, KENNETH D., AND R. JOSEPH MONSEN. "State-Owned Business Abroad: New Competitive Threat," (March), p. 160.

WEICHMANN, ULRICH E., AND LEWIS G. PRINGLE. "Problems That Plague Multinational Marketers," (July), p. 118.

1978

DYMENT, JOHN J. "International Cash Management," (May), p. 143.

FRANKO, LAWRENCE G. "Multinationals: The End of U.S. Dominance," (November), p. 93.

GALBRAITH, JOHN KENNETH. "Defense of the Multinational Company," (March), p. 83.

GOLDMAN, MARSHALL I. "Office in Moscow," (November), p. 153.

KILLOUGH, JAMES. "Improved Payoffs from Transnational Advertising," (July), p. 102.

NEVIN, JOHN J. "Can U.S. Business Survive Our Japanese Trade Policy?" (September), p. 165.

RUMMEL, R. J., AND DAVID A. HEENAN. "How Multinationals Analyze Political Risk," (January), p. 67.

VOGEL, EZRA F. "Guided Free Enterprise in Japan," (May), p. 161.

1977

APGAR, MAHLON, IV. "Succeeding in Saudi Arabia," (January), p. 14.

BARRETT, EDGAR M. "Case of the Tangled Transfer Price," (May), p. 20.

GROSS, PHILLIP J. "How to Make That Trip Abroad More Exciting," (March), p. 14.

HERTZFELD, JEFFREY M. "New Directions in East-West Trade," (May), p. 93.

WEIGAND, ROBERT E. "International Trade Without Money," (November), p. 23.

WELLS, LOUIS T., JR. "Negotiating with Third World Governments," (January), p. 72.

1976

DELAFON, J. C. "For Business, the True EEC Is Taking Shape," (March), p. 6.

JONES, ROBERT T. "Executive's Guide to Antitrust in Europe," (May), p. 106.

KENNY, ROGER M. "Helpful Guidance from International Advisory Boards' Ideas for Action," (March), p. 14.

PRAHALAD, C. K. "Strategic Choices in Diversified MNCs," (July), p. 67.

SEARBY, DANIEL M. "Doing Business in the Mideast: The Game Is Rigged," (January), p. 56.

VOGT-LIOTARD, PIERRE. "Nestlé—At Home Abroad," (November), p. 80.

1975

SORENSON, RALPH Z., AND ULRICH E. WEICHMANN. "How Multinationals View Marketing Standardization," (May), p. 38.

SPENCER, WILLIAM I. "Who Controls MNCs?" (November), p. 97.

WELLS, LOUIS T., JR. "Social Cost/Benefit Analysis for MNCs," (March), p. 40.

Journal of International Business Studies
1986

DOYLE, PETER, JOHN SAUNDERS, AND VERONICA WONG. "A Comparative Study of Japanese Marketing Strategies in the British Market," (Spring), pp. 27–46.

JOHANSSON, JOHNY K., AND ISRAEL NEBENZAHL. "Multinational Production: Effect on Brand Value," (Fall), pp. 101–126.

MIRUS, ROLF, AND BERNARD YEUNG. "Economic Incentives for Countertrade," (Fall), pp. 27–39.

TANSUHAJ, PATRIYA S., AND JAMES W. GENTRY. "Foreign Trade Zones in Global Marketing and Logistics," (Spring), pp. 19–33.

WALTERS, PETER G. P. "International Marketing Policy: A Discussion of the Standardization Construct and its Relevance for Corporate Policy," (Summer), pp. 55–69.

1985

COOPER, ROBERT G., AND ELKO J. KLEINSCHMIDT. "The Impact of Export Strategy on Export Sales Performance," (Spring), pp. 37–55.

DENIS, JEAN-EMILE, AND DEPELTEAU. "Market Knowledge, Diversification and Export Expansion," (Fall), pp. 77–89.

GRAHAM, JOHN L. "The Influence of Culture on Business Negotiations," (Spring), pp. 81–96.

JOHANSSON, JOHNY K., AND HANS B. THORELLI. "International Product Positioning," (Fall), pp. 57–75.

SARATHY, RAVI. "Japanese Trading Companies: Can They Be Copied?" (Summer), pp. 101–119.

1984

SUDIT, EPHRAIM F. "The Role of Comparative Productivity Accounting in Export Decisions," (Spring/Summer), pp. 105–118.

1983

DOUGLAS, SUSAN P., AND C. SAMUEL CRAIG. "Examining Performance of U.S. Multinationals in Foreign Markets," (Winter), pp. 51–62.

LUTZ, JAMES M., AND ROBERT T. GREEN. "The Product Life Cycle and the Export Position of the United States," (Winter), pp. 77–94.

MULLOR-SEBASTIAN, ALICIA. "The Product Life Cycle Theory: Empirical Evidence," (Winter), pp. 95–106.

1982

AYAL, IGAL, AND SEEV HIRSCH. "Marketing Factors in Small Country Manufactured Exports: Are Market Share and Market Growth Rate Really Important?" (Fall), pp. 73–86.

BILKEY, WARREN J. "Variables Associated with Export Profitability," (Fall), pp. 39–56.

1981

BODDWEYN, J. J. "Comparative Marketing: The First 25 Years," (Spring–Summer), pp. 61–80.

DAVIES, GARY J. "The Role of Exporter and Freight Forwarder in the United Kingdom," (Winter), pp. 99–108.

SCHIFFMAN, L. G., W. R. DILLON, AND F. E. NGUMAH. "The Influence of Subcultural Factors on Consumer Acculturation," (Fall), pp. 137–144.

TERPSTRA, V., AND N. AYDIN. "Marketing Know-how Transfer by MNCs," (Winter), pp. 35–48.

1980

BURNS, JANE O. "Transfer Pricing Decision in U.S. Multinational Corporations," (Fall), pp. 23–39.

FARLEY, JOHN U., T. D. J. LOWS, AND SRINIVAS REDDY. "Joint 'Social Marketing' of a Weaning Food and a Contraceptive in Sri Lanka," (Winter), pp. 73–80.

GREEN, ROBERT T., AND JAMES M. LUTZ. "U.S. High-Technology Import/Export Performance in Three Industries," (Fall), pp. 112–117.

KIRPALANI, V. H., AND N. B. MACINTOSH. "International Marketing Effectiveness of Technology-Oriented Small Firms," (Winter), pp. 81–90.

LEFF, NATHANIEL H., AND JOHN V. FARLEY. "Advertising Expenditures in the Developing World," (Fall), pp. 64–79.

RABINO, S. "Tax Incentive to Exports,"(Spring–Summer), pp. 74–85.

SUZUKI, N. "The Changing Pattern of Advertising Strategy by Japanese Business Firms in the U.S. Market: Content Analysis," (Winter), pp. 63–72.

1979

BRADY, DONALD L., AND WILLIAM O. BEARDEN. "The Effect of Managerial Attitudes on Alternative Exporting Methods," (Winter), pp. 79–84.

BUCKLEY, PETER J., AND RICHARD D. PEARCE. "Overseas Production and Exporting by the World's Largest Enterprises: A Study in Sourcing Policy," (Spring–Summer), pp. 9–20.

KEEGAN, WARREN J. "The Future of the Multinational Manufacturing Corporation: Five Scenarios," (Spring–Summer), pp. 98–104.

STERNITZKE, DONALD L. "The Great American Disadvantage: Fact or Fiction?" (Fall), pp. 25–36.

WHITE, PHILLIP D. "Attitudes of U.S. Purchasing Managers Toward Industrial Products Manufactured in Selected Western European Nations," (Spring–Summer), pp. 81–90.

1978

ANDERSON, RONALD D., JACK L. ENGLEDOW, AND HELMUT BECKER. "Advertising Attitudes in Germany and the U.S.: An Analysis over Age and Time,"(Spring–Summer), pp. 27–38.

BILKEY, WARREN J. "An Attempted Integration of the Literature on the Export Behavior of Firms," (Spring–Summer), pp. 33–46.

BRASCH, JOHN J. "Export Management Companies," (Spring–Summer), pp. 59–72.

———, AND WOO-YOUNG LEE. "The Adoption of Export as Innovative Strategy," (Spring–Summer), pp. 85–94.

COCCARI, RONALD L. "Alternative Models for Forecasting U.S. Exports," (Spring–Summer), pp. 73–84.

FOWLER, D. J. "Transfer Prices and Profit Maximization in Multinational Enterprise Operations," (Winter), pp. 9–26.

LOMBARD, FRANCOIS. "The Foreign Direct Investment Screening Process: The Case of Colombia," (Winter), pp. 66–80.

MOUSTAFA, MOHAMED E. "Pricing Strategy for Export Activity in Developing Nations," (Spring–Summer), pp. 95–102.

TOYNE, BRIAN. "Procurement-Related Perceptions of Corporate-Based and Foreign-Based Purchasing Managers," (Winter), pp. 39–54.

WIEDERSHEIM-PAUL, FINN, HANS C. OLS, AND LAWRENCE S. WELCH. "Pre-Export Activity: The First Step in Internationalization," (Spring–Summer), pp. 47–58.

1977

BILKEY, WARREN J., AND GEORGE TESAR. "The Export Behavior of Smaller-Sized Wisconsin Firms," (Spring–Summer), pp. 93–98.

BROCK, JOHN R., AND P. RONALD TARULLO. "Estimation of Incremental Import Potentials in the Soviet Union," (Fall–Winter), pp. 55–62.

BRUNNER, JAMES A., AND GEORGE M. TAOKA. "Marketing and Negotiating in the People's Republic of China: Perceptions of American Businessmen Who Attended the 1975 Canton Fair," (Fall–Winter), pp. 69–82.

ELLIOT, JAMES S. "Estimates of Export Sales to Eastern Europe and the USSR by U.S. Subsidiaries Located in Western Europe," (Fall–Winter), pp. 63–68.

JOHNSON, JAN, AND JAN-ERIK VAHLNE. "The Internationalization Process of the Firm—A Model of Knowledge Development and Increasing Foreign Market Commitments," (Spring–Summer), pp. 23–32.

RUSHING, FRANCIS W. "The Role of U.S. Imports in the Soviet Growth Strategy for the Seventies," (Fall–Winter), pp. 31–48.

SAMLI, A. COSKUN. "An Approach for Estimating Market Potential in East Europe," (Fall–Winter), pp. 49–54.

STOBAUGH, ROBERT B. "Multinational Competition Encountered by U.S. Companies That Manufacture Abroad," (Spring–Summer), pp. 33–44.

TOREE, JOSE DE LA, JEFFREY S. ARPRAN, MICHAEL JAY JEDEL, ERNEST W. OGRAM, JR., AND BRIAN TOYNE. "Corporate Adjustments and Import Competition in the U.S. Apparel Industry," (Spring–Summer), pp. 5–22.

WEINSTEIN, ARNOLD K. "Foreign Investments by Service Firms: The Case of the Multinational Advertising Agency," (Spring–Summer), pp. 83–92.

1976

BECKER, H. "Is There a Cosmopolitan Information Seeker?" (Spring), pp. 77–90.

GREEN, RICHARD T., AND PHILLIP D. WHITE. "Methodological Considerations in Cross-National Consumer Research," (Fall–Winter), pp. 81–87.

HACKETT, D. W. "The International Expansion of U.S. Franchise Systems: Status and Strategies," (Spring), pp. 65–76.

VOGEL, R. H. "Uses of Managerial Perceptions in Clustering Countries," (Spring), pp. 91–100.

1975

BILKEY, WARREN J. "An Analysis of Advertisements for Positions in International Business," (Fall), pp. 75–78.

LEFF, NATHANIEL H. "Multinational Corporate Pricing Policy in the Developing Countries," (Fall), pp. 55–64.

WHICH COMPANY IS TRULY GLOBAL?[1]

Four senior executives of companies operating in many countries speak:

Company A: "We are a truly global company. We sell our products in over 100 countries, and we manufacture in 15 countries. Some of our divisions have worldwide responsibility for their business, and others focus on the huge U.S. market. In the latter case, we rely upon our country subsidiaries to pursue business opportunities in their territory.

"We're proud of our international reach, but we are concentrating on defending our position in the U.S. market. This doesn't mean that we are trying to defend all of our threatened positions in the United States. I admit that we've lost market share in many of our traditional manufacturing businesses both in the United States and in overseas markets. But the United States is still where it's at, and the United States is a service economy. Even though we started out as an electrical equipment manufacturer, today we're very excited about our success in financial services. There's no point in fighting city hall and trying to hang on to the old manufacturing businesses like power generation and power distribution. It's just too hard to compete in those industries. Services are where it's at, and we want to be a leader in the fast growing financial services industry."

Company B: "We are a global company. We are a unique media company. We do not dominate any particular area, but we have an important presence on three continents, in magazines, newspapers, and television. We have a global strategy. We are a global communications and entertainment company. We're in the business of informing people around the world on the widest possible basis. We know how to serve the needs of our customers who are readers, viewers, and advertisers. We transfer people and money across national boundaries, and we know how to acquire and integrate properties as well as how to start up a new business. We started out as Australian, and then the weight of our effort shifted to the U.K. and today our main effort is in the United States. We go where the opportunity is because we are market driven.

"Sure, there are lots of Australians in the top management of this company, but we started in Australia, and those Aussies know our business and the company from the ground up. And, look around and you'll see more and more Americans and Brits taking the top jobs. We stick to English because I don't believe that we could really succeed in foreign print or broadcast. We know English, and so far the English speaking world is big enough for us. The world is shrinking faster than we all realize, and to be in communications is to be at the center of all change. That's the excitement of what we're doing—and also the importance"

Company C: "We're a global company. We are committed to being the number one company in our industry worldwide. We do all of our manufacturing in our home country because we have been able to achieve the lowest cost and the highest quality in the world by keeping all engineering and manufacturing in one location. The constantly rising value of our home currency is forcing us to invest in overseas manufacturing in order to maintain our cost advantage. We are doing this reluctantly, but we believe that the essence of being global is dominating markets and we plan to do whatever we must do in order to maintain our position of leadership.

"It is true that all of our senior managers at home and in most of our foreign markets are home country nationals. We feel more comfortable with our own nationals in key jobs because they speak our language and they understand the history and the culture of our company and our country. It would be difficult for an outsider to have this knowledge which is so important to smooth working relationships."

Company D: "We are a truly global company. We have 24 nationalities represented on our headquarters staff, we manufacture in 28 countries, we market in 92 countries, and we are committed to leadership in our industry. It is true that we are backing off on our commitment to develop business in the Third World, but as you may know we have found it extremely difficult to increase sales and earnings in the Third World, and we have been criticized for our aggressive marketing in these countries. It is also true that by law, only home country nationals may own voting shares in our company. So, even though we are global, we do have a home and a history and we respect the traditions and sensibilities of our home country.

"We want to maintain our number one position in Europe, and over time achieve the same position of leadership in our target markets in North America and Japan. We are also keeping a close eye on the developing countries of the world, and whenever we see a country make the move from LDC (less developed country) to DC (developing country) we commit our best effort to expand our position, or, if we don't have a position, to establish a position. Since our objective is to achieve an undisputed leadership position in our industry, we simply cannot afford *not* to be in every developed and advanced country market.

"We have always had a European CEO, and this will probably not change. The executives in this company from Europe tend to serve all over the world, whereas the executives from the United States and Japan serve only in their home countries. They are very able and valuable executives, but they lack the necessary perspective of the world required for the top jobs here at headquarters."

QUESTIONS

1. Which company is truly global?
2. What are the attributes of a truly global company?
3. Why quibble about the extent to which a company is global?

2

UNDERLYING FORCES AND CONCEPTS

Grey are all theories,
And green alone Life's golden tree.

Johann Wolfgang von Goethe,
1749–1832, Faust, *I, iv*

INTRODUCTION

International trade, investment, and markets have been the fastest-growing sectors of the world economy since the end of World War II. The dynamic growth of international markets and global marketing has occurred in a context of fundamental underlying forces and concepts. This chapter identifies and explains these forces and concepts and presents a basic conceptual scheme to provide an understanding of the distinctive character of international marketing.

THE THEORY OF THE CASE

There are three basic theories that the student and practitioner of global marketing should understand. The oldest, and most basic, is the theory of comparative advantage which goes back to Adam Smith's *The Wealth of Nations* and the work of David Ricardo. A more recent and equally important theory is the trade or product trade cycle theory discovered by Dr. Raymond Vernon of Harvard Business School. A third, even more recent theory, which identifies business orientations, was discovered by Dr. Howard Perlmutter of the Wharton School of the University of Pennsylvania.

The Theory of Comparative Advantage

The theory of comparative advantage is a demonstration (under assumptions) that a country can gain from trade *even* if it has an absolute disadvantage in the production of all goods, or, that it can gain from trade *even* if it has an absolute advantage in the production of all goods. In other words, if the United States is better (more efficient) in the production of everything than Tanzania, the United States can still gain from specialization and trade. If Tanzania is inferior (less efficient) in the production of everything than the United States, Tanzania can still gain from specialization and trade. How can this be so?

The simplest demonstration of the theory of comparative advantage is a two country–two product model, such as the one shown in Table 2–1. In this example, the two countries are the United States and France. The two products are apples and oranges. There is no money, the products are undifferentiated, and they are produced with production units which are a mixture of land, labor, and capital.

If you take any production mix between the two limits (A) and (E), you will find that the total world production is less at these production mixes than it is when there is a concentration of production units on the product in which the country has the greatest comparative advantage. For the United States, this is oranges. For France, it is apples. How do you know that the United States' comparative advantage is the greatest in oranges? To determine that greatest *comparative* advantage you must compare the production ratios for the two products. For apples, the United States has an advantage of 1.25 (100/80). For oranges, the United States has an advantage of 3.0 (60/20). In other words, you simply compare what each country can produce under total specialization.

Table 2–1 concludes with a set of questions. Make sure that you are comfortable with the answers. The fourth question raises the matter of price. Since there is no money, you must determine prices on the basis of barter. How much is an apple worth in oranges, and how much is an orange worth in apples?

Does this still seem a little hard to comprehend? A good illustration of comparative advantage is the classic example of the famous impresario, Billy Rose, who was also the world's fastest typist. He faced a decision: "Should I do my own typing or should I pursue a career as a typist?" The answer to both questions was no, because even though he had an absolute advantage as a typist over all other typists in the world, his *comparative* advantage was as an impresario. If the objective is to maximize material well-being, both individuals and countries are better off specializing in their area of *comparative* advantage and then trade and exchange with others in the marketplace.

Any literate international marketer should be familiar with both the existence and the demonstration of the theory of comparative advantage. However, the theory itself does not relate to the situation faced in the firm. The problem with the theory of international trade, as is so often the case with economic theories, is that reality is far more complex than the limiting assumptions upon which the theory is based. A firm's costs are based not only on factor costs such as wages and materials but

TABLE 2–1   Comparative Advantage—An Example

1. Production Possibilities of United States and France (1,000 production units)

	BEFORE SPECIALIZATION AND TRADE (000 bu)			
	UNITED STATES		FRANCE	
	Apples	Oranges	Apples	Oranges
Use of Production Units				
or Production Possibilities				
A 1,000 in apples, 0 in oranges	100	0	80	0
B 750 in apples, 250 in oranges	75	15	60	5
C 500 in apples, 500 in oranges	50	30	40*	10*
D 250 in apples, 750 in oranges	25*	45*	20	15
E 0 in apples, 1,000 in oranges	0	60	0	20

*Production in isolation.

II. Production and Consumption After Total Specialization and Trade

	UNITED STATES			FRANCE		
	Produces	Trades: Imports (+) Exports (−)	Consumes	Produces	Trades: Imports (+) Exports (−)	Consumes
Apples (000 bu)	0	+30	30	80	−30	50
Oranges (000 bu)	60	−12	48	0	+12	12
Trading price 30:12 = 2.5 apples = 1 orange						
12/30 = 4 oranges = 1 apple						

QUESTIONS

1. Who has the greater advantage in the production of apples? _____ of oranges? _____
2. What is the apple advantage? _____
3. What is the orange advantage? _____
4. What is the price of apples in the United States? _____ of oranges? _____
5. What is the price of apples in France? _____ of oranges? _____
6. What is the maximum price the United States will pay for apples? _____ for oranges?

7. What is the maximum price France will pay for apples? _____ for oranges? _____
8. Can both countries gain from trade? Why? How?

also on the volume of production. It has been conclusively demonstrated in hundreds of observations of actual cost behavior that there is a relationship between cost and volume that results in a typical decline in costs of 20–30 percent with each doubling of accumulated volume in the production of manufactured items. This empirical observation, which was first suggested by the Boston Consulting Group, is now widely known as experience theory.

Thus, even though a firm may be paying higher wages and experiencing other higher-factor costs than it would encounter in other parts of the world, if it has a volume advantage over competitors in lower-cost areas, its net cost position may still be lower.

Another limitation of classical trade theory is that it ignores product and program differentiation. A company's ability to compete in national or international markets is only partly determined by its cost position. Of great importance is the actual product and program differentiation and the effectiveness of the company's customer offering in relation to competitive offerings. For example, the extraordinarily robust and appreciating deutsche mark that has contributed to the rising prices of Mercedes automobiles has not resulted in a displacement of Mercedes from the high-priced segment of the U.S. automobile market. Clearly, demand for the Mercedes and other ''quality'' products is so great that customers are prepared to pay a significant price differential to obtain what they perceive to be a superior product.

The Product Trade Cycle Model

The theory of comparative advantage is a pure theory based upon a set of assumptions which are an abstraction from the complexities of the real world. The theory is a powerful idea and a constant and major influence on the thinking and action of public policy makers in governments around the globe. Nevertheless, it has limiting assumptions. For example, the demonstration of the theory is based on the assumption that the products are undifferentiated (one auto is exactly like the next, an orange is an orange is an orange), *and* in the two country–two product demonstration, there is no money or complication of foreign exchange rates.

In the real world, products are highly differentiated in the customer's mind and in physical expression. Consumers do not go out to purchase an auto, for example, in a market where all cars are the same. The success of international competitors is based on creating value for the customer by differentiating their product. Indeed, one of the important maxims of marketing is that you can differentiate anything. Also, in the real world exchange rates exist and change, and have a major impact on the cost position of competitors.

The international product life cycle model,[1] discovered by Professor Raymond

[1]Raymond Vernon, "International Investment and International Trade in the Product Cycle," *Quarterly Journal of Economics,* May 1966, pp. 190–207. See also Louis T. Wells, Jr., "A Product Life Cycle for International Trade?" *Journal of Marketing,* July 1968, pp. 1–6; and Sak Onkvisit and John J. Shaw, "An Examination of the International Product Life Cycle and Its Application within Marketing," *Columbia Journal of World Business,* Fall 1983, pp. 73–79.

Vernon of the Harvard Business School and the Harvard department of government, is, in contrast to the pure theory of comparative advantage, based on empirical actual patterns of trade. As such, it is a valuable complement to the theory of comparative advantage because it helps us understand what is actually happening in the real world of international competition. The model describes the relationship among the product life cycle, trade, and investment. Vernon's initial work was based on an analysis of U.S. trade in products during the 1950s and 1960s. The international product life cycle model suggests that many products go through a cycle during which high-income, mass-consumption countries are initially exporters, then lose their export markets, and finally become importers of the product. At the same time other advanced countries shift from the position of importers to exporters later in time, and still later, less developed countries shift from the position of being importers to being exporters of a product. These shifts correspond to the three stages in the product life cycle: introduction, growth and maturity, and decline. These stages are represented graphically in Figure 2–1.

The pattern from the point of view of the high-income country is as follows: Phase 1, export strength is exhibited; phase 2, foreign production begins; phase 3, foreign production becomes competitive in export markets; and phase 4, import competition begins. The model suggests that new products are initially introduced in high-income markets. There are two main reasons for this. First, high-income markets offer the greatest potential demand for new products, both consumer and industrial. Second, it is useful to locate production facilities close to the product's markets because of the need in the early stages of a product's life to respond quickly and fully to the customer in adjusting and adapting the design and performance of the product. Thus it is typical for products to initially be produced in the market where they will be sold. The first manufacturers of the new product have a virtual monopoly in world markets. Foreigners who want the new product must order it from companies in the high-income country. At this point, unsolicited orders begin to appear from overseas; high-income-country exports begin to grow from a trickle to a steady stream as active export programs are established. Markets for the new product exist not only in the high-income country but also in foreign countries that are supplied by high-income-country exports.

In the relatively high-income foreign countries, entrepreneurs are quick to note the growing markets in the new product and are relatively swift in taking advantage of lower labor costs and factor costs in many foreign markets. Production is then initiated abroad in the new product. In the second stage of the cycle, foreign and high-income-country production supply the same export markets. As foreign producers gain experience and expand, competition from the lower-cost foreign production increasingly displaces the high-income-country export production source for the product. At this point high-income-country companies often decide to invest in foreign markets to retain market shares acquired via export sourcing.

As foreign manufacturers expand production to supply home markets, their growing economies of scale make them a competitive source for third-country markets where they compete with high-income-country export marketers.

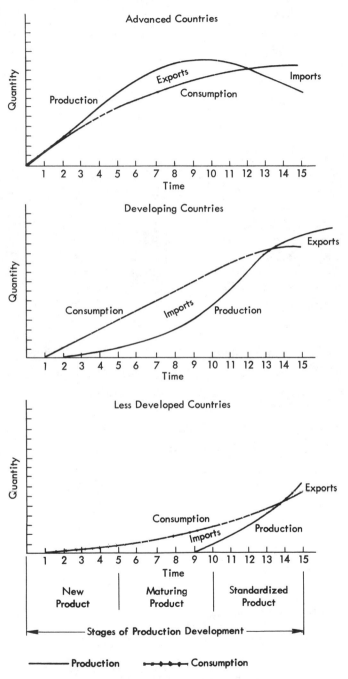

FIGURE 2–1 International Product Life Cycle

The final phase of this cycle occurs when the foreign manufacturer achieves mass production based on home and export markets and, due to lower factor costs, is able to produce at a lower cost than his or her American counterpart. The foreign manufacturer then begins to export to the high-income-country market. The cycle is now complete, and high-income-country companies that once had a virtual monopoly in the product find themselves facing foreign competition in their home market.

The cycle continues as the production capability in the product extends from the other advanced countries to less developed countries of the world that eventually displace the other advanced countries first at home, then in international trade, and finally in the other advanced countries' home market. Textiles are an example of a product that has gone through the complete cycle for the investing country (Britain), other industrialized countries, and finally for less developed countries.

The international product life cycle is basically a "trickle down" model of world trade and investment. First, products are introduced to the home market, then to other advanced countries, and finally to developing and less developed countries. It is an accurate description of the behavior of investors during the period from 1950 to the early 1970s, and it still describes the behavior of many U.S. firms who have abandoned efforts to maintain the United States as world low-cost producer by shifting production to lower-cost countries or by giving up market share to lower-cost producers in other countries. Unconsciously, many U.S. executives have acted as if the international product life cycle of consumption, trade, and investment was inevitable. Under this assumption, the advanced countries are doomed (or blessed with the opportunity) to constantly discover and introduce new products because they cannot compete with the lower-wage competitors in mature, established products.

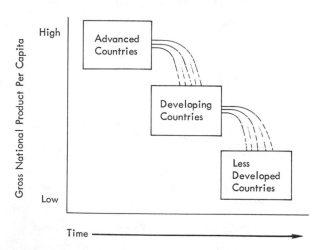

FIGURE 2–2   International Product Life Cycle—Trickle Down or Waterfall Approach

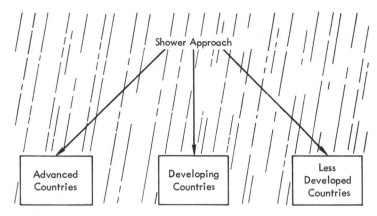

FIGURE 2–3 International Product Life Cycle—Shower Approach

An alternative to the trickle down approach (or what one writer has called the "waterfall" model[2] approach) is the "shower" approach. This strategy is to develop a product and simultaneously introduce it in world markets (a shower instead of a trickle). These contrasting approaches are illustrated in Figures 2–2 and 2–3. The difference between the two approaches begins with assumptions about the nature of world markets. The waterfall strategy, which is obsolete, assumes that markets develop sequentially over time. The shower approach recognizes that we live in a global village, and that markets develop simultaneously around the globe.

Nevertheless, there is still an opportunity for competitors to take advantage of lower factor costs in less developed and developing countries to gain an advantage in serving world markets. At the same time, companies with production capacity in advanced countries must always be on the alert for competitive threats that are based on taking advantage of lower-wage rates in developing countries and less developed countries. Production may be goods or services. India, for example, is a major production location for software programming. The product is "exported" via satellite signals. You can't see, taste, touch, or feel it, but it is a real export.

Orientations of Management

Howard Perlmutter of the Wharton School first identified the distinctive "orientations" of management of international companies. His EPRG schema (ethnocentrism, polycentrism, regiocentrism, geocentrism) identifies four types of attitudes or orientations toward internationalization that are associated with successive stages in the evolution of international operations. *Ethnocentrism* is associated with a home country orientation, *polycentrism* with a host country orientation, *regiocentrism* with a regional orientation, and *geocentrism* with a world orientation. This typology is the basis for the stages of corporate development framework outlined in Chapter 1.

[2] Kenichi Ohmae, *Triad Power* (New York: The Free Press, 1985), p. 21.

In the ethnocentric company, overseas operations are viewed as being secondary to domestic and primarily as a means of disposing of surplus domestic production. Plans for overseas markets are developed in the home office utilizing policies and procedures identical to those employed at home. There is no systematic marketing research conducted overseas, there are no major modifications to products, and there is no real attention to consumer needs in foreign markets.

In the polycentric stage, subsidiaries are established in overseas markets. Each subsidiary operates independently of the others and establishes its own marketing objectives and plans. Marketing is organized on a country-by-country basis, with each country having its own unique marketing policy.

In the regiocentric and geocentric phases, the company views the region or entire world as a market and seeks to develop integrated regional or world market strategies. The ethnocentric company is centralized in its marketing management, the polycentric company is decentralized, and the regiocentric and geocentric companies are integrated.

A crucial difference between the orientations is in the underlying assumption for each orientation. The ethnocentric orientation is based on a belief in home country superiority. This leads to an extension of home country products, policies, and programs. The underlying assumption of the polycentric approach is that there are so many differences in cultural, economic, and market conditions in each of the countries of the world that it is impossible to attempt to introduce any product, policy, or program from outside or to integrate any country's program in a regional or world context.

The regiocentric and geocentric assumptions hold that it is possible to identify both similarities and differences and to formulate an integrated regional or world marketing strategy on the basis of actual as opposed to imagined similarities and differences. While there can be no question that the geocentric orientation most accurately captures market reality, it does not follow that the geocentric orientation requires an integrated world structure and strategy. To implement the geocentric orientation, experienced international management and a great deal of commitment are required. For companies with limited experience, it may be wiser to adopt a centralized or a decentralized strategy and wait until experience accumulates before attempting to design and implement integrated marketing programs.

To underline this point, the case of a basically ethnocentric U.S. company is instructive. Several years ago this company, after reviewing the international business literature, decided that its ethnocentric corporate international division structure was not the most advanced way of operating internationally. Management decided therefore to abandon or dissolve the corporate international division and establish each of the company's product divisions as worldwide product divisions. This was implemented by top-management edict, and overnight each of the formerly domestic product divisions was responsible for its products on a worldwide basis. The consequences of this move were disastrous. In one typical division, managers acquired a European company and neglected to retain the seller as general manager. The seller proceeded to go to Switzerland for a ski holiday, and the American company proceeded to run the acquired company into the ground. Eighteen months after the acquisition, the seller publicly announced his willingness to repurchase his own company at one-half the price the American company had paid for it. To add insult to injury, he also publicly announced that each day the American company waited the price would go down. The American company accepted the offer! This case illustrates the consequences of adopting a design or approach without giving full consideration to the capabilities of existing management.

DRIVING AND RESTRAINING FORCES

The remarkable growth of the international economy over the past 40 years has occurred because the balance of driving and restraining forces has shifted significantly in favor of the driving forces. It is useful to identify these forces to gain an insight into the foundations of the international economy and international markets as they exist today and as they can be expected to develop in the decade ahead.

Driving Forces

These are the forces that are contributing to the growth of international business.

1. MARKET NEEDS. As you will see in Chapter 4, there are cultural universals as well as cultural differences. There is a common element in human nature and in the human psyche that is the underlying basis for the opportunity to create and serve global markets. The word *create* is deliberate. Most global markets do not exist in nature: They must be created by marketing effort. For example, soft drinks, one of the biggest successful global industries, are not needed by anyone and yet today in some countries soft drink consumption per capita *exceeds* the consumption of water. Marketing has driven this change in behavior.

Advanced global companies have discovered that the same basic segment need can be met with a global approach in selected product markets. Successful global strategies are based on performing a global function or serving a global need. Any industry which addresses these universals is a candidate for globalization. The advertising campaign for a global product may be a global appeal which is adapted to each national culture. For example, Debeers, the South African diamond company, is running a campaign to promote the giving of a diamond ring to announce an engagement in Japan, where a diamond is not a traditional engagement custom. The ads are humorous sketches showing a male suitor getting nowhere with flowers, but winning the girl with a diamond. The strategy is logical and sound and has been quite successful because the emotions that surround engagement and marriage are universal, and Debeers believes that these universal emotions or needs can be attached to a new want, the diamond.

The advertising campaign for a global product may be a single global execution such as a recent Camel cigarette television commercial showing the macho Camel man repairing a broken bridge across a jungle stream so he can cross in his Jeep and then enjoy a Camel. This campaign ran in every country in the world except Brazil (where they have too many jungles to get excited about the feat), with the only adaptation being the translation of the voice into the target market language. This type of campaign is possible because there are universal appeals for universal needs. In the case of Camel the brand is positioned to appeal to a masculine macho image. Marlboro is another enormously successful global brand. Targeted on urban smokers around the world, the brand appeals to the spirit of freedom, independence, and open space symbolized by the cowboy in beautiful, open western settings. The need addressed by Marlboro is universal, and therefore the basic appeal and execution of its advertising and positioning are global.

2. TECHNOLOGY.   Professor Theodore Levitt of Harvard Business School, perhaps the best known exponent of global marketing, wrote in his celebrated *Harvard Business Review* article of a "new commercial reality—the emergence of global markets for standardized consumer products on a previously unimagined scale." According to Levitt, "A powerful force drives the world toward a converging commonality, and that force is technology. It has proletarianized communication, transport, and travel. It has made isolated places and impoverished peoples eager for modernity's allurements. Almost everyone, everywhere wants all the things they've heard about, seen, or experienced via the new technologies."[3]

Technology is a universal, uniform, consistent factor across national and cultural boundaries. A 256K memory device is a 256K memory device. There are no cultural boundaries limiting the application of technology. Once a technology is developed, it immediately becomes available everywhere in the world. If a company knows how to manage a technology in one country, it has experience that is relevant for the rest of the world. Witness the growth and expansion of international publishing in books, magazines, and newspapers. The next step is television. One of the reasons that The News Corporation is a strong contender to succeed with its Fox Broadcasting Company in the United States is because it can draw upon its broadcasting experience in Australia in managing stations and in creating a network.

3. COST.   Uniformity can drive down research, engineering, design, creative, and production costs across business functions, from engineering and manufacturing to marketing and administration.

The pressure for globalization is intense when new products involve major investments and long periods of development. This is true for pharmaceuticals, where new products typically cost $50–$100 million to develop over a period of six to ten years. The enormous cost and risk of new product development must be recovered in the global marketplace, as no single national market is large enough to support investments of this size.

[3]Theodore Levitt, "The Globalization of Markets," *Harvard Business Review,* May–June 1983, p. 92.

4. QUALITY. Global volume generates greater revenue and greater operating margins to support design and manufacturing quality. A global and a local company may each spend 5 percent of sales on research and development, but the global company may have two, three, or even ten times the total revenue of the local. With the same percentage of sales spent on research and development, the global will outspend the local by a factor of two, three, or ten times, as the case may be. The same advantage applies also to manufacturing and marketing. Focusing on one marketing strategy, as opposed to letting each country develop its own, can result in greater marketing effectiveness and efficiency and therefore greater value for the consumer.

5. COMMUNICATIONS AND TRANSPORTATION. The information revolution contributes toward the emergence of global markets. Everybody wants the best, latest, and most modern expression of a product. In regional markets such as Europe, the increasing overlap of advertising across national boundaries and the mobility of consumers have created a pressure on marketers to align product positioning and strategy in adjacent markets. You see this in companies like Nestlé who have a tradition of decentralized country marketing efforts and who operate in markets where local tastes have developed over centuries. Even this combination of local preferences and decentralized marketing is subject to the pressure of overlapping communications and travel: It is increasingly difficult to position the same brand differently in countries where the customers are frequently exposed to brand communications from other markets. When there are overlapping communications the positioning message and the marketing impact are diluted, and there is a strong pressure to align positioning and brand image.

6. LEVERAGE. One of the unique advantages of a global company is the opportunity to develop "leverage," or advantages that it has because it operates simultaneously in more than one national market. A global company can develop five types of leverage.

1. Experience Transfers. A global company can leverage its experience in any market in the world. It can draw upon strategies, products, advertising appeals, sales management practices, promotional ideas, and so on that have been tested in actual markets and apply them in other comparable markets. There is nothing "automatic" about this, and it can be misused if the experience transferred is not relevant, but the potential to draw on world experience is a part of the leverage of a global company. An example of a positive experience transfer is RJR Nabisco's transfer of its successful positioning of Camel in Germany to Spain and then to the world market. An example of negative leverage in experience transfer was Nestlé's application of its European coffee strategy based upon flavor blends to the U.S. market. The result of this transfer was a decline in market share of 1 percent, a real disaster in the coffee business.

2. Systems Transfers. A global company can refine its planning, analysis, research, control, and other systems and apply the refinements worldwide. The leveraging of systems improvements also makes it possible for company staff to communicate with each other.

3. Scale Economies.   In manufacturing, the global company can take advantage of its greater volume to obtain the traditional single plant scale advantages and it can also combine into finished products those components manufactured in scale-efficient plants in different countries.

Just as a national company can achieve economies in staffing by eliminating duplicate staff after an acquisition, a global company can achieve the same economies on a global scale by centralizing functional activities. The larger scale of the global company also creates opportunities to increase the level of competence and quality of corporate staff and expand its role.

4. Resource Utilization.   A major strength of the global company is its ability to scan the entire world to identify people, money, and materials (or, as economists would put it, land, labor, and capital) that will enable it to compete most effectively in world markets. For a global company, it is no disaster if the value of the "home" currency rises dramatically, because for this company there really is no such thing as a home currency. The world is full of currencies, and a global company seeks financial resources on the best available terms and uses them where there is the greatest opportunity to serve a need at a profit.

5. Global Strategy.   The global company's greatest single advantage is its global strategy. A global strategy is based on scanning the world business environment to identify opportunities, threats, trends, and resources. The global company searches the world for markets that will provide an opportunity to apply its skills and resources to create value for customers that is greater than the value created by its competitors. The global strategy is a design to create a winning offering on a global scale. This takes great discipline, great creativity, and constant effort, but the reward is not just success—it's survival.

An example of a company that consciously elected to adopt a global strategy and thereby create one of the elements of leverage advantage is Merrill Lynch, the American financial services company. Merrill Lynch, by adopting a strategy of being a services supermarket, had expanded beyond its traditional securities brokerage business into a wide range of investment banking activities. In brokerage and investment banking, Merrill Lynch operated globally with major investments and operations in all major financial markets of the world. In addition to this geographic diversification of its financial services business, Merrill Lynch had also diversified into the real estate brokerage and relocation services business in the United States alone. When the company realized that it was operating globally in financial services and locally in real estate and relocation, it decided to divest itself of the nonfinancial services businesses and concentrate all of its resources and efforts on its global financial services business. As the Merrill Lynch CEO put it at the time the decision to sell was announced, "This is a statement about where we're going in the 1990s. It boils down to a long-term fit: Real estate is not where we should be now. Greater opportunities for us lie in our traditional businesses, such as global merchant banking, trading, securities underwriting, and consumer markets activities.''[4]

Restraining Forces

MARKET DIFFERENCES. In every product category, differences are still great enough across national and cultural boundaries to require adaptation of at least some elements of the marketing "mix" (product, price, advertising and promotion, and channels of distribution). Companies that have ignored these differences and who have tried to implement a global brand strategy without taking differences into account have met with disaster. Global marketing does not work without a strong local team who can adapt the product to local conditions. The list of failures ranges from Christianity to writing instruments. Five centuries of Christian missionary effort in Japan has led to almost no success. The reason is the fact that foreign products do not succeed in Japan unless they are adapted, and Christianity has been offered in an undiluted, unadapted form. Parker pen recently attempted to implement a tops-down global marketing strategy which ignored local market inputs. The result was a total failure and a sale of the company to the managers of the former U.K. subsidiary.

HISTORY. Even in cases where the product itself may be a good candidate for globalization, a brand's history may require a distinct and different marketing strategy and positioning in each country. This is true even for high potential products such as the image-driven brands. If a brand has an established identity in national markets, it may not be possible to achieve a single global position and strategy.

MANAGEMENT MYOPIA. In many cases, products and categories are candidates for globalization, but management does not seize the opportunity. A good example of management myopia is any company that does not maintain leadership in creating customer value in an expanding geographical territory. A company that looks backward will not expand geographically.

ORGANIZATIONAL CULTURE. In companies where subsidiary management knows it all, there is no room for vision from the top. In companies where headquarters management knows it all, there is no room for local initiative and in-depth knowledge of local needs and conditions. The successful global companies are marketers who have learned how to integrate global vision and perspective with local market initiative and input. The most striking theme of my interviews with executives of the most advanced global marketing companies was the respect for local initiative and input by headquarters' executives and the corresponding respect for headquarters' vision by local executives.

[4]"Merrill Lynch Set to Quit Real Estate," *The New York Times,* September 30, 1986, p. D1.

NATIONAL CONTROLS/BARRIERS TO ENTRY.   Every country protects local enterprise and interests by maintaining control over market access and entry. This control ranges from the low-tech tobacco monopoly control of access to tobacco markets to the high-tech national government control of broadcast, equipment and data transmission markets. This has been a major barrier, and the worldwide movement toward deregulation and privatization is a development that removes one of the major barriers to global marketing and advertising.

UNDERLYING FORCES OF INTERNATIONAL BUSINESS

Behind the remarkable growth of the international economy in the post–World War II decades are six basic factors that were not present before the war. It is useful to identify these underlying forces to gain further insight into the foundations of the global economy as it exists today.

The International Monetary Framework

The rapid growth of trade and investment in the post–World War II era has created an increasing need for international liquidity (i.e., money or a means of payment) to facilitate the exchange of goods and services between nations. Until 1969 the world economy limped along, with gold and foreign exchange as the entire source of international liquidity. Since 1969 the liquidity available to nations has been supplemented by the agreement of International Monetary Fund members to accept the SDRs (special drawing rights) in settling reserve transactions. For the first time an international reserve asset is available. The inherent limitations on liquidity expansion through the use of gold and foreign exchange have been overcome. The essential fact concerning the international monetary framework is that for over three decades it has functioned adequately. This evolving structure has every prospect of continuing to function adequately, thus making it possible for companies to finance trade and investment between nations, and to continue their global marketing efforts.

The World Trading System

The post–World War II world trading system was constructed out of a common desire to avoid a return to the restrictive and discriminatory trading practices of the 1920s and the 1930s. There was a commitment to the creation of a liberal world in which there would be a free flow of goods and services between countries. The system that evolved out of this commitment included the General Agreement on Tariffs and Trade (GATT), which provided an institutional framework and a set of rules and principles for efforts to liberalize trade. The most favored nation (MFN) principle whereby each country agrees to extend to all countries the most favorable terms that it negotiates with any country is an example of a GATT rule that contributed to the reduction of high tariff levels. Major reductions of tariff levels were accomplished by multilateral negotiations such as the Kennedy Round of the 1960s and the Tokyo Round of the 1970s. The Tokyo Round, when implemented, will bring industrial country tariff levels down to roughly 4 percent by 1987, less than the sales tax in most U.S. states.

One of the complications of the world trading system is that governments tend to encourage and support exporters with subsidies and assistance of various kinds. (One of the most common subsidies is export credit at below-market rates of interest.) This leads to efforts by target market countries to protect their own industry from "unfair" competition. In the United States, for example, law provides [Sections 731 and 733(a) of the 1930 Trade Act and Sections 201, 301, and 406(a) of the Trade Act of 1974] an apparatus through which American manufacturers or workers can ask the government to determine whether they are the victims of unfair trade practices and to prescribe a remedy for them. The U.S. laws, which are administered by the Department of Commerce and the International Trade Commission, follow international agreements that permit remedies against injurious dumping, subsidization, and other unfair practices.

The major challenge to the trading system in the 1980s is not tariff levels but, rather, the so-called "nontariff barriers" (NTBs). These include safeguard actions to protect industries, exclusion orders, standards (requiring, for example, that products admitted to the country meet exact specifications that either cannot be met in the case of some natural products or that are very expensive to meet in the case of manufactured products), exclusionary distribution, and administrative delays. (When the French decided that Japanese imports of automobiles were excessive, they simply "applied the rules" and gave each automobile a complete inspection before admitting it to France. Needless to say, this inspection took time, and an enormous backlog of Japanese automobiles accumulated in French ports.) Another nontariff barrier to trade is voluntary restraint, or the agreement by the exporting country to limit its exports of product to provide relief to the domestic industry in that country. This has been frequently used by the Japanese in response to requests from the U.S. government.

Global Peace

Since 1945 the world has remained free of the major world conflicts that marked the first half of the century. Although postwar geopolitics has been characterized by an abundance of regional and low-intensity conflict, battles continue to be localized and limited to conventional weapons. Although these conditions are not, to be certain, entirely peaceful, they provide a relatively stable foundation for the healthy and rapid growth of the international economy. We live in a paradoxical world which, although in constant bitter conflict, is at peace on a global basis.

Not only is the conflict localized, but it also takes place entirely in the countries outside the advanced country markets which account for over 70 percent of world market potential. World Wars I and II were essentially advanced country conflicts. Today, the wars in the world are between countries that are in the developing and less developed categories.

Domestic Economic Growth

Behind this growth are the more basic factors of technology and managerial skill, which have created growing markets in those domestic economies that have been receptive to the entry of international firms. When a country is growing rapidly, receptiveness is encouraged because a growing country means growing markets and therefore expanding opportunities. Under this condition it is possible for an outside or international company to enter a domestic economy and to establish itself without taking business away from local firms. The growing economy is a classic illustration of the so-called "nonzero-sum game" whereby players can participate and "win" without doing so at the expense of others because their "play" enlarges the size of the total gains to be distributed. Without economic growth, international participation in countries could occur only if the firms were able to take business away from local enterprise (assuming of course that local enterprise was not deliberately liquidating its position). If this kind of competition between international and domestic enterprise existed, it is more likely that domestic enterprise would seek governmental intervention to protect its local position.

Thus there are two reasons why economic growth has been an underlying force in the expansion of the international economy. First, growth has created market opportunities. The existence of market opportunities has been the major reason for the international expansion of enterprise. Of course, international enterprise has itself contributed to the process of development in host countries. Second, economic growth has reduced the resistance that might otherwise have developed in response to the entry of foreign firms into domestic economies. The worldwide recession of the early 1980s created a predictable pressure in most countries to limit foreign access to domestic markets.

Communications and Transportation Technology

Developments that have increased the speed and capacity and lowered the cost of communications have been a major force underlying international business expansion. The jet airplane has revolutionized the communications field by making it possible for people to travel around the world in less than 48 hours. One of the essential characteristics of the effective business enterprise is the face-to-face meeting of those responsible for directing the enterprise. Without the jet airplane, the face-to-face contact so essential to business management would not have been possible because the amount of time required to travel the distance involved in international operations would be too great. The jet aircraft has made it possible for executives to be in face-to-face contact at regular intervals throughout the year.

A second major communications develement has been the enormous improvement in the ability to transmit data electronically. The cost of transmitting voice, facsimile, television, and data has declined continuously since the end of World War II. The declining cost and increasing availability of transportation and electronic communications have made it possible to manage geographically dispersed operations.

A similar revolution has occurred in transportation technology. A letter from China to New York is now delivered in eight days—faster than domestic mail in many countries. The cost of shipping automobiles from Japan and Korea by specially designed auto-transport ships is less than the cost of shipping from Detroit to either U.S. coast over land. The time and cost barriers of distance have fallen tremendously over the past 50 years.

The Global Corporation

The global corporation, or any business enterprise that pursues global business objectives by relating world resources to world market opportunity, is the organization that has responded to the driving, restraining, and underlying forces in the world. Within the international financial framework and under the umbrella of global peace, the global corporation has taken advantage of the expanding communications technologies to pursue market opportunities and serve needs and wants on a global scale.

KEY CONCEPTS

There are six key concepts that contribute toward a better understanding of the opportunity and challenge of global marketing. The first, and most important, is the concept of strategy.

Strategy

Strategy has been defined as the considered response of an organization to the realities of organization stakeholders and the realities of the business environment.

Table 2–2 presents a conceptual framework for strategy formulation. Phase 1 of this framework identifies three strategic dimensions: the external environment of the firm, the organization or the internal environment, and values and aspirations. The strategic planning process requires an assessment of the facts and assumptions concerning the firm's external environment. This assessment can be organized around the macro dimensions of economic, sociocultural, political, and technological factors, and the micro factors of markets, costs, competitors, customers, and government. This assessment should cover the entire world and should ensure that no significant competitor, market, or trend is overlooked.

The second dimension identified in phase 1 is the organization. Here, it is necessary to single out the particular strengths and weaknesses of the organization

TABLE 2–2   Strategy Formulation—A Conceptual Framework

	ENVIRONMENT	ORGANIZATION	STAKEHOLDER VALUES
1. Strategic dimensions	Economic Sociocultural Political Technological Markets Costs Competitors Customers Government	Human resources/capabilities Marketing Finance Manufacturing Engineering R&D	Size/growth Profitability/return Geographic Social responsibility Aesthetic Style Ethics

2. Strategic process
  a. Identify
  b. Assess
  c. Determine
	Key assumptions, opportunities, threats, trends	Key assumptions, strengths/weaknesses	Relative importance

	Alternatives—What is possible?		Relative importance
3. Determine	Objectives and Goals		

4. Identify driving force of the business; distinctive competence.

CATEGORY	STRATEGIC AREA
Products, markets	Products offered, markets served; knowledge of customers. Financial resources/structure new product development
Capabilities	Technology Production capability Method of sale Method of distribution Natural resources
Results	Size/growth Profitability/return

5. Develop integrated plans and programs for

Control	Manufacturing
Engineering	Marketing
Finance	R&D
Human resources	Social responsibility

6. Plan implementation. Obtain and commit resource to plans and programs. Manage resources.
7. Control. Compare implementation results with plans. Compare environmental, organizational, and value assessment with key assumptions. Recycle to phase 1.
8.   Timing

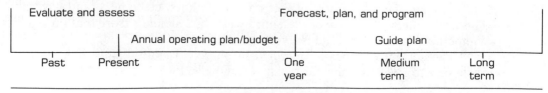

Evaluate and assess		Forecast, plan, and program		
	Annual operating plan/budget		Guide plan	
Past	Present	One year	Medium term	Long term

The line of time
strategy links past, present, and future.

so that these can be considered in the light of identified opportunities, threats, and trends.

The third dimension of phase 1 is stakeholder values. Stakeholders are any person or group with an interest in the outcome of an organization's activity. They include the stockholders, managers, employees, customers, members of the community, state, and country in which the business operates, and so on. As stakeholders often have conflicting values and interests, resolving these conflicting values is a management task that requires political skills and talents.

Phase 2 of the strategy formulation process is the assessment of the opportunities, threats, and trends in the environment; the strengths and weaknesses of the organization; and the desires of the stakeholders, leading to a formulation of what is possible or of the alternatives open to the organization. Phase 3 continues with a decision about objectives and goals based on the organization's alternatives.

Phase 4 is the identification of the driving force of the business, a critical stage of the process. Each of the identified strategic areas is important, and every successful business must be strong in each of the identified areas. The truly successful business, however, will identify its own particular area of distinctive competence that will be the "driving force" of the business. For example, IBM is strong in each of the strategic areas, but the driving force of IBM is now, and always has been, market needs. Everyone at IBM knows that the organization's true strength is based on its commitment to serving customer needs.

Phase 5 of the process is the preparation of integrated plans and programs in each of the functional areas of the business. The process continues with plan implementation and control and recycles to phase 1, where the results of the strategy are compared with objectives and goals and with the facts and assumptions about environment, organization, and stakeholder values. To the extent that the results of the strategy are consistent with objectives, goals, facts, and assumptions, the strategy can be maintained as is. If there are deviations, it must of course be adapted.

Phase 6 is plan implementation. This calls for obtaining and committing resources to the plans and programs.

Phase 7 of the framework—control—overlaps with strategy implementation. In this phase implementation results are compared with plans, and any deviation from plans is reviewed to determine whether this requires an adjustment in the strategy or improvement in the implementation effort. Another aspect of control, and critically important as a part of strategy formulations, is the scanning of the external and internal environment as well as stakeholder values to compare environmental, organizational, and value assessment with key assumptions that were established at the beginning of the strategy formulation process.

Phase 8—timing—indicates the relationship of the past, present, and future to the strategy formulation process. As indicated in Table 2–1, strategy formulation cuts across the time line. It requires an evaluation and assessment of past events, an assessment and identification of present realities, and an anticipation or forecast of future conditions. Since the past is history, and the future has not yet occurred, the only time period in which we can actually have an impact on the external world is the present. Thus strategy, even though it has a profound impact on a company's future, is implemented in the present. What a manager does on Monday morning is as much a part of the overall strategy of the organization as any thinking about what the organization might be 5, 10, or 15 years from now. Many managers fall into the trap of assuming that there is some magical distinction between future thoughts and present actions. Nothing could be further from the truth. The future is nothing more or less than an accumulation of actions in the present. Indeed, in a changing world the future is a creation of people's egos, and egos operate not only in thought but also in the action of the moment.

The Company in the World

There are, in addition to the basic universal concept of strategy, several aspects of international marketing that are distinctive. The first is the context or environment of international marketing. Figure 2–4 suggests the major characteristics of the environment of global marketing. At the center of the diagram is the company, which is defined by four major dimensions: its products, markets served, resources, and skills. The company exists in a world of more than 180 different countries and territories, each of which is in some respects similar to and in other respects different from the other countries in the world. Although each of the countries and territories

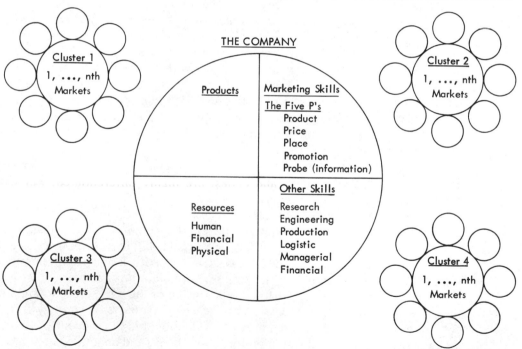

FIGURE 2–4   A Conceptual Framework for Global Marketing: The Company in a World of Clusters of National Market Environments

is in fact unique, both statistical analysis of the major environmental dimensions and managerial judgment agree that it is possible to cluster national different market environments to establish groups of countries that result in clear within-group similarities and between-group differences.[5]

Clustering

The characteristics of markets served differ considerably around the globe on many key dimensions. For example, the income per capita of world markets varies from a low of $120 per capita per annum in Ethiopia to a high of $23,770 in the United Arab Emirates.[6] At the extremes there is no question that income is a differentiating influence in world markets today. The similarities between the U.S. market and, say, the market in Mali are so small as to be unimportant. Nevertheless, within this wide range of global per capita income, there are clusters of countries at the bottom, in the middle, and at the top that are so similar in income that it becomes a unifying influence rather than a differentiating one.

Another important market characteristic is size. The U.S. market, with $4 trillion in annual income, is enormous. Other industrialized countries with incomes on a per capita basis quite similar to that of the United States are still quite small in the aggregate. A good example is Sweden, whose per capita GNP (gross national product) in 1982 was $13,840 but whose GNP was only $115 billion. At these extremes, the size of markets is a highly differentiating influence. The structure, staffing, information, and control system that is appropriate for the Swedish marketing organization would be grossly inadequate for an organization that obtains a similar share of the U.S. market. A company that is simultaneously marketing in large and small markets must be flexible in its approach to organization, staffing information, and control lest it find itself in the position of enforcing some unified approach to each of these system areas—and as a consequence having organizations, information systems, and control systems that are either inadequate to the size of the market or too elaborate for a smaller market.

Governmental influences in the company's global environment, including tariffs, taxes, laws, regulations, and codes, are highly differentiated. For example, companies marketing equipment used in the construction and building trades must face the complete welter of codes and regulations that exist not only internationally but also within a particular national environment in various local political jurisdictions. Consider, for example, the situation faced by a crane manufacturer. In many countries in the world, cranes must have a free-fall capability for instantly releasing their load. This requirement has been established to make the cranes safer. A crane with the capability of a free-fall displacement of its load is difficult to tip over. In other countries, however, there is a requirement that a crane not have a free-fall

---

[5]See, for example, S. Prakash Sethi, "Comparative Cluster Analysis for World Markets," *Journal of Marketing Research,* August 1971, p. 348.

[6]Data source: *1986 World Bank Atlas,* International Bank for Reconstruction and Development/The World Bank, 1818 H. Street, N.W., Washington, D.C. 20433, 1986.

capacity. The prohibition against free fall is also motivated by a desire to increase the safety of crane operation. The rationale behind the prohibition of free-fall capability is that any crane with this capability is liable to lose its entire load accidentally. In other words, considerations of safety for this particular product have motivated opposite conditions in the area of free fall, and any company that wishes to market this product internationally must be able to respond to these conditions and to offer products that do not have such a capability.

Environmental Sensitivity

A very useful way of looking at products internationally is to place them on a continuum of environmental sensitivity. At one end of the continuum are the environmentally insensitive products, which do not require significant adaptation to the economic and social environments of markets around the world. At the other end of the continuum are those products that are highly sensitive to differences in economic, sociocultural, physical, and governmental factors in world markets. A company with environmentally insensitive products is going to have to spend relatively less time determining the specific and unique conditions of local markets because the product the company offers is basically universal.

The sensitivity of products can be represented on a scale as in Figure 2–5. At the left of the scale are the environmentally insensitive products. An integrated circuit is an example of an environmentally insensitive product. Moving to the right on the scale is a computer that must be sensitive to the environmental variable of voltage and cycles. In addition, the computer's software documentation must be in the local language. At the far end of the continuum are the products with high environmental sensitivity. Food products fall into this category because they are a part of culture, but power generation systems also fall into this category because it happens that in many countries the local power generation manufacturing companies have a de facto

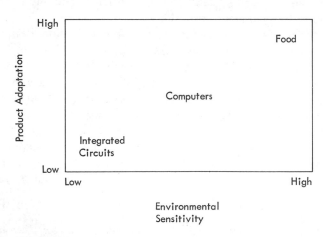

FIGURE 2–5 Environmental Sensitivity-Product Adaptation Matrix

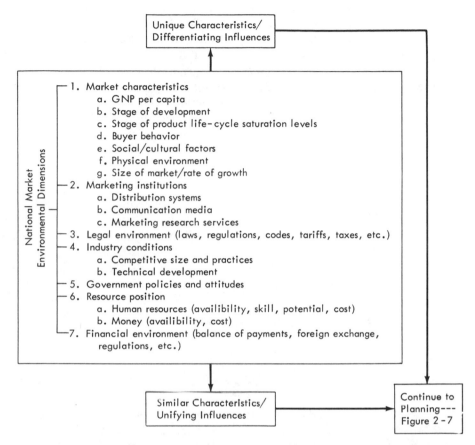

FIGURE 2–6 A Conceptual Framework for Multinational Marketing: Major Dimensions of a National Market Environment: Absolute and Compared with Other Nations

monopoly on national purchases. The greater the environmental sensitivity of a product, the more necessary it is for a company to learn about the way in which its products interact with the specific economic, social and cultural, physical, and prescriptive environmental conditions that exist throughout the world.

Unifying and Differentiating Influences

Figure 2–6 illustrates the application of the concept of unifying and differentiating influences to the task of environmental and market analysis.[7] This concept is based on the fact that in every situation there are both unique and similar aspects. The

[7]The concept of unifying and differentiating influences was first suggested by John Fayerweather in *International Business Management: A Conceptual Framework* (New York: McGraw-Hill, 1969).

unique aspects are "differentiating" influences; the similar aspects are the "unifying" influences. If the analysis of a market focuses on only the unique or only the similar aspects, it will be one-sided, and if followed in developing a marketing program, it will result in a program that is either too standardized or too differentiated. For example, a totally standardized program, based on analysis that recorded only the unifying influences, might establish a single price worldwide for an identical product and not take into account the ability to pay or the competitive situation in the various world markets. This would be simple to design and administer, but it would be costly in terms of lost business and profits that might have been obtained by a more differentiated pricing policy. At the other extreme, if a unique price is calculated for each country, there might be serious transshipment problems as dealers and distributors seek the lowest possible price for their supplies.

Information and conclusions resulting from this scanning feed into the analysis, planning, and control process shown in Figure 2–7, which is concerned with relating opportunities and threats in the world market environment to the basic strengths

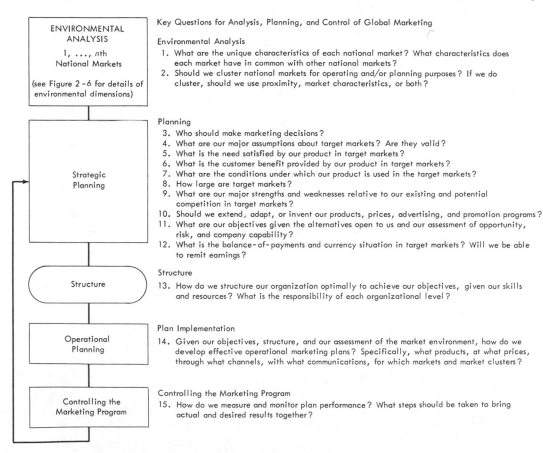

FIGURE 2–7   A Conceptual Framework for Multinational Marketing

and weaknesses of the company. The planning process results in the selection of objectives among the alternatives open to the company. Given objectives, companies decide upon an organization appropriate to the company's basic skills and resources. Within the framework of a specified organizational structure, the implementation of decisions about objectives must be accomplished. In marketing this requires the design and specification of products, prices, channels, and communications. Given specified marketing plans, the next step is implementation. The final phase of the global marketing process is control, that is, the measurement and evaluation of performance. The results of this control activity feed back to the planning process and become an important input to the planning cycle.

The process of global marketing requires the marketing manager to answer a number of basic questions to plan and implement a global marketing strategy. The marketing manager must identify opportunities and threats and must know where global markets are located today and where they will be in the future. The remarkable success in recent years of countries such as Japan, Brazil, and Spain is a reminder that opportunity is constantly shifting in the world. The global marketer needs to identify similarities and differences to know what to change and what not to change. To do this, an organization must be structured to respond to the unique aspects of country markets and at the same time be capable of identifying any relevant experience and applying it across all pertinent national boundaries.

Product Life Cycle/Market Life Cycle

The concept of the PLC (product life cycle) is well established in marketing. The general notion of the PLC is that a product has a characteristic or normal life with a beginning, or birth, and rapid growth (the growth stage), followed by a declining rate of growth, no growth, decline, and eventually, to complete the metaphor, death. This typical PLC is illustrated in Figure 2–8.

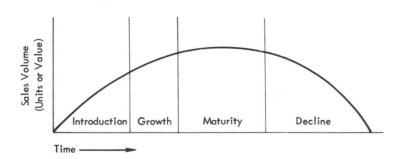

FIGURE 2–8   The Product Life Cycle

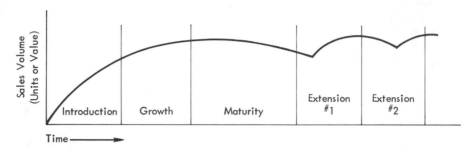

FIGURE 2–9 Extending the Product Life Cycle

Of course, the concept of the PLC does not provide a basis for predicting or forecasting the actual rate of sales growth or the timing of the shifts in rate. In practice, the rate of growth and the timing of change in rate varies across a vast spectrum. Indeed, the whole concept of the PLC is based upon a notion of product that is quite obsolete in today's markets: the notion that a product is launched and that is it. Today, in order to succeed, it is absolutely essential to constantly improve products and to increase the value offered to customers. When this is done, the PLC can be extended, as shown in Figure 2–9.

The market life cycle is a related concept. Markets have a beginning, growth stage, maturity, and decline. A company engaged in global marketing will find that not all markets are at the same stage of development. It is important to recognize the stage of market development and match the marketing strategy for the product to that stage. For example, the same product may be at the mature stage in one country and at the growth stage in another. The appropriate marketing strategy for the product will be different for each market: perhaps greater emphasis will be on price in the mature market, while in the growth stage market explaining and gaining acceptance will be emphasized. The twin dangers in the global company are that each country will operate in autonomy without the benefit of experience from the rest of the world, or that inappropriate experience will be imposed on the world.

SUMMARY

The tremendous growth in world business is a result of the interaction of specific driving and restraining forces. Clearly, the driving forces, which include market needs, the communications and transportation revolutions, and the leverage of the global company, have overcome the restraining forces that include market differences, management myopia, and national barriers to entry.

The major underlying forces that support the growth of international markets and international business include the international monetary framework, the world trading system, global peace, domestic economic growth, and last but certainly not least, the global corporation.

The chapter concludes with a list of key concepts for global marketers which includes the concept of business strategy.

DISCUSSION QUESTIONS

1. Why have trade and investment grown faster than national income since the end of World War II?
2. If a country has an absolute disadvantage in the production of everything, can it gain anything from trade? How?
3. What would happen to a country that decided to protect all local industry from international competition?
4. What are the major underlying forces supporting the growth of international business? What is the current direction and strength of these forces, and what do you see as the short-term future of international opportunity for companies based in (a) the United States, (b) France, (c) Japan, (d) Tanzania?
5. What are the major dimensions of the strategy formulation conceptual framework? Do these dimensions apply to the past, the present, or the future?
6. What is the meaning of the term "environmentally sensitive"? Cite an example of an environmentally sensitive product.
7. Which type of product provides a greater opportunity for the global company: the low or high environmentally sensitive product?

BIBLIOGRAPHY

Books

AHARONI, YAIR. *The Foreign Investment Decision Process*. Boston: Division of Research, Graduate School of Business Administration, Harvard University, 1966.

BEHRMAN, JACK N. *Some Patterns in the Rise of the Multinational Enterprise*. Chapel Hill: Graduate School of Business Administration, University of North Carolina, 1969.

DANIELS, JOHN D., AND LEE H. RADEBAUGH. *International Business: Environments and Operations*. Reading, Mass.: Addison-Wesley, 1986.

FAYERWEATHER, JOHN. *International Business Management: A Conceptual Framework*. New York: McGraw-Hill, 1969.

GLADWIN, THOMAS N., AND IAN H. GIDDY. *A Survey of Foreign Direct Investment Theory*. Ann Arbor: Division of Research, Graduate School of Business Administration, University of Michigan, November 1973.

GROSSE, ROBERT. *The Theory of Foreign Direct Investment*. South Carolina Essays in International Business, No. 3, December 1981.

KINDLEBERGER, CHARLES P. *Foreign Trade and the National Economy*. Westport, Conn.: Greenwood Press, 1975.

———, AND PETER LINDERT. *International Economics*, 7th Ed. Homewood, Ill.: Richard D. Irwin, 1982.

KNICKERBOCKER, F. T. *Oligopolistic Reaction and Multinational Enterprise*. Boston: Division of Research, Graduate School of Business Administration, Harvard University, 1973.

MASON, R. HAL, ROBERT R. MILLER, AND DALE R. WEIGEL. *The Economics of International Business*. Melbourne, Fla.: Krieger, 1981.

OHLIN, BERTIL. *Interregional and International Trade,* rev. ed. Cambridge, Mass.: Harvard University Press, 1967.

OHMAE, KENICHI. *Triad Power: The Coming Shape of Global Competition*. New York: The Free Press, 1985.

ROBOCK, STEFAN, AND KENNETH SIMMONDS, *International Business and Multinational Enterprises,* 3rd Ed. Homewood, Ill.: Richard D. Irwin, 1983.

WILKINS, MIRA. *The Emergence of Multinational Enterprise: American Business Abroad from the Colonial Era to 1914*. Cambridge, Mass.: Harvard University Press, 1970.

————. *The Maturing & Multinational Enterprise: American Business Abroad from 1914 to 1970*. Cambridge, Mass.: Howard University Press, 1974.

Articles

HOY, HAROLD J., AND JOHN J. SHAW. "The United States' Comparative Advantage and Its Relationship to the Product Life Cycle Theory and the World Gross National Product Market Share." *Columbia Journal of World Business,* (Spring 1981), pp. 40–50.

KORBIN, STEVE. "The Environmental Determinants of Foreign Direct Investment: An Ex Post Empirical Analysis." *Journal of International Business Studies,* (Fall–Winter 1976), pp. 29–42.

ONKVISIT, SAK, AND JOHN J. SHAW. "An Examination of the International Product Life Cycle and Its Application Within Marketing." *Columbia Journal of World Business,* (Fall 1983), pp. 73–79.

PERLMUTTER, HOWARD J. "Social Architectural Problems of the Multinational Firm." *Quarterly Journal of AIESEC International,* Vol. 3, no. 3 (August 1967).

SIMMONDS, KENNETH. "Multinational? Well, Not Quite." *Columbia Journal of World Business,* (Fall 1966), pp. 115–122.

WIND, YORAM, SUSAN P. DOUGLAS, AND HOWARD V. PERLMUTTER. "Guidelines for Developing International Marketing Strategy." *Journal of Marketing,* Vol. 37 (April 1973), pp. 14–23.

LAUNDROWASH S.p.A. (A)[1]

Mr. Mario Paino, owner of Laundrowash[2] S.p.A., was wondering what price schedules he should set for his new Turin automatic laundry. Laundrowash S.p.A., which was scheduled to open May 9, 1961, was to be the first American-style automatic coin-operated laundry in Italy.

Mr. Paino, a successful Italian investor living in Rome, had recently acquired the Speed Wash coin-operated laundry equipment franchise for Italy. After acquiring the franchise, he had made many attempts to interest Italian investors in coin-operated laundries, but each time these attempts were

[1]Copyright 1962 by l'Institut pour l'Etude des Méthodes de Direction de l'Entreprise (IMEDE), Lausanne, Switzerland. Reprinted by permission. This case was written by the author. This case has been voted a marketing classic by readers of earlier editions of this book and is included here in response to reader demand. Although the specific market conditions described in the case are closer to those in a country like Portugal than to Italy today, the application of the general lessons of the case apply as fully today as they did in 1961.

[2]All names and locations are disguised.

greeted with skepticism. Many investors were interested, but felt the market risks of this radical new service were too great to justify their making the first move. After a number of unsuccessful attempts to interest investors, Mr. Paino decided to form a corporation called Laundrowash S.p.A. and open his own Speed Wash coin-operated laundry. Although his main objective remained to distribute coin-operated equipment, he felt that a successfully operating laundry would provide the evidence he needed to convince investors that coin-ops could be profitable in Italy.

DEFINITION AND DEVELOPMENT OF COIN-OPS IN THE UNITED STATES

The term "coin-op" developed in the United States. It was used there to describe unattended (or attended by one clerk) laundries where customers operated automatic washers, dryers, and soap and bleach dispensers themselves by dropping coins in the appropriate slots. In a coin-operated laundry, each machine was equipped with a coin meter that automatically operated the machine when the correct amount of change was inserted.

In the United States the forerunners of coin-ops were "launderettes." The launderette was a laundry where customers' clothes were washed by laundry attendants. This type of laundry offered a same-day, rough-dry service in which the clothes were simply washed by machine, and dried in an automatic dryer. They also usually offered a more expensive "semi-finished" service in which clothes were hand folded after drying. Although most launderettes used automatic equipment, their labor cost for attendants limited their ability to compete on a price basis with coin-ops. It also limited the hours per day that they could remain open, so that their costs were not spread over a twenty-four-hour day. Because

of their higher cost structure, the cost per pound to the housewife was greater than that of the coin-ops.

Coin-ops were first introduced in the United States at the close of World War II. Their installation was on a small scale, however, and made little market impression. Initial attempts to establish them on a large scale failed, partly because then-existing machines and metering devices were unreliable.

With rising labor costs, and the development of effective coin-metering equipment and more reliable machines, the way was open for the installation of self-service laundries in America. The business got its start in California, where people were more accustomed to self-service facilities. By 1958, coin-ops were spread over the entire country, and new ones were being established at the rate of one per day.

In early 1960 *Coin-Op Magazine* estimated that there were 25,000 automatic laundries in the U.S., and that during the year another 3,000 would open their doors. Using an average figure of 20 machines per laundry, this meant that there were 500,000 coin-operated machines in the U.S. in January of 1960, and expectations were that an additional 60,000 would be installed during the year. Throughout the rise of the coin-ops, annual sales of four million automatic machines for home use remained steady.

One of the reasons for this rapid growth, according to *Barron's*,[3] was the lower cost to the housewife.

A housewife can wash a load of clothes in one (coin-operated machine) for 10 or 20 cents, and she can use a dryer which will take up to four loads of washing for one cent per minute. Indeed, all her laundering for a week can be done in an hour for no more than $1.25, or far less than the payments on a washing machine of her own.

[3]November 10, 1958. *Barron's* is a well-known U.S. financial publication.

In 1960, the average prices in the U.S. were less than 25 cents per wash, and 10 cents per five-minute drying cycle.

In America, small investors were attracted to coin-ops by the low initial cash outlay, the small claim on their time, and the prospect of a high return on investment. ALD, Inc., the largest equipment supplier to the trade, estimated that a laundry containing 20 regular 9 lb. (4 kilos) automatic machines and one large 25 lb. (11 kilos) machine for rugs, eight dryers, and all necessary auxiliary equipment such as changemakers, water softeners, boilers, heaters, and sinks would cost, completely installed, $23,000. Another estimate of laundry costs was made by an appraisal bulletin published in January, 1959, which suggested that on the average the total cost of all equipment and installation charges averaged about $700 per washer. Using this guide, the total investment for the average 20-machine laundry in the U.S. was around $14,000. It further reported:

Income and operating information is rather sketchy but we have obtained figures in St. Louis from what we consider reliable sources. A good average sized coin-op in the St. Louis area will gross about $15,000 during this year. In order to do this volume of business, the laundry would have to be in a good location and should operate 24 hours a day, 365 days a year. We found a few coin-ops gross as high as $30,000 per year.

Insofar as the expenses are concerned, on a coin-op doing an annual gross of $15,000, the breakdown will be about like this:

	Monthly	Yearly
Rent	$100	$1,200
Utilities	200	2,400
Maintenance	50	600
Insurance (including vandalism coverage)	30	360
Taxes	10	120
Miscellaneous	150	1,800
	$540	$6,480

THE ITALIAN MARKET

After forming Laundrowash S.p.A. in 1960 to operate the first coin-op laundry in Italy, Mr. Paino's first step was to investigate potential cities as sites for his automatic laundry. In checking market statistics, he quickly found that considerable variations existed in different regions. For example, average per capita Gross National Product for 1959 in Italy was listed as $545. In the same year a survey in the industrial north[4] revealed a much different figure: a sample of 97,000 workers in metallurgical and mechanical firms showed that payments to them averaged $2,200 per year including direct payments, indirect payments, and charges for social welfare. Statistics for the province of Turin, in the north, showed one car owner for every 22 persons, while this figure for Nuovo, in comparatively backward Sardinia, was 272. The average figure for Italy of 77 (1956) was anything but indicative of the real picture. A close look at the figures confirmed Mr. Paino's conclusion that Italy was economically two countries: the highly-developed north and the relatively under-developed south.

Because of the much higher living standards there, Mr. Paino decided to concentrate his search in northern Italy. In the north, Turin seemed the best choice for a number of reasons. Since 1946, the city had grown from 700,000 to over one million in population. With less than 4 percent of the country's population, it paid almost 20 percent of the national tax bill. It was the fourth largest city in Italy, located in the heart of the industrial Po Valley, where workers enjoyed a standard of living rivalling that of the most advanced European countries. After several visits to Turin, Mr. Paino concluded that it was a dynamic modern city, whose population was

[4]Turin Industrial Association, May 1959. Results published in *Setting Up a Business in Italy*. Investment Information Office, Rome, 1960.

receptive to new ideas. Therefore, when he was offered a chance to sign a two year lease for a 5 × 13 metre shop on Via Rosselli, he accepted with the thought of setting up his first coin-op laundry there.

THE SITE

Via Rosselli was a wide, tree-lined street at the southwest edge of Turin. A street plan of Turin showing the location of the automatic laundry and the other shops in the block is given in Figure 1. The area was predominantly residential, with most families living in apartment buildings ranging from four to seven stories in height. All buildings within approximately 2,000 metres of the laundry appeared to be of post-war construction. The apartments in the immediate area were of excellent quality and had been constructed within the last five years. The average four-room apartment was renting for around $65 per month. There were no single unit dwellings in the area.

The inhabitants were mainly middle-class families, with a few professionals and managers. Occupationally they were about evenly divided between office workers and skilled factory workers, with most families having more than one wage earner. Mr. Paino estimated that average family income was around $200 per month, and that there was about one car for every 20 people in the area.

Turin was divided into 20 zones for statistical reporting. The automatic laundry site was located at the southern end of zone 17. Table 1 shows population statistics for zone 17, and total figures for all 20 zones.

AVAILABLE LAUNDRY FACILITIES

For the Turin housewife, there were three ways of getting her wash done. She could have it done by a "charwoman," do it herself at home, or send it to a commercial laundry. A great deal of washing was done by "charwomen" who charged from 200 ($0.32) to 250 lire ($0.40) per hour plus soap. These women would come into homes and wash or would do the laundry in their own homes.

The housewife did her laundry at home by machine if she owned one, but since this was rare, the more usual method was by hand. Table 2 shows washing machine sales and market saturation figures for Italy. Mr. Paino estimated that the saturation index for Turin was double the national average.

There were approximately 200 com-

VIA ROSSELLI

├──────────────── One city block ────────────────┤

FIGURE 1   Street Plan Showing the Site of the Automatic Laundry

TABLE 1 Population Statistics for the Proposed Laundrowash Zone* (30th January, 1959)

	Blue Collar Workers Number	%	Office Workers Number	%	Managers Number	%	Self-Employed Number	%	Self-Employed Professionals Number	%	Part-Time Workers Number	%	Non-Working Population Number	%
LAUNDROWASH Zone (17)	26,232	24.0	17,682	16.0	790	0.7	6,033	5.0	391	0.3	2,162	2.0	57,395	52.0	110,685	100
City Total (percentages only)		21.0		14.0		1.0		7.0		1.0		2.0		54.0		100

*Note: For statistical reporting purposes, Turin was divided into 20 zones.

Source: Citta di Torino.

TABLE 2   Washing Machine Sales and Saturation in Italy

| | | SALES | | HOUSEHOLD SATURATION INDEX | | |
Year	Number (000)	Average Price in Lire	Total Value in Lire (000)	Household Units (000)	Number with Machines (000)	Percentage with Machines
1950	10	80,000	800,000	5,910	11	.18
1951	20	80,000	1,600,000	6,260	30	.49
1952	23	85,000	1,955,000	6,560	50	.76
1953	30	85,000	2,550,000	6,810	80	1.17
1954	40	90,000	3,600,000	7,300	115	1.57
1955	52	90,000	4,680,000	7,600	160	2.10
1956	74	100,000	7,400,000	8,000	225	2.80
1957	90	100,000	9,020,000	8,350	300	3.60
1958	120	110,000	13,200,000	8,700	400	4.60
1959	190	110,000	20,900,000	9,100	570	6.25

Source: Apparecchi Elettrodomestici, anno 111, No. 8, Agosto 1960, page 64.

mercial laundries in Turin. Their per kilo rates for unfinished dry laundry ranged from 110 to 160 lire, while finished rates per kilo were from 170 to 235 lire. Average finished piece rates ranged from 160 to 200 lire per shirt and from 130 to 150 lire per sheet.

Although confident that his laundry would succeed, Mr. Paino recognized that the success in the United States of coin-op laundries did not necessarily mean that they would be successful in Italy. The standard of living, for example, was different and there were definite customs and cultural patterns in Italy that might retard the early acceptance of the automatic laundry idea. Several people had pointed to the disappointing sales of supermarkets which had recently opened in Turin as an example of what was in store for other American ideas that were transplanted to Italy. Mr. Paino, however, felt that lessons learned from the supermarket experience supported his belief in the future of automatic laundries. He noted that especially among middle and upper middle class housewives it was a "status symbol" to be seen in a su-

permarket. By going to a supermarket, the housewife proved that she was "modern" and "up to date."

Housewives did not continue to trade in supermarkets, according to Mr. Paino, because the great majority were without cars and found supermarkets too inconvenient. He reasoned that the need to feel "modern" which motivated many women to try supermarkets would also motivate them to try an automatic laundry. Once they had tried them, he was convinced women would continue to use the laundries.

INVESTMENT COSTS

Table 3 was Mr. Paino's estimation of the cost of equipping and installing a laundry with sixteen 9 lb. (4 kilos) machines, one 25 lb. (11 kilos) rug washer, six dryers and all necessary auxiliary equipment, leasehold improvements, and furniture. The estimated total investment cost of $30,900 shown in Table 3 was almost double that of the average cost of an equivalent sized U.S. laundry.

TABLE 3   Investment Required for Turin Automatic Laundry

Equipment	No. of Units	Cost per Unit	Total Cost
Four-kilo Speed Wash washers with meter	16	$ 524	$ 8,384
11-kilo washer with meter	1	1,179	1,179
Speed Wash dryers with meter	6	758	4,548
Water Extractor, with meter	1	758	758
Hot water storage tank	1	1,400	1,400
Water softener	1	2,213	2,213
Water heater	1	2,710	2,710
Soap and bleach dispenser	1	758	758
Outdoor electric sign	1	454	454
Indoor instructions signs		252	252
Furniture		179	179
Equipment Total:			22,835
Installation Costs and Leasehold Improvements			8,605
Total Investment Required			$30,900

Mr. Paino observed that "clearly the reason for the high investment cost is the expensive imported auxiliary equipment." A typical example of the cost of importing was the hot water storage tank shown below:

Cost of Imported Hot Water Storage Tank	
U.S. Factory Cost	$592
Freight: Factory to New York	62
Freight: New York to Genoa	300
Duty and Misc. Import Taxes	406
Total Landed Cost in Italy	$1,360

All equipment in Table 3 was imported. For the type of equipment necessary, no Italian source existed. Although Mr. Paino was concerned about the high costs, he was not completely discouraged. He did observe that "it is quite evident that if I am ever going to make a success of my Speed Wash franchise, I must find a cheaper Italian source of auxiliary equipment." He reasoned that investors would be concerned with the total cost of opening a laundry, and that lowering this figure by bringing down auxiliary equipment costs would lower the cost of entering the business, and therefore make it more attractive as an investment.

The cost of importing washers was not as high as the cost of the auxiliary equipment. The landed cost in Genoa of a $215 (factory price) Speed Wash automatic washer was $325. Mr. Paino planned to sell these machines to coin-op investors at the landed price plus a 38 percent markup.

Mr. Paino's estimate of monthly operating expenses is shown below:

Estimated Monthly Operating Expenses

Fixed Expenses	
Rent	$175
Maintenance	80
Salaries (attendant & janitor)	140[1]
Insurance	30
Depreciation	500
	$925

Variable Expenses

Utilities (gas, fuel, oil and electricity).
$ 0.04 per 20-min. washer cycle
$0.015 per 5-min. dryer cycle

---

[1]Assumes that there will be one attendant and that the laundry will be open 8 hours per day, 5 1/2 days per week. Attendant's salary was estimated at $110 per month. The janitor would work part time and would receive $30 per month.

TABLE 4

Italian Coins	U.S. $ Value (620 lire = $1)
5 lire	$0.008
10 "	0.016
20 "	0.032
50 "	0.08
100 "	0.16
500 "	0.80

The depreciation figure was based on five-year straight-line (20%) rates applied against the estimated total investment of $30,900. The variable expense for utilities was taken from an estimated income statement which ALD, Inc. (the largest U.S. coin-op distributor) mailed to prospective investors. Italian electricity costs were about the same as those in America, but gas costs were slightly higher. However, for estimating purposes, the figures given were considered satisfactory, although Mr. Paino felt they might be a bit on the low side.

EQUIPMENT CAPACITY

The four kilo washers had a 20-minute cycle, while the 11 kilo washer had a 30-minute cycle. The dryers had 5-minute cycles and were capable of drying the average four kilo load in two cycles. With a 24-hour operation, therefore, the theoretical capacity of each washer was 72 loads per day, while each dryer had a theoretical capacity of 144 four kilo loads per day. Loading time was the limiting factor on theoretical capacity. One estimate of actual washer capacity was published by ECON-O-WASH, a U.S. installer of coin-ops, who advised investors that a 20-minute cycle could produce about 60 loads per day.

The supply vending machine was designed to sell packets of soap and bleach. An American laundry detergent could be imported and put up in individual wash packets at a total cost of 20 lire ($0.032) per packet. There was a possibility that an Italian manufacturer might be able to deliver an equivalent soap for 15 lire ($0.024) per package. Bleach was available at a price of 20 lire per packet.

Coin meters were available and capable of accepting any combination of Italian coins, except five 100 lire coins or a single 500 lire coin.

PRICING

A critical problem for Mr. Paino was to decide what prices to charge for washing, drying, and supplies. Table 4 below shows Italian coins and their exchange value in U.S. dollars.

In his attempt to select prices that would maximize long run profitability, Mr. Paino was having considerable difficulty appraising elasticity of demand for his new service. He was aware of U.S. prices, but felt they were only a very rough guide in Italy, especially because of much higher Italian investment costs.

LAUNDROWASH S.p.A. (B)[1]

In August 1961, Mr. Mario Paino reviewed his first few months of operation and was concerned about what he could do to increase sales in his new laundry.[2] Mr. Paino had, three months earlier, opened in Turin what he believed to be the first American-style coin-operated automatic laundry in Italy. Initial results were extremely disappointing.

Mr. Paino had equipped the Turin laundry with 16 Speed Wash 4-kilo washers, one 11-kilo washer, six dryers, one water extractor, and a soap and bleach dispenser. The laundry opened on May 9, 1961. Prices were L.200 for the 4-kilo washers, L.400 for the 11-kilo washer, L.50 for each five-minute dryer cycle, and L.50 per packet for the soap and bleach. The water extractor, which was equipped with a L.50 coin meter, was not used due to mechanical difficulties.[3] Hours of operation were from 8:00 to 12:00, and from 15:00 to 19:00, Monday through Saturday. Local regulations made it illegal to operate on Sunday.

ADVERTISING AND PROMOTION

Pre-opening advertising and promotion consisted of movie slides announcing Laundrowash, two pamphlets describing the new laundry, and free wash coupons which were inserted with the two pamphlets into 1,000 mail boxes in the Via Rosselli area. Several days after the laundry opened, the slides were discontinued, and no more free wash coupons were distributed.

One of the pamphlets opened to three pages printed on both sides. An English translation of this pamphlet is reproduced in Appendix 1. The second pamphlet was larger and opened to two pages printed on both sides. In addition to a large two-colour picture of the interior of the laundry, it repeated most of the text of the three page pamphlet.

There were 86 redemptions of free wash coupons during the first week of business. In the second week this number fell to 20, and in successive weeks it dropped to 10, six, and one. The last coupon was redeemed in July, bringing the total redemption to 123.

OPERATING RESULTS

Laundrowash sales, including free washes, for the first 13 weeks are shown in Table 1. Although complete expense reports were not available, preliminary data indicated that fixed expenses were as expected ($925 per month, including $500 for depreciation), while variable expenses were around $0.04 per twenty-minute washer cycle and $0.015 per five-minute dryer cycle.

Mr. Paino was extremely discouraged by the laundry's performance. He estimated that for the month ending August 6th, 1961, his "out-of-pocket" expenses exceeded income by almost $100, and that including depreciation, operating losses were at least $600.

As a rough estimate, Mr. Paino calculated that sales would have to increase to L.676,000 per month in order for the store to break even.[4] His break-even calculation, which

---

[2]See Laundrowash S.p.A. (A)

[3]As of mid-August, Mr. Paino had not been able to locate a mechanic who could repair the machine.

[4]Break even: the point at which fixed plus variable cost equals total revenue.

TABLE 1 Laundrowash Sales

1961, Week Ending	WASHING OPERATIONS			INCOME			TOTAL	
	Paid	Free	Total	Washers (Lire)	Dryers (Lire)	Soap (Lire)	Lire	U.S.$ Equivalent*
May 14	51	86	137	10,200	3,700	3,400	17,300	28.00
May 21	124	20	144	24,800	5,650	10,000	40,450	65.00
May 28	133		133	26,600	6,450	12,350	45,400	73.00
June 4	159	10	169	31,800	6,450	13,800	52,050	84.00
June 11	171	6	177	34,200	7,200	15,200	56,600	91.00
June 18	217	1	218	43,400	6,200	19,200	68,800	110.00
June 25	217		217	43,400	7,350	17,600	68,350	109.00
July 2	216	1	217	43,200	6,850	19,100	69,150	111.00
July 9	232		232	46,400	4,150	19,800	70,350	113.00
July 16	176		176	35,600	4,400	14,250	54,250	88.00
July 23	162		162	32,400	5,000	13,300	50,700	82.00
July 30	226		226	45,200	6,700	14,300	66,200	107.00
August 6	225		225	45,000	7,300	14,750	67,050	108.00

*One U.S.$ = L.620.

Source: Company records.

is reproduced in Table 2, was figured on the basis of washer and dryer operation only.

Mr. Paino was puzzled by the laundry's failure to achieve a profitable sales level. Although he was unhappy about the continuing losses, he remained firm in his belief that coin-ops could be profitable in Italy. He felt that a major problem was educating people to accept coin-ops. For example, women were observed entering Laundrowash with their laundry concealed in suitcases because they were afraid of being seen on the street with dirty laundry.

Mr. Paino wondered if an advertising and promotion campaign was needed to overcome the public's resistance to coin-ops. One promotion possibility was a formal opening ceremony with the dignitaries from the U.S. Consulate and Italian Foreign Trade Department as guests of honour.

TABLE 2 Break-Even Calculation for Laundrowash S.p.A.*

Break-even: the point at which fixed plus variable expenses = total revenue.

Assumption: Each wash load L.200 ($0.32) is matched with 10 minutes drying time L.100 ($0.16), producing a total revenue of $0.48 per "load".

Lex X = the number of break-even "loads" per month.

(Revenue per load × No. of loads = Fixed Costs + variable costs)

$0.48(X) = $925 + $0.07(X)

$0.41X = $925

X = 2256

No. of break-even "loads" per month = 2256

Break-even revenue per month = $1083 (L.676,800)

*Excluding soap, bleach, water extractor, and 11-kilo washer sales.

Source: Mr. Paino's records.

Appendix 1: Text of Laundrowash Pamphlet

(Translation from the Italian by Miss G. Schori.)

Page 1: Announcing a shop for Automatic Laundry equipped with commercial laundry machines.

Welcome neighbors!! to your Speed Wash automatic laundry, open every day of the week.

Page 2: Welcome neighbors!

To your Speed Wash self service laundry, designed and furnished only for you, yes, it is your shop, and you should feel right at home.

Now you can do your own laundry just as you do at home, with the assurance that there are plenty of machines, big dryers, and unlimited hot and soft water. You can save 50 percent doing your laundry this way.

Finished are the days when you have to do laundry in small loads. Now you can use as many washing machines as you need, and you will be through with your laundry in less than an hour.

The cost is so little that it would be more expensive to do it at home even if you had a free washing and drying machine. We can save you money, because we do not need to pay personnel. We offer you this saving and reduce the cost of your laundry.

Page 3: The 4 ingredients of a good wash:

A really good wash requires:

—a good plant
—a good detergent
—plenty of hot water
—soft water

Our laundry is furnished with the best equipment available, constructed with the utmost care by Speed Wash. The Speed Wash washer does not have an agitator that damages your laundry, and dirty water is removed so that it does not go through your laundry as it does in conventional machines. You need 77 litres of water at 80°C to wash 4 kilograms dry weight. The heaters you have in your house have a capacity ranging from 80–120 litres, of which only 45 to 50 litres are warm enough to provide a good wash. You would need at least 6 hours to wash a weekly laundry of 20 kilos because you would have to wait for your boiler to heat the water. The Speed Wash laundry has enough water to provide continuous washing for each machine in the laundry.

Page 4: To dry your laundry at home you need many hours. Instead your Speed Wash laundry has big commercial dryers which circulate your laundry in a big cylinder, drying it quickly and giving a soft dry wash. The water used on the Speed Wash automatic laundry is as filtered and soft as rain water. We use soft water because hard water minerals make the soap less efficient and leave deposits. The Speed Wash machine NEEDS LESS THAN ONE CUP OF DETERGENT. The reason this is so is that with soft water you get a better wash with less soap. This is another saving for you.

DO NOT USE TOO MUCH DETERGENT: you will only get too many bubbles. Your Speed Wash automatic laundry was created to lighten your work and lessen your fatigue, from the boring days you spent doing laundry. Remember that this is your neighborhood washing place. Cooperate with your neighbors to make it and keep it a nice and gay place where you can do your weekly laundry.

Page 5:   You will obtain a whiter and cleaner wash using the Speed Wash commercial laundry. This laundry uses purified soft water that is as soft as rain.

Page 6:   The woman who wants the best of everything uses the Speed Wash Laundrowash.

* You will get a better wash than you get at home.

* You can do your entire weekly wash in an hour by using several machines.

* You will get scientifically clean, deodorized clothes with machines that are frequently sterilized.

* You can dry your clothes cheaply and quickly.

* You can do the laundry yourself with all the advantages, and none of the disadvantages of home.

* You will reduce the cost of your wash by 50 percent and do your wash in a pleasant atmosphere with your friends and neighbors.

3

ECONOMIC ENVIRONMENT

Free trade, one of the greatest blessings which a government can confer on a people, is in almost every country unpopular.

Lord Macaulay, 1800–1859

INTRODUCTION

A major characteristic of the global marketers' world is the diversity of marketing environments in which they conduct their operations. The economic dimensions of this world market environment are of vital importance. This chapter examines the characteristics of the world economic environment from a marketing perspective.

The global marketer is fortunate in having a substantial body of data available that charts the nature of the environment on a country-by-country basis. Every country has national accounts data indicating, at a minimum, estimates of gross national product. Also available on a global basis are demographic data indicating the number of people, their distribution by age category, and the rates of population growth. National accounts and demographic data do not exhaust the types of economic data available. A single source, *The Statistical Yearbook of the United Nations,* contains global data on labor force, agriculture, mining, manufacturing, construction, energy production and consumption, internal and external trade, railroad and air transport, wages and prices, health, housing, education, communications (mail, telegraph, and telephone), and mass communications by book, film, radio, and television. In general, all these data are available for the richer industrialized countries. The less developed a country is, the scarcer is the availability of economic data. In the least developed countries of the world, one cannot be certain of obtaining anything more than basic national accounts and demographic and external trade data. Nevertheless, in considering the world economic environment, the initial problem is not one of an absence of data but rather of an abundance. This chapter will identify the most salient characteristics of the economic environment to provide the framework for further consideration of the elements of a multinational marketing program.

THE WORLD ECONOMY—AN OVERVIEW[1]

The world economy has undergone revolutionary changes during the past 50 years. Perhaps the greatest and most profound change is the emergence of global markets and global competitors who have steadily displaced their local competitors. The integration of the world economy has increased from less than 10 percent at the turn of this century to approximately 50 percent today. Even as recently as 25 years ago, the world was far less integrated than it is today. As a young man working in Europe and in Africa in the 1960s, I was struck by how *different* everything was. There were many companies, many products, and great differentiation. Take automobiles, for example. In 1960, the European Renault, Citroen, Peugeot, Morris, Volvo, and others were radically different than the American Chevrolet, Ford, or Plymouth, or the Japanese Toyota or Nissan. These were different cars for different markets. Today, the world car is a reality. A few companies offer the same cars to world customers.

The changes continue. Within the past decade, there have been four major changes:

- Capital movements rather than trade have become the driving force of the world economy.
- Production has become "uncoupled" from employment.
- Primary products have become "uncoupled" from the industrial economy.
- The world economy is in control. The macroeconomics of the nation-state are no longer in control.

These remarkable changes are contrary to much of the received doctrine of economic theory, and they are of great significance and importance to government and business practitioners. Practitioners cannot wait until there is a new theory—the likelihood of success is much greater when actions are based on the new reality of the changed world economy.

The first change is the increased volume of capital movements. World trade is greater than ever before. Trade in goods and so called "invisibles" (services) is running at roughly $3 trillion per year. But the London Eurodollar[2] market turns

---

[1] See the excellent article "The Changed World Economy" by Peter F. Drucker, *Foreign Affairs,* Spring 1986.

[2] A Eurodollar is a U.S. dollar held outside the United States. The difference between a Eurodollar and a U.S. dollar is that the latter is subject to U.S. banking regulations while the former is not.

over $300 billion each working day or $75 trillion per year—25 times that of world trade. In addition, foreign exchange transactions are running at approximately $150 billion per day worldwide, which is $35 trillion per year or 12 times the volume of world trade in goods and services. There is an inescapable conclusion in these data: Capital movements far exceed the volume of trade finance. This explains the recent bizarre episode of U.S. trade deficits and a continually rising dollar. In the past, when a country ran a deficit on its trade accounts, its currency would depreciate in value. Today, it is capital movements rather than trade that determine currency value. Capital seeks a return, and the U.S. interest rates and safety have attracted enough capital to substantially increase the value of the dollar in spite of the U.S. trade deficit.

The second change is that although employment in manufacturing remains steady or has declined, production continues to grow. The pattern in agriculture where fewer and fewer produce more and more continues. In the United States manufacturing holds a steady 23–24 percent of GNP. This is true of all the other major industrial economies as well. Manufacturing is not in decline—it is employment in manufacturing that is in decline. Countries like the U.K., which have tried to hold onto blue-collar employment in manufacturing, have lost both production and jobs for their efforts, a bitter fruit indeed.

The third change is the "uncoupling" of the primary products economy from the industrial economy. Commodity prices have collapsed to levels that are as low as during the Great Depression. There is a major depression in the primary products economy, and it seems as if it has had almost no impact on the industrial economy, in contrast to the past when a sharp drop in raw material prices would bring on a worldwide depression in the industrial economy.

Finally, the greatest change of all, and the reason for this book, is the emergence of the world economy as the dominant economic unit. Simply put, this means that companies and countries that recognize this fact have the greatest chance of success. The real secret of the success of Germany and Japan is their focus on the world economy and world markets; the first priority of their governments and businesses has been their competitive position in the world. In contrast, the U.K. and to a lesser extent the United States have focused upon domestic objectives and priorities to the exclusion of global competitive position. The difference is that private and public policy makers in the United States and U.K. have not really understood the new reality, while those in Japan and Germany have.

MARKET CHARACTERISTICS

The Location of Income

In charting a plan for multinational market expansion, the single most valuable economic variable for most products is income. For some products, particularly those that have a very low unit cost, population is a more valuable predictor of market potential than income. Cigarettes are an excellent example of this type of product. Nevertheless, for the vast range of industrial and consumer products in international markets today, the single most valuable and important indicator of potential is income.

Income is not an accurate or a precise measure of potential; it is only an approximate indicator. For example, the United States per capita GNP is approximately 10 times that of Brazil. This figure is of initial interest to a manufacturer of light sockets and light bulbs and suggests a U.S. market 10 times larger on a per capita basis. However, the average number of light sockets per home in Brazil is 5 versus 27 in the United States, a difference of 5.5 times. When market potential is estimated on the basis of the number of Brazilian homes, the size of the Brazilian market can be estimated more precisely. With additional data on the average utilization of light bulbs in Brazilian households, the light-bulb marketer with data on the number of homes could identify the exact potential in Brazil. Without the household data, the marketer could estimate roughly on the basis of total GNP.

Gross national product and other measures of national income converted to U.S. dollars or any other numéraire should ideally be calculated on the basis of purchasing power parities (i.e., what the currency will buy in the country of issue) or through direct real product comparisons. This would provide an actual comparison of the standards of living in the countries of the world. Since these data are not available in regular statistical reports, throughout this book we use, instead, conversion of local currency measured at the year-end U.S. dollar foreign exchange rate. The reader must remember that exchange rates equate, at best, the prices of internationally traded goods and services. They often bear little relationship to the prices of those goods and services not entering the international trade, which form the bulk of the national product in most countries. Agricultural output and services, in particular, are generally priced lower in relation to industrial output in developing countries than in industrial countries. Furthermore, agriculture typically accounts for the largest share of output in developing countries. Thus the use of exchange rates tends to exaggerate differences in real income between less developed and more developed countries.

The United Nations' International Comparison Project (ICP) developed a sophisticated method for measuring total expenditure, which has been used to derive more reliable and directly comparable estimates of per capita income. The World Bank has published a comparison of ICP findings with its own *Atlas* figures based on exchange rate conversion. Table 3–1 compares World Bank GNP data based on exchange rate conversion of local currency GNP with the ICP's more sophisticated measure. India's real income, for example, is three times greater than that indicated by the exchange comparison. The ICP income figure is one and one-half times greater than that indicated by the exchange comparison. In short, the use of exchange rates tends to distort real income or standard-of-living measures. Nevertheless, the use of exchange rates does provide a rough measure of income levels and has the merit of being an easily obtainable figure.

Beyond the exchange distortion, there is the distortion of money itself as an indicator of the welfare and standard of living of a people. A visit to a mud house

**TABLE 3–1 Per Capita Currency Conversion Method (*Atlas* GNP)
Compared with International Comparison Project Method
(ICP-GDP), 1970 and 1974 (indices U.S. = 100)**

	1970		1974	
Country	GDP ICP (1)*	GNP Atlas (2)†	GDP ICP (3)‡	GNP Atlas (4)§
Kenya	5.72	2.94	6.84	3.03
India	7.12	2.31	6.28	2.02
Colombia	15.90	7.12	17.57	7.55
Hungary	40.30	30.60	58.20	32.70
Italy	45.80	42.00	47.40	42.30
United Kingdom	60.30	53.40	62.00	53.80
Japan	61.50	55.40	64.00	61.00
Germany, Federal Republic of	74.70	94.00	75.40	93.90
France	75.00	76.00	77.30	81.60
United States	100.00	100.00	100.00	100.00

*GDP ICP.

†*Atlas* 1970 current price estimates based on 1973–1975 prices and exchange rates.

‡CP 1970 estimates updated using gross domestic product deflators and 1974 exchange rates.

§*Atlas* 1974 current price estimates based on 1973–1975 prices and exchange rates.

All data except 1970 ICP are special World Bank estimates not based on *Atlas* method.

Source: *1976 World Bank Atlas*, p. 21.

in Tanzania will reveal many of the things that money can buy: radios, an iron bed frame, a corrugated metal roof, factory-made beer, bicycles, shoes, snap-shots, soft drinks, and razor blades. But Tanzania's per capita income of $250 does not reflect the fact that instead of utility bills, Tanzanians have the local well and the sun. Instead of nursing homes, tradition and custom ensure that elderly are cared for by their relatives. Instead of expensive doctors and hospitals, there is the witch doctor and healer. Much of the wealth of the rich industrialized countries is really only a free good or service in a poor country that has been "monetized."

With these qualifications in mind, the reader is referred to Table 3–2, which indicates the location of world income by region in 1984. The striking fact revealed by this table is the concentration of income in the three large regions of the world—North America, Europe, and Japan, which accounted for 69 percent of global income but only 17 percent of the world's population.

The concentration of wealth in a handful of large industrialized countries is the most striking characteristic of the global economic environment. This characteristic appears again if one examines the world regions and again if one examines the distribution of wealth and income within countries. The United States is, of course,

TABLE 3–2 Global Income and Population, 1984

MARKETS	GDP $ BILLION	GDP PER CAPITA	PERCENTAGE OF WORLD GDP	POPULATION (MILLION)	PERCENTAGE OF WORLD POPULATION
North America	3959	15,086	35	262	6
Western Europe	2777	6553	24	424	9
Japan	1233	10,315	11	120	3
Sub Total	7968	9890	69	806	18
Asia (Excl. Japan)	901	359	8	2507	54
USSR	699	2536	6	276	6
South America 1	699	1758	6	398	9
Middle East 2	414	2867	4	144	3
Africa 3	322	793	3	406	9
Eastern Europe	279	2462	2	113	2
Oceania	190	10,188	2	19	0
Sub Total	3503	907	31	3862	83
Global Total	11,471	2,457	101*	4668	101**

EXPANSIONS OF MARKETS 1,2,3	GDP $ BILLION	GDP PER CAPITA	PERCENTAGE OF REGION GDP	POPULATION (MILLION)	PERCENTAGE OF REGION POPULATION
South America 1					
Argentina	76	2680	11	28	7
Brazil	209	1562	30	134	34
Mexico	175	2243	25	78	20
R.O.S.A.*	238	1518	34	157	39
South America	699	1758	100	398	100
Middle East 2					
Egypt	38	824	9	46	32
Iran	122	2840	30	43	30
Saudi Arabia	108	10,404	26	10	7
R.O.M.E.*	145	3246	35	45	31
Middle East	414	2867	100	144	100
Africa 3					
Algeria	38	1725	12	22	5
Libya	30	8486	9	4	1
Nigeria	88	953	27	92	23
South Africa	73	2848	23	33	8
R.O.A.*	94	368	29	255	63
Africa	322	793	100	405	100

*Rest of South America, Middle East, Africa.

**Error due to rounding.

Sources: *Business International, Indicator of Market Size 1986; World Bank Atlas, 1986*; table prepared by author.

a colossus in North America, as is the Soviet Union in Eastern Europe. These countries accounted for 91 percent and 68 percent, respectively, of their region's GDP (gross domestic products) in 1980. In Western Europe, France, West Germany, and the United Kingdom accounted for almost three-quarters of that region's GDP. In Asia, Japan accounted for 58 percent of the 1980 GDP. In Latin America, Argentina, Brazil, and Mexico accounted for 72 percent of LAFTA (Latin America Free Trade Area) GDP in 1980 and so on.

An examination of the distribution of wealth within countries again reveals patterns of income concentration, particularly in the less developed countries outside the Communist bloc. Adelman and Morris found that the average share of GNP accruing to the poorest 20 percent of the population in less developed countries included in their study was 5.6 percent as compared with 56.0 percent going to the top 20 percent. The income of the bottom 20 percent was about one-fourth of what it would have been had income been distributed uniformly throughout the population. Their study suggests that the relationship between the share of income at the lowest 20 percent and economic development varies with the level of development. Economic development is associated with increases in the share of the bottom 20 percent only after relatively high levels of socioeconomic development have been attained. At the early stages of the development process, economic development works to the *relative* disadvantage of the lowest income groups. In Brazil, for example, the poorest 20 percent of the population received 3.5 percent of total national income, while the top 20 percent received 61.5 percent.[3]

Adelman and Morris found that countries with a higher share of national income accruing to the poorest 20 percent were characterized by low or moderate degrees of dualism in their economies and by the pursuit of agriculturally oriented foreign trade policies. Countries in which the smallest portion of national income (2 percent) accrued to the lowest 20 percent were characterized by sharp dualism in their economies, which were centered on foreign finance and foreign-managed exploitation of natural resources.

Throughout the ages, people have spent most of their energy making a living—finding food, clothing, and shelter. An old Armenian folk saying, "Making a living is like taking food out of a lion's mouth," captures this reality. Although the problem of poverty has not been eliminated in all the industrialized countries, those countries with homogeneous populations and an advanced collective social conscience have indeed eliminated poverty within their borders.

Today a different type of inequality has impressed itself on the conscience of the world—the vast and growing gap between the rich and the poor nations. There are several crucial questions concerning the present economic distance between these nations. When did it evolve? How large is it? What were the dimensions of time and space that brought it about? Can it be bridged in the foreseeable future?

---

[3]Irma Adelman and Cynthia Taft Morris, "An Anatomy of Income Distribution Patterns in Developing Nations—A Summary of Findings," International Bank for Reconstruction and Development, International Development Association, Economic Staff Working Paper No. 116, September 23, 1971.

At the beginning of the Industrial Revolution 200 years ago, the economic landscape of the world was relatively flat in contrast to the present uneven world where there are very high mountains and very low plains. Even as late as 1860 more than half the population of northwestern Europe and the United States was engaged in agriculture—not much different from the share of the population engaged in agriculture in the preindustrial countries at present. Yields per hectare of land, share of industries in total output, and illiteracy ratios were only marginally different. The peoples of Western Europe, for example, did not have the means to be much better off economically than the rest of the world. World output of pig iron in 1850 was only 4.6 million tons, and half of it was produced in Great Britain. The most advanced countries were still in the last days of the Iron Age. Even by 1870, world output of steel was no more than 700,000 tons—less than one-fifth of India's output in 1961.

Empirical evidence about the income levels in industrialized countries supports this picture. Professor S. S. Kuznets has, by applying known rates of growth, extrapolated backward the per capita income of the industrial countries in the early 1950s. The data in the following list show the years when such regression (extrapolation backward) yields a per capita income of $200 in comparable 1952–1954 prices:

United States	1832	Sweden	1889
United Kingdom	1837	Italy	1909
France	1852	Japan	1955
West Germany	1886		

A weighted average and straight-line extrapolation suggest that the average per capita income in industrial countries as a group was about $170 in 1850, or only 70 percent higher than that of the preindustrial countries in the early 1960s. If the United Kingdom and the United States are excluded, the average income in the rest of this group would have been $150 in 1850.

Although these estimates make no allowance for free sunshine and the lower requirements for survival in the warmer climates, it seems clear that the economic landscape of the 1850s was relatively flat. The actual conditions of life for the masses of the two worlds could not have been significantly different. This is in sharp contrast to the condition of today's world economic landscape with the sunny mountaintops of the industrial countries and the dark valleys of the preindustrial world.

Since 1850 the distribution of population between the industrial and the preindustrial countries has not altered significantly. But between 1850 and 1980, the industrial countries' share of world income increased from 39 to 82 percent. The annual compound rates of growth during this period, which have so profoundly altered the world's distribution of income, were 2.7 percent in total output, and 1.8 percent in per capita output. The magnitude of change as compared with the previous 6,000 years of our civilized existence is enormous; over one-third of the real income and about two-thirds of the industrial output produced by people throughout civilized history were generated in the industrialized countries in the last century. The significance of these growth figures is that relatively small average annual rates of growth have transformed the economic geography of the world. What the industrial countries have done is to systematize economic growth, or, put another way, they have established a process of continuous, gradual change. Patel has calculated that India, one of the poorest countries in the world, could reach U.S. income levels by growing at an average rate of 5 to 6 percent in real terms for 40 to 50 years. This is no more than the lifetime of an average Indian, and much less than half the lifetime of an average American. To point out the possible does not of course make it a probable event, but it does underline the fact that economic distance created by sustained growth can also be removed by sustained growth, as Japan has so dramatically demonstrated in recent years.

The world has changed enormously from biblical times when Saint Matthew observed, ''For ye have the poor always with you.'' Today, much more than was true 2,000 years ago, wealth and income are concentrated regionally, nationally, and within nations. The implications of this reality are crucial for the global marketer. A company that decides to diversify geographically can accomplish this objective by establishing operations in a handful of national markets. The 10 largest countries in the world account for 70 percent of world income, and the 5 largest account for 63 percent (see Table 3–3). These data underline the fact that a company can be global in the sense that its income is derived from a number of countries instead of being concentrated in a single national market, and at the same time be operating in ten or fewer countries. Another inescapable implication of these data is that any company that decides to enter a large number of national markets is going to find itself managing small-scale operations.

TABLE 3–3 1982 GNP of the Ten Most Populous Countries in the World

	1982 GNP AT MARKET PRICES (U.S. $ MILLIONS)	PERCENT OF TOTAL
1. United States	3,047,490	28.91
2. U.S.S.R.	na	na
3. Japan	1,190,650	11.30
4. Germany, Federal Republic of	757,210	7.18
5. France	627,210	5.95
6. United Kingdom	536,790	5.09
7. Italy	382,230	3.63
8. China, People's Republic of	302,630	2.87
9. Brazil	274,610	2.61
10. Canada	278,960	2.65
11. Other	3,141,711	29.81
TOTAL:	7,397,780	70.19
World Total:	10,539,491	100.00%

Data Source: *World Bank Atlas,* Washington, D.C., 1985. Table prepared by author.

The Location of Population

For products whose price is low enough, population is a more important variable than income in determining market potential. Although population is not as concentrated as income, there is, in terms of size of nations, a pattern of considerable concentration. The 10 most populous countries in the world account for roughly two-thirds of the world's population today.

People have inhabited the earth for over 2.5 million years. The number of human beings has been small during most of this period. In Christ's lifetime there were approximately 300 million people on earth, or roughly one-third of the number of people on Mainland China today. World population increased tremendously during the eighteenth and nineteenth centuries. By 1850 world population had reached 1 billion. Between 1850 and 1925 it had increased to 2 billion, and from 1925 to 1960 it had increased to 3 billion. World population is now approximately 4 billion and at the present rate of growth will reach 7 billion by the end of the century. There is no necessary correlation between country population and income level. India and China, the two most populous countries in the world, have low incomes. The United States and the Union of Soviet Socialist Republics, the third and fourth most populous countries, have high incomes.

BALANCE OF PAYMENTS

The balance of payments is a record of all of the economic transactions between residents of a country and the rest of the world. The U.S. and the Japanese balance of payments for the period 1980–1985 is shown in Tables 3–4 and 3–5.

The balance of payments is divided into a so-called "current" and "capital" account. The current account is a record of all of the recurring merchandise and service trade and private gifts and public aid transactions between countries. The capital account records all of the direct investment (investments that involve control, which for balance-of-payments reporting purposes is defined as any investment that involves 20 percent or more of the equity of a company), portfolio investment (investments that involve less than 20 percent of the equity of a company), and other short- and long-term capital flows. The changes in reserves and the so-called net errors and omissions are the accounts that make the balance of payments balance. In general, a country accumulates reserves when it is in surplus above the line (i.e., the net of the current and capital account transactions) and it gives up reserves when it is in deficit above the line.

The important fact to recognize about the overall balance of payments is that it is always in balance. Imbalances occur in subsets of the overall balance. For example, a commonly reported balance is the balance on merchandise trade or, in short, the trade balance (line 3 in Tables 3–4 and 3–5.)

As you can see in Tables 3–4 and 3–5, since 1980, Japan has had an increasing surplus on its merchandise trade balance while the United States has had an increasing deficit. Japan has offset its growing trade surplus with an outflow of capital (see line 14) while the United States has offset its trade deficit with an inflow of capital (see line 14). For both countries, the balance of payments balances, but the two countries have ended up in a different position vis a vis each other as a result of the different balances they have generated. The United States owns an increasing quantity of Japanese consumer and industrial products, while Japan owns more U.S. land, real estate, and equity in both marketable and nonmarketable securities. The United States has been a spender, and Japan has been a saver.

TABLE 3–4   U.S. Balance of Payments 1980–85

	CURRENT ACCOUNT					
	1980	*1981*	*1982*	*1983*	*1984*	*1985*
1. Merchandise: Export F.O.B.	224.27	237.10	211.20	201.83	219.90	214.41
2. Merchandise: Import F.O.B.	−249.77	−265.07	−247.70	−268.91	−332.41	−338.86
3. Trade Balance	−25.50	−27.97	−36.50	−67.08	−112.51	−124.45
4. Other Goods, Services, and Income: Credit	118.21	138.69	138.82	129.90	140.24	144.10
5. Other Goods, Services, and Income: Debit	−83.29	−96.91	−101.63	−101.96	−122.05	−122.45
6. Services Balance	34.92	41.78	37.19	27.94	18.19	21.65
7. Private Unrequited Transfers	−1.03	−.92	−1.17	−.99	−1.43	−1.61
8. Official Unrequited Transfers	−6.55	−6.52	−7.70	−8.49	−10.74	−13.37
9. Net current Account = 3+6+7+8	1.84	6.37	−8.18	−48.62	−106.49	−117.78
	CAPITAL ACCOUNT					
10. Direct Investment	−2.30	15.57	16.09	11.59	21.50	−.90
11. Portfolio Investment	2.85	2.84	−.69	4.96	28.66	64.26
12. Other Long-Term Capital	−9.03	−18.97	−22.68	−17.84	−13.11	7.64
13. Other Short-Term Capital	−27.43	−27.33	−17.77	31.70	42.68	29.38
14. Net Capital Account	−35.91	−27.89	−25.05	30.41	79.73	100.38
15. *Total Change in Reserves*	−7.64	−3.21	−3.86	.45	−.97	−8.21
16. Net Errors and Omissions	25.01	20.28	35.26	14.16	27.28	23.03

Data Source: International Financial Statistics, August, 1986.

TABLE 3–5   Japan Balance of Payments 1980–85

	CURRENT ACCOUNT					
	1980	*1981*	*1982*	*1983*	*1984*	*1985*
1. Merchandise: Export F.O.B.	126.74	149.52	137.66	145.47	168.29	173.93
2. Merchandise: Import F.O.B.	−124.61	−129.56	−119.58	−114.01	−124.03	−117.92
3. Trade Balance	2.13	19.96	18.08	31.46	44.26	56.00
4. Other Goods, Services, and Income: Credit	31.49	39.78	41.09	37.59	42.10	45.55
5. Other Goods, Services, and Income: Debit	−42.84	−53.35	−50.94	−46.70	−49.85	−50.64
6. Services Balance	−11.35	−13.57	−9.85	−9.11	−7.75	−5.09
7. Private Unrequited Transfers	−0.24	−0.21	−0.09	−0.18	−0.13	−0.28
8. Official Unrequited Transfers	−1.29	−1.41	−1.29	−1.37	−1.38	−1.37
9. Net current Account = 3+6+7+8	−10.75	+4.77	+6.85	20.80	34.99	49.26
	CAPITAL ACCOUNT					
10. Direct Investment	−2.11	−4.71	−4.10	−3.20	−5.97	−5.87
11. Portfolio Investment	9.43	7.67	0.84	−2.90	−23.96	−41.74
12. Other Long-Term Capital	−4.93	−9.41	−12.99	−12.63	−20.07	−16.08
13. Other Short-Term Capital	16.49	4.89	0.05	−2.59	13.44	10.09
14. Net Capital Account	18.88	−1.56	−16.2	21.32	−36.56	−53.6
15. *Total Change in Reserves*	−5.11	−3.57	4.87	−1.27	−1.83	−0.28
16. Net Errors and Omissions	−3.10	.43	4.65	2.07	3.68	3.92

Data Source: International Financial Statistics, August, 1986.

TRADE PATTERNS

Since the end of World War II, world merchandise trade has grown faster than world production. The faster rate of growth in merchandise trade is more pronounced for manufacturing than for mining or agriculture (see Table 3–6).

The regional pattern of merchandise trade is dominated by industrial area country exports to other industrial area countries (47 percent in 1985). The second largest share of world trade is developing area exports to industrial areas (15 percent in 1985). The third largest share is industrial area exports to developing areas (13 percent

TABLE 3—6   Value of World Merchandise Trade by Areas (Billion dollars and percentages)

	EXPORTS (F.O.B)	IMPORTS (C.I.F.)
	Value 1985	Value 1985
WORLD	1 910	1 990
of which:		
Industrial area	1 230	1 333
Developing area	440	410
Fuels	196	69
Other products	244	341
Eastern trading area	202	205

Sources: IMF, *International Financial Statistics;* UN, *Monthly Bulletin of Statistics;* OECD, *Monthly Statistics of Foreign Trade;* national statistics.

TABLE 3—7   The Regional Pattern of World Merchandise Trade in 1984 and 1985 (Percentages)

Importing area	Exporting area	CHANGE OVER PREVIOUS YEAR		Share in 1985[a]
		1984	1985	
World	World	5½	½	100
Industrial area	Industrial area	9	5	47.0
	Developing area	4½	−4	15.1
	Eastern trading area	5	−7	3.0
Developing area	Industrial area	−1½	−6	12.7
	Developing area	1	−7	6.3
	Eastern trading area	3	−7	2.0
Eastern trading area	Industrial area	5	11	3.1
	Developing area	6½	10	1.4
	Eastern trading area	3½	1	5.5

[a]Shares do not add to 100 percent because trade of Australia, New Zealand, and South Africa is not covered in regional trade flows.

Source: GATT Secretariat estimates.

in 1985). A summary of regional patterns of world merchandise trade is shown in Table 3–7.

The top 10 leading exporters and importing countries of the world are the advanced industrialized countries. However, the second 10 countries include developing and less developed countries such as Taiwan, Korea, China, and Brazil. The twenty leading exporters and importers in world merchandise trade in 1985 are shown in Table 3–8.

**TABLE 3–8 Twenty Leading Exporters and Importers in World Mechandise Trade in 1985
(Billion dollars and percentages)**

EXPORTS (F.O.B.)	VALUE	1985 OVER 1984	IMPORTS (C.I.F.)	VALUE	1985 OVER 1984
United States (1)	206	− 2.2	United States (1)	359	+ 6.0
Germany (Fed. Rep.) (2)	182	+ 7.0	Germany (Fed. Rep.) (2)	157	+ 3.5
Japan (3)	176	+ 3.3	Japan (3)	129	− 5.1
France (5)	102	+ 4.2	United Kingdom (4)	109	+ 3.9
United Kingdom (4)	101	+ 7.4	France (5)	106	+ 2.6
Canada (7)	88	+ 1.5	Italy (6)	90	+ 7.3
USSR (6)	86	− 6.0	Canada (8)	82	+ 7.1
Italy (8)	78	+ 6.7	USSR (7)	79	− 0.9
Netherlands (9)	68	+ 3.2	Netherlands (9)	65	+ 4.0
Belgium-Luxembourg (10)	53	+ 2.7	Belgium-Luxembourg (10)	55	+ 0.1
Taiwan (12)	31	+ 0.8	China (19)	40	+ 54.9
Korea (Rep. of) (14)	30	+ 3.6	Korea (Rep. of) (12)	31	+ 1.9
Sweden (13)	30	+ 2.9	Switzerland (13)	31	+ 4.0
Hong Kong (15)	30	+ 6.6	Spain (14)	30	+ 3.6
Switzerland (17)	27	+ 6.1	Hong Kong (16)	30	+ 4.0
China (18)	27	+ 6.7	Sweden (18)	28	+ 7.2
Brazil (16)	26	− 5.0	Singapore (15)	26	− 8.3
Spain (23)	24	+ 2.6	Saudi Arabia (11)	[25]	[− 26]
Saudi Arabia (11)	24	− 35.0	Australia (17)	24	− 1.0
Singapore (20)	23	− 5.1	Taiwan (20)	20	− 8.5

Note: Figures in parentheses ( ) indicate rank in 1984.

Sources: IMF, *International Financial Statistics*; UN, *Monthly Bulletin of Statistics*; GATT Secretariat estimates.

Table 3–9 shows the relationship between the growth of real gross domestic product and export volume in the period 1973–1984 for the 20 leading exporters listed in Table 3–9. The positive relationship between export growth and economic growth is quite pronounced. The reason for the relationship is that export growth represents the ability to penetrate foreign markets. This ability must be based on more than a protected home market: It requires a competitive advantage and the ability to project this advantage into a competitive market. The ability to compete is a reflection of applied energy, superior skills, organization, and effectiveness. This combination of elements creates wealth and economic growth.

Table 3–10 shows global exports and imports by country or region for 1983. The importance of the triad countries (North America, Western Europe, and Japan) is quite pronounced: They accounted for 66 percent of world exports and 68 percent of world imports.

Table 3–11 shows United States exports and imports for 1984 and 1985. The balances are shown at the end of the table. The striking fact about U.S. trade in

TABLE 3–9 Export and Economic Growth of Leading Exporters, 1973–1984 (Average annual percentage change)

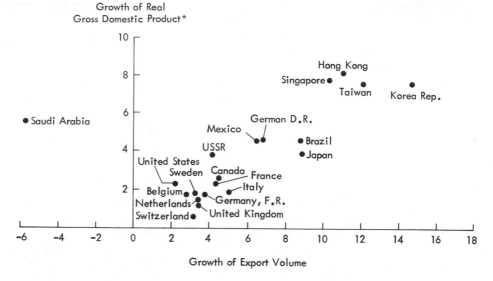

*USSR and German Democratic Republic: net material product.

Source: General Agreement on Tariffs and Trade (GATT), *International Trade,* 1984–85, p. 19.

TABLE 3–10 Global Exports and Imports, 1983[1]

	GDP ($Millions)	% World GDP	TOTAL EXPORTS		TOTAL IMPORTS	
			F.O.B. ($Millions)	% World Exports	C.I.F. ($Millions)	% World Imports
Triad Markets:						
North America	$ 3,583	32%	$ 277,283	16%	$ 333,035	19%
Western Europe	2,873	26	700,737	41	736,124	42
Japan	1,156	10	146,958	9	126,434	7
SUB TOTAL	7,612	69%	$1,124,978	66%	$1,195,593	68%
Rest of the World:						
Africa	353	3%	75,997	4%	65,410	4%
Asia (excl. Japan)	853	8	180,816	11	194,265	11
Eastern Europe (incl. USSR)	1,005	9	76,133	4	79,041	5
Latin America	666	6	98,504	6	72,323	4
Middle East	397	4	124,718	7	121,071	7
Oceania	178	2	25,987	2	24,736	1
SUB TOTAL	3,452	32%	$ 584,155	34%	556,846	32%
GLOBAL TOTAL	$11,064	100%	$1,707,133	100%	$1,752,439	100%

[1] 1982 data.

Source: Prepared by author.

TABLE 3–11 U.S. Merchandise Trade, 1984–1985 [Millions of dollars]

Balance of payment adjustments to Census trade data:

EXPORTS

	1984	1985[p]
Merchandise exports, Census basis[1] including reexports and excluding military grant shipments	218,722	212,360
Adjustments:		
Private gift parcel remittances	223	251
Gold exports, nonmonetary	330	406
Inland U.S. freight to Canada	1,541	1,484
U.S.-Canadian reconciliation adjustments, n.e.c., net[2]	4,962	5,198
Merchandise exports transferred under U.S. military agency sales contracts identified in Census documents[3]	−5,719	−5,823
Other adjustments, net[4]	−143	114
Equals: Merchandise exports, adjusted to balance of payments basis excluding "military" (table 1, line 2).	219,916	213,990

IMPORTS

	1984	1985[p]
Merchandise imports, Census basis[1] (general imports)	330,514	335,127
Adjustments:		
Electric energy	1,074	1,035
Gold imports, nonmonetary	474	559
Inland freight in Canada	1,504	1,479
U.S.-Canadian reconciliation adjustment, n.e.c., net[2]	775	−1,097
Merchandise imports of U.S. military agencies identified in Census documents[3]	−795	
Other adjustments, net[5]	478	1,177
Equals: Merchandise imports, adjusted to balance of payments basis, excluding "military" (table 1, line 16).	334,023	338,279

Merchandise trade, by area and country, adjusted to balance of payments basis, excluding military[6]—Continued:

IMPORTS

	1984	1985[p]
Total, all countries	334,023	338,279
Western Europe	72,054	77,234
European Communities (10)	57,774	62,387
Belgium and Luxembourg	3,089	3,263
France	7,957	8,876
Germany, Federal Republic of	17,426	19,478
Italy	8,056	9,350
Netherlands	4,126	4,079
United Kingdom	14,418	14,406
Other	2,702	2,936
Westeren Europe, excluding EC (10)	14,280	14,847
Canada[2]	69,229	71,180
Japan	60,211	65,536
Australia, New Zealand, and South Africa	5,633	5,582
Eastern Europe	2,217	1,830
Latin America and Other Western Hemisphere	48,366	46,003
Brazil	7,754	7,196
Mexico	18,076	19,051
Venezuela	6,660	6,509
Other	15,874	13,248
Other countries in Asia and Africa	76,313	70,914
Asia	64,423	60,919
Members of OPEC	11,629	8,417
China	3,114	3,821
Hong Kong	8,355	7,954
Korea, Republic of	9,857	9,970
Singapore	3,959	4,126
Taiwan	15,429	15,466
Africa	11,793	9,880
Members of OPEC	6,801	5,934
International organizations and unallocated		
Memoranda:		
Industrial countries[6]	207,127	219,532
Members of OPEC[6]	26,852	22,617
Other countries[6]	100,043	96,130

79

	EXPORTS		BALANCE (EXCESS OF EXPORTS +)	
Total, all countries	219,916	213,990	-114,107	-124,289
Western Europe	56,866	55,997	-15,188	-21,237
European Communities (10)	46,379	45,171	-11,395	-17,216
Belgium and Luxembourg	5,194	4,836	2,105	1,574
France	6,055	6,102	-1,902	-2,774
Germany, Federal Republic of	8,773	8,948	-8,653	-10,530
Italy	4,310	4,480	-3,746	-4,870
Netherlands	7,486	7,229	3,360	3,151
United Kingdom	12,201	11,102	-2,217	-3,304
Other	2,360	2,475	-342	-462
Western Europe, excluding EC (10)	10,487	10,826	-3,793	-4,021
Canada²	53,067	54,053	-16,162	-17,127
Japan	23,240	22,146	-36,971	-43,390
Australia, New Zealand, and South Africa	7,849	6,962	2,216	1,380
Eastern Europe	4,290	3,252	2,073	1,422
Latin America and Other Western Hemisphere	29,767	30,441	-18,599	-15,562
Brazil	2,744	3,334	-5,010	-3,862
Mexico	12,020	13,262	-6,056	-5,789
Venezuela	3,386	3,023	-3,274	-3,486
Other	11,616	10,822	-4,258	-2,426
Other countries in Asia and Africa	44,447	40,844	-31,866	-30,070
Asia	39,006	35,192	-25,417	-25,726
Members of OPEC	8,419	6,216	-3,210	-2,201
China	3,016	3,950	-97	129
Hong Kong	3,118	2,753	-5,236	-5,201
Korea, Republic of	5,887	5,711	-3,970	-4,259
Singapore	3,686	3,453	-273	-673
Taiwan	4,765	4,232	-10,663	-11,234
Africa	5,526	5,528	-6,267	-4,353
Members of OPEC	1,316	1,503	-5,485	-4,431
International organizations and unallocated	390	295	390	295
Memoranda:				
Industrial countries⁶	141,021	139,157	-66,106	-80,375
Members of OPEC⁶	13,771	11,327	-13,081	-11,291
Other countries⁶	64,734	63,210	-35,310	-32,920

Source: *Survey of Current Business*, March 1986, pp. 37–38. Please note that references in the table above can be found in this source.

1985 is the deficit balances with almost every country and region in the world. If the United States were a creditor country with earnings from investments abroad, it could afford to be in a net deficit on the merchandise trade account. Unfortunately, the United States has become a net debtor nation, and must earn a surplus to pay the interest and dividends on foreign holdings of U.S. assets.

The trade data shown in Tables 3–6 through 3–11 are merchandise trade. Probably the fastest growing sector of world trade is trade in services. Unfortunately, the statistics and data on trade in services are not as comprehensive as those for merchandise trade. In 1983, U.S. service sales were approximately $55 billion, or 25 percent of exports. When income on investments is included, the United States had a net balance on services of +$25 billion to offset the net balance of merchandise trade of −$60 billion. This is shown in Figure 3–1.

U.S. trade balance on services transactions and on merchandise trade; both in billions of dollars

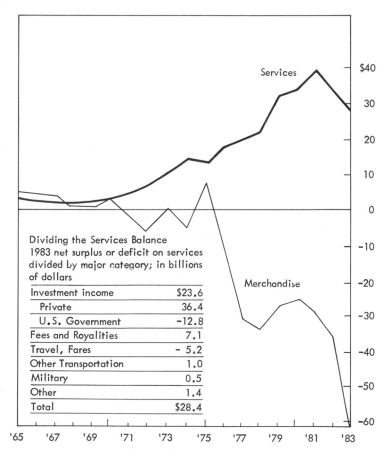

Dividing the Services Balance
1983 net surplus or deficit on services
divided by major category; in billions
of dollars

Investment income	$23.6
Private	36.4
U.S. Government	−12.8
Fees and Royalties	7.1
Travel, Fares	− 5.2
Other Transportation	1.0
Military	0.5
Other	1.4
Total	$28.4

FIGURE 3–1   The Role of Services in U.S. Trade—U.S. trade balance on services transactions and on merchandise trade; both in billions of dollars

Source: *The New York Times*, Oct. 24, 1984.

CONSUMPTION PATTERNS

Engel's Law

Income is the single most important variable affecting market potential for most products. How does income affect consumption? Every marketer is aware of the relationship between income level and consumption patterns and, therefore, frequently uses income segmentation in defining a market. The nature of income elasticity (the relationship between demand changes and changes in income) for food was first observed and formulated by the nineteenth-century Prussian statistician Ernst Engel. Engel discovered a uniform condition in European countries that he surveyed: When income grew above a certain minimum, expenditures on food as a percentage of total income decreased, although the absolute amount of food expenditures was maintained or increased. This pattern of expenditures on necessities is referred to as Engel's law and has been confirmed by empirical budget studies. One survey, published by the United Nations Food and Agricultural Organization in Rome, recorded the elasticities of demand for food along with per capita incomes in dollars. This survey revealed that Asia, the poorest area, had an income elasticity of demand for food of .9, whereas North America, the richest area, had an income elasticity of demand for food of .16. This means that 90 cents out of every additional dollar in income in Asia was expended on food, as compared with 16 cents for North America. By and large there is an inverse correlation between GNP per capita and income elasticity of demand for food. As incomes rise, the elasticity of demand for food declines.

Product Saturation Levels

In general, product saturation levels, or the percentage of potential buyers or households who own a particular product, increase as national income per capita increases. However, in markets where income is sufficient to enable consumers to buy a particular product, other factors may be determinant. For example, the sale of air conditioners is explained by income and climate. Average-income-level people in an underdeveloped country cannot afford an air conditioner no matter how hot it is. High-income people in a northern climate can easily afford an air conditioner but have no need for one.

In a survey made during the 1960s, the ownership of electric vacuum cleaners in the European Common Market ranged from a high of 95 percent of households in The Netherlands to a low of 7 percent of households in Italy. The differences in ownership of this appliance in Europe are explained only partially by income. A much more important factor in explaining ownership levels is the type of floor covering used in the homes of the country. Almost every home in The Netherlands contains rugs, whereas in Italy the use of rugs is uncommon. This illustrates the importance of a companion product in determining the sale potential for a product.

Income is a major determinant of ownership of consumer durable goods. The effect of rising incomes in Japanese households is dramatic. For products that are major labor-saving tools, such as washing machines and refrigerators, rising incomes increase ownership to more than 95 percent. See Table 5–1, page 163, for an example of this phenomenon.

The average Japanese household owns a refrigerator and washing machine. Over 90 percent have color televisions and vacuum cleaners and keep warm in winter using kerosene stoves and keep cool in summer using electric fans. Even though well supplied with consumer durables, Japan is more energy efficient than other nations. Appliances tend to be smaller, fit the size of the home, and use less power. Ownership of central heating, a major energy consumer, is very low. Although air conditioner sales show high rates of growth, total ownership remains relatively low. Energy consumption has been increasing as more families purchase cars and add to their stock of appliances. To reduce their household energy bills, many consumers are replacing present durables with larger and more efficient models.

MARKET DEVELOPMENT

Marketing and Economic Development

An important concern in marketing is whether or not it has any relevance to the process of economic development. It is widely asserted that marketing is a field that is relevant only to the conditions that apply in wealthy, industrialized countries where the major problem is one of directing society's resources into ever-changing output or production to satisfy a dynamic marketplace. In the less developed country, it is argued, the major problem is the allocation of scarce resources into obvious production needs. The important focus in the less developed countries is on production and how to increase output, not on customer needs and wants.

It can also be argued that the marketing process of focusing an organization's resources on environmental opportunities is a process that has no relevance in the less developed country, that the needs and wants in less developed countries so far exceed the productive capability of these societies that it is superfluous to focus societal resources on considering these needs. If the existing stock of goods and services available in the world is fixed, this argument has merit. On the other hand, if the existing stock of goods and services is not considered fixed, this argument can be challenged on the grounds that it does not allow for the possibilities of dynamic response to needs within less developed countries. The application of the marketing process to the less developed country would involve an appraisal of the list of wants and needs in the country and an appraisal of the productive capabilities of the society. Combined with the creative application of the marketing process, this would lead to the formulation of new products that matched the wants and needs with the true productive capabilities of the society. Indeed the possibilities for the application of the marketing process to market conditions in less developed countries are unlimited. For example, less developed countries have a need for washing and cleaning. Because of the low-income levels, this washing is done by hand. It is not feasible for less developed countries to engage in the production and sale of automatic, electrically operated washing machines because the expense and the complexity of these devices far exceed the economic and productive capabilities of these societies. The application of the marketing process under these conditions should lead to the development of a washing device that is appropriate to the economic capability of the society. The possibilities for the development of an inexpensive hand-operated washing machine are considerable.

The economics literature places a great deal of emphasis on the role of "marketing" in economic development when marketing is defined as distribution. In his book *West African Trade*,[4] P. T. Bauer considered the question concerning the number of traders and their productivity. The number and variety of traders in West Africa had been much criticized by both official and unofficial observers. Traders were condemned as wasteful and were said to be responsible for wide distributive margins both in the sale of merchandise and in the purchase of produce. Bauer examined these criticisms and concluded that they stemmed from a misunderstanding. He argued that the West African system economized in capital and used resources that were largely redundant, such as labor, and therefore that it was a productive system by rational economic criteria.

A simple example illustrates Bauer's point. A trader buys a package of 20 cigarettes for 1 shilling and resells them one at a time for 2 cents each, or for a total of 2 shillings. Has this man exploited society to the extent of 1 shilling, or has he provided a useful service? In a society where consumers can afford to smoke only one cigarette at a time, the trader has provided a useful service in substituting labor for capital. In this case, capital would be the accumulation of an inventory of cigarettes by a consumer. The first obstacle to this accumulation, which is the possession of a shilling, is paramount. However, even if a consumer were able to accumulate a shilling, his standard of living would not allow him to smoke the 20 cigarettes at a rate that would allow them to be consumed in a fresh condition. Thus, even if he were able to save and accumulate a shilling, he would end up with a package of spoiled cigarettes. The trader in this case, by breaking bulk, serves the useful function of making available a product in a quantity that a consumer can afford and in a condition that is attractive. As income levels rise, the purchaser will smoke more frequently and will be able to buy an entire package of cigarettes. In the process, the amount of local resources consumed by distribution will decline and the standard of living will have risen. Meanwhile, in the less developed condition where labor is redundant and cheap and where capital is scarce, the availability of this distributive function is a useful one and a rational application of society's resources.

[4]Peter T. Bauer, *West African Trade* (London: Routledge and K. Paul, 1963).

Another function of distribution in economic development, which Peter Drucker identifies, is the important business experience provided by distribution.[5] Both Bauer and Drucker argue that experience in the distributive sector is valuable because it generates a pool of entrepreneurial talent in a society where alternatives for such training are scarce. Adam Smith in *The Wealth of Nations* observed, "The habits besides, of order, economy, and attention, to which mercantile business naturally forms a merchant, render him much fitter to execute with profit and success, any project of improvement."

Product, price, and communications are also marketing decision areas that can be crucial in the process of economic development. This is well illustrated by the role that these decision areas in marketing have played in the economic integration and development of the Central American Common Market (CACM). Local manufacturers of paint in Central America applying the marketing concept and focusing on the needs of the customer decided to offer a medium-quality paint at a price that was 40 to 50 percent lower than that of the formerly available high-quality imported paint. This product proved to be much more oriented toward the true needs of the Central American consumer, as demonstrated by the tremendous response of the market to the product. The local companies with their lower-priced paint quickly gained over 80 percent of the market.

A more controversial aspect of marketing is its ability to stimulate and direct demand through merchandising and advertising programs. Until recently marketers in industrialized countries were given complete license to employ marketing to promote any legal product—even products such as cigarettes, which had been known for some time to be harmful to the health or welfare of consumers. Less developed countries have not been sympathetic to the expenditure of societal resources on stimulating and directing demand, again because of the general position that demand and wants so far exceed the availability of resources that stimulation or direction is unnecessary. In recent years both the license of the industrialized countries and the rejection of the less developed countries have come into question. In the industrialized countries it is now recognized that complete license to merchandise products is an excess. The most notable example of this revised thinking concerns cigarette advertising, which was banned from television in the United States as of January 1, 1971. In less developed countries the usefulness of merchandising and advertising to stimulate and promote desired behavior has been recognized in at least some circles. For example, the widely heralded high-protein foods that became available in the latter half of the 1960s were not quickly adopted by the inhabitants of the less developed countries. This came as a great surprise to many people, since the nutritional value of these foods was clearly superior to that of the traditional diet. Unfortunately, high-protein foods were not what the consumers had accustomed themselves to and developed preferences for, and therefore they needed to be carefully formulated, recognizing taste and texture preferences, and skillfully promoted and merchandised. The use of marketing communications and marketing skills to

---

[5] Peter Drucker, "Marketing and Economic Development," *Journal of Marketing*, January 1958, pp. 252–259.

shift consumer food consumption into more nutritional types of food is an example of an extremely useful application of marketing to the needs of less developed countries.

Stages of Market Development

Global markets are at different stages of development which can be divided into five categories based on the criterion of gross national product per capita. Although the exact division is arbitrary, countries in the five categories have similar characteristics, so the stages provide a useful basis for global strategic planning.

PREINDUSTRIAL COUNTRIES. Preindustrial countries are those with 1983 incomes of less than $400 per capita. The characteristics shared by countries at this income level are:

1. Limited industrialization and a high percentage of the population engaged in agriculture and subsistence farming
2. High birth rates
3. Low literacy rates
4. Heavy reliance on foreign aid
5. Political instability and unrest
6. Concentration in Africa south of the Sahara

These countries are limited markets for all products, and are not significant locations for competitive threats.

LESS DEVELOPED COUNTRIES. Less developed countries are those with a 1983 GNP per capita between $401 and $1,635. These countries are at the early stages of industrialization. Factories are erected to supply a growing domestic market with such items as batteries, tires, building materials, packaged foods, automobiles and trucks. These countries are also locations for the production of standardized or mature products such as clothing for export markets.

Consumer markets in these countries are expanding, and they represent an increasing competitive threat as they mobilize their abundant resources and cheap and highly motivated labor.

DEVELOPING COUNTRIES. Developing countries are those with 1983 GNP per capita between $1,636 and $5,500. In these countries, the percentage of population engaged in agriculture drops sharply as people move from the agricultural to the industrial sector and the degree of urbanization increases. These countries are rapidly industrializing. They have rising wages and high rates of literacy and advanced education, but they still have significantly lower wage costs than the advanced countries. With the capability of the advanced countries and the lower wage rates, they frequently become formidable competitors and experience rapid economic growth led by exports.

INDUSTRIALIZED COUNTRIES. Industrialized countries are those with a 1983 GNP per capita of $5,500 to $10,000. They are positioned to make the transition from their industrial base to a so-called postindustrial or advanced status, where rising wages and costs, infrastructure, and a highly educated population allow them to take their place in the select group of high income countries in the world.

ADVANCED COUNTRIES. Advanced countries are those with 1983 GNP per capita in excess of $10,000. Most of the countries in this category reached their present income level through a process of sustained economic growth. The category also includes oil-producing nations such as Kuwait and the United Arab Emirates. This group of countries is also referred to as postindustrial countries, a term which has been advanced by Daniel Bell of Harvard. Bell suggests that the main difference between the industrial and the postindustrial society is that the sources of innovation in a postindustrial society are derived increasingly from the codification of theoretical knowledge rather than from "random" inventions. Other characteristics, summarized in Table 3–12, are the importance of the service sector (more than 50 percent of GNP); the crucial importance of information processing and exchange; and the ascendancy of knowledge over capital as the key strategic resource, of intellectual technology over machine technology, of scientists and professionals over engineers and semiskilled workers, and of theory and models over empiricism.

Other aspects of the postindustrial society are an orientation toward the future and the importance of interpersonal and intragroup relationships in the functioning of society.

The United States, Sweden, and Japan are examples of postindustrial or advanced societies. Japan is a particularly interesting case of a postindustrial society. The Japanese in many respects are uniquely suited in their basic cultural orientation to adapt to the basic requirements of a postindustrial society. Cooperation and harmonious interaction, for example, are important keystones of the Japanese culture. This is in marked contrast to Britain, which has experienced difficulty in emerging from the industrial stage of development largely because of the inability of labor and management to find mutually acceptable ways of adapting to the adjustments required by technological, organizational, and managerial modernization.

The Japan Computer Usage Development Institute has prepared a document called "The Plan for Information Society—A National Goal Toward Year 2000," which is a conscious statement of the qualities and goals of a postindustrial society. The introduction to the report states

> During almost a century, since the Imperial Restoration, Japan endeavored to build a modernized industrial society, and has almost reached this goal. However, Japan is now confronting multitudes of social and economic problems that include pollution problems, excessively dense population problems in urban areas, economic depression resulting from industrial and economic structures, increases in aged population, etc.
>
> In the advanced countries, de-industrialization is now under way, and the world is generally and steadily shifting from the industrialized society to the information society. Therefore, this committee proposes the establishment of a new national target, "Realization of the Information Society."

TABLE 3–12 The Postindustrial Society: A Comparative Schema

MODES (Mode of Production)	PREINDUSTRIAL (Extractive)	INDUSTRIAL (Fabrication)	POSTINDUSTRIAL (Processing, Recycling Services)
Economic sector	Primary Agriculture Mining Fishing Timber Oil and gas	Secondary Goods producing Manufacturing Durables Nondurables Heavy construction	Tertiary Transportation Utilities Quaternary Trade Finance Insurance Real estate Quinary Health Research Education Government Recreation
Transforming resource	Natural power Wind, water, draft animals, human muscle	Created energy Electricity—oil, gas, coal Nuclear power	Information Computer and data transmission systems
Strategic resource	Raw materials	Financial capital	Knowledge
Technology	Craft	Machine technology	Intellectual technology
Skill base	Artisan, manual worker, farmer	Engineer, semiskilled worker	Scientist, technical, and professional occupations
Methodology	Common sense, trial and error, experience	Empiricism, experimentation	Abstract theory: models, simulations, decision theory, systems analysis
Time perspective	Orientation to the past	Ad hoc adaptiveness, experimentation	Future orientation, forecasting, and planning
Design	Game against nature	Game against fabricated nature	Game between persons
Axial principle	Traditionalism	Economic growth	Codification of theoretical knowledge

Source: *Physics Today*, February 1976, p. 47.

The ultimate goal of the information society is the realization of a "society that brings about a general flourishing state of human intellectual creativity." Intellectual creativity may be defined as a process of exploring into future possibilities by fully employing information and knowledge with the aim of materializing such possibilities.

Product and market opportunities in the postindustrial society are more heavily dependent upon new products and innovations than in industrial societies. All the basic products are already owned. Household saturation levels are extremely high, and a marketer seeking to expand his or her business must either expand the share of existing markets, which is always difficult, or create a new market. This situation explains the very high incidence of new product development and innovation that takes place in the postindustrial society.

Table 3–13 identifies the five stages of development and the number of countries, population, and income in each stage as of 1984.

NATIONAL CONTROLS OF INTERNATIONAL TRANSFERS

The nation-states of the world exercise control over a broad range of international transfers. Items transferred include not only goods and services but also money, people, technology, and rights. All these elements are important aspects of the multinational marketing mix, particularly goods, money, and people.

There are several motives for controlling international transfers. A major motive is to accomplish economic goals. The earliest economic goal of controls over international transfers was revenue production. Today, only in the less developed countries is the revenue motive a principal factor guiding national policy in this area.

TABLE 3–13 Stages of Market Development

CATEGORIES	INCOME GROUP BY PER CAPITA GNP	1982 POPULATION (Millions)	1982 GNP (Billions)	1982 GNP PER CAPITA	NUMBER OF COUNTRIES
1	$400 or less	2163	594	270	32
2	$401 to $1,635	633	532	840	48
3	$1,636 to $5,500	486	1330	2740	42
4	$5,500 to $10,000	77	554	7168	14
5	$10,000 and more	572	6964	12159	24

Categories:
1. Preindustrial countries
2. Less developed countries
3. Developing countries
4. Advanced countries: A. Industrialized countries
                        B. Postindustrial countries.

Source: *1985 World Bank Atlas;* table prepared by author.

More common motives today are protection of local industry and the corollary of fostering the development of local enterprise. In less developed countries these three motives work together. A country can increase national revenues by increasing tariffs and duties on transfers of goods and at the same time can provide protection for local infant industries or for local enterprise that has obtained political influence.

Employment is a major economic goal influencing controls over international transfers. When the free play of economic forces results in heavy competitive pressure, which in turn creates domestic unemployment, political forces activated by management, as well as workers in the affected industry, are often capable of bringing pressure to control international transfer. The controls may be in the form of higher tariffs or import quotas that place an absolute quantity limit on the quantity by weight, value, or volume of goods that may enter the country.

Although economic goals are the prime cause of the imposition of controls on international transfers, political goals and values are a major reason for controls. The barriers between Eastern Europe and the West, for example, are very real; they exist because of differences between the values and objectives of eastern and western countries.

Why Identify Control Motives?

The identification of motives for controlling international transfers is important because this is the first step in the formation of a behavioral model of nation-states in the economic policy area. Admittedly any behavioral model of a nation will be an extremely rough approximation of the reality it attempts to describe. Nevertheless, moves by nations have as great an impact on the success of international marketing programs as do moves of individual competitors. It is essential that the international marketing planner account for and attempt to forecast possible moves by nation-states that would affect marketing programs being designed.

The current Japanese situation is a good example of how motives influence national controls over international transfers. The Japanese have established a world-wide reputation for the stringency of their barriers to direct entry into the Japanese economy and market. In general, it was impossible for most enterprises to obtain permission to begin independent direct operations in Japan. Every company wishing to enter the Japanese economy had to obtain the approval of the National Planning Authority, and all applications were carefully scrutinized and considered in the light of the national plan for Japanese economic development. In most cases the Japanese have permitted entry of foreign firms only on a joint venture basis. In many industries, automobiles, for example, the Japanese have resisted any form of foreign entry until their own industry established a strong base both in Japan and in the international economy.

The major controlling factor that has forced the Japanese to admit foreign companies into the Japanese economy has been the fact that Japan has a major stake in markets in the industrial countries of the world. Because the Japanese are committed to developing a position in international markets, they are responsive to the positions of the national governments who control access to these markets. In a real sense, then, Japan has been a hostage to its own market position in other countries when companies based in these countries have sought permission to enter the Japanese market. Concurrently, the Japanese position has led to a substantial balance-of-payments surplus and the accumulation of large reserves that have created further pressure for allowing greater access to the Japanese markets both of imported goods and of direct operations by foreign companies. The consequence of these pressures has been a major liberalization of the Japanese investment law, which today permits 100 percent foreign ownership in all but four industry areas.

In taking this example one step further, there is considerable pressure today in some sectors in the United States for restrictive measures to reduce the quantity of Japanese goods imported into the United States. As the U.S. market position, both in terms of direct operations and in terms of export markets, develops in Japan, the companies that hold these markets in Japan will naturally be anxious to preserve them. It is likely, then, that these interests will bring pressure upon the U.S. government to maintain amicable relations with Japan, and if their judgment is that the restriction of Japanese imports in the United States would harm United States-Japanese relationships, they would protest these restrictions. In this example the United States would, in a real sense, be a hostage to its interests in Japan.

The hostage framework applies very well to advanced countries because all advanced countries today are involved in symmetrical relationships with other advanced countries. They are at the same time both importers and exporters of manufactured goods, both recipients of direct investments and foreign operations, and both direct investors and foreign operators. The relationships between advanced countries and less developed countries, on the other hand, are not nearly so symmetrical. In general, less developed countries export raw materials to the advanced countries and import manufactures from them. Moreover, the flow of direct investment and foreign operations is one way—from the advanced countries to the less developed countries. As a result, the companies from advanced countries have an economic stake in the less developed countries that is not reciprocated. This lack of symmetry in the relationship between advanced countries and less developed countries creates a less stable economic and political environment in the underdeveloped country because there is no hostage motive controlling pressures to restrict or constrain the operations of foreign investors and foreign-based exporters. Without the constraint of hostage investments and market positions, the behavior of less developed countries responds to a matrix of economic, social, political, cultural, and security motives that must be established and forecast by the marketing planner to estimate the general level of environmental conditions that will exist in the less developed country over the company's planning horizon. In general, if a country is economically successful, as defined by sustained real growth and the absence of balance-of-payments pressures, the business environment will typically remain favorable. If a country gets into difficulty, pressures will develop to deal with problems. These pressures may take the form of restricting the operations and access of all companies to foreign exchange, making it difficult, expensive, or impossible to import components or repatriate dividends and capital. Another form of response to local frustration may be the requirement that foreign companies localize management and ownership.

SUMMARY

The economic environment is a major determinant of market potential and opportunity. Since the single most important indicator of market potential is income, the first step in determining the potential of a country or region is to identify the total and, even more significantly, the per capita income. In general, as people's incomes rise, they spend less on necessities and more on discretionary purchases. One of the ways of determining market potential for a product is to evaluate product saturation levels in the light of income levels. In general, it is appropriate to compare the saturation levels of countries or of consumer segments with similar income levels.

Countries and markets go through typical stages of market development. Although development is on a continuum, it is possible to identify distinct stages and formulate general estimates about the type of demand that will be found in a country or market at a particular stage of development. In advanced countries, for example, more than half the gross national product is accounted for by services as opposed to goods, and the market for services reflects this mix in the value of GNP. In a preindustrial country, the market for services and goods is very small because, by definition, the country has very low income levels.

DISCUSSION QUESTIONS

1. What is the pattern of income distribution in the world today? How do developing countries' markets compare with postindustrial markets in the proportion of income going to the bottom and the top 20 percent of the population?
2. A manufacturer of long-range radios is assessing the world market potential for his products. He asks you if he should consider developing countries as potential markets. How would you advise him?
3. Are income and standard of living the same thing? What is meant by the term "standard of living"?
4. The saturation level of kerosene heaters in Japan was 92.2 percent in 1978. The founder of Kerosun noticed this high saturation level and concluded that there was a huge untapped market for kerosene heaters in the United States and Western Europe where saturation levels were less than 1 percent. Is this scientific marketing or just wild guessing?

BIBLIOGRAPHY

Books

GALBRAITH, JOHN KENNETH. *The Nature of Mass Poverty*. Cambridge, Mass.: Harvard University Press, 1979.

JAFFE, EUGENE D. *Grouping: A Strategy for International Marketing*. New York: American Management Association, 1974.

KRAVIS, IRVING B., ET AL. *A System of International Comparisons of Gross Product and Purchasing Power*. Washington, D.C.: International Bank for Reconstruction and Development, 1975.

Article

LEWIS, ARTHUR W. "The Slowing Down of the Engine of Growth." *American Economic Review*, September 1980, pp. 555–564.

INTERNATIONAL FOODS INCORPORATED (A)[1]

In early 1982, International Foods Incorporated (IFI) was evaluating its plan for Boor Concentrated Soups in the U.S. market. IFI had marketing subsidiaries in 112 countries and manufacturing plants in 30 countries. Over half the company's sales of $2 billion came from outside the United States. Consumer sales accounted for over 60 percent of worldwide sales, up from 25 percent only 10 years earlier. Forty percent of the company's sales were of refined corn products sold in bulk form to a wide range of industries. The company was pursuing an aggressive program of taking successful products from a single national market to its international markets. Many U.S. companies had launched U.S. products abroad, but IFI was determined to extend products in all directions, from foreign markets to the United States.

In 1974, IFI acquired the H.C. Boor Company, the largest European producer of dehydrated packaged soups. This acquisition extended IFI's product line into soups for the first time. Boor produced soups in 20 countries, and held a major share of the market for dehydrated soups in most of these mar-

kets. The European market for soup in which Boor participated was characterized by a level of per capita consumption that was four times higher than that in the United States. There were four types of soup consumed in the European market: homemade, which accounted for 45 percent of all soup consumption; bouillon; dehydrated; and canned. Bouillon, which accounted for 30 percent of soup consumption, was the main commercially produced soup in Europe. It was a concentrated extract cube that dissolved into bouillon when dropped into boiling water. Dehydrated soups, which accounted for 15 percent of soup consumption, were the second most important commercially produced soups in Europe. These were made from dehydrated vegetables, noodles, and other ingredients. A user made soup by adding the dehydrated powder to water and boiling for approximately 10 minutes. Canned soups in both concentrated and ready-to-serve form accounted for only 10 percent of European soup consumption. Canned concentrated soups were prepared by mixing the contents of the can with an equal quantity of water and heating. Ready-to-serve canned soup was prepared by simply heating the contents of the can. The 1975 European market share and expected growth by 1995 are shown

[1]This case was prepared by Professor Warren J. Keegan. All figures, dates, and names are disguised.

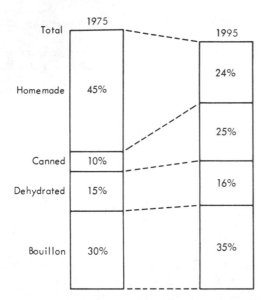

FIGURE 1 **European Soup Consumption: 1975 Market Share and Estimated Market Shares in 1995**

in Figure 1. Overall, as shown, total soup consumption was expected to decline in Europe. Homemade soups were expected to drop to 25 percent of the total market, while canned soups were expected to increase to 25 percent of the market. This was part of a general convenience foods revolution expected to occur in Europe as a result of rising income levels.

THE U.S. SOUP MARKET

Prior to the introduction of Boor in 1981 by IFI, the U.S. soup market totaled about $1 billion in annual sales, almost double the size of the market in 1956. Wet or canned soups accounted for over 90 percent of the market. Campbell was the major supplier in the wet soup area with close to 90 percent of the market. The dry soup market was a more or less static $70–80 million, about 8 percent of the overall market. The major factors in the industry were as follows:

1. Campbell's, by far the leader in the household market, with almost 90 percent of the canned soup market.
2. H. J. Heinz, a distant second in the canned wet soup field with a 7–10 percent market share. Heinz was, however, the leader in institutional sales.
3. Thomas J. Lipton, Inc., a division of Unilever, the biggest and oldest maker of dehydrated soups. Lipton dominated the dry soup market with almost 95 percent of sales.
4. Wyler Co., a division of Borden Co., a Chicago-based manufacturer of dry soup mixes.

By 1981, the domestic per capita consumption of canned soups had climbed from 10 to 15 pounds annually since 1950, although this was still only about one-fourth that of European consumption. It was estimated that 25 percent of the nation's families served canned soup on an average day. The sales of soup accounted for roughly 1 or 2 percent of food store sales.

Before 1981 Boor was sold in the United States as an imported European soup. Sales were very low and represented an insignificant factor in the U.S. soup market. Carried by a few specialty stores and delicatessens, Boor was perceived as a gourmet's food. Prior to International Foods Incorporated's introduction of Boor soups, the 1981 Market Research Corporation of America (MRCA) figures for the total soup sales in the United States were as shown in Table 1. Dehydrated soup sales made up about 8 percent of total sales by volume and 7.8 percent of the total dollar sales.

DECISION TO INTRODUCE BOOR

In 1980 a virtually autonomous team was established to manage Boor's soups in the United

TABLE 1 1981 U.S. Soup Sales

	CASES (millions)	DOLLARS (millions)
Canned soups	100.7	$382.8
Dehydrated soups	8.7	32.4
Total	109.4	$415.2

Source: Company records.

States. This new product development team was to create and introduce a new line of Americanized Boor soups. This concept of management, it was felt, would be a stimulus to hard work and initiative and would encourage the team to operate like an aggressive new company.

Market Research

Boor's soups were European products tailored to suit continental tastes. The new soups had to be adapted to fit American tastes and images. International Foods Incorporated undertook this task of translating its recipes very carefully through extensive product development and product tasting tests. Psychological studies were conducted to determine the image American women held of soup. The American housewife was found to have a somewhat vague and negative attitude toward dehydrated soups. Particular findings of importance regarding dehydrated soups were

1. Not as convenient
2. Made thin soups
3. Only limited flavors available
4. Were less fresh
5. Were economical
6. Were easy to carry

IFI was anxious to convince the consumer that Boor soups were easy to make and that they were of the highest quality available at the grocery store or supermarket. The product development task was basically to create recipes that were similar in processing to Boor's other soups but that were, in flavor and body, typically attractive to Americans.

Product Testing and Adoption

Nearly two years were spent (1980 and 1981) in developing recipes for the new Boor soup line. A Swiss master chef sent sample after sample to the International Foods Incorporated Home Service Department for evaluation. Every sample was tested by four panels of 20 to 30 people. According to their feedback replies, the master chef altered his soup formulas to suit their tastes. An outside research firm was hired to test family preferences and responses to the more nearly final forms. This research was conducted in homes throughout the country. Ten thousand home consumer tests were used to perfect the taste to American standards. The result of all these efforts was a seven-product line of which only one was totally new to American consumers (leek soup). Every one of the Boor soups had, however, at least one ingredient feature not found in other American manufacturers' versions of that particular flavor. The product offering was to be as follows: beef and noodle, golden onion, cream of mushroom, chicken and noodles, smoky green pea, garden vegetable, and cream of leek.

Package Design

Package development and research was carried out with much care and awareness of current marketing techniques. Basically, the International Foods Incorporated marketing team required that the package express all the following characteristics of Boor soups:

1. The ideal image as defined by the team
   a. Uniqueness—not a "me-too" product
   b. Broad appeal—all customers, families, and gourmets
   c. Convenience—easy to carry, store, prepare
   d. Value—best quality ingredients
2. Serve as an advertisement
3. Stack easily
4. Lend itself to various types of external and internal promotions

Extensive in-depth studies were conducted to appraise the two most popular of the many package designs developed. One used an ingredient motif and illustrated only the ingredients that went into the soup. The other showed a large bowl of soup superimposed against a European landscape background. The study's results indicated to the development team that the ingredient design was superior to the European landscape background in meeting the requirements. They felt that it said

> This is a soup.
>
> This is a modern product from Europe designed for American tastes and preferences.
>
> This soup is made from the best and freshest ingredients.
>
> This is a light soup with a rich body.
>
> This is a high-quality soup, easy to prepare.
>
> This soup satisfies the discriminating consumer.

After the ingredient design was chosen for the outer box, a design was needed for the individual packets that held the soup itself inside the box (two to a carton). The inner packets were designed to follow the European motif and to represent the seven countries associated with the different flavors. The packets said, for example, "Take a kettle cruise to Sweden with Boor smoky green pea soup . . . smaklig." Following the determination of the product offering and the package design, the necessary equipment was ordered for limited production and four test markets were selected.

TEST MARKETING AND RESULTS

Starting in January 1981 the new Boor soups were testmarketed in four cities: Syracuse, New York; Providence, Rhode Island; and Columbus and Dayton, Ohio. The combined population of these cities was 3.5 million, or approximately 1.5 percent of total U.S. population. Prices were made competitive, and the usual channels of distribution for soups were selected. In Columbus and Providence, IFI undertook an enormous free-sampling program in which pouches of soup were mailed to 57 percent of the local families. Included with each sample was a certificate that, when coupled with a store-bought box top from a Boor carton, was redeemable for a free soup carton.

Backing the sampling efforts were TV spots and color spreads in local Sunday newspaper supplements. In Syracuse and Dayton, International Foods Incorporated decided to concentrate on preprint color advertisements in newspapers. In these cities there was no free-sample program, but the newspaper advertisements carried coupons similar to those used in the mailings. Expenses for the four test markets ran close to $1 million. Surprisingly, the sales resulting from the promotions in the four cities ran proportionately about the same, the free samples notwithstanding.

Results from the test markets showed

that the volume of dry soup sales doubled after the new Boor soups got to the stores. Data further revealed that Boor's promotional efforts did not cause a decrease in total sales by Lipton, Heinz, and Campbell's, although the market share percentages changed. All the companies benefited from the increased market activity of dehydrated soups resulting from the promotion. The test markets were continued for a full year. By the end of 1981, the company was convinced that an attempt at achieving greatly increased nationwide distribution was in order.

PRODUCTION DECISION

After the decision to begin a new sales effort was reached, IFI built a modern new manufacturing and packaging plant with an annual one-shift capacity of 5.8 million cases in Centrallia, Kansas. Construction of the plant was completed on October 25, 1981. The technology and machinery employed were the most modern available but were so specialized that they were not transferable to alternative uses. The plant and equipment investment in the Centrallia plant amounted to $20 million.

NATIONAL ADVERTISING CAMPAIGN

IFI's introductory magazine advertising campaign for Boor soups was described as "the largest single grocery advertisement in history." The main vehicle for the introduction was the use of seven-page spreads in magazines conveying the theme of the campaign: "Take a kettle cruise to Europe." A full page was devoted to each of the seven flavors with an accompanying national motif. Approximately $750,000 was allotted for each of these seven-page spreads. Another 60 percent of the advertising budget was spent on television advertisements. The budget for the first six months of 1982 was to be $10 million. This was considered to be the advertising cost of "launching" the new Boor soups.

TOTAL COMPANY COMMITMENT

Fifteen million dollars was committed to the new investment in Boor soups in an effort to capture a 30 percent share of the dehydrated soup market, which was expected to triple over the next two years (from $64 million to $192 million).

IFI hoped that by the time Campbell's Soup Co. made a countermove in dry soup, the Boor line would be firmly entrenched on the grocers' shelves and in the consumers' memory.

National distribution was achieved by the beginning of 1982. IFI hoped to reach its proposed break-even point by October of 1982 and to achieve pay back by 1984. Projected sales by the end of 1982 were $64 million.

QUESTIONS

1. What are the major assumptions that underlie IFI's decision to introduce Boor soups in the United States?
2. Evaluate these assumptions—which are well grounded in evidence and which are doubtful?
3. In what ways would you adjust IFI's program for Boor soups in the United States based on assumptions that you believe are reasonable?

INTERNATIONAL FOODS INCORPORATED (B)[1]

In July 1985 a special committee presented a report to top management of International Foods Incorporated (IFI) on possible courses of action for Boor Soups. In 1974, IFI had acquired the A. C. Boor Company, a leading European producer and marketer of dehydrated dry, packaged soups. In 1981, IFI introduced Boor soups to the U.S. market with the largest single grocery advertising campaign in history. Backing up heavy advertising and promotional budgets was an intensive product testing program and an investment in a modern, fully automated manufacturing facility in Centrallia, Kansas. See International Foods Incorporated (A) for a full description of the planning for Boor's introduction to the U.S. market.

In late 1981, Boor was joined in the dehydrated soup market by Red Kettle, a new dehydrated soup developed by Campbell, the country's largest producer of canned concentrate soups.

During 1982 the dry soup industry achieved sales of 12.2 million cases, an increase of 40 percent over the 1981 level (see Table 1). This was short of the tripled market that International Foods Incorporated had expected. In addition, as the year progressed, it became apparent that there was not enough room in the dehydrated soup market for two new entrants.

Furthermore, as can be seen in Table 1 and Figure 1, Boor sales failed to maintain the new expanded levels projected for the following years. Sales achieved through extensive promotional activities in 1982 were not repeated in 1983 and 1984 when volume

fell back to 125 percent of the 1981 sales level from 140 percent. Of added significance is the fact that this lagging performance of the dry soups in the marketplace occurred during a general expansion of total soup sales.

During these circumstances each brand performed in a particular manner, each of which will be described here and in Tables 2 and 3 and Figures 2 and 3. Lipton's market share rapidly yielded to the Boor attack on the market. (See Figure 3, third and fourth quarters, 1981.) Following this initial decline, Lipton successfully protected its market share against new efforts from both Boor and Red Kettle. It is of interest to note that Lipton's sales were not permanently harmed by Red

TABLE 1   Total Soup Market Trends 1978–1984

YEAR	CANNED	DRY	TOTAL	DRY AS A PERCENTAGE OF TOTAL
Sales Volume (millions of cases)				
1978	101.4	7.9	109.3	7.2%
1979	98.7	8.2	106.9	7.6
1980	104.4	8.3	112.7	7.5
1981	100.7	8.7	109.4	8.0
1982	102.5	12.2	114.7	10.6
1983	103.2	11.5	114.7	10.0
1984	105.2	10.9	116.1	9.4
Sales Volume (millions of dollars at retail)				
1978	$770	$58	$828	7.1
1979	750	61	810	7.5
1980	798	61	859	7.3
1981	766	65	831	7.8
1982	780	93	873	10.7
1983	776	83	859	9.1
1984	780	80	860	9.3

Source: Market Research Corporation of America (MRCA).

[1]This is an actual case history. All figures, dates, and names are disguised.

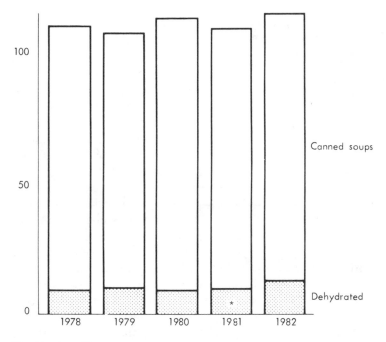

*Introduction of Boor.

FIGURE 1 Total Soup Sales Volume in the United States, 1978–1982
(in millions of cases)

TABLE 2 Brand Shares in the Dry Soup Market, 1981–1985

QUARTER		BOOR	LIPTON	RED KETTLE	WYLER	OTHERS
1981:	3	8.3%	67.1%	—	9.9%	14.7%
	4	29.0	49.3	1.1%	8.9	11.7
1982:	1	34.6	40.8	6.3	8.7	9.6
	2	29.4	39.6	9.8	10.9	10.3
	3	26.4	42.1	14.3	8.7	8.5
	4	21.7	36.6	22.6	10.7	8.4
1983:	1	20.5	40.9	18.2	10.8	9.6
	2	N.A.	—	—	—	—
	3	N.A.	—	—	—	—
	4	16.3	43.5	17.5	15.7	7.0
1984:	1	21.5	43.4	12.7	15.7	6.7
	2	18.4	44.7	10.5	17.0	9.4
	3	15.6	51.0	9.0	16.4	7.9
	4	15.9	47.0	10.4	17.5	9.2
1985:	1	19.1	42.4	12.8	17.0	8.7

N.A.—Not available.

TABLE 3 Advertising and Measurable Media Expenses, 1981–1984 (in millions of dollars)

BRAND	1981	1982	1983	1984
Boor	$ 3.8	$10.4	$ 5.6	$ 5.2
Lipton	7.6	6.8	5.6	6.2
Red Kettle	6.8	6.8	5.4	2.8
Wyler	N.A.	N.A.	.4	.6
Total dry soup	18.2	24.0	17.0	14.8
Campbell's	26.8	30.4	28.6	30.0
Total soup	$45.0	$54.4	$45.6	$44.8

N.A.—Not available.

Kettle's record performance through the second to fourth quarters of 1982. In fact, during the first half of 1983, Lipton soup sales rebounded and returned to the level from which they had so rapidly fallen during the end of 1982. In absolute terms, Lipton's decline in 1982 is not nearly as dramatic as is indicated by the market share analysis, the reason being that this decline occurred in a market that had expanded by 140 percent. One Lipton executive had this to say about the events of 1982 and 1983: "We developed a strategy and we stuck to it. If a company has a good franchise to start with, which we always have had, it's able to withstand the onslaughts of competition. You've got to start with the basic product. A housewife doesn't remember promises about a glorious trip to Moscow or Finland. We offered them an excellent value and taste sensation the other products just didn't have."

The introduction of Red Kettle dehydrated soups by the Campbell Soup Co. was purely defensive. An International Foods Incorporated executive described Red Kettle as "a bad product, with bad packaging, promoted by excessively high advertising." This quick move was aimed to put Campbell's in a market that some feared would be the future supplier of soup for American housewives. Red Kettle was developed and marketed with such speed that it reached the national marketplace at the same time as Boor. In fact, more advertising dollars were spent in 1981 on Red Kettle than on Boor.

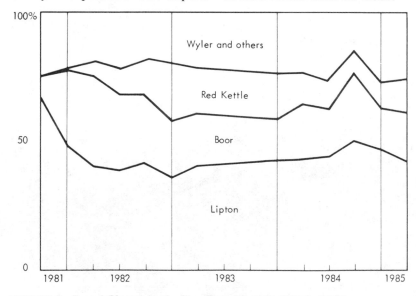

FIGURE 2 Brand Shares in the Dry Soup Market, 1980–1985

Source: Quarterly publication of Market Research Corporation of America (MRCA).

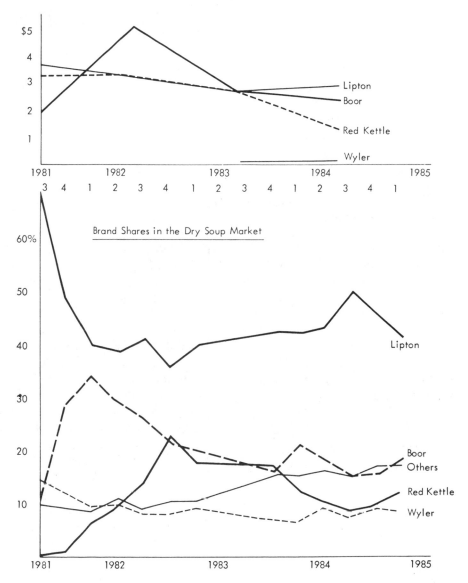

FIGURE 3 **Advertising and Measurable Media Expenses, 1981–1985 (in millions of dollars)**

When sales of Red Kettle developed in the second quarter of 1982, they cut mainly Boor's growing market share. This relationship is shown quite clearly in Figure 2. Red Kettle so effectively squeezed Boor soup sales that by the end of 1982 Boor had fallen below them in share of market figures. Red Kettle's soups had a year of declining sales in 1984. Campbell's eventually decided to discontinue the Red Kettle brand when it became obvious that there was no real future for them in the dry soup market.

Boor soups began 1982 with a promising increase in sales, but the breakeven point was never reached. The sales peak was attained in the first quarter of 1982. This was followed by a steady decline during the rest of 1982, after which Boor saw its market share settle between 15 percent and 20 percent.

Advertising expenditures, with a peak of $10.4 million in 1982, *did* successfully introduce the product and create awareness, but repeat purchases failed to materialize as the successive quarters of 1982 progressed. Promotions during the following years continued to emphasize the foreign appeal of Boor. During 1983 a box top from any of the nine Boor soups was exchangeable for a cash refund in coinage from any of the following countries: France, Italy, England, Holland, Denmark, Sweden, Switzerland, Austria, and Norway. Color-page spreads in magazines supported this premium promotion. In October 1983 IFI undertook another premium promotion, this time offering dolls representing the nine nations.

At an interview an International Foods Incorporated executive summed up the events of these three years with three points:

1. The market only achieved half the expected volume.
2. Advertising expenses were much higher than originally expected.
3. Boor achieved a higher than expected market share. In its *1973 Annual Report,* IFI had this to say about the venture:

Despite the general trend to increased sophistication in consumer tastes, strongly ingrained habits have not been overcome in the dehydrated soup market. Although the company's Boor Soups are increasingly popular in overseas markets, U.S. sales of Boor soup and the entire dried-soup market have not yet met expectations.

The company chairman admitted that "International Foods Incorporated had stubbed its toe on the introduction of Boor soups.'' Following a review by top-level management it was decided that, in the future, advertising expenditures would be pulled back, a new policy of retrenchment would be practiced, and the Boor soups would be allowed to seek their own level of sales.

THE DISINVESTMENT DECISION

In July of 1985, a special committee presented a report to top management of IFI on possible courses of action with regard to Boor Soups. The report considered the merits of two alternatives: complete disinvestment or continuing in the business of producing and marketing Boor Soups in the United States.

1. *Disinvestment.* This involved ceasing production, ending the sale of the products, liquidating the finished goods inventory, and selling surplus equipment for realizable value. A conservative estimate of the cash gain resulting from such disinvestment was $5.2 million resulting from $2.6 million of nontaxable income and a $2.6 million tax credit.

2. *Continuation in the business.* The decision to continue Boor operations in the United States was compared with the cash gain of $5.2 million from disinvestment. Top management felt that since International Foods Incorporated had already been badly burned in an attempt to sell Boor to U.S. housewives, the decision to continue in the business at this time would have to be accompanied by the development of major new marketing and product strategies.

The committee presented a sales forecast for the next eight years (1986–1993) based on the following assumptions:

TABLE 4   Pro Forma Cash Flow Statement (in thousands)

Sales (cases)	2,000	
Gross sales (dollars)		$ 7,200
Freight	$ 220	
Cash discount	132	
Breakage and spoilage	200	552
Net sales		$ 6,648
Raw materials	$2,400	
Packaging	940	
Other direct manufacturing	1,020	4,360
Gross margin		$ 2,288
Factory overhead	$ 125	
Factor margin		$ 2,163
Advertisement and promotion	$2,500	
Marketing (other)	40	
Brokerage and warehousing	200	
General and administration expense	50	
Marketing and selling (est.)	100	−2,890
Net cash flow		$ −727

1. Average total soup market would be between 124 million and 127 million cases per year.
2. The dry soup market would average between 9.4 percent and 10.6 percent of the average total soup market.
3. The Boor share of the dry soup market would range between 15 percent and 20 percent.

Using these assumptions, the committee predicted the most likely sales volume for Boor would be 2.2 million cases per year, with a 10 percent probability that 1.7 million cases would be sold (the minimum) and a 10 percent probability that 2.7 million cases would be sold (the maximum). Top management was known to favor staying in business even if the return on investment was as low as 5 percent per year after taxes (10 percent pre-tax). Cash flows of at least $800,000 per year would thus be required to make staying in business at least as attractive as disinvestment (the present value, assuming a 5 percent discount rate, of $800,000 a year for eight years is approximately $5.2 million).

As Table 4 indicates, even if 2 million cases could be sold in 1986, the Boor operation would run a cash flow loss of something over $1.4 million, or more than $2 million below the required cash flow. From this it was clear that the chances were minimal that staying in business could ever be as profitable as disinvestment.

QUESTIONS

1. What were the major reasons for Boor's failure in the U.S. market?
2. Could these reasons have been predicted on the basis of IFI's market research prior to launching Boor? If not, what additional research would have been needed?
3. What are the major lessons to be learned from IFI's experience with Boor?

4

SOCIAL AND CULTURAL ELEMENTS OF THE WORLD MARKET ENVIRONMENT

In spite of difference of soil and climate, of language and manners, of laws and customs—in spite of things silently gone out of mind, and things violently destroyed, the Poet binds together by passion and knowledge the vast empire of human society, as it is spread over the whole earth, and over all time.

William Wordsworth, 1770–1850, Lyrical Ballads *(2nd ed., 1800)*

INTRODUCTION

This chapter focuses on the social and cultural forces that shape and affect individual behavior in the world market environment. Every person in the world reflects the interaction of his or her own unique personality with the collective forces of the culture and milieu in which he or she has developed and experienced life. The approach of this chapter expresses the book's conceptual orientation, which is based on the assumption that individuals and cultures of the world are characterized by both differences and similarities.

The task of the global marketer is to recognize both the similarities and the differences and incorporate this perception into the marketing planning process so that strategies, products, and marketing programs are adapted to significant and important differences. At the same time, the global marketer must also perceive relevant similarities and avoid unnecessary and costly adaptations to marketing strategies and programs. The objective of this chapter is to provide an analytical approach to understanding cultural dynamics in the marketplace.

The popular definition of *culture* is, "What I've got and you haven't." "My taste in clothing, music, food, and so forth is cultured, and yours, of course, is not." This is confusing taste with nature. For the anthropologist, culture is, "the ways of living built up by a group of human beings that are transmitted from one generation to another." Culture includes both conscious and unconscious values, ideas, attitudes, and symbols that shape human behavior and that are transmitted from one generation to the next. In this sense, culture does not refer to the instinctive responses of people, nor does it include one-time solutions to unique problems.

BASIC ASPECTS OF CULTURE

Anthroplogists agree on three characteristics of culture: (1) It is not innate, but learned; (2) the various facets of culture are interrelated—touch a culture in one place and everything else is affected; (3) it is shared by the members of a group and defines the boundaries between different groups.[1]

Because culture has such an important influence on customer behavior, it is useful to outline some of the major assumptions concerning the nature of culture. The following assumptions are drawn from recent anthropological literature and have fairly general acceptance among anthropologists.

Culture consists of learned responses to recurring situations. The earlier these responses are learned, the more difficult they are to change. Many aspects of culture influence the marketing environment. Taste, for example, is a learned response that is highly variable from culture to culture and has a major impact on the market environment. Preference for such things as colors and styles is culturally influenced. For example, ". . . green is a highly regarded color in Moslem countries, but has negative connotations in Southwest Asia, where it is associated with disease, while white, usually associated with purity and cleanliness in the West, signifies death in Asian countries. Red, a popular color in most parts of the world, is poorly received in some African countries."[2] Attitudes toward whole classes of products can be a function of culture. For example, in the United States there is a high cultural predisposition to be interested and intrigued by product innovations that have a "gadgety" quality. Thus the electric knife, the electric toothbrush, the Water-Pik (a dental appliance that cleans teeth and gums with a pulsating stream of water under high pressure), and a host of appliances find a ready and very quick market in the United States even though many of these products are often purchased, used for a period of time, and then quietly put away and never used again. There is unquestionably a smaller predisposition to purchase such products in other developed country markets such as Europe.

A reasonable hypothesis is that this difference is partially a result of cultural differences. Nevertheless, because incomes in other industrial country markets and the United States are different, the influence of income on behavior and attitudes is also at work. Indeed the basic question that must be answered by marketers seeking to understand or predict behavior is, "To what extent do cultural factors influence behavior independent of income levels?" The profusion of automobiles, convenience

---

[1]Edward T. Hall, *Beyond Culture* (Garden City, N.Y.: Anchor Books, 1977), p. 16.
[2]Richard R. Still and John S. Hill, "Multinational Product Planning: A Meta Market Analysis," *International Marketing Review*, Spring 1985, p. 60.

foods, disposable packages, and other articles in the trial markets of the United States, Europe, and Japan suggests that many or perhaps even most consumer products have universal appeal and will be purchased in any country, regardless of cultural differences, when consumer disposable income reaches a high enough level.

The Search for Cultural Universals

For the international marketer the search for cultural universals provides a valuable orientation. A *universal* is a mode of behavior existing in all cultures. To the extent that aspects of the cultural environment are universal as opposed to unique, it is possible for the international marketer to standardize such aspects of his or her marketing program as product design and communications, which are two of the major elements of a marketing program. Fortunately for the international marketer, much of the apparent cultural diversity in the world turns out to be different ways of accomplishing the same thing.

A partial list of cultural universals was developed by George P. Murdock and includes the following:

> Age grading, athletic sports, bodily adornment, calendar, cleanliness training, community organization, cooking, co-operative labor, cosmology, courtship, dancing, decorative art, divination, division of labor, dream interpretation, education, ethics, etiquette, family feasting, firemaking, folklore, food taboos, inheritance rules, joking, kin groups, kinship, language, law, magic, marriage, mealtime, medicine, modesty concerning natural functions, mourning music, nomenclature, obstetrics, penal sanctions, personal names, population policy, postnatal care, pregnancy usage, property rights, propitiation of supernatural beings, puberty customs, religious rituals, residence rules, sexual restrictions, soul concepts, status differentiation, superstition, surgery, toolmaking, trade, visiting, weaning, and weather control.[3]

Let us consider music as an example of how these universals apply to marketing decision making. Music as an art form is part of all cultures; thus the musical songtype commercial is universally feasible. Although music is culturally universal, its style is not internationally uniform. Therefore, the type of music that is appropriate in one part of the world may not be acceptable or effective in another part. A campaign might utilize a bossa nova rhythm or "cha-cha-cha" beat for Latin America, a rock rhythm for North America, a "high life" for Africa, and so on. In this way the universal forms can be adapted to cultural styles in each region.

With increasing travel and communications many of the national attitudes toward style in clothing, color, music, and food and drink are becoming international and even universal. This internationalization of culture has been significantly accelerated by multinational companies that have recognized an opportunity to extend their product/communications strategies into international markets. Coke and Pepsi, Levi Straus, Kentucky Fried Chicken, IBM, and Apple are just a few examples of

[3]George P. Murdock, "The Common Denominator of Culture," in *The Science of Man in the World Crisis,* ed. Ralph Linton (New York: Columbia University Press, 1945), p. 145.

U.S. companies breaking down cultural distinctiveness by their expansion into new international markets. As Professor Levitt points out in his celebrated article on the globalization of markets,

> Ancient differences in national tastes or modes of doing business disappear. The commonality of preference leads inescapably to the standardization of products, manufacturing, and the institutions of trade and commerce. Small nation-based markets transmogrify and expand. Success in world competition turns on efficiency in production, distribution, marketing, and management, and inevitably becomes focused on price.[4]

The Anthropologist's Standpoint

As Ruth Benedict points out in her classic *The Chrysanthemum and the Sword,* no matter how bizarre one's act or opinion, the way a person thinks, feels, and acts has some relation to his experience. Successful international marketers must adopt this assumption if they are to understand the dynamics of a foreign market.

Any systematic study of a foreign market requires a combination of tough-mindedness and generosity. The appreciation of another way of life cannot develop when one is defensive about one's own way of life; it is necessary to be secure in one's own convictions and traditions. In addition, generosity is required if one is to appreciate the integrity and value of other ways of life and points of view. The international marketer needs to develop an objective standpoint that recognizes diversity, seeks to understand its origins, and avoids the pitfalls of both rejection and identification. There are many paths to the same end in life—the international marketer knows this and rejoices in life's rich diversity.

Communication

The ability to communicate in one's own language is, as everyone knows, not an easy task. Whenever languages change, there is an additional communications challenge. This is especially so when the language and the culture are different. For example, "yes" and "no" are used in an entirely different way in Japanese than in Western languages. This has caused much confusion and misunderstanding. In English, the answer "yes" or "no" to a question is based on whether the answer is affirmative or negative. In Japanese, this is not so. The answer "yes" or "no" may refer to whether or not the answer affirms or negates the question. For example, in Japanese if you were asked, "Don't you like meat?" you would answer "yes" if your answer is negative. You might say, for example, "Yes, I don't like meat."

Perhaps the most challenging form of communication is not verbal communications, but nonverbal. The West tends to be verbal, and the East more nonverbal. The American anthropologist W. Caudill conducted a study to compare American and Japanese mothers' attitudes toward child rearing. One of the most significant

---

[4]Theodore Levitt, "The Globalization of Markets," *Harvard Business Review,* May–June 1983, pp. 93–94.

differences that he found was that American mothers talked to their babies even before they reached the babbling stage, whereas Japanese mothers seldom talked to theirs. There is a greater expectation in the East that people will pick up nonverbal cues and understand intuitively without being told.[5] Many a business and government executive has learned to his chagrin that when the Japanese executive said yes to a proposal, what he really meant was "yes, I hear you," not, "yes, I agree."

ANALYTICAL APPROACHES TO CULTURAL FACTORS

Introduction

The reason cultural factors are a challenge to global marketers is that they are hidden from view. Culture is learned behavior passed on from generation to generation and is difficult for the inexperienced or untrained outsider to fathom. Unless we learn how to let go of our cultural assumptions, we will be limited in our understanding of the meaning and significance of the statements and behaviors of the people from a different culture whom we are trying to do business with.

For example, if you come from a culture that encourages responsibility and initiative, you could experience misunderstandings with a client or boss from a culture that encourages people to remain in personal control of all activities. Your boss would expect you to keep him advised in detail of what you were doing when you might be taking initiative assuming that he would appreciate your willingness to assume responsibility.

To transcend cultural myopia it is important to know that there are cultural differences and that they can be learned and incorporated into your experience base. There are several basic facts that will accelerate your ability to learn about other cultures:

1. The beginning of wisdom is to accept that we will never fully understand ourselves or others—people are far too complex to be "understood." As Carl Jung pointed out, "There are no misunderstandings in nature . . . misunderstandings are found only in the realm of what we call 'understanding.'"[6]
2. Our perceptual systems are extremely limited. We "see" almost nothing. Our nervous systems are organized on the principle of negative feedback (i.e., our nervous system operates so smoothly that the only time our control system is brought into play is when input signals deviate from what we expect).
3. We spend most of our energy managing perceptual inputs.
4. When we experience or perceive bizarre behavior, there is something behind this behavior (i.e., a cultural system of beliefs and values that we do not understand).
5. If we want to be effective in a foreign culture, we must attempt to understand beliefs, motives, and values. This requires an open attitude, one that transcends our own culture.

[5]Tsune Shirai, "What Is an 'International Mind'?" *PHP* (June 1980), p. 25.

[6]C. G. Jung, *Critique of Psychoanalysis*, Bollingen Series XX (Princeton, N.J.: Princeton University Press, 1975), par. 776, p. 228.

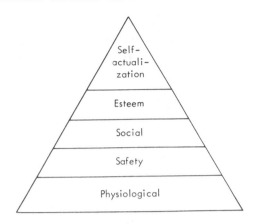

FIGURE 4–1 Maslow's Hierarchy of Needs

The Need Hierarchy

In the search for cultural universals, an extremely useful theory of human motivation was developed by the late A. H. Maslow.[7]

Maslow hypothesized that people's desires can be arranged into a hierarchy of needs of relative potency. As soon as the "lower" needs are filled, other and higher needs emerge immediately to dominate the individual. When these higher needs are in turn satisfied, new and still higher needs emerge. Figure 4–1 illustrates the hierarchy identifying the major needs formulated by Maslow.

Physiological needs are at the bottom of the hierarchy because they are most fundamental. They include food, water, air, protection from the elements, comfort, sex, and so on. For the person who is extremely hungry, no other interest except food exists. The individual thinks only about food, wants only food, and has little interest in writing poetry, reading a good book, or acquiring a new automobile or anything other than satisfying an overwhelming need for food. Once these physiological needs are gratified, a new set of needs emerges that Maslow categorizes as safety needs. Safety, in general, refers to a feeling of well-being and a sense that danger is not present in the environment. A person whose physiological and safety needs are satisfied will feel the need for friendships and love relationships and will strive to gratify these needs, which Maslow called social needs.

Once these "lower" needs have been satisfied, two higher needs emerge. First is a need for esteem. This is the desire for self-respect, self-esteem, and the esteem of others and is a powerful drive creating demand for status-improving goods. The status symbol exists across the spectrum of stages of development. In developing East Africa women who owned bras always wore them with straps exposed to show the world that they owned a bra. In the United States a more expensive automobile was for decades a standard form of status improvement.

[7]A. H. Maslow, "A Theory of Human Motivation," in *Readings in Managerial Psychology,* eds. Harold J. Leavitt and Louis R. Pondy (Chicago: University of Chicago Press, 1964), pp. 6–24.

The final stage in the need hierarchy is self-actualization. When all the needs for sex, safety, security, friendship, and the esteem of others are satisfied, discontent and restlessness will develop unless one is doing what one is fitted for. A musician must make music, an artist must paint, a poet must write, a builder must build, and so on. As Albert Einstein said when asked how he withstood the acclaim he received for his accomplishments and the peril of corruption by praise, "One is tempted to stop and listen to it. The only thing is to turn away and go on working. Work, there is nothing else."[8] There is a possibility that demand for material goods declines at this point.

The hierarchy of needs proposed by Maslow is, of course, a simplification of the complexity of need feelings in people. A person's needs do not progress neatly from one stage of a hierarchy to another. A person who is fulfilling self-actualization needs is also in need of love, sex, and food. One may be restless and dissatisfied before approaching self-actualization. Nevertheless, the hierarchy does suggest a hypothesis for relating higher levels of consumption to basic psychological drives.

The usefulness of the need hierarchy hypothesis to the international marketer is its universality. The more highly developed a market, the greater the proportion of goods and products that will be filling social and esteem needs as opposed to physiological. As countries continue to develop, it appears that self-actualization needs begin to affect consumer behavior. In the United States, for example, the automobile is no longer a universal status symbol, and many younger consumers are turning away from material possessions. As countries progress through the stages of economic development, more and more members of a society are operating at the esteem need level and higher, having satisfied physiological, safety, and social needs.[9]

The expression of these higher needs takes some surprising forms. In Los Angeles, for example, a company called Rent-A-Wreck has discovered a thriving market among affluent Hollywood residents who are reacting to what they consider to be a low-brow esteem for expensive cars and who assert their cultural values by driving "wrecks." This is an example of a growing tendency in the United States to reject material objects as "status symbols." This mass rejection of materialism is not so advanced in other leading industrialized countries. For example, in Germany today, the automobile remains a supreme status symbol. Germans give their automobiles loving care, even going so far as to travel to distant locations on weekends to wash their cars in spring water.

Although there are abundant sources of stereotypes that suggest enormous differences in the basic nature of different nationalities and races, increasing evidence is accumulating to dispute these stereotypes. In a study of 25 overseas operations of a large manufacturing company, Sirota and Greenwood found considerable similarity in the work goals of employees:

[8]Ronald W. Clark, *Einstein: The Life and Times* (New York: World, 1971).

[9]An anomaly of modern times is the emergence of need in the safety area in the United States, one of the richest countries in the world. Indeed, the high incidence of violence in the United States may leave U.S. residents with a lower level of satisfaction of this need than in many so-called "poor" countries.

The implications of our study may be considered at a number of different levels . . .

Perhaps most relevant to the managers of international organizations is the considerable similarity we have found in the goals of employees around the world. This finding has an extremely important policy implication: since the goals of employees are similar internationally, corporate policy decisions, to the extent that they are based on assumptions about employee goals, can also be international in scope.

It is not only Americans who want money, or Frenchmen who want autonomy, or Germans who want their work skills utilized and improved. A management whose policies and practices reflect these stereotypes (for example, providing few advancement opportunities in some countries or using certain countries as dumping grounds for routine, unchallenging work) should be prepared to suffer the consequences of managing a frustrated and uncommitted work force.

In this respect, it would be interesting to determine how much of the difficulty experienced in managing employees in other countries is due not to cultural differences at all but, rather, to the automatic and psychologically self-serving assumption of differences that, in reality, may be minor or even nonexistent.[10]

✗ The Self-Reference Criterion

A way of systematically reducing the extent to which our perception of market needs is blocked by our own cultural experience was developed by James Lee. Lee terms the unconscious reference to one's own cultural values the *self-reference criterion,* or SRC. He addresses this problem and proposes a systematic four-step framework for eliminating this form of myopia.[11]

1. Define the problem or goal in terms of home country cultural traits, habits, and norms.
2. Define the problems or goal in terms of the foreign culture, traits, habits, and norms.
3. Isolate the SRC influence in the problem and examine it carefully to see how it complicates the problem.
4. Redefine the problem without the SRC influence and solve for the foreign market situation.

Lce provides the following example of an application of this analytical approach. An automobile manufacturer withdrew its assembly operation from Karachi under government pressure to manufacture automobiles or to sell out. Taking this pressure as the beginning of a product design problem, how might the company have proceeded at the time of its entry into the Pakistani market?

Step 1. *Define the business problem or goal in terms of domestic cultural traits, habits, or norms.* Western countries are characterized by transportation needs geared to speed, promptness, comfort, and style. Advanced country highways demanded a cruising speed of 60 to 70 miles an hour and 80- to 100-octane gasoline was available. Manufacturing techniques were very sophisticated; foreign exchange was not a businessman's problem.

[10]David Sirota and Michael J. Greenwood, "Understand Your Overseas Workforce," *Harvard Business Review,* January–February 1971, p. 60.

[11]James A. Lee, "Cultural Analysis in Overseas Operations," *Harvard Business Review,* March–April 1966, pp. 106–114.

Step 2. *Define the business problem or goal in terms of the foreign cultural traits, habits, or norms. Make no value judgments.* Pakistan was a culture characterized by a strong desire to be mobile but with a low technological skill level. There was extreme pressure on foreign exchange. Consumer credit was a future hope.

Step 3. *Isolate the SRC influence in the problem and examine it carefully to see how it complicates the problem.* The significant differences between steps 1 and 2 suggest strongly that the needs upon which the advanced country model were originally based did not exist in Pakistan and that a modification of these models was needed by the market.

Step 4. *Redefine the problem without the SRC influence and solve for the foreign market situation.* This would require the design of a car to fit Pakistan's cultural and economic specifications. Lee maintains that such a car would be made of angle, channel, and strap iron. The capital investment in Pakistan would be about $100,000 in hard currency and in the equivalent amount in the local currency for each 1,000 units of annual capacity. The car would sell for approximately $2,000, would have a cruising speed of 40 miles an hour, and would travel 80 miles on a gallon of low-octane gasoline.

Diffusion Theory

Since the late 1930s hundreds of studies have been directed toward achieving and understanding the process through which an individual adopts a new idea.[12] In his book *Diffusion of Innovations,* Everett Rogers reports on 506 diffusion studies that suggest some remarkably similar findings. This enormous body of research has suggested concepts and patterns that are extremely useful to international marketers because they are involved in introducing innovations in the form of their products into markets.

An *innovation* is something new or different, either in an absolute sense or in a situational sense. In an absolute sense, once a product has been introduced anywhere in the world, it is no longer an innovation because it is no longer new to the world. However, a product introduced in one market may be an innovation in another market because it is a new and different product for the new market. Thus, in international marketing, companies are in the position of marketing products that may be simultaneously new product innovations in some markets and mature, postmature, or declining products in other markets. Thus the findings from studies of the diffusion of innovations have great relevance to the various circumstances in which the international marketer finds himself or herself.

THE ADOPTION PROCESS.   One of the basic elements of the theory of the diffusion of innovations is the concept of an adoption process—the mental process through which an individual passes from the time of his or her first knowledge of an innovation to the time of adoption or purchase of the innovation. Research suggests that an individual passes through five different stages in proceeding from first knowledge of

[12]This section is drawn from Everett M. Rogers, *Diffusion of Innovations* (New York: Free Press, 1962).

a product to the final adoption or purchase of that product. These stages are as follows:

1. *Awareness*. At this stage the customer becomes aware for the first time of the product or innovation. Studies have shown that at this stage impersonal sources of information such as advertising are most important. Frequently one of the major objectives of advertising in international marketing is to create product awareness where the product is an innovation in the new market.

2. *Interest*. During this stage the customer knows of the product and, because of an interest in the product, seeks additional information. In the information gathering, the customer has shifted from a viewing position to a monitoring position. He or she will incorporate any information on the product in question if information on it should come into his or her possession. Additionally, because of an interest in the product, the customer will engage in research activities to acquire additional information.

3. *Evaluation*. In this stage the individual mentally applies the product or innovation to the present and anticipated future situation and decides whether or not to try the product.

4. *Trial*. After learning of the product, obtaining information about it, and mentally deciding whether or not to try the product, the customer's next stage is trial or actual purchase depending on the cost of the product. If the product is expensive, then a customer will not purchase it without trial, although the trial may be mental or theoretical rather than actual. A good example of an actual trial that does not involve purchase would be the automobile demonstration ride. For the inexpensive product, trial often involves purchase, but can also involve a free sample. In inexpensive products, adoption is defined as repeat purchase as opposed to a single purchase that is defined as trial.

5. *Adoption*. In this stage the individual either purchases the more expensive product that has been tried without purchase or continues to purchase (repeat purchase) the less expensive product, such as a razor blade. As a person moves from the evaluation to the trial to the adoption stage, studies show that personal sources of information are more important than impersonal sources. It is during these stages that the representative and, perhaps even more important, word of mouth come into play as major persuasive forces affecting the decision to buy.

CHARACTERISTICS OF INNOVATIONS. One of the major factors affecting the rate of adoption of an innovation is the characteristics of the innovation itself. Rogers suggests five characteristics that have a major influence on the rate of adoption of an innovation. They are as follows:

1. *Relative advantage*. How does a new product compare with existing products or methods in the eyes of customers? The perceived relative advantage of a new product versus existing products is a major influence on the rate of adoption. An example of a product with a high perceived relative advantage is the transistor radio vis-à-vis the tube-type radio. If a product has a substantial relative advantage vis-à-vis the competition, it is at a great advantage in the market.

2. *Compatibility*. This is the extent to which a product is consistent with existing values and past experiences of adopters. The history of product failures in international marketing is replete with examples that were caused by the lack of compatibility of the new products in the target market. The fluffy frosted cake mixes were introduced by U.S. companies into the United Kingdom where cake was eaten at teatime with the fingers rather than as a dessert with a fork. The result was lack of sales and failure. The Renault Dauphine was introduced into the United States in 1959 to a market that subjected

automobiles to driving conditions far more rigorous than those encountered in France. The result was product breakdowns and failure. The Jolly Green Giant attempted to market corn in Europe where the prevailing attitude is that corn is a grain that is fed to hogs and not to people. The result was a lack of sales and severe losses on investments in European corn production. These products did not succeed in international markets because of the lack of compatibility with existing values and patterns of behavior.

3. *Complexity.* This is the degree to which an innovation or new product is difficult to understand and use. If a product has a high coefficient of complexity, then this is a factor that can slow down the rate of adoption, particularly in developing country markets with low rates of literacy.

4. *Divisibility.* This is the degree or extent to which a product may be tried and used on a limited basis. In the international market, wide discrepancies in income levels result in major differences in acceptable levels of divisibility. Hellmann's mayonnaise, a product of CPC International, was simply not selling in U.S.-size jars in Latin America. The company then placed the mayonnaise in small plastic packets and immediately sales developed. The plastic packets were within the food budgets of the local consumers, and they required no refrigeration, another plus.

5. *Communicability.* This is the degree to which results of an innovation or the value of a product may be communicated to a potential market.

The major dimensions of the product that determine the rate of its adoption or penetration of international markets are its relative advantage vis-à-vis other products, its compatibility with existing values and patterns of behavior, and the price of the product relative to the price of competing or substitute products. A fourth major factor is the availability of the product. Finally, the communicability and the effectiveness of communications concerning the product are a major influence affecting the rate of adoption.

ADOPTER CATEGORIES. Adopter categories are classifications of individuals within a market on the basis of their innovativeness. The hundreds of studies of the diffusion of innovation demonstrate that adoption is a social phenomenon and therefore is characterized by the normal distributions. If the number of adopters is plotted on the Y axis and time on the X axis, the adopters of an innovation are those shown in Figure 4–2.

Five categories have been assigned to the segments of this normal distribution. The first 2.5 percent of people to purchase a product are defined as *innovators*. The

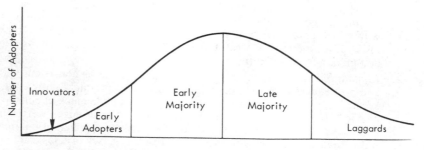

FIGURE 4–2 Adopter Categories

next 13.5 percent are defined as *early adopters*, the next 34 percent as the *early majority*, the next 34 percent as the *late majority*, and the final 16 percent as *laggards*. Studies show that innovators tend to be venturesome, more cosmopolitan in their social relationships, and wealthier than those who adopt later. Earlier adopters are the most influential people in their communities, even more than the innovators. Thus the early adopters are a critical group in the adoption process, and they have a great influence on the majority, who make up the bulk of the adopters of any product. Several characteristics of early adopters stand out. First, they tend to be younger, have higher social status, and are in a more favorable financial position than later adopters. They must be responsive to mass-media information sources and must learn about innovations from these sources because they cannot simply copy the behavior of earlier adopters.

One of the major reasons for the normal distribution of adopter categories is the so-called "interaction effect." This is the process through which individuals in a social system who have adopted an innovation influence those who have not yet adopted. Adoption of a new idea or product is the result of human interaction. If the first adopter of an innovation or new product discusses it with two other people, and each of these two adopters passes the new idea along to two other people, and so on, the resulting distribution follows a binomial expansion. This mathematical function follows a normal shape when plotted.

From the point of view of the marketing manager, steps taken to persuade innovators and early adopters to purchase a product are critical because these innovators must make the first move and are the basis for the eventual penetration of a product into a new market because the majority copy their behavior.

High- and Low-Context Cultures

Edward T. Hall has suggested the concept of high and low context as a way of understanding different cultural orientations.[13] In a low-context culture, messages are explicit; words carry most of the information in communication. In a high-context culture, less information is contained in the verbal part of a message, since much more information is in the context of communication, which includes the background, associations, and basic values of the communicators. Who you are—that is, your values and position or place in society—is crucial in the high-context culture, such as in Japan or the Arab countries. In these cultures, a bank loan is more likely to be based upon who you are than upon formal analysis of pro forma profit and loss statements and balance sheets. In a low-context culture, deals are made with much less information about the character and background and values of the participants and much more reliance upon the words and numbers in the loan application. Examples of low-context cultures would be the United States or, perhaps even more distinctly, the Swiss-Germans.

[13] See Edward T. Hall, *Beyond Culture* (Garden City, N.Y.: Anchor Press/Doubleday, 1976), and "How Cultures Collide," *Psychology Today*, July 1976, pp. 66–97.

In general, high-context cultures get along with much less legal paperwork than is deemed essential in low-context cultures such as the United States. In a high-context culture, a person's word is his or her bond. There is less need to anticipate contingencies and provide for external legal sanctions in a culture that emphasizes obligations and trust as important values. In these cultures, shared feelings of obligation and honor take the place of impersonal legal sanctions—thus the importance of long and protracted negotiations that never seem to get to the point. Part of the purpose of negotiating for a person from a high-context culture is to get to know the potential partner.

For example, insisting on competitive bidding can cause complications in low-context cultures. In a high-context culture, the job is given to the person who will do the best work and whom you can trust and control. In a low-context culture, one tries to make the specifications so precise that a builder is forced by the threat of legal sanction to do a good job. According to Hall, a builder in Japan is likely to say, "What has that piece of paper got to do with the situation? If we can't trust each other enough to go ahead without it, why bother?"

Although countries can be classified as high or low context in their overall tendency, there are of course exceptions to the general tendency. These exceptions are found in subcultures. The United States, for example, is a low-context culture with subcultures that operate in the high-context mode.

Charles A. Coombs, senior vice president of the Federal Reserve Bank of New York in charge of the Fed's foreign exchange operations, provides such an example in his book *The Arena of International Finance*. The world of the central banker, as he describes it, is a gentleman's world, that is, a high-context culture. Even during the most hectic days in the foreign exchange markets, a central banker's word is sufficient for him to borrow millions of dollars. During the rioting and political upheavals in France in 1968, the confidence of central bankers in one another was dramatically demonstrated. Except for telephones, all communications between France and the United States were cut off. Consequently, the New York Fed agreed that it would follow instructions received by telephone from the Bank of France for intervening on its behalf in support of the franc. Within eight days the New York Fed had bought more than $50 million of francs without a single written confirmation for any part of the purchase. The Fed was far out on a limb. A couple of weeks later the daughter of the governor of the Bank of France came to New York on personal business. She brought written confirmations with her. "Our legal department heaved a sigh of relief," Coombs remembers. The legal department was operating in a low-context culture with all the assumptions that go with this culture (everything must be spelled out and confirmed in writing—you can't trust anyone), but the central bankers, who were obviously much more relaxed about the matter, were operating within a high-context culture (a person's word is his or her bond). Another U.S. high-context subculture is the Mafia, which has imported the high-context culture of Sicily to the United States and has maintained this culture with language, ritual, separation, and a strong sense of distinct identity.

Bernard Sloan, a U.S. advertising executive, recounts the following story of his introduction to high-context culture in Australia.

TABLE 4–1   **High- and Low-Context Cultures**

FACTORS/DIMENSIONS	HIGH CONTEXT	LOW CONTEXT
Lawyers	Less important	Very important
A person's word	Is his or her bond	Is not to be relied upon; "get it in writing"
Responsibility for organizational error	Taken by highest level	Pushed to lowest level
Space	People breathe on each other	People carry a bubble of private space with them and resent intrusions
Time	Polychronic—everything in life must be dealt with in terms of its own time	Monochronic—time is money. Linear—one thing at a time
Negotiations	Are lengthy—a major purpose is to allow the parties to get to know each other	Proceed quickly
Competitive bidding	Infrequent	Common
Country/regional examples	Japan, Middle East	United States, Northern Europe

> While living in Australia, I discovered that banks do not return canceled checks. Having tossed away receipts on the assumption that our checks would come back, I asked the teller what evidence we would have for the tax department.
>
> "Not to worry," he said with a smile, "you just show the stubs in your checkbook."
>
> "But I could write in any amount," I said.
>
> He pondered for a moment and replied, "I suppose one could, couldn't one?"

Sloan goes on to recount dozens of other examples of Australian behavior that would dumbfound Americans: return bottles that are returned without a deposit, prices at public events for food and drink that are no higher than everyday prices in the shops, packaged products that are sold in uniform sizes, and even electric bills that are mailed to overseas destinations when people are moving.[14]

All these examples illustrate the ways of a high-context culture in which there is trust, a sense of fair play, and a widespread acceptance of the rules of the game as it is played.

Table 4–1 summarizes some of the ways in which high- and low-context cultures differ.

Perception

The vital, critical skill of the global marketer is perception, or the ability to see what is so in a culture. Although this skill is as valuable at home as it is abroad, it is of particular importance to the global marketer because of the widespread tendency to rely on the self-reference criterion or SRC. The self-reference criterion is the *un-*

---

[14]"Dumb Aussies, They Say," *The New York Times,* April 24, 1979, p. A19.

conscious tendency to draw on memory and assumptions about people instead of perceptions of how they actually behave and think.[15]

The SRC is a powerful negative force in global business, and one of the major causes of failure and misunderstanding. To avoid the SRC, you must suspend your experience and be prepared to acquire new knowledge about human behavior and motivation.

It would be easy to get paranoid about the hazards of doing business across cultures, but in fact, the main obstacle is attitude. If you are sincere, and truly want to learn about a culture, you will find that people respond to your sincerity and interest and will help you acquire the knowledge you need to be effective. If you are arrogant and insincere and believe that you are right and "they" are wrong, you can expect a full measure of trouble and misunderstanding. The best antidote to the problem of misperceiving a situation is constant vigilance and an awareness that there are many opportunities to err. This should create an attitude of openness to see what is so. Every global marketer should strive to suspend judgment and simply perceive and take in the facts.

NEGOTIATIONS—CROSS-CULTURAL CHALLENGES

One of the best opportunities to apply a knowledge and understanding of cross-cultural differences is in negotiations as negotiation style reflects assumptions about the values and assumptions of one's negotiating partner. In international negotiations the international marketer faces partners from diverse cultural backgrounds.

Americans bring their cultural ethnocentrism to the negotiating table. According to two experts on international negotiations, there are ten uniquely American tactics or approaches to negotiations. They may be effective with other Americans, but when used with people from other cultural backgrounds, they require modification. The approaches and the corrections required are:

1. "I can go it alone." Americans are typically outnumbered in negotiations. Solution: greater reliance on teamwork and division of negotiating labor.
2. "Just call me John." Americans place a high value on informality and equality of participants in negotiations. This may conflict with the customs and class structures of foreign cultures. Solution: Respect the customs and class structure of other cultures. Obtain information from self study and local agents on local attitudes and values.
3. "Pardon my French." Americans are culturally monolingual. Solution: Forget everything you ever heard about how difficult it is to learn a foreign language and accept that you have a talent for language (you read, speak, and write English!). If you are going to be regularly doing business with a country, take the time, make the effort, and learn their language. If your contact with a culture is too limited to justify the time and effort required to learn their language, make sure that you select and develop a good working relationship with a competent interpreter.

---

[15] See discussion of SRC on p. 111.

4. "Get to the point." Americans are, in comparison to people from other cultures, blunt and impatient. Solution: Understand that people from other cultures *need* to develop a sense of connection and personal trust in order to feel comfortable about doing business. This takes time. Take time to get to know your negotiating partner.

5. "Lay your cards on the table." Americans like to state the case up front, and are not accustomed to "feeling out" prospective partners. Solution: Slow down, and recognize the need to ask the same question in different ways. Prepare to spend double the time you think is needed to get the information you need.

6. "Don't just sit there, speak up." Americans are uncomfortable with silence during negotiations and often deal with their discomfort by "running at the mouth." Solution: Recognize that silence is golden. You do not have to keep a constant stream of chatter. If there is silence, let it be. Reflect. Take in information that comes from body posture and facial expression. Reflect on the words that have been spoken and on your own objectives and values. In other words, *value* the silence. Take advantage of it.

7. "Don't take no for an answer." Persistence and the "hard sell" are highly valued in the United States. Solution: If the answer is no, stop selling and find out why. Respond to the reasons for the no answer.

8. "One thing at a time." Americans favor a linear, organized, "left brain" style of negotiating. This is not a universal approach. Solution: Recognize your own right brain capability. Embrace a more holistic approach toward negotiations.

9. "A deal is a deal." This is a projection of an expectation which may not be shared. Solution: Accept a more gradual, supplemental view of negotiations and joint effort.

10. "I am what I am." Solution: Adopt a more flexible standpoint. Be willing to change your mind and to adapt to your opposite.[16]

INDUSTRIAL PRODUCTS

Cultural factors are important influences on the marketing of industrial products and must be recognized in formulating an international marketing plan. Different conventions regarding specifications are an important variable internationally. For example, U.S. specifications typically contain a margin of error so that a buyer will obtain the specifications plus some margin of error that varies from industry to industry. In the United States if you need a metal bar to carry 20,000 pounds with an occasional load of 25,000 pounds, then you can specify 20,000 pounds and get a bar that will have a sufficient safety factor built in to cover overload situations. In Europe specifications are exact. Typically, in Europe if you buy a bar to carry 20,000 pounds, this is the maximum weight that the bar can carry. If you want a safety factor up to 25,000 pounds, you must buy a bar with specifications of that point.

One of the major requirements of a successful industrial marketing effort internationally is persistence. Motorola, Inc., a U.S. company, decided that it wanted to penetrate the Japanese market. It proceeded realistically to implement this objective. First, the company hired a former U.S. government assistant trade representative who had the experience and skill to guide the company's campaign to

[16]This section is adapted from John L. Graham and Roy A. Heberger Jr., "Negotiators Abroad—Don't Shoot From the Hip," *Harvard Business Review*, July-August 1983, pp. 160–168.

penetrate the Japanese market. The company decided to focus upon Nippon Telephone and Telegraph, the public telecommunications monopoly. The company had a strong competitive position in pagers, and to secure Nippon's business, the company built a special assembly line to build pagers to Nippon's specifications. The next thing Motorola did was to seek certification to supply mobile telephone equipment. Getting certification is a difficult process and usually takes at least 18 months. This is time consuming and costly, which makes it important for a company to know what it is doing and why it is doing it to underline the commitment to the effort. Otherwise, it is more than likely that difficulties will cause companies to give up and go home. Motorola was successful in getting this commitment, which was a virtual guarantee that it would get a piece of this business.[17]

A Case Example: Marketing an Industrial Product in Latin America

Much has been written about specific cultural differences in various regions of the world. The cultural variety of the world is so great that it is neither feasible nor prudent to attempt to capture these differences in a single volume. The following actual case suggests, however, the way in which cultural differences influenced the marketing of an industrial product in Latin America.

A Latin American republic had decided to modernize one of its communication networks at a cost of several million dollars. Because of its reputation for quality, the government approached American company ''Y.''

The company, having been sounded out informally, considered the size of the order and decided to bypass its regular Latin American representative and send instead its sales manager. The following describes what took place.

> The sales manager arrived and checked into the leading hotel. He immediately had some difficulty pinning down just who it was he had to see about his business. After several days without results, he called at the American Embassy where he found that the commercial attaché had the up-to-the-minute information he needed. The commercial attaché listened to his story. Realizing that the sales manager had already made a number of mistakes, but figuring that the Latins were used to American blundering, the attaché reasoned that all was not lost. He informed the sales manager that the Minister of Communications was the key man and that whoever got the nod from him would get the contract. He also briefed the sales manager on methods of conducting business in Latin America and offered some pointers about dealing with the minister.
>
> The attaché's advice ran somewhat as follows:
> 1. You don't do business here the way you do in the States; it is necessary to spend much more time. You have to get to know your man and vice versa.
> 2. You must meet with him several times before you talk business. I will tell you at what point you can bring up the subject. Take your cues from me. (Our American sales manager at this point made a few observations to himself about ''cookie pushers'' and wondered how many payrolls had been met by the commercial attaché.)

---

[17]''Motorola Hurdles a Japanese Barrier,'' *Business Week,* June 7, 1982.

3. Take that price list and put it in your pocket. Don't get it out until I tell you to. Down here price is only one of the many things taken into account before closing a deal. In the United States, your past experience will prompt you to act according to a certain set of principles, but many of these principles will not work here. Every time you feel the urge to act or to say something, look at me. Suppress the urge and take your cues from me. This is very important.

4. Down here people like to do business with men who are somebody. In order to be somebody, it is well to have written a book, to have lectured at a university, or to have developed your intellect in some way. The man you are going to see is a poet. He has published several volumes of poetry. Like many Latin Americans, he prizes poetry highly. You will find that he will spend a good deal of business time quoting his poetry to you, and he will take great pleasure in this.

5. You will also note that the people here are very proud of their past and of their Spanish blood, but they are also exceedingly proud of their liberation from Spain and their independence. The fact that they are a democracy, that they are free, and also that they are no longer a colony is very, very important to them. They are warm and friendly and enthusiastic if they like you. If they don't, they are cold and withdrawn.

6. And another thing, time down here means something different. It works in a different way. You know how it is back in the States when a certain type blurts out whatever is on his mind without waiting to see if the situation is right. He is considered an impatient bore and somewhat egocentric. Well, down here you have to wait much, much longer, and I really mean much, much longer, before you can begin to talk about the reason for your visit.

7. There is another point I want to caution you about. At home, the man who sells takes the initiative. Here, they tell you when they are ready to do business. But most of all, don't discuss price until you are asked and don't rush things.

THE PITCH. The next day the commercial attaché introduced the sales manager to the Minister of Communications. First, there was a long wait in the outer office while people kept coming in and out. The sales manager looked at his watch, fidgeted, and finally asked whether the minister was really expecting him. The reply he received was scarcely reassuring, "Oh yes, he is expecting you but several things have come up that require his attention. Besides, one gets used to waiting down here." The sales manager irritably replied, "But doesn't he know I flew all the way down here from the United States to see him, and I have spent over a week already of my valuable time trying to find him?" "Yes, I know," was the answer, "but things just move much more slowly here."

At the end of about thirty minutes, the minister emerged from the office, greeted the commercial attaché with a *doble abrazo,* throwing his arms around him and patting him on the back as though they were long-lost brothers. Now, turning and smiling, the minister extended his hand to the sales manager, who, by this time, was feeling rather miffed because he had been kept in the outer office so long.

After what seemed to be an all too short chat, the minister rose, suggesting a well-known café where they might meet for dinner the next evening. The sales manager expected, of course, that, considering the nature of their business and the size of the order, he might be taken to the minister's home, not realizing that the Latin home is reserved for family and very close friends.

Until now, nothing at all had been said about the reason for the sales manager's visit, a fact which bothered him somewhat. The whole setup seemed wrong; nor did he like the idea of wasting another day in town. He told the home office before he left that he would be gone for a week or ten days at most, and made a mental note that he would clean this order up in three days and enjoy a few days in Acapulco or Mexico City. Now the week had already gone and he would be lucky if he made it home in ten days.

Voicing his misgivings to the commercial attaché, he wanted to know if the minister really meant business, and if he did, why could they not get together and talk about it? The commercial attaché by now was beginning to show the strain of constantly having to reassure the sales manager. Nevertheless, he tried again: "What you don't realize is that part of the time we were waiting, the minister was rearranging a very tight schedule so that he could spend tomorrow night with you. You see, down here they don't delegate responsibility the way we do in the States. They exercise much tighter control than we do. As a consequence, this man spends up to 15 hours a day at his desk. It may not look like it to you, but I assure you he really means business. He wants to give your company the order; if you play your cards right, you will get it."

The next evening provided more of the same. Much conversation about food and music, about many people the sales manager had never heard of. They went to a night club, where the sales manager brightened up and began to think that perhaps he and the minister might have something in common after all. It bothered him, however, that the principal reason for his visit was not even alluded to tangentially. But every time he started to talk about electronics, the commercial attaché would nudge him and proceed to change the subject.

The next meeting was for morning coffee at a café. By now the sales manager was having difficulty hiding his impatience. To make matters worse the minister had a mannerism that he did not like. When they talked he was likely to put his hand on him; he would take hold of his arm and get so close that he almost "spat" in his face. As a consequence, the sales manager was kept busy trying to dodge and back up.

Following coffee, there was a walk in a nearby park. The minister expounded on the shrubs, the birds, and the beauties of nature, and at one spot he stopped to point at a statue and said: "There is a statue of the world's greatest hero, the liberator of mankind!" At this point, the worst happened, for the sales manager asked who the statue was of and, being given the name of a famous Latin American patriot, said, "I never heard of him," and walked on.

THE FAILURE.   It is quite clear from this that the sales manager did not get the order, which went to a Swedish concern. The American, moreover, was never able to see the minister again. Why did the minister feel the way he did? His reasoning went somewhat as follows:

"I like the American's equipment and it makes sense to deal with North Americans who are near us and whose price is right. But I could never be friends with this man. He is not my kind of human being and we have nothing in common. He is not simpático. If I can't be friends and he is not simpático, I can't depend on him to treat me right. I tried everything, every conceivable situation, and only once did we seem to understand each other. If we could be friends, he would feel obligated to me and this obligation would give me some control. Without control, how do I know he will deliver what he says he will at the price he quotes?"

Of course, what the minister did not know was that the price was quite firm, and that quality control was a matter of company policy. He did not realize that the sales manager was a member of an organization, and that the man is always subordinate to the organization in the United States. Next year maybe the sales manager would not even be representing the company, but would be replaced. Further, if he wanted someone to depend on, his best bet would be to hire a good American lawyer to represent him and write a binding contract.

In this instance, both sides suffered. The American felt he was being slighted and put off, and did not see how there could possibly be any connection between poetry and doing business or why it should all take so long. He interpreted the delay as a form of polite brush-off. Even if things had gone differently and there had been a contract, it is doubtful that the minister would have trusted the contract as much as he would a man whom he considered his friend. Throughout Latin America, the law is made livable and contracts workable by having friends and relatives operating from the inside. Lacking a friend, someone who would look out for his interests, the minister did not want to take a chance. He stated this simply and directly.[18]

CONSUMER PRODUCTS

Consumer products are probably more sensitive to cultural difference than are industrial products, and among consumer products food is probably the most sensitive of all. In West Germany, Campbell's reportedly lost over $10 million trying to change the wet soup habits of the German consumer from dehydrated soup to a canned soup concentrate. In the United States CPC International faced the same problem in reverse in trying unsuccessfully to significantly penetrate the U.S. soup market (90 percent canned) with Knorr dehydrated soups. Knorr was a Swiss company acquired by CPC that had a major share of the European prepared soup market where bouillon and dehydrated soups accounted for 80 percent of commercial soup sales.

A major cultural factor in food marketing is the attitude and practice of housewives toward food preparation. Campbell Soup discovered in a study conducted in Italy that Italian housewives were spending approximately 4.5 hours per day in food preparation in contrast to the less than 60 minutes a day spent in food preparation by U.S. housewives. These differences in time spent in food preparation reflect not only a cultural pattern but also the different income levels in the two countries.

Indeed Campbell's discovered how strong the feeling against convenience food in Italy was by asking a random sample of Italian housewives the following question: "Would you want your son to marry a canned soup user?" The response to this question was sobering. Ninety-nine and six-tenths percent of the respondents answered, "No!" Rising incomes will affect Italian attitudes toward time and convenience and will have a major effect on the market for convenience foods. Meanwhile the habits and customs of people continue to affect food markets independently of income levels.

Thirst is a universal physiological need. What people drink, however, is very much culturally determined. The market for coffee presents an interesting demonstration of the effect of culture on drinking habits. In the United Kingdom instant coffee has 90 percent of the total coffee market as compared with only 15 percent in Sweden. The other countries in the Atlantic community fall between these two extreme points. Instant coffee's large share of the British market can be traced to the fact that in hot beverage consumption Britain has been a tea-drinking market. Only in recent times have the British been persuaded to take up coffee drinking.

[18]Edward T. Hall, "The Silent Language in Overseas Business," *Harvard Business Review*, May–June 1960, pp. 93–96. © 1960 by the President and Fellows of Harvard College; all rights reserved.

Instant coffee is more like tea than regular coffee in its preparation, and so it was natural that when the British did begin to drink coffee they should adopt instant rather than regular coffee. Another reason for the popularity of instant coffee in Britain is the practice of drinking coffee with a large quantity of milk, so that the coffee flavor is masked. Differences in the coffee flavor are thus hidden, so that a "better cup" of coffee is not really important. Sweden, on the other hand, is a coffee-drinking country. Coffee is the leading hot beverage. The product tends to be consumed without large quantities of milk, and therefore the coffee flavor is not masked.

A study of consumption patterns of soft drinks in Western Europe and the United States demonstrated, however, that there are conspicuous differences in the demand for soft drinks in Western Europe and the United States. Although the population of the United States is only 20 percent greater than the combined population of France, Germany, and Italy, sales of soft drinks in the United States are approximately four times greater than the combined sales of these three countries. The average American drinks about five times as many soft drinks as the average Frenchman, three times as many as the average Italian, and two and one-half times as many as the average German.

The U.S. preference for soft drinks has developed continuously since the middle of the nineteenth century. In 1849, for example, U.S. consumption of soft drinks was 1.1 12-oz containers per capita. In 1949, 100 years later, it had increased 9,800 percent to 108 12-oz containers per capita. In 1979, 30 years later, it was up *another* 370 percent to 400 12-oz containers, and in 1980, it was up to 410 12-ounce containers per capita.[19]

The differences in soft drink consumption are associated with much higher per capita consumption of other kinds of beverages in Europe. In France and Italy, for example, 30 to 40 times as much wine is consumed as in America on a per capita basis. The French prefer mineral water to soft drinks, whereas few Americans have tasted mineral water. German per capita consumption of beer exceeds by far the equivalent figure in the United States. Why the difference then between the popularity of soft drinks in Western Europe and the United States? The following factors are responsible for the differences:

$$C = f(A, B, C, D, E, F, G)$$
$$C = \text{consumption of soft drinks}$$

where

f = function of

A = influences of other beverages' relative prices, quality, and taste

B = advertising expenditure and effectiveness, all beverage categories

C = availability of products in distribution channels

D = cultural elements, tradition, custom, habit

E = availability of raw materials (particularly of water)

F = climatic conditions, temperature, and relative humidity

G = income levels

[19]Beverage Industry, *1982 Annual Manual,* p. 32.

Culture is an important element in determining the demand for soft drinks. But it is important to recognize that it is only one of seven factors and, therefore, is an influencing rather than a determining factor. If aggressive marketing programs (including lower prices, more intensive distribution, and heavy advertising) were placed behind soft drinks, the consumption of this product would increase more rapidly than it would otherwise. However, it is also clear that any effort to increase the consumption of soft drinks in Western Europe would be pitted against cultural tradition and custom and the competition of widely available alternative beverages. Culture in this case is a restraining force, but because culture is changing so rapidly, there are many opportunities to accelerate changes that favor a company's product.

The world's champion drinkers, as measured by percentage of personal income spent on alcoholic beverages, are the Irish, followed closely by the Hungarians, Poles, and Russians. The differences, shown in Table 4–2, are dramatic.

The penetration of the U.S. beverage market by bottled water is an excellent example of the impact of a creative strategy on a firmly entrenched cultural tradition. The U.S. culture, until recently, did not include drinking bottled water. The general attitude in the United States was, "Why pay for something that is free?" Perrier, the French bottled water firm, decided to take a shot at the U.S. market by hiring Bruce Nevin, an experienced American marketing executive, and giving him a free hand to formulate a creative strategy.

TABLE 4–2 Percentage of Personal Income Spent on Alcoholic Beverages, 1971

COUNTRY	PERCENTAGE
Ireland	12.6%
Hungary	11.6
Poland	11.5
Soviet Union	9.0
Portugal	8.1
United Kingdom	7.8
Yugoslavia	7.0
Australia	6.3
Finland	5.7
Sweden	4.7
Belgium	3.5
Canada	3.5
West Germany	3.0
Japan	3.0
France	2.3
Italy	2.3
United States	1.4

Source: Beverage Industry, *1982 Annual Manual*, p. 159.

Nevin decided to reposition Perrier from an expensive imported bottled water (which no red-blooded *sane* American would touch) to a competitively priced lo-cal beverage in the soft drink market. To back up this positioning, Nevin launched a major consumer advertising campaign, lowered prices, and moved the product from the gourmet section of the supermarket to the soft drink section. That marketing strategy involved the significant adjustment or adaptation of three of the four P's: price, promotion, and place. Only the product was left unchanged.

The campaign succeeded beyond even the most optimistic expectations. The success of this strategy stemmed from the facts that undoubtedly the market was ready for bottled water and the marketing strategy of Perrier was brilliant. It is impressive to see how a well-executed campaign got people to pay for what they had been getting for free. The results illustrate how culture can be changed by a creative marketing strategy that is grounded in market possibilities.

Eating habits are changing all over the world in response to rising incomes. The basic trends in a country with rising incomes are toward the increasing consumption of packaged, convenience foods that save time for the housewife and add variety to menus. This is the basic and unmistakable trend, but companies have discovered that specific discrete changes are not always easy to accomplish. In the early 1960s General Mills decided to be one of the first companies to profit from the increasing sales of dry breakfast cereals in Japan. By the time General Mills had organized to move into this market, the cereal boom had leveled off. General Mills discovered that not enough Japanese families were willing to order the extra milk that dry cereals require—and even when they did increase the quantities of milk they purchased, they preferred to drink the extra amount without cereal.

NATIONALISM

Nationalism is a term which describes the powerful influence of collective forces that are unleashed by the social, economic, and cultural group that we call the nation. The world today is swept by the forces and passions of nationalism. As Tom Farer has pointed out, for decades France occupied Vietnam with an army of less than 20,000 troops, but once the dormant idea of national independence came round again, the United States could not hold half the country with a force of 500,000 troops and the most modern arsenal of arms ever assembled in the history of the world.[20]

We live in an age in which the currents of nationalism seem to be running in two directions. Among the advanced countries, there is an unmistakable tendency and direction toward the affirmation of a world community and interdependence. Indeed, in Sweden, one of the most advanced social democracies in Europe, there is even a conscious expression of the national goal of strengthening the sense of community within the nation and affirming through international cooperation and

[20]Tom J. Farer, "The United States and the Third World: A Basis for Accommodation," *Foreign Affairs,* October 1975, p. 90.

support the role of Sweden in the world community. Although these goals may not be as clearly articulated in other industrial nations, the implicit national objectives are clear. When difficulties develop in the economic relations between industrialized countries, negotiations since the end of World War II have always led to a resolution of the problem. This occurs because the negotiations take place within the framework of a shared commitment to cooperation and interdependence.

The interdependence of the industrialized or advanced countries is based upon a perception of mutual advantage. Although industries that are exposed to strong foreign competition will often strongly disagree with national free trade and open market policies, the business community recognizes that the nation gains more than it gives up in participating in the international economy. Moreover, each advanced country is exposed to overseas risk because it has its own investors and assets abroad. If it should decide to discriminate against foreign investors, the home countries of the foreign investors can always "return the favor" and retaliate against its overseas investors. This is in effect a mutual hostage situation where each side is restrained by its asset and business interest exposure. If The Netherlands decides to expropriate IBM, the United States could retaliate by taking similar action against Philips.

This mutual hostage restraint does not exist in relations between advanced and less developed countries. If India should decide to nationalize IBM, the United States cannot retaliate by nationalizing the Indian equivalent of IBM because such a company does not exist.

As a consequence, investors in companies operating in less developed countries must be prepared to justify on a continuing basis the contribution they are making to the perceived welfare of the less developed state. Since most companies are unable to demonstrate a continuing unique advantage over local enterprise, this typically requires a very flexible attitude and willingness to adjust the terms and conditions of participation in the developing country. Only enterprises that have a unique advantage technologically or in some other way are able to resist efforts on the part of less developed states to appropriate equity and management participation in their operations.

CROSS-CULTURAL COMPLICATIONS AND SUGGESTED SOLUTIONS[21]

Business is conducted in an ever-changing environment, a blend of economic, political, cultural, and personal realities and events. Different understandings of the respective obligations of the parties to a commercial transaction will often occur even when the parties belong to the same low-context society and the transaction

[21]This section draws heavily on the experience of Paul M. Flowerman, president, P. L. Thomas & Co., Inc.

is embodied in a legal document, which can seldom anticipate all contingencies. Further negotiation between parties who have contracted with each other is often needed, and practical considerations will usually be given greater weight than strict legal interpretation, because only legal counsel really wins when there is business litigation.

Business relationships between parties of different cultures and/or nationalities are subject to additional challenges. Parties from different countries may have trouble coming to contract terms because of differences in the laws governing their respective activities and problems of enforcement across international boundaries. No matter what is stated in a contract, it is usually extremely difficult and costly to sue a party for breach of contract except on his or her home turf, which may be an insurmountable advantage for the home country participant.

When a party from a high-context culture takes part in a business understanding, the factors discussed in the preceding two paragraphs may be even further complicated by very different beliefs about the significance of formal business understandings and the ongoing obligations of all parties. Hall's anecdote about the American sales manager in Latin America describes a basic implicit disagreement about what is important for a business relationship. The sales manager sincerely believed that a well-written contract was all that would be required for his firm to comply fully with its obligations. The minister failed to understand this. But the sales manager failed to understand that in many parts of the world, things can be accomplished only if personal ties exist (personal ties will also sometimes be important for getting things done in the low-context environments).

Natural and human-induced catastrophes, political problems, foreign exchange inconvertibility, widely fluctuating exchange rates, depressions, and changes in national economic priorities and tariff schedules dominate the business environment in many of the countries outside the triad markets. One cannot predict precisely how the most carefully laid plans will go awry, only that they will. The marketing executive dealing with a foreign market must build mutually felt trust and empathy with business contacts, because they will be required to sustain an enduring relationship. Appointing a host national as foreign sales representative will not eliminate the issue. The "rep" must act as the company's surrogate and therefore adhere to company philosophy while building the personal relationships necessary to achieve the company's business objectives. The corporation that moves around its international staff or otherwise impedes the formation between its people and host nationals of what we might call "high-context subcultures" diminishes its chances to overcome business crises.

In 1986, Mexico imposed severe foreign exchange restrictions. Companies that had sold products or services to Mexican parties with selling terms other than "confirmed irrevocable international letter of credit" learned they would have to wait for very long periods of time before receiving payment in a "hard" currency such as U.S. dollars. Mexican companies dependent on certain critical foreign supplies (essential ingredients, spare parts, etc.) were subjected to a rationed supply of the foreign exchange for new orders. In this situation personal relationships superseded contractual obligations. Perhaps policymakers/administrators needed to be convinced that a certain transaction deserved a priority allocation of foreign exchange. Perhaps the foreign seller decided to accept payment in Mexican products (barter) or in pesos that had to be invested in Mexico. Perhaps a foreign seller needed the best guarantees obtainable in a difficult situation that his or her clients would fulfill their obligations as soon as they could find ways to do so. All these matters have become almost routine problems in international business. Although there are standard approaches, most solutions emerge from taking creative advantage of opportunities available through personal links.

India is an important supplier of crude and processed agricultural and forest product raw materials to the United States and many other countries. Collectors and processors, usually small family-owned enterprises, are typically required to offer, months before the crop is in, processed product for later delivery to foreign buyers who must make long-term contractual commitments to their own customers. It is not possible for the Indian firms to hedge reliably by making forward crop purchases because typically the farmers or sellers of forest products do not have the resources to cover their sales if the crop fails and there are no regulated commodity exchanges for these products. Nearly every year there are major problems because (1) natural disaster or insufficient plantings result in short crops; (2) strikes, protracted power shortages, or the lack of spare parts results in excessive shipment delays and reduced capacity; (3) business downturns or unexpected changes in the buyers' required inventory levels (or consumption) lead buyers to request or even insist that shipments be held back or prices be reduced even though such action will cause the supplier severe financial hardship; and (4) the supplier is unable for some reason to comply precisely with the contract and therefore provides a substitute order (usually without preadvising the buyer), hoping that the buyer will inadvertently pay before discovering the switch and then reluctantly accept the merchandise with only minor adjustment.

Ongoing business between India and its foreign clients is, of course, spurred on by mutual interest, but personal relationships are what make it possible. False rumors, supplier defaults, and customer cancellations are prevalent, and therefore the greatest importance is assigned to contacts and business associates who can be fully trusted and whose culture-influenced perceptions are understood and predictable. Indian society is at least as ethnically and culturally diverse as that in Europe, and business practices are probably even more varied than in Europe.

Personal relationships are an essential ingredient for the international businessperson. One-third of a Peace Corps volunteer's training is devoted to learning about ways things are done in the host country (particularly personal relationships). The international businessperson should have comparable preparation and a willingness to at least consider the merits of accommodating to the host culture's ways of doing business.

SUMMARY

Culture has both a pervasive and changing influence on each national market environment. International marketers must recognize the influence of culture and must be prepared to either respond to it or change it. International marketers have played an important and even a leading role in influencing the rate of cultural change around the world. This is particularly true of food, but it includes virtually every industry, particularly in consumer products. Soap and detergent manufacturers have changed washing habits, the electronics industry has changed entertainment patterns, clothing marketers have changed styles, and so on.

In industrial products culture does affect product characteristics and demand but is more important as an influence on the marketing process, particularly in the way business is done. International marketers have learned to rely upon people who know and understand local customs and attitudes for marketing expertise. Often, but not always, these are local nationals.

DISCUSSION QUESTIONS

1. Marketing is a universal discipline. There is no such thing as American marketing, French marketing, Japanese marketing, and so on. Do you agree or disagree? Why? Why not?
2. It is a mistake to label the United States a low-context culture. There are many aspects of the U.S. business world that are extremely high context. Do you agree or disagree?
3. The world is becoming more and more monocultural. Today you can get Japanese noodles in the United States and McDonald's hamburgers in Japan. Cultural factors are simply not as important as they were 50, even 10, years ago. Discuss.

BIBLIOGRAPHY

Books

ABEGGLEN, JAMES C., AND GEORGE STALK, Jr. *Kaisha, The Japanese Corporation*. New York: Basic Books, Inc., 1985.

BENEDICT, RUTH. *Patterns of Culture*. Boston: Houghton Mifflin, 1959.

————. *The Chrysanthemum and the Sword*. Rutland, Vt.: Charles E. Tuttle, 1972.

de TOCQUEVILLE, ALEXIS. *Democracy in America*. New York: New American Library, 1956.

ENGEL, J. F., R. D. BLACKWELL, AND D. T. KOLLAT. *Consumer Behavior,* 3rd ed. New York: Holt, Rinehart and Winston, 1978.

FIELDS, GEORGE. *From Bonsai to Levis*. New York: Mentor, New American Library, 1983, 1985.

HAGEN, E. *On the Theory of Social Change*. Homewood, Ill.: Dorsey Press, 1962.

HALL, EDWARD T. *Beyond Culture*. Garden City, N.Y.: Anchor Press/Doubleday, 1976.

McCLELLAND, D. *The Achieving Society*. New York: Van Nostrand, 1961.

McKINSEY & COMPANY, INC. *Japan, Business Obstacles and Opportunities,* 1983.

REISCHAUER, EDWIN O. *The Japanese*. Cambridge, Mass.: The Belknap Press of Harvard University Press, 1977.

Articles

BECKER, HELMUT. "Is There a Cosmopolitan Information Seeker?" *Journal of International Business Studies,* Vol. 7, no. 1 (Spring 1976), pp. 77–89.

DAVIS, STANLEY M. "U.S. versus Latin America: Business & Culture." *Harvard Business Review,* November–December 1969, pp. 88–89.

DICHTER, ERNST. "The World Customer." *Harvard Business Review,* July–August 1962, pp. 113–122.

KROEBER, ALFRED L., AND CLYDE KLUCKHOHN. "Culture: A Critical Review of Concepts and Definitions," Vol. 47. Papers of the Peabody Museum, 1952.

LEE, JAMES A. "Cultural Analysis in Overseas Operations." *Harvard Business Review,* March–April 1966, pp. 106–114.

SCHIFFMAN, LEON G., WILLIAM R. DILON, AND FESTUS E. NGUMAH. "The Influence of Subcultural and Personality Factors on Consumer Acculturation." *Journal of International Business Studies,* Fall 1981, pp. 137–143.

CHOUFONT-SALVA, INC.[1]

On January 10, 1966, the marketing committee[2] of Choufont-Salva, Inc., the Philippine subsidiary of A. L. Choufont et Fils, S.A., decided to add to the company's product line an oral contraceptive developed by the laboratories of the parent company. Choufont-Salva's marketing division (see Figure 1) now was faced with the task of designing a marketing plan that would effectively sell this product.

THE COMPANY

Choufont-Salva, Inc., was founded in 1948 by Mr. Lorenzo J. Salva. The company was known as the L. J. Salva Drug Company until 1959, when the company became a subsidiary of A. L. Choufont et Fils, S.A., of Belgium, the second largest drug company in Europe and a company with operations in 39 countries, including the Philippines. Many of the subsidiaries of A. L. Choufont et Fils, S.A., marketed both ethical[3] and proprietary[4] drugs. Choufont-Salva, however, had followed the policy established by Mr. Salva when he founded the company of dealing only in ethical drugs.

---

[1] This case was prepared by Dr. Ralph Z. Sorenson, president and chief executive officer, Barry Wright Corporation, Newton Lower Falls, Mass. Used by permission.

[2] The marketing committee was composed of the general manager, the marketing manager, the sales manager, and the manager of marketing services.

[3] Ethical drugs were promoted directly to the medical profession, whose members in turn recommended or prescribed the drugs to the ultimate consumers. Ethical drugs could be divided into two groups: (1) prescription pharmaceuticals, which were ethical products that legally were available only by prescription, and (2) over-the-counter drugs, which were ethical products that could be purchased legally without prescription, although physicians frequently did write prescriptions for these drugs. Over-the-counter products typically were manufactured by firms that specialized in prescription pharmaceuticals.

[4] Proprietary drugs were promoted directly to the consumers; the manufacturers of proprietary products usually engaged in heavy consumer advertising and promotions, including extensive in-store display advertising.

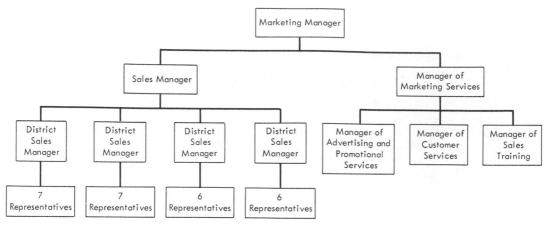

FIGURE 1 Organizational Chart of the Marketing Division

In 1965 Choufont-Salva marketed 67 different drug products and had sales of approximately ₱6,900,000.[5] Penicillin accounted for 47 percent of the sales and streptomycin, 16 percent. Thirteen other products were responsible for an additional 21 percent of the company's income.

For all products, Choufont-Salva had three prices: the retail price,[6] the semiwholesale price, which was 5 percent less than the retail price, and the wholesale price, which was 10 percent less than the retail price. Because of the difficulty in determining whether a purchaser was functioning primarily as a wholesaler or a retailer. Choufont-Salva used the volume of business done annually with the company as the basis for determining which of the price lists was applicable to the customer. Approximately 30 percent of the company's sales were retail; 10 percent, semiwholesale; and 60 percent, wholesale.

[5]One peso = U.S.$.256.

[6]Retail price, as used by Choufont-Salva and other drug companies, referred to the price charged to retail drug outlets and similar purchasers, not to the price paid by the ultimate consumers. The price paid by the ultimate consumers generally was about 10 percent higher than this retail price.

In 1965 Choufont-Salva realized an average gross profit of 59 centavos on every peso of sales. Five centavos of this gross profit was paid out in commissions,[7] 9.5 centavos was spent on advertising and promotions, and 21.5 centavos was expended on other marketing and administrative expenses. However, the gross profit that the company received on sales of a particular product and the expenditures made in promoting the sale of a product frequently varied greatly from this average.

SALES ACTIVITIES

Choufont-Salva had divided the Philippines into 26 sales territories. In each territory, there were between 150 and 300 doctors in private practice on whom the sales representative assigned to the territory called once per month.

Since Choufont-Salva dealt only in ethical drugs, management believed that the doctor was the most important person to reach

[7]Sales representatives received commissions of 4.5 percent, and district sales managers received commissions of .5 percent on all sales made in their respective territories.

in the company's marketing activities. Sales representatives in the provinces spent approximately 70 percent of their time calling on physicians. Sales representatives in Manila and other large cities devoted an estimated 80 percent of their time to this activity.

Because of the busy schedules of the doctors, most visits with physicians did not last longer than 15 minutes. During this time a sales representative normally made two product presentations. During each presentation, the sales representative described how the drug being discussed had been developed, noted the benefits of the product, pointed out how this drug differed from comparable products on the market, and presented clinical evidence attesting to the effectiveness of the drug. At the close of the visit, the sales representative left samples of the two products he had discussed and also of two or three other drugs that the company marketed.

Approximately 40 percent of the doctors on whom Choufont-Salva salespersons called dispensed their own drugs. During visits to these doctors, the salesperson also took orders and made collections for previous purchases.[8] Approximately 10 percent of Choufont-Salva's sales in 1965 were made to this group of doctors, most of whom were located in the provinces.

A sales representative who had a territory in Manila or another large city and devoted his day exclusively to calling on doctors could make 15 to 18 calls if the doctors had their offices at a hospital, and 12 to 15 calls if the doctors had private offices away from a hospital. A provincial sales rep calling only on doctors could average 10 to 12 calls per day.

Choufont-Salva sales reps called on an estimated 25 percent of the doctors in the Philippines. Management believed, however, that these doctors were the ones with the highest professional standing and with the largest and most important practices.

In addition to the doctors, Choufont-Salva salespersons called monthly on 1,500 of the estimated 5,000 drugstores in the Philippines. Approximately 85 percent of the company's sales were made to these pharmaceutical outlets. When calling on drugstores, the sales reps answered any questions that the personnel had about different products, discussed with the employees new or improved products that the company was introducing, took back old stocks of drugs, accepted orders, and made collections.

Drugstores in the Philippines were free to dispense pharmaceutical products without prescriptions. According to one expert in the field, the Philippines probably had the least restrictive drug laws of any major country in the world. It was not uncommon for antibiotics and similar drugs to be promoted directly to the consumer through media advertising, posters, and point-of-purchase displays.

The sales reps also called each month on approximately 50 clinics. Sales to these clinics, which were either government health centers or industrial clinics attached to large manufacturing facilities, were responsible for 5 percent of Choufont-Salva's sales. During the visits to the clinics, the sales representatives promoted Choufont-Salva products, left samples, took orders, and received payments for previous orders.

Choufont-Salva supported the activities of its sales representatives with advertising and promotional efforts. The company spent ₱8,000 on advertising in 1965. Since Choufont-Salva dealt only in ethical drugs, the entire advertising expenditure was for ads placed in the three leading professional medical journals—*The PMA[9] Journal, Family*

---

[8]Commissions on a sale were not paid until the company had received payment.

[9]Philippine Medical Association.

TABLE 1   Journals in Which Choufont-Salva Advertised

JOURNAL	FREQUENCY OF PUBLICATION	CIRCULATION	COST PER PAGE*
Family Physician	Quarterly	3,000	225
The Philippine Journal of Surgeons	Quarterly	3,000	225
The PMA Journal	Monthly	7,000	675

*The journals accepted only full-page advertisements.

Physician, and *The Philippine Journal of Surgeons*. (See Table 1.)

In 1965 Choufont-Salva also spent ₱650,000 on promotional activities. Of this amount ₱550,000 was invested in samples given to physicians. This reflected management's belief that samples were the most effective way of promoting the company's drugs. When samples of drugs were left with doctors it reminded them of the products and encouraged them to prescribe them to their patients. Also, the company believed that doctors like samples because samples enabled them occasionally to give away medicine free to patients, thus generating goodwill among the recipients.

The remaining ₱100,000 spent on promotions in 1965 was used to print cards, folders, and booklets about various drugs sold by Choufont-Salva. These printed materials were used by the sales representatives in discussing the products with the doctors and were left with the doctor at the close of the call.

THE PHILIPPINE MARKET FOR CONTRACEPTIVES

When Choufont-Salva decided to enter the contraceptive market in 1966, the population of the Philippines was approximately 33,000,000. The country had an estimated 5,600,000 households, 85 percent of which were located in rural areas. According to government statistics, the population was increasing at the rate of 3.2 percent per year, one of the highest population growth rates in the world. If this rate of population growth continued, the country would have 53,000,000 inhabitants by 1980.[10] (See Tables 2 through 5.)

In early 1965 the Family Planning Association of the Philippines, Inc. (FPAP), was organized by a group of Catholic laypersons. Although three small Protestant family planning groups already were in existence, the FPAP was the first nationwide family planning movement in the Philippines, a country in which 84 percent of the population was Catholic.[11]

By the time that Choufont-Salva decided to enter the market in 1966, the management of the company estimated that there were approximately 100 government or private clinics from which persons could receive information on family planning and, if they desired, birth control products. The majority of these centers were affiliated with either the

[10] See Tables 2, 3, and 4 for selected demographic data based on the 1960 Census and Table 5 for a summary of the results of a Family Limitation Survey taken by the Bureau of the Census and Statistics in 1965.

[11] See Appendix I for a statement of the position of the Roman Catholic Church concerning family planning and Appendix II for additional information on the FPAP.

TABLE 2 Population by Marital Status, 1960* (10 years and over)

Individuals 10 Years Old and Over	TOTAL PHILIPPINES		GREATER MANILA ONLY	
	Population	Percent	Population	Percent
Single	8,323,157	45.9%	452,040	54.6%
Married	8,918,739	49.2	339,061	41.0
Widowed	822,412	4.5	33,032	4.0
Divorced or separated	81,175	.4	3,022	.4
Total	18,145,483	100.0%	827,155	100.0%

*Rate of marriages per 1,000 persons: 13.56.

Source: Based on data from the Bureau of Census and Statistics.

FPAP or the Planned Parenthood Movement of the Philippines. Birth control products were also available at most drug outlets.

The management of Choufont-Salva estimated that in 1965 Filipinos spent ₱5,000,000 on contraceptive products. Approximately 70 percent of these products were dispensed through drugstores, 25 percent through clinics, and 5 percent directly by doctors. Management predicted that in 1966 the market for contraceptives would be ₱7,500,000 and that the market would continue to grow at least 50 percent per year for the next three years.

In 1965 an estimated ₱4,000,000 was spent on oral contraceptives in the Philippines. The popularity of this method of birth control was attributed to the fact that oral contraceptives were virtually 100 percent effective and extremely easy to use. Although there were 15 brands of oral contraceptives on the Philippine market, 5 brands controlled 75 percent of the market. (See Table 6.)

The second most popular contraceptive product in the Philippines was the intrauterine contraceptive device (I.U.D.). Filipinos in 1965 spent an estimated ₱750,000 on I.U.D.s, including fees paid to doctors for inserting the devices. The charges made by private doctors for this service ranged from a low of ₱5 to a high of ₱100 per patient.

Planned parenthood clinics, on the other hand, had a policy of inserting I.U.D.s completely free or at a charge of ₱5 or less.

I.U.D.s were in strong favor with governmental and private agencies in the Philippines who promoted planned parenthood to

TABLE 3 Female Population in the Philippines, 10 Years and Over, 1960 (in thousands)

Age (years)	LAST CENSUS (1960)		CURRENT
	Total No. of Women	No. of Ever Married Women*	Estimated No. of Women
10–14	1,705	2	2,146
15–19	1,401	174	1,802
20–24	1,158	689	1,472
25–29	959	792	1,208
30–34	796	691	996
35–39	675	664	822
40–44	580	497	689
45–49	489	464	585
50–54	384	312	493
55–59	288	218	389
60–64	214	180	284
65+	409	334	462
Total	9,058	5,017	11,348

*Women who currently were married or had been married at one time. Choufont-Salva executives believed that common law marriages were included in these data.

Source: Bureau of Census and Statistics.

TABLE 4   Distribution of Households by Income, 1960

| | PERCENT OF FAMILIES | | |
Annual Income	Greater Manila	Other Metropolitan Areas	Rural Areas
Under ₱500	.9%	11.3%	21.2%
₱500 to ₱999	4.6	20.0	36.0
₱1,000 to ₱1,499	13.2	16.8	18.0
₱1,500 to ₱1,999	12.2	15.7	10.5
₱2,000 to ₱2,499	10.8	8.8	5.4
₱2,500 to ₱2,999	8.1	6.2	2.8
₱3,000 to ₱3,999	13.3	7.8	2.8
₱4,000 to ₱4,999	7.8	4.4	.9
₱5,000 to ₱5,999	6.8	2.9	.7
₱6,000 to ₱7,999	9.4	2.9	.6
₱8,000 to ₱9,999	4.0	1.0	.1
₱10,000 +	8.7	2.3	.2
Number of families	361,000	1,444,000	2,921,000
Total number of families:	4,726,000		

Source: Based on data from the Bureau of Census and Statistics.

TABLE 5   Summary of Family Limitation Survey

A total of 4,207 women representing approximately 59 percent of the 7,148 ever-married women* in the Philippines covered in the inquiry indicated not wanting more children than what they had in 1965. A significant 39 percent of the total knew how to go about limiting the number of children. In fact, 31 percent of such women had already done something† about the matter. The survey further indicated that of women aged below 45 years and who did not know anything about children limitation, 24 percent welcomed the idea of learning possible means of limiting their number of offspring. These indications were revealed by the sample survey conducted in May 1965, covering 7,148 ever-married women from 6,646 sample households throughout the country.

In terms of the level of education attained by the ever-married women included in the inquiry, 32.0 percent belonged to the primary level; 29.5 percent, intermediate; 13.6 percent, high school; 7.0 percent, college; and no grade completed, 16.7 percent. Those whose level of education was not stated represented only 1.2 percent.

According to religious affiliation, on the other hand, 86.5 percent comprised Roman Catholics; 3.4 percent, Aglipayans; 1.2 percent, Iglesia ni Kristo; 2.5 percent, Protestants; and "Others" representing Moslems, Buddhists as well as those not reporting any religion at all, 6.4 percent.‡

Among the questions asked of the women were: "If all of your children are living, do you think you would like to have more?" "Do you know or have you heard of certain ways by which the number of children in the family may be limited?" "Have you and your husband done anything to limit the number of your children?" And for women aged below 45 years only, the question, "Are you willing to learn any means to limit the number of your children?" was asked. Less than .5 percent did not give answers to any of the four questions.

Answers to the inquiries showed that in all the sectors of the ever-married women there was widespread refusal to have a bigger size of family and that a sizable portion was practicing means of limiting their number of children.

To the first question, an appreciable 60 percent of the women in the urban areas did not want more children than what they had at the time of the survey; meanwhile, 57.4 percent of the rural ever-married women

136

TABLE 5 *continued*

included in the inquiry were of the same opinion. The desire to have more children was concentrated among women of ages below 30 years—a common finding to both the urban and rural sectors. It seems that the desire for more children among these young ever-married women is geared toward acquiring a family—to them, the number of children is rather uncertain.

By religious affiliation, 66.7 and 62.9 percent of the Aglipayan respondents in the urban and rural communities, respectively, did not want to have more children. This indication was followed by the Roman Catholic group with 61.0 and 59.3 percent and the Iglesia ni Kristo group with 56.9 and 50.0 percent for the urban and rural sectors, in that order.

It is interesting to note that the desire not to have more children than what they actually have is inversely related to the level of education and this holds true to both the urban and rural ever-married women.

In the urban sector, 72.4 percent, 64.1 percent, 60.1 percent, 55.8 percent, and 43.5 percent of the ever-married women with corresponding level of education of no grade completed, primary, intermediate, high school, and college, respectively, expressed not wanting more children as compared with the rural ever-married women with 65.0 percent, 61.1 percent, 49.6 percent, 46.9 percent, and 33.8 percent, in the same order of level of education.

The survey further revealed that 45.1 and 31.6 percent of the urban and rural ever-married women, respectively, knew or have heard ways of family limitation. Some 45.4 percent of the Roman Catholic group, 45.6 percent of Aglipayan, 44.8 percent of Iglesia ni Kristo, and 45.3 percent of Protestant ever-married women in the urban areas knew ways of limiting family sizes as compared with the women in the same order of religion in the rural areas with only 32.4 percent, 32.6 percent, 20.8 percent, and 25.3 percent, respectively. It was noted that the Aglipayan women in both urban and rural areas alike proved to be most apprised regarding ways of family limitation than women belonging to the other religious affiliations. This observation was followed by the Roman Catholic, Protestant, and Iglesia ni Kristo groups.

The survey also showed that the higher the level of education, the greater is the number of women knowing about family limitation. And this pattern is common in both urban and rural areas. However, in the urban areas, women with high school educations exercised the least family limitation practice, while in the rural areas it was found that the women with no grade completed manifested the same attitude.

It was observed from the answers to the inquiries that a sizable portion among those who knew means of limiting their number of children were actually practicing or doing something to limit their family size. Some 32.5 percent[§] in the urban areas were practicing family limitation compared to 27.1 percent represented by the rural sector. From among the four major religious groups, 38.5 percent for both Aglipayan and Iglesia ni Kristo groups in the urban centers were noted doing something about family limitation. In the rural areas, however, 38.1 percent of the Protestant women practiced family limitation followed by the Roman Catholic with 27.9 percent, Iglesia ni Kristo with 20.0 percent, and Aglipayan with 18.6 percent.

Finally, among those women aged below 45 years who did not know ways of family limitation, many signified intentions of learning about it. This number represented 24.3 percent among the urban women and 23.2 percent from the rural group.

* * *

Special Note to Readers from the Bureau: Readers should bear in mind that these data were gathered from a sample survey conducted simultaneously last year with the annual labor force survey made by the Bureau of Census and Statistics. This being a sample survey, it should, therefore, be treated with certain limitations in mind.

*Includes common law marriages.

†Includes both artificial and natural methods of birth control.

‡The Aglipayan and Iglesia ni Kristo religions were both relatively minor religious sects indigenous to the Philippines. Neither sect objected to artificial means of birth control on theological grounds.

§That is, 32.5 percent of those women who knew about family limitation.

Source: This summary was prepared by the Bureau of Census and Statistics and is based on a survey conducted by the Bureau in May 1965.

TABLE 6   Five Leading Brands of Oral Contraceptives

BRAND	USUAL PROGESTIN STRENGTHS (mg)	EST. MARKET SHARE	RETAIL PRICE*,† (Pesos)	COMMENTS
Brand A	2.5 or 5.0	35%	₱3.25	Company concentrated on drug outlets for promotion and distribution.
Brand B	4.0	17	3.00	Company concentrated on family planning centers for distribution.
Brand C	2.0 or 10.0	10	4.50	
Brand D	3.0	8	5.50	An improved version of Brand B; made by same company.
Brand E	10.0	5	8.00	

*Price per course of medication.

†Retail price refers to the price charged by the drug firms to retail drug outlets and similar purchasers. The prices to the ultimate consumer generally were 10 percent higher than these prices.

low-income groups. This method of birth control was inexpensive and did not require instructions that women had to remember. Yet, I.U.D.s had a major drawback. Approximately 20 percent of all women were unable to retain I.U.D.s. This method of birth control, however, was 98 percent effective in preventing pregnancy among the other 80 percent of the women.

Condoms, diaphragms, and spermicidal jellies and creams were not widely used in the Philippines. In 1965 these products together accounted for only an estimated ₱250,000 of the total contraceptive market.

CHOUFONT-SALVA'S ORAL CONTRACEPTIVE

Choufont-Salva's oral contraceptive was developed in the A. L. Choufont laboratories in Belgium. In early 1965 the product was first introduced on the market in Canada. By 1966 it was being marketed in 14 countries. The parent company had not yet published for its subsidiaries any detailed information on the market performance of the contraceptive. The bits of data that had been received from the company's Brussels headquarters indicated that the acceptance of the new contraceptive by the market had ranged from fair in Brazil to excellent in Mexico and Denmark.

Oral contraceptives were manufactured in the form of tablets that were taken by women for 20 to 22 days during each menstrual cycle. Most oral contraceptive tablets were a combination of a progestin and an estrogen, and tablets containing these two hormonal products were virtually 100 percent effective as contraceptives.

Oral contraceptives, however, produced in one out of every five women undesirable side effects, such as weight gain, nausea, and headaches. In general the incidence of these side effects was related to the dose of the progestin in the oral contraceptive. As a result, pharmaceutical companies had been trying to develop new progestational agents that could be given in dosages of 1 milligram or less but still be effective in controlling fertility.

A. L. Choufont et Fils, S.A., was the first to achieve this breakthrough in steroid research. The company in its laboratories developed a new, totally synthesized and extremely potent progestational hormone. By using this new progestational agent, Choufont et Fils was able to produce a new oral contraceptive that combined in each daily dose only 1 milligram of progestin with one-tenth of a milligram of an estrogenic agent.

There was only one oral contraceptive compound available in the Philippines that contained as little as 1.5 milligrams of progestin per daily dose. This was a new contraceptive that had been on the market for less than three months. The strength of the progestin in the other compounds on the market varied from 2 to 10 milligrams per tablet.

The low dosage of progestin in the Choufont-Salva contraceptive lessened the chance that a patient would experience undesirable side effects from taking the medication. Clinical data compiled by A. L. Choufont et Fils, S.A., indicated that in only 4 percent of the patients taking the oral contraceptive developed by the company did the patient experience nausea, headaches, or similar unpleasantness. No other oral contraceptive had such a low incidence of side effects.

The Choufont-Salva oral contraceptive consisted of 21 tablets per course of medication. The woman was to take the first tablet on the fifth day of her menstrual cycle and take one tablet daily for 21 days. She was then to stop taking tablets for 7 days. On the eighth day she was to start the next 21-day series of tablets. This meant that each new course of medication started on exactly the same day of the week as the initial course. Always starting the medication on the same day of the week lessened the chance of a woman forgetting to begin the cycle anew. Choufont-Salva felt that this attribute would give the product a slight competitive advantage over most of the other oral contraceptives on the market. Only two other contraceptives on the market had dosages of 21 tablets per 28-day period.

Because of the heavy financial investment in equipment required for producing oral contraceptives, Choufont-Salva had signed a contract with Companie Nationale de Pharmacie, S.A., the French subsidiary of A. L. Choufont et Fils, S.A. According to the contract, the French company would supply Choufont-Salva with the contraceptive tablets at a cost equivalent to ₱.71 per course of medication. This price included shipping to Manila but did not include packaging.

DEVELOPING A MARKETING PLAN

In 1965, 63 percent of Choufont-Salva's revenue came from the sales of penicillin and streptomycin. Management wanted to lessen the company's dependence on these two products and felt that its new oral contraceptive had the potential of developing into a major drug in the company's product line. The marketing manager said that to help achieve this goal, the sales representatives would devote at least 15 percent of their time to promoting the contraceptive during the first 18 months that it was on the market.

The task of developing a marketing plan that would effectively promote Choufont-Salva's oral contraceptive was the responsibility of the company's marketing committee. Deciding on a name for the tablets, selecting the packaging that would be used, determining the price that would be charged, and deciding on what advertising and promotional activities to employ were among the decisions facing the committee.

Name

The oral contraceptive developed by A. L. Choufont et Fils, S.A., was marketed by the company's Canadian subsidiary under the brand name Controva. This name was formed by combining the prefix *contra,* which makes

TABLE 7 Kinds of Packaging Being Considered

DESCRIPTION OF THE PACKAGE*	ESTIMATED COST†	MAJOR ADVANTAGES	MAJOR DISADVANTAGES
Glass bottle with label on the outside.	₱0.13	Very low cost Adequate protection to the tablets	Not attractive Little room on label for product description or instructions on usage Impossible to mark the package; the woman cannot easily ascertain the number of pills she has taken
Aluminum strip 5" long and 1¾" wide to which the tablets would be affixed by being encased in thin plastic. Strip would be packaged in aluminum foil.	₱0.22	Relatively low cost Permits instructions on a separate sheet to be enclosed with the strip Strip can be marked with the days of the week so the woman can easily ascertain the number of pills she has taken	Inadequate protection to the tablets—would have some breakage
Comb case in which tablets would be affixed (by being encased in plastic) to an aluminum strip 5" long and 1¾" wide; the strip would be placed in a comb carrying case 5½" long and 2¼" wide. The aluminum strip and carrying case would be packaged in a cardboard container 6" × 2¾" × ½".	₱0.29	Excellent protection to the tablets Relatively attractive carrying case Permits ample room for instructions to be enclosed separately and/or printed on the package Aluminum strip can be marked so woman can easily ascertain the number of pills she has taken	Relatively high cost
Compact case in which tablets would be affixed (by being encased in plastic) to an aluminum disc 2¾" in diameter; disc would be placed in a compact 3¼" in diameter; perforated holes in the bottom of the compact would permit the woman to push the label through the bottom of the compact, separating the tablet from the aluminum disc; compact would be packaged in a cardboard container 3¾" × 3¾" × ¾".	₱0.76	Very attractive carrying case Excellent protection to the tablets Permits ample room for instructions to be enclosed separately and/or printed on the package Aluminum disc can be marked so woman can easily ascertain how many pills she has taken	Very high cost

*Each package would contain 21 tablets.

†This estimated cost includes the price of the container and the cost of labor and other expenses involved in packaging the tablets.

140

up the first half of the word *contraceptive* and means against, with *ova*, the plural of *ovum*, which means egg. Since entering the market in Canada, the product had been introduced in three other English-speaking countries— Great Britain, the United States, and Australia. In all three countries the product was also being sold under the name Controva.

Because *contraceptive* and *ovum* were not words commonly used by Filipinos, some in the marketing organization at Choufont-Salva felt that the company should select another brand name for the product. These persons felt that the name should be easy to remember, be suggestive of a characteristic of the product, and sound western. Two names had been suggested: Combitabs, which was formed from the words *combination* and *tablets* and suggested that the tablets were a combination of progestin and estrogen, and Periodez, which suggested that the tablets were taken during a definite period in the menstrual cycle.

Packaging

Management was considering four packaging possibilities for the oral contraceptive: a glass bottle, a simple aluminum strip, a comb case, and a compact case. (See Table 7.) The company was also faced with the question of what color combinations to use on the packaging. Three combinations had been suggested: black and white, gold and white, and light pink and pale green. An advocate of the pastel colors claimed that they were "feminine and inviting to the woman."

Price

Primarily because of its lower progestin content, the progestin-estrogen compound developed by Choufont et Fils cost less to manufacture than did other oral contraceptives.

Since the tablets were costing Choufont-Salva only ₱.71 plus packaging for each dosage of 21 tablets, management was considering making the company's retail price for the medication ₱2.50 or ₱2.75 per bottle or package. This would give the company a competitive advantage in price since the retail price[12] of other oral contraceptives on the market ranged from ₱3.00 to ₱10.00 per course of medication.

Advertising and Promotional Activities

Choufont-Salva did not engage in consumer advertising. The company had the policy of advertising only in medical journals because management wanted Choufont-Salva to have the image of being a responsible pharmaceutical organization that worked closely with and through the medical profession. Some members of management, however, felt that the company should advertise its oral contraceptive directly to the general public. The decision made regarding this matter would influence the theme of the advertising campaign as well as the size of the advertising budget for the product.

Management also was undecided about how to promote Choufont-Salva's oral contraceptive. (A memo from the company's advertising and promotional staff containing suggestions regarding promotional activities is reproduced in Table 8; representative consumer-oriented media costs are shown in Table 9.)

NEW COMPETITION

A week after Choufont-Salva decided to enter the oral contraceptive market, the com-

---

[12]Price charged to retail drug outlets and similar purchasers.

TABLE 8   Memo on Possible Promotional Activities

DATE: February 16, 1966

TO: Mr. Jose J. Lim, Manager of Marketing Services
FROM: Mr. Manuel D. Pineda, Manager of Advertising and Promotional Activities
RE: Possible Promotional Activities for the Oral Contraceptive Product

The sales promotional staff submits the following sales promotional ideas for consideration in the formulation of the marketing plan for the new oral contraceptive product.

I.   Sampling. The sales promotion staff suggests that the following sampling activities be considered:

A. Comprehensive sampling of all the doctors upon whom Choufont-Salva salesmen call. Almost every doctor in the Philippines has patients who are potential customers for our oral contraceptive. Extensive sampling will give broad coverage to our product.

To get the desired penetration and to develop brand loyalty among doctors, it might be desirable for the company to engage in heavy sampling for at least six months. This could be accomplished:

1. By giving to gynecologists, obstetricians, and general practitioners with clientele likely to use contraceptives from one to four dozen sample packets per month, depending upon the doctor's location and practice. (We estimate that this group of doctors constitutes no more than one-fourth of the doctors on whom our salesmen call.)

2. By giving to all other doctors upon whom our salesmen call four sample packets of our oral contraceptive during the product's introductory month and two packets per month for the next five months.

B. That the approximately one hundred government and private clinics disseminating birth control information and products be heavily sampled. Most of these clinics recommend—and often insert either free or for a very nominal charge—I.U.D.s. For example, at one Manila family planning clinic last year, only 2 percent of the couples that came to the clinic decided to take oral contraceptives. The others are using I.U.D.s. To help alter this situation, the company might give one to four dozen samples monthly to each of the clinics, the number of samples depending upon the size of the clinic.

II.   The printing of both brochures and posters that will be used by the salesmen in describing to physicians our oral contraceptives and will be left with the physicians at the end of the visit. A five-color, eight-page brochure measuring 8″ × 11″ will cost approximately ₱590.00 per 1,000 with a minimum order of 5,000 required. A five-color 12″ × 15″ poster will cost approximately ₱500.00 per 1,000 with a minimum order of 5,000 required.

III.   Mailing to all physicians on whom our salesmen do not call the eight-page brochure mentioned above. The cost of printing a cover letter and mailing the brochure would be approximately ₱0.20 per physician, not counting the cost of the brochure.

IV.   Engaging in outlet promotions. Because of the nature of the product and the large number of potential consumers, the company might consider altering its policy against outlet promotions and engage in the following subtle promotional activities:

A. Encourage the salesclerks in drugstores to recommend our oral contraceptive to contraceptive customers. This could be accomplished (1) by the sales representatives discussing with the clerks both the characteristics of the product and its advantages over similar products on the market and (2) by giving the clerks a sample packet of our contraceptive.

B. Print small booklets on family planning and have them displayed on the sales counter in an attractive heavy cardboard rack. The booklet would define family planning, discuss the various methods of birth control, give the answers to the questions people most frequently ask about family planning, and contain semihumorous illustrations. Printing a three-color, thirty-page booklet that would be 5″ × 3½″ in size would cost approximately ₱250.00 per 1,000 with a minimum order of 5,000 required. Each display rack would cost approximately ₱5.00. Consideration might also be given to placing these racks in the offices of doctors. Both the booklets and the display racks would carry the name and trademark of Choufont-Salva.

TABLE 9   Consumer-Oriented Media Costs

PRINT

Publication	Circulation	Percent of Copies to Households Earning ₱15,000 and Above	Rates per Column Inch
Newspapers			
Evening News	29,000	N.A.	₱ 8.00
Manila *Chronicle*	72,000	22%	11.00
Manila *Daily Bulletin*	59,000	71	9.50
Manila *Times*	120,000	31	19.00
Mirror	24,000	N.A.	6.00
Philippine Herald	47,000	18	8.50
The Sunday Times	155,000	48	21.00
Weekly magazines			
Free Press	86,000	42	15.00
Graphic	88,000	55	12.00
Weekly Women's Magazine	93,000	65	14.00
Woman & the Home	81,000	22	13.00

N.A. = Not available.

RADIO
Class A Time: 6:00 A.M.–9:00 A.M.

Units	60 Seconds (per spot)	30 Seconds (per spot)	5–10 Seconds (per spot)
1– 12	₱12.50	₱9.37	₱3.12
13– 25	11.88	8.91	2.97
26– 38	11.25	8.44	2.81
39– 51	10.63	7.97	2.66
52–103	10.00	7.50	2.50
104–259	9.30	7.03	2.34
260+	8.75	6.56	2.19

Class B Time: 5:00 A.M.–6:00 A.M.,
9:00 A.M.–2:00 P.M., and 5:00 P.M.–6:00 P.M.

Units	60 Seconds (per spot)	30 Seconds (per spot)	5–10 Seconds (per spot)
1– 12	₱7.50	₱5.62	₱2.28
13– 25	7.13	5.35	1.87
26– 38	6.75	5.06	1.69
39– 51	6.38	4.78	1.59
52–103	6.00	4.50	1.50
104–259	5.63	4.23	1.41
260+	5.25	3.89	1.31

TABLE 9 *continued*

	Class C Time: 2:00 P.M.–5:00 P.M., 6:00 P.M.–12:00 *Midnight, and* 4:00 A.M.–5:00 A.M.		
Units	60 Seconds (per spot)	30 Seconds (per spot)	5–10 Seconds (per spot)
1– 12	₱4.50	₱3.37	₱1.12
13– 25	4.28	3.21	1.07
26– 38	4.05	3.04	1.01
39– 51	3.83	2.87	0.96
52–103	3.60	2.70	0.90
104–259	3.38	2.53	0.85
260+	3.15	2.36	0.79

	Class D Time: 12:00 Midnight–4:00 A.M.		
Units	60 Seconds (per spot)	30 Seconds (per spot)	5–10 Seconds (per spot)
1– 12	₱3.00	₱2.25	₱0.75
13– 25	2.85	2.14	0.71
26– 38	2.70	2.03	0.67
39– 51	2.55	1.91	0.64
52–103	2.40	1.80	0.60
104–259	2.25	1.69	0.56
260+	2.10	1.57	0.52

PRODUCTION COSTS*

Length	Estimated Costs
60 seconds	₱500
30 seconds	500
10 seconds	400
5 seconds	400

TELEVISION
1. RATES

Midprogram breaks	Prime Time 6:30 P.M.–10:00 P.M. (per spot)	Class B Time (all other hours) (per spot)
60 seconds	₱500	₱250
30 seconds	250	125
10 seconds	125	65
5 seconds	65	35

TABLE 9 *continued*

Station breaks (between programs)		
60 seconds	₱400	₱200
30 seconds	200	100
10 seconds	100	50
5 seconds	50	25

2. PRODUCTION COSTS

a. *A 30-second film commercial would cost approximately ₱5,000 to produce.*
b. *The estimated costs of producing a T.V. slide commercial are as follows:*

Length	Estimated Costs
60 seconds	₱350
30 seconds	325
10 seconds	310
5 seconds	305

*In estimating costs, it was assumed that (1) two announcers would be used in producing a 30- or 60-second ad and that only one announcer would be used in producing a 5- or 10-second ad and (2) a combo would furnish simple background music for the ads. The estimated costs also include the studio fees, the costs of tapes, and similar expenses.

pany learned that within a year a competing Philippine drug company probably would be marketing an oral contraceptive containing only .5 milligram of progestin. North American Drugs, Inc., the American parent company of the Philippine company, had just developed the new oral contraceptive in its laboratories. The American company planned to test market the product in the United States. If the test marketing was successful, North American Drugs would then release the product to its subsidiaries. Because of the test marketing, Choufont-Salva's management felt that it would be at least 9 months and probably 12 months before North American Drug's oral contraceptive would appear on the Philippine market.

Appendix I: Position of the Roman Catholic Church Concerning Contraception

At the present time (1966), the Church holds the position stated by Pope Pius XI in *Casti Connubii*, an encyclical issued in 1930. This excerpt is a summary of it:

Any use whatsoever of matrimony exercised in such a way that the act is deliberately frustrated in its natural power to generate life is an offense against the law of God and nature, and those who indulge in such are branded with the guilt of a great sin. (para. 56)

The only methods of family limitation which meet with the approval of the Church are continence and periodic continence, or the rhythm method. The Catholic Church does, however, permit the use of artificial contraception for medical (as distinct from birth control) reasons.

Appendix II: Excerpts from "The Family Planning Association of the Philippines— Its Performance and Program of Activities"[1]

The present status of the family planning movement in the Philippines has been very favorable and progressing in spite of its predominantly Catholic population, about 84 percent of the total population. Because of this strong religious affiliation, before the year 1965 although there were about three Protestant family planning groups already existing, the mere mention of birth control was strongly tabooed and no public forum on the subject was allowed even by a private organization. Any press publication on family planning and birth control materials was censured and not permitted to enter the country and be transmitted through mails (old custom and postal laws).

In the early part of 1965, the Family Planning Association of the Philippines, Inc. (FPAP), organized by progressive Catholic leaders, launched a nationwide family planning movement which was never done before. Since this concept was very new to the general public, the FPAP's intensified and relentless efforts have been concentrated on dissemination of informative knowledge of family planning methods and motivation programs to change the attitude and behavior of the people through continuing series of lectures and speaking tours in public meetings and forums all over the country, and through extensive use of mass media communications, such as endless publication of articles and news in newspapers, magazines, medical journals, nationwide distribution of pamphlets, handouts, brochures, and lately the use of TV and radio. Note that the first article in the Graphic-Kislap magazine was censured, but the favorable public opinion changed the attitude of authorities which later just ignored the old law, and which was recently repealed "by implication" by the Republic Act No. 4729 of June, 1966.

Training seminars to create man-power are being conducted locally for physicians, nurses, and health educators. Family planning leaders and workers, including those of other allied organizations (PPMP, RPA, PFPA, Manila Health Dept., Municipal Health Officers) were sent through the FPAP under IPPF and other foreign grants to attend training seminars, international conferences, university studies, and observation tours of family planning programs in other countries. To date, the FPAP

---

[1] Published by the FPAP, May 1967.

has 162 assisted clinics and 3 fully supported and maintained clinics in different areas of the country. Including the Manila Health Department, PPMP, RPA, and the Pathfinder Fund to which the FPAP is closely associated, there are now about 300 family planning clinics all over the country. The strongly conservative Catholic sector is starting to establish rhythm clinics, and there are strong indications that other institutions, especially the educational, may follow soon.

The present population of the Philippines is about 33 million, with an annual rate of growth of 3.2 percent, the highest in Asia. The annual birth rate is 45 to 46 per thousand and the annual death rate is 12 to 14 per thousand. The average family size is 6.7. The land area is 115,700 sq. miles. The population density is 280 persons per sq. mile which is already five times the world average. The city of Manila has 80,000 persons per sq. mile. The country cannot feed its population adequately; therefore, it is over-populated. Food supply and increasing unemployment are two very serious major problems. The annual net income per capita is only ₱390.-. or about $100.-. Two-thirds of the population are in poverty and medically indigent, and depend very much on government agencies which, at this time, cannot give family planning services. In spite of FPAP efforts in creating more public demand for family planning services and in participation of private medical sectors, without the participation of government health agencies, it would be far from its goal—the promotion of the well-being of the Filipino family and helping in the socioeconomic development of this country.

There is at present increasing awareness and demand from government health officers and agencies relative to the knowledge and methods of family planning. Cognizant of this, the Family Planning Association of the Philippines, Inc. is also exerting its efforts to offer its help to introduce a family planning program in the Maternal and Child Health agencies of the government.

DISCUSSION QUESTIONS

1. Formulate a marketing strategy for Choufont-Salva. Identify your objectives, target markets, product, price, promotion, and distribution policies and your research plan.
2. Would you respond to the North American Drug announcement? How and why, or why not?

5
REGIONAL MARKET CHARACTERISTICS

This is the place!

*Brigham Young, 1801–1877,
on first seeing the Valley
of the Great Salt Lake,
July 24, 1847*

INTRODUCTION

It is not necessary to be an expert on every country in the world to manage a global marketing program. Obviously, in-depth market and country knowledge must be applied to the country marketing effort by members of the business team, but team members may be local agents, representatives, or employees. The critical skill of the global marketer is working with this team. The purpose of this chapter is to give you a better understanding of world market characteristics so you can work effectively with the marketing team in serving customers in the different countries of the world.

This chapter, which is organized around world regions, presents a broad overview of the markets of the world. The first half of the chapter outlines economic cooperation and preferential trade arrangements. The second half describes the characteristics of the major regional markets of the world and concludes with an in-depth study of one country market.

ECONOMIC SYSTEMS

There are three types of economic systems in the world today: capitalist, socialist, and mixed. These classifications are based essentially on the method of resource allocation in the system. The three methods of resource allocation are *market allocation, command* or *central plan allocation,* and *mixed allocation.*

Market Allocation

A market allocation system is one which relies upon the customer or consumer to allocate resources. Consumer choice or purchase under a market system decides what will be produced by whom. The United States, Western Europe, and Japan (the triad countries which account for almost three-quarters of gross world product) are examples of market allocation systems.

Command Allocation

In a command allocation system, resource allocation decisions (i.e., which products to make and how to make them) are made by government planners. The number of automobiles, shoes, shirts, motorcycles, television sets, and so on, and the size, color, quality, features, and so on, of every product are determined by government planners whereas in a market system, these decisions are made by consumers who in effect write the economic plan with their purchase decisions and purchase intentions. These two systems are profoundly different methods of allocating resources, and reflect fundamentally different views about the role of the individual in society. The market system is an economic democracy—money gives you the right to vote for the goods of your choice. Under the command system, consumers are free to spend their money on what is available, but the decisions about what is produced and therefore what is available are made by the state planners.

Mixed System

There are no pure market or command allocation systems. The market systems of the West have a command sector and the command systems of the East have a market sector. The economic systems on both sides of the Iron Curtain are mixed. All capitalist market systems are "mixed" (i.e., they have elements of market *and* command allocation). The command allocation of the market economy is the proportion of gross national product that is taxed and spent by government. This proportion for the 24 OECD (Organization for Economic Cooperation and Development) member countries ranges from 25 percent of gross national product in Japan to 57 percent in Sweden.[1]

One of the profound changes that is taking place in the world today is the move toward "privatization," which is another way of describing the move within a mixed economy toward greater reliance upon the market to allocate resources. When the U.S. Post Office became the U.S. Postal Service (USPS), it was a move toward deregulation and privatization of mail services. Although the USPS still has mo-

[1]The OECD Member Countries, 1982 Ed., The OECD Observer, no. 115 (March 1982).

nopoly rights to basic first-class mail service, it competes with a number of vendors in the overnight letter and package markets. The allocation of resources for this service is now determined by consumers rather than by post office executives.

Just as the market economies have command sectors, command economies have market sectors where production and prices are set by forces of supply and demand. Farmers in most socialist countries, for example, are permitted to offer part of their production in a free market.

Based on economic performance to date, there is absolutely no question about the superiority of the market system from a material point of view. This superiority has led voters and governments responding to voter wishes to support initiatives to move toward the privatization of services that are financed by tax revenues.

ECONOMIC COOPERATION AND PREFERENTIAL TRADE ARRANGEMENTS

Since World War II there has been a tremendous interest in economic cooperation. The enthusiasm for international cooperation has been stimulated by the success of the European community, which was itself inspired by the success of the U.S. economy. There are many degrees of economic cooperation, ranging from the agreement of two or more nations to reductions of barriers to trade, to the full-scale economic integration of two or more national economies. In the nineteenth century the German Zollverein and the British imperial preference system were the two most important agreements leading to the reduction of internal tariff barriers in Germany and international barriers in the British Empire.

The best known preferential arrangement of this century was the British Commonwealth preference system, known as the imperial preference system before World War II. This system was important in trade between such countries as the United Kingdom, Canada, Australia, New Zealand, India, and certain other former British colonies in Africa, Asia, and the Middle East. The decision by the United Kingdom to join the European Economic Community resulted in the demise of this system. This development illustrates the constantly changing nature of international economic cooperation.

GATT

The General Agreement on Tariffs and Trade (GATT) is a 92-country organization whose objective is to promote trade among members. To achieve this aim, GATT has over the years provided a forum where countries have met to negotiate on tariffs and trade. As the name implies, GATT has focused on tariffs and it has been quite successful in reducing tariff barriers to trade. In recent years, however, the basic technique of protectionism has shifted from tariffs to subsidies and market sharing agreements. Market sharing goes against one of the basic tenants of GATT—non-discrimination (i.e., a tariff against one country must be a tariff against all, or a concession for one country must be a concession for all).

Free Trade Area

A free trade area is a group of countries that have agreed to abolish all internal barriers to trade between the member countries. Country members of a free trade area can and do maintain independent trade policies vis-à-vis third countries. To avoid trade diversion in favor of low-tariff members (for example, importing goods in the member country with the lowest tariff for shipment to countries within the area with higher external tariffs), a system of certificates of origin is used.

Customs Union

The customs union is the logical evolution of the free trade area. In addition to eliminating the internal barriers to trade, members of a customs union agree to the establishment of common external trade barriers. Today there is no significant form of customs union in operation, although a union is a logical stage of development in the transition from a free trade area to a common market. Belgium, Luxembourg, and The Netherlands, for example, were participants in a customs union that dates to 1921 before becoming members of the European Economic Community.

Economic Union

The economic union builds upon the elimination of the internal tariff barriers and the establishment of common external barriers. It also seeks to coordinate economic and social policy within the union to allow free flow of capital and labor from country to country. Thus an economic union is a common marketplace not only for goods but also for services and capital. The full evolution of an economic union would involve the creation of a unified central bank, the use of a single currency, and common policies on agriculture, social services and welfare, regional development, transport, taxation, competition, and mergers. A fully developed economic union requires extensive political unity, which makes it similar to a nation. The further integration of nations that were members of fully developed economic unions would be the formation of a central government that would bring together independent political states into a single political framework. The best-known and most successful example of an economic union is the European Community.

REGIONAL ECONOMIC ORGANIZATIONS

Andean Group

This group, officially known as the Acuerdo de Cartagena (from the Cartagena Agreement which established it in 1969) and also known as the Grupo Andino (Andean Group) or the Pacto Andino (Andean Pact), aims to accelerate the harmonious development of its member states through economic and social integration. The members of the group are Bolivia, Colombia, Ecuador, Peru, and Venezuela. The organization consists of a Commission, a Council, a Junta (a technical body responsible for the agreement's implementation), a Parliament, a Court of Justice, a Reserve Fund, and a Development Corporation.

The operations of the group have frequently been hindered by political problems. Trade among the members was $1,400 million in 1980, or approximately 4.5 percent of their foreign trade, compared with $111 million (2.5 percent) among the same countries in 1970. By 1980, tariff reduction on manufactured goods traded among Colombia, Peru, and Venezuela was almost complete.

Since 1971, in accordance with a Commission directive (Decision 24), foreign investors are required to transfer 51 percent of their shares to local investors in order to qualify for the preferential trade arrangements. Transfers were to be completed by 1989 for Colombia, Peru and Venezuela, and by 1994 for Bolivia and Ecuador. Foreign owned companies are not to repatriate dividends of more than 20 percent except with approval of the Commission.

Association of South East Asian Nations— ASEAN

The Association of South East Asian Nations (ASEAN) was established in 1967 at Bangkok to accelerate economic progress and to increase the stability of the South-East Asian region. The member countries are Brunei, Indonesia, Malaysia, the Philippines, Singapore, and Thailand. The ASEAN industrial complementation program, begun in 1981, encourages member countries to produce complementary products in specific industrial sectors for preferential exchange among themselves (for example, components to be used in the automobile industry). Member countries have negotiated tariff reductions within the association and a customs code of conduct has been adopted.

Although the six countries of ASEAN are geographically close, they are divided in most other respects. One of the reasons the association has remained in existence is because it does almost nothing. In mid-1987 President Aquino of the Philippines was urging the association to become a real political and economic force, and proceed with real economic integration. They have a long way to go, as can be seen in Figure 5–1.

Caribbean Community and Common Market— CARICOM

The Caribbean Community and Common Market (CARICOM) was formed by the Treaty of Chaguaramas in 1973 as a movement toward unity in the Caribbean. The members are Antigua and Barbuda, Barbados, Belize, Dominica, Grenada, Guyana, Jamaica, Montserrat, St. Christopher and Nevis, Saint Lucia, Saint Vincent and the Grenadines, and Trinidad and Tobago.

The Caribbean Community's main field of activity is economic integration by means of a Caribbean Common Market which replaced the Caribbean Free Trade

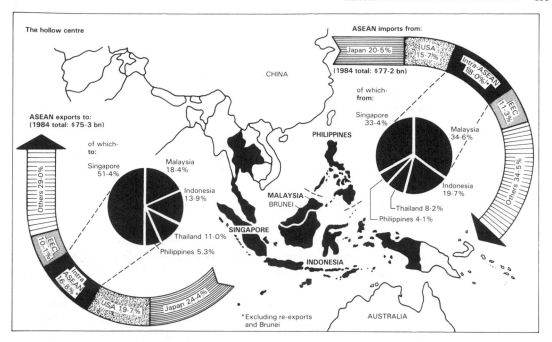

FIGURE 5–1 ASEAN Imports and Exports

Source: Institute of South-East Asian Studies, and *The Economist,* August 30, 1986, p. 31.

Association (CARIFTA). The goal of integration has been limited by problems and obstacles. A Multilateral Clearing Facility (MCF) collapsed after it exceeded its credit limit. There have also been difficulties in applying CARICOM Rules of Origin which attempt to verify that imported goods genuinely come from within the community.

The principal organ of the Common Market, the Council, consists of a minister of government designated by each member state. It is responsible for the development and smooth running of the Common Market, and for the settlement of any problems arising out of its functioning. However, the Conference may issue directives to the Council. The Council generally takes decisions unanimously.

Under the treaty, the following bodies are associate institutions of the Community: Caribbean Development Bank, Caribbean Examinations Council, Caribbean Investment Corporation, Caribbean Meteorological Council, Council of Legal Education, Regional Shipping Council, University of Guyana, University of the West Indies, and Organisation of Eastern Caribbean States.

Central American Common Market (Mercado Común Centro Americano)

Established under the aegis of the Organization of Central American States (ODECA), the main formal instrument of the Central American Common Market (CACM) is the General Treaty of Central American Economic Integration (Tratado General de Integración Económica Centroamericana) signed in Managua on December 15, 1960. It was ratified by all countries by September 1963. The members are Costa Rica, Guatemala, El Salvador, Honduras, and Nicaragua.

The General Treaty envisages the eventual liberalization of intraregional trade and the establishment of a free trade area and a customs union. By 1969, 95 percent of customs items had been awarded free trade status. The remaining 5 percent consisted of goods covered by international agreements and other special arrangements. A CACM common external tariff was also created. By 1980 it covered 99 percent of all customs sections.

Council of Arab Economic Unity

The Council, which held its first meeting in 1964, is composed of Iraq, Jordan, Kuwait, Libya, Mauritania, Palestine Liberation Organization, Somalia, Sudan, Syria, United Arab Emirates, Yemen Arab Republic, Yemen, and People's Democratic Republic.

The Council has approved a five-year coordination plan and has resolved to create, in stages, an Arab common market. Members have initiated multilateral agreements aimed at achieving economic unity and have established a number of joint ventures.

Council for Mutual Economic Assistance[2]

The Council (COMECON) was founded in 1949 to assist the economic development of its member states through joint utilization and coordination of efforts. The Mongolian People's Republic was admitted in 1962, the Republic of Cuba in 1972, and the Socialist Republic of Vietnam in 1978. The members are Bulgaria, Cuba, Czechoslovakia, German Democratic Republic, Hungary, Mongolia, Poland, Romania, U.S.S.R. and Vietnam. Albania ceased to participate in the activities of the Council at the end of 1961.

In accordance with Article XI of the Charter, the Council may invite participation of nonmember countries in the work of its organs or in spheres agreed by arrangement with the relevant countries. Delegations from Afghanistan, Angola, Ethiopia, Laos, Mozambique, and the People's Democratic Republic of Yemen were invited to send observers to the session of the Council held in Berlin in 1983.

In 1964 an agreement was concluded whereby Yugoslavia can participate in certain defined spheres of the Council's activity, where a mutual interest with member countries prevails. The agreement also envisaged Yugoslavia attending meetings of the Council's standing commissions and other organs where matters of mutual interest are discussed.

---

[2]*The Europa Year Book, 1982,* Europa Publications Limited, London, p. 171.

COMECON has cooperation agreements with Finland (signed May 1973), Iraq (July 1975), and Mexico (August 1975).

COMECON's aims are to unite and coordinate the efforts of the member countries to improve the development of socialist economic integration; to promote planned economic development; to achieve more rapid economic and technical progress in these countries, and particularly a higher level of industrialization in countries where this is lacking; to achieve a steady growth of labor productivity; to work gradually toward a balanced level of development in the different regions; and to achieve a steady increase in standards of living in the member states.

Economic Community of West African States (ECOWAS)

The Treaty of Lagos establishing ECOWAS was signed in May 1975 by 16 states with the object of promoting trade, cooperation, and self-reliance in West Africa. The members are: Benin, Burkina Faso, Cape Verde, The Gambia, Ghana, Guinea, Guinea-Bissau, Ivory Coast, Liberia, Mali, Mauritania, Niger, Nigeria, Senegal, Sierra Leone, and Togo.

The European Community

Germany, France, Italy, Belgium, Luxembourg, The Netherlands, the United Kingdom, Ireland, and Denmark are being welded into an economic union within the framework of the European Community (EC). The EC was established by the Treaty of Rome, which came into force on January 1, 1958. A step-by-step reduction of internal customs duties on industrial goods resulted in their complete removal by July 1, 1968. Simultaneously the duties applied to imports from third countries were gradually aligned, and the common external tariff within the EC also came into force on July 1, 1968, and there is a target of removing all internal barriers to the movement of goods and services by 1992.

A common agricultural policy has been adopted. The removal of internal agricultural duties has been completed. The external customs duties for the majority of agricultural products, which are subject to EC regulations, were suspended and replaced by variable import levies designed to bring the price of products imported from third countries in line with those prevailing inside the community. The community has made progress in abolishing restrictions on the movement of capital, in the alignment of taxes, in developing a community policy on competition, restrictive practices such as price fixing, and company mergers. In addition, EC companies have achieved freedom for workers from member countries to obtain employment anywhere in the community and freedom for firms to establish and operate anywhere in the community.

Association with the community is open to all countries under the Rome Treaty. Greece and Turkey became associate members of the community in 1962 and 1963, respectively. Under these agreements, upon the completion of the customs union between the two countries and the community, it is expected that they will move toward full economic union with the other countries in the EC.

The Rome Treaty also provided for links between the European community and the colonies and other dependencies in Africa and elsewhere of France, Belgium, The Netherlands, and Italy. The first association agreement signed in 1963 known as the Yaounde Convention, which was renewed in July 1969, specifies duty-free entry for industrial goods to the common market and also specifies that agricultural products subject to EC market regulations and some tropical products will enjoy a slightly improved preferential treatment in the EC. The associated African States may reimpose duties or other restrictions on imports for the EC if it is necessary for their economic development.

In 1975 the EC entered into a new trade and economic cooperation agreement with 46 African, Caribbean, and Pacific countries (ACP). The agreement, known as the Lomé Convention, allows the EC duty-free access to all the industrial goods and 96 percent of the agricultural products of the ACP. Included in this agreement is an Export Revenue Stabilization Plan through which the EC provides development assistance to the ACP countries.

European Free Trade Association

The European Free Trade Association (EFTA) was established by the Stockholm convention of 1959. The members are Austria, Finland (associate member), Iceland, Norway, Portugal, Sweden, and Switzerland. EFTA's objective is to bring about free trade in industrial goods and an expansion of trade in agricultural goods. Internal EFTA tariffs on industrial products were abolished in 1966.

The European Free Trade Association does not maintain a common external tariff; instead each member country retains its own tariff structure applicable to non-EFTA countries. To prevent the import of non-EFTA goods into one EFTA country by way of another with a lower external tariff, a system of declaration of origin is in operation by which goods can be shown to be EFTA origin and therefore entitled to the tariff reductions.

Total exports of the seven member countries in 1983 to each other were US $14.5 billion as compared with exports to the European Economic Community of $54 billion, $6.8 billion to the United States, $7.1 billion to Eastern Europe, and $19.9 billion to the rest of the world.

Latin American Integration Association
(Asociación Latino-Americana de Integración)

The Latin American Integration Association[3] (LAIA) was established in August 1980 to replace the Latin American Free Trade Association, set up in February 1960. The

---

[3]*The Europa Year Book, 1982. A World Survey,* Vol. I (London: Europa Publications, 1982), p. 232.

members are Argentina, Bolivia, Brazil, Chile, Colombia, Ecuador, Mexico, Paraguay, Peru, Uruguay, and Venezuela.

The Latin American Free Trade Association (LAFTA) was an intergovernmental organization, created by the Treaty of Montevideo in February 1960 with the object of increasing trade between the contracting parties and of promoting regional integration, thus contributing to the economic and social development of the member countries. The treaty provided for the gradual establishment of a free trade area, which would form the basis for a Latin American Common Market. Reduction of tariffs and other trade barriers was to be carried out gradually up to 1980.

Unfortunately, LAFTA made little progress. By 1980 only 14 percent of annual trade among members could be attributed to LAFTA agreements, and it was the richest states that were receiving most benefit. In June 1980 it was decided that LAFTA should be replaced by a less ambitious, more flexible organization, the Latin American Integration Association (ALADI), established by the 1980 Treaty of Montevideo, which came into force in March 1981. Instead of across-the-board tariff cuts, a system of bilateral preference agreements would be set up, taking into account the different stages of development of the members, and with no definite timetable for the establishment of a full common market.

Organisation Commune Africaine et Mauricienne

The Organisation (OCAM) was founded in February 1965 as the successor of the *Union africaine et malgache de coopération économique* (UAMCE) to accelerate the economic, social, technical, and cultural development of member states within the framework of the OAU. The members are Benin, Central African Republic, Ivory Coast, Mauritius, Niger, Rwanda, Senegal, Togo, and Upper Volta.

The objectives proposed in 1965 included customs reform, possibly leading to the establishment of an African Common Market, and common economic policies covering investment, insurance of trade, and restrictions on double taxation. A stabilization fund was projected, to support commodity prices.

REGIONAL MARKET CHARACTERISTICS

There are innumerable ways of dividing the countries of the world into different regional markets. In effect, defining regional markets is an exercise in clustering countries where, it is hoped, both within-cluster similarities and between-cluster differences will be maximized. Clustering can be accomplished with the use of mathematical programs that determine the spatial relationship of objects (countries), defined by variables (market measures), or by judgmental analysis on the basis of both explicit and implicit criteria. In the section that follows, national markets are clustered judgmentally on the basis of geographic proximity. A brief survey of each region is presented. Japan is examined in greater detail as an example of a more in-depth analysis.

Western Europe

Europe is the second smallest of the world's continents; only Australia is smaller. All Europe, including the USSR, accounts for only 7 percent of the land surface of the earth. Western Europe, which could be fitted into Australia or more than twice over into Brazil, generated 24 percent of global income in 1984.

The 16 countries and 423 million people of Western Europe are distinguished by a wide range of different customs, tastes, and traditions. Their populations range from more than 60 million people in West Germany to less than 300,000 people in Luxembourg. The biggest country in area, France, is more than twice the size of the United Kingdom or Germany but has fewer people than either of these countries. The most densely populated country, The Netherlands, has more than 30 times as many people per square kilometer as Norway, the least crowded country.

There are 11 major languages spoken in Europe, a fact that presents a special challenge to the international marketer.

The countries of Europe are among the most prosperous in the world, although their income is unevenly distributed. The average per capita annual income in Portugal is only $1,857 as compared with $12,577 in Switzerland. In the judgment of many observers, each of these countries has a higher standard of living than the United States. The different levels of prosperity across Europe are the basis for many other differences, such as the different proportions of ownership of various consumer durable goods and the different ways in which homemakers do their work. These income differences also reflect radically different societies. For example, in Portugal 29 percent of the population is still employed on the land as compared with 7 percent of Sweden's population and less than 2 percent of Britain's.

Eastern Europe

Eastern Europe includes Bulgaria, Czechoslovakia, East Germany, Hungary, Poland, Rumania, and the USSR. The region has been dominated economically and militarily by the USSR, which accounts for two-thirds of the region's net national product. The Eastern European economy is not fully compatible with the Western market economic system. For many years the USSR, and to a lesser extent the other East European countries, were basically committed to self-sufficiency and a centrally planned economic organization. In recent years Russia, and especially the smaller East European countries, have made substantial moves toward economic decentralization and a shift from the control of resources at the state plan level to control at the enterprise level, with increasing reliance on the market as a mechanism both for establishing production priorities and for allocating resources. Nevertheless, the ability of East European enterprise to compete in world markets remains limited. The discipline of competitive markets revealed the limitations of state planning and state control of the resource allocation and resource management process. The simple fact is that the East Europeans, especially the Russians, must employ controls to ensure that their purchases from the West do not exceed their sales and credit receipts. There is no free exchange or convertibility of East European currency because this would violate their decision to rely upon state planning instead of the market as a resource allocation mechanism.

Marketing is undoubtedly the key to expanded participation of the East European economies in the international economic order, as well as the key to the standard-of-living aspirations of the East Europeans. Without improved marketing performance, East European enterprises will continue to turn in lackluster performance in the competitive market economies of the West. This will result in continued shortages of foreign exchange, which will of course put limits on the ability of East Europeans to import and purchase products and services from the West. Thus it is no exaggeration to conclude that the key to expanded economic cooperation between East and West is marketing. To the extent that economic cooperation and exchange promote understanding and create conditions that support world peace, it follows that marketing in this part of the world is contributing to world peace.

The potential for close economic ties between global corporations and East European socialist economies is expanding. The markets are there and skilled labor is available. A major limiting factor is the East European countries' position on foreign ownership. Most companies are reluctant to undertake long-term commitments involving a substantial transfer of technology, know-how, and skill unless they can have a major ownership and control. Opposed to this, most of the East European socialist economies have difficulties in permitting even minority equity ownership by capitalist corporations.

The trend in Eastern Europe is toward increased contact and closer relations with the West. In the view of many experts, global corporations will play a major role in the transfer of technology and know-how to East European countries. Rumania and Hungary, for example, now permit 49 percent equity ownership by foreigners, which is a gesture of encouragement to companies who are concerned about control and equity participation in a profit stream as an incentive to invest in any country.

The political and economic stability of the East European countries is relatively high due to the permanence of the governments and the general tightness of the political situation. The quality of the labor force in East Europe is high, literacy is high, and production costs are relatively low.

In late 1986, the Soviet Union announced ambitious measures to decentralize and enhance its foreign trade by giving more than 20 ministries and 70 major enterprises the right to make deals directly with foreign entities and to maintain their own accounts in convertible currencies. Observers agree that if these changes are actually implemented they could have a tremendous impact on trade volume and also on political relations. These moves were linked to the Soviet effort to join the 92-nation General Agreement on Tariffs and Trade (GATT).[4]

[4] "Trade Rights Expanded for Soviet Enterprises," *The New York Times*, September 25, 1986, p. D1.

North America

The North American market is a distinctive world regional market. In the United States there is a concentration of wealth and income within the framework of a single national economic and political environment that presents unique marketing characteristics. Per capita GNP in the United States in 1984 was $12,677.

The distinctive characteristic of the U.S. market is the unique combination of high per capita income, large population, vast space, and plentiful natural resources. High product ownership levels are associated with a high income and relatively high receptivity to innovations and new ideas both in consumer and industrial products.

The U.S. industrial product market is particularly receptive to innovations and products that reduce labor hours required in production. The intensive application of computers and automated equipment in the United States reflects the high cost of labor, which creates an incentive to manufacture, process, and control as much activity as possible with machines. In general, U.S. industry is the most automated and efficient in the world, although there are notable exceptions. The U.S. steel industry, for example, is believed by many experts to be at least 15 years behind the industry in other parts of the world, especially Japan.

The United States presents a unique foreign market opportunity for companies based outside the United States. It is, in a single national market, an opportunity as large as that presented by all the countries of Western Europe, and is twice as large as the Japanese market. Indeed the size of the U.S. market is so great that most foreign companies wisely enter the U.S. market with regional strategies where they focus their program on target regions and eventually go national.

The United States was formerly a unique market also in terms of product saturation levels for consumer products, receptiveness to consumer product innovation, and receptiveness to innovative industrial products. Although these are no longer unique U.S. market qualities, the United States is still a market that is receptive to innovative ideas, especially in the consumer products area.

Another distinctive feature of the U.S. market is that because of the size of the United States, there is to an unusual degree an arm's-length—even an adversary—relationship between business and government. This relationship grows out of a long and complex history, which we do not have time or space to go into in this book. However, for the non-U.S.-based marketer, the arm's-length relationship provides greater opportunities for competing as a foreign firm than is true in most countries of the world, where closer partnership between government and business often excludes foreign suppliers from major product categories, especially industrial products. For example, the United States is one of the few industrial countries in the world where foreign manufacturers can bid on and obtain orders for power generation equipment. In almost every other country with a major power generation industry, either formal or informal collaboration between power generation companies and national equipment manufacturers excludes foreign competitors.

Canada, with a population of 26 million and a 1986 per capita income of $11,048, only $1,629 below that of the United States, shows many similar marketing characteristics. Canada also maintains the closest trading ties with the United States: In 1985, 25 percent of U.S. exports went to Canada and 21 percent of U.S. imports came from Canada. U.S. direct investment in Canada is the largest of any investor country. The close economic cooperation between the two countries has led to the conclusion of unique agreements such as the automotive agreement that provides for the economic integration of the U.S. and Canadian auto industries. The intention of the act is to make it possible for auto companies to specialize in the manufacture and assembly of autos on each side of the border and to import and export components and assembled cars freely with tariff barriers. Although there are strains in the economic relations between the two countries, on balance the degree of economic cooperation and integration is quite high by international standards.

Asia

The 21-country Asian market is a colossus, with 55 percent of the world's population. The region accounted for 19 percent of global income in 1984. Fifty-eight percent of the region's income was concentrated in Japan, which has only 5 percent of the region's population. Many of the smaller countries in the region—South Korea, Taiwan, and Hong Kong—are developing rapidly, and no company can afford to ignore China, a country with 1,047 million potential customers. There are many political and cultural constraints operating in this most dynamic and fastest growing market area of the world.

BASIC CHARACTERISTICS OF THE JAPANESE MARKET. Population density and geographic isolation are the two crucial and immutable factors that cannot be discounted when discussing Japan as a world market. It is interesting to note that while Japan's territory occupies only .28 percent of the world total, and its population makes up only 2.56 percent of the world total, Japan shares some 10.75 percent of the GNP of the free world, and its trade volume represents 10 percent of overall world trade. The base for this amazing economic strength rests on a narrow stretch of land.

Since 72 percent of Japan's land area is mountainous, the cultivated land area encompasses about 15 percent, the residential area represents only 3 percent, and the industrial area is merely 1.4 percent. As for its relative geographical position, Japan sits at the opposite side of the Pacific separated from the other major economic powers.

The needs of Japanese consumers are rather uniform because Japan is a mono-racial country and because, particularly since the end of World War II, information is transmitted very rapidly. At the same time, however, the Japanese consumers have multifaceted tastes in their daily living, as is exemplified in their consumer response to the three basic needs of food, clothing, and shelter.

The Japanese enjoy every kind of dish in the world. They wear Western-style clothes for most occasions, yet still sometimes wear their traditional kimono. The typical Japanese house has a construction style that mixes both traditional Japanese and modern Western elements. In other words, the Japanese life-style is really very versatile.[5]

The success of the Japanese economy has resulted in a growing interest in the underlying factors, forces, and methods that have enabled the Japanese to perform so impressively in raising their own standard of living and in competing worldwide across a broad range of products. Marketing has been a key factor in the Japanese success. It creates as well as fits needs in a society.

One of the most striking aspects of the Japanese marketing system as compared with the U.S. system, particularly in view of the cultural differences, is the remarkable similarity of the processes of change in the two countries. Japanese food retailing today has been dominated by small establishments. These small establishments have been threatened by larger chains, and each year the total number of food stores is declining. The reduction parallels one that started almost 40 years ago in the United States.

In addition to rising incomes there is a process of diffusion of wealth that is reducing inequalities in income distribution. For example, in 1958 the average cash wage of a blue-collar worker with a secondary education was 64 percent of that paid a white-collar worker. By 1968 the difference was narrowed to 74 percent. This current prosperity and diffusion of wealth is more remarkable when viewed in the light of the great disparity in income distribution that existed in prewar Japan. As late as 1930 nearly 90 percent of Japanese families earned less than $150 annually. Collectively they received only half the total national income.

One of the major marketing implications of the rapidly rising income level of Japanese consumers has been the "Shohi Kakumai," or consumption revolution. Every aspect of daily life has been affected. The effect of improved diet has had a marked change on the physical size of the Japanese. Since World War II the average height of a 20-year-old Japanese woman has risen 2 inches to 5 feet 3 inches. The same is true for men. Before World War II the average 20-year-old male in Japan was 5 feet 3½ inches. Today he is almost 5 feet 8 inches tall. Arms are longer, feet are bigger, and so are necks. The average weight of Japanese youngsters has increased more than 15 pounds since the 1930s.

The average Japanese woman owns over 16 kimonos. The large number of kimonos reflects both the rising income and wealth of Japanese consumers as well as the love of the traditional Japanese culture. Japanese dress reflects in many ways the national response to the difficult choice between modernization and traditional practices. The Japanese prefer Western dress for business because it is more efficient, but they prefer the traditional dress for social and family occasions because they feel it reflects the style and elegance of traditional Japanese culture.

By 1981, refrigerators, washing machines, color television sets, and electric vacuum cleaners all had a diffusion or household ownership rate of more than 95 percent. Table 5–1 summarizes data on the diffusion of a cross section of consumer goods in Japan in 1981.

[5] Adapted from Yasuo Ōki, "Some Prerequisites for Entering the Japanese Market," *Look Japan*, October 10, 1982, p. 1.

TABLE 5–1 Diffusion Rates of Durable Consumer Goods in Japan, February 1970 versus March 1981*

No. of Surveyed Households			Electric Ovens	T.V.s		Stereos	Living Sets	Cameras
				Mono	Color			
All households								
1970	8,338	100.0%	2.1%	90.2%	26.3%	31.2%	22.6%	64.1%
1981	5,814	100.0	37.4	20.0	98.5	58.5	40.7	85.2
Farming households								
1970	1,792	100.0	0.6	91.6	18.1	18.6	14.4	45.3
1981	715	100.0	35.5	21.4	98.2	54.5	40.4	80.6
Nonfarming households								
1970	6,546	100.0	2.5	89.8	28.6	34.6	24.8	69.3
1981	5,099	100.0	37.7	19.7	98.5	59.2	40.7	86.0
Cities‡								
1970	5,113	100.0	—	90.1	30.4	36.6	26.1	72.1
1981	3,971	100.0	38.3	21.0	98.6	59.1	40.9	86.2

No. of Surveyed Households			Cars	Refrigerators	Washing Machines	Vacuum Cleaners	Oil Stoves
All households							
1970	8,338	100.0%	22.1%	89.1%	91.4%	68.3%	79.1%
1981	5,814	100.0	58.5	99.2†	99.2	95.4	91.3
Farming households							
1970	1,792	100.0	22.4	83.1	90.6	48.3	69.7
1981	715	100.0	76.4	99.0†	98.9	91.3	95.9
Nonfarming households							
1970	6,546	100.0	22.0	90.8	91.6	73.8	81.6
1981	5,099	100.0	55.4	99.3†	99.3	96.1	90.5
Cities‡							
1970	5,113	100.0	22.6	92.5	92.1	75.4	82.2
1981	3,971	100.0	51.6	99.2†	99.0	96.1	88.6

No. of Surveyed Households			Electric Fans	Air Conditioners	Tape Recorders	Gas Burners	Pianos
All households							
1970	8,338	100.0%	83.2%	5.9%	30.8%	37.4%	6.8%
1981	5,814	100.0	95.0	41.2	62.7	77.3	16.7
Farming households							
1970	1,792	100.0	74.8	0.7	18.9	24.8	1.1
1981	715	100.0	96.0	17.3	56.8	69.0	10.3
Nonfarming households							
1970	6,546	100.0	85.5	7.3	34.1	40.9	8.4
1981	5,099	100.0	94.9	45.3	63.7	78.7	17.8
Cities‡							
1970	5,113	100.0	88.5	8.4	35.3	42.7	9.1
1981	3,971	100.0	94.9	49.7	63.6	79.7	17.7

*The percentage of households with goods to the total surveyed households.

†The figures for refrigerators in 1981 include gas refrigerators.

‡With more than 50,000 inhabitants.

SOURCE: "Survey on Domestic Consumption" by Business Statistics Research Division, Economic Planning Agency.

Japanese firms widely accept the critical importance of marketing. A major reason for the frequent reorganization of Japanese firms is to improve their marketing capability. The product division has been widely adopted to allow full implementation of a marketing orientation. The distinctive organizational feature of Japanese companies is that there is no marketing department. The absence of a marketing department and marketing specialists contributes to the creation of an organization with a total commitment to marketing. The marketing concept is fully implemented only when the entire organization is oriented by marketing and the marketing concept. Unless marketing is everybody's business, there is no true marketing emphasis in an organization. The Japanese have been protected from the dilution of marketing that occurs whenever it is the responsibility of a marketing department.

In distribution, modern merchandising with emphasis on self-service, lower gross margins and prices, and rapid turnover has been introduced by a pioneering group of new entrepreneurs who have carefully studied the U.S. model. They have built successful and rapidly growing chains in Japan. There are only a handful of suburban shopping centers in Japan, but they are expected to grow rapidly in the coming years. Interestingly, the primary mode of transportation to the existing centers is public transportation. For example, one major center conducted a study and estimated that only 30 percent of its shoppers travel to the center by automobile.

Three hundred major trading firms are responsible for 80 percent of Japanese imports and exports. A dozen large firms account for 60 percent of total trading company volume. There are two types of Japanese trading companies. One type handles diversified merchandise lines; the other specializes on a product basis. The trading companies act as both purchasing and sales agents for the companies they represent. For example, a company might purchase iron ore and coal as agent for a steel mill and sell its finished product. Recently, trading companies have been moving into mass merchandising in Japan. With their resources some observers predict that they will emerge as a dominant force in this field.

The most striking thing about Japan is the similarity of the impact of wealth and mass consumption on both the society and marketing system in Japan and the United States. The U.S. influence on Japanese marketing has been profound, not directly but through Japanese borrowings and adaptations of U.S. practices. The Japanese have not merely copied, but the major environmental differences have required systematic adaptation. Nevertheless, the Japanese experience suggests that wealth and mass consumption have a similar impact on societies of fundamentally different cultural traditions. Japan exemplifies the fact that as the world grows richer, it becomes more homogeneous in its consumption patterns.

Perhaps the best illustration of this point is the growing appetite in Japan for U.S. fast foods. The American fast-food craze in Japan began around 1970 and has been on a fast growth track ever since. It is a response to the basic changes in Japanese life that parallel those in the United States. Automobile ownership has reached over 50 percent saturation of households, disposable incomes are up, television promotions are aimed at small children who lead the family to the hamburgers and milkshakes. In short, Japanese families in circumstances that are in many respects similar to those in the United States are responding similarly to the availability

**TABLE 5–2 Comparisons and Contrasts in Culture, Tradition, and Behavior
Japan–United States**

	JAPAN	UNITED STATES
Myth/hero emphasis	Group	Individual
Attitude	Self-denial dependence	Self-expression independence
Emphasis	Obligations	Rights
Style	Cooperation	Competition
Assumptions	Interdependence	Independence
View of self	Organization man	Individual with a skill
Worker identification	Company	Craft/function
Management	Generalist	Specialist
Trust in	Feeling connection	Contract/words
Structure of society	Vertical	Horizontal
Cultural atttitude-1	We are unique	Everyone is just like us
Cultural attitude-2	Willing to borrow/adopt/adapt	Nih Syndrome
Organization goal-1	Share of market jobs/employment	Profitability financial success
Organization goal-2	World market/global competition	National market national competition
Organization goal-3	Quality/customer value	Production/financial return
Government/business relations	Cooperation	Separation
Public sector/private sector career moves	Government to business	From business to government
Financial structure	Debt/equity 80:20	40:60
Key stakeholder	Employees	Stockholders
Key value/goal	Harmony, consensus	Success, winning

Note: The author is indebted to Chikara Higashi, member of the Japanese Diet and President, Recia, Tokyo, for assistance in preparing this table.

of the fast-food-away-from-home alternative.

U.S.-Japanese Contrast. Table 5–2 summarizes the major contrasts in U.S. and Japanese cultural values and orientation. At the top of the table is the overall orientation in the two societies. The United States is oriented by the ideal of individualism, whereas Japan is oriented by the ideal of the collective. Of course, each society recognizes the importance of both the individual and the collective, but a very fundamental difference between the two countries is the fact that the United States is oriented by the myth of the importance of the individual, whereas Japan is oriented by the myth of the importance of the collective.

In the United States the ideal is independence, whereas in Japan there is an affirmative attitude toward dependence.[6] The U.S. traditional culture prefers authoritative decision making, whereas the Japanese culture prefers participative decision making. The United States emphasizes competition, and Japan values and celebrates cooperation. There is in the U.S. culture a style preference for confron-

[6]See, for example, T. Doi, *The Anatomy of Dependence* (Tokyo: Kodansha International, 1973).

tation as opposed to the very definite preference in Japan for compromise.

Americans are quick in decision making but slow and hesitating in implementation, whereas the Japanese are very slow due to the consensus process in decision making but quick and steady in implementation. The U.S. cultural style is direct, whereas the Japanese is indirect.

In the eyes of many observers, the United States is more short term oriented than is Japan where the more interactive and participative style of decision making, because it is so deliberate and incorporates so many inputs, is necessarily more long-term.

A review of the 18 contrasting items in Table 5–2 demonstrates that the United States and Japan are fundamentally different cultures. And yet, as we have already observed, the Japanese consumer exhibits behavior that is remarkably similar to that of the U.S. consumer when income levels are similar. Thus the ultimate paradox of the Japanese market is the striking and fundamental dissimilarity of the Japanese and U.S. cultures, and at the same time the rather remarkable similarity in customer behavior. The international marketer needs to be responsive both to the widespread requirements for adaptation in Japan and to the widespread opportunity of supplying needs that express cultural universals. For example, American fast-food franchisers have found Japan to be a remarkably fertile market opportunity. On the other hand, American manufacturers of doormats have had no success at all in Japan.[7]

Negotiating in Japan.[8]   The success or failure of a foreign business executive's efforts in Japan will be largely determined by myriad negotiations with Japanese businesspeople and government officials. These negotiations involve a number of important steps and actions.

Planning the Talks.   Once a company has decided to negotiate in Japan, it should prepare its representatives for a long stay and arm them with thorough and exhaustive explanations of what the company has to offer and what the company is seeking. Experienced negotiators in Japan report that on the average it takes six times longer and is three times more difficult to reach an agreement in Japan than in the United States. There are many reasons for this including the need for interpreters and the fact that neither the Japanese nor the Westerners understand very much about each other's thinking processes.

Because interpreters are used, it is wise to follow some basic rules when dealing with them:

1. Brief the interpreter in advance and provide him or her with a copy of the material to be discussed.
2. Speak clearly and avoid the use of unusual or rare words.
3. Assume that all numbers over 10,000 will be mistranslated. Write them down for all to see and repeat them carefully. Avoid using the number billion because it means "1" with 12 zeros in Europe, and "1" with 9 zeros in the United States.

[7]A Japanese purchasing delegation visiting the U.S. had to explain politely to a doormat manufacturer that the Japanese remove their shoes before entering their houses and that there was no market for doormats.

[8]Adapted from Howard F. Van Zandt, "How to Negotiate in Japan," *Harvard Business Review,* November–December, 1970.

4. Avoid the use of slang terms, such as "right on." Say "very good" or "good."
5. Do not expect an interpreter to work more than an hour or two without a rest. If nonstop discussions are planned over a day, arrange for two interpreters.
6. Be understanding if it develops that the interpreter has made a mistake, because these are difficult to avoid given the great dissimilarities between European languages and the Japanese language.

Personal Relations. The Japanese go to great lengths to establish a warm personal relationship as the basis for business activities. Entertainment is a very important part of the process of establishing a relationship. Gift giving is customary and a definite factor in business relations. Gifts need not be expensive. Foreigners visiting Japan are advised to bring souvenirs from their country to give to Japanese contacts. The cost of these items should not be excessive because it is the sentiment rather than the value that is important.

Making a Presentation. The Japanese, like businesspeople everywhere, are looking for sincerity and honesty in potential partners, customers, or suppliers. One useful way to obtain credibility in Japan is to show information in print that supports a presentation. The Japanese feel that when a person is willing to put his or her case in print where all may challenge what has been said, it is likely that the presenter will be as accurate as possible so as not to lose face. Material appearing in a respected technical or trade publication is especially valuable.

Closing Discussions. The final stage of negotiations should include the joint drawing up of a contract that reaches agreement on points at issue. It is important for foreigners, particularly Americans, to recognize that the Japanese have a custom of being silent for what seems to Westerners as an excessively long time. The Westerner should not become excited and feel a compulsion to speak during these periods of silence because it often results in a concession on a disputed point by the Westerner when he simply tries to keep the conversation going. It is common for the Japanese to insist that negotiations end by gathering large amounts of data to justify the action being taken. Some of the data will be needed for internal company use, and a considerable amount of data will be required to satisfy the Japanese government. Besides the need to satisfy government requirements, one of the reasons for requiring supporting data is that, should the venture fail, no one in the Japanese company can be rebuked for having proceeded on a project without sufficient evidence to justify the action. In America this kind of documentation is called "alibi paper."

SOUTH KOREA. The miracle economy of the 1980s has been South Korea. In little more than 20 years a country torn apart by war has emerged as an important new economic power. Korea is an outstanding example of a country making the transition from a less developed to developing country. If the growth pattern of the past 20 years is maintained, Korea will achieve advanced country status before the end of this century.

Korea and Japan both have hard-working, well-educated labor forces and a history of strong government aid to business, but the differences between the two countries are as striking as the similarities. Korea is much smaller, with 40 million people as compared to Japan's 120 million, and Korea's history includes a period of foreign domination (Korea was a Japanese colony before World War II). As Korea has continued to develop and grow, it has moved into new markets and fields including computers and automobiles. Its success in industrializing has resulted in its overtaking Argentina in per capita income. Table 5–3 presents statistics on the Korean economy as compared to other countries.

TABLE 5–3 South Korea—Economic Comparisons

Living Standards
1983 population and per capita gross
national product for selected countries

	Population (millions)	Per Capita G.N.P.
United States	234.5	$14,110
Japan	119.3	10,120
Singapore	2.5	6,620
Hong Kong	5.3	6,000
Mexico	75.0	2,240
Argentina	29.6	2,070
South Korea	40.0	2,010
Brazil	129.7	1,880
Thailand	49.2	820
North Korea	19.2	.....

...Not available

Economic Growth
Average annual change in real gross
national product

	1965–73	1973–83
United States	3.2%	2.3%
Japan	9.8	4.3
Singapore	13.0	8.2
Hong Kong	7.9	9.3
Mexico	7.9	5.6
Argentina	4.3	0.4
South Korea	10.0	7.3
Brazil	9.8	4.8
Thailand	7.8	6.9
North Korea	...	...

Sources: World Bank, International
Monetary Fund

Composition of Exports
Share of South Korea's merchandise
exports, in percent

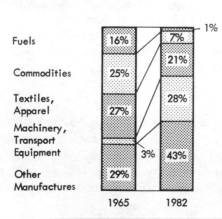

Where the Exports Go
Destination of South Korea's
exports, 1984

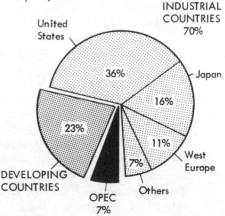

Source: "Ebb Tide for the Korean Miracle," *The New York Times*, October 6, 1985, p. F8.

Latin America

Latin America, with 6 percent of the world's wealth and 8.5 percent of its population, is a developing region with an average per capita income that is 70 percent of the world average. It is a region of great contrasts. Argentina, one of the richest countries in the world at the turn of the century, had a per capita income of only $2,680 in 1984, far behind the $9,000–12,000 range of today's top-income countries. This relatively low income reflects the years of industrial conflict that arrested the country's growth.

Brazil, Argentina's very near neighbor, is one of the most rapidly developing countries in the world, with real growth in most recent years running at 8 percent per annum. In contrast to Argentina, Brazil has demonstrated its capability to adjust to adversity and in very unorthodox ways to manage the process of economic growth successfully. The distinctive characteristics of Brazil are its vast territory and resources, a diversity of racial background in the population that is perhaps unique in the world, and the country's almost unique ability to utilize the inputs of foreign investors (including almost every multinational company in the world) in a way that does not sap the national esprit de corps or the sense of identity. Many observers believe that Brazil's enormous resources and capacity to adjust to adversity indicate acceptable risks for foreign investors over the long pull.

Today most Latin American countries have made significant progress in coping with balance-of-payments problems and sustaining the industrialization process. Restrictive policies and administrative practices with respect to foreign enterprises are gradually being liberalized. Markets are growing. For these reasons, many observers consider the countries less risky now than they were a decade ago.

Although the Latin American countries have made substantial efforts to create a more regionally integrated economy, these countries are highly differentiated and this very pronounced diversity (geographic, economic, and social) encourages both nationalism and what appears to be a trend toward more independent actions. Realistically, international marketers should approach Latin American integration efforts as more aspiration than fact.

Africa

It is not really possible to treat Africa as a single economic unit. The continent is divided into three distinct areas: the Republic of South Africa, North Africa, and, between the Sahara Desert in the north and the Zambezi River in the south, Black Africa. The economy of the Republic of South Africa is rapidly developing, with a well-diversified manufacturing base and with a demand for goods and services that is much more comparable to the poorer countries in Western Europe or the richer countries in Latin America than it is to other African nations. In North Africa the 78 million Arabs are differentiated politically and economically. They are richer and more developed, with many of the states benefiting from large oil resources. The

Arab states have been independent for a longer period than have the Black African nations.

Nigeria is the largest developing nation of Black Africa, with a gross domestic product of $88 billion. The sixth largest producer of crude oil in the world, Nigeria has replaced Venezuela as the second largest oil exporter to the United States. Per capita income in 1987 was $953.

Although many of the nations in Black Africa are poor and underdeveloped both politically and economically, the expectations of the people are very high. President Nyerere of Tanzania has said that the standard of living in the United States is part of the reality of Tanzania. Although he regrets that this is the case, modern communications and information have created a situation in the world where nearly everyone knows how other people live. The expectations of Tanzanians are based partly on what they know about the rest of the world.

The challenge to marketing in this type of market is not to stimulate demand for products but to identify the most important needs of the society and to develop products that fit these needs. There is much opportunity for creativity in developing unique products that fit the needs of the people in developing countries rather than merely giving copies of products that have been developed for richer countries and therefore may not be the most suitable product for a poorer country.

Oceania[9]

Australia and New Zealand are island economies in the Asian region that have been settled by Europeans. The combined population of these countries is only 19.3 million, or less than .5 percent of the world total. The income level in both countries is relatively high at approximately $10,188.17 per capita, which means that the region accounts for over 1.65 percent of global income. The real rate of growth in Australia, which has been stimulated by the enormous mineral resources of the continent, has exceeded 3 percent per annum. Australia is important to the international economy as a source of mineral wealth, and because of its high income level and its similarity to United States and European markets, many Japanese and other Asian country companies test market products in Australia before introducing them to the U.S. and European markets.

AUSTRALIA.   In world terms, Australia ranks twenty-third in the value of world trade. In 1986, the ratio of Australia's exports to GDP was 13.5 percent, while the ratio of imports to GNP was about 15 percent. Despite Australia's relatively modest role in aggregate world trade, it is a key world supplier of many agricultural and mineral commodities. More than 50 percent of the nation's output of rural and mineral industries is exported.

Australia's population, 16 million in 1986, is expected to grow to 19.3 million by the year 2000 and to 23 million by 2020. There is a high degree of urbanization:

[9]The author is indebted to Professor Donald Gibson, Graduate School of Management, Macquarie University, Sydney, Australia for the section on Oceania.

Approximately 85 percent of the population live in urban areas and 60 percent of its people reside in eight major cities. A high rate of immigration since 1947 has accounted for more than half of Australia's substantial post-World War II population growth, and transformed the country into one of the most heterogeneous contemporary, industrial-based societies.

Australia's middle-sized economy (US$ 170 billion in 1986) is very dependent on trading conditions in world markets for its major exports of low value-added agricultural and mineral products. As the prices received for its exports have not kept pace with the prices paid for its imports (mainly industrial raw materials and capital equipment), Australia has suffered a long-term decline in trade (a 43 percent drop between 1955 and 1985) that has contributed to a slide in its relative standard of living from third highest per capita GDP in the 1950s to sixteenth in 1986.

Over the past 30 years Australia has primarily developed inward looking manufacturing and service sectors to provide employment and meet domestic needs. Because of the changed international situation, and the resulting deterioration in its balance of payments (US$ 9.8 million current deficit or 6 percent of GDP in 1985-1986), the country's revised economic policies are attempting to improve its balance of payments and introduce new directions for industry. Australia's emphasis on raw material exports, at a time when the strongest growth in international trade has been in manufactures and services, has caused its share of world trade to drop from 2.6 percent to 1.3 percent over the last 30 years. Now the country is facing up to the problems of an inappropriate composition of exports and the need for structural adjustment of its economic base.

The Australian government's industry policy aims to restructure the country's manufacturing sector into an export-oriented and internationally competitive sector. To increase exports, the government has consolidated its various export assistance agencies into one body, the Australian Trade Commission, known as Austrade. Austrade's major role is to target the industries and markets which show the greatest potential for export growth, and to provide marketing support for the export of manufactures and services. The Austrade strategy includes the development of a global marketing plan which seeks to match export markets with Australian industry capabilities.

In comparison with most industrialized countries Australia relies heavily on imports of capital equipment and lightly on imports of foods, beverages, fuels, and lubricants. In the remaining broad categories—industrial supplies (25 percent), transport equipment (13 percent), and consumer goods (15 percent)—Australia's composition of imports is comparable to other industrial countries'. Despite a historic reliance on tariff policy to protect local manufacturing, effective rates of protection have been diminishing since the 1970s for all but the most highly protected sectors, and are now at 15 percent. The major issue of protection is how fast and in what ways protective barriers for the most highly protected sectors can be reduced.

Australia's new industrial policy has encouraged a progressive expansion of its domestic economy into the international economy. The floating of the Australian dollar in 1984 provided a boost to price competitiveness, and trade exposed sectors have been strengthened by the large real depreciation of the currency (about 35 percent against Australia's main trading partners). Deregulation of the finance sector, the entry of foreign banks, and the freeing of restrictions on foreign investment supplemented the gradual withdrawal of protection for Australian manufacturing and given further impetus to industry restructuring.

In 1987 Australian society and its economy were going through a unique period of structural change and painful transition. The national debate is about how quickly the changes occur and in what direction, not *if* they occur. Devaluing the currency is not sufficient to correct Australia's balance of payments deficit. The devaluation needs to be supported by appropriate fiscal, wage, and monetary policies to ensure that resources are redirected into the export/import competing sectors.

Australia has started to develop its own multinational companies, with the initial impetus coming from firms in the mineral, publishing, brewing, transport, and construction material fields. New sources of growth are coming from increased processing of natural resources available within the Australian economy, increased use of technology in manufacturing, and a stronger marketing focus to develop product innovations and new markets. Many of the main elements of policies for economic growth had begun by 1987, including development of facilitative policies, specific industry plans, and adoption of broad industry policies for redirecting resources. For example, specific plans have been developed for the automotive, steel, and heavy engineering industries and are in prospect for the textile, clothing, and footwear industries. The object of these plans is to help these industries adjust to changing market circumstances and become less reliant on government.

Major internal markets in Australia are separated by considerable distances, but there is a highly developed and efficient infrastructure of transportation and communication systems. The workforce is mainly employed in tertiary industries (76 percent), with 17 percent employed in secondary industries, and 7 percent in primary industries. This employment structure is reflected in the declining proportion of household expenditure on the consumption of goods compared to services (which have absorbed an increasing proportion of household budgets in the last 30 years).

The domestic marketing environment in Australia is serviced by product and marketing mix strategies comparable to advanced Western and Japanese markets. The relatively small size of the Australian market often means product ranges are narrower than those available in larger markets. However, retail distribution systems are dominated by department store and supermarket chains which make extensive use of leading edge electronic technologies to process customer transactions. In 1985 employment in wholesale and retail trade occupations represented about 26 percent of service sector employment, while sales workers accounted for 9 percent of employment among all occupations.

As there is a very high density of television ownership in Australia, broadcast television (including three commercial channels in each of the major markets of Sydney and Melbourne) has excellent access to target markets. There is increasing use of direct mail, and growing interest in telemarketing selling methods. A major challenge facing all marketers in Australia is the spread out location of the eight major markets across a vast continent. This presents distribution and communication considerations which tend to increase national marketing costs.

NEW ZEALAND. New Zealand is a small, developed country with a population in 1986 of 3.3 million and a land area approximately the size of Japan or the United Kingdom. In the 1950s New Zealand was one of the third or fourth richest countries in the world, but by 1980 its international rankings had slipped below the twentieth position. In 1986 the country had a GDP of US$ 23 billion and GDP per capita of US$ 7,000. Real GDP growth in the decade to 1985 was a low 1.2 percent per annum due to the economy's failure to adapt to the reduction in its international trade as a result of the government's pre-1984 policies to suppress inflation.

Following a change in government in July 1984, New Zealand embraced a major program of economic liberalization. The NZ dollar was devalued by 20 percent against a basket of currencies, and policy reforms were introduced to improve resource utilization within the domestic economy. These reforms included the removal of many restrictions and distortions concerning the international trade in goods and services. A scheduled phasing out of nontariff barriers was accelerated, tariffs were reduced, and subsidies and other forms of assistance to exporters were removed. Constraints on investment flows between New Zealand and other countries were relaxed.

These policy changes have made the economy more responsive to a changing international environment. The primary sector of the economy accounts for about 10 percent of GDP; the manufacturing sector represents around 20 percent of GDP; and various services, including construction, public utilities, transport, communication and tourism account for the rest. The sectoral distribution of employment is similar to these industry shares of GDP.

The New Zealand economy is very dependent on international trade, and exports 28 percent of GDP. Although farm-based industry products are still major earners of foreign exchange, efforts to diversify exports and develop new export markets away from traditional destinations have been fairly successful. For example, the United Kingdom accounted for only 9 percent of New Zealand exports in 1986, compared to 15 percent for Japan. A major part of manufacturing activity is divided between further processing of primary products for export and production or assembly of products for the domestic market. By 1986 there was a significant trend towards the production of more technology-intensive products, particularly for export. The rapid development of the tourist industry by 1985 had made this sector also an important earner of foreign exchange.

The Closer Economic Relationship (The CER) Agreement between Australia and New Zealand, which came into force in 1983, is designed to strengthen and foster economic links between the two countries by establishing free trade between Australia and New Zealand. All tariffs between them (except for specified exclusions) are to be phased out by 1988, while quotas (which are almost all New Zealand's) are to be phased out no later than 1995. Initial developments indicated the gains from trade appeared fairly evenly matched, and investment between the two countries had grown since CER, although not a lot faster than third-country investment. New Zealand investment has been mainly in import, distribution, servicing, and wholesale/retail outlets to place their products into the larger Australian market whereas Australian investment has been directed to cheap production facilities in New Zealand. Consumer effects are probably not large compared to producer effects; however, some gains to consumers are likely due to lower prices and a wider product range.

New Zealand has developed local manufacturing and distribution systems to meet the diverse needs of a small population scattered over a wide area. The factor dominating the country's markets is the rapid pace of economic liberalization. Restructuring of industry and agriculture in response to changing prices and the removal of subsidies and tax shelters have caused an inevitable degree of dislocation, particularly in rural and provincial areas outside the main population centers. The immediate prospect in 1986 was for a continuation of the flatness in economic activity which started in mid-1985. However, the medium-term outlook for the New Zealand economy promises improved growth opportunities resulting from the more flexible policy environment.

Middle East

The Middle East has been going through a sudden and dramatic transformation since the energy crisis of 1973. The Middle East includes 15 countries: Bahrain, Egypt, Iraq, Iran, Israel, Jordan, Kuwait, Lebanon, Oman, Qatar, Syria, Saudi Arabia, the United Arab Emirates, and the two Republics of Yemen.

In a total population of approximately 144.4 million the majority, 67.0 percent, are Arabs, with 29.8 percent Persians and 2.9 percent Israelis. However, Persians and Arabs share the same religion, beliefs, and Islamic traditions, making the population 95 percent Muslim and 5 percent Christian and Jewish. Despite this apparent homogeneity, heterogeneity exists within each country and within religious groups. The differences are deeply rooted and are as ancient as the history of the area itself.

Seven of the countries have high oil revenue: Bahrain, Iraq, Iran, Kuwait, Oman, Qatar, and Saudi Arabia hold more than 75 percent of free world oil reserves. Recent increases in oil revenue have widened the gap between poor and rich nations of the Middle East, and income disparities contribute to political and social instability in the area. Shantytowns stand side by side with plush palacelike buildings and fancy villas in most Middle Eastern cities. At one extreme, Saudi Arabia, Israel, Kuwait, and the United Arab Emirates (UAE) with 11 percent of the population share 40 percent of the area's wealth. At the other extreme, Egypt, Oman, and the Arab Republic of Yemen with 49 percent of the population have only 14 percent of the area's income. These disparities are expected to increase as income rises with the demand for Middle Eastern crude.

The Palestinian dilemma has had serious repercussions on the economy of the region. Communication, the lifeline of economic activity, does not exist between Israel and its Arab neighbors. The negative effect of such a situation on business and economic activities is obvious and influences the daily life of most foreign businesspeople operating in the region.

Most local Middle Eastern markets are still primitive and fragmented. Marketers cannot apply the latest schemes and techniques of marketing. On one hand, market surveys and studies are costly; on the other hand, necessary data are totally lacking. In addition, impulsive buying is very common and market behavior is often unpredictable. There does not exist a societal type with a typical belief, behavior, and tradition; each capital and major city in the Middle East has a variety of social groups differentiated by their religion, social classes, educational fields, degree of wealth, and so forth. In general, however, Middle Easterners are warm, friendly, and clannish. Tribal pride and generosity toward guests are basic beliefs. Decision making is by consensus, and seniority has more weight than educational expertise. Life of the individual centers on the family. Leadership emanates from the clan, and the bigger the clan, the stronger the leadership. Ideological revolution never existed; rather, clannish uprise is more frequent in the Middle East. Authority is acquired by aging, and power is related to family size and seniority. Marrying a leader's daughter makes one a leader, and the more powerful her family, the more powerful the leadership.

Important decisions in the Middle East are often made quickly on the basis of feeling or intuition, and management is politic, in its broad sense, and family oriented. Honor is put above all, and a good reputation is a Middle Easterner's most valuable asset.

According to a *Business International* report, the success of the Japanese in penetrating Middle Eastern markets is based on

1. Realizing that technical competence and good reputation count more than money.
2. Being prepared for hard bargaining and bargaining hard in return.
3. Being flexible in trading off short-term profits for a longer-term but steadier flow of profit.
4. Taking time in negotiations and use of same social and traditional methods by applying the informal personal approach rather than the formal organizational approach. Put another way, the Japanese emphasize "feeling" connections in their business dealings.

These matters are of great importance when dealing in the Middle East. Business is typically mixed with pleasure, and time is viewed as well spent when shared with people who are valued and trusted. For the typical Western businessperson, it is especially important to realize that the Western (especially the U.S.) view of time and approach to life is in a fundamental sense a shared value. The difference lies in the Middle East belief that you should do business with those you trust and their need to take time to develop rapport and trust. Thus, in both cultures, time is money.

MARKETING IN LESS DEVELOPED COUNTRIES

Does marketing have a role in less developed countries? Many government officials and planners have asked this question and have concluded that it does not. They point out that a shortage of goods and services is the central-problem of developing countries and that the most pressing need is to expand production. Needs are well known, almost anything produced can be sold, and marketing with its focus on identifying needs and wants is really quite out of place in an environment characterized by scarcity.

Certainly, marketing that focuses on creating new needs and wants, which is very important in a developed, mass-consumption economy, is out of place in a poor developing country. But dynamic, modern marketing is more than a search for new needs and wants. It is, fundamentally, a system of concepts, tools, and skills that enables managers to match the capability of organizations to the needs of society. As such, marketing science can be directed toward the needs of the less developed country[10] as well as the needs of the nonprofit organization.

For example, there is a need in every developing society for clean laundry. The human desire for cleanliness is universal. However, the automatic electric washing machine, which is the ideal solution to the problem of dirty clothes in a developed country, is not going to be the appropriate solution in an underdeveloped country. Between the extremes of washing clothes in a stream of running water, or on a rock, and using a fully automatic electric washing machine lie many possibilities. For example, a small plastic washing machine that is handpowered has been developed with the conditions of developed countries as a constraint, and the result has been a handpowered washing machine that is most efficient.

Another example of the importance of marketing to a developing country is in the communications or persuasion area. Marketers have long been associated with their skill in stimulating or even creating demands for products. There are many products or items whose use should be encouraged in underdeveloped countries. For example, in many African countries there are plentiful supplies of fish from lakes and the sea. Fish is an extremely nutritious and desirable food from a health point of view. However, Africans are not accustomed to eating fish and do not consume it in any significant quantity. A program of persuading Africans to consume fish would be highly beneficial to the health and welfare of the African people. Marketers with skills in the advertising and promotion area clearly have a contribution to make in this kind of program.

The important role of marketing in the less developed countries is to focus societal resources in organizations on the creation and delivery of products that best serve the needs of the people. The conditions of scarcity in less developed countries make it imperative that products designed for developed country markets are not automatically copied. Basic marketing concepts can and should be applied to design a product that fits the needs and ability to buy of the less developed country market. These concepts must also be applied to educate the taste and preferences of the people to accept these products. Marketing in the dynamic sense can relate resources to opportunity and satisfy needs on the consumer's terms.

[10]Peter F. Drucker, "Marketing and Economic Development," *Journal of Marketing,* January, 1958.

SUMMARY

One of the ways of dealing with the complexity of a world with over 180 national markets is to focus upon world regions. Each country in the world is sovereign and unique, but there are similarities among countries in the same region that make a regional approach to marketing planning a sound approach. In this chapter, the organization of the material is around geographic regions. It could just as well be organized around stage of economic development or some other criterium. It is important to have a broad overview of the nature of world regions so that there will not be any serious oversights in developing the marketing plan.

DISCUSSION QUESTIONS

1. What are the differences among a free trade area, a customs union, and an economic union?
2. What do you feel are the most fundamental differences between the United States and Japan? What are the implications of these differences for economic relations between the two countries?
3. Many experts believe that the fastest growing region in the world will be the Pacific Basin. Where is the Pacific Basin? Do you agree with this forecast?
4. Why has the EC been so successful while so many other regional economic cooperation agreements have failed to amount to anything?

BIBLIOGRAPHY

Books

Concise Guide to International Markets, ed. Leslie Stinton. Surrey: Leslie Stinton, 1982.

DREW, JOHN. *Doing Business in the European Community.* London: Buherworths, 1979.

FIELDS, GEORGE. *From Bonsai to Levis.* New York: Mentor, 1983.

REISCHAUER, EDWIN O. *The Japanese.* Cambridge, Mass.: The Belknap Press of Harvard University Press, 1977.

The Europa Yearbook, 1985. A World Survey, Vol. 1. London: Europa Publications, 1985.

The World in Figures, 3rd ed. Detroit: Gale Research, 1982.

Articles

GREEN, ROBERT T., AND ERIC LANGEARD. "A Cross-National Comparison of Consumer Habits and Innovator Characteristics." *Journal of Marketing,* Vol. 39, no. 3 (July 1975), pp. 34–41.

HAYDEN, ERIC W., AND HENRY R. NAU. "East-West Technology Transfer." *Columbia Journal of World Business,* Vol. 10 (Fall 1975), pp. 70–82.

HEENAN, DAVID A. "Moscow Goes Multinational." *Harvard Business Review,* May–June 1981, pp. 48, 52.

HERTZFELD, JEFFREY M. "Setting up Shop in Moscow." *Harvard Business Review*, September–October 1974, pp. 137–142.

———. "New Directions in East-West Trade." *Harvard Business Review*, May–June 1977, pp. 93–99.

LANGE, IRENE, AND JAMES S. ELLIOTT. "U.S. Role in East-West Trade." *Journal of International Business Studies*, Fall–Winter 1977, pp. 5–16.

LAUTER, G. PETER. "The Changing Role of Marketing in the Eastern European Socialist Economies," *Journal of Marketing*, October 1971, pp. 16–21.

———, AND PAUL M. DICKIE. "Multinational Corporations in Eastern European Socialist Economies." *Journal of Marketing*, October, 1975, pp. 40–46.

OZAWA, TERUTOMO, MOYES PUCIENNIK, AND K. NAGARAJA RAO. "Japanese Direct Investment in Brazil." *Columbia Journal of World Business*, Vol. 11 (Fall 1976), pp. 107–116.

SORENSON, RALPH Z., II. "U.S. Marketers Can Learn from European Innovators." *Harvard Business Review*, September–October 1972, pp. 89–99.

VAN ZANDT, HOWARD F. "How to Negotiate in Japan." *Harvard Business Review*, November–December 1970.

———. "Learning to Do Business with 'Japan, Inc.'." *Harvard Business Review*, July–August 1972, pp. 83–92.

FRIED CHICKEN IN JAPAN[1]

In summer, 1975, Yamashita, Managing Director of Kentucky Fried Chicken (Japan), KFCJ, had just reached his mid-30s, an unusually young age for such a responsible position in a seniority-conscious country like Japan. Total sales of KFCJ were expected to pass 6 billion yen (US$20 million) for the fiscal year 1975, almost a 100 percent growth in sales from the previous fiscal year. Reflecting upon the past five years, which Yamashita had devoted to establishing KFCJ's toe-hold in the growing "fast food" market in Japan, he felt relieved that KFCJ's past trial-and-error approaches to the Japanese market had imbedded in him a sense of confidence as well as an aspiration for new challenges in the years to come. Challenges indeed were there for him to seek.

The "fast-food" market, which is merely a portion of the total "eating-out and catering service" industry in Japan had come by 1975 to attract new foreign and Japanese entrants. From the United States, MacDonalds, Burger Chef, A&W, Dairy Queen, Dunkin' Donuts, Mr. Donuts, Pizza Hut, Golden Pioneer and an assortment of ice-cream chains, had already followed KFC into Japan. Like KFC, these U.S.-based fast-food firms had invariably chosen a joint venture or straight licensing agreement with Japanese firms(s). In the years to come, not only would other U.S.-based fast-food firms specializing in fried chicken enter the Japanese markets, but the existing ones might well attempt to add fried chicken to their product lines. In addition, Japanese restaurants and food companies as well as assortments of textile, mining and chemical firms, were already entering into growing fast-food markets in Japan as their traditional lines of business continued to decline.

If the intensifying market competition was challenging enough, Yamashita knew that the task of maintaining and building KFCJ's employees' morale would become all the more crucial for its future success. Perhaps because of KFCJ's affiliation with Mitsubishi Corporation, a leading trading firm in Japan and perhaps because of KFCJ's product image as "modern, American, and stylish," KFCJ had been able to attract many young, ambitious and entrepreneurial employees. And the rapid spread of KFCJ's stores to major cities had enabled the firm to place these young and ambitious employees in challenging and growing situations. From 1974 to 1975 alone, KFCJ added 30 new stores, bringing the total to 130. About one-half of these stores were run directly by KFCJ: franchises had never constituted more than one-half of KFCJ stores. Yamashita knew, however, that in the years to come, KFCJ's growth tempo would continue, but not as spectacularly as in the past. Would KFCJ be able to satisfy the career aspirations of store manager candidates and other hard-working young employees who had been drawn to the growth potentials of KFCJ? With a spread of fast-food chains, centralized operations like central kitchen and depot systems were feared as reducing store operators from "chefs" to "waiter and assemblers." Perhaps because of demoralizing effects of such modern fast-food service systems on young employees, labor unions appeared, spreading from one large restaurant chain to the next.

The growth of KFCJ also brought the problem of procuring an increasing supply of such necessary ingredients as chicken, vegetable oil, flour and assortments of fresh food items. Japan, which possessed about 110 million people in 1975, was already importing over 30 percent of all her food and animal

feed requirements combined. As more and more countries came to fear a worldwide food and feed shortage, the Japanese government was looking into the whole question of procuring food and feed items worldwide. The Japanese dietary habit changed drastically from 1950 to 1975. By 1975, on the average, the Japanese daily intake of protein had almost doubled to about 80 grams, about 43 percent of which came from animal protein including dairy products and fish. But fish and shellfish accounted for less than-one-half of the Japanese intake of animal protein.

Meanwhile, especially since the early 1960s, broiler farms in Japan had rapidly increased in number, and by 1975 their rapid production had come to surpass the demand. While this overproduction appeared to be temporary, the broiler farmers were already organizing the drive to "regulate" the total supply of broilers in their favor. From 1965 to 1975, the total number of broiler farms declined from about 20,000 to 13,000. By 1974, over 40 percent of all broilers were supplied by about 700 farms, each of which at the time was supplying over 100,000 broilers to markets. A sign of further concentration among broiler farms was seen in 1975.

Table 1 shows the broiler production and consumption levels in Japan. The Japanese government was expected to be drawn into the rescue operations of prefectures and farmers' associations which had already exhausted their financial means of keeping stockpile "surplus" broiler meats or of continuing to guarantee broiler farmers the "minimum floor price" for their broilers. The increasing importation of frozen broilers might well become a "political" focal point in the "chicken debate" to come. Even without the organizing attempts of broiler farmers, the Ministry of Agriculture and Forestry, the Ministry of Welfare and Health, and the Ministry of International Trade and Industry were all closely

TABLE 1 Production and Consumption of Chicken 1960–1973

| | CHICKEN PRODUCTION (TON) | | | CONSUMPTION | |
Year	Broiler	Other Chicken	Total	Per Household	Per Capita
1960	17,496	57,154	74,650	1,566g	382g
1965	89,253	115,087	204,340	4,699	1,108
1970	353,913	136,162	490,075	8,655	2,715
1971	400,689	139,276	539,965	8,799	2,222
1972	482,154	140,074	622,228	9,582	2,420
1973	546,050	140,283	686,333	10,233	2,617

Source: Ministry of Agriculture and Forestry, Tokyo, 1975.

watching the growing fast-food market to see which ministry should be put in charge of administering the industry.

HOW FRIED CHICKEN FLEW TO JAPAN

Mitsubishi Corporation, a leading trading firm, was in the mid–1960s the leading Japanese importer (and domestic distributor) of animal and chicken feeds, corn and milo. With a rapid increase in the living standard of the Japanese population, their consumption of animal protein, eggs, beef, pork and chicken was also increasing. Since the production lead-time of chicken was shorter than that of other animal meats, and the raising of broilers was technically the easiest, Mitsubishi Corporation took the initiative in starting large-scale broiler farms in Japan, at first mainly as the captive customers of Mitsubishi's corn and milo feeds. In order to find captive markets for their increased chicken feed businesses, the trading firm continued to open broiler farms around the major cities in Japan. Originally, over three-quarters of all broiler breeds were imported from the United States, and the remainder from Canada, the United Kingdom and Europe. The indigenous breeds were improved through cross-breeding with imported breeds.

TABLE 2 Projection of Production and Consumption of Meats and Eggs in Japan, 1972–1985 (In thousands of tons except for Per-Capita Consumption)

| | CONSUMPTION | | PRODUCTION | | PER-CAPITA CONSUMPTION | |
	1972	1985	1972	1985	1972	1985
Total Meats	2,147	3,193	1,730	2,747	14.2Kg	18.6Kg
Beef	367	625	290	508	2.4	3.6
Pork	883	1,335	793	1,325	5.6	7.5
Chicken	668	915	640	914	4.7	5.7
Eggs	1,848	2,206	1,811	2,205	14.6	15.0

Source: The Ministry of Agriculture and Forestry, Tokyo, 1975.

TABLE 3   Supply of Chicken and Wholesale Price of Chicken 1974–1975

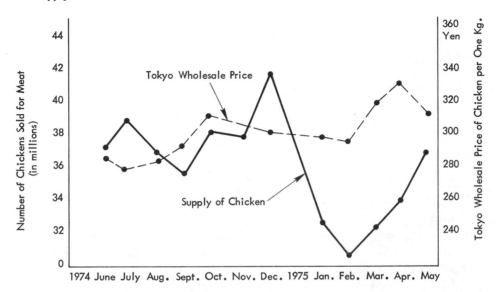

Mitsubishi's broiler farms continued to increase the supply of broilers so much so, that by around 1967, the trading firm was saddled with surplus broiler meats. One logical way out of this problem was to create an expanding and new demand for broilers.

At that time supermarket chains such as Seiyu and Jasco were expanding their networks in Tokyo and other major cities. Since the boning of broilers required cumbersome handling and was an extremely costly operation (the weight ratio of bone to meat being the greatest for chicken than for steer and hog), the supermarkets tried to sell their chicken packaged without boning. While this package offered chicken at a much lower price than filleted chicken, the Japanese housewives had long considered good chicken to be "boned" and did not purchase chicken packages sold "bone, stock and barrel."

The Tokyo Headquarters of Mitsubishi then cabled its Chicago office to get suggestions for new ways of increasing chicken consumption in Japan. They requested in effect, that their Chicago office "identify the largest broiler consuming firm in the United States." The man who received this request was Aso, in his early forties. Aso had long been familiar with American food chains and supermarkets, having sold to them in the past an assortment of canned foods and other food-related items. Being stationed in Chicago, the center of agri-business in the United States, Aso had watched from around 1965 the opening of Kentucky Fried Chicken franchises in the Midwest. Aso's intuitive reply was: the greatest single user of broilers in the United States must be Kentucky Fried Chicken. Aso's children had long been converted to Colonel Sanders' fried chicken, and Aso himself had found it "sporty" to munch on.

In order to confirm his hunch, Aso went to a Chicken Farmers' Convention in Kansas City in 1967. There, he witnessed Colonel Sanders receive a standing ovation from the chicken farmers. Being convinced of the wisdom of bringing Kentucky Fried Chicken (KFC) to Japan, Aso went immediately to

Nashville and implored KFC to come to Japan. KFC's reception was, Aso recalled, worse than his worst expectation. The firm was totally preoccupied with expanding in the United States. Besides, as Aso did not know then, an American with Japanese ancestry had obtained KFC's franchise for Japan in 1962 and his initial entry proved to be a total disaster and a discouraging experience for KFC. No individual KFC manager was receptive to international expansion.

Undaunted, Aso kept sending feelers to KFC, even after he returned to Japan in 1968. The year 1969 saw a faint change in KFC's attitude against going international. At that time, KFC was exhausting its expansion possibilities in the United States and was turning its attention to Canada. In addition, KFC's corporate counsel, who was subsequently fired by KFC's owner and president, appeared unusually international-minded and was urging KFC to accept Aso's offer.

Having persuaded KFC to form a joint venture with Mitsubishi, Aso needed to convince the top management of Mitsubishi Corporation that they ought to get involved in the "fried chicken" business. The initial response of the board members was overwhelmingly skeptical. "You imagine that our Mitsubishi is going to run a restaurant?" "You dare call this quaint taste a marketable meal?" "No Japanese would buy it."

Aso's replies were in essence that "KFC is not a conventional restaurant but a modern manufacturing plant." "The younger generation of the Japanese will like KFC-flavored fried chicken." "KFC will use lots of our broilers." "Increase in broiler sales means increase in our feed sales." Thus, Kentucky Fried Chicken (Japan) was born early in 1970, 50 percent owned by Mitsubishi and 50 percent by KFC (U.S.A.). KFCJ was to pay a royalty of 4 percent of total sales to KFC (U.S.A.). The initial capitalization of KFCJ

was 70 million yen (US$200,000). And more important, Aso secured from the top echelon of Mitsubishi Corporation two basic rules concerning the operation of KFCJ: namely, (1) not to treat KFCJ as a dumping ground for Mitsubishi's retiring managers and employees: and (2) not to obligate KFCJ to buy broilers, equipment and other necessary materials exclusively from Mitsubishi.

KFCJ'S EARLY MARKETING EXPERIENCE

Just after KFCJ was established, EXPO'70 was opened in Osaka, an industrial and commercial center. This international event was expected to attract over 30 million visitors, including thousands from abroad. The United States sent "Moon Stone" to its gigantic exhibition hall and she was already the talk of the town before EXPO opened.

Near the United States Pavilion stood the "Kentucky Fried Chicken" store with all the authentic appearance and decorum of the "finger lickin' good" store found in the United States. This EXPO store was opened and managed by KFC (U.S.A.), assisted and closely watched by KFCJ personnel including Aso and Yamashita.

From the outset until EXPO'70 closed, the popularity of the KFC booth kept rising among the visitors. All the necessary ingredients of KFC items were procured in Japan. A slight change in menu was made along the way when mashed potatoes were abandoned in favor of French fries. Soft drinks and ice cream were added to the menu. Likewise, cole slaw was down-played as few Japanese indicated a preference for it. In sum, KFC in EXPO'70 proved to be a resounding success.

Immediately after the EXPO'70, KFC (U.S.A.) suggested to KFCJ that in order to exploit the success of EXPO'70 in Osaka, two or three test stores be opened in the Osaka area. These KFCJ test stores were to be located in the newly emerging shopping centers or in near suburban housing developments, whose residents were predominantly the families of white collar employees and lower to middle management. The test store was to be a free-standing building, occupying 4,400 square feet and was to cater to take-out orders. In short, a typical KFC store found in the suburbs of the United States was to be transplanted, practically as is, to the Osaka area.

Yamashita and Aso had a hunch that the Toyko area, not Osaka, should be the first test place. They thought that KFCJ should capitalize on the stylish image of "fashionable fast foods" fresh from the United States. As with any other "fashion products," Tokyo should be the starting point. Historically, new fashions and new ways of life have spread invariably from Tokyo to other areas, not the other way around. The Japanese staff of KFCJ and Mitsubishi also had intuitive skepticism about the size of the proposed store, about KFC's overemphasis on take-out service and the specific store location (in shopping areas near new housing developments). But they decided to go along with KFC's proposal simply because "too much revision of the KFC know-how and manuals from the outset was feared to destroy the original KFC know-how." According to Aso, "there will be ample time later, to fiddle with KFC (and American) know-how, once we know how to pick and choose."

During eighteen months of test operations, two of the three initial KFCJ stores in the Osaka area never registered sales above calculated break-even points and were subsequently closed. The remaining store barely stayed above the break-even point. Each store's sales (production) capacity was 15 million yen per month. But actual monthly sales hovered around 2 million yen. During the first nine months of operation, KFCJ ran up accumulated accounting losses of over 220 million yen ($600,000). In short, the test stores were less than a resounding success. Middlefield, who was sent in 1970 by KFC (U.S.A.) to manage KFCJ, recalled in 1975, "We wanted to make mistakes during the initial test period, in Osaka, not in Tokyo, so that the Tokyo market would be left undamaged."

"KFC" COMES TO TOKYO

The Osaka experience demonstrated a need for radical change in KFC's "marketing approach" à la American if KFCJ was to succeed. Aso, Yamashita, Middlefield and Takagi (who was Aso's assistant on the KFCJ project inside Mitsubishi) debated the necessary adaptations of the KFC know-how to the Japanese market. They agreed upon the following premises which the KFCJ should use to promote Kentucky Fried Chicken:

1. Product to be promoted as "new fashion" from the United States.

2. The Japanese children and youth, ranging from kindergarten to university ages, to be the principal target customers, along with housewives in their late 20s and early 30s;

3. The family background of the target customers to be the upper-middle and the upper class of corporate executives and professionals who have gone abroad or are capable, of going abroad;

4. With a slight sign of success of test stores, KFCJ's direct-owned stores to be increased in number as rapidly as possible;

5. Price and product appeal to be competitive with an eat-out or home-delivered

meat meal popular with Japanese customers.

In order to adapt the KFC product and marketing package to the market attributes mentioned above, KFCJ came up with the following marketing and product package. The experience of the first three test stores in the Osaka area was amply woven into the renewed "marketing package" to be tested in the Tokyo market:

1. *Brand:* "Kentucky Fried Chicken" to be spelled out both in Japanese phonetics (Katakana) and English.
2. *Price:* Most popular three-piece tray to be competitive with a popular Japanese meat dish, "Katsudon" (sirloin pork cutlet placed over spiced rice).
3. *Location of test stores:* Near key stations of the Toyoko Commuter Line stretching from Shibuya, a southwest leisure center of Tokyo, through the southwest suburban area of Tokyo, to Yokohama where upper middle class and high-income families reside. Residents within a radius of 2 kilometers ($1\frac{1}{4}$ mile) from the store to be considered "potential customers" of the store.
4. *Store size:* Standard size to be reduced to 66 square meters (about 2,100 square feet) from 132 square meters (about 4,400 square feet) specified in the KFC manual so that rent and other maintenance expenses be reduced.
5. *Store space:* Tenant store in the existing building.
6. *Advertisement and sales promotion:* Leafletting all the houses within market coverage of each store. Promote "KFC Booth" to the "Bazzar," "Rummage Sales," "Picnic," "Athletic Meeting" and "Excursion Tour" of PTAs, schools, and kindergartens within the market coverage of each test store. These direct promotional campaigns to be supplemented with spot commercials on TV and radio between 2 p.m. and 4 p.m. when school children come home and desire afternoon snacks.
7. *Store function:* Eat-on-premises to be promoted as well as take-out services.
8. *Store decoration:* Red and white striped appearance to be maintained, together with Colonel Sanders' "real-size" statue in front of the store.
9. *Menu:* Luxurious looking menu to be printed in color matching store decoration.

In particular, these marketing and product approaches were considered necessary because the cost of TV commercials in Japan was about three times as great as in the United States, and because store rents and key money deposits were also two to three times as great in Japan. Costs of various ingredients were just about the same as those in the United States. In order to make maximum use of limited space, the cooking and kitchen equipment were also reduced in size and redesigned to be arranged vertically with much of the equipment being used for multiple purposes. All key equipment was to be leased rather than purchased outright. In this way, the initial cash outlays were kept to a minimum and each store was expected to "pay as it goes." The Food Processing Equipment Division of Mitsubishi Corporation, to which Takagi formally belonged, became the key leasor of the kitchen equipment. The break-even sales level of the new standard store of KFCJ was reduced to about 3.5 million yen ($12,000) per month.

The promotion of eat-on-premises was considered absolutely necessary in order to draw potential customers. The idea to promote the KFCJ store as a "fashionable place to eat in," which also provides take-out services. The ratio of eat-on-premises sales to take-out sales was expected to vary from 70 percent for a downtown store to 40 percent for a store in a residential area. In addition to six stores in the Tokyo area, one test store was opened inside the fashionable shopping arcade called "Toa Road" in Kobe further west of Osaka. Unlike the Osaka area, the Kobe area has traditionally attracted the residences of upper middle class and professional families and has formed the "Toyoko Line Resident" of the west. In particular, the shopping arcade, "Toa Road" is frequented by the housewives and children of the upper middle class.

When the seven test stores showed a sign of success, twelve new stores were opened early in 1972. All of them were under the direct management of KFCJ and were located along the Toyoko Line and the Odakyu Line to the north of the Toyoko Line. A number of residential areas along the Odakyu Line possessed many similar socioeconomic attributes of the Toyoko Line.

The overall break-even number of KFCJ stores in 1972 was estimated to be around 25. Thus, KFCJ wanted to accelerate the momentum of expanding the store networks. From mid–1971 to 1972, the Japanese economy plunged into the "borrowers' market" in capital and loan markets. This "extraordinary liquidity" of the financial institutions, as the Japanese called it, was mainly brought about by the combination of increased export sales and the levelling-off of the capital investment needs of Japanese manufacturing firms. Manufacturing firms were trying to repay their past debts to banks and other financial institutions. And financial institutions were scurrying around in search of potential borrowers. As a result, banks relaxed their

past reluctance to lend funds to "entertainment and restaurant" businesses. Being associated with Mitsubishi Corporation, the KFCJ found it easy to borrow money from the financial community.

Meanwhile, toward the end of 1971, KFC (U.S.A.) was acquired by Heublein Co., Hartford, Connecticut. And the 50 percent ownership of KFCJ was transferred to Heublein. Recognizing a need for increasing the number of KFCJ stores in the Tokyo and Osaka-Kohe area, Aso persuaded Heublein to agree to increasing the paid-in equity base of KFCJ from $200,000 to $2 million. Armed with increased equity funds as well as additional borrowed funds, KFCJ rented "whatever appropriate store spaces" were available in target market areas. During 1972, altogether sixty new stores were opened under the management of KFCJ. In December alone, fourteen new stores were opened. This time, KFCJ also ventured to downtowns and other "leisure centers" in the Tokyo and Osaka areas, catering to both "eat-on-premises" and take-out customers.

During 1973, KFC continued to open new stores and at the same time, called for KFCJ franchises in remote areas of Japan. Starting with nominating franchisees in Hokkaido (northernmost island) and the Sanin area (southwest facing Japan Sea) in 1973, KFCJ added new franchisees in 1974 in Kyushu (southernmost areas). The areas were selected primarily on the basis of the trend of per-capita income of each prefecture as well as on the basis of the urban population in regional cities. Learning from the success of Coca-Cola in Japan, KFCJ carefully selected the franchisees. The franchisees were also established and leading regional firms. The franchise fee was 4 percent of total sales.

When the year 1974 ended, KFCJ had 122 stores which evenly divided between the direct management of KFCJ and the franchisees. Meanwhile, Mitsubishi Corporation renegotiated successfully with Heublein for a reduction of the royalty fee from the initial 4 percent to 3 percent of sales of KFCJ. Aso maintained that KFCJ needed to plough as much profit as possible into expanding store networks and that KFCJ was totally operated and managed by the Japanese portion of KFCJ including Mitsubishi. As a result, by the end of 1973, KFCJ began to register an annual profit. With the continued growth of sales and profits, it was expected that by the beginning of 1976, even accumulated accounting losses would be totally cleared. In 1974, on the average, each store was producing profits corresponding to about 13 to 20 percent of sales.

THE "FAST FOOD" MARKET IN JAPAN

In 1975 there were about 450,000 stores and restaurants throughout Japan engaged in one form or other of retailing meals, snacks, alcoholic and non-alcoholic beverages for "eat-on-premises" and "take-out" customers. The bulk of these operations were a single store operated by members of the owner family. While these stores tended to feature one of three menus, "Japanese food," "Chinese food" and "Western food," there were many menus which consisted of the stores' own combinations of these three categories. These small-sized, family-owned single stores had long existed in Japan. In their operational format and behavior, however, these stores were to the fast growing chain restaurants of the "food-service industry" what small-sized craftsmen's workshops were in the past to the growing sector of the modern manufacturing firm.

As the Japanese economy grew, especially from the early 1960s, not only individ-

uals' disposable income but also leisure time increased. Five-day work week and paid holidays were spreading from one firm to the next. Furthermore, young work forces and student populations, both male and female, emerged as the big spenders on fashions, sporting goods, entertainment, travelling and eating out. These spenders thronged to the large cities as the urbanization of the Japanese populace progressed. Fashions of the American youth culture, such as hair style, attire and taste for music were quickly being taken up by young consumers in Japan.

Around 1965, the total annual sales of "eating out" and "catering services" was estimated to be less than 1,000 billion yen ($2.7 billion). Most people associated eating out with such special occasions as weddings, company-sponsored outings, athletic meetings and other recreational events of schools and family gatherings. From the mid–1960s, the "eating-and-drinking-out" market began to grow at an exponential rate. Generally, the "Americanization" of the Japanese drinking taste progressed, as was witnessed by the rapid growth of Coca-Cola sales after 1965. In 1975, the "eating out" and "catering services" market was in total passing 4,000 billion yen per year. And the market was growing at an annual rate of over 10 percent. The growing fast-food market alone was estimated to pass 30 billion yen in 1975.

For instance, in 1963, the average monthly expenditure on eating out was about 1,000 yen per household. In 1971, the same expenditure was over 2,700 yen. Needless to say, the monthly expenditure per household for eating out in 1963 was twice as large for Tokyo as the national average. This trend remained the same in 1971. From 1963 to 1971 other large cities like Osaka, Nagoya, Yokohama and Kobe moved much closer to Tokyo in terms of respective city household's monthly expenditure on eating out. Figure 1

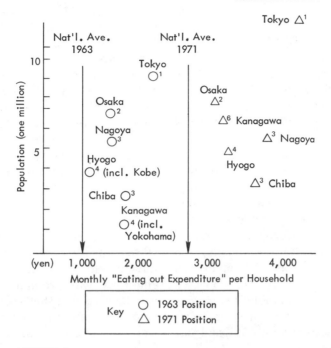

FIGURE 1

schematically shows the trend of a household's monthly expenditure for eating out purposes from 1963 to 1971 by respective prefectures.

From the early 1960s to the early 1970s, the amount of eating-out consumers' "one-time-expenditure" on a meal or snack also increased from 200 yen to 600 yen. This rate of increase was significantly greater than the general rate of inflation during the period. As consumers' "one-time-expenditure"—the amount eating-out consumers were financially and psychologically prepared to spend—increased from 200 yen to 600 yen consumers' preference for specific items also changed. While income elasticity of demand for such conventionally popular items as Japanese and Chinese noodle dishes remained low (less than the unity), income elasticity of demand for more prestigious dishes such as "sushi" (raw fish fillet with rice), coffee shop items, "Western foods," bar and beer-hall items registered large value (significantly greater than the unity); indicating that the "eating- and drinking-out" markets of "westernized" or "traditional but prestigious" Japanese dishes expanded far more quickly than conventionally popular dishes.

KFC's entry into Japan simply coincided with the time when Japanese urban consumers were about to embrace the idea of "eating- and drinking-out" and were about to loosen their purse strings upon fashionable fast-food items. In retrospect, the initial growth phase of KFCJ could not have better coincided with the Japanese economy. After the oil crisis hit Japan in October 1973, the financial markets again became "lenders' markets." As money became tighter, even blue-chip manufacturing firms found it difficult to borrow much from the financial communities. Fledling fast-food and entertainment firms were literally squeezed out of the capital and loan markets.

ECONOMICS
OF THE KFCJ OPERATIONS

Tables 4 and 5 show the financial statements of KFCJ for the fiscal year 1974 ending on May 31, 1974. Overall costs of goods sold were about 50 percent of the total sales of stores under the direct management of KFCJ. About 80 percent of these costs were ingredients and raw materials purchased from outside suppliers. Mitsubishi Corporation supplied about one-half of KFCJ's total purchases.

To open a store with approximately 3,000 square feet of rented space, the key-money deposit in 1975 was about 10 million yen ($32,000). In addition, about 15 million yen were needed to make improvements on leased space and equipment. Each KFCJ store was urged to aim at 13 to 20 percent as the minimum profit after costs of goods sold and various expenses. The KFCJ stores began first with four to five regular storekeepers. But the number of regular KFCJ employees was reduced on the average in May 1973 to 2.7 per store. It was left to each store manager to hire part-time and non-regular helpers depending on the sales fluctuations by day and by month. Store hours were ordinarily from 11:00 a.m. till 9:00 p.m. seven days a week. However, a store manager could petition the KFCJ Headquarters to lengthen his store hours. Some stores were open until midnight.

From 1972 to 1975, KFCJ experienced a very low rate of employee turnover (about 10 percent for the first three years). After a three month "training period," a regular store employee was promoted to assistant store manager. Some high-performing assistant managers, after six months in that position, were promoted to store manager. The mini-

TABLE 4   Balance Sheet of the Kentucky Fried Chicken (Japan) As of May 31, 1974 (In thousands of yen)

Current Assets		Current Liabilities	
Cash	549,422	Notes payable	30,125
Accounts Receivable	32,114	Accounts Payable	134,313
Inventory	61,925	Short-term-debts	1,161,396
Pre-paid expenses	120,993	Reserve for employees' bonus	50,539
Loan	31,719	Long-term Liabilities	
Fixed Assets		Long-term debts	493,630
Land	262,641	Capital	
Buildings	18,202	Paid-in capital	600,000
Improvements on leased		Earned surpluses	71,085
equipments	337,640		
Equipment and machinery	102,185		
Automobiles and trucks	3,637		
Prepaid construction	26,100		
Invisible Assets			
Leased Property Rights	120,946		
Long-term prepaid expenses	74,188		
Investments	599,932		
Deferred Assets			
Royalties	55,469		
Issuing expenses of new stock	1,805		
	2,398,918		2,398,918

Source: Corporation Annual Report.

TABLE 5   Profit and Loss Statement of the Kentucky Fried Chicken (Japan) From June 1, 1973 till May 31, 1974 (In thousands of yen)

Sales	¥ 2,101,996	
Franchise Royalties	84,544	¥ 2,186,540
Costs of Goods Sold	1,081,062	
Sales and Administrative expenses including payments*	1,003,430	2,084,492
Gross profits		102,048*
Interests earned	11,922	
Other non-sales profits	5,603	17,525
Interest expenses	100,472	
Other expenses	2,124	102,596
Profit before tax		¥ 16,977

*Including depreciation expenses of 35,682,000 yen.

Source: Corporation Annual Report.

mum salary of the store manager in 1975 was about 130,000 yen ($440) per month, approximately twice that of assistant store managers. In addition, according to the Japanese salary system, regular employees were paid about a six-months' salary equivalent of "bonus" per year. Promotion was determined on the basis of written and field tests on KFCJ's operational manual plus superiors' evaluations of employees' working attitudes. Annually, five or six employees were selected to go on a month-long "study tour" abroad (mainly in the United States) at KFCJ's expense.

A store manager was evaluated on the basis of his store's sales and profit records. All stores under the direct management of KFCJ were ranked monthly according to actual sales and profits (their growth rate and actual amounts), containment of costs and expenses against the targeted members. This ranking was published in the KFCJ monthly newsletter distributed to all KFCJ personnel. Supervisors, each of whom oversaw eight to ten stores, were asked to help store managers improve their performance. If store managers' performance was not improved in six months, they were demoted and sent back to work within the store.

Accordingly, aggressive and imaginative store managers improvised various ways to increase their sales and profits. For example, one store happened to be located right across from a television station in Tokyo. Every afternoon, there appeared a long queue of visitors to live-filmings of popular programs. The store manager walked up and down the queue and sold ice cream and soft drinks. Another manager in Tokyo noticed that the second floor of one store was being used as the storage space for the KFCJ store downstairs. He persuaded Yamashita to open a restaurant and bar on the second floor instead of the storage space. This new establishment was to cater to two different groups of customers: daytime, to young office girls and college coeds; and at night, to young male customers and their dates. The menu was changed twice a day according to the target customers. At night a female singer and a guitarist provided live music. This store proved to be a hit. And a KFCJ decided to institute discount services in this store to the KFCJ employees as a fringe benefit for them. Soon, many young KFC employees were seen frequenting this store with their dates. The store manager of this special restaurant was rotated among KFCJ store managers so that he could enjoy a change of air from selling KFC items.

Another employee suggested to Yamashita that surplus chicken drumsticks could be smoked and vacuum-packed. Intrigued by this suggestion, Yamashita sent this young graduate in agricultural chemistry from Hokkaido University to the laboratory of his alma mater, together with 200,000 yen. Three months later, he came back with the perfected methods of smoking and vacuum-packing chicken. This new product was sold in the store as a "delicacy" to KFCJ customers. The KFCJ store managers pushed smoked chicken to other restaurants and bars in the neighborhoods of their stores. In the summer 1975 "smoked chicken" was contributing sales and profits to KFCJ stores.

Each store was also selling fried drumsticks by piece as well as a "mini-pack" of one fried drumstick and a child's portion of french fries. These items were popular with children. Coleslaw, potato salad, home rollbreads, and french fries were sold in addition to milk shakes, ice cream, coffee, cola, and orange juice. Some downtown stores in Tokyo were in, summer 1975, selling bottled wines to take-out customers.

PRIVATE THOUGHTS OF YAMASHITA AND MIDDLEFIELD

In summer 1975, Yamashita recounted his experience with KFCJ as follows:

. . . Right now, our first problem is how to reduce the interest payments. The required compensating balances on the borrowed funds bring the effective rate of interest to about 13 percent a year . . . We have a tough time in explaining this Japanese peculiarity to Heublein . . . Ever since Heublein took over KFC (U.S.A.), Heublein has placed us on strict Heublein's reporting and control system. They want tons of information on the Japanese market.

This is all right. But their emphasis on ROI per store and per whatever does not take into consideration the "human side" of KFCJ operations . . .

. . . For example, in order to maintain and cultivate the comradeship among our employees, we often sit down on the floor almost half-naked after store hours and pass drinks among us. We rap about many things and keep encouraging one another. I doubt Heublein would understand the precious need for such things as this . . .

. . . Japanese consumers' taste for fast foods is rapidly broadening. In order to maintain and expand our market share, we will have to keep broadening our menu . . . Up until six months ago, Heublein kept telling us to think only chicken. Mitsubishi is no problem. They recognize a need for exploiting changes in Japanese consumers' taste . . .

. . . Last year, Heublein took KFC to Hong Kong. It changed KFC to a Chinese name and added spring rolls to its menu . . . I thought that the venture was totally misconceived. I understand that Heublein spent about $2 million and retreated from Hong Kong. No two markets look alike . . .

. . . Naturally, I have enjoyed my work with KFCJ . . . I came to KFCJ in order to sell posters and other paper products from my former employers, a printing firm. They asked me to join the firm. I am glad that I did . . .

Middlefield, the sole American (or foreigner) in KFCJ reminisced in summer, 1975:

. . . I was fascinated by Japan when I commanded an all-Japanese crew transport ship during my active duty in the Korean War . . . They saved my face by covering up my mistakes. And I wanted to come back to Japan . . .

. . . I joined IBM as a salesman but I did not have any hope of being sent to Japan. I worked for IBM for about sixteen years. Then I was sent to Nashville. I happened to live next door to the owner and president to KFC (U.S.A.) . . . As far as he was concerned, I was the "Japan expert" . . . When he asked me to go to Japan in 1970, I did not hesitate to take the job . . .

I decided to visit Europe on my way to Japan. In Greece, one day when I was sightseeing, I ran into a Japanese executive. I told him that I was on my way to KFCJ . . . He asked me to look up

Yamashita of his printing company because his firm would be interested in doing business with KFCJ . . . Being fluent in English and bright, Yamashita would be a nice person for me to know, anyhow, he said.

. . . I don't recall in which books and articles I read on doing business in Japan. But I recalled, then, that a Japanese and foreign joint venture often failed because the Japanese partner used it as the dumping ground for his own reject employees. So I thought that if Yamashita was a good person, I would cultivate personal friendship with him and would ask him to join KFCJ. I was going to demand that Mitsubishi respect KFCJ's own Japanese personnel . . . As it turned out, Mitsubishi was thinking along the same line . . .

. . . Yamashita showed me around Tokyo and showed me how Japanese eat-on-premises fast-foods were sold and served . . . Eventually, I convinced Yamashita to join KFCJ . . .

. . . When Heublein bought KFC (U.S.A.), I was scared of being fired. Unlike Japanese firms, American firms have a habit of firing managers associated with the previous firm just acquired . . . As it turned out, I was one of the few who survived . . . When Heublein people came to Japan, Mitsubishi people went out of their way to tell them that I was doing a good job . . . Mitsubishi people even assured me that if and when Heublein fired me, they would find a job for me . . .

. . . In order to get free but good publicity for KFCJ I made it a rule to appear on radio and television shows featuring "peculiar" foreigners in Japan . . . We got lots of free publicity this way. And it was useful when we were starting up our business. Television air time costs a lot more here than in the States . . .

. . . When we asked in 1972 Heublein to increase the equity base of KFCJ, I pointed it out to them that the Japanese yen was going to be revalued again . . . Heublein paid its increased share before the yen became 15 to 17 percent dearer vis-à-vis the U.S. dollar . . .

. . . I am hoping that American businesses will recognize the positive correlation between market share and profit. Japanese businesses have intuitively known this and have attempted to expand sales and market share . . . Growth is in essence a deferred profit for a firm . . .

. . . American marketing techniques and manuals have to be adapted to Japanese situations . . . Compare MacDonald's success with Burger Chef's failure . . . Both of them came later than us. MacDonalds watched us closely and duplicated our own adaptations . . . Burger Chef insisted on and continued with mechanical application of its American manuals in Japan . . . Burger Chef had to sell its business back to its Japanese partner . . .

. . . I understand that the American fast food chains are now moving back to downtown and eat-on-premises markets. Perhaps Heublein could use the operational know-how of KFCJ.

6

LEGAL DIMENSIONS

When you are at Rome live in the Roman style; when you are elsewhere live as they live elsewhere.

St. Ambrose, A.D. 340–397
advice to St. Augustine

INTRODUCTION

The field of international law is complex and fascinating, but far beyond the scope of this book. This chapter (1) examines the development of international law as it relates to global marketing and (2) considers the most pressing current issues and the rules and organizations now in existence to deal with them.

INTERNATIONAL LAW

International law as it exists today dates from the late sixteenth century. Early international law was concerned with the waging of war, the establishment of peace, and other such political issues as diplomatic recognition of new national entities and governments. Thus, while elaborate international rules gradually emerged—covering, for example, the status of neutral nations—the creation in the nineteenth century of laws governing commerce was done on a state-by-state basis. This perpetuated the major split in legal systems between those areas under English influence founded on common law (such as Great Britain, the United States, and Canada) and those under the influence of the old Roman law and, later, the Napoleonic Code based on civil or code law. Under civil law, the judicial system is divided into civil, commercial, and criminal law. Thus, commercial law has its own administrative structure, and property rights, for example, are established by a formal registration of the property. Under common law, on the other hand, the law is established by the creation of precedents from previous rulings, and commercial law until recently was not recognized as a special entity. Property rights, under common law, are based on ownership established by use. A significant recent development is the Uniform Commercial Code, now recognized by 49 U.S. states, which brings together a body of specifically designed rules covering commercial conduct.

International law has the function of upholding order. While at first, as we have noted, this referred to preventing war or dealing with problems arising from war, with the growing trade among nations, order in commercial affairs came to assume increasing importance. While the law had originally dealt only with nations as entities, a growing body of law rejected the idea that only states can be subjects of international law. *Reparation for Injuries Suffered in the Service of the United Nations* (International Court of Justice Reports, 1949, p. 179), for example, recognized the claims of an individual. The Nuremberg International Tribunal in its trial of Nazi war criminals reiterated this concept:

> It was submitted that international law is concerned with the actions of sovereign states, and provides no punishment for individuals; and further that where the act in question is an act of state, those who carry it out are not personally responsible, but are protected by the doctrine of the sovereignty of the state. In the opinion of the Tribunal, both these submissions must be rejected. Crimes against international law are committed by men, not by abstract entities, and only by punishing individuals who commit such crimes can the provisions of international law be enforced.

International law may be defined as the rules and principles that states and nations consider binding upon themselves. This raises the first of two unique characteristics of international law: Those areas in which law has been written are those that have always belonged to individual states or nations—property, trade, immigration, and so on—and the law now exists only to the extent that individual states are willing to relinquish their rights in these areas. Even today there is very little one nation can do if another refuses to submit to arbitration or to recognize an unfavorable judgment against it. This deficiency is increased by the second characteristic of international law: the lack of an adequate international judicial and administrative framework or a body of law that would form the basis of a truly comprehensive international legal system.

In this situation multinational marketers face a multitude of legal environments. They will discover that simply finding out what the law is, or whose law prevails, in a given situation is a difficult task. First, laws of various states, rulings, and local customs must be identified and classified. Then it must be decided whether enough states have actually followed a rule over sufficient time so that it may be considered binding. The twentieth century has seen an increase in international judiciary organizations paralleled by a growing body of international case law. The complex background of this new body of law was aptly summed up in a 1900 fishing case:

where there is no treaty and no controlling executive or legislative act or judicial decision, resort must be had to the customs and usages of civilized nations, and, as evidence
of these, to the work of jurists and commentators who by years of labor, research, and
experience have made themselves peculiarly well acquainted with the subjects of which
they treat.

The court goes on to rule that

By the general consent of civilized nations of the world, and independently of any
express treaty or other public act, it is an established rule of international law, founded
on considerations of humanity.[1]

Notice the important precedent emphasized here; there *is* an established rule
of international law per se. Thus, while the law was at first an amalgam of treaties,
convenants, codes, and agreements, there is an increasing codification of law starting
with the formation by the United States in 1947 of the International Law Commission.
To this may be added the rulings of the Permanent Court of International Justice
(1920–1945); the International Court of Justice, founded in 1946; and the results of
various other organizations and conferences—for example, the Geneva Conference
on the Law of the Sea, which began in 1958 and is still meeting regularly.

RELEVANT BUSINESS ISSUES

While it becomes clear in such a situation that the best course to follow is to get
expert legal help, an astute marketer, by being aware of the complexity of the legal
environment, may do a great deal to avoid situations in which a conflict might arise.
Most issues center on the following major questions.

Establishment

Under what conditions am I allowed to establish trade? To transact business, citizens
of one country must be assured that they will be treated fairly in another country.
Treaties of friendship, commerce, and navigation give U.S. citizens the right to
nondiscriminatory treatment in trade, the reciprocal right to establish a business,
and particularly to invest in the 43 countries with which the United States has signed
these agreements. There are, however, important exceptions: the Coelso Doctrine
in Latin America, for example, insists that foreigners, by entering Latin America,
agree to being treated as nationals. This can create problems for business managers
who may still be under the jurisdiction of their own laws even when they are out of
their native country. U.S. citizens, for example, are forbidden by the Foreign Corrupt
Practices Act to bribe an official of a foreign government or political party, even if

[1]Gerard F. Mangor, *The Elements of International Law* (Homewood, Ill.: Dorsey Press, 1967),
p. 14.

bribes or "payments" are customary and almost essential for conducting business elsewhere.

Patents and Trademarks

Will my patents and trademarks be protected? There is no international patent. Patents and trademarks that are protected in one country are not necessarily protected in another, so international marketers must ensure that every product is registered in each country they intend to trade in. There are a number of separate patent agreements, the most important of which is the International Convention for the Protection of Industrial Property, first signed in 1883 and now honored by 45 countries. This treaty provides that if you file in a signatory country within one year of the first filing, you will be afforded the date of the first filing for priority purposes.[2]

A patent cooperation treaty (PCT) and a European Patent System are also currently in effect. The PCT, which now numbers 39 countries, includes Australia, Brazil, France, Germany, Japan, Korea (DPR), Korea (ROK), The Netherlands, Switzerland, USSR, and the United States. These states constitute a union for cooperation in the filing, searching, and examination of applications for the protection of inventions and for the rendering of certain technical services.

The European patent convention, effective in 11 countries, enables a patent applicant to file a single application covering all of the convention states designated by the applicant and thus achieve the advantage that the application will be subject to only one procedure of grant. National patent laws remain effective under this system. In fact, the procedure does not result in the existence of one single unitary patent but rather leads to a bundle of national patents.

Recourse

Lawsuits in other countries may be long, costly, and aggravating and may create an unfavorable public image, while at the same time subjecting a company to a court that is unfamiliar with international law or unfavorably disposed toward foreign companies. For these reasons, most business executives prefer to arbitrate disputes. Arbitration generally involves efforts at conciliation, a hearing of all parties before a three-member panel, and a judgment that the parties agree in advance to abide by. The decades since World War II have seen an increase in the numbers and scope of arbitration groups. Some of the most widely used and respected of these are the International Chamber of Commerce, the American Arbitration Association, the London Court of Arbitration, and the Inter-American Commercial Arbitration Committee.

Lawyers advise that arbitration clauses should be written into all contracts. They also advise that all contracts should contain a clause that establishes jurisdic-

---

[2]Private communication, John Kurucz, Kane, Dalsimer, Kane, Sullivan, and Kurucz, Attorneys at Law, New York, New York.

tional rules in the event of a conflict. Jurisdiction is generally established on the basis of (1) a jurisdictional clause, (2) where a contract was entered into, and (3) where the provisions of a contract are to be performed.

Still another consideration should be the site of incorporation, with its implications for taxes and other economic and legal issues. Some countries consider incorporation to be the location of main business activity, others look at the location of the central management, while still others, including the United States, decide on the basis of place of incorporation.

A final concern, lawyers advise, is the need for extreme care in the writing of all contracts and in having them translated with infinite pains so that all parties are absolutely clear on their obligations.

Taxes

What taxes will my company face abroad? Taxes are an area in which states fiercely retain their national rights. U.S. companies pay taxes to the country in which the income is earned and receive tax credits in the United States on taxes paid abroad. Credits in the United States are limited by a ceiling determined by the ratio of foreign profits to total profits. Because of differing tax rates, it is often advantageous for a company to have as much income taxed abroad as possible.

Dilution of Equity—Control

Political pressure for national control of foreign owned companies is a constant factor in international business.[3] Legislation that requires companies to dilute their equity is never popular in the boardroom, yet the consequences of such legislation are often surprisingly favorable. Dennis J. Encarnation and Sushil Vachani examined corporate responses to India's Foreign Exchange Regulation Act (FERA) of 1973 which restricts foreign equity participation in local projects to 40 percent. They identified four options.

1. Follow the law to the letter. Colgate Palmolive (India) took this course and became an Indian Company and maintained its dominant position in a growing market.

2. Leave the country. This was IBM's response after several years of negotiations. IBM concluded that it would lose more in shared control than it would gain from continued operations under the new rules.

3. Negotiate under the law. Some companies used the equity dilution requirement to raise funds for growth and diversification. In most cases this was done by issuing fresh equity to local investors. Ciby-Geigy increased its equity base 27 percent to

---

[3]This section is based on Dennis J. Encarnation and Sushil Vachani, "Foreign Ownership: When Hosts Change the Rules," *Harvard Business Review,* September–October 1985, pp. 152–160.

$17.7 million, for example, and also negotiated an increase in production that doubled the sales of Hindustan Ciby-Geigy.

4. Take preemptive action. Some MNCs initiated defensive strategies well before FERA's passage. These included preemptive diversification to take advantage of investment incentives, phased Indianization, and continuously updating technology and maintaining export sales.

The experiences of MNCs in India teach some important lessons.

1. First, look at the range of possibilities. There is no single best solution, and each company should look at itself and at the country situation as it decides on strategy.

2. Use the law to achieve your own objectives. The experiences of many companies demonstrate that by satisfying government demands, it is possible to take advantage of government concessions and subsidies and market protection.

3. Anticipate government policy changes. Companies that take initiatives are prepared to act when the opportunity arises. It takes time to implement changes and the sooner a company identifies possible government directions and initiatives, the sooner it is in a position to propose its own plan to help the country achieve its objectives.

4. Listen to country managers. Country managers should be encouraged to anticipate government initiatives and to propose company strategy for taking advantage of opportunities created by government policy. Local managers understand the political environment and experience suggests they are in the best position to know when issues arc arising and how to turn potential adversity into opportunity through creative responses.

Expropriation

The ultimate threat of the nation-state is expropriation. The incidence of manufacturing company expropriations is widely exaggerated by the business community, especially among those without international experience. In fact, the total expropriation loss to American companies during this century not only is trivial compared with the total amount of American foreign direct investment but is concentrated entirely outside of the Western industrialized states.

Franklin Root identified 187 U.S. companies that had experienced expropriation since the end of World War I.[4] These companies were involved in 240 separate acts of expropriation—171 in Communist countries and 69 in non-Communist countries. Cuba alone accounted for 137 seizures of American business property. As can be seen in Table 6–1, the total value of major expropriations of U.S. business property

---

[4]Franklin R. Root, "The Expropriation Experience of American Companies," *Business Horizons*, April 1968, pp. 69–74.

TABLE 6–1 Major Expropriation of U.S. Business Property by Foreign Governments (in millions of dollars)

COUNTRY	DATE	ESTIMATED AMOUNT OF U.S. ASSETS EXPROPRIATED
Soviet Union	1917–20	$ 175
Mexico	1983	120
Eastern Europe	1945–48	240
Cuba	1959–60	1,400
Argentina	1963	237
Indonesia	1965	160
		$2,332

Source: Franklin R. Root, "Expropriation Experience of American Companies," *Business Horizons*, April 1968, p. 71.

by foreign governments from 1917 to 1965 was less than $2.5 billion, or only 5 percent of the total U.S. foreign direct investment base of $49 billion in 1965.

Although the risk of expropriation may be exaggerated it is still quite real, especially in certain industries. As can be seen in Table 6–2, between 1960 and 1974, 12 percent of all U.S. oil properties and 18 percent of all U.S. mining concessions were expropriated. Other sectors with relatively high rates of expropriation were utilities and transportation, which experienced a 4 percent rate of expropriation. By contrast, only 1.2 percent of U.S. manufacturing properties have been expropriated since 1960.

A regional analysis of expropriation between 1960 and 1976 revealed that Latin American countries were responsible for 49 percent of all U.S. expropriations, the Arab states for 27 percent, the Black African states for 13 percent, and the Asian states for 11 percent.[5]

When governments that are frustrated by lack of economic development expropriate foreign property, they are taking a step that conflicts directly with the property and income concerns of the highly developed nations of Western Europe and the United States. Industrial countries are committed to "prompt, adequate, and effective compensation" and support the establishment of an international consultation procedure in cases of expropriation. Nevertheless, there are bars to action to reclaim a national's property based on the Act of State Doctrine, which assumes that the acts of foreign states are legal. As U.S. Chief Justice Fuller said in 1897, "Every sovereign state is bound to respect the independence of every other sovereign state, and the courts in one country will not sit in judgment on the acts of government of another done within its territory" (*Underhill* v. *Hernandez,* 168 U.S. 250 [1897]). This policy has been upheld as recently as the reversal of *Banco Nacional de Cuba* v. *Sabbatino* (U.S. Supreme Court, 1964, 376 U.S. 398). The expropriation of the copper companies in Chile shows most clearly, perhaps, the impact that companies

[5]David G. Bradley, "Managing Against Expropriation," *Harvard Business Review*, July–August 1977.

TABLE 6–2 Expropriation by Industry Group, 1960–1974

INDUSTRY	NUMBER OF EXPROPRIATIONS	PERCENTAGE OF TOTAL
Oil	84	12.0%
Extractions	38	18.0
Utilities and transportation	17	4.0
Insurance and banking	33	4.0
Manufacturing	30	1.2
Agriculture	19	N.A.
Sales and service	16	N.A.
Land, property, and construction	23	N.A.

N.A.—Not available.

Source: David G. Bradley, "Managing Against Expropriation," *Harvard Business Review*, July–August 1977, p. 79.

can have on their own fate. Companies that strenuously resisted government efforts to introduce nationals into the company management were expropriated outright while other companies that made genuine efforts to follow Chilean guidelines were allowed to remain under joint Chilean-U.S. management.

Expropriated companies may have recourse to arbitration at, for example, the World Bank Investment Dispute Settlement Center. They may also seek protection by buying expropriation insurance, offered both by private companies and, to an extent limited to new investment in needy countries, by the U.S. government's Overseas Private Investment Corporation (OPIC).

Antitrust

Antitrust laws, a legacy of the nineteenth-century U.S. "trust-busting" era, are intended to maintain free competition by limiting the concentration of economic power. Long a part of the U.S. legal environment, they are taking on increasing importance outside the United States as well. For example, the European Community Commission prohibits agreements and practices that prevent, restrict, and distort competition. The interstate trade clause of the treaty includes trade with third countries, so that a company must be aware of the conduct of its affiliates.

The international marketer should be aware that the European Community Commission also exempts large categories of "good" cartels from Articles 85 and 86 in an effort to encourage the growth of certain businesses so they can compete on an equal footing with Japanese and U.S. companies and also permits selective distribution in some cases.[6]

[6]Robert T. Jones, "Executive's Guide to Antitrust in Europe," *Harvard Business Review*, May–June 1976, pp. 106–118.

Bribery

As Walter Guzzardi points out, history does not record a burst of international outrage when Charles M. Schwab presented a $200,000 diamond and pearl necklace to the mistress of Czar Alexander's nephew, although in return for that consideration, Bethlehem Steel won the contract to supply the rails for the Trans-Siberian railroad.[7] Today, far less crass sales inducements are quickly and universally denounced when used by U.S. companies doing business abroad. We now are living in a post-Watergate age that requires continuous investigation, discovery, and condemnation.

The recent discussion of payments by international companies has demonstrated that there are enormous differences around the globe in judgments about what is right and what is wrong. What emerges from this discussion is that even in the remotest cultures there are rights and wrongs on the extremes. This is not really a problem. The problem arises in the question of how you judge the gray areas—where most companies work.

In a report made by the SEC (Securities and Exchange Commission) to the Senate Committee on Banking, Housing, and Urban Affairs, the commission recognized the difference between payments made to government officials "to procure special and unjustified favors" and those made "to persuade low-level government officials to perform functions that they are obliged to perform as part of their governmental responsibilities but which they may refuse or delay unless compensated." The SEC efforts at making practical distinctions in the type of payments involved in foreign operations are certainly a step in the right direction.

In 1977 the U.S. government passed the Foreign Corrupt Practices Act (FCPA), which makes it a crime for U.S. corporations to bribe an official of a foreign government or political party to obtain or retain business in a foreign country. The law requires publicly held companies to institute internal accounting controls and makes it a crime to make payments to any person when the company has reason to believe that part of the money will go to a foreign official. The law excludes government employees who are essentially clerical and therefore permits so-called "grease" payments to low-level officials to avoid red tape—for example, expediting shipments through customs, securing permits, or even getting airport passport clearance to leave a country.

When companies operate abroad in the absence of home country legal constraints, they face a continuum of choices concerning company ethics. At one extreme they can maintain home country ethics worldwide with absolutely no adjustment or adaptation to local practice. At the other extreme they can abandon any attempt to maintain company ethics and adapt entirely to local conditions and circumstances as they are perceived by company managers in each local environment. Between these extremes companies may select varying degrees of extension of home country ethics, or alternatively they may adapt in varying degrees to local customs

---

[7]Walter Guzzardi, Jr., "An Unscandalized View of Those 'Bribes' Abroad," *Fortune*, July 1976, pp. 118 ff.

and practices. For companies that are headquartered outside the United States, this theoretical range of choice is indeed the actual choice because with the exception of the United States no major industrial country attempts to establish the extraterritorial sovereignty of its laws. The United States has—either happily or regrettably depending on your point of view—an imperial tendency to impose U.S. laws and therefore U.S. values and mores on American companies and citizens worldwide. Most observers feel that while this tendency is not without merit, when it is rigidly applied it often puts American companies in a difficult position vis-à-vis foreign competitors.

The strongest criticism of the Foreign Corrupt Practices Act (FCPA) is that it has had a negative impact on U.S. companies vis-à-vis Japanese and European competitors. While it is probably impossible to ever prove or disprove this charge, a recent macroeconomic study found that the FCPA had no negative effect on the export performance of U.S. industry.[8] While the findings of this study are in no way conclusive, they do not provide any support for those who argue that the FCPA has damaged the U.S. trade position. In the meantime, even though the U.S. Justice Department has endorsed proposed changes in the law that would limit the criminal liability provisions of the law, it has made steady use of the law's provisions. Since 1980, at least 20 individuals and corporations have been convicted or pleaded guilty to bribery or related offences.[9]

The fact of bribery in world markets will not change because it is condemned by the American Congress. What should you do if you are unwilling to offer a bribe and your competitors are willing? Two approaches may be employed. One is to ignore bribery and act as if it does not exist. The other is to recognize the existence of bribery and evaluate its effect on the purchase decision as if it were just another element of the marketing mix.

If your competitor is offering a bribe, your own marketing mix and offering must be as good or better than the competitor's overall offering, bribe included. You might offer a lower price, a better product, better distribution, or better advertising to offset the benefit of the bribe to the decision influencer.

Table 6–3 illustrates a marketing offering evaluation of a company offering a product without a bribe versus that of a company that is offering a bribe. In this illustration, each company makes an equal P-1 to P-4 offering. The quantitative value of the offering is identical for each company for P-1 to P-4, but the non-U.S. company makes a bribe offer with a value of 15 points, which tips the balance in its favor. In this example, the U.S. company will lose the business *unless* it comes up with a way to counteract the bribe offering of the bribing company.

Clearly, merely increasing the price points from 25 to 40 will not counteract the competitor's offer because the bribe is going entirely to one or more decision influencers who would not be as well off personally with an equivalent total offer.

[8]John L. Graham, "The Foreign Corrupt Practices Act: A New Perspective," *Journal of International Business Studies,* Winter 1984, pp. 107–121.

[9]"Recent Charges of Payoffs by Companies Coincide with Bid to Relax Law Barring Overseas Bribes," *Wall Street Journal,* July 10, 1986, p. 54.

TABLE 6–3 Marketing Offering Evaluation—With and Without a Bribe

	U.S. COMPANY (Points)	BRIBING COMPANY (Points)
P-1: Product	25	25
P-2: Price	25	25
P-3: Promotion	25	25
P-4: Place	25	25
P-5: Bribe	0	15
Total	100	115

The essence of a bribe is that it diverts value from the organization (company or country) to the pocket of the individual.

Space does not permit a detailed discussion of how to balance the offer to counteract a bribe, but it can be done in one or several of the marketing mix elements. The easiest way is to have a product that is so superior to that of the competition that a bribe will not sway a decision. If this is not possible, clear superiority in service and in local representation may tip the scales.

REGULATORY AGENCIES

One of the most important influences on business affairs concerns the actions of regulatory agencies that address such matters as price control, valuation of imports and exports, trade practices, labeling, food and drug regulations, employment conditions, collective bargaining, advertising content, competitive practices, and so on. The influence of regulatory agencies is pervasive, and an understanding of how they operate is essential to protecting business interests and the advancing of new programs. As an example, in the United States, the International Trade Commission administers the Tariff Act of 1930. Section 337 of this act prohibits "unfair methods of competition" if the effect of this competition is to destroy or substantially injure an industry, efficiently and economically operated, in the United States. To seek relief or defend access to the U.S. market if it is challenged under this act requires the services of specialized legal talent supported by technical expertise in patents and in international marketing. If regulatory agencies are blocking access to a market, the firm should seek out the assistance of competent local counsel and advice. Normally, it is useful to call on the assistance of home country diplomatic staff to assist and support the effort to obtain a favorable ruling.

The GATT Legal System

GATT (the General Agreement of Tariffs and Trade) is a set of norms and procedures which 92 governments have accepted to create order and predictability in international trade relations. There are three basic principles in the GATT: (1) nondiscrimination, whereby each member country must treat the trade of all other member countries equally; (2) open markets which are encouraged by the GATT through a prohibition of all forms of protection except customs tariffs; and (3) fair trade, which prohibits export subsidies on manufactured products and limits the use of export subsidies on primary products. None of these principles is fully realized.

The real function of GATT is to enable countries to defend national economic interests not against the national interests of other countries but against sectional interests within their own and other countries. Thus GATT is formally an international agreement among countries, but functionally it is part of the domestic legal order of each country. It serves as a defense that governments can refer to in defending themselves against pressure groups.[10]

SUMMARY

Astute marketers use their awareness of the complexity of the legal environment to avoid situations that might result in conflict, misunderstanding, or outright violation of national laws. Clearly, there is no substitute for competent legal advice. This is especially true when operations extend internationally because it is less possible to rely on knowledge of law gained from personal experience.

DISCUSSION QUESTIONS

1. You are travelling on business in the Middle East. As you are leaving country X, the passport control officer at the airport tells you there will be a delay of 12 hours in the "processing" of your passport. You explain that your plane leaves in 30 minutes, and the official suggests that a contribution of $50.00 would probably speed things up. What would you do? Why?

2. You are negotiating with an agent who will represent you in a developing country that offers a huge potential market for your telecommunications product line. The agent explains that your traditional 10 percent commission is far short of what he will require to represent you adequately in this highly "competitive" market. He suggests that a commission of $33\frac{1}{3}$ percent would be adequate to cover his selling expenses. You have every reason to believe that this agent is capable of obtaining at least 50 percent of the potential market of $200 million for your products over the next five years. He tells you that he could obtain the market share objective of 50 percent with a $33\frac{1}{3}$ percent commission and a price increase that would include his commission. Would you agree to his request? Why? Why not?

3. Should a company operating internationally adhere to a single standard of conduct, or should it adapt to local conditions? Why?

---

[10]For an excellent description of the GATT Legal System, see Frieder Roessler, "The Scope, Limits and Function of the GATT Legal System," *World Economy,* September 1985, pp. 287–298.

BIBLIOGRAPHY

Books

JACOBY, NEIL H., PETER NEHMENKIS, AND RICHARD EELLS. *Bribery and Extortion in World Business*. New York: Macmillan, 1977.

MANGONE, GERARD J. *The Elements of International Law*. Homewood, Ill.: Dorsey Press, 1967.

Articles

BRADLEY, DAVID G. "Managing Against Expropriation." *Harvard Business Review*, July–August 1977.

GRAHAM, JOHN L. "The Foreign Corrupt Practices Act: A New Perspective." *Journal of International Business Studies*, Winter 1984, pp. 107–121.

HAWKINS, ROBERT B., NORMAN MINTZ, AND MICHAEL PROVISSIERO. "Government Takeovers of U.S. Foreign Affiliates." *Journal of International Business Studies*, Spring 1976.

KAIKATI, JACK, AND WAYNE A. LABEL. "The Foreign Antibribery Law: Friend or Foe?" *Columbia Journal of World Business*, Spring 1980, pp. 46–51.

ROESSLER, FRIEDER. "The Scope, Limits and Function of the GATT Legal System." *World Economy*, pp. 287–298.

WORLD ELECTRIC[1]

TO: Officers, General Managers and Managers at Department Level and Higher

At our recent Division General Managers meeting, I called attention once again to the need for all Company employees to comply with the standards of proper business practices set forth in Policy Number 40.0.

In summary, that policy provides that no employee of World Electric or of any of its subsidiaries will arrange or make payments in the nature of kickbacks or bribes, nor will the Company and its subsidiaries use intermediate parties such as sales representatives for such purposes.

The wisdom of following such a policy has been borne out in the recent headlines and by the investigations conducted by various governmental agencies.

As in the case of other fundamental Company policies, such as those governing employees conflicts of interest and compliance with the antitrust laws, each of you has a dual responsibility, first, to comply personally with the policy and, second, to promote full compliance by Company and subsidiary employees.

This latter responsibility entails a broad teaching function plus effective monitoring of the component for which you are responsible. In the execution of these functions it is, I believe, essential that your associates know that you stand unequivocally in support of the policy, and further that you are available to assist them in maintaining full compliance. We shall emphasize this subject in

---

[1]This case is based on the policy statement of a company that prefers to remain anonymous.

connection with annual strategic planning reviews.

Justin Balance
President

WORLD ELECTRIC
POLICY NUMBER 40.0

Subject: Business Ethics: Payments to Sales Representatives

Need for a Policy

It is the policy of World Electric Company to conduct its business affairs in strict compliance with all applicable laws. In particular, this policy requires a constant awareness and vigilance on the part of every employee to avoid violations of said laws arising out of a transfer directly or indirectly through commission payments or otherwise of anything of value (in the form of compensation, gift, contribution, or otherwise) to any employee, representative, person or organization in any way connected with or designated by any customer, private or governmental. Because of the severe penalties and severe consequences to the company that participation in any such practice could produce under the laws of the United States and foreign countries, it is deemed necessary to single out such activity for clear and detailed prohibition by way of a division policy.

Policy

1. No employee of the division or an affiliate company acting on behalf of the division shall offer, or commit to the making of, or make a transfer of anything of value (in the form of compensation, gift, contribution, or otherwise) to any employee, representative, person, or organization in any way connected with any customer, private or governmental. No such offer or commitment made by such employee will be honored, and the employee making the offer or commitment will be removed from his or her position and subject to further disciplinary action, including possible discharge.

2. No employee of the division or an affiliate company acting on behalf of the division shall make any offer or commitment for, or concur in the payment of, or pay any sales commission where the fact is made known to such employee that all, or some part, of such commission will be transferred to any employee, representative, person, or organization in any way connected with any customer, private or governmental. Such offer or commitment will not be honored, and any employee making such offer, commitment, or concurrence shall be removed from his or her position and subject to further disciplinary action, including possible discharge.

3. Where any employee is requested to make, authorize, or concur in any commitment or payment contrary to this policy, the employee shall promptly report to his or her manager full details of such request.

4. The provisions of paragraphs 1, 2, and 3 are not intended to apply to (a) reasonable business entertainment or to personal gifts of nominal value, provided that such business entertainment or nominal value gifts are of the type customary in the particular commercial environment and do not violate any applicable law or regulation, or (b) financial support or payments provided in accordance with company policy.

5. The contents of this policy shall be communicated to all applicable personnel by

operation, section, and/or unit managers in meetings conducted to explain and clarify the intent of this policy and to answer any questions that may arise. These managers shall advise the manager of financial operation by memorandum when their communications program is complete.

Responsibility and Counseling

Each manager is responsible for the compliance of his or her personnel with this policy.

The financial operation shall be responsible for auditing compliance by all employees with this policy. The division counsel will counsel on application and interpretation of this policy.

QUESTION

1. Do you agree with Justin Balance concerning the wisdom of policy number 40.0? Why? Why not?

Appendix: Guidelines for Multinational Enterprises: Organization for Economic Cooperation and Development (OECD)[1]

Member countries set forth the following guidelines for multinational enterprises with the understanding that member countries will fulfill their responsibilities to treat enterprises equitably and in accordance with international law and international agreements as well as contractual obligations to which they have subscribed:

General Policies

Enterprises should

1. Take fully into account established general policy objectives of the Member countries in which they operate;

2. In particular, give due consideration to those countries' aims and priorities with regard to economic and social progress, including industrial and regional development, the protection of the environment, the creation of employment opportunities, the promotion of innovation and the transfer of technology;

3. While observing their legal obligations concerning information, supply their entities with supplementary information the latter may need in order to meet requests by the authorities of the countries in which those entities are located for information relevant to the activities of those entities, taking into account legitimate requirements of business confidentiality;

[1] Source: Organization for Economic Cooperation and Development, "Declaration by the Governments of OECD Member Countries and Decisions of the OECD Council on Guidelines for Multinational Enterprises," 1976.

4. Favour close cooperation with the local community and business interests;
5. Allow their component entities freedom to develop their activities and to exploit their competitive advantage in domestic and foreign markets, consistent with the need for specialisation and sound commercial practice;
6. When filling responsible posts in each country of operation, take due account of individual qualifications without discrimination as to nationality, subject to particular national requirements in this respect;
7. Not render—and they should not be solicited or expected to render—any bribe or other improper benefit, direct or indirect, to any public servant or holder of public office;
8. Unless legally permissible, not make contributions to candidates for public office or to political parties or other political organisations;
9. Abstain from any improper involvement in local political activities.

Disclosure of Information

Enterprises should, having due regard to their nature and relative size in the economic context of their operations and to requirements of business confidentiality and to cost, publish in a form suited to improve public understanding a sufficient body of factual information on the structure, activities and policies of the enterprise as a whole, as a supplement, in so far as necessary for this purpose, to information to be disclosed under the national law of the individual countries in which they operate. To this end, they should publish within reasonable time limits, on a regular basis, but at least annually, financial statements and other pertinent information relating to the enterprise as a whole, comprising in particular:

i. The structure of the enterprise, showing the name and location of the parent company, its main affiliates, its percentage ownership, direct and indirect, in these affiliates, including shareholdings between them;
ii. The geographical areas[2] where operations are carried out and the principal activities carried on therein by the parent company and the main affiliates;
iii. The operating results and sales by geographical area and the sales in the major lines of business for the enterprise as a whole;
iv. Significant new capital investment by geographical area and, as far as practicable, by major lines of business for the enterprise as a whole;
v. A statement of the sources and uses of funds by the enterprise as a whole;
vi. The average number of employees in each geographical area;
vii. Research and development expenditure for the enterprise as a whole;
viii. The policies followed in respect of intra-group pricing;

---

[2] For the purposes of the guideline on disclosure of information the term "geographical area" means groups of countries or individual countries as each enterprise determines is appropriate in its particular circumstances. While no single method of grouping is appropriate for all enterprises or for all purposes, the factors to be considered by an enterprise would include the significance of operations carried out in individual countries or areas as well as the effects on its competitiveness, geographic proximity, economic affinity, similarities in business environments, and the nature, scale, and degree of interrelationship of the enterprises' operations in the various countries.

ix. The accounting policies, including those on consolidation, observed in compiling the published information.

Competition

Enterprises should, while conforming to official competition rules and established policies of the countries in which they operate,

1. Refrain from actions which would adversely affect competition in the relevant market by abusing a dominant position of market power, by means of, for example,
    a. Anti-competitive acquisitions,
    b. Predatory behavior toward competitors,
    c. Unreasonable refusal to deal,
    d. Anti-competitive abuse of industrial property rights,
    e. Discriminatory (i.e., unreasonably differentiated) pricing and using such pricing transactions between affiliated enterprises as a means of affecting adversely competition outside these enterprises;
2. Allow purchasers, distributors, and licensees freedom to resell, export, purchase, and develop their operations consistent with law, trade conditions, the need for specialisation, and sound commercial practice;
3. Refrain from participating in or otherwise purposely strengthening the restrictive effects of international or domestic cartels or restrictive agreements which adversely affect or eliminate competition and which are not generally or specifically accepted under applicable national or international legislation;
4. Be ready to consult and co-operate, including the provision of information, with competent authorities of countries whose interests are directly affected in regard to competition issues or investigations. Provision of informaton should be in accordance with safeguards normally applicable in this field.

Financing

Enterprises should, in managing the financial and commercial operations of their activities, and especially their liquid foreign assets and liabilities, take into consideration the established objectives of the countries in which they operate regarding balance of payments and credit policies.

Taxation

Enterprises should

1. Upon request of the taxation authorities of the countries in which they operate, provide, in accordance with the safeguards and relevant procedures of the national laws of these countries, the information necesssary to determine correctly the taxes to be assessed in connection with their operations in other countries:

2. Refrain from making use of the particular facilities available to them, such as transfer pricing which does not conform to an arm's length standard, for modifying in ways contrary to national laws the tax base on which members of the group are assessed.

Employment and Industrial Relations

Enterprises should, within the framework of law, regulations, and prevailing labour relations and employment practices, in each of the countries in which they operate,

1. Respect the right of their employees to be represented by trade unions and other bona fide organisations of employees, and engage in constructive negotiations, either individually or through employers' associations, with such employee organisations with a view to reaching agreements on employment conditions, which should include provisions for dealing with disputes arising over the interpretation of such agreements, and for ensuring mutually respected rights and responsibilities;

2. a. Provide such facilities to representatives of the employees as may be necessary to assist in the development of effective collective agreements,
   b. Provide to representatives of employees information which is needed for meaningful negotiations on conditions of employment;

3. Provide to representatives of employees where this accords with local law and practice, information which enables them to obtain a true and fair view of the performance of the entity or, where appropriate, the enterprise as a whole;

4. Observe standards of employment and industrial relations not less favourable than those observed by comparable employers in the host country;

5. In their operations, to the greatest extent practicable, utilise, train and prepare for upgrading members of the local labour force in co-operation with representatives of their employees and, where appropriate, the relevant governmental authorities;

6. In considering changes in their operations which would have major effects upon the livelihood of their employees, in particular in the case of the closure of an entity involving collective lay-offs or dismissals, provide reasonable notice of such changes to representatives of their employees, and where appropriate to the relevant governmental authorities, and co-operate with the employee representatives and appropriate governmental authorities so as to mitigate to the maximum extent practicable adverse effects;

7. Implement their employment policies including hiring, discharge, pay, promotion and training without discrimination unless selectivity in respect of employee characteristics is in furtherance of established governmental policies which specifically promote greater equality of employment opportunity;

8. In the context of bona fide negotiations[3] with representatives of employees on conditions of employment, or while employees are exercising a right to organise, not threaten to utilise a capacity to transfer the whole or part of an operating unit from the country concerned in order to influence unfairly those negotiations or to hinder the exercise of a right to organise;

9. Enable authorised representatives of their employees to conduct negotiations on collective bargaining or labour management relations issues with representatives of management who are authorised to take decisions on the matters under negotiation.

[3] Bona fide negotiations may include labour disputes as part of the process of negotiation. Whether or not labour disputes are so included will be determined by the law and prevailing employment practices of particular countries.

Science and Technology

Enterprises should

1. Endeavour to ensure that their activities fit satisfactorily into the scientific and technological policies and plans of the countries in which they operate, and contribute to the development of national scientific and technological capacities, including as far as appropriate the establishment and improvement in host countries of their capacity to innovate;
2. To the fullest extent practicable, adopt in the course of their business activities practices which permit the rapid diffusion of technologies with due regard to the protection of industrial and intellectual property rights;
3. When granting licenses for the use of industrial property rights or when otherwise transferring technology do so on reasonable terms and conditions.

QUESTIONS

1. Evaluate the OECD guidelines from the following perspectives:
   a. As the minister of finance of a developing country
   b. As the chief executive officer of a global manufacturing company
2. What, in your view, should be added to the guidelines? What should be deleted?

7

FINANCIAL RESOURCES AND DECISIONS

Money alone sets all the world in motion.

Maxim 656
Publilius Syrus
First Century B.C.

INTRODUCTION

Many aspects of global marketing, when compared to domestic marketing, are matters of degree rather than kind. For example, cultural differences exist among nations, but they also exist within nations. Indeed, it can be argued that the differences among people within countries or cultures are greater than the differences among countries and cultures.

Foreign exchange is another matter. When business is conducted within a single country, with domestic customers and suppliers in the domestic currency, there is no exchange risk. All prices, payments, receipts, assets, and liabilities are in the national currency. When a company operates outside the home country, it must deal in foreign exchange. This thrusts the company into the wonderful world of exchange risk which impacts financial resources and decisions, and even more importantly, pricing strategy. The global marketer is exposed to exchange risk whenever business involves payments or receipts in foreign currencies or the ownership of assets in foreign countries.

The basic function of money in global marketing is no different than its function in domestic marketing. Money facilitates the specialization of production and exchange of goods. Without money, international business would be reduced to a pure barter system. However, foreign exchange makes it possible to do business across the boundary of a national currency.

Customers, the ultimate judges of the success of a company's marketing effort, are seeking value. Value is a function of the relationship between the package of measurable and intangible benefits that customers get from a product and the price of the product. Price is, in part, a function of cost, and the foreign exchange rate is an important determinant of a company's cost position. Therefore, foreign exchange rates directly impact the quality and effectiveness of a company's marketing effort.

This chapter outlines the history and dimensions of the present international financial framework, a designation for the formal and official as well as the informal and private arrangements and agreements that make up the international financial system. The global marketer should be familiar with the international financial system and understand currency risk and exposure in order to formulate a global sourcing and financial strategy that will support the global marketing strategy. The driving force and energy of the successful company must be marketing because it is marketing that is focused upon creating value for customers. The real purpose of money is to apply it to achieve marketing objectives.

A BRIEF HISTORY OF THE INTERNATIONAL FINANCIAL SYSTEM

1944–1971

At Bretton Woods, New Hampshire, in 1944, the Allied powers met to create an international financial framework that would encourage and support postwar reconstruction and economic growth. To encourage trade and investment, the architects of the postwar system decided that it should provide for currency convertibility and orderly adjustment of currency values to maintain an ongoing equilibrium in exchange rate values. Lord Keynes, who participated in this conference, urged the adoption of the Bancor, his name for an international reserve asset to supplement foreign exchange and gold. His recommendations were not adopted at Bretton Woods; the world was not yet ready for "paper gold" as the international reserve asset was known.

The financial system which emerged from this conference included the International Bank for Reconstruction and Development (IBRD or the World Bank), which was chartered to promote reconstruction of war-torn countries and economic development, and the International Monetary Fund (IMF), which was chartered to oversee the management of the international financial system.

The main elements of the system, summarized in Table 7–1, were: fixed or pegged rates for all currencies; tight bands of fluctuation around the pegged rates; a dollar that was defined in terms of its gold value and which was exchangeable for gold; and controlled adjustment in fixed exchange values.

In 1971 the old system collapsed under the weight of U.S. balance of payments deficits. The world was accumulating dollars, and official reserves held by central

TABLE 7–1   The Old International Monetary System 1944–1971

1. Fixed or "pegged" exchange rates. All currencies were "pegged" to the U.S. dollar.
2. Country commitments to maintain fixed or "pegged" exchange within + or − 1 percent of the fixed rate.
3. Valuation of the U.S. dollar for official transactions at $35 = one troy ounce of gold. The U.S. government committed to exchange official dollars for gold at a price of $35.00 = one troy ounce of gold. "Official" dollars, that is dollars held by the central bank of IMF members, could be exchanged for gold at this price. Under this system, the dollar was literally better than gold because you could earn interest on dollar holdings *and* exchange dollars for gold at any time. If you held gold, you had storage costs, and of course, earned no interest.
4. Official reserves of gold, U.S. dollars, and the IMF position (the latter being a small technical element).
5. Control of adjustment in fixed exchange values by prescribed IMF procedures. In practice, there were infrequent, large devaluations under this system as opposed to smaller percentage adjustments through revaluations as well as devaluations.

banks around the world far exceeded the U.S. supply of gold. Because it was clear the United States could not honor its commitment to redeem official dollars for gold (the United States had some $40 billion of gold in official reserves and, under the old system, a liability of over $200 billion in official reserves to foreign holders of official dollars), President Nixon announced that the United States was unilaterally withdrawing its promise to redeem official dollars for gold. At this moment, the old system collapsed, and the world moved to a new system.

Today's System: Managed Dirty Float with SDRs

The system which emerged following the collapse of the old system is known as a managed dirty float with SDRs. What does this mean? The *dirty float* refers to the present system of floating or fluctuating exchange rates. Rates are "floating" or adjusting in the foreign exchange market subject to all of the forces of exchange supply and demand. *Dirty* refers to the fact that governments participate in the foreign exchange market in an effort to influence the exchange rates. *Managed* refers to the efforts of governments to influence exchange rates with the various instruments of fiscal and monetary policy.

Special Drawing Rights or *SDRs* were created by the IMF to supplement the dollar and gold as reserves. The SDR is an owned reserve asset, created by the IMF and allocated to member countries on the basis of a formula which takes into account factors such as share of gross world product and share of world trade. As of 1986, there were 21.4 billion SDRs (none had been allocated or created since January 1, 1981). Participants in the IMF with a balance of payments need can use SDRs to obtain currency from other participants designated by the fund. The fund also permits a variety of additional uses among participants including settlement of financial obligations, swaps, donations, and security for performance of financial obligations. In 1985–1986 there were 46 such transfers totaling SDR 111 million.

The International Monetary Fund has a total membership of 151 countries (as of 1986), which includes virtually every country in the world except the Union of Soviet Socialist Republics, most East European countries, Cuba, and North Korea. The fund oversees the operation of the international monetary system; exercises surveillance over the exchange rate policies of members; monitors developments in the field of international liquidity and manages the SDR system; provides temporary balance of payments assistance to members in external difficulties; and a variety of other functions including technical assistance designed to promote effective cooperation in international financial relations.

FOREIGN EXCHANGE

What is foreign exchange? Is the U.S. dollar foreign exchange? Is the French franc foreign exchange? The answer, of course, is that it depends. If the U.S. dollar is used in the United States it is not foreign exchange. If it is traded for another currency, it becomes, in that transaction, foreign exchange. Similarly, the French franc in France, or for that matter anywhere else in the world, is still a French franc. It becomes foreign exchange when it is traded for any other currency. Foreign exchange is a currency other than the national or home country currency that is purchased or sold in the foreign exchange market.

What is the foreign exchange market? All the people and institutions who buy and sell currency are the foreign exchange market. The *spot* market is for immediate delivery or, in the interbank market, for delivery within two business days of the transaction. The market for future delivery is called the *forward* market. The principal players in the foreign exchange market are the banks who create the so-called interbank market. Other players include the International Monetary Market (IMM) in Chicago, the London International Financial Futures Exchange (LIFFE), and the Philadelphia Stock Exchange (PSE) which is an options market for foreign exchange (an option is the right to buy or sell within a specific period of time or at a specific date).

The volume of trading in the foreign exchange market is enormous. In any two weeks, foreign exchange traders do as much business as importers and exporters of goods and services do in a year. According to estimates, turnover in the market is at least $200 billion a day, making it the world's largest financial market. The three major markets and their average daily turnover in late 1986 were: London ($90 billion), New York ($50 billion) and Tokyo ($48 billion). Each market has its own focus: London is $/L (30 percent), New York is $/DM (34 percent), and Tokyo is $/Y (82 percent).[1]

Thus the foreign exchange market consists literally of a buyer's and a seller's market where currencies are traded for both spot and future delivery on a continuous basis. As such, this market represents one example of a true market where prices

[1]"The Currency Carousel," *The Economist*, August 23, 1986, p. 64.

are based on the combination of forces of supply and demand that come into play at the moment of any transaction. A currency in this market is worth what people are willing to pay for it, or, put another way, it is worth what people are prepared to sell it for.

Foreign Exchange Market Dynamics

Figure 7–1 shows a supply curve of U.S. dollars and two demand schedules for dollars by holders of German deutsche marks. In the example, demand moves from D_1 to D_2, with a resultant increase in the price of dollars from 2.5 to 5.0 deutsche marks. In this example, we assume that the supply of dollars is constant and that for various reasons the demand for dollars by holders of deutsche marks increases from quantity C to quantity E. Such an increase in demand could result from a multiplicity of factors, for example, a major shift in German consumer automobile preferences from domestic and other foreign cars to cars imported from the United States, or a desire on the part of German investors to shift their assets and wealth from Germany to the United States because of concerns about the political stability and future security of investments in Germany, or a response by German investors

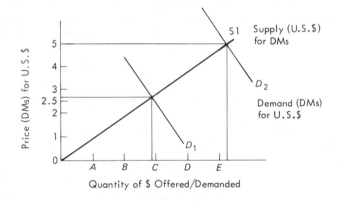

C = Supply and demand for U.S. \$

D_1 = 2.5 DMs = \$1.00
D_2 = 5.0 DMs = \$1.00

Exchange Risks and Gains in Foreign Transaction

Foreign Exchange Rates	\$1M Contract U.S. Seller Receives	Germany Buyer Pays	DM 4M Contract U.S. Seller Receives	Germany Buyer Pays
DM5 = \$1	\$1M	DM5	\$0.8M	DM4
DM4 = 1	1M	DM4	1.0M	DM4
DM3 = 1	1M	DM3	1.33M	DM4
DM2 = 1	1M	DM2	2.0M	DM4

FIGURE 7–1   The Foreign Exchange Market (DM = deutsche marks)

to high interest rates in the United States, or a belief by holders of DMs that the dollar is strong and the DM is weak, or a host of other factors. If the net effect of such factors is an increase in demand for dollars, all other things being equal, the price of the dollar will rise. This is known as a revaluation of the dollar and a devaluation of the deutsche mark.

The price of one currency in any other currency is the result of the forces of supply and demand expressed in the foreign exchange market. The foreign exchange market itself consists of traders operating principally by telephone engaging in transactions to meet customer requirements with their counterparts in banks and foreign exchange trading houses around the world. These foreign exchange traders are operating during normal business hours in every world time zone, with the result that foreign exchange trading activity is being conducted on a 24-hour basis every day of the year. When the traders on one side of the world conclude their work at the end of their working day, the basis of prices for their trading on the following working day will be established on the other side of the world while they are sleeping.

The purchases and sales in the foreign exchange market represent supply and demand of each of the world's traded currencies deriving from actual trade in goods and services, as well as short- and long-term capital flows and speculative purchases and sales. To the extent that a country sells more than it buys, there will be a greater demand for its currency and a tendency for it to appreciate in value. If the foreign exchange market were influenced only by purchases and sales to support actual trade in goods and services, it would be a rather simple matter to forecast foreign exchange rates. Unfortunately, there are many other forces and motives for buying and selling currencies. Short- and long-term capital flows and speculative purchases and sales are a major source of supply and demand for foreign exchange. Short-term capital is sensitive to interest rates, long-term capital to return expectations, and both are sensitive to perceptions of risk.

Governments intervene regularly in the foreign exchange market to either support or depress the price of their own or other currencies. Government intervention is normally aimed at dampening the fluctuations in foreign exchange rates or attempting to influence over the short and medium term the actual exchange rate. For example, many governments are reluctant to see the value of their currency appreciate because their exporters fear the effects that rising exchange value will have on their price competitiveness in foreign markets. In response to this basic domestic pressure, governments engage in extensive trading to stem the rise in their own currency value.

While government efforts in the long run will not prevail against fundamental economic or political factors, they can have a definite effect on exchange values in the short and medium run.

Forecasting Foreign Exchange Rates

Foreign exchange rate forecasting is one of the most hazardous tasks imaginable. The reason for the difficulty in forecasting foreign exchange rates is simple: There are a multitude of factors and forces which determine rates, and many of these factors and forces are not quantifiable. *Any* forecast of exchange rates is necessarily a combination of economic analysis and judgment.

PURCHASING POWER PARITY. One of the most important and durable of all the economic fundamentals that must be considered in forecasting foreign exchange rates is purchasing power parity (PPP). This venerable concept holds that from an equilibrium exchange rate, a change in the relationship between domestic and foreign price levels will require an adjustment in the currency exchange rate to offset the price level difference. In plain English, PPP says that one unit of a currency should buy the same amount of goods and services as it bought in a base or "equilibrium" period, regardless of differential rates of inflation.

The lower a contry's rate of inflation as compared to the world's, the greater will be the purchasing power parity effect. If prices in local currency rise faster or more slowly than prices in the rest of the world, an equal adjustment of the exchange value of the currency in the opposite direction will restore equilibrium to relative price levels. For example, if a Mercedes 190 costs DM 40,000 and the U.S. dollar exchange rate is DM2 = $US 1, the Mercedes 190 will cost $US 20,000. If there is a zero rate of inflation in Germany and a 20 percent rate of inflation in the United States, an exchange rate of DM 1.6666 = US$ 2 would restore equilibrium because the Mercedes 190 at this exchange rate would cost $US 24,000 or $US 20,000 × 120 percent (the U.S. rate of inflation). Since the U.S. money supply would have expanded by 20 percent, the new exchange value of the DM would insure that 2.4 units of the depreciated dollar could buy the same amount of goods that 2 units of the preinflationary dollar could purchase.

For example, assume that the rate of exchange between Germany and the United States is DM 2 = US$ 1. Assume that the rate of inflation in the U.S. is 10 percent per annum, and that the rate of inflation in Germany is zero. According to PPP, the exchange rate after one year (*t* + 1) would be DM 1.8 = US$ 1 or DM 2 = US$ 1.10. To a German, what could be purchased in the U.S. at *t* for DM 2 would cost DM 2.2 *if* there were no adjustment in the exchange rate. An appreciation of the DM in the foreign exchange market by 10 percent would exactly offset the U.S. 10 percent rate of inflation so that the U.S. inflation would have no effect on the purchasing power of the DM in the U.S. Similarly, in *t* an American could purchase DM 2 worth of goods in Germany for U.S. $1.00. One year later, at *t* + 1, DM2 would cost an American or a holder of dollars US$ 1.10. The German would receive a dollar amount which would exactly offset the differential or different inflation rate in the two countries. This is PPP. The formula to calculate the PPP impact on an exchange rate is

$$S_{t+1} + (S_t)\left(\frac{1 + i_h}{1 + i_r}\right)$$

where

S = the spot exchange rate quoted in the number of units of the home currency equal to one unit of the foreign currency

i_h = the inflation rate in the home country

i_r = the inflation rate in the foreign country

t = the base period or the present time

$t + 1$ = the future time period as defined

In the example above, the calculation of the exchange rate after one year would be:

$$St_1 = 0.5\frac{(1.1)}{(1.0)}$$
$$= 0.5(1.1)$$
$$St_1 = 0.55$$

or,   U.S. \$0.55 = $DM1$
or,   U.S. \$1.10 = $DM2$

If the only foreign exchange transactions were concluded solely to provide exchange for purchases of goods and services (i.e., the current account of the balance of payments) and if rates of inflation were easily predictable, PPP would be a reliable and useful predictor of the foreign exchange rate. To forecast exchange rates, one would need only to forecast differential rates of price inflation. Unfortunately, the current account of the balance of payments is not the sole measure of demand and supply of foreign exchange, and rates of inflation are not easy to predict.

This was illustrated during the 1980–85 period when in spite of growing deficits on the current account of the U.S. balance of payments, the U.S. dollar continued to soar in value in foreign exchange markets. This was contrary to PPP theory, and foreign exchange traders who based their purchases on PPP suffered major losses. During this period, it was a case of the dog's tail (capital movements) wagging the dog (current account of the balance of payments). According to PPP, the dog is the current account of the balance of payments, and the capital account is the tail.

FACTORS INFLUENCING CURRENCY VALUE IN FOREIGN EXCHANGE MARKETS.   There are a host of factors that impact the foreign exchange rate of currency. They include, in addition to PPP, economic factors related to a country's fiscal, monetary, and economic policies. Economic policy and performance that create a rate of economic growth that is higher than the world average will over the long run increase the exchange value of a country's currency. The best examples of currencies reflecting this fact are the Japanese yen and the West German deutsche mark. Although it is not yet apparent, this fundamental economic law will be reflected in the exchange value of the Korean won, the Taiwan dollar, and the currency of any other country that is growing in real terms faster than the world's average rate of growth.

Another important economic factor is interest rates as compared to world averages. If the *real* rate of interest in a country (real interest is the nominal rate of interest minus the rate of inflation) is higher than the interest rate in comparable countries, this will attract capital, create demand for the country's currency, and will put upward pressure on the currency value in the foreign exchange market.

Another economic factor is the importance of a currency in the world financial system. A "key" currency, such as the U.S. dollar, is less subject to economic "laws," such as purchasing power parity, because it is held by individuals, companies, and countries for many purposes. The willingness to hold the dollar creates a demand source that impacts its exchange market value.

Political factors are important determinants of currency value. These include the country's political situation, especially the philosophy of the party in power and the proximity of elections.

In the short run, perhaps the single most important factor impacting currency value are expectative or psychological factors, or what analysts and traders *believe* is going to happen. This is a psychological/speculative factor because it really amounts to what analysts and traders believe other analysts and traders believe is going to happen. This is why most traders of foreign exchange do not pay a great deal of attention to the so-called fundamentals. They believe that all information about the value of a commodity can be read on the screen or tape.

Notwithstanding the short-run factors and the attitudes of traders that influence exchange rates, the fundamentals cannot be avoided. A country's ability to purchase foreign goods and services is based on its ability to earn foreign exchange. If that ability is limited, its ability to maintain its exchange value will be limited. This is illustrated in Table 7–2, which is a memorandum the Central Bank of Nigeria circulated to creditors outlining its plan to deal with the reduction of foreign exchange available to service overseas debts as a result of the severe decline in oil revenue.

Table 7–3 is a partial list of factors that impact foreign exchange rates.

INDEX MEASURES OF EXCHANGE VALUE. One of the issues in analyzing a country's competitive position is the actual adjustment of the exchange value of a country's currency. In late 1986, according to the IMF, the dollar's trade-weighted index (an index which weights currencies based upon their share of world trade) dropped 30 percent from its peak in February 1985, with a fall of 40 percent against the yen and the deutsche mark. However, the IMF index overstated the dollar's fall because it included only the currencies of 17 advanced countries and almost half of the U.S. trade deficit was with countries whose currencies remained stable or even fell against the dollar. The Manufacturers Hanover index, which includes the 17

TABLE 7–2   Central Bank of Nigeria: US Dollar Promissory Notes ("Notes") issued or to be issued pursuant to the Circular dated 18th April, 1984

Foreign exchange revenues of Nigeria have fallen sharply following the steep decline in world oil prices in 1986. Whereas in 1984 and 1985 oil revenues amounted to some U.S.$11.9 billion and U.S.$12.5 billion respectively, estimated receipts in 1986 are not expected to exceed U.S.$6.5 billion. Nigeria's financing requirements remain large, notwithstanding a massive domestic adjustment effort, involving severe cutbacks in government expenditure and reductions in imports. The enforced reduction in foreign exchange available to service overseas debts has compelled Nigeria to enter into discussions with its international creditors to seek a rationalisation of its external debt on a comprehensive and realistic basis. The object on all sides is to achieve an enduring solution which will enable Nigeria henceforward to meet all its obligations within the framework of the Structural Adjustment Programme announced by the President on 26th June, 1986.

Substantial progress has been made in negotiations entered into concurrently with the World Bank, the International Monetary Fund, the export credit agencies of Nigeria's trading partners and international commercial banks in connection with medium and long term debt and confirmed letters of credit.

Pursuant to procedures set out in the Circular dated 18th April, 1984, the Central Bank has verified and accepted exporter claims totalling approximately U.S.$1.95 billion, of which approximately U.S.$1.5 billion relates to uninsured claims for which Notes have been issued. A further substantial volume of claims has been reconciled by Chase Manhattan Bank and is in process of verification by the Central Bank. **It remains the intention of the Central Bank to complete the verification of all creditor claims reconciled by Chase Manhattan Bank so that all qualifying creditors will receive Notes as soon as possible.**

As an integral part of the comprehensive restructuring of its external debt outlined above, the Central Bank wishes to place before Noteholders proposals which would have the effect of deferring repayment of principal under the Notes according to an agreed schedule. For this purpose the Central Bank, acting in conjunction with the Trustee, proposes to convene a meeting of Noteholders in London. Formal notice of the meeting, including the detailed proposals, will be given to Noteholders in early November.

In the light of the foregoing, the Central Bank is not in a position to make the payment of principal due to Noteholders on 6th October, 1986. In all the circumstances Noteholders are asked to exercise their forebearance in respect of such non-payment.

Nigeria greatly appreciates the continued understanding and cooperation shown by all her creditors.

Source: Central Bank of Nigeria; Lagos, September 29, 1986.

biggest trading partners of the United States (eight of which are developing countries in Asia and Latin America), dropped only 2 percent for the same period. The dollar's adjustment for this period is shown in Figure 7–2.

FINANCIAL RESOURCES AND THE EXPANDED ROLE OF THE CHIEF FINANCIAL OFFICER (CFO)

Technology and the world wide trends of deregulation, privatization, and globalization or unification of financial markets and services have created an entirely new

TABLE 7–3   **Factors Influencing Currency Value in Foreign Exchange Markets**

ECONOMIC

1. Balance of Payments:
   a. Current account. Trade surplus or deficit for goods, services, investment income and payments, and so on.
   b. Capital account. Surplus or deficit of demand for short- and long-term financial instruments.
2. Nominal and real interest rates.
3. Domestic inflation.
4. Monetary and fiscal policies.
5. Estimate of international competitiveness, present and future.
6. Foreign exchange reserves.
7. Attractiveness of country currency and assets, both financial and real.
8. Government controls and incentives.
9. Importance of currency in world finance and trade.

POLITICAL FACTORS

10. Philosophies of political party and leaders.
11. Proximity of elections or change in leadership.

EXPECTATIVE OR PSYCHOLOGICAL FACTORS

12. Expectations and opinions of analysts, traders, bankers, economists, and businesspeople.
13. Forward exchange market prices.

THE BOTTOM LINE

The bottom line for all of the above factors is that foreign exchange rates are determined by transactions which reflect the sum total of all of the motives, reasons, and beliefs behind currency supply and demand. The intersection of the supply and the demand *is* the rate.

financial environment. The old boundaries among bankers, brokers, underwriters, and investment bankers have broken down. The comfortable cartel arrangements that fixed commissions for services have collapsed in one country after another. Today, financial services are provided by a new breed of firm whose success is based upon performance, ability, and willingness to take risks.

The job of the chief financial officer (CFO) of a company has never been more complex. Today, credit and equity markets are global. Whereas companies used to raise capital in the country of operation, a company today might float a Euro-yen swap to finance operations in many countries. For example, in early 1986, American Express raised 20 billion yen which were then swapped into $109 million dollars. The dollars were then swapped into debt securities of eight different currencies. In 1985, Avon issued a Euro-yen bond (a Eurobond denominated in yen) that saved

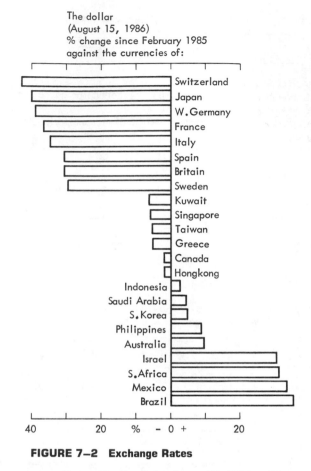

The dollar
(August 15, 1986)
% change since February 1985
against the currencies of:

FIGURE 7–2   Exchange Rates

Source: *The Economist,* August 23, 1986, p. 82.

about a half percentage point in interest and raised 26 billion yen which was worth about $100 million dollars. This deal also involved a currency swap so that Avon would repay in dollars.[2]

Never before in history have financial resources techniques and instruments been more plentiful and available to support and sustain creative marketing strategies. The robust and creative financial markets of the world have demonstrated that there is virtually an infinite supply of financial resources in the world to support the creative business strategy. The core of a business strategy is the marketing strategy. If you have a sound marketing plan, you or your company can get the financial resources you need to implement the plan.

[2]"Finance Officers' Wider Role," *The New York Times,* October 20, 1986, p. D1 ff.

SUMMARY

The international financial system is continually evolving. Today's system is based on floating exchange rates where exchange values are established by the market forces of supply and demand. The factors that determine the ultimate levels of supply and demand for exchange are numerous, interrelated, and in a word, complex. Forecasting foreign exchange value is extremely difficult in the present financial environment. Companies who do not wish to expose themselves to exchange risk can in effect sell off the risk by purchasing forward contracts which lock in a known contractual rate of exchange.

The financial resources of the world are truly an example of the principle of infinite supply. Any company that has a sound marketing strategy and plan should be able to obtain the financial resources needed to implement them.

DISCUSSION QUESTIONS

1. You are exporting to Country X. Assume that you have an operating profit on sales of 30 percent. If the exchange rate for Country X's currency appreciates, what, if anything, would you do to your export prices in your home currency? If you do nothing, your prices will rise in Country X. If you reduce your prices by the percentage amount of the devaluation of your currency, your prices in Country X will remain unchanged. Prepare a brief memo outlining your position and the assumptions underlying your position.
2. What causes foreign exchange rates to change? Are exchange rates predictable? Why? Why not?
3. If over the course of a year prices rise 100 percent in Argentina and 1 percent in Germany, what would you expect to happen to the value of the DM and the Astral, all other things being equal?
4. In your own words, what does Purchasing Power Parity mean?

BIBLIOGRAPHY

Books

RODRIGUEZ, RITA M., AND E. EUGENE CARTER. *International Financial Management,* 3rd. Ed. Englewood Cliffs, N.J.: Prentice-Hall, Inc., 1984.

Articles

LESSARD, DONALD. "Finance and Global Competition." Unpublished working paper prepared for Colloquium on Competition in Global Industries, Harvard Business School, Boston, Mass., April 1984.

8

MARKETING INFORMATION SYSTEMS AND RESEARCH

Knowledge is of two kinds. We know a subject ourselves, or we know where we can find information upon it.

Samuel Johnson, 1709–1784
from Boswell, Life of Johnson, 1763

INTRODUCTION

Information, or useful data, is the raw material of executive action. The global marketer is faced with a dual problem in acquiring the information needed for decision making. In the advanced countries the amount of information available far exceeds the absorptive capacity of an individual or an organization. The problem is superabundance, not scarcity. While advanced countries all over the world are enduring an information explosion, there is relatively little information available on the marketing characteristics of less developed countries. Thus the global marketer is faced with the problem of information abundance and information scarcity. The global marketer must know where to go to obtain information, the subject areas that should be covered, and the different ways that information can be acquired. The process of information acquisition is known as *scanning*. The section that follows presents a scanning model for multinational marketing. The chapter continues with an outline of how to conduct global marketing research.

ELEMENTS OF A GLOBAL INFORMATION SYSTEM

Information Subject Agenda

A subject agenda, or list of subjects for which information is desired, is a basic element of a global marketing information system. Because each company's subject agenda should be developed and tailored to the specific needs and objectives of the company, it is not possible to suggest an ideal or standard agenda. Therefore any framework such as that proposed in Table 8–1 is only a starting point in the construction of a specific agenda for any particular organization.

The general framework suggested in Table 8–1 consists of 6 broad information areas with 31 information categories. The framework satisfies two essential criteria. First, it is exhaustive: It accepts all the subject areas of information encountered by a company with global operations. Second, the categories in the framework are mutually exclusive: Any kind of information encompassed by the framework can be correctly placed in one and only one category.

Prescriptive information covers the rules for action in the foreign market. This category incorporates information from guidelines to regulations, rulings, and laws by public and private groups and authorities.

Scanning Modes: Surveillance and Search

Once the subject agenda has been determined, the next step in formulating a systematic information-gathering system in the organization is the actual collection of information. There are two important modes or orientations in information collection or scanning: surveillance and search.

In *surveillance* the scanner is oriented toward acquiring relevant information that is contained in messages that cross his or her scanning attention field. In *search* the scanner is deliberately seeking information, either informally or by means of an organized research project. The two orientations and their components are briefly described in Table 8–2.

The significance of determining scanning mode is the measure it offers (1) of the extent that a scanner actively seeks out information, as contrasted to the more passive acquisition of information, and (2) of the scanner's attention state at the time of acquiring information.

Table 8–3 shows that the bulk of information acquired by headquarters' executives of major U.S. multinational firms is gained through surveillance as opposed to search (73 percent versus 27 percent). However, viewing (general exposure), the least oriented of the surveillance modes, generates only 13 percent of important external information acquired, where monitoring generates 60 percent.[1]

This paucity of information generated by viewing is the result of two factors. One is the extent to which executives are exposed to information that is not included in a clearly defined subject agenda. The other is their receptiveness to information outside of this agenda. Both factors operate to limit the relative importance of viewing as a scanning mode. Every executive limits his or her exposure to information that will not have a high probability of being relevant to the job or company. This is a rational and necessary response to the basic human mental limitations. A person

[1] Warren J. Keegan. "Scanning the International Business Environment: A Study of the Information Acquisition Process," doctoral dissertation, Harvard Business School, 1967.

TABLE 8—1 Thirty-One Categories for a Global Business Intelligence System

CATEGORY	COVERAGE
I. Market Information	
1. Market Potential	Information indicating potential demand for products, including the status and prospects of existing company products in existing markets.
2. Consumer/customer attitudes and behavior	Information and attitudes, behavior, and needs of consumers and customers of existing and potential company products. Also included in this category are attitudes of investors toward a company's investment merit.
3. Channels of distribution	Availability, effectiveness, attitudes, and preferences of channel agents.
4. Communications media	Media availability, effectiveness, and cost.
5. Market sources	Availability, quality, and cost.
6. New products	Nontechnical information concerning new products for a company (this includes products that are already marketed by other companies).
II. Competitive Information	
7. Competitive business strategy and plans	Goals, objectives. Definition of business; the "design" and rationale of the company.
8. Competitive functional strategies, plans, and programs	Marketing: Target markets, product, price, place, promotion. Strategy and plan; finance, manufacturing, R&D, and human resource strategy, plans, and programs.
9. Competitive operations	Detailed intelligence on competitor operations. Production, shipments, employee transfers, morale, etc.
III. Foreign Exchange	
10. Balance of payments.	Government reports.
11. Nominal and real interest rates.	Expert estimation.
12. Inflation rate compared to weighted trading partner average.	PPP theory.
13. Estimate of international competitiveness.	Expert judgment.
14. Attractiveness of country currency and assets to global investors.	Currency demand.
15. Government policy re: country competitiveness.	Expert assessment.
16. Country monetary and fiscal policy.	Expert assessment.
17. Spot and forward market activity.	Market reports.
18. Expectations and opinions of analysts, traders, bankers, economists, business people.	General assessment.
IV. Prescriptive Information	
19. Foreign taxes	Information concerning decisions, intentions, and attitudes of foreign authorities regarding taxes upon earnings, dividends, and interest.
20. Other foreign prescriptions and laws	All information concerning local, regional, or international authority guidelines, rulings, laws, decrees other than foreign exchange and tax matters affecting the operations, assets, or investments of a company.
21. Home country prescriptions	Home country incentives, controls, regulations, restraints, etc., affecting a company.

TABLE 8–1 (continued)

CATEGORY	COVERAGE
V. Resource Information	
22. Human resources	Availability of individuals and groups, employment candidates, sources, strikes, etc.
23. Money	Availability and cost of money for company uses.
24. Raw material	Availability and cost.
25. Acquisitions and mergers	Leads or other information concerning potential acquisitions, mergers, or joint ventures.
VI. General Conditions	
26. Economic factors	Macroeconomic information dealing with broad factors, such as capital movements, rates of growth, economic structure, and economic geography.
27. Social factors	Social structure of society, customs, attitudes, and preferences.
28. Political factors	"Investment climate," meaning of elections, political change.
29. Scientific technological factors	Major developments and trends.
30. Management and administrative practices	Management and administrative practices and procedures concerning such matters as employee compensation, report procedure.
31. Other information	Information not assignable to another category.

TABLE 8–2 Scanning Modes

MODES	COVERAGE
Surveillance Orientation	
Viewing	General exposure to external information where the viewer has no specific purpose in mind other than exploration.
Monitoring	Focused attention, not involving active search, to a clearly defined area or type of external information.
Search Orientation	
Investigation	A relatively limited and informal seeking out of specific information
Research	A formally organized effort to acquire specific information usually for a specific purpose.

TABLE 8–3 Relative Importance of Scanning Modes in Acquiring Global Information

	Percent of Information Acquired	
Surveillance		73
Viewing	13	
Monitoring	60	
Search		27
Investigation	23	
Research	4	
Total		100

TABLE 8—4   Sources of Information (in percent)

LOCATION OF SOURCES		TYPES OF SOURCES	
Inside organization	34%	People	67%
Outside organization	66	Documentary	27
		Physical phenomena	6

can handle only a minute fraction of the data available to him or her. Because exposure absorbs limited mental resources, exposure must be selective.

Nevertheless, receptiveness by the organization as a whole to information not explicitly recognized as important is vital. The effective scanning system must ensure that the organization is viewing areas where developments that could be important to the company might occur. This may require the creation of a fulltime scanning unit that would have explicit responsibility for acquiring and disseminating information on subjects of importance to the organization.

SOURCES OF INFORMATION

Human Sources

As can be seen in Table 8–4, people are the most important source of information for headquarters executives of global companies.[2] The most important human source of external information is company executives based abroad in company subsidiaries, affiliates, and branches. The importance of executives abroad as a source of information about the world environment is one of the most striking features of the modern global corporation. The general view of headquarters executives is that company executives overseas are the people who know best what is going on in their areas. Typical comments of headquarters executives are

> Our principal sources are internal. We have a very well informed and able overseas establishment. The local people have a double advantage. They know the local scene and they know our business. Therefore, they are an excellent source. They know what we are interested in learning, and because of their local knowledge they are able to effectively cover available information from all sources.

The presence of an information network abroad in the form of company people is a major strength of the global company. It may also be a weakness in the scanning posture of a company that has only partially extended the limits of its geographical operations because inside sources abroad tend to scan only information about their own countries or region. Although there may be more attractive opportunities outside exisiting areas of operation, the chances of their being noticed by inside sources in

[2]Ibid.

TABLE 8–5 Comparison of Personal and Impersonal Human Sources (in percent)

SOURCE RELATIONSHIP	INSIDE SOURCES	OUTSIDE SOURCES	ALL HUMAN SOURCES
Personal sources	97%	80%	86%
Impersonal sources	3	20	14
Total	100%	100%	100%
Number of instances	$\Delta = 33$	$N = 60$	$N = 93$

a domestic company are very low because the horizons of domestic executives tend to end at national borders. In his book on foreign trade, Kindleberger identifies the impact of horizons upon trade patterns:

> A man may be perfectly rational, but only within a limited horizon. As a consumer, he will normally restrict his expenditures to those goods offered to him through customary channels. As a producer, he will sell his goods typically in a given ambit. Over his horizon there may be brilliant opportunities to improve his welfare as a consumer or his income as a producer, but unless he is made aware of them, they will avail him nothing.[3]

Distributors, consumers, customers, suppliers, and government officials are also important information sources. Information from these sources is largely obtained by country operating personnel as opposed to headquarters' staff. Other sources are friends, acquaintances, professional colleagues, "free-lance" university consultants, and candidates for employment, particularly if they have worked for competitors. As shown in Table 8–5, personal human sources of information far exceed impersonal sources in importance.[4] Eighty-six percent of the human sources utilized by respondents are personal. Interestingly, when human sources inside and outside the company are compared, 97 percent of sources inside the company are personal. The comparison suggests that lack of acquaintanceship is a barrier to the flow of information in an organization, thus underlining the importance of travel and contact.

Significantly, three-quarters of the information acquired from human sources is gained in face-to-face conversation. Why is face-to-face communication so important? There are many factors involved. Some information is too sensitive to transmit in any other way. Political information from government sources, for example, could be damaging to the source if it were known that the source was transmitting certain information. In such cases word of mouth is the most secure way of transmitting information. Information that includes estimates of future developments or even appraisals of the significance of current happenings is often considered too uncertain to commit to writing. One executive in commenting upon this point said

[3]Charles P. Kindleberger, *Foreign Trade and the National Economy* (New Haven, Conn.: Yale University Press, 1962), p. 16.

[4]*Personal* is defined as either a friend or an acquaintance and *impersonal* as a person not known.

People are reluctant to commit themselves in writing to highly "iffy" things. They are not cowards or overly cautious; they simply know that you are bound to be wrong in trying to predict the future, and they prefer to not have their names associated with documents that will someday look foolish.

Other information does not have to be passed on immediately to be of value. For example, a division president said

Information of relevance to my job [strategic planning] is not the kind of information which must be received immediately. Timeliness is not essential; what is more important is that I eventually get the information.

The great importance of face-to-face communication lies in the dynamics of personal interaction. Personal contact provides an occasion for executives to get together for a long enough time to permit communication in some depth. Face-to-face discussion also exposes highly significant forms of communication, such as the tone of voice, the expression of a person's eyes, movements, and many other forms of communication that cannot be expressed in writing. One executive expressed the value of face-to-face contact in these terms:

If you really want to find out about an area, you must see people personally. There is no comparison between written reports and actually sitting down with a man and talking. A personal meeting is worth four thousand written reports.

The greatest technological contribution to face-to-face communication of information has been the jet aircraft, which has made it possible for executives in a far-flung organization to maintain personal contact with one another. A measure of the importance of travel in international operations is provided by the size of travel budgets. The average travel budget of international executives (area directors, department heads, and key executives) is in excess of $30,000 per annum. It is not unusual to find executives whose travel budgets exceed $75,000 per annum.

Documentary Sources

Of all the changes in recent years affecting the availability of information, perhaps none is more apparent than the outpouring of documentary information. The outpouring has created a major problem, the so-called "information explosion." The problem is particularly acute for international marketers who must be informed about numerous national markets.

Although executives are overwhelmed with documentary information, only a handful of companies employ a formal system for monitoring documentary information. The absence of formal monitoring systems has resulted in a considerable amount of duplication. A typical form of duplication is the common practice of an entire management group reading one publication covering a particular subject area when several excellent publications covering the same area are available.

The best way to identify unnecessary duplication is to carry out an audit of reading activity by asking each person involved to list the publications he or she reads regularly. A consolidation of the lists will reveal the reading attention of the group. In a surprisingly large number of instances, the reading attention of the group will be limited to a handful of publications to the exclusion of other publications of considerable merit. An elaboration of this procedure could involve consultation with experts outside the company regarding the availability and quality of publications in relevant fields.

External documentary sources are a valuable source of information for part of every company's international information requirement, and they are also a particularly valuable source of information for the student who typically does not have the human and written sources available to a long-time professional working in the field.

Perception Sources

Direct perception is the source of a very limited proportion of the information acquired by executives as measured by message volume. However, it provides a vital background for the information that comes from human and documentary sources. There are three types of direct perception. One type is information easily available from other sources, but it requires sensory perception of the actual phenomena to register the information in the respondent's mind. An example is the case of the executive who realized the distance between Australia and New Zealand on a flight that took three hours.

Another type of direct perception is information not readily available from alternative sources. An example is the information that a company is erecting a plant in a country capable of producing a competitive product. Local executives in the country drove by the new plant every day on their way to their offices but were unaware of the product X potential of the plant under construction. The company erecting the plant had announced that it was for product Y, and local executives accepted this announcement. The headquarters executive realized immediately as he was being driven by the plant that it was potentially capable of producing product X. He possessed technical knowledge that enabled him to perceive information in a physical object (the plant) that his local executives were unable to perceive.

These two types of direct perception account for the messages obtained from this source. The third type of direct perception is perhaps the most important. This is the background information that one gets from observing a situation. It is one thing to receive a report or hear a description of, say, a new type of retail outlet such as the European *hypermarché*. It is another thing actually to visit such an outlet. Of course, in multinational marketing, direct perception requires travel. Thus the independent variable in the use of this source is travel. Travel should be seen not only as a tool for management control of existing operations but also as a vital and indispensable tool in information scanning.

TABLE 8–6   Global Marketing Information: Perception and Media

PERCEPTION	MEDIA/TECHNOLOGY
Sensation (five senses)	*Electronic*
Sight	Telephone
Reading text	Telex
Viewing images	Facsimile (Fax)
Direct perception	Electronic mail
Hearing	Television
Smell	Radio
Taste	Cable
Touch	*Print*
	Letters
Intuition (sixth sense)	Reports/memos
Holistic perception	Magazines
	Newspapers
	Books
	Transportation
	Land
	Sea
	Air

Information Perception and Media

The medium is the channel through which information is transmitted. Any marketing information system is based on three basic media: the human voice for transmitting words and numbers, printed words and numbers, and direct perception through the senses of sight, hearing, smell, taste, and touch. Each of these basic information system media has been extended in recent years by important innovations in electronic and travel technologies. Of particular importance to the marketing information system have been the impressive developments in telephone, telex, satellite communication networks for voice and data, and transportation via jet aircraft. The basic media of a global marketing information system are summarized in Table 8–6.

The telephone, telex, and facsimile are important media for the transmission of information internationally: In one study 67 percent of all important international information acquired by international executives was from human sources, and 81 percent of this information was transmitted by voice.[5] Moreover, of the human information transmitted by voice, 94 percent was communicated in face-to-face conversation. This finding underlines the importance of the jet aircraft as a communications device because a large proportion of the important information transmitted in international marketing is accomplished by people who have come together in a face-to-face situation as a result of the high-speed travel of jet aircraft.

[5] Keegan, "Scanning the International Business Environment."

MARKETING RESEARCH

Information is a critical ingredient in formulating and implementing a successful marketing strategy. Marketing research is the gathering of information in the search scanning mode. There are two modes of search:

Investigation—a relatively limited and informal seeking out of specific information
Research—a formally organized effort to acquire specific information for a specific purpose

There are two ways to conduct marketing research. One is to design and implement a study with in-house staff. The other is to use an outside firm specializing in international marketing research. Regardless of whether the study is conducted in or out of house, there are several factors and issues that must be addressed.

Comparability of International Data

International statistics are subject to more than the usual number of caveats and qualifications concerning comparability. An absence of standard data-gathering techniques is the basis for some of the lack of comparability in international statistics. In Germany, for example, consumer expenditures are estimated largely on the basis of turnover tax receipts, whereas in the United Kingdom consumer expenditures are estimated on the basis of data supplied not only by tax receipts but also from household surveys and production sources.

Even with standard data-gathering techniques, definitional differences would still remain internationally. In some cases, these differences are minor; in others, they are quite significant. Germany, for example, classifies the purchase of a television set as an expenditure for "recreation and entertainment, whereas the same expenditure falls into the "furniture, furnishings, and household equipment" classification in the United States.

Survey data are subject to perhaps even more comparability problems. When Pepsico International, a typical user of international research, reviewed its data it found a considerable lack of comparability in a number of major areas. Table 8–7 shows how age categories were developed in seven countries surveyed by Pepsico.

While flexibility may have the advantage of providing groupings for local analysis that are more pertinent (14 to 19, for example, might be a more pertinent "youth" classification in one country, whereas 14 to 24 might be a more useful definition of the same segment in another country), Pepsico's headquarters marketing research group pointed out that if data were reported to the company's headquarters in standard five-year intervals, it would be possible to compare findings in one country with those in another. Without this standardization, such comparability was not possible. The company's headquarters marketing research group recommended, therefore, that standard five-year intervals be required in all reporting to headquarters, but that any other intervals that were deemed useful for local purposes be

TABLE 8—7 Age Classifications from Consumer Surveys, Major Markets

MEXICO	VENEZUELA	ARGENTINA	GERMANY	SPAIN	ITALY	PHILIPPINES
14–18	10–14	14–18	14–19	15–24	13–20	14–18
19–25	15–24	19–24	20–29	25–34	21–25	19–25
26–35	25–34	25–34	30–39	35–44	26–35	26–35
36–45	35–44	35–44	40–49	45–54	36–45	36–50
46+	45+	45–65	50+	55–64	46–60	
				65+		

Source: Pepsico International.

perfectly allowable. Pepsico also found that local market definitions of consumption differed so greatly that it was unable to make intermarket comparisons of brand share figures. Representative definitions of consumption are shown in Table 8–8.

One important qualification about comparability in multicountry survey work is that comparability does not necessarily result from sameness of method. A survey asking the same question and using the same methods will not necessarily yield results that are comparable from country to country. For example, if the data were recorded by household, the definition of *household* in each of these countries could vary. The point is that comparability of results has to be established directly; it does not simply follow from the sameness of method. Establishing that results will be comparable depends upon either knowing that methods will produce identical measurements or knowing how to correct any biases that may exist.

Assessing Market Opportunity

The vice presidents of finance and marketing of a shoe company were traveling around the world to estimate the market potential for their products. They arrived in a very poor developing country and both immediately noticed that no one in this country was wearing shoes. The vice president-finance of the company said, "We might as well get back on the plane. There is no market for shoes in this country." The vice president of marketing replied, "What an opportunity! Everyone in this country is a potential customer!"

This story underlines the difference between existing and potential markets.

TABLE 8—8 Definition of Consumption Used by Pepsico Market Researcher

Mexico	Count of number of occasions product was consumed on day prior to interview.
Venezuela	Count of number of occasions product was consumed on day prior to interview.
Argentina	Count of number of drinks consumed on day prior to interview.
Germany	Count of number of respondents consuming "daily or almost daily."
Spain	Count of number of drinks consumed "at least once a week."
Italy	Count of number of respondents consuming product on day prior to interview.
Philippines	Count of number of glasses of product consumed on day prior to interview

The existing market for shoes in the country was zero. The potential market was zero in the eyes of the vice president-finance but it was enormous in the eye of the vice president-marketing.

There are three basic categories of demand and therefore of market opportunity: existing demand, latent demand, and incipient demand. *Existing* markets are as the term suggests—those in which customer needs are being served by existing suppliers. At least in theory, the size of existing markets can be measured. The task of measurement is one of devising a method for identifying the rate of purchase or consumption of the product.

Latent demand is demand which would be expressed *if* a product were offered to customers at an acceptable price. Latent demand is the demand for any new product which succeeds. Before the product is offered, demand is zero. After the offer, there is existing demand. Personal computers are an example of a product for which there was enormous latent demand. The PC revolution sparked by Apple is an outstanding example of tapping a latent market.

Incipient demand is demand that will emerge if present trends continue. If you offer a product to meet incipient demand before the trends have had their impact, you will have no market response. After the trends have had a chance to unfold, the incipient demand will become latent demand. An outstanding example of incipient demand is the impact of rising income on demand for consumer durables, automobiles, etc. You can be absolutely certain that as income per capita rises in a country the demand for automobiles will also rise. Therefore, if you can predict a country's future rate of income growth, you can also predict the growth rate of its automobile market. Table 8–9 summarizes the different types of demand.

Assessing a market opportunity requires a measure of both the overall size of a market and the competitive conditions in the market. It is the combination of total size and competitive conditions that determines sales opportunity and profit. In global marketing, companies focusing on existing markets must first estimate the size of these markets and then assess their overall competitiveness as compared with their competitors' by measuring product appeal, price, distribution, advertising, and promotional coverage and effectiveness. Cameras are a good case in point. Before 1960, German companies dominated the 35mm camera market with their rangefinder design. Enter the Japanese. The Japanese offered a superior design (they were the first to develop the single-lens reflex design in the 35mm camera). While the overall quality and design of Japanese cameras was high, prices were relatively low, distribution was intensive, and communications were at least as good as those of the competition (mainly German companies). The results of this Japanese tour de force were dramatic. In 1960 Germany exported $42 million and Japan $16 million. By 1970 Japanese exports had increased from approximately 40 percent to 270 percent of German exports during this period. The Japanese have continued to innovate in this area and today they virtually monopolize the market.

A second market objective in international marketing is to identify and exploit latent markets. These markets present a very different challenge from those presented by existing markets, where the main challenge is the competition. The major

TABLE 8–9 Three Categories of Demand

	EXISTING	LATENT	INCIPIENT
Definition	Customer needs are being served by existing products/suppliers.	Customer needs are not being served by existing products/suppliers.	Customer needs do not exist now but will emerge in future if present trends continue.
Characteristics	Can be precisely measured or estimated.	Cannot be precisely measured or estimated. Will materialize if the marketing mix combination that meets the need is offered. Examples include market for instant pictures tapped by Polaroid in 1947; market for personal computers in 1976, or fast food franchises in the USSR.	If trends continue, will become a latent market. Is not an existing market; would not respond if product were offered.

The author is indebted to H. Igor Ansoff for suggesting the terms *existing, latent,* and *incipient demand* in his *Corporate Strategy* (New York: McGraw-Hill, 1965), p. 191.

236

challenge in successfully exploiting latent markets is the identification of market opportunity. Initial success will not be competitiveness, but rather ability to identify opportunity and launch a marketing program to supply the latent demand. Of course, if there are other companies producing the same or equivalent products, it is important to assess the likelihood and expected timing of competitive entry into latent markets. An example of a latent market is the demand for small refrigerators in the United States for the vacation trailer or caravan. European and Japanese companies were producing small refrigerators for the household market and their smallest models were well suited to the needs of the U.S. camper. The same type of U.S. market developed for the subcompact car. People wanted small inexpensive transportation, and Detroit would not offer a U.S. product to fill this need. Foreign companies exploited an existing latent market and positioned themselves in an emerging incipient market. Because of their leadership in exploiting this market, foreign manufacturers held roughly 30–35 percent of the U.S. market in 1986.

The British and Japanese motorcycle industries provide an example of different approaches to market demand. The British industry was well established before World War I and had attained a leading position in world markets. In 1969 the British industry sold 30,000 motorcycles (more than 450 cc) in the United States as compared with Japanese sales of 27,000. In 1973, British sales remained at 30,000 units while Japanese sales had increased to 218,000 units. The Japanese had, in the short space of four years, opened up entirely new markets with products that attracted an entirely new segment of the population to motorcycle riding. Japanese machines were cheaper and more reliable than were the British machines. The combination of product design, quality, price, and aggressive advertising and promotion resulted in a 430 percent increase in market size, which was entirely captured by the Japanese. In 1969 the British industry held a 49 percent share of the U.S. market for motorcycles in the 450- to 749-cc size class. Four of 8 available models were British. In 1973 the British share of this market was down to 9 percent, and only 2 of 10 available models were British. Today, the British industry is defunct.

Incipient international markets are those that will emerge as a consequence of known conditions and trends. Internationally these are important for planning purposes. In advanced countries, because of high wages, there is a ready market for any product that saves labor and thereby reduces costs. Because domestic labor is scarce and incomes are high, there is also a ready market for household labor-saving devices. The same pressures or forces operate throughout the world. Companies marketing labor-saving products can predict with reasonable accuracy when demand will emerge in a country as wages and incomes rise and can plan to deploy their resources to tap these markets as they emerge.

Special Problems
in International Marketing Research

The objectives just outlined are not unique to international marketing. However, international market researchers do face special problems and conditions that differentiate their task from that of the domestic market researcher. First, instead of analyzing a single national market, the international market researcher must analyze many national markets. Each national market has unique characteristics that must be recognized in analysis. And for many countries, the availability of data is limited. This limitation is particularly true of less developed countries where statistical and research services are relatively primitive.

The small markets around the world pose a special problem for the international researcher. The relatively low-profit potential in smaller markets permits only a modest marketing research expenditure. Therefore the international researcher must devise techniques and methods that relate the expenditures on research to the profit potential of markets. The smaller markets put a premium on discovering economic and demographic relationships that permit demand estimation from a minimum of information and on inexpensive survey research that sacrifices some elegance to achieve results within the constraints of the smaller market research budget.

Another frequently encountered problem in developing countries is that data may be inflated or deflated for political expediency. For example, a Middle Eastern country revised its balance of trade in a chemical product by adding 1,000 tons to its consumption statistics. It did this to encourage foreign investors to install domestic production facilities. Consumer research is inhibited by a greater reluctance on the part of people to talk to strangers, greater difficulty in locating people, and an absence of telephones. Both industrial and consumer research services are less developed, although the cost of these services is much lower in a high-wage country.

Five Rules for International Research

Experience suggests that there are five rules that, if followed, will contribute to the preparation of research reports that will be effective management tools.

1. Before you begin your research, ask yourself these six questions:
   a. What information do I need? What will I do with the information when I get it?
   b. Where can I get this information? Is it available in files, a library, or on line from a data base?
   c. Why do I need this information?
   d. When do I need the information?
   e. What is this information worth to me in dollars (or yen, etc.)?
   f. What would be the cost of not getting the information?
2. Start with desk research. Use the available information in your own files, libraries, on-line data bases, trade associations, and so on. Refer to the information appendix of this book for guidance on information sources. Quite often, the information you are looking for is in your own files or in an easily obtainable public source.
3. Identify the type of information that is available from overseas sources. Just because the information is or is not available at home does not mean that it is or is not available abroad. The general rule: the more developed the country, the greater the information available.
4. Know where to look. If you do not know, go to someone who does. Your embassy staff or commercial attaché may be able to offer help.

5. Do not assume that the information you get is comparable or accurate. Check everything. Use common sense and logic to evaluate the comparability and accuracy of the information obtained from overseas sources.

Survey Research

When data are not available through published statistics or studies, direct collection is necessary. One of the most important means of collecting market data is via survey research. Survey research involves interviewing a target group, for example, potential customers, to obtain the desired information. Normally a questionnaire is essential to ensure a successful survey. Many good textbooks suggest how to design and administer questionnaires. The following is not intended to be a complete guide to questionnaires but, rather, a summary of design with particular reference to conditions in developing countries.

A good questionnaire has three main characteristics:

1. It is simple.
2. It is easy for respondents to answer and for the interviewer to record.
3. It keeps the interview to the point and obtains desired information.

To achieve this, the following principles should be observed:

1. *Single-element questions.* An apparently simple question may have many elements. Questions should focus on a single element.
2. *Expected replies.* Wherever possible, expected replies should be listed on the questionnaire where the interviewer can check the answer. This eliminates a difficult coding task of trying to decide what people meant by replies that are written out on the questionnaire.
3. *Ambiguity in questions.* Carelessly worded questions can be ambiguous, as can questions with words that are not understood by respondents. Therefore, questionnaires must be carefully stated in language that even the least educated respondents will understand.
4. *Leading questions.* Leading questions suggest answers and should be avoided. For example, "Do you prefer brand X because of its high quality?" is an assertion that provides its own answer.
5. *Personal and embarrassing questions.* This is a difficult area to deal with. One rule is to rely upon local managers and experts who are familiar with local customs and mores. It is important to ensure, however, that the local adviser is not excessively conservative in his or her judgments about what can be asked. Therefore, the use of several judges is advisable to ensure that a single bias is not determining the questionnaire design.
6. *Pretesting.* A pretest is invaluable in determining whether or not a questionnaire accomplishes what is desired. No matter how much thought and effort go into questionnaire design, there are always unanticipated problems or ambiguities that are often identified in a pretest.

Sampling

Sampling is the selection of a subset or group from a population that is representative of the entire population. The two basic sampling methods in use today are probabilistic and non-probabilistic sampling. In a probabilistic sample, each unit chosen has a known chance of being included in the sample. In a random sample, which is one type of probabilistic sample, each unit has an *equal* chance of being selected. The results of a probabilistic sample can be projected to the entire population with statistical reliability.

The results of a non-probabilistic sample cannot be projected with statistical reliability. For example, a quota sample is the selection of the proportions that are known to exist in the universe. Since the units that are selected in a quota sample do not have an equal or even a known chance of being selected, the results of a quota sample cannot be projected with any statistical reliability to the universe. However, if there are no reasons to expect that the quota is significantly different from the universe, then it is assumed that the sample will be representative of other characteristics. Thus only the random or probabilistic sample produces results of statistically measurable accuracy. This is the major advantage of a probability sample. The disadvantage of a probability sample is the difficulty of selecting elements from the universe on a random or probability basis. The quota sample does not require selection on a probability basis and is therefore much easier to implement. Its main disadvantage is the possible bias that may exist in the sample because of inaccurate prior assumptions concerning population or because of unknown bias in selection of cases by field workers.

Three key characteristics of a probability sample determine the sample size:

1. The permissible sampling error that can be allowed, e.
2. The desired confidence in the sample results. In a statistical sense the confidence is expressed in terms of the number of chances in 100 tries that the results obtained could be due to chance. Confidence is usually desired at the 99 percent level and is expressed as three standard errors, t.
3. The amount of variation in the characteristic being measured. This is known as the standard deviation, s.

The formula for sample size is

$$n = \frac{(t^2)\,(s^2)}{e^2}$$

where

n = sample size
t = confidence limit expressed in standard errors (three standard errors = 99 percent confidence)
s = standard deviation
e = error limit

The important characteristic of this formula from the point of view of international marketers is that the sample size, n, is not a function of the size of the universe. Thus, a probability sample in Tanzania requires the same sample size as one in the United States if the standard deviation in the two populations is the same. This is one of the basic reasons for scale economies of marketing research in larger markets.

A quota sample is designed by taking known characteristics of the universe and including respondents in the sample in the same proportion as they occur in the known characteristic universe. For example, population may be divided in six categories according to income as follows:

Percent of population	10%	15%	25%	25%	15%	10%
Earnings per month	0–10	10–20	20–40	40–60	60–70	70–100

If it is assumed that income is the characteristic that adequately differentiates the population for study purposes, then a quota sample would include respondents of different income levels in the same proportion as they occurred in the population, that is, 15 percent with monthly earnings from 10–20, and so on.

ANALYTICAL TECHNIQUES FOR RESEARCHING INTERNATIONAL MARKETS

Demand Pattern Analysis

Industrial growth patterns provide an insight into market demand.[6] Production patterns, because they generally reveal consumption patterns, are helpful in assessing market opportunities. Additionally, trends in manufacturing production indicate potential markets for inputs to the manufacturing process. Figure 8–1 illustrates patterns of growth in large industry categories. It relates the percentage of total manufacturing production accounted for by major industrial groups to gross domestic product per capita. At the early stages of growth in a country, when per capita incomes are low, manufacturing centers on necessities: food, beverages, textiles, and light manufacturing. As incomes grow, these industries decline relatively and are replaced in importance by heavy industries.

Income Elasticity Measurements

Income elasticity describes the relationship between demand for a good and changes in income. Symbolically, it can be expressed as

$$\frac{\Delta Q_A / Q_A}{\Delta Y / Y} = \text{income elasticity of demand for product } A$$

[6]This section is adapted from Reed Moyer, "International Market Analysis," *Journal of Marketing Research*, November 1968.

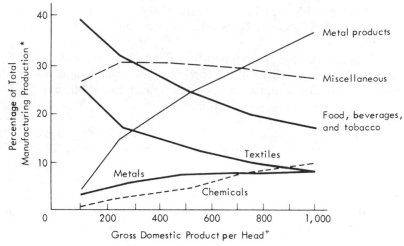

*Based on time series analysis for selected years, 1899–1957, for 7 to 10 countries depending on commodity.

⁺Dollars at 1955 prices.

FIGURE 8–1   Typical Patterns of Growth in Manufacturing Industries

where Q represents the quantity demanded and Y represents income. When the elasticity coefficient is <1, it is said to be inelastic. If a 10 percent increase in Y results in a 20 percent increase in the quantity A demanded or consumed, the income elasticity coefficient is 2.0. In this relationship A is said to be income elastic, because the coefficient is >1. If a 10 percent increase in Y results in only a 5 percent increase in quantity A demanded or consumed, the income elasticity coefficient is .5. Since it is less than 1, the coefficient of elasticity is said to be inelastic.

Income elasticity studies covering both consumer and industrial products show that necessities such as food and clothing tend to be income inelastic; that is, expenditures on products in this category increase but at a slower percentage rate than do increases in income. This is the corollary of Engel's law, which states that as incomes rise, smaller proportions of total income are spent on basic necessities such as food and clothing. Demand for durable consumer goods such as furniture, appliances, and metals tends to be income elastic, increasing relatively faster than increases in income.

REGIONAL LEAD-LAGS.   A regional lead-lag analysis assumes that demand patterns in a leading country are predictive of those that will occur in a country under consideration. The positing of a lead-lag relationship requires that economic, social, and cultural conditions in the two countries be analogous and separated only by time. There is empirical evidence to support the hypothesis that regional lead-lags exist. Two examples are television sets and automobiles.

Figures 8–2 and 8–3 show the diffusion of television sets in the United States, England, and Germany from 1946 to 1970.

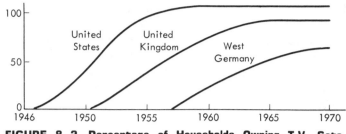

FIGURE 8–2 Percentage of Households Owning T.V. Sets, 1946–1970

Television was introduced into the United Kingdom and the United States at approximately the same time and into the German market about six years later. The yearly increase in penetration (Figure 8–2) in the United States was much greater than that in the United Kingdom. Thus, although there was no lag in the initial introduction of the product in the two countries, the initial market development of the product was quite different. The U.S. penetration levels have been approached by the United Kingdom with a time lag and with a less rapid growth pattern.

Comparing the ownership and growth data for England and West Germany shows the initial German imitation lag of six years remained almost constant during the complete pattern and that German sales patterns have almost duplicated U.K. patterns in every way except in time. This constant time lag allows the forecasting of future development in West Germany by simply taking the percentage figures for England six years earlier and multiplying them by the number of households.

On the basis of the data, it is clear that market forces influencing television demand are similar in England and West Germany but different in the United States. The usefulness of this lead-lag analysis using the United Kingdom as a predictor for West Germany exists because the time series of data for the two markets is long enough to allow formulation of a lead-lag hypothesis. Lead-lag analysis is analytic strategy appropriate for comparing markets that have developed over some period of time.

Estimation by Analogy. Estimating market size with available data presents challenging analytic tasks. When data are unavailable, as is frequently the case in

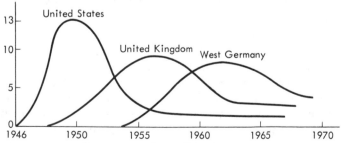

FIGURE 8–3 Yearly Increase in Household Ownership of T.V. Sets, 1946–1970

both less developed and industrialized countries, resourceful techniques are required. One resourceful technique is estimation by analogy. There are two ways to use this technique. One way is to make cross-section comparisons, and the other is to displace a time series in time. The first method, cross-section comparisons, amounts simply to positing the assumption that there is an analogy between the relationship of a factor and demand for a particular product or commodity in two countries. This can best be explained as follows:

Let

$$X_A = \text{demand for product } X \text{ in country } A$$
$$Y_A = \text{factor that correlates with demand for product } X \text{ in country } A, \text{ data from country } A$$
$$X_B = \text{demand for product } X \text{ in country } B$$
$$Y_B = \text{factor that correlates with demand for product } X \text{ in country } A, \text{ data from country } B$$

If we assume that

$$\frac{X_A}{Y_A} = \frac{X_B}{Y_B}$$

and if X_A, Y_A, and Y_B are known, we can solve for X_B as follows:

$$X_B = \frac{(X_A)\,(Y_B)}{Y_A}$$

Basically, estimation by analogy amounts to the use of a single factor index with a correlation value obtained from one country applied to a target market. This is a very simple method of analysis, but in many cases it is an extremely useful, rough estimating device whenever data are available in at least one potentially analogous market for product sales of consumption and a single correlation factor. Some researchers have been quite creative in identifying analogous products. A major U.S. chemical company, for example, found that soup consumption was the only reliable index forecasting chemical sales in Asia.

Displacing time is a useful method of market analysis when data are available for two markets at different levels of development. This method is based on the assumption that an analogy between markets exists in different time periods or, put another way, that the markets in question are going through the same stages of market development. The method amounts to assuming that the demand level for product X in country A in time period one was at the same stage as demand for product X in time period two in country B. This can be illustrated as follows:

Let

X_{A_1} = demand for product X in country A during time period 1

Y_{A_1} = factor associated with demand for product X in country A during time period 1

X_{B_2} = demand for product X in country B during time period 2

Y_{B_2} = factor or factors correlating with demand for product X in country A and data from country B for time period 2

Assume that

$$\frac{X_{A_1}}{Y_{A_1}} = \frac{X_{B_2}}{Y_{B_2}}$$

If X_{A_1}, Y_{A_1}, and Y_{B_2} are known, we can solve for X_{B_2} as follows:

$$X_{B_2} = \frac{(X_{A_1})\,(Y_{B_2})}{Y_{A_1}}$$

The use of the method of displacing time involves arriving at an estimate of when two markets were at similar stages of development. One might assume on the basis of analyzing factors associated with demand that the market for product X in Mexico in 1986 was comparable to the markets for the same product in the United States in 1946. If this assumption were valid, by obtaining data on the factors associated with demand for product X in the United States in 1946 and in Mexico in 1986, as well as actual U.S. demand in 1946, one could solve for the unknown, that is, potential demand for product X in Mexico in 1986.

Any technique as simple as estimation by analogy is subject to substantial limitations. The following factors should be kept in mind in using this technique.

1. Are the two countries for which the analogy is posited really similar either in cross section or in displaced time? To answer this question, the analyst must understand the similarities and differences in the cultural systems in the two countries if a consumer product is under investigation and in the technological systems if an industrial product is being considered.

2. Have technical and social developments resulted in a situation where demand for a particular product or commodity will leapfrog previous patterns, skipping entire growth patterns that occurred in more developed countries? For example, it is clear that washing machine sales in Europe leapfrogged the pattern of sales in the United States. In the United States the consumer went from hand-washing machine methods to nonautomatic washing machines and then, when they were finally available and reliable, to semiautomatic and fully automatic machines. In Europe many consumers are skipping the

entire progression from nonautomatic to semiautomatic machines and are moving from hand washing to fully automatic equipment. Thus it is clear that the simple analogy between the growth in sales for nonautomatic, semiautomatic, and automatic machines does not exist between the United States and Europe. Nevertheless, the analyst might conclude that one could lump together the nonautomatic and semiautomatic equipment in the United States market and use this growth pattern as the basis for estimation by analogy of potential demand in Europe.

3. The distinction between potential demand for a product based on underlying factors, and actual sales based on the combination of potential demand, and the offering conditions of a product should be kept clearly in mind. If there are differences among the availability, price, quality, and other factors associated with the product in two markets, potential demand in a target market will not develop into actual sales of a product because the offer conditions are not comparable.

Comparative Analysis

One of the unique opportunities in international marketing analysis is to analyze comparatively market potential and marketing performance. Three basic categories of comparison can be drawn in international marketing. The first are national comparisons, both intracompany and intercompany. These comparisons are a basis for much analysis in domestic marketing and also are applicable in single-country situations in international marketing. A second major form of comparative analysis is the intracompany cross-national comparison. This comparison is based upon the conclusion that there is enough similarity between two or more countries to justify cross-national comparison of performance and potential. For example, if the general market conditions in country X on such matters as income, stage of industrialization, and other relevant factors are similar to those in country Y, it is valuable to raise the question of why any discrepancy between per capita sales in the two countries might exist. There may be good explanations for discrepancies or there may not be. Comparative cross-national analysis raises questions and suggests areas for investigation and is therefore a valuable analytical tool.

A third form of comparative analysis is based on national-subnational markets. Table 8–10 is a 1982 comparison between France, a national market, and California, a subnational market. The two markets are substantially different in terms of total population and total income. France's population was more than twice that of California, although it was growing much more slowly. French gross national product is double that of California. Although these differences in the microeconomic dimensions of the two markets exist, there are striking similarities in the area of specific products. Indeed, for many products, such as microwave ovens and dishwashers, California is a bigger market than is France. As the data available within company management information systems become increasingly available on a worldwide basis, the possibility of analyzing marketing expenditure effectiveness on a market basis that cuts across national boundaries becomes a reality. Companies can then decide where they are achieving the greatest marginal effectiveness for their marketing expenditures and can adjust expenditures accordingly.

TABLE 8–10   National Submarket Comparisons, 1982

	FRANCE	*CALIFORNIA*
GNP	$569 billion	$333.7 billion at 1983 price
GNP per capita	$10,552	$12,617
Real GDP growth (1980–1982)	0.5 approx.	
Demographic Data		
Population	54,085,000	24,698,000
Population growth (1976–1982)	4%	8.3% (1980–1984)
Population density	99.4/Km²	164 per square mile
Urban rural distribution	78/22	91.3/8.7
Principal city	Paris	Los Angeles
Population of principal city	2,230,000	2,812,000
Selected Statistics		
Road mileage	802,407 Km	174,000 miles
Total area	543,965 Km²	411,049 Km²
Passenger cars total	20,300,000	14,730,000
Telephones per 100 people	45.9	86.99
Newspapers	106 dailies	118 dailies

Source: *European Marketing Data & Statistics 1984*, Euromonitor Publications, Ltd.; U.S. Bureau of the Census, *Statistical Abstract of the United States, 1984*. Washington D.C., 1984.

Cluster Analysis

The objective of cluster analysis is to group variables into clusters that maximize within-group similarities and between-group differences. This objective is well suited to international marketing research because the national markets of the world are made up of similarities as well as differences that are clustered within regions and across income levels or stages of economic development. A number of computer programs are available for cluster analysis.

Multiple Factor Indexes

A multiple factor index measures potential demand indirectly by using as proxies variables that either intuition or statistical analysis suggests can be closely correlated with the potential demand for the product under review.

Gross indicators such as GNP, net national income, or total population are useful in constructing an index, but wherever possible the analyst should restrict the use of factors to variables that are closely related to product demand. For example, an analyst interested in the potential demand for small electrical appliances might conclude on the basis of cross-national analysis and the time-series analysis within single countries that personal disposable income was the best proxy measure of expenditures on small appliances. If the analyst is attempting to measure demand for coffee-making appliances of all types, an essential additional proxy would be the number of coffee drinkers in the country and the type of coffee preferred.

Ordinarily, market indexes are constructed not to measure total potential but to rank submarkets or to assign potential shares of the total market to each submarket. An index of this kind can be used to establish sales quotas or evaluate sales performance. A Brazilian index assigns a potential to the state of Sao Paulo of 30 percent of the nation's total. If sales of the company's product fall below 30 percent, and the product sales are related to the three-factor index, management would have reason to question the performance in that submarket. Obviously such a tool must be used with great care. Full investigation may show that the sales performance in Sao Paulo is satisfactory but that the index is an inaccurate measure of potential.

Regression Analysis

Regression analysis can be a powerful tool for predicting demand in international markets. If the researcher elects to use multiple regression tactics, which is the use of independent or predictor variables to estimate a dependent variable, there are computer programs available today that follow a stepwise procedure. The procedure selects the independent variable that accounts for the most variance in the dependent variable, and then the variable that accounts for most of the remaining variance, and so on until the user decides to stop. Using these tactics the analyst can select from a set of potential predictor variables those variables that explain the greatest amount of variance in the dependent variable under investigation.

Table 8–11 summarizes regression results that relate consumption of various commodities to single macroeconomic indicator, GNP per capita. A linear simple regression model of the form $Y = A + BX$ was used, where Y is the amount of product in use per thousand population and X is GNP per capita. As can be seen from the unadjusted R^2 in Table 8–11, this single macroeconomic variable explains from 50 to 78 percent of the variation in the dependent variables.

The results in Table 8–11 can be interpreted as follows: an increase in $100

TABLE 8–11   Regression of Amount of Product in Use per 1,000 Population on Gross National Product

PRODUCT	NUMBER OF OBSERVATIONS	REGRESSION EQUATION	UNADJUSTED R^2
Autos	37	$-21,071 + .101x$	.759
Radio sets	42	$8.325 + .275x$	.784
Television sets	31	$-16.501 + .074x$	.503
Refrigerators	24	$-21.330 + .102x$	.743
Washing machines	22	$-15.623 + .094x$	.736

Source: Reed Moyer, "International Market Analysis," *Journal of Marketing Research*, November 1968.

per capita GNP will result on the average in an increase of 10 automobiles, 10 refrigerators, 9 washing machines, 7 television sets, and 27 radio sets per thousand population.

The variance in the dependent variable under investigation could be reduced by adding variables that are related to demand. For example, in the case of automobiles, in addition to looking at income, data could be obtained on the road system availability, on the price of automobiles, on the availability of public transportation, on the cost of keeping and operating an automobile, and on other relevant factors that could affect the sale of automobiles. With these additional variables, it is possible to follow a stepwise progression analysis strategy and select that combination of variables that explains the greatest amount of variance in automobile sales consistent with an acceptable level of statistical significance. The demand for automobiles in New York City, for example, is far less than the income variable would suggest because of the negative influence on automobile sales of high insurance rates, lack of availability, high cost of parking, and the availability of extensive public transportation systems.

Many products do not lend themselves to simple single variable regression analysis. Moyer, for example, found a very poor fit for a regression of cement consumption per capita on gross disposable product per capita. Fortunately, however, the consumption of many products can be estimated reasonably accurately by a knowledge only of income for GNP per capita in the market under investigation.

To use regression to estimate demand, analysts must first compute the regression using those "predictor" variables that are expected to explain variation in the dependent variable. If the unexplained variation is reasonbly low, the analyst may use the results of these calculations to estimate current demand in countries for which no demand data are available. Getting the estimate of demand requires that the data on the predictive or independent variable be available. Assume, for example, that we want to estimate the ownership of refrigerators in country X where data on ownership are unavailable. Through regression analysis of 24 countries we have the equation $Y = -21.330 + .102X$, $R^2 = .743$, which is statistically significant at the .01 level where Y equals refrigerators in use per thousand population and X equals GNP per capita. GNP per capita in country X is $1,000. Using this equation we calculate the number of refrigerators in use to be 80.67 per thousand population. If we expect GNP per capita in country X to grow to, say, $1,300 during the next five years, and if our regression equation is valid over this range of incomes, using the same equation the number of refrigerators per thousand population in five years in country X will be roughly 111.

HEADQUARTERS CONTROL
OF GLOBAL MARKETING RESEARCH

An important issue for the global company is where to locate control of the organization's marketing research capability. The difference between the multinational,

TABLE 8-12   Worldwide Marketing Research Plan

RESEARCH OBJECTIVE	COUNTRY CLUSTER A	COUNTRY CLUSTER B	COUNTRY CLUSTER C
Identify market potential			X
Appraise competitive intentions		X	
Evaluate product appeal	X	X	X
Study market response to price	X		
Appraise distribution channels	X	X	X

stage three company and the global stage four company on this issue is profound.[7] The multinational delegates responsibility for research to the operating subsidiary. The global company delegates responsibility for research to operating subsidiaries but retains overall responsibility and control of research as a headquarters' function. In practice, this means that the global company will, whenever possible, conduct research which is comparable. Comparable data based on experience in other parts of the world provide more possibilities for insight into market dynamics.

Comparability requires that scales, questions, and research methodology be standardized. To achieve this, the company must inject a level of control and review of marketing research at the global level. The director of worldwide marketing research must respond to local conditions as he or she searches for a research program that will be implementable on a global basis. It is most likely that the marketing director will end up with a number of programs tailored to clusters of countries that exhibit within-group similarities. The agenda of a coordinated worldwide research program might look like that in Table 8-12.

The director of worldwide research should not simply "direct" the efforts of country research managers. It is his or her job to ensure that the corporation achieves maximum results *worldwide* from the total allocation of its research resources. To achieve this, the director will need to ensure that each country is aware of research being carried out in the rest of the world and that each country is involved in influencing the design of its own country as well as the overall research program. Although each subsidiary will influence the country and the overall program, the director of worldwide research must be responsible for the overall research design and program. It is his or her job to take inputs from the entire world and produce a coordinated research strategy that generates the information needed by managers to achieve global sales and profit objectives.

SUMMARY

One of the most basic ingredients of a successful marketing strategy is information. The global marketer must scan the world for information about oportunities and

---

[7] A study of 10 large U.S. based multinational companies revealed that only one was making any effort to direct country research efforts. See Warren J. Keegan, "Multinational Marketing Management," Marketing Science Institute Working Paper, January 1970.

threats. The two equally important modes of scanning are surveillance by keeping in touch with an area of information, and search by actively seeking out information. Both are important and require conscious attention to design and management. This chapter outlines a conceptual framework for organizing the scanning activity of individuals and organizations.

DISCUSSION QUESTIONS

1. What is the major source of information for headquarters' executives of global companies?
2. What are the different modes of information acquisition? Which is the most important for gathering strategic information?
3. What determines the horizons of managers? Why do some managers seem to see farther and more clearly than others?
4. Assume that you have been asked by the president of your organization to come up with a systematic approach to scanning. The president does not want to be surprised by major market or competitive developments. What would you recommend?
5. What is the difference between latent and existing demand?
6. What are some examples of countries that might lend themselves to the use of lead-lag analysis?
7. What is the rationale for the use of the technique of estimation by analogy?

BIBLIOGRAPHY

Books

DOUGLAS, SUSAN P., AND C. SAMUEL CRAIG. *International Marketing Research.* Englewood Cliffs, N.J.: Prentice-Hall, 1983.

JAFFE, EUGENE D. *Grouping: A Strategy for International Marketing.* New York: AMA, 1974.

KRAVIS, IRVING B., ZOLTAN KENESSEY, ALAN HESTON, AND ROBERT SUMMERS. *A System of International Comparisons of Gross Product and Purchasing Power.* Baltimore: Johns Hopkins University Press, 1975.

MANVILLE, RICHARD. *Steps in Conducting a Marketing Research Study.* Westport, Conn.: Richard Manville Research, 1978.

Articles

ADLER, LEE. "Managing Marketing Research in the Diversified Multinational Corporation." In *Marketing in Turbulent Times and Marketing: The Challenges and Opportunities— Combined Proceedings,* ed. Edward M. Mazze. Chicago: American Marketing Association, 1975, pp. 305–308.

DOUGLAS, SUSAN P., C. SAMUEL CRAIG, AND WARREN J. KEEGAN. "Approaches to Assessing International Marketing Opportunities for Small- and Medium-sized Companies." *Columbia Journal of World Business,* Fall 1982, pp. 26–30.

GREEN, ROBERT, AND ERIC LANGEARD. "A Cross-National Comparison of Consumer Habits and Innovator Chracteristics." *Journal of Marketing,* July 1975, pp. 34–41.

————, AND P. D. WHITE. "Methodological Considerations in Cross-National Consumer Research." *Journal of International Studies*, Fall–Winter 1976, pp. 81–88.

LINDBERG, BERTIL C. "International Comparison of Growth in Demand for a New Durable Consumer Product." *Journal of Marketing Research*, August 1982, pp. 364–371.

MOYER, REED. "International Market Analysis." *Journal of Marketing Research*, November 1968.

SETHI, S. PRAKASH. "Comparative Cluster Analysis for World Markets." *Journal of Marketing Research*, Vol. 8 (August 1971), p. 350.

STOBAUGH, ROBERT B., JR. "How to Analyze Foreign Investment Climates." *Harvard Business Review*, September–October 1969, pp. 100–108.

VOGEL, R. H. "Uses of Managerial Perceptions in Clustering Countries." *Journal of International Business Studies*, Spring 1976, pp. 91–100.

PARKER PEN CO. (A) INTERNATIONAL MARKETING STRATEGY REVIEW[1]

It is circumstance and proper timing that give an action its character and make it either good or bad.—Agesilaus

INTRODUCTION

The meeting at sunny Palm Beach concluded with nary a whimper of dissent from its participants. After years of being run as a completely decentralized company whose managers in all corners of the world enjoyed a high degree of flexibility, Parker Pen Co., of Janesville, Wisconsin, was forced to reexamine itself. The company had enjoyed decade after decade of success until the early 1980s. By this time, Parker faced strong competitive threats and a deteriorating internal situation. A new management team was brought in from outside the company—an unprecedented step for what had been until then an essentially family-run business. At the March, 1984 Palm Beach meeting, this new group of decision makers would outline a course of action that would hopefully set Parker back on a path to success.

The men behind the new strategy were supremely confident of its chances for success—and with good reason. Each was recognized as a highly skilled practitioner of international business and their combined extensive experience gave them an air of invincibility. They had been recruited from larger

[1]Cases (A), (B), and (C) were prepared by Charles J. Anderer, research associate, under the supervision of Warren J. Keegan, Professor of International Business and Marketing, as part of the International Business Case Study Project, Center for International Business Studies, Pace University. This project was funded in part by a grant from the United States Department of Education. Copyright © 1986 by the Board of Trustees, Pace University.

companies, had left high paying, rewarding jobs and each had come to Janesville with a grand sense of purpose. For decades, Parker had been a dominant player in the pen industry. In the early 1980s, however, the company had seen its market share dwindle to a mere 6 percent and, in 1982, net income plunged a whopping 60 percent.

To reverse this decline, Parker recruited James Peterson, an executive vice president at R.J. Reynolds, as the new president and CEO. Peterson hired Manville Smith as president of the writing instruments group at Parker. Smith, who was born in Ecuador and had a broad international background, came from 3M where he had been appointed division president at the tender age of 30. Richard Swart was vice president/marketing of the writing instruments group. He spent 11 years at the advertising agency BBDO and was an expert on marketing planning and theory. Jack Marks was head of writing instruments advertising. Marks came to Parker from Gillette, where, among other things, he assisted in the worldwide marketing of Paper Mate pens. Rounding out the team was Carlos Del Nero, manager of global marketing planning, who brought with him considerable international experience at Fisher-Price. Each of these men was convinced that Parker would right itself by following the plan they unveiled at Palm Beach.

A BRIEF HISTORY OF PARKER PEN

The "Rolls Royce" of the Pen Industry

The Parker name has been identified with pens since 1888 when George S. Parker delighted ink-splotched pen-users everywhere by introducing a leakproof fountain model called the Parker Lucky Curve. Parker Pen would eventually blossom into America's, if not the world's, largest and best-known pen maker. Parker's products, which would eventually include ballpoint pens, felt-tip pens, desk sets, mechanical pencils, inks, leads, erasers, and, or course, the fountain pen, were also known for their high price tags. In 1921, for example, Parker introduced the Duofold pen. The Duofold, even though it was comparable to other $3 pens on the market, was extravagantly priced a $7. Parker was able to charge a premium price because of its reputation for quality and style, and its skill in positioning products in the top price segment.

Parker's position as America's leading pen maker was solidified during the years when the pen was mainly viewed as a gift item. High school and college graduates in the forties and fifties, for example, were quite likely to receive a Parker "51" fountain pen (priced at $12.50) commemorating their achievement. Indeed, it was with a "51" that General Douglas MacArthur signed the Japanese Peace Treaty in 1945. Parker's stylish products and high profile name would keep it at the top of the pen market until the late sixties when American competitors A.T. Cross and Sheaffer, as well as a few foreign brands, knocked them out of first place once and for all.

Of course, Parker would not have lost its hold on the market had it not made some oversights along the way. In addition to a more competitive environment, Parker failed to come to terms with a fundamental change in the pen market— the development of the disposable, ballpoint pen. When Parker unveiled the $25 "75" pen in 1963, it showed that it remained committed to supplying high-priced pens to the upper end of the market. As the sixties wore on, a clear trend toward cheap ballpoint and soft-tip pens developed. Meanwhile, Parker's only ultimately successful addition to its product range in the late sixties was the "75" Classic line, yet another high-priced pen.

A Brief Flirtation With Low-Priced Pens

Parker did, however, make an effort to compete in the lower price segment of the market in the late sixties only to see it fail. In an attempt to capitalize on the trend toward inexpensive pens, Parker produced the T-Ball Jotter, priced at $1.98. The success of the Jotter led it to move even further down the price ladder when it acquired Eversharp. Whereas the Jotter had given Parker reason to believe it could make the shift from pricy pens to cheap pens with little or no difficulty, the Eversharp experience proved to be different. George Parker, a grandnephew of the company's founder and president of Parker Pen at the time, stated the reasons for the Eversharp failure, as well as its consequences:

All the market research surveys said go lower, go lower, go lower, that's where the business is. So I said, 'Go lower? Fine. But we don't know how.' We bought Eversharp and tried to run it ourselves, and we couldn't do it. Our people just couldn't think in terms of big units, and they didn't know how to sell people on the lower-priced end of the business—grocers, supermarkets, rack jobbers. The result was, Bic and Paper Mate were cleaning up in the lower-priced end, Cross in the high, and Parker was getting squeezed in the middle. Volume was going up, but our costs went up faster, and our profits were squeezed. (*Forbes*, 10/1/73)

The 1970s: The Illusion of Success

Despite the difficulties Parker encountered when it left its niche in the upper end of the pen market, the company experienced a healthy period of growth and profitability for most of the 1970s. Demand for its products remained strong, and its worldwide markets expanded significantly due to a rise in consumer income and increasing literacy rates in much of the Third World. Parker also chose to diversify during this decade, and its most noteworthy acquisition, Manpower, Inc., proved to be a very strong asset. In 1975, when it acquired Manpower, a temporary-help firm, Parker was the slightly more profitable of the two. With the boom in temporary services in the late seventies and early eighties, however, Manpower eclipsed Parker in sales and earnings and eventually subsidized its parent company during down periods.

Why did Parker fall from its position of leadership in the writing instrument market? There were many reasons, and one of the most important was the weakening of the U.S. dollars. At its peak, Parker accounted for half of all U.S. exports of writing instruments and 80 percent of its total sales came from 154 foreign countries. Parker was especially strong in Europe, most particularly in the United Kingdom. When sales in the strong European currencies were translated into dollars, Parker earned huge profits.

The downside of a weak dollar, however, was that it gave Parker the illusion that it was a well-run company. In fact, throughout the seventies, Parker was a model of inefficiency. Manufacturing facilities were dated and inefficient. Production was so erratic that the marketing department often had no idea what type of pens they would be selling from year to year or even month to month. Under the leadership of George Parker, nothing was done by company headquarters to update these facilities or to develop new products. As a result, subsidiaries and distributors around the world saw fit to develop their own products. By the end of George Parker's reign, the company's product line included 500 writing instruments.

That distant subsidiaries would have the leeway to make such decisions was not at all unusual at Parker, for it had long been known as one of the most globally decentralized companies in the world. Decentralization, in fact, was something that Parker took pride in and considered to be vital to its success as a multinational. Yet it was this very concept that Peterson and his new management team would hold to be responsible for much of what ailed Parker Pen.

PARKER'S GLOBAL OPERATIONS BEFORE PETERSON

In addition to having a hand in manufacturing and product line decisions, Parker's subsidiaries developed their own marketing strategies. More than 40 different advertising agencies promoted Parker pens in all the corners of the globe. When Peterson came to Parker, he was proudly informed that the company was a "federation" of autonomous geographical units. The downside to the "federation" concept, Peterson thought, was that home country management often lacked the information needed to make and coordinate basic business decisions. Control was so completely decentralized that Parker didn't even know how many pens it was selling by the time Peterson and his group arrived.

On the other hand, decentralization obviously had its positive aspects, most noticeably in the field of advertising. Pens mean different things to different people. Whereas Europeans are more likely to choose a pen based on its style and feel, a consumer from a lesser developed country in the seventies viewed the pen as nothing less than a badge of literacy. In addition, tastes varied widely from country to country. The French, for example, remained attached to the fountain pen. Scandanavians, for their part, showed a marked preference for the ballpoint. The logic behind having so many different advertising agencies was that, even if it appeared to be somewhat inefficient, in the end the company was better off from a sales standpoint.

Some of the individual advertising agencies were able to devise excellent, imaginative campaigns that struck a responsive chord among their local audiences. One example was the Lowe Howard-Spink agency in London. The Parker U.K. division became the company's most profitable during the tenure of the Lowe agency. An example of its creativity is an ad entitled "Rediscover the lost art of the insult." Gracing the ad is a picture of a dead plumber, on his back, with a giant Parker pen protruding from his heart. Part of the text is as follows:

Do you know plumbers who never turn up?
Hairdressers who missed their vocations as butchers?
Drycleaners who make your stains disappear—and your clothes with them?
Today, we at Parker give you the chance to get your own back.
Not only are we offering a beautiful new pen called the Laque which owes its deep lustre to a Chinese technique 2000 years old, but we are attempting to revive something that went out when the telephone came in.
The well-armed, witty, malicious dart. (*Ad Age*, 6/2/86)

While the Parker U.K. division was a success, however, the company's general inefficiencies, loss of market share, and lack of strategic direction were finally revealed in the early eighties with the rise of the U.S. dollar. Parker's financial decline was even more precipitous than the dollar's increase. When the huge 1982 losses were registered, Peterson was brought in from R.J. Reynolds to try and turn things around for Parker. He decided that every aspect of the company needed to be closely examined, not the least of which was Parker's decentralization of global operations.

QUESTIONS (A)

1. What would you do if you were in James Peterson's shoes in January of 1982?
2. What changes, if any, would you make in Parker's marketing strategy?
3. Which aspects of Parker's structure would you discard? Which would you keep?
4. Assume that you are James Peterson and you have just hired a new management team composed of highly qualified executives from outside companies. You and your new team are convinced that you have the solution to Parker's problems but there are many holdovers who disagree with you. How would you implement your plan? To what extent would you incorporate the views of Parker management into your plan?

PARKER PEN CO. (B)
PARKER GOES GLOBAL

We will be creating more news in the next two years than we have in the past ten.—James Peterson. July, 1982

James Peterson relished the chance to be the top man at Parker Pen. He spent 24 years at Pillsbury and had a taste of what it was like to be at the helm of a corporation when he rose to the rank of president, the number two power spot in the company. At R.J. Reynolds, he was an executive vice president—an influential position, to be sure, but not one that afforded him the freedom of movement that he would have liked. When he was brought to Parker in January of 1982, Peterson, then 54, finally had the chance to run a company. All the theories he held to be true would be tested. All the lessons he had learned after some 30 years of practical business experience—much of it in international operations—would now be applied.

His years at R.J. Reynolds had convinced him of the superiority of global marketing, which he understood to mean standardized product and promotion strategies the whole world over. This view made him unalterably opposed to the loose structure that had characterized Parker Pen before his arrival. In the opinion of Peterson, there was absolutely no way that any company operating in the modern world would be able to survive such disarray. That a subsidiary thousands of miles away could decide not only what products it would manufacture but also how they would market them ran counter to everything Peterson believed.

Peterson quickly moved to remold Parker Pen in his own image. In addition to too much decentralization, Peterson thought Parker lacked "a good enunciation of business philosophy." According to Peterson, "every good company has to have one." In order to correct this problem, Peterson devised an eight-point statement of his management philosophy and had it translated into more than 40 languages and sent in letter form to Parker managers all over the world. The statement contained such phrases as, "There is no substitute for quality," and, "Like most managers, I don't like surprises." The letters concluded by saying: "As I get to meet each of you in the months ahead, I will be discussing this business philosophy with you and asking you how you have used it." (*Ad Age*, 7/26/82)

THE DISMANTLING OF DECENTRALIZATION: FROM 40 AGENCIES TO 1

The core of Peterson's revitalization efforts would be directed at dismantling the geographical organization that Parker had evolved into over the years. He slashed the product line from 500 to the 100 most profitable items. The manufacturing function was consolidated, greatly reducing the number of units produced overseas. As for what products would be manufactured, that was to be strictly decided by the management team at the Janesville headquarters. Of course, the manufacturing facilities themselves would have to be updated, for no longer could the production department be allowed to dictate to marketing executives exactly what kind of products it would be selling. None of these measures in and of themselves was startling—each addressed problems that needed to be corrected. However, when Peterson decided to get rid of Parker's 40-odd advertising agencies in favor of one "world-class agency," more than a few eyebrows were raised.

The logic behind the decision to go with one advertising agency (Ogilvy & Mather) was consistent with Peterson's desire to make Parker Pen a global marketing corporation. With one agency instead of 40, not only could money be saved, but strategies could be coordinated on a global scale. One problem, however, was that formerly productive agencies such as Lowe Howard-Spink in London were fired. This had a devastating effect on morale at Parker U.K., the company's most profitable subsidiary which had in effect been

subsidizing the same American division that was now telling it how to advertise.

"THE WORLD'S NO. 1 PEN COMPANY"

Even though Parker had experienced many problems before Peterson arrived, the company was still very proud of its tradition as a leading producer of "quality writing instruments." Of course, this pride was sometimes translated into overblown statements such as, "Parker is the world's No. 1 pen company." This indeed was the party line at Parker even though it was paid little more than lip service. When Manville Smith arrived in 1982, he commissioned a study to see just how important Parker was. His findings shocked him: Parker had only a 6 percent share of the global pen market and it didn't even attempt to participate in a segment that was responsible for 65 percent of all sales of pens in the world— that is pens that sold for less than $3.

The new management team wanted to make Parker more than just a fictitious No. 1 company. In order to recapture market share, Parker would have to participate in the lower end of the market—the same area that George Parker himself had so hastily abandoned in the late sixties. A new $15 million state-of-the-art plant would be built whose main function would be to manufacture the Vector, a roller-ball pen selling for $2.98. The Vector was Manville Smith's pet project. Using a new automated line at Parker's new plant, Smith calculated that the Vector could be produced for 27 cents per unit and therefore generate huge profits for the company. After the Vector, Smith planned to plunge even deeper into the low-price market with the Itala. An even cheaper model that would be Parker's first disposable pen.

THE FIRST RUMBLINGS OF DISSENT: GEORGE PARKER

Although George Parker was still formally the chairman of Parker Pen, he was expected to lead a quiet, charmed life in Marco Island, Florida and never to be heard from again. In fact, George Parker was paying very close attention to the new developments in the company that bore his name, and he was none too happy. As his above remarks might suggest, he was scornful of a strict market research approach to the pen business. He also took pride in Parker Pen's autonomous federation" system that provided a high degree of flexibility to the company's many subsidiaries. Even more disturbing to him was the planned foray into the lower depths of the marketplace, as he might put it. Cheap pens were beneath Parker Pen, in his opinion, and nothing could be more disgraceful than a disposable pen bearing his name. What were they manufacturing anyway, garbage bags?

Compounding George Parker's displeasure was his sincere dislike for James Peterson, whom he dubbed "motormouth." To him, Peterson was the embodiment of everything that was wrong with the new Parker Pen. The grandnephew of the company's founder still had many well-placed friends in the company, and his constant criticism of the new management team probably did little to aid their cause.

PROBLEMS: FINANCIAL LOSSES, SMITH GETS FIRED, ONE WORLD MARKETING FAILS

Despite all the complaints from George Parker, Peterson's major problems lay elsewhere. The strong dollar that had exposed so many of his company's weaknesses got even stronger. Recession was a worldwide plague. The costs of new plant development were not absorbed by profits and the company lost $13.6 million in fiscal 1983. Still, Peterson had the luxury of time on his side, since he had little more than one full year under his belt. One more year like 1983, however, and he was gone.

In Peterson's opinion, only a full-fledged global marketing effort could save Parker. At the March, 1984 Palm Beach meeting, it was decided that Parker would participate "in every viable segment of the writing instrument business." In addition, it was declared that, "The concept of marketing by centralized direction has been discussed and consensus was reached." The management team, filled with a sense of purpose, then set out to achieve its lofty goals.

There remained one major problem: Parker's new plant was proving to be a failure. The plant was not functional for the 1983 Christmas season, costing the company millions of dollars in sales. Even as Peterson and his group were working round-the-clock to see its strategy through, the computer-automated plant which was supposed to spearhead Parker's drive into the lower end of the market, broke down repeatedly. With automation having failed, the company was forced to hire labor again and its costs skyrocketed. Manville Smith, who had placed his name next to the fully automated Vector project, was fired by Peterson as a result.

Smith's departure was important because he was the only member of the management team that held out for local advertising flexibility. Smith had worked closely with Ogilvy & Mather (O & M) on Parker's first worldwide advertising campaign. At Smith's urging O & M devised a campaign that allowed for some degree of local flexibility. When Smith left, however, Peterson took over the advertising reins and pushed very hard for "one-look" advertising and the results were disastrous.

The fashion in which Peterson promoted his advertising policy was enough to alienate once and for all those remaining managers that supported his efforts. A proclamation issued from the Janesville office and sent across the globe headquarters stated that: "Advertising for Parker pens [no matter model or mode] will be based on a common creative strategy and positioning. . . . The worldwide advertising theme, 'Make your mark with a Parker,' has been adopted. . . . [It] will utilize similar graphic layout and photography. It will utilize an agreed-upon typeface. It will utilize the approved Parker logo/graphic design. It will be adapted from centrally supplied materials. . . ."

The new advertising campaign was indeed rigidly controlled. Subsidiaries were sent their materials and told to get on with it. Managers abroad were seen as simple implementers of the global marketing strategy with little or no input. The problem was that many of them realized right away that the new advertising campaign wouldn't work in their markets. In fact, the campaign really didn't work anywhere. Jack Marks would later qualify it as "lowest-common denominator-advertising," that "tried to say something to everybody, and didn't say anything to anybody."

The last to admit failure was Peterson himself, who ignored all evidence and tried to move forward with a second wave of global advertising in January of 1985, this time for the Vector, which had finally made it off the production line. By this time, however, Peterson's position was terminally weakened. Production problems persisted, morale was low, resentment of the management team was high and reaction to yet another generic campaign was so negative that Peterson felt compelled to resign.

POSTSCRIPT: "GLOBAL MARKETING IS DEAD."

The successor to Peterson as CEO was Mitchell Fromstein, president of what once was Parker's Manpower subsidiary. Since it

TABLE 1 Parker Pen Co. Selected Operating Results

YEAR ENDED FEB. 28	REVENUES (MILLIONS)	NET INCOME (MILLIONS)	EARNINGS	DIVIDENDS (PER SHARE)	RANGE
1985	$843.7	$5.4	$0.32	$0.52	21–13
1984	708.8	11.8	0 70	0.52	21–12
1983	635.3	d13.6	d0.80	0.52	17–11
1982	679.1	15.7	0.92	0.50	24–14
1981	723.2	37.7	2.23	0.44	26–14

d-Deficit

Balance sheet as of June 30, 1985:
  Current assets: $284.5 million
  Current liabilities: $239.5 million
  Current ratio: 1.1–to–1
  Long-term debt: $27.1 million
  Common shares: 17,635,000
  Book value: $7.65

Source: Annual reports.

was purchased in 1975 by Parker, Manpower continued to grow to the point where it was far more profitable than its parent and, indeed, subsidized it for several years. Manpower would wind up taking over Parker, finally selling it to a group of British investors in 1986.

Fromstein was an implacable foe of Peterson's. Manpower was as international as Parker Pen, and Fromstein had his own views as to how an international business should be run. When he assumed control of Parker in January 1985, he gathered the company's country managers in Janesville and told them: "Global marketing is dead. You're free again." (*Ad Age*, 6/2/86)

QUESTIONS (B)

1. Why did Peterson's global strategy fail?
2. What lessons can be drawn from the decline and fall of Parker Pen?

PARKER PEN CO. (C)
GLOBAL MARKETING STRATEGY:
AN INTERVIEW WITH DR. DENNIS THOMAS

President, The Berol Corporation,[1]
Danbury, Conn. 06810

Charles Anderer[2]: I would first like to thank you for taking the time to share your views on global marketing and Parker Pen in this interview.

Dennis Thomas[3]: It's my pleasure.

CA: I would like to start out by asking you a question about an article that we both have read.[4] Do you agree with the notion that the big issue today is not whether to go global

[1] The Berol Corporation manufactures a variety of office products including a wide range of writing instruments.

[2] Case writer and researcher, the Leading Edge Case Study Project, Lubin Graduate School of Business, Pace University.

[3] President, The Berol Corporation, Danbury, Conn.

[4] J. A. Quelch and E. J. Hoff, "Customizing Global Marketing," *Harvard Business Review*, May–June 1986, pp. 59–68.

but how to tailor the global marketing concept to each business?

DT: If it's an either or proposition, I am broadly in agreement with the proposition. I believe that there are relatively few major markets where the local conditions are so self-contained, so capable of being kept self-contained, and so different, either for cultural or other kinds of reasons, that the underlying, increasing level of similarity that is coming into most major marketplaces, as opposed to the nuances of necessary local difference, cannot form the bedrock of acceptable product offerings, positionings and what you have. Also, the economies of scale and the relative size of self-contained markets, in and of themselves, are of decreasing appeal other than for a small business which chooses to remain small. But in many industries and many marketplaces, the products which adequately serve market needs increasingly have within them either outright commodities or commodity-like ingredients if they are likely to be products that are positioned in a marketplace over a period of decades rather than over a few fashion cycles of a few months or a few years. . . . The real question is: What is the appropriate international scale for the business and what is the appropriate international scale for the underlying marketplace?

CA: What forces do you see behind the increasing similarities of markets? Telecommunications is one that comes to mind. . . .

DT: Sure. We are much more aware, whether we are conscious of it or not, of what other parts of the world look like. . . . Broadly speaking, people behave as consumers who may be appealed to in the same kinds of ways. Whether they are at level two or level four of a Maslow hierarchy or any kind of structure you would like to adopt, we are becoming more steadily accepting of the fact that they are likely to go through the same kinds of progressions. The form that a status need may take in one society as opposed to another may be somewhat different, but status needs exist in both. How well developed they are, whether people may exercise them, how many people, in what kinds of ways, and what they will be looking for—those are all to my mind subsidiary kinds of questions, but you know its going to be there.

You do, also, have the fact of increasing international communities. People travel, they go from one culture and from one history to another. The world is becoming more interrelated, either directly through people transfer or indirectly through visual transfer, on a much more regular basis. Something that has already happened in Tokyo will be there for you to see on the six o'clock news. It sounds as though its a long way between that phenomenon and whether or not you can sell the same pen in Japan and the United States. But I don't think it's as far-fetched as many have

historically supposed when you stop and think about it.

There is no reason why the intervention of water should be a cutoff point between groups of people and their often similar characteristics.

CA: When you look at recent developments in the global business arena such as Rupert Murdoch's bid to establish a global communications empire and the growing concentration of the world's advertising agencies as evidenced by the rash of mergers and acquisitions which culminated with Saatchi & Saatchi's purchase of Ted Bates Worldwide, do you see an irreversible trend toward the globalization of business and, if so, what do you make of it?

DT: There probably is a trend and, certainly, the existence of a large number of international unifiers in various forms of communication is going to make it more possible for companies to entertain the notion of doing business internationally. Whether, however, businesses will look for over-homogenization and try to bring it about to make their own lives easier or simply to see a reflection of their own set of values cast on a worldwide stage remains to be seen. That's an area where I'm a little puzzled and, perhaps, a little concerned at this point in time. There are important shades, colors, and nuances in individual countries or regions or cultures whether those cultures happen to coincide or not with international boundaries. I am also not so sure that there won't be an encouragement or an enticement to make Parker pen type mistakes.

The economic incentive to homogenize the world is indeed very strong. It is also probably the natural route for the northern hemisphere in particular to counter demographics and broad scale cultural differences. There is more appeal to continue to do as you have done particularly if [the firm] has evolved to a "higher level." To look to do the same thing somewhere else is somehow more appealing than to go back two or three paces and start over in an emerging country or society and be successful doing the things you did ten or fifteen years ago.

Pure volume and demographic growth is likely to be much more concentrated in the southern hemisphere and the far east over the next twenty years or so. However, there are more concerns about political and societal stability in those kinds of arenas. They are more prone to political and economic volatility than they once were and they are no longer easy to colonize in the economic sense. They're more likely to pinch whatever technology they need, start their own businesses, and kick you out than used to be the case. You can't sit back and control the world from New York or London or Frankfurt as once you could. It's a more unruly place, therefore, we prefer to deal with safer and more secure boundaries which are spread across the northern hemisphere with digressions into the south when we consider it relatively safe. The trend that you've identified is partly a response to this way of thinking and that's how you can make the economic case for continuing to do what you are doing.

CA: In addition to making developing nations more technologically sophisticated, what are the broader implications of worldwide availability of and easy access to advanced technologies?

DT: Since there is more access to technology and much less in the way of protection and security around technologies and, because of the sheer length of life of many technologies and many basic product categories, the opportunity for capital substitution in place of human substitution has to a large extent already taken place. Therefore, there is a more even access to the various forms of production advantage—whether it be economies of

scale, optimum size of plant and configuration, or an optimum form of technology. Quite simply, the thresholds for entry into many kinds of industries are not that great. And, certainly, the ability to maintain exclusivity or erect boundaries is nowhere near what it used to be. You cannot keep people out.

CA: Static demographics and markets, worldwide technological parity and converging product quality make it more important than ever to have a handle on your costs and to be efficient. Are we moving toward the day when only the largest and most highly efficient firms can afford to compete internationally?

DT: Yes. Unless you set out to be, and deliberately restrain your ambitions to very clearly identified and defensible niches of one kind or another. It's a very, I think, competent strategist and manager who can make a success of a totally niche-based strategy. Not many people can do that. Most companies simply cannot afford to.

I think you can afford to internationally extend some of the segmentation that you have already domestically achieved. For example, if you've got a particular product portfolio that has appeal in a certain market segment that you've historically concentrated on within your domestic base, it is sometimes easier to transfer that segmentation geographically than to add other segments to it domestically. By the same token, it is perhaps easier to extend yourself horizontally than to move vertically. Certainly to move up. It may not be easier to move down, as many people point out when evaluating Parker Pen's strategy.

I don't think that many people operating in product fields where differentiation is possible yet not, for very long, sustainable either in terms of an individual product or a product category could follow a niche-based strategy. It's only the real late arrival to a market that, by default, has to pursue such a strategy. For the other players, I think there has to be a combination of capability to operate at the low-cost end and forms of niche-differentiation either in terms of market boundaries (segmentation) or in terms of product characteristics. Although the latter, as I say, are more difficult to sustain over time.

CA: Besides the problem of moving down the product line in the case of Parker Pen, many observers felt that the company's drastic shift from a largely decentralized organization to the more tightly controlled version that is necessary when implementing a classic global marketing strategy automatically ruled out the strategy's chances for success because it resulted in too much loss of employee morale on the local level. Do you see this as a problem in any company undergoing that same shift from a decentralized to a centralized organization?

DT: A lot depends on how you do it. The time scale that you negotiate to achieve [the strategic shift] with, either with your board or with your stockholders as opposed to with your managers, goes a long way toward determining success or failure. To achieve some of those things in terms of internal human scale often requires a longer commitment than might be available in terms of an external financial scale. There is probably an underlying sentiment that says, satisfy those external audiences and see if you can't sit on top of the internal ones. . . and, yes, if these guys don't like it, presumably there are others that are prepared to operate within that kind of a changed culture.

But I believe that, in Parker's instance, they probably put an impossible time scale on themselves to achieve the desired degree of change in acceptable human terms without precipitating unnecessary turnover. You see, a certain amount of turnover is not only to be expected but is probably necessary be-

cause the kinds of values and skills that you've looked for and rewarded in the truly decentralized operation may not be as valid or as useful in the more integrated approach. Particularly if you give the pendulum a big yank and a swing towards the other end you can expect the sheer momentum to throw people off from side to side. It's really a question of how many people did you lose that you didn't want to or that, at the end of the day, you couldn't afford to? This is more the measure of success or failure in implementing that kind of strategy.

And, finally, by what audacity do you believe that your insights, analytical abilities, creative talents, administrative skills and business acumen combine to make such a decision failure-proof? For the decision to come from an individual or a very small group of individuals, some of whom might be very new to that industry and to that marketplace. . . you've got to have a lot of reasons to justify having self-confidence in that small a pool of talent than what might have been available out of a goodly proportion of your previously successful decentralized managers. But if you have a French operation, for example, that had been losing money for quite a period of time or about whose management you have questions concerning their capability, you would have those questions whether the company was centralized or decentralized. The question is: How flexible are some of those domestic managers? They may learn, grow, and develop in some extraordinary ways by being exposed to the international world. So it's not that they're always right and the center is always wrong either.

CA: It seems as if Parker not only gave itself very little time to accomplish its transition from decentralization to centralization but that it also engaged in draconian measures on the operational side. I speak here of dropping all 40 of its advertising agencies in favor of a single "world class" agency. Can a single agency hope to be all things to all people or, in the case of Parker, do the job more effectively than a multitude of agencies?

DT: It depends on the advertising program that they come up with, which in turn depends on the degree of internationalism within the agency. I think one of the difficulties is that, historically at least, some of the worldwide agencies have been strongly oriented to their home countries—that is, wherever they started—be it the United States or Japan. There is a substantial difference between an American agency operating in France and a French agency, that has been fused to an American agency through acquisition, operating in France. Some advertising agencies, just like some multinationals, are unmistakably ethnocentric.

It's also a question of the extent to which certain appeals in relation to a product themselves are international. Some products lend themselves to a high degree of uniformity in terms of what it is that they will do and in terms of what it is that will appeal in relation to what they do. From one country to the next, you may well be able to have very easy local adaptation as long as you avoid some of the major cultural pitfalls. If, for example, there are visual symbols that are somewhat obscene in certain cultures and perfectly O.K. in others and you screen for those adequately, you may be able to get away with a high degree of uniformity. If you can, then I would think that the proportional level of local resistance would be that much lower. The question is whether local management thinks the program will work in terms of its market segment.

CA: Can a pen in the Parker price range, which was generally moderate to expensive, be successfully marketed in uniform fashion from country to country?

DT: Let's try and pick it apart a little bit. You might have some elements of appeal in terms of a relatively uniform visual configuration. Whether that product performs as a fountain pen or a ballpoint or a felt-tip or a roller ball—that's easily variable from the inside out. You can have a common external configuration with a fair variety of tip, and therefore, performance variation coming out of it. So you could have an element of design uniformity that, given a fair degree of demand in whatever geographically international market segment you are targeting, should not compromise the product's appeal to different people.

The higher up you go in terms of price, the closer you get to a piece of personal jewelry or adornment, and the easier it is to market the product uniformly. In the higher segments it is purely an issue of cosmetics—whether the product, which you would want to be slim and elegant no matter the country, would be better in silver for that market or in gold for this market—these are second order questions. The real question is: Do people regard personal adornment with writing instruments as a way of expressing a level of achievement and status in their local community? If the answer is yes, then you can very easily market that product on an international scale. An interesting example might be Dunhill. Admittedly, their success has been on a limited international scale. Still, it is interesting to think how a tobacco seller gets into writing instruments and the fact that the same Dunhill pens are available in world-class, cosmopolitan cities. This is a good example of a totally uniform product and presentation on an international scale in a particularly narrow market segment.

At the other end of the scale, you go right down to the commodity product and the same argument prevails for slightly different reasons. If what you are interested in is a very basic writing instrument to make a mark on paper you have two choices: Do you want to be able to make that mark and subsequently be able to change it, in which case you go predominantly for a wood-case pencil, or, do you want to be able to make it and have a certain amount of longevity associated with it, in which case you go for a ballpoint pen? These products are fairly basic, straightforward, and, I would say, uniform. As long as you take into account the lower, if not the lowest, common denominator in terms of writing surface and your ballpoint is able to operate on lower-quality paper as opposed to the finest bond, you can probably make, sell, and present the same product in India as you can in Ghana or in Peru because the basic consumer's need is uniform on a worldwide basis.

CA: Let's switch from marketing the product to producing it. As you know, Parker was beset by production woes before and after it marketed its products globally. How important is the production process in the pen industry in general and how far do you think faulty production went toward the undermining of its global marketing plan?

DT: Reliable consistency is important in that industry as in most. In Parker's instance, I think the very marked contrast between the new Parker and the old Parker in terms of production had as much of a disruptive effect as anything else. Secondly, I believe that very often people coming into any industry new, or relatively new, tend to shortchange the need to understand manufacturing and technological processes. Such understanding enables managers to know with confidence what kinds of future commitments they can make and expect to meet. Historically, company takeover or turnaround specialists don't usually have strong personal background or interest in the manufacturing function. They tend to have spent their time in either marketing or finance rather than in manufacturing, so that function gets shortchanged.

I would suspect that the new Parker management didn't have the ability to look at the projections for the rationalization and re-equipment program and say: "Come on guys, you say you can do that in 15 months. Where is your Kentucky Windage Factor? Where are the critical delivery bottlenecks? How reliable are those suppliers? What has been their track record in terms of on-time delivery? What allowance has been made for de-bugging? Do we have people experienced with that kind of equipment? Are we getting equipment that's new to the suppliers as well as new to our own production people? In which case, you should probably build a safety factor into the de-bugging period rather than just the shortest possible time to get it done." I'm probably beginning to sound like a cracked record, but it points out the need to know what is realistic and achieveable. This is never going to be satisfactory, but at least you know how much time things should be taking and then how much you're compromising, as opposed to how much you don't know you're overpromising to yourself or to other people.

Appendix: Global Marketing Research[1]

Global marketing research is a complex and demanding task. Unilever's experience illustrates some of the problems and opportunities on conducting international research in Europe. For example,

1. We still have a number of local products and brands that are marketed in just one or two countries—for example, jam or canned vegetables. Unless there is a serious interest in the possibility of extending their marketing to a number of other countries, the consumer research involved will by definition be purely locally planned and probably limited. However, by far the main weight of our consumer research nowadays is naturally on international brands, actual or potential.

2. A substantial minority—probably over a third—of market research expenditure in Europe generally is on continuous research, primarily market measurement. In our case, the proportion varies quite a lot by product field and country, but our overall average would not be radically different from the general European picture. Such background research is obviously vital for planning and monitoring marketing activities, both strategic and tactical. However it hardly calls for special comment here, beyond saying that in our case the decision about what, and how much, data of this kind to buy is normally the responsibility of the local company. Europe is on the whole very well served by retail audits and consumer panels.

3. In the case of an international brand that is "master minded" by a lead country, the latter will probably need to carry out much more intensive consumer research than will a receiver country. Where a country is responsible for developing a particular new product, considerable concept, product development, and marketing mix research is likely to be called for before other countries become heavily involved with the new product. The laboratories themselves will also usually be carrying out a great deal of consumer research guidance work.

4. Especially where technical product development work is an important element in a brand, we may nevertheless need at an early stage a broader geographical picture of consumer habits, needs, and responses to formulation variables. This may necessitate detailed habit surveys across a number of the major countries, although increasingly international data banks have been built up of such basic information. It may sometimes also call for some product testing across several countries to provide guidance for technical development programs. Such work may or may not be carried out simultaneously in different countries.

5. If the new development goes well in the lead country, then research elsewhere will naturally start by checking out reactions to the already developed mix. Only if this throws up some problem is it likely that any more basic work will be called for in the receiver country. This incidentally is one factor that increases the importance of having effective but not too expensive laboratory test market facilities fairly widely available in the different countries.

6. Unilever's decentralized structure means that the funds for, and decisions about, market research are primarily at local level. Product coordinations have only very limited central

[1]Contributed by John Downham, head of market research, Marketing Division, Unilever PLC, London. Adapted from a paper presented to the American Marketing Association Annual Marketing Conference, New York City, May 1982.

budgets for such work. This means that whenever research on an international scale is called for, it will be paid for mainly (or most likely totally) out of the local companies' research budgets in the countries concerned. This may sometimes lead to problems if a particular local company has only very limited immediate interest in a particular project or has already largely committed its annual research budget to other studies. On the other hand the approach has the very great merit of making sure that the participating countries are closely involved in the project and committed to its success.

7. In practice it is nowadays very unusual for Unilever to carry out a multicountry study in Europe, in the sense of the same survey being carried out in a number of countries simultaneously. Such studies were if anything more common 10 to 15 years ago than they are today. There are several reasons for this, including, for example,

   a. The fact that more of the key background data are already available for the major countries.

   b. Greater emphasis on lead country work.

   c. Evidence that for many nonfood products a fairly standard (but not necessarily identical) mix is appropriate across a range of countries. Where this is not the case, for example, with certain food products, then we are likely to have to fall back anyway on individual country research to work out the best local solution.

However, a situation where formal multicountry studies are less frequent means that (a little paradoxically) standard international research methods become *more* important. International comparability of research data has then to arise out of the general use of a common research approach rather than from the coordinated planning of a specific international project.

Standardization of Research Methods

Standardization for the sake of standardization is a trap if it leads in practice to results that are in fact not comparable or even misleading. In the case of Europe, however, the differences in culture are sufficiently small today to make it possible to apply similar techniques very widely—although even now not quite universally. We would not, for example, use mail questionnaires in Italy. Compared with the situation described 10 years ago, we have therefore moved considerably farther down this route.

Standardization has developed in various directions and to varying extents. It has gone farthest, as you might expect, in fields (such as detergents) where there are the most noticeable similarities between the different markets and also where expenditure on market research tends to be highest. It has also developed more quickly and intensively in the case of research providing inputs to basic technical and R&D operations—where in certain cases specifically technical measurements of in-the-home activities and performance are needed in parallel with the more traditional forms of consumer research. In certain product fields we now have extremely detailed manuals covering basic habits and product development research. More latitude is still allowed in other areas of research where there is less agreement about the merits of alternative approaches and/or where these are continuing to evolve fairly rapidly (for example with laboratory test markets of various kinds).

The Organization of Unilever's Marketing Research

Unilever has always been a major user of marketing research. Today we probably spend roughly $40 million per year on market research worldwide. With the development of local manufacturing facilities in a growing number of countries, Unilever followed a policy of setting up its own local full-service market research departments in many of these countries. During the 1960s and early 1970s, these departments were increasingly turned into separate profit centers and were encouraged to compete for third-party business.

The present position in Western Europe is that we have local Unilever research companies in 13 countries—the exceptions being Ireland (where our U.K. unit can provide help when required), Luxembourg, Norway, and Switzerland. The 13 European units operate under the umbrella title of Research International, although for historical and legal reasons, they tend to have different local company names. Of the 13, all but 2 (Portugal and Greece) are now fully coordinated within a European Market Research Group, based in London. This functions in much the same way as the product coordinations referred to earlier. Well over half of Research International's business now comes from non-Unilever clients.

This background obviously affects the way in which we handle our market research requirements. There is in fact no obligation on Unilever companies to buy their research from our own units. The latter must compete with outside suppliers for the work that Unilever commissions. As you are doubtless aware, there is no shortage of such suppliers. The current European Society of Marketing Research ESOMAR Handbook lists some 500 market research agencies in the 17 Western European countries, as follows:

Austria	12	Greece	9	Portugal	5
Belgium	25	Holland	57	Spain	20
Denmark	15	Ireland	5	Sweden	24
Finland	12	Italy	45	Switzerland	30
France	59	Luxembourg	1	United Kingdom	93
West Germany	72	Norway	15		

This ESOMAR list is by no means the total story: It has a natural bias toward the larger research companies and those interested in international business. The current *Market Research Society Directory* in the United Kingdom, for example, lists 210 companies in that country alone—over twice as many as the ESOMAR Handbook.

Even today, however, there are relatively few *international groups or chains* that can offer direct coverage of all the countries in Western Europe and fewer still that have common ownership. This consideration is an important one for us in research just as it is in advertising. In our experience the international standardization of research approaches is easier when the research agencies involved are closely linked through common ownership. We have learned by bitter experience over the years how easy it is even within Europe for misunderstandings to arise over the design of a multicountry survey—and even in the case of research units that know one another well.

Effective international briefing obviously means tremendous attention to detail right from the outset. In the case of Research International, for example, the group has a standard initial briefing form for use in communicating with other units during the early stages of a multicountry survey. The full checklist of points to be covered runs to 77 items under the following headings:

Executive tasks	18	Production	11	Commercial	5
Data collection	20	Timing	7	Other general points	3
Data processing	13				

The briefing checklist is designed to cover the main issues of design and administration that need to be specified by the master unit appointed to control the study. No system of this kind can completely eliminate errors and misunderstandings. The approach has certainly helped to reduce them as executives in the different units have become familiar with the issues listed, and it also helps in pinning down the client's requirements fairly early on. But even so, it is ultimately no substitute for having detailed agreement in advance on standard methodology for general use.

There is one final issue to which to refer that also influences international research planning: the costs of research. Market research costs in Europe have risen steeply in recent years, and the squeeze on margins and profits generally has put the squeeze on research also. Although Unilever does not carry out many multicountry surveys, one consideration that can on occasion influence our research strategy is the wide difference in costs between countries. Table 1 is an index of market research costs for 14 European countries:

TABLE 1 Quantitative/Qualitative Studies Comparison of Market Research Costs

QUANTITATIVE (average of four indices)		QUALITATIVE (average of two indices)	
Country	Index	Country	Index
Switzerland	147	France	134
Sweden	125	Norway	132
France	123	The Netherlands	126
West Germany	116	Switzerland	112
The Netherlands	109	Denmark	107
Italy	106	Sweden	105
Norway	101	Spain	101
Great Britain	96	Great Britain	99
Denmark	94	West Germany	89
Spain	93	Italy	89
Finland	76	Belgium	87
Austria	75	Finland	84
Belgium	73	Austria	73
Greece	68	Greece	63

Source: ESOMAR.

We should not attach too much importance to the precise figures—and a different set of research specifications might show a slightly different ranking. However, the table does help to make two points. First, when considering a multicountry study in Europe, the budget required will depend not only on how many but *which* countries are to be included. Second, to emphasize once again an earlier line of argument, despite its growing similarities in various respects, the Common Market still has many facets that are very far from common.

9

SOURCING DECISIONS AND GLOBAL PRODUCTION STRATEGY

If there is but little water in the stream, it is the fault, not of the channel, but of the source.

St. Jerome, c. 342–420
Letter 17

INTRODUCTION

A global business strategy has four legs: marketing, research and development, engineering and design, and sourcing. Although this book focuses upon the task of formulating and implementing a global marketing strategy, it goes without saying that without a competitive global sourcing strategy even the most brilliant global marketing strategy is doomed to failure. This chapter addresses the decisions of whether to make or buy product and where to make or buy product that is required to satisfy demand identified in the marketing plan.

MARKETING REVISITED

Since marketing is applied economics, it is useful to relate marketing to the world as seen from the perspective of the economist. The economist's world is illustrated in Figure 9–1. Macroeconomics recognizes the importance of aggregate demand and supply by identifying aggregate supply as part of the equation that determines overall output (real GNP), employment levels, prices, and inflation. The relationship between marketing and the economist's world is direct: Aggregate demand is the sum of all customer and market segment demand identified by marketers.

The "new" concept of marketing shifted the focus of marketing from the product to the customer. This shift led some marketers to act as if they believed

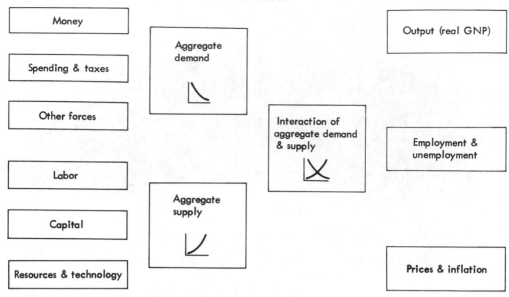

FIGURE 9–1   Macroeconomics—The World According to Paul A. Samuelson, Economist and Nobel Laureate

Source: *The Economist*, March 14, 1987.

that focusing upon the customer would insure success. This is analogous to the macroeconomics perspective of the 1930s and 1940s that ignored the importance of supply in the equation (Figure 9–1) that described the determination of real GNP. Focusing upon the customer will, if it is done with sensitivity and skill, lead to knowledge of needs that must be satisfied by a business plan that creates a competitive advantage. Sourcing is a critical element of the business plan. For example, Honda may have a plan to deliver 1,000,000 cars per year to Japanese consumers. As exchange rates shift, Honda may decide that in order to achieve the greatest possible competitive advantage in the Japanese market it should shift its sourcing for certain models from Japan to the United States.

The modern view of marketing recognizes that product, price, and distribution are vital and coequal elements in the marketing equation which determines market share and competitive performance. There are four essential elements of marketing, and *needs* are only one of them (see Table 9–1).

TABLE 9–1   The Four Key Elements of Marketing

1. Needs
2. Product, price, place (channels of distribution)
3. Value
4. Communications

Focusing upon the customer's *needs* and *communicating* the way in which the firm's product can satisfy those needs are two of the four elements of marketing. Both are critically important and essential for success. Equally important and essential for success are four additional elements: the *product, price, place* (channels of distribution), and *value*. A company's success is based on delivering greater value to customers than competitors can. This requires a product that customers want and value, *and* a sourcing or production strategy that delivers competitive value.

THE SOURCING CHALLENGE

The challenge of sourcing is to materialize the value that will meet customer needs. This requires a decision on *whether* to make or buy, and then a decision about where to make or buy. The aim in reaching this decision should be to achieve a quality cost combination of value that maximizes both customer benefits and company profits.

Value

Customer value is defined by the following equation:

$$V = \frac{Q + F}{P}$$

where

 V = customer value
 Q = product quality as perceived by the customer
 F = product features valued by customer
 P = price of product to customer

An increase in the numerator factors quality and features (as defined by the customer) will increase value. Similarly, a decrease in the denominator factor, price, will increase value.[1] It is this formula that defines the parameters of the sourcing decision. If customers are nationalistic, they may put a value on the feature "made in the home country." If this is the case, this preference must be measured to solve for value in the above equation. One of the reasons companies outside the United States

---

[1]There are, of course, notable exceptions to the rule that a decrease in the denominator of this equation will increase value. To the extent that price is perceived as an indicator of quality and value, an *increase* in price may increase value. This requires no change in the formula because in these situations, an increase in the denominator results in an increase in the quality element (as perceived by the customer) of the numerator which is greater than the increase in the denominator. The formula as presented applies to situations where customer perceptions of value and quality are influenced by price.

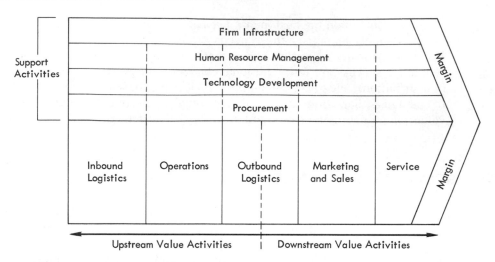

FIGURE 9–2   The Value Chain

have had such great success in penetrating the U.S. market is because competitors from many countries have convinced U.S. customers that products from their country are of high quality. The mark "Made in Japan" or "Made in Germany" is a plus while "Made in U.S.A." for many products is a minus. All of Chrysler's attempts to wave the flag over their product line have not stopped American consumers from storming the showrooms of the Hyundai dealers. Indeed, Hyundai is getting more benefit from the halo effect of the general perception of quality associated with Japan and the Pacific basin than Chrysler is from its flag waving attempt to add value by appealing to a U.S. consumer preference for "Made in the U.S.A."

The Value Chain

Figure 9–2 is a diagram of a value chain.[2] A value chain is a representation of a business. At the top are support activities. At the bottom are value activities. Downstream activities are closer to the customer and are principally marketing and service. Upstream activities begin with the extraction of raw materials or the production of food and fiber, and continue with operations which include research and development, engineering, manufacturing, and the logistics of delivery. Every firm is positioned in a value chain: The integrated firm covers a wide range of activities and support services. An extreme example was Henry Ford's decision to "fully" integrate the upstream activities in the automobile business. This led Ford into the rubber

[2] For a full description of the value chain, see Michael Porter, *Competitive Advantage* (New York, The Free Press, 1985), pp. 33–61.

plantation business and could have led him into the auto-dealer business if it had been pushed downstream. The specialized firm covers only a limited range of value activities.

The sourcing decision is really a decision about where and how to position a company on the value chain. The first decision is whether to make or buy, and the second is where to make or buy. As suggested in Figure 9–2, the ultimate purpose of all value chain activity and the firm is to create value for customers. One measure of the value created is the margin that the firm enjoys (margin is the difference between all value chain costs and the price to the customer). The greater the value, the greater the potential margin.

SOURCING AND THE TRADE CYCLE

The product trade cycle (see page 49) posits a relationship among production, consumption, trade, and the product life cycle. In brief, this model shows how production of mature products with stabilized technologies has relocated from the advanced to the developing to the less developed countries of the world to take advantage of lower wage and other factor costs.

A vast number of products have gone through the trade cycle in the United States. Black and white television, AM and FM radios, textiles, hand-sewn shoes, motorcycles, auto parts, home entertainment products such as sound and video playback machines, and specialty steel are examples of products that are produced entirely outside the United States today. In 1987, automobile imports, including parts and components, exceeded 50 percent of the U.S. market for the first time in history according to one estimate.

The record of the trade cycle in the United States might be taken as an indication that it is inevitable that any mature, standardized product will be produced in a lower-wage country. Is it in fact inevitable that as a product matures world production will shift to less developed countries? Certainly not! Indeed, what is abundantly clear is that production of goods and services is concentrated primarily in the advanced countries of the world in spite of the fact that the Third World contains vast supplies of ''cheap'' labor. The key variable is the cost and quality of the finished product and not exclusively the cost of a single factor of production, labor. As Peter Drucker has pointed out, wage levels for blue-collar workers are becoming increasingly irrelevant in world competition. The reason is that blue-collar labor no longer accounts for a high enough percentage of total costs to give much competitive advantage to low wages. In the U.S. manufacturing blue-collar costs are 181 of total costs and declining.

As U.S. manufacturing efficiency and quality improve in response to the ''Japan Shock'' of the 1980s, and as the U.S. dollar adjusts (i.e., declines in value in foreign exchange markets in response to a new government policy and strategy), the balance of trade between the United States and the rest of the world will shift. Once again, U.S. manufacturers will be in a position to compete in world markets if they choose to do so.

There is an unresolved debate about whether or not an advanced country needs to have a strong basic manufacturing sector in order to remain economically healthy. One school of thought argues that as a country develops economically, it moves from agriculture to manufacturing to services and that a natural and inevitable part of the development process is the decline of the manufacturing sector and the development of the services sector. Another school of thought argues that basic manufacturing is essential for economic health and welfare. If this latter view is sustained, countries like the United States will need to ensure that there are economic incentives for companies to invest in manufacturing in the United States. For example, the decline in the value of the dollar and the threat of import restrictions have been strong incentives for Japanese companies to invest in U.S. manufacturing.

In the meantime, companies in developing countries that have the ability to produce a quality product can take advantage of their lower-wage costs to carve out a niche in world markets for their products. Advanced countries like the United States must decide whether or not they want to allow the location of manufacturing to shift to low-wage countries. One sure way to maintain a manufacturing base is to support company investment to reduce the percentage of blue-collar labor in total value added.

DECISION CRITERIA

Clearly, there are no simple rules. Indeed, the sourcing decision is one of the most complex and important decisions faced by the global enterprise. As shown in Table 9–2, six factors must be taken into account in the sourcing decision.

Factor Costs

Factor costs are land, labor, and capital costs (remember Economics 101!). Labor includes the cost of workers at every level: manufacturing and production, profes-

TABLE 9–2 Sourcing Decision Factors

---

1. Factor costs and availability
2. Logistics: time required to fill orders, security and safety, and transportation costs
3. Country infrastructure
4. Political risk
5. Market access (tariff and nontariff barriers to trade)
6. Exchange rate, availability, and convertibility

---

sional and technical, and management. Basic manufacturing direct labor costs today range from $0.50 per hour in the typical LDC to $6.00 to $12.00 per hour in the typical developed country. In certain industries in the United States, direct labor costs in manufacturing exceed $20.00 per hour without benefits, which can equal the hourly rate.

Labor costs include not only the cost of direct manufacturing labor but all other labor categories as well, including management. The cost differences for management are often greater than for labor. This is certainly true for the U.S. automobile industry. While the U.S. autoworker has a wage rate that is roughly double that of his Japanese counterpart, U.S. executives, especially those at the top of the executive hierarchy, have rewarded themselves with an average level of compensation that is 10 times greater than that received by their Japanese counterparts (in spite of the fact that some would argue that they are probably less than 50 percent as effective as their Japanese counterparts).

The other factors of production are land, materials, and capital. The cost of these factors depends upon their availability and relative abundance. Often, the differences in factor costs will offset each other so that on balance companies have a "level field" in the competitive arena. For example, the United States has abundant land and Japan has abundant capital. These advantages partially offset each other. When this is the case, the critical factor is management, professional, and worker team effectiveness.

The application of advanced computer and laser-optic machine motion controls has shifted the ratio of labor to capital in manufacturing in favor of capital. A major current that needs to be recognized in formulating any company's sourcing strategy is the declining importance of direct manufacturing labor as a percentage of total product cost. The average percentage of blue-collar labor cost in the United States today is less than 20Y. The most advanced global companies are no longer blindly chasing cheap labor manufacturing locations. The great differences in wage rates in manufacturing do not dictate the location of manufacturing activity because blue-collar labor may be a very small percentage of total cost, and, as a result, it may not be worthwhile to incur the costs and risks that are part of establishing a manufacturing activity in a distant location. Another reason is that cheap labor attracts demand and that drives up wage rates which erodes the initial advantage.

Transportation Costs

In general, distance means greater time delay and transportation costs. However, a plant located near a deep water port may be able to supply customers on the coast of the United States at a lower transportation cost than a plant located in Ohio or Michigan. New technologies and regulations are constantly impacting the transportation cost factor, so it is important to obtain up-to-date data on transportation costs before proceeding with a plan. For example, the cost of transporting data by satellite is declining so that distance is no longer a significant factor in the cost of moving data. On the other hand, the cost of moving steel containers from Korea to the United States is roughly two-thirds of the ex-factory price in Korea. This cost gives local suppliers in each country a significant advantage.

Country Infrastructure

In order to present an attractive setting for a manufacturing operation, it is important that the country's infrastructure be sufficiently developed to support a manufacturing operation. The required infrastructure will vary from company to company, but in general, a country must offer reliable access to foreign exchange for the purchase of necessary material and components from abroad as well as a physically secure setting where work can be done and product can be shipped to customers.

A country may have cheap labor, but does it have the necessary supporting services or infrastructure to support a manufacturing activity? Minimally, these include power, transportation, communications, service and component suppliers, a labor pool, civil order, and effective governance. Many countries offer these conditions: Hong Kong, Taiwan, and Singapore, for example. There are also many other countries that do not: Lebanon, Uganda, and El Salvador, for example.

Political Risk

Political risk, or the risk of a change in government policy that would adversely impact a company's ability to operate effectively and profitably, is a deterrent to investment. Conversely, the lower the level of political risk, the less likely it is that an investor will avoid a country of market. The job of assessing political risk is inversely proportional to the stage of a country's economic development. In other words, the less developed a country, all other things being equal, the more difficult it is to predict political risk. The political risk of the triad countries, for example, is quite limited as compared to a less developed pre-industrial country in Africa, Latin America, or Asia.

Market Access

A key factor in locating production facilities is market access. If a country or a region decides to limit market access for balance of payments or any other reason, a production facility within the country itself is a way of overcoming this barrier to market access. The Japanese automobile companies are investing in U.S. plant capacity because of their concern about market access. With U.S. production, they have a source of supply that is not exposed to the threat of tariff, nontariff, or other barriers. In the 1950s and 1960s U.S. companies created production capacity abroad in order to insure continued access to markets that had been established with supply exported from U.S. plants.

The U.S. tax laws provide incentives for U.S companies to locate manufacturing in the Caribbean because production from Caribbean plants has full access to the U.S. market, including the military procurement market which is subject to security clearances.

Foreign Exchange

In deciding where to locate a manufacturing activity, the cost of production supplied by a country source will be determined in part by the prevailing foreign exchange rate for the country's currency. Exchange rates are so volatile today that for most companies it is prudent to diversify production locations. At any point in time, what has been an attractive location for production may become much less attractive due to exchange rate fluctuation. For example, the exchange value of the U.S. dollar declined almost 50 percent vis-à-vis the Japanese yen between 1985 and 1987. Of course, the flip side of this adjustment is that the yen appreciated by almost 50 percent in the same period.

The company with flexible sourcing alternatives is much better able to adapt to extreme exchange rate fluctuations. While there is talk of agreements and actions that would stabilize exchange rate fluctuations, there is little action. The prudent company will incorporate exchange volatility into its planning assumptions and be prepared to prosper under a variety of exchange rate relationships.

SOURCING STRATEGY ALTERNATIVES

Stage 1: International

International sourcing relies upon the home country manufacturing capability or home country service group to supply product for customers worldwide. This strategy is normally the best initial sourcing for a product since it does not place any demands upon the organization to transfer know-how and capability in manufacturing. With domestic sourcing, a company can concentrate upon the marketing challenge of identifying target markets, prioritizing markets, and developing country marketing plans.

The arguments against domestic sourcing are twofold. The first is that it is too expensive, and the second is that it will not deliver a product that is adapted to the specific needs and conditions of target markets. Both of these arguments are unique to the United States, and both are without merit. On the issue of cost, U.S. labor costs used to be significantly higher than those anywhere else in the world. This is no longer true. The rise in real incomes in the other advanced countries of the world combined with the devaluation of the dollar has created a world in which the United States is no longer the highest labor cost location in the world.

Even if a country has higher costs than other potential production locations, labor costs are a single element in the overall production cost equation and for most products and industries direct labor, as a percentage of total cost, is declining. Taking into account overall costs and the trend of declining direct labor costs, it may make sense to concentrate on manufacturing excellence (defined as increasing reactive quality and decreasing relative costs) in the home country and total commitment to market penetration in target markets.

Stage 2: Multinational

Whereas the international sourcing strategy concentrates production in the home country and focuses resources upon market penetration, the multinational sourcing strategy establishes production in each operating country. The advantages of this strategy are many. First, it locates production inside barriers to entry. In many countries, barriers to entry preclude any other sourcing approach. Second, it takes advantage of local factors of production and shortens supply lines. Third, by locating closer to customers, the production will be responsive to country customer needs and wants.

The disadvantage of this approach is that multiple production facilities limit the possibilities of economies of scale in manufacturing and that dispersion of the production activity adds distance and complexity to the task of managing manufacturing.

Stage 3: Global

The international strategy limits sourcing alternatives to the home country. The multinational sourcing strategy locates production in each operating country. A global approach avoids any prior conclusion about sourcing strategy. The global approach to sourcing seeks a balance between the advantages and disadvantages of the international and the multinational approaches. It also recognizes that when exchange rates and market access conditions change the flexible company is best suited to adapt to the changing circumstances.

The global approach locates production activity in a way that maximizes quality *and* availability and minimizes cost. An example of a company with a global production strategy is IBM. The IBM production plan relies primarily on country and regional production to supply market needs in each country. The location of IBM production activity seeks to balance the gains from specialization of production with a limit on the risks that go with specialization. IBM's strategy also recognizes the importance to countries of full participation in the economic life of the country and the value that countries place on local production and research and development. This also gives IBM access to research talent on a global basis. One of the breakthrough discoveries in superconductive materials occurred in IBM's Zurich R&D lab. In Japan, IBM has 18,000 employees, annual sales of $6 billion, and more engineering graduates vying to enter the company than any other corporation in Japan. It is quite conceivable that in our lifetime, the CEO of IBM might be a European or a Japanese national.

SUMMARY

Sourcing is the what, where, and how of production to supply the customers targeted in the marketing plan. A global marketing plan requires a global sourcing plan whose objective is to supply customers with the highest quality at the lowest cost. The factors which determine quality and cost include factor costs, logistics, country infrastructure, political risk, market access, and exchange rates.

The declining proportion of direct labor as a cost element for most products is reducing the importance of wage rates in the sourcing decision. Clearly, there is no simple formula for sourcing decisions. A global approach to sourcing takes into account all of the variables that impact the company's ability to create and deliver value to customers over the long term. Since many of the variables, such as foreign exchange rates, fluctuate, most companies devise sourcing plans that will enable the company to meet customer needs under a variety of conditions.

DISCUSSION QUESTIONS

1. What is sourcing?
2. How does the trade cycle impact the sourcing decision?
3. What are the major criteria that must be taken into account in making a sourcing decision?

BIBLIOGRAPHY

Books

OHMAE, KENICHI. *Triad Power,* New York: The Free Press, 1985.

PORTER, MICHAEL E., ed. *Competition in Global Industries.* Boston, Mass.: Harvard Business School Press, 1986.

PORTER, MICHAEL E. *Competitive Advantage.* New York: The Free Press, 1985.

ODYSSEUS, INC.[1,2]
(THE DECISION TO "GO INTERNATIONAL")

She faced him, waiting. And Odysseus came, debating inwardly what he should do: embrace this beauty's knees in supplication? Or stand apart, and, using honeyed speech, inquire the way to town, and beg some clothing? In his swift reckoning, he thought it best to trust in words to please her—and keep away: he might anger the girl, touching her knees.

Homer, *The Odyssey*
Book Six, *The Princess*
at the River,
Robert Fitzgerald translation

In early 1981, Mr. Donald R. Odysseus, president of the Odysseus Manufacturing Company of Kansas City, Kansas, was actively considering the possibilities of major expansion of the firm's currently limited international activities and the form and scale such expansion might take.

Odysseus was founded in 1916 by Edward Odysseus as a small machine shop. By 1981, the head office and production facilities of the company were located in a 500,000-square-foot modern factory on a 30-acre site near the original location. Odysseus products were sold throughout the United States and Canada. In 1980, net sales were over $52,000,000 while after-tax profits were about $3,000,000. In early 1981, Odysseus em-

ployed just over 1,000 people, and its stock was held by 1,000 shareholders. (The company's 1980 income statement and balance sheet are given in Tables 1 and 2.)

Odysseus produced a line of couplings and clutches including flange, compression, gear type, flex pin, and flexible disc couplings, and overrunning and multiple disc clutches. In all, the company manufactured about 600 different sizes and types of its eight standard items. The company's single most important product was the Odysseus Flexible Coupling, which its research department had developed in 1975 and which, produced in about 70 different sizes and combinations, now accounted for one-third of Odysseus' sales. Odysseus held patents throughout the world on its flexible coupling as well as several other devices. By 1981, Odysseus had carved itself a secure niche in the clutch and couplings market, despite the competition in this market of larger firms with widely diversified product lines.

Odysseus was not dependent on any single customer or industry. Sales were made through distributors to original equipment manufacturers for use in small motor drives for a wide range of products including machine tools, test gear, conveyors, farm implements, mining equipment, hoisting equipment, cranes, shovels, and so on. No more than 10 percent of its output went to any single industry; its largest single customer took less than 4 percent of production. Speaking generally, Odysseus couplings and clutches were used more by small- and medium-sized producers of general-purpose equipment than by large manufacturers of highly automated machines. Odysseus' sales manager believed that demand for the company's couplings and

[1]Copyright © 1984 by the President and Fellows of Harvard College. This case was prepared by Warren J. Keegan under the supervision of Professor Charles M. Williams as a basis for class discussion rather than to illustrate either effective or ineffective handling of an administrative situation. Reprinted by permission of the Harvard Business School.

[2]All names and places have been disguised.

TABLE 1   Consolidated Income Statement, Year Ending December 31, 1980 (in thousands of dollars)

Income		
Net sales	$52,552	
Royalties, interest, and other income	108	
Costs and expenses	$52,660	$52,260
Cost of goods sold	$33,516	
Depreciation	1,100	
Selling, administrative, and general expense	11,692	
Interest on long-term debt	136	
	$46,444	$46,444
Income before income taxes		6,216
Federal taxes on income (est.)		3,200
Net income		$ 3,016

clutches would benefit from continuation of a long-term trend toward increased installation of labor-saving equipment in medium-sized enterprises. This trend and the breadth of its market had provided some protection against cyclical fluctuations in business activity. During the period 1967 to 1980, sales had increased from $20 million to $52 million; the largest annual decline during the period had been 8 percent, while in the most recent recession year sales had actually increased by 5 percent.

The company's commercial objective was to operate as a specialist in a product

TABLE 2   Balance Sheet, December 31, 1980 (in thousands of dollars)

Assets		
Cash	$ 3,516	
Marketable securities	2,288	
Accounts receivable	3,970	
Inventories	15,870	
Total current assets	$25,644	$25,644
Investments and other assets		838
Property, plant, and equipment (net)		14,380
Total assets		$40,862
Liabilities		
Accounts payable	$ 1,250	
Dividends payable	462	
Accruals	2,106	
Federal income tax liability (estimated)	2,328	
Installment on long-term debt	172	
Total current liabilities	$ 6,318	$ 6,318
Long-term debt (20-year $6\frac{7}{8}\%$ notes, final maturity 1977)		3,134
Preferred stock		3,952
Common stock and retained earnings		27,458
Total liabilities		$40,862

field in which its patents and distinctive skills would give it a strong competitive position. In the past, the company had experimented with various products outside its coupling and clutch line; it had tried to make components for egg candling machinery, among other things. The investment in these products was initially considered a means of more efficiently utilizing the company's forging and machining capacity, but the firm had not been particularly successful. The Odysseus management had come to the conclusion that it should concentrate its efforts on its line of couplings and clutches; and in 1981, Mr. Odysseus stated the company's corporate objectives explicitly as being a coupling and clutch manufacturer. New investments were made to develop better products within this field, and to open new markets for Odysseus products.

Odysseus' production and assembly facilities were located in its modern factory near Kansas City, Kansas. The site offered ample room for expansion and was well located for both rail and highway transportation. The company maintained warehousing facilities in Boston, Jersey City, Atlanta, Columbus, Ohio, and Oakland, California. The scale economies stemming from concentrating production in one factory can be seen from the following examples. One of the company's largest selling items, product K-2A (a flexible coupling component) produced in lots of 750, cost $3.22 each; in lots of 1,200, $2.62 each. The incremental 450 units produced after the initial 750, therefore, cost only $1.62 each. Put differently, on this particular product, a 50 percent cost saving could be realized on the marginal production from the 750-unit level to the 1,200-unit level. Although specific cost savings from higher volume varied among its products, a fundamental characteristic of Odysseus' cost structure was that marginal cost typically was significantly less than average cost and that important economies of scale could be obtained by achieving larger lot sizes and longer production runs.

Odysseus' cost structure was, of course, dictated by its manufacturing process. In the first of three major steps in the manufacture of couplings or clutches, steel bars or tubing were cut and forged. Apart from the unit cost reductions stemming from more complete utilization of the existing forging facilities, economies of scale in this department were limited. Second, the forged steel pieces were machined to close tolerances in the machine shop. Here costs varied significantly with lot sizes. For most products, the choice among two or three alternative methods of production depended on the lot size. If a large lot size were indicated, special-purpose automatic machines with large setup costs and lower variable unit costs were used. Smaller lot sizes were produced on general-purpose turret and engine lathes where setup time was less but unit costs were higher. Typically, production of smaller lot sizes was more labor intensive than the larger runs. For example, one operator running three automatic machines could perform all the boring and cutting operations on 300-$2\frac{1}{2}$-inch coupling flange units in an hour. The same output on general-purpose lathes and boring machines would require about six person-hours. To set up the automatic machines required a day and a half, however, while the lathes could be set up in about two hours. Furthermore, the burden charge on the automatics was considerably higher. On the other hand, the cost of the third step, assembly, did not vary under different lot sizes. (Table 3 presents a breakdown of the costs of some representative components.)

Mr. Odysseus regarded Odysseus' U.S. and Canadian market position as a strong one. The patented Odysseus Flexible Coupling possessed unique characteristics that no other

TABLE 3 Typical Variation of Production Costs with Lot Sizes Product N-15C1

OPERATION	LOTS OF 150	LOTS OF 400
I. Foundry	$ 32.06	$ 32.06
II. Machine shop		
1. Boring	34.54	20.28
2. Turning	8.78	7.10
3. Facing	12.28	10.08
4. Drilling	20.00	16.32
5. Turning	11.76	9.56
6. Facing	12.38	9.16
7. Finishing	11.64	11.64
8. Finishing	11.14	11.32
III. Assembly	4.94	4.94
	$159.52	$132.46

Product L-36G:
Lots of 3: $67.40 each
Lots of 4: $56.20 each

coupling device duplicated, and many other Odysseus products served special functions not performed by competitive devices. Of course, other coupling and clutch systems competed with Odysseus, but no single company could be said to compete directly by producing an identical product line. Mr. Odysseus estimated that Odysseus accounted for roughly 10 percent of total sales of its products in the American market and that there was ample room for Odysseus to expand its sales in this domestic market as the total market grew and through an increase in its share of industry sales. Odysseus products were sold by distributors who generally, but not always, carried the entire line of Odysseus couplings and clutches. These distributor organizations were complemented by a 45-person Odysseus sales force.

In 1980, export sales were $840,000 on which the company made a $100,000 operating profit. Although export sales had never been actively solicited, a small but steady stream of orders for export trickled into the Kansas City sales office. These orders were always filled expeditiously, but the active exploitation of export markets was considered too difficult in view of the barriers of language, custom, and currency. Furthermore, although he recognized that foreign wages were increasing more rapidly than those in the United States, Mr. Odysseus had always believed that Odysseus could not compete in export markets because its costs in Kansas City were too high. Also, tariffs imposed on Odysseus products by foreign governments were typically 10 percent ad valorem[3] or higher. (See Appendix for data on world markets and costs).

Odysseus sold all products on flat price basis (F.O.B. warehouse) to all customers. In competing with other suppliers of similar products, Odysseus stressed delivery time, quality, service, and merchandising, but not price.

In its management's view, improvements in its products or in delivery or service promised more than temporary competitive advantage. Price cutting moves, in contrast, would likely be matched by competitors the same day. No added sales would be gained, and total revenues would be cut. The company's export pricing policy was identical to its domestic policy. This meant that the foreign importer paid the U.S. F.O.B. price plus freight and import duties.

Along with filling orders, Odysseus' activities outside the United States and Canada consisted of a licensing agreement with an English coupling manufacturer. In 1975, on

---

[3]Duties may be *specific, ad valorem,* or *compound.* Specific duties are assessed on the weight or quantity of an article without reference to its monetary value or market price. Ad valorem duties are expressed as a percentage of the dutiable value of an article without reference to weight or quantity. Compound duties combine both specific and ad valorem valuations; for example, in 1976, the U.S. duty on polyethylene resins amounted to 1.3 percent per pound plus 10 percent ad valorem. The U.S. tariff on clutches and couplings was 9.5 percent ad valorem.

a vacation trip in England, where Odysseus' vice president in charge of engineering had spent his youth, he met the chairman of Siren Ltd. of Manchester. Siren, a manufacturer of related equipment with sales of $7 million in 1974, was anxious to diversify by adding other power transmission products. Consequently, Siren became interested in several Odysseus patents, particularly those on the Odysseus Flexible Coupling. In late 1975, Odysseus granted the English concern an exclusive 15-year license to manufacture and sell all present and future Odysseus products in the United Kingdom. The licensing arrangement specifically defined the United Kingdom to include England, Scotland, Wales, and Northern Ireland. Siren was granted also a nonexclusive license to sell products produced from Odysseus patents in all other countries except the United States, Canada, Mexico, and France. The terms of the license agreement stipulated a $1\frac{1}{2}$ percent royalty on the ex-factory sales price of all products in which devices manufactured from Odysseus patents were incorporated. The 1980 royalty income from Siren amounted to $80,000 and was expected to rise to $100,000 in 1981.

Mr. Odysseus had noted Siren's success with considerable interest. The royalty payments were a welcome addition to Odysseus income, especially since they had not necessitated any additional investment. Mr. Odysseus felt that the licensee was receiving very generous profits from this deal, as Siren had almost tripled its sales (which by 1980 were equivalent of $22 million) during its five-year association with Odysseus and its equity had appreciated many times the total royalties of about $300,000 that Odysseus had received.

During the five years Odysseus and Siren had worked together, however, the English firm had made it understood that in general it considered its territory to be the Eastern

Hemisphere, while Odysseus' was in the Western Hemisphere. Siren was especially interested in the West German market for couplings and clutches and was a licensee of a West German brakeshoe manufacturer.

In addition, Odysseus had a licensing agreement on the same terms ($1\frac{1}{2}$ percent royalty) with Scylla, S. A. Scylla was a medium-sized French manufacturer of clutches and complementary lines, located near Paris. The company was financially sound and was headed by a young and aggressive management team. Scylla had been granted an exclusive license in France and a nonexclusive license in Belgium to sell products incorporating Odysseus-patented devices. Odysseus had entered the agreement during 1979 for an initial period of 10 years. Royalty income in 1980, the first full year of operation in France, had totaled roughly $20,000. Odysseus expected a doubling of this figure in 1981.

In February 1981, M. Scylla, the president of the French firm, had proposed to Mr. Odysseus a closer association of their two companies. M. Scylla was anxious to expand his operations and needed capital to do this. He, therefore, proposed that Odysseus form a joint venture with Scylla. According to the terms of the proposal Odysseus would bring $400,000 into the joint venture, paid in cash, while Scylla would provide a 40,000-square-foot plant, equipment, a national distribution system, and managerial personnel. Scylla, S.A., would cease to exist as a corporate entity; its expanded organization and plant would become Scylla Odysseus, S.A. (SOSA). The original owners of Scylla, S.A. (the Scylla family) would own 60 percent of SOSA, and their return would be in the form of dividends plus salaries of members of the Scylla family employed by SOSA. Odysseus would own 40 percent of SOSA and, for tax reasons, would receive fees and royalties rather than dividends totaling 5 percent of the ex-factory price of all products incorporating Odysseus patents.

Mr. Odysseus thought that he should give this proposal serious attention. The French market for couplings looked very attractive. Moreover, the geographical location of SOSA and the formation of the European Economic Community would make it theoretically possible to supply the even larger German market from the SOSA plant near Paris. M. Scylla had indicated that he considered Germany as a primary target for future expansion.

So far, Odysseus had not actively pursued business leads in West Germany, in spite of several inquiries about licensing from West German companies. Odysseus even had the possibility of acquiring an existing German manufacturer of couplings, Charybdis Metallfabrik GmbH (CMF) of Kassel. Mr. Odysseus had learned that CMF's aging owner-managers were anxious to sell their equity interest in the company but would stay on in a managerial capacity. Odysseus' British licensee, Siren, had made it clear, however, that although it had no sizable business in Germany, it considered this market to be in Siren's sales territory and a move into Germany by Odysseus without Siren an "unfriendly act." In the light of Odysseus' growing royalty income from Siren, Mr. Odysseus did not want to antagonize the British licensee.

Mr. Odysseus had no ready means of precisely quantifying the market potential for clutches and couplings in Germany and in France. He knew, however, that the total market for Odysseus' "type L" couplings in the United States was $45 million a year. Odysseus' U.S. sales of type L couplings were $6.4 million in 1980, or 14 percent of the U.S. market. Odysseus assumed that the coupling market in France was correlated with sales of durable equipment in France, which were

12 percent of the U.S. total. The French type L coupling market, therefore, would be $5.4 million a year, of which SOSA should expect to capture 14 percent, or $756,000. Similarly in Germany, durable equipment sales were 20 percent of those in the United States. The type L coupling market could therefore be expected to be about $9 million, of which a company using Odysseus patents and know-how should obtain between 10 percent and 15 percent. Sales of comparable lines by both Scylla, S.A., and CMF appeared to justify these estimates; Scylla had sold $560,000 of a device closely comparable to the type L coupling, or 10 percent of the assumed French market, and CMF had sold $750,000 of virtually the same device, or 8 percent of the assumed German market.

In 1981, the European market with its accelerating pace of industrial development and mechanization appeared to offer great opportunities for Odysseus. Mr. Odysseus, therefore, was most anxious to capitalize on these opportunities, presumably by manufacturing in Europe in cooperation with a European firm. He saw three reasons why Odysseus should expand its foreign operations.

First, the corporate objectives of focusing on a single line of products sold in as large a market as possible—the policy of area instead of product diversification—dictated expansion into markets outside the United States and Canada. The nature of the demand for Odysseus' products appeared to limit near-term sales potential in less developed areas; but in Europe, especially, Odysseus couplings and clutches appeared to find ready acceptance. Proof of this seemed to be contained in Siren's success in the United Kingdom.

Second, an important improvement on Odysseus' multiple disc clutch had been the result of European research. Mr. Odysseus felt that by becoming an active participant in the European market, the company could obtain valuable recent innovations that would be important to its competitive position in the United States. There was considerable activity in the clutch and coupling field in Europe, and Mr. Odysseus wanted to be in touch with the latest developments in the industry.

Third, Mr. Odysseus was seriously worried about the trend of costs in his Kansas City plant. He knew that a French firm could sell its gear-type coupling in Kansas City, Kansas, cheaper than Odysseus' current list price. How could Odysseus, paying its workers $6.69 an hour, compete with French firms paying $3.77 an hour? Ultimately Odysseus might have to follow the lead of United States watch and bicycle firms and perform much of its manufacturing abroad and import parts, or even finished products, into the United States. At the present time, Mr. Odysseus felt that there was some reluctance on the part of American manufacturers to buy foreign couplings and clutches, and foreign competition was virtually nil in this market in 1980. But Mr. Odysseus was worried about the future and wanted to preserve Odysseus' competitive position by assuring a foreign source of supply. Also, the company would be in a better position to withstand exorbitant demands from the local labor union if it possessed alternative manufacturing facilities.

Before definitely deciding whether Odysseus should become more deeply involved in foreign operations, Mr. Odysseus wanted to review the ways this might be done. First, Odysseus could establish foreign markets by expanding export sales. Mr. Odysseus believed, however, the Odysseus' costs might be too high for it to compete successfully on this basis. Second, the company could enter into additional licensing agreements. This it had done with Siren in England and Scylla in France, but there was a definite ceiling on the possible profit potential from exclusive use of this method. Third, the company could enter "joint ventures" with a firm already established in foreign markets. Presumably, Odysseus would supply capital and know-how and the foreign firms would supply personnel (both local managerial skill and a labor force), market outlets, and familiarity with the local business climate. This approach appeared particularly promising to Mr. Odysseus. Finally, the company could establish wholly owned foreign subsidiaries. Mr. Odysseus saw formidable barriers to such action, since Odysseus lacked managerial skill in foreign operations. They were unfamiliar with foreign markets and business practices. They did not have executives to spare from the Kansas City operations who might learn the intricacies of foreign business and the development of wholly owned operations from scratch would require significant investment of time and money.

Mr. Odysseus recognized that certain deep-seated ideas of his tended to make him predisposed toward active development of overseas business. These included a view that his business should not shrink from difficult tasks—organizations, he believed, couldn't stand still—the choice was one of moving forward or falling backward. He considered "taking the plunge" into less familiar areas and learning from the experience was generally preferable to long-extended and expensive inquiry before taking action. Nonetheless, he wanted to be sure that the most basic issues related to expansion overseas by Odysseus were thought through before firm decisions were made.

QUESTIONS

1. Should Odysseus expand international business operations?
2. Rightly or wrongly, Odysseus management has decided in the affirmative. What *form*

should these operations take? What *scope* will be required for Odysseus' international activities to achieve success? (Possible forms, which in turn may be combined, include (a) exporting, (b) licensing, (c) joint ventures, and (d) wholly owned subsidiaries, either by starting them from scratch or by acquiring one or more existing companies.) This decision should take into account Odysseus' capabilities (as determined, for example, by its products, its capital and manpower strength, and its marketing and research needs) as well as the industry's competitive requirements and foreign conditions, such as trade and business barriers, the number and sizes of countries to be covered, and political and business risks.

3. Evaluate the arrangement with Siren, particularly the following questions:

   a. What assumptions were in Mr. Odysseus' mind when he concluded the licensing arrangement with Siren?

   b. Do you consider it a success?

   c. How does the timing of this arrangement fit into Odysseus' overall business strategy?

4. Evaluate the Scylla, S.A., proposal and the Charybdis possibility.

5. Recommend an international strategic plan to Mr. Odysseus.

Appendix I: Global Income and Population—1979

	GNP PER CAPITA (US$)	GNP (US $000 MILLIONS)	PERCENT OF WORLD GNP	POPULATION (MILLIONS)	PERCENT OF WORLD POPULA- TION
North America	$10,500	$ 2,597	25%	247	6.0%
Japan	8,730	1,010	10	116	3.0
Oceania	7,000	154	2	22	1.0
Europe (excluding USSR)	6,760	3,546	35	524	13.0
USSR	4,040	1,067	11	264	6.0
Middle East[1]	4,310	207	2.0	48	1.0
South America	1,730	404	4.0	233	6.0
Central America[2]	1,620	172	2.0	106	3.0
Africa	700	322	3.0	456	11.0
Asia (excluding Japan and Middle East)	310	677	7.0	2,165	52.0
World	$ 2,430	$10,156	101.0[3]	4,181	102.0[3]

[1]Consists of Bahrain, Iraq, Israel, Jordan, Kuwait, Oman, Qator, Saudi Arabia, Synah Arab Republic, United Arab Emirates, Yemen Arab Republic, and Yemen (People's Democratic Republic of).

[2]Includes Mexico.

[3]Columns do not add up to 100 due to rounding.

Data Source: *1981 World Bank Atlas,* pg. 10.

Appendix II: Odysseus Manufacturing Company

	NATIONAL INCOME ($ BILLION)	1980 POPULATION (MILLION)	NATIONAL INCOME (PER CAPITA)	EXPORTS ($ BILLION)	IMPORTS ($ BILLION)	AVERAGE HOURLY EARNINGS IN MANUFACTURING 1979	% OF WORLD NATIONAL INCOME
United States	$2,250.0	226.5	$ 9,934	$ 220,706	$ 252,997	$6.69	24.7%
Western Europe	3,124.5	416.3	7,505	820,208	929,264		34.3
France	580.9	53.4	10,878	116,016	134,874	3.77	6.4
West Germany	724.0	60.9	11,888	192,861	188,002	6.74	8.0
United Kingdom	455.8	55.9	8,148	115,137	120,077	4.12	5.0
Eastern Europe	1,016.7*	376.7	N.A.	61,770	67,991		11.2
Japan	901.9	116.4	7,748	130,435	141,291	(USSR) 1.44	9.9
Oceania and Canada	341.3	41.9	8,146	95,025	90,348	(Australia) 4.33	3.7
Latin America	625.7†	367.6	1,702	99,031	110,087‡	(Mexico) 1.74	6.9
Asia (excluding Japan)	419.7	285.7	184	155,521	173,921	(Hong Kong) .99	4.6
Middle East	167.8	127.8	1,313	173,954	86,407§	(Israel) 2.70	1.8
Africa	254.1	410.5	619	209,362	64,555§	(Nigeria) 0.48	2.8
Global total	$9,101.7	4,369.4	$ 2,355‖	$1,966,012	$1,916,864		100%

N.A.—not available.

*Net material product.

†Estimate, data missing for parts of Caribbean.

†Totals do not include missing country data for Caribbean.

‡Totals do not include missing country data.

§Totals do not include missing country data.

‖Global average.

Source: "Indicators of Market Size for 131 Countries," *Business International*, December 1981 (and 1979 for wage data).

10

STRATEGY ALTERNATIVES FOR ENTRY AND EXPANSION

The best Strategy is <u>always to be very strong</u>, first generally then at the decisive point . . . there is no more imperative and no simpler law for Strategy than to <u>keep the forces concentrated</u>.

Karl von Clausewitz, 1780–1831
Vom Kriege (1833), Book III, Chapter XI,
"Assembly of Forces in Space"

INTRODUCTION

Every firm, at every point in its history, faces a broad range of strategy alternatives. In far too many cases, companies fail to appreciate the range of alternatives open to them and therefore employ, often to their grave disadvantage, only one strategy. The same companies also fail to consider the strategy alternatives open to their competitors and leave themselves vulnerable to the dreaded "Titanic" syndrome, or the thud in the night that comes without warning and sinks the ship.

INTERNATIONAL ENTRY, EXPANSION, AND POSITIONING

A company which has decided to "go international" or expand its share of world markets faces three basic issues:

- *Marketing*. Which markets should we target in which sequence? Which countries, and which segments in target countries? How should we manage and implement our marketing effort? Should we establish direct marketing operations in the target market or use agents or reps? If we use agents or reps, how much support should we give them, and how should we communicate with them (i.e., how do we insure that we get accurate and timely market feedback from our agents, and how do we insure that we transfer to the agents and reps all of the information they will need to represent us effectively in the market)?

- *Sourcing*. How and where should we obtain or produce the product to supply customer demand? Should we make or buy? Where and from whom?
- *Investment and Control*. Should we joint venture with a local, regional, or global partner or operate directly without a partner? If the decision is to operate directly, should we do this through an acquisition or a direct start up?

The value chain, (see Chapter 9, page 274) shown in Figure 10–1, focuses upon the marketing task. The strategy alternatives for entry and expansion must insure that the necessary value chain activities are performed and integrated. The simplest solution is to configure the value chain abroad exactly as it is at home, but this may not be the most effective solution because the organization may lack the necessary skill and experience to conduct all of the value chain activities in target markets.

Marketing

Global strategy must begin with marketing. Which markets should we target in which sequence? What objectives should we establish for volume, share of market, sales, and earnings? How should we implement our marketing effort?

```
Purchasing
In-bound Logistics
R&D
Assembly & Manufacturing
Out-bound Logistics
Marketing
   Target Market Selection
   Product Policy and Strategy
   Pricing Policy and Strategy
   Distribution Policy and Strategy
   Communications Policy and Strategy
      Messages, Appeals
      Media Strategy and Plan
         Advertising Plan
         Promotion Plan
         Direct Marketing Plan
            Personal Selling
            Direct Mail
            Telemarketing
   Information and Research
Installation and Testing
Service
Margin
```

FIGURE 10–1 *Value Chain*—**Marketing Function Detail**

Sourcing

Exporting is a well-established basis for sourcing product for a foreign target market. To establish a local manufacturing operation prior to learning about the real needs and wants of the market is often premature and unwise. Today, with average tariffs on manufactured goods at all-time low levels, exporting is often the lowest-cost, lowest-risk method of supplying customers in a country market.

The real, basic sourcing question is: From what source should we supply customers in target market 1 . . . nth? The answer to this question will depend upon a host of factors that fall under three categories: cost, quality, and risk. Since labor costs for most manufactured goods today are less than 15 percent of total costs, the mere availability of cheap labor is not a basis for locating a plant. The advantages of using cheap labor may be offset by the cost of transporting critical components to the production site from developed countries and the cost of transporting the finished products to markets.

And, as many companies have found to their chagrin, today's cheap labor can become more expensive as the law of supply and demand drives up the price of labor. Wages in Singapore, for example, increased from $0.25 to $1.25 per hour between 1973 and 1983.

The dramatic shifts in price levels of commodities and currencies (which are a commodity) are a major characteristic of the world economy today. This volatility argues for a sourcing strategy that provides alternative platforms for supplying markets. Thus, if the dollar or the yen or the DM becomes seriously overvalued, a company with production platforms in other locations can take advantage of these locations by shifting production to the alternative locations.

Volkswagen followed this approach when it established manufacturing capacity in Brazil and Mexico to supply the local and export markets. Indeed, Volkswagen planned in the early 1970s to build Beetle engines in Germany, bodies in Brazil and Mexico, and a new small car in Germany. The failure of Volkswagen to hold its world small-car market leadership position in the face of Japanese competition illustrates that in the end there is no substitute for the right product at the right price. Indeed, Peter Drucker has argued that Volkswagen's failure illustrates "that a 'clever' innovative strategy *always* fails, particularly if it is aimed at exploiting an opportunity created by a change in industry structure. Then only the very simple, specific strategy has a chance of succeeding."[1]

Investment and Control

A third issue which must be considered is that of investment and control. Do we want to control our own fate, or do we want to join with partners and jointly pursue mutual objectives? Answers to these questions will depend upon our attitudes and

[1] Peter F. Drucker, *Innovation and Entrepreneurship* (New York: Harper & Row, 1985), p. 87.

preferences concerning risk and our assessment of our ability to achieve our objectives in target markets. Do we need partners to complement our own lack of market knowledge and experience or our own limited human and financial resources? Are partners a requirement for access to markets (as is true in India and Mexico with their investment laws limiting foreign investors to minority positions)? Answers to these questions will determine our choices concerning the major investment tools available for entry and expansion: exporting, licensing, joint ventures, and direct investment.

EXPORTING

Exporting is the most traditional and well-established form of operating internationally. It is often identified as a low-investment alternative, but this perception is a gross and unfortunate misconception. Exporting does indeed require no investment in manufacturing operations abroad, but if it is done effectively and well, it requires significant investments in marketing.

The advantages of exporting are that it allows the manufacturing operations to be concentrated in a single location. Many companies in a variety of industries have concluded that concentrated manufacturing operations give them cost and quality advantages over the alternative of decentralized manufacturing.

Part of the export versus global manufacture decision is an exercise in cost analysis and forecasting, which can be facilitated by advanced management science techniques in linear programming. Indeed a number of companies have developed sourcing models that take into account all cost factors and compute the lowest-cost source for supplying markets. Another part of the export versus local manufacture decision is estimating political risk and conditions affecting the access to target markets. For example, many companies have decided to invest in foreign market manufacturing facilities even though they could more cheaply supply target markets from home country manufacturing operations because their access to the target markets is blocked by formal or informal trade barriers or the threat of such barriers. Local manufacturing then is a strategy for obtaining or retaining market access.

The decision to export or manufacture should not change the basic marketing program for the product in a market. Indeed it is essential to differentiate clearly the sourcing plan and the marketing plan so that each is given full attention regardless of the source of product supply for a market. Serious exporters invest in marketing in target markets. This investment begins with intensive market study leading to the development of a country marketing strategy. The hallmarks of this strategy are products that have been adapted to customer needs and preferences in the market (or in some cases left unchanged if this fits the strategy) and price, distribution, and communication policies that are an integrated part of the country marketing strategy. Each marketing strategy is of course unique so it is impossible to generalize, but the following examples illustrate the principles of export marketing.

Examples

AUTOMOBILES. The spectacular penetration of the U.S. auto market by Japanese manufacturers began with the adaptation of the basic domestic product targeted upon the home mass market for the low-priced compact and subcompact segments of the U.S. market. The initial cars exported to the United States by Toyota were so ugly and underpowered that they were unsellable. This was Japanese export marketing research: introduce a product, and if it is not successful, find out why, make the necessary changes, and return to the market with what the customers want.

The initial competitive focus of the Japanese manufacturers was on the compact and subcompact segment. After penetrating this segment, the Japanese companies found themselves with higher wage costs at home and a rising yen in the foreign exchange market, and growing protectionist sentiment in the United States. They responded by shifting the location of part of their production to the United States and by targeting the middle and then the upper price segments of the market. By moving up the market, they were able to obtain greater operating margins, which enabled them to continue to operate profitably in spite of their rising wage costs and the appreciating yen.

WATER. Perrier was able to accomplish a major increase in sales by simply repositioning their home market product from an imported water to a no-cal beverage. This required a change in pricing, in positioning in the channels and in the channels themselves, and in advertising and promotion. After the success of the repositioning, Perrier proceeded to introduce new products in the form of flavored water. All Perrier products are exported. Indeed, an important part of the positioning of the product is that the water is imported from the "Source."

The lesson from these examples is that marketing can drive a very successful export strategy, which over time may evolve into a different sourcing strategy, as in the Japanese auto case. Or it may remain tied to a home country manufacturing base, as in the Perrier water example.

Factor Costs

World factor costs in manufacturing are in three tiers. The first tier consists of the industrialized countries where factor costs are tending to equalize. The second tier consists of the industrializing countries that offer significant factor costs savings as well as an increasingly developed infrastructure and political stability, making them extremely attractive manufacturing locations. The third tier consists of those countries that have not yet become significant locations for manufacturing activity and that present the combination of lower factor costs (especially wages) offset by limited infrastructure development and greater political uncertainty.

Most companies conclude that exporting is the best way to source product for a market because of the importance of developing a sound marketing plan and strategy prior to investing in bricks and mortar. A marketing plan cannot be developed in "dry dock." It must be tested and refined under live conditions. The best way to do this is to apply the maxim

Always separate the marketing and the sourcing plan.

What this means is simply that entering a market and manufacturing should never be *automatically* tied to each other. The decision to invest in bricks and mortar should rest on considerations of cost, market access, political risk, and quality. If you can supply a country with quality product, at a lower cost, with reliable access from an export source, why invest? If any of these conditions is not met, you should consider investing in the country to create a source of supply.

LICENSING

Licensing is an alternative strategy with considerable appeal. A company with technology and know-how can, through licensing agreements, attractively supplement its bottom-line profitability with no investment and very limited expenses. Indeed, licensing offers an infinite return on investment. The only cost is the cost of signing the agreements and of policing their implementation. Of course, anything so easily attained has its disadvantages.

The principal disadvantage of licensing is that it can be a very limited form of participation. There are risks in following the licensing approach, particularly for those who do not know what they do not know. The potential returns from marketing and manufacturing may be lost, and the agreement may have a short life if the licensee develops its own know-how and capability to stay abreast of technology in the licensed product area.

Even more distressing, licensees have a troublesome way of often turning themselves into competitors. Thus many companies have found that the upfront easy money obtained from licensing turns out to be a very expensive source of revenue. One way of avoiding the danger of strengthening a competitor through a licensing agreement is to ensure that all licensing agreements provide for a cross-technology exchange between licenser and licensee.

On the positive side, it is possible to establish license arrangements that create export market opportunities and open the door to low-risk manufacturing relationships. Trademarks can be an important part of the creation and protection of opportunities for lucrative licenses.[2]

For companies that do decide to license, agreements should anticipate the possibility of extending market participation and, insofar as is possible, keep options and paths open for expanded market participation. One path is joint venture with the licensee.

[2]Private communication, E. M. Lang, President, REFAC Technology Development Corporation, 122 East 42nd Street, New York, N.Y.

JOINT VENTURES

A more extensive form of participation in foreign markets than either exporting or licensing is a joint venture with a local partner. The advantages of this strategy are the sharing of risk and the ability to combine strength in a joint venture. Thus a company with in-depth knowledge of a local market might combine with a foreign partner who lacks market knowledge but has considerable know-how in the area of technology and process applications.

Technology and Process Applications

Partners that lacked sufficient capital resources might get together to jointly finance a project. A venture might link up manufacturing resources and skill with an international marketing capability. Finally, a joint venture may be the only way to remain or enter a country if the country has a law that prohibits foreign control but permits joint venture. Mexico is an example of this type of country.

It is possible to use a joint venture as a source of supply for third-country markets. This must be carefully thought out in advance. One of the main reasons for joint venture divorce is disagreement about third-country markets where partners face each other as actual or potential competitors. To avoid this, it is essential to work out a plan for approaching third-country markets as part of the venture agreement.

The disadvantages of joint venturing are not insignificant. Of course, a joint venture requires the sharing of rewards as well as risks. The main disadvantage of this form of international expansion is the very significant costs of control and coordination associated with working with a partner. These difficulties have actually become so great that more than one-third of the 1,100 joint ventures of 170 multinational firms studied by Franko were unstable, ending in "divorce" of a significant increase in the U.S. firm's power over its partner.[3] Wright found that 65 joint ventures were either liquidated or transferred to the Japanese interest in 1976. This was up from 6 in 1972, a 600 percent increase. The most fundamental problem was the different benefits that each side expected to receive.[4,5]

OWNERSHIP

The most extensive form of participation in international markets is 100 percent ownership. This form of participation requires the greatest commitment of capital

---

[3]Lawrence G. Franko, "Joint Venture Divorce in the Multinational Company," *Columbia Journal of World Business,* May–June 1971, pp. 13–22.

[4]Richard W. Wright, "Joint Venture Problems in Japan," *Columbia Journal of World Business,* Spring 1979, pp. 25–31.

[5]Richard W. Wright and Colin S. Russel, "Joint Ventures in Developing Countries: Realities and Responses," *Columbia Journal of World Business,* Summer 1975, pp. 74–80.

and managerial effort and offers the fullest means of participating in a market. In addition, there is the not insignificant advantage of avoiding through 100 percent ownership any of the potential problems of communication and conflict of interest that may arise with a joint venture or coproduction partner.

One hundred percent ownership may be attained by either direct expansion or acquisition. Direct expansion is expensive and involves a major commitment of managerial time and energy. Alternatively, the acquisition route creates an instant position in a market but presents a demanding and challenging task of integrating the acquired company into the worldwide organization.

The four alternatives—exporting, licensing, joint ventures, and ownership— are in fact points along a continuum of alternative strategies or tools for international expansion and operation. There are an infinite number of possible combinations of these four basic alternatives. For example, a firm may decide to enter into a joint venture or coproduction agreement for purposes of manufacturing and may either market the products manufactured under this agreement in a wholly owned marketing subsidiary or sell the products from the coproduction facility to an outside marketing organization. Joint ventures may be 50:50 partnerships or minority or majority partnerships. Ownership may range anywhere from 51 percent to 100 percent. There may be in addition combinations of exporting, licensing, joint ventures, and ownership in the overall design of the international strategy and in relationships with particular foreign enterprises.

MARKET EXPANSION STRATEGIES[6]

Companies must decide whether to expand by seeking new markets in existing countries or, alternatively, seeking new country markets for already identified and served market segments. These two dimensions in combination produce four strategic options, as shown in Figure 10–2. Strategy 1 concentrates on a few segments in a few countries. This is typically a starting point for most companies. It matches company resources and market investment needs. Unless a company is large and resource rich, this strategy may be the only realistic way to begin.

In strategy 2, country concentration and segment diversification, a company serves many markets in a few countries. This strategy was the design of many European companies that remained in Europe and sought growth by expanding into new markets. It is also the approach of the American companies that decide to diversify in the U.S. market as opposed to going international with existing products.

Strategy 3, country diversification and market segment concentration, is the classic global company strategy that seeks out the world market for a product and serves the world customer. The rationale of this strategy is that by serving the world

---

[6]This section draws on Igal Ayal and Jehiel Zif, "Market Expansion Strategies in Multinational Marketing," *Journal of Marketing,* Vol. 43 (Spring 1979), pp. 84–94, and "Competitive Market Choice Strategies in Multinational Marketing," *Columbia Journal of World Business,* Fall 1978, pp. 72–81.

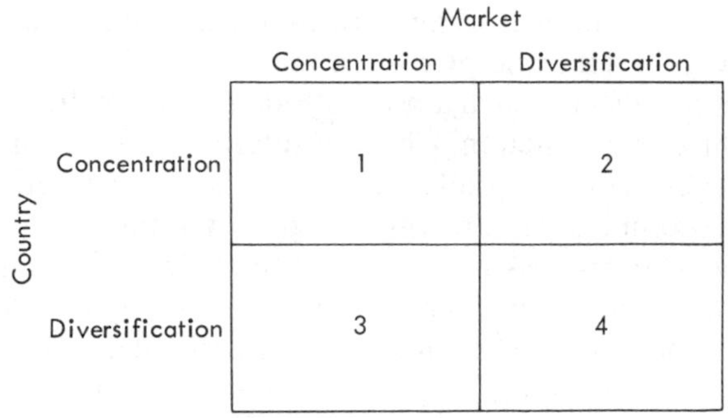

Market

	Concentration	Diversification
Concentration	1	2
Diversification	3	4

Country

FIGURE 10–2 Market Expansion Strategies   ANSOFF GRID.

customer, a company can achieve a greater accumulated volume and lower costs than any competitor and therefore have an unassailable competitive advantage. This is the strategy of the well-managed business that serves a distinct need and customer category.

Strategy 4, country and segment diversification, is the corporate strategy of a large multibusiness company such as GE or Matsushita. These companies are multicountry in their scope, and because they include many departments, business units, and groups, they are multisegment. The combination of these elements produces corporate strategy 4. It is important to recognize, however, that at the operating business level, management is focused on the needs of the world customer in a global market or, in this schema, strategy 3: country diversification and market segment concentration.

MARKET POSITION—A STRATEGIC GUIDE

An increasing number of firms all over the world are beginning to see the importance of market share not only in the home or domestic market but also in the world market. Since experience effects are independent of where a product is sold, overseas markets are as important as domestic markets in determining a company's total volume and cost position.

The pricing implications of experience theory are profound indeed. Low export prices enable a firm to penetrate foreign markets rapidly and keep potential competitors from gaining a foothold. They keep competitors out of the market and frustrate the competitor's ability to gain experience and lower costs. At the same time, a dominant producer can profit from a large share of a mature home market by maintaining profit margins at a level that stabilizes market shares.

This strategy preserves the dominant domestic position by frustrating potential foreign and domestic competition and by preserving the domestic base. It enables the company to fund overseas growth from domestic sales. An export pricing policy of "domestic price plus freight and insurance" is inappropriate and dangerous from this perspective.

If a foreign competitor penetrates a firm's domestic market, the domestic firm should lower its domestic prices. In the United States, this could be a problem for a dominant producer if such a price cut damaged smaller U.S. producers and invited government antitrust action. This consideration makes an aggressive export pricing policy an even more desirable strategy for U.S. competitors.

The recommended strategic program for the single-product, single-plant firm is investment in process as well as product improvement and the maintenance of world market dominance from the single source by developing and dominating new segments of markets and keeping cost competitive in old ones. Exports are absolutely critical to the single-plant firm's continued competitiveness. Thus the single-plant firm needs an overseas marketing system and strategy. It must seek to reduce overseas marketing costs through integrated logistical systems, and it must invest in country marketing programs to ensure that it reaches customers with an integrated marketing mix.

MARKETING STRATEGIES OF U.S., EUROPEAN, AND JAPANESE MULTINATIONAL SUBSIDIARIES

Brandt and Hulbert found distinct national influences in subsidiary strategies in management practices in their study of subsidiaries of multinational companies in Brazil.[7] The American subsidiaries in their sample were characterized as mature, established firms operating within a well-defined management system under the watchful eye of the home office. In contrast to the European and Japanese, the American procedures for planning, reporting, and control and evaluation were much more formalized and clearly defined.

According to Brandt and Hulbert, American subsidiaries rely on product innovation as the key to continued growth. European strategies, they found, were much more defensive. European subsidiaries, for example, demonstrated a strong preference for penetration of existing or closely related markets rather than entry via new products into new markets. The Japanese companies adopted a strategy of low-cost, high-volume production in limited product lines, which enabled them to use price as a major competitive tool for achieving the number one goal, which was sales growth. The Japanese concern is with sales volume. One manager described this as a "profit-neglecting selling strategy" and pointed out that his company profits resulted as much from concern over production efficiencies as from profit margins. According to Brandt and Hulbert, Japanese companies seemed to operate with less overhead. Their offices were typically spartan, and organizational structures were lean.

[7]William K. Brandt and James M. Hulbert, "Marketing Strategies of American, European and Japanese Multinational Subsidiaries;" Paper presented at the Academy of International Business Meeting, Fountainebleau, France, July 7–9, 1975.

ALTERNATIVE STRATEGIES

Table 10–1 suggests three basic alternative international business strategies: Stage 1—international—and stage 2—multinational—strategies correspond to ethnocentric and polycentric orientations, respectively; stage 3—global strategy—corresponds with the geocentric orientation. The basic design of the stage 1, international strategy, is extension. Companies following this approach seek either consciously or unconsciously to extend their products and programs as much as possible. The basic design of stage 2 multinational is decentralization where insofar as possible responsibilities for local operations are delegated to subsidiary management. The stage 3 global design is an integration model that seeks to synthesize inputs from world and regional headquarters and the country organization.

As can be seen from Table 10–1, there is an evolution from stage 1 to stage 3 in all the major elements that make up the overall organization and its approach to international business. Structurally, the evolution is from an international division to regional organization to the matrix. The planning process is top-down in stage 1, bottom-up in stage 2, and interactive in stage 3. The interaction is a dialogue on objectives and programs between corporate and country management. The marketing process is not standardized in stage 1, partially standardized in stage 2, and standardized in stage 3. In other words, in stage 3 each person and organization approaches marketing with the same process: a common vocabulary and approach to marketing planning, for example.

In stage 1, the typical product sourcing plan is an export arrangement where, as in stage 2, the most frequent or preferred sourcing arrangement is local manufacture. In stage 3, product sourcing is based on a sourcing plan that takes into account cost, delivery, and all other factors affecting competitiveness and profitability and produces a sourcing plan that maximizes both competitive effectiveness and profitability. In stage 1, companies' key jobs go to home country nationals in both the subsidiaries and the headquarters. In stage 2, key jobs in host countries go to country nationals, whereas headquarters management positions are usually held by some country nationals. In stage 3 the best person is selected for all management positions regardless of nationality. Research and development in stage 1 is conducted in the home country and in stage 2 becomes decentralized and fragmented. In stage 3, research is part of an integrated worldwide research and development plan and is typically decentralized taking advantage of resources as well as responding to local aspirations to produce a worldwide decentralized research and development program.

Control and measurement standards are usually in stage 1 based on home country experience, whereas in stage 2 they become highly decentralized. In stage 3, control and measurement standards are circumstantial and take into account both local conditions and international experience.

The three alternatives for international business strategy are in fact an idealization of actual behavior. No company ever aligns each of the elements of strategic

TABLE 10–1 International Business Strategy: Three Alternatives

STRATEGIC DIMENSION	STAGE 1 INTERNATIONAL	STAGE 2 MULTINATIONAL	STAGE 3 GLOBAL
Management assumptions	Ethnocentric	Polycentric	Geocentric
Design	Extension	Decentralization	Integration
Structure	Internation division	Regional divisions	Matrix/grid
Planning process	Top-down	Bottom-up	Interactive
Decision making	Centralized	Decentralized	Circumstantial/interactive
Marketing process	Not standardized	Partially standardized	Standardized
Marketing programs	Standardized	Unique	Circumstantial/interactive
Product sourcing	Export	Local manufacture	Lowest cost
Human resources			
Key job nationality			
Country management	Home country	Host country	Best person
Headquarters management	Home country	Home country	Best person
R&D, product development	Home country	Decentralized, fragmented	Circumstantial/interactive
Control/measurement	Home country standards	Decentralized	Circumstantial

TABLE 10–2 The Evolution of Fleetguard, Inc.

STRATEGIC DIMENSION	STAGE 1 INTERNATIONAL Years 1–4	STAGE 2 MULTINATIONAL Years 5–8	STAGE 3 GLOBAL Years 9–11
Management assumptions	70% Ethnocentrism 30% Polycentrism	80% Polycentrism 20% Ethnocentrism	60% Polycentrism 40% Geocentrism
Design	Extension	75% Decentralized 25% Extension	80% Integration 20% Decentralized
Structure	Regional	Regional	20% Matrix 80% Regional
Planning process	Bottom-up	Bottom-up	20% Interactive 80% Bottom-up
Decision making	70% Decentralized 30% Centralized	80% Decentralized 20% Centralized	80% Decentralized 20% Centralized
Marketing process	Not standardized	Partially standardized	Standardized
Marketing programs	Standardized	30% Unique 70% Standardized	Unique
Product sourcing	Export	Construct plant Export	60% Local manufacturing 40% Export
Human resources	Extension	Extension, local	Host country
Key job Nationality			
Country management	Home Country	Host country	Host Country
Headquarters management	N.A.	Host Country	Best person
R&D, product	Home Country	60% Home country 40% Decentralized	70% Integrated 30% Decentralized
Central/measure	50% Home standardized 50% Decentralized	60% Decentralized 40% Home standardized	75% Decentralized 25% Integrated

N.A.—not available.

This example was provided by Jon Adamson.

focus in exactly the fashion shown in Table 10–1. As companies evolve, unique combinations of the strategic dimensions make up the actual strategy. Nestlé, for example, has stage 2 management assumptions and human resource policies in its subsidiaries and is a stage 3 company in its marketing process and structure. The most effective firms are unique combinations of the elements of Table 10–1 rather than clear stage 1, 2, or 3 companies.

Many experienced managers feel that stage 3 makes sense only after one has experienced the behavioral characteristics and attitudes of stages 1 and 2. The mere fact that you have read this chapter will not make it possible for you to jump to stage 3. On the other hand, knowing that stage 3 exists can accelerate the evolution of an organization to the most effective combination of strategic dimension stages.

Table 10–2 shows an example of how Fleetguard, Inc., a wholly owned subsidiary of Cummins Engine Company, evolved over an 11-year period.

SUMMARY

Companies face a wide range of alternative ways of participating in international markets. Those who have had experience in international marketing realize that it is necessary to practice marketing regardless of sourcing arrangements. Companies committed to marketing study the foreign customer and in effect become so knowledgeable about the "foreign" market that it is no longer foreign but rather a market in a geographical location as are all other markets. This is a fundamental application of the marketing concept and if applied leads to the formulation of a unique and adapted marketing strategy that integrates product, price, place, and promotion elements in an appropriate way consistent with corporate and product strengths and weaknesses as well as competitive reality.

Companies that have developed an appropriate marketing strategy are then able to reach a decision about the most effective sourcing arrangements. Sourcing plans must take into account organizational resources, strengths and weaknesses, factor costs, transportation costs, conditions of market access and entry, and realistic assessments of political risk and future conditions at entry, as well as security of investments. The choice of an appropriate strategy is complex and always involves an element of risk and uncertainty. In this chapter, we have outlined the major alternative tools and have highlighted factors and conditions that should influence the choice of these tools.

DISCUSSION QUESTIONS

1. What are the alternative tools or strategies for expanding internationally? What are the major advantages and disadvantages of each tool?
2. The president of XYZ Manufacturing Company of Buffalo, New York, comes to you with a license offer from a company in Osaka. In return for sharing the company's patents and know-how, the Japanese company will pay a license fee of 5 percent of the ex factory

price of all products sold based on the U.S. company's license. The president wants your advice. What would you tell him?

3. What are the differences among an international, multinational, and a global company? Can you think of examples of companies that fit the characteristics of each of these types of companies?

4. What are the differences, if any, among the typical U.S., Japanese, and European company?

5. What is the difference between the strategic options of a small versus a large company?

BIBLIOGRAPHY

Articles

BERLEW, F. KINGSTON. "The Joint Venture—A Way Into Foreign Markets." *Harvard Business Review,* July-August 1984, pp. 48–54.

DAVIDSON, KENNETH. "Strategic Investment Theories." *The Journal of Business Studies,* Vol. 6, no. 1 (Summer 1985), pp. 16–28.

DOZ, YVES L. "Strategic Management in Multinational Companies." *Sloan Management Review,* Winter 1980, pp. 27–46.

———, AND C. K. PRAHALAD. "How MNC's Cope with Host Government Demands. *Harvard Business Review,* Vol. 58, no. 2 (March–April 1980), pp. 149–160.

———, CHRISTOPHER A. BARTLETT, AND C. K. PRAHALAD. "Global Competitive Pressures and Host Country Demands." *California Management Review,* Spring 1981, pp. 63–73.

FRANKO, LAWRENCE G. "Pattern in the Multinational Spread of Continental European Enterprise." *Journal of International Business Studies,* Fall 1975, pp. 41–54.

GULLANDER, STEFFAN. "Joint Ventures and Corporate Strategy." *Columbia Journal of World Business,* Vol. 11, no. 1 (Spring 1976), pp. 104–114.

HAMEL, GARY, AND C. K. PRAHALAD. "Do You Really Have A Global Strategy?" *Harvard Business Review,* July-August 1985, pp. 139–148.

HARRIGAN, KATHRYN RUDIE. "Joint Ventures and Global Strategies." *Columbia Journal of World Business,* Summer 1984, pp. 7–16.

HAWKINS, R. G., N. MINTZ, AND M. PROVISSIERO. "Government Takeovers of U.S. Foreign Affiliates." *Journal of International Business Studies,* Spring 1976, pp. 3–16.

JATUSRIPITAK, SOMKID, LIAM FAHEY, AND PHILIP KOTLER. "Strategic Global Marketing: Lessons From the Japanese. *Columbia Journal of World Business,* Spring 1985, pp. 47–53.

JOHANSSON, J. K., AND JAN-ERIK VAHINE. "The Internationalization of the Firm: A Model of Knowledge Development and Increasing Foreign Commitments." *Journal of International Business Studies,* Spring-Summer 1977, pp. 23–32.

KOGUT, BRUCE. "Designing Global Strategies: Comparative and Competitive Value-Added Chains." *Sloan Management Review,* Summer 1985, pp. 17–27.

———. "Designing Global Strategies: Profiting from Operational Flexibility." *Sloan Management Review,* Fall 1985, pp. 27–38.

MCINTYRE, DAVID R. "Multinational Positioning Strategy." *Columbia Journal of World Business,* Vol. 10, no. 3 (Fall 1975), pp. 106–110.

MAZZOLINI, RENATO. "European Corporate Strategies." *Columbia Journal of World Business,* Vol. 10, no. 1 (Spring 1975), pp. 98–108.

NIELSEN, RICHARD P. "Should a Country Move toward International Strategic Market Planning?" *California Management Review*, Vol. 15, no. 2 (January 1983, pp. 34–44.

PERLMUTTER, HOWARD V., AND DAVID A. HEENAN. "How Multinational Should Your Top Managers Be?" *Harvard Business Review*, November–December 1974, pp. 121–132.

PETERSON, RICHARD B., AND HERMANN F. SSCHWIND. "A Comparative Study of Personnel Problems in International Companies and Joint Ventures in Japan." *Journal of International Business Studies*, Spring–Summer 1977, pp. 45–56.

PORTER, MICHAEL E. "The Strategic Role of International Marketing." *The Journal of Consumer Marketing*, Vol. 3, no. 2 (Spring 1986), pp. 17–21.

PRAHALAD C. K. "Strategic Choices in Diversified MNC's." *Harvard Business Review*, July–August 1976, pp. 67–78.

RONSTADT, ROBERT, AND ROBERT J. KRAMER. "Getting the Most Out of Innovation Abroad." *Harvard Business Review*, March–April 1982, pp. 94–99.

SHEARER, JOHN C. "The External and Internal Manpower Resources of Multinational Corporations." *Columbia Journal of World Business*, Vol. 9, no. 2 (Summer 1974), pp. 9–17.

STOPFORD, J. M. "Changing Perspectives on Investment by British Manufacturing Multinationals." *Journal of International Business Studies*, Fall–Winter 1976, pp. 15–28.

VAN WOLFEREN, KAREL G. "The Japan Problem." *Foreign Affairs*, Vol. 6, no. 2 (Winter 1986–1987), pp. 288–303.

WELLS, LOUIS T., JR. "Social Cost/Benefit Analysis for MNC's." *Harvard Business Review*, March–April 1975, pp. 40–50.

———, "Negotiating with Third World Governments." *Harvard Business Review*, January–February 1977, pp. 72–80.

WIND, YORAM, AND SUSAN DOUGLAS. "International Portfolio Analysis and Strategy: The Challenge of the 80s." *Journal of International Business Studies*, Fall 1981, pp. 69–82.

———, SUSAN P. DOUGLAS, AND HOWARD V. PERLMUTTER. "Guidelines for Developing International Marketing Strategies." *Journal of Marketing*, April 1973, pp. 14–23.

———, AND THOMAS S. ROBERTSON. "Marketing Strategy: New Directions for Theory and Research." *Journal of Marketing*, Vol. 47 (Spring 1983), pp. 12–25.

GLOBAL COMPETITION— MOTORCYCLES, 1955–1985[1]

INTRODUCTION

The first form of a motorcycle was built during the 1860s when a German inventor attached a steam driven engine to a bicycle. It was not until the 1890s, however, when gasoline powered engines were introduced, that the first real motorcycle was built. The practical nature of the machine quickly led to its development on both sides of the Atlantic Ocean. In the first decade of this century, companies such as Harley-Davidson and Triumph, names that were to become syn-

[1]This case was prepared by Charles J. Anderer, research associate, under the supervision of Warren J. Keegan, Professor of International Business and Marketing. Copyright © 1986 by the Board of Trustees of Pace University.

onomous with the production of motorcycles, came into existence. At the same time, a host of other manufacturers engaged themselves in the motorcycle business, sparking a wide range of technological development. By 1913, there were 179,926 motorcycles registered in England while the United States was producing 70,000 machines annually.

Motorcycles distinguished themselves as particularly useful machines during the two World Wars. In fact, the first American soldier to enter Germany in 1918 did so aboard a Harley-Davidson. After each of the wars, a proliferation of small companies occurred, taking advantage of the gaps left by the larger companies whose production had been diverted overseas. By the 1950s, most of these small companies had disappeared, leaving the production of motorcycles in the hands of a few, well-recognized names.

The decade of the 1950s was a period of calm and stability for the major motorcycle makers of the world. The British manufacturers, Norton, BSA, Triumph, and Enfield, and America's Harley-Davidson enjoyed solid reputations and steady, if unspectacular, success. The German manufacturer BMW and the Italians Moto-Guzzi, Benelli, and Ducati also produced quality motorcycles for markets in Europe. Motorcycles were still being used primarily as substitutes for cars, and they were especially popular among gangs of young toughs and the police who pursued them. Motorcycle makers seemed happy enough to remain confined to relatively narrow markets, which no doubt explains the modest sales levels of the era.

These companies had no idea what was in store for them. In 1955, sales in the United States were about 50,000 units, by 1965, this figure would increase tenfold, and, in 1975, sale levels flirted with the one-million mark for the third consecutive year. The shift of market share from Western producers to Eastern producers was accomplished in a relatively brief space of time. The Japanese, who entered the global market in 1959, would control 85 percent of the American market by 1966.

1966 US Motorcycle Market Shares

Honda	63%
Yamaha	11
Suzuki	11
Harley-Davidson	4
Other	11

Source: Japanese Automobile Manufacturers Association.

The balance of power having shifted eastward, the leading motorcycle producers of Great Britain and America entered a period of steady decline. Between 1955 and 1970, Harley-Davidson would see its share of the American market drop from nearly 70 to 5 percent. Triumph was in even worse shape; it fell hopelessly into debt in the 1970s and has since ceased to exist. As of 1984, the top four Japanese producers controlled just over 95 percent of the American market (Table 1).

HISTORICAL BACKGROUND

One of the main reasons why demand for motorcycles soared was that the product's usage underwent a fundamental change. Throughout the first half of the twentieth century, motorcycles had been used as a means for transportation, for military purposes and by enthusiasts who raced them. Until the early 1960s, nobody had envisioned the motorcycle as a recreational product or as a secondary form of transportation for automobile owners. Sales in the 1950s were also limited by the fact that motorcycles had an image problem. In the 1954 Marlon Brando film, *The*

TABLE 1 New Motorcycle Registrations of 10 Leading Brands by Market Share, 1979–1984

Make	1984 Rank	1984 Mrkt. Share	1983 Rank	1983 Mrkt. Share	1982 Rank	1982 Mrkt. Share	1981 Rank	1981 Mrkt. Share	1980 Rank	1980 Mrkt. Share	1979 Rank	1979 Mrkt. Share
Honda	1	57.7%	1	54.8%	1	45.1%	1	39.1%	1	39.5%	1	39.7%
Yamaha	2	18.6	2	19.0	2	22.2	2	24.9	2	23.5	2	23.0
Suzuki	3	10.0	3	11.8	3	14.2	4	13.6	4	14.9	4	13.3
Kawasaki	4	8.9	4	9.8	4	12.7	3	15.7	3	15.4	3	14.7
Harley-Davidson	5	3.7	5	3.3	5	4.5	5	5.0	5	4.7	5	6.1
BMW	6	0.6	6	0.6	6	0.5	7	0.4	7	0.4	6	0.7
Husqvarna	7	0.2	7	0.3	8	0.2	9	0.2	9	0.2	10	0.3
Moto Guzzi	8	0.1	9	0.1	10	0.1	—	—	—	—	—	—
Can Am	9	*	—	—	9	0.1	10	0.1	10	0.1	—	—
Vespa	10	*	8	0.1	7	0.3	6	0.5	6	0.8	7	0.7
Triumph	—	—	10	*	—	—	8	0.2	8	0.3	8	0.6
Hodaka	—	—	—	—	—	—	—	—	—	—	9	0.3

*Less than 0.05%.

R. L. Polk new registrations include the three most current model years. Some off-highway motorcycle and all-terrain vehicle new registrations are included:

California new off-highway motorcycle and ATV registrations have been added to 1983 and prior year new registrations, so that comparisons can be made with 1984 and subsequent years which include California off-highway registrations.

New York new registrations were not available from October 1983 through December 1984.

Oklahoma new registrations are not available.

Source: *New Motorcycle Registrations*, R. L. Polk & Co., Detroit, Michigan.

308

Wild One, a gang of bikers riding Harley-Davidsons struck fear into the hearts of a small town (and moviegoers everywhere). This movie gave Harley-Davidson a reputation that, it must be said, it did little to dispel. In fact, Harley-Davidson used to take pride in the notion that its machines were the choice of motorcycle gangs everywhere, for this was viewed as the ultimate seal of approval.

The first suggestion that motorbikes might be marketed to a broader mainstream of the marketplace came in the late fifties when several Italian manufacturers, led by Innocenti, decided to try and take advantage of the rage for European automobiles by introducing the motor scooter to the United States. The product did surprisingly well with urban residents and women, a previously untapped target market. Outside of the Italians, nobody paid any attention to the popularity of the motor scooter and it was quickly dismissed as a fad.

The arrival of Honda, the first Japanese motorcycle maker to seriously export, took place in 1959. Although Honda was a newcomer to the international scene, its domestic sales figures made it the world's largest producer of motorcycles. Honda would use its size to develop economies of scale that neither its Western, nor its Japanese, competitors could match. From the start, however, both Harley-Davidson and the Europeans chose to minimize the importance of the Japanese challenge:

In that complacent decade (the 1950s), people joked about the groups of "little yellow men" at the Isle of Man TT motorcycle races nursing their entries to the small cc events. When they were spoken to, the Japanese would lower their eyes modestly and say they were "learning." Few guessed that in the next decade they would virtually wipe the British out of the motorcycle market (*The Sunday Times,* June 1, 1970).

JAPANESE MARKETING STRATEGY

The most important reason for all four of the Japanese motorcycle manufacturers' successes is that they offered quality products at competitive prices. Furthermore, the Japanese aggressively marketed the notion that it was both smart and chic to ride a motorcycle. Honda ads featured blond, suburban types on small, unimposing machines and the slogan "You meet the nicest people on a Honda." The company offered a wide range of models in the aim of meeting the needs of every potential rider, and they would proceed to outspend all their competitors in terms of advertising:

US Advertising Expenditure of Major Competitors ($000)

	1961	1965	1970	1974
Honda	$95	$1,376	$2,365	$5,509
Yamaha		266	885	2,187
Kawasaki			258	2,932
Suzuki		129	699	1,572
Ducati		107		
Triumph		29		
Harley-Davidson	75	162	539	1,508

Source: National Advertising Investments.

The Japanese companies, led by Honda, also afforded the American consumer a wider range of products. By 1965, they offered 14 motorcycles between the sizes of 50 cc and 450 cc. This by far exceeded the selection of any single Western manufacturer. By reducing the financial "barrier to entry" into the world of cycling to a mere $245 for a 50 cc bike (it cost $1,395 for a 650 cc Triumph), Honda created a new market and spawned a new generation of enthusiasts. The result was an unprecedented boom in motorcycle sales, which increased by 35 percent in 1962 and averaged increases of 18 percent for the following ten years.

In addition to competitive prices and creative advertising, all four Japanese companies, Honda, Kawasaki, Suzuki, and Yamaha, were able to adhere to a long-term strategy that stressed gains in market share and sales volume even at the expense of short-term profitability. The Boston Consulting Group (BCG), which was hired by the British government to analyze its motorcycle industry in 1975, observed that each of the Japanese motorcycle producers followed four basic principles in the pursuit of their growth goals:

1. Update or redesign products whenever a market threat or opportunity is perceived;

2. Set prices at levels designed to achieve market-share goals, and reduce them if necessary;

3. Establish effective marketing systems in all markets where serious competition is intended, regardless of short-term costs; and

4. Take a long-term perspective in planning and defining objectives.

By concentrating on market share, the Japanese were able to boost productivity levels to previously undreamed of heights. In his *Illustrated History of Motorcycles,* Erwin Tragatsch remarks that a factory having an annual rate of production of 20,000 motorcycles used to be considered "big." In 1970, four Japanese companies made over 2,800,000 motorcycles. In that same year, the entire British industry produced 64,521 machines. In 1984, over 4,000,000 motorcycles were produced in Japan (Table 2). Such disparities in productivity levels enabled the Japanese to develop economies of scale and built-in

TABLE 2 Japanese Motorcycle Production 1956–1984

YEAR	TOTAL PRODUCTION
1956	332,760
1957	410,064
1958	501,332
1959	880,629
1960	1,473,084
1961	1,804,371
1962	1,674,925
1963	1,927,970
1964	2,110,335
1965	2,212,784
1966	2,447,391
1967	2,241,847
1968	2,251,335
1969	2,576,873
1970	2,947,672
1971	3,400,502
1972	3,565,246
1973	3,763,127
1974	4,509,420
1975	3,802,547
1976	4,235,112
1977	5,577,359
1978	5,999,929
1979	4,475,956
1980	6,434,524
1981	7,412,582
1982	7,063,178
1983	4,807,379
1984	4,026,307

Source: Japanese Automobile Manufacturers Association.

cost advantages that the smaller Western companies found difficult to contend with. Furthermore, these companies were as preoccupied with short-term goals as the Japanese were concerned with the long term. Each time the Japanese entered a market segment (a given cc level), Harley-Davidson or Triumph, to name just two companies, would deem the costs of competition too high. Instead of fighting the Japanese by developing global marketing strategies of their own, segment after segment was conceded:

British Producers' Segment Retreat

	450–749cc		750cc +	
	1969	1973	1969	1973
Number of models	4	2	3	3
US sales (000)	25	12	4	21
US market share (%)	49	9	49	19

Source: Boston Consulting Group.

Perhaps this strategy of abandonment was adopted because it was wrongly assumed that the Japanese would forego an opportunity to enter the heavy bike sector. Eric Turner, chairman of the board of BSA Ltd., in the 1960s, went so far as to say that the Japanese were doing his company a favor:

The success of Honda, Suzuki and Yamaha in the States has been jolly good for us. People here start out buying one of the little low priced Japanese jobs. They get to enjoy the fun and exhiliration of the open road and frequently end up buying one of our more powerful and expensive BSA or Triumph machines. (*Ad Age,* 12/27/65)

The assumption was that the Japanese would not extend their product line to large bikes. In reality, the Japanese companies were each waiting for the moment when they could apply the same comparative advantage they possessed in the production of smaller bikes to the production of large bikes. Steadily they climbed the product ladder and, because of their sheer size, it was only a matter of time before they successfully mounted a challenge in the big bike sector. Predictably, the Japanese entry into this sector resulted in market share decreases for all those who thought themselves protected. Harley-Davidson, for example, saw its share of "heavyweight" sales in the United States drop from 99.6 percent in 1972, to 44.4 percent in 1975.

COMPETITIVE ADVANTAGE OF THE JAPANESE

In its report entitled "Strategy Alternatives for the British Motorcycle Industry," the Boston Consulting Group made an extensive study of the cost-volume relationship and its effect on Japanese motorcycle production. The BCG report notes that, in any industry, real unit costs decline at a fairly constant rate each time production experience doubles. "Costs decline because of various factors, including greater use of standardized parts, longer production runs, improved work methods and accumulated managerial experience. . . . Also, if a company accumulates production experience at a faster rate than its competitors, its real unit costs will fall more rapidly."

The BCG report underlines the fact that the Japanese were able to accumulate vast amounts of production experience because of the diligence with which they pursued their market share goals:

. . . Japanese emphasis on market share objectives has led in the longer term not only to high output volumes, but also to improved productivity, lower costs and higher profitability . . . Low share competitors inevitably now operate under substantial economic disadvantages relative to the Japanese (Boston Consulting Group 1975).

The growth of the Japanese companies also made them more cost effective in areas such as advertising and research and development. In the early 1970s, for example, each of the major producers of motorcycles spent about 2 percent of sales on advertising. For Honda, this represented an expense of $8,100,000 in 1972, while the entire British industry only spent $1,300,000. By spending the same percentage of money, Honda was outspending the competition. The Japanese were also able to develop large R&D facilities

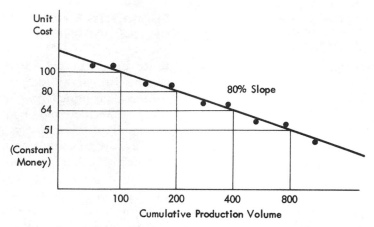

Note: Each point plotted represents the data for a particular year in the product history.

The Experience Curve (Schematic)

Source: Boston Consulting Group.

at comparatively low costs. While Honda, Yamaha, and Suzuki each boasted large research and development departments, all of them had fewer such employees as a percentage of sales than did the British:

Company	R&D Employees Per L1 Million of Sales	Total Research and Development Employees
Honda	1.8	1300
Suzuki	2.7	1000
Yamaha	3.2	800
Triumph	4.0	100

Source: Boston Consulting Group.

The end result of the enormous cost advantages for the Japanese was that they were able to build better quality products at lower cost. When their competitors realized that the Japanese were offering superior products at lower prices, they naturally assumed that it was the work of "Japan, Inc." or that there was collusion among the four Japanese producers. Besides being inconsistent with the industrial economic principles outlined above, this point of view was factually off base. BCG's research showed that Japanese motorcycles were actually being sold *at a premium* in the United States relative to their price to the Japanese consumer.

Premium on Retail List Prices, 1974

	Japan Price	U.S. Price	Premium
CB 750	$1411	$2024	43%
CB 550	1268	1732	37%
CB 450	1082	1471	36%
CB 360	904	1150	26%
CB 350	982	1363	39%
MT 250	779	965	24%
MT 125	564	743	32%
CB 125	593	640	8%

Source: Boston Consulting Group.

U.S.A. MARKET: PROTECTIONISM

The enormous success of the Japanese was explained in a different way by the American company, Harley-Davidson. Having lost a huge portion of its market share in the heavyweight segment, the company accused the Japanese of "dumping" their products in the American marketplace at artificially low prices. In 1977, depending on the exchange rate for the dollar, Harley-Davidson's bikes sold anywhere from $500 to $1,000 more than similarly sized Japanese bikes. In that same year, the company unsuccessfully petitioned the government for a tariff relief program that would shield it from the pressures of Japanese imports.

Honda and Kawasaki, perhaps in antic-ipation of the possibility of protectionist measures, both established production facilities in the United States. This undoubtedly helped these two companies to overcome Harley-Davidson's second and successful bid for a tariff in 1983. In that year, the International Trade Commission imposed a five-year tariff on bikes with an engine displacement of 700 cc or more in an effort to get the floundering Harley-Davidson back on its feet. Because of Honda's and Kawasaki's U.S. based production facilities, they were able to better absorb the impact of the tariff than Yamaha and Suzuki. The result of the tariff from the

TABLE 3   U.S. Total Motorcycle Registrations, 1945–1984

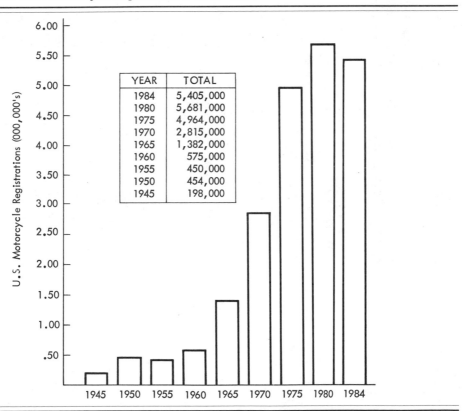

YEAR	TOTAL
1984	5,405,000
1980	5,681,000
1975	4,964,000
1970	2,815,000
1965	1,382,000
1960	575,000
1955	450,000
1950	454,000
1945	198,000

Source: U.S. Department of Transportation, Federal Highway Administration for 1945–1975 motorcycle registrations. Motorcycle Safety Foundation, Costa Mesa, California for 1980 and subsequent year motorcycle registrations.

TABLE 4 1984 Motorcycle Accident Statistics

	REGISTRATIONS	REPORTED ACCIDENTS	ACCIDENTS PER 10,000 REGISTRATIONS	FATALITIES	FATALITIES PER 10,000 REGISTRATIONS	FATALITIES PER 100 ACCIDENTS
National						
1984	5,405,453	169,685	313.91	4,584	8.48	2.70
1983	5,484,552	168,439	307.12	4,396	8.02	2.61
State Data—1984						
Alabama (1, 2, 10, 18, 23)	71,502	2,439	341.11	48	6.71	1.97
Alaska (1, 2, 12, 18, 23)	15,094	343	227.24	9	5.96	2.62
Arizona (12, 15, 23)	84,093*	4,405	535.72	119	14.15	2.64
Arkansas (4, 10, 18, 23)	28,119	747*	265.66	22	7.82	2.95
California (14, 15, 22)	695,251	28,444	409.12	866	12.46	3.04
Colorado (5, 14, 18, 23)	120,000*	3,464*	288.67	73	6.08	2.11
Connecticut (1, 13, 15, 20)	79,854	3,669	459.48	88	11.02	2.40
Delaware (5, 14, 18, 23)	8,573*	380*	443.25	14*	16.33	3.68
Dist. of Col. (5, 14, 18, 23)	5,599*	377*	673.33	3*	5.36	0.80
Florida (5, 14, 18, 23)	221,339	12,423	561.27	309	13.96	2.49
Georgia (10, 15, 20)	114,234	2,512	219.90	80	7.00	3.18
Hawaii (3, 11, 18, 20)	10,199	404	396.12	15	14.71	3.71
Idaho (1, 2, 10, 15, 20)	50,595	903	178.48	27	5.34	2.99
Illinois (1, 2, 4, 10, 15, 22)	309,807*	8,178	263.97	182	5.87	2.23
Indiana (1, 2, 9, 15, 19)	135,729	4,154	306.05	85	6.26	2.05
Iowa (2, 12, 18, 23)	183,687	2,589*	140.95	45	2.45	1.74
Kansas (1, 2, 11, 15, 23)	83,744	1,835	219.12	47	5.61	2.58
Kentucky (2, 9, 18, 23)	50,355	1,619	321.52	51	10.13	3.15
Louisiana (1, 2, 9, 16, 23)	104,000	2,947	283.37	68	6.54	2.31
Maine (1, 4, 11, 15, 19)	40,361	1,216	301.28	35	8.67	2.88
Maryland (14, 15, 22)	71,761	3,051	425.16	75	10.45	2.48
Massachusetts (12, 18, 23)	103,000	4,596*	446.21	83	8.06	1.81
Michigan (9, 15, 22)	200,609	3,400	169.48	140	6.98	4.12
Minnesota (4, 12, 15, 22)	153,851	2,768	179.91	63	4.09	2.28
Mississippi (5, 14, 18, 23)	26,116	769	294.48	40	15.32	5.20
Missouri (1, 4, 12, 15, 22)	111,106	2,603	234.28	75	6.75	2.88
Montana (10, 15, 22)	37,371*	525	140.48	27	7.22	5.14
Nebraska (2, 10, 15, 22)	46,532	1,274	273.79	26	5.59	2.04
Nevada (14, 15, 22)	20,780	639	307.51	16	7.70	2.50

State	Registrations	Accidents		Fatalities		
New Hampshire (5, 14, 18, 23)	35,543	1,196	336.49	26	7.32	2.17
New Jersey (5, 14, 18, 23)	115,303	4,631	401.64	57	4.94	1.23
New Mexico (5, 14, 18, 23)	56,148	2,289	407.67	50	8.91	2.18
New York (2, 12, 15, 22)	174,911	8,085	462.24	183	10.46	2.26
North Carolina (12, 16, 23)	67,615	2,957	437.33	99	14.64	3.35
North Dakota (4, 12, 15, 19)	31,480	386	122.62	7	2.22	1.81
Ohio (1, 2, 8, 15, 23)	280,297	7,649	272.89	206	7.35	2.69
Oklahoma (1, 14, 16, 23)	105,963	2,350	221.78	72	6.79	3.06
Oregon (1, 12, 15, 23)	78,166	1,461	186.91	67	8.57	4.59
Pennsylvania (1, 2, 14, 15, 23)	207,170	5,217	251.82	171	8.25	3.28
Rhode Island (2, 11, 16, 22)	27,907	264	94.60	7	2.51	2.65
South Carolina (5, 14, 18, 23)	37,119	2,593	698.56	92	24.79	3.55
South Dakota (1, 12, 18, 23)	38,956	559	143.50	10	2.57	1.79
Tennessee (9, 18, 23)	100,879	3,052	302.54	110	10.90	3.60
Texas (1, 2, 3, 4, 10, 15, 22)	306,578	11,365	370.71	370	12.07	3.26
Utah (5, 14, 18, 23)	67,603*	1,393	206.06	38*	5.62	2.73
Vermont (5, 14, 18, 23)	25,724*	459*	178.43	10	3.89	2.18
Virginia (1, 12, 15, 22)	81,825	2,808	343.17	63	7.70	2.24
Washington (11, 15, 23)	136,679*	3,477	254.39	75	5.49	2.16
West Virginia (2, 10, 15, 19)	33,432	280	83.75	28	8.38	10.00
Wisconsin (1, 2, 18, 23)	190,612	4,085	214.31	98	5.14	2.40
Wyoming (2, 12, 15, 20)	22,282	356	159.77	14	6.28	3.93

*Estimated

Registrations:
1. Includes motorbikes (UVC motor driven cycles less than 5 NHP)
2. Includes mopeds and other motorized bicycles of 50 cc or less
3. Includes scooters
4. Other
5. Description not available

Accidents-Damage Threshold:
6. $0-$25-$50 property damage threshold
7. $100 property damage threshold
8. $150 property damage threshold
9. $200 property damage threshold
10. $250 property damage threshold
11. $300 property damage threshold
12. $400–$500 property damage threshold
13. $800 property damage threshold
14. No property damage figure specified/ available

Accident-Description:
15. Accident listed as "property damage, personal injury or fatality"
16. Accident listed as "any reported motorcycle accident"
17. Only records accidents investigated by State Highway Patrol

18. Other/Not available
Fatalities:
19. Number of fatal accidents in which a motorcycle was involved
20. Number of motorcyclists and passengers fatally injured in a motorcycle accident
21. Motorcycle operators only
22. Number of motorcyclists, passengers, and others (such as pedestrians) fatally injured in a motorcycle accident
23. Description not available

Source: Cycle Safety Info, Motorcycle Safety Foundation, Costa Mesa, California, 1985. Compiled by Motorcycle Safety Foundation and American Motorcyclist Association.

standpoint of Harley-Davidson's performance in terms of market share and sales has
been uneven at best—the four Japanese companies still account for more than 80 percent
of the U.S. "big-bike" market.

MARKET TRENDS

End of the Boom (1973)

The boom period of the 1960s carried into the
following decade, albeit not for the right reasons. Sales in the United States reached an
all-time high in 1973 with 1.5 million units
sold in the wake of an energy crisis. Not surprisingly, motorcycle manufacturers were
quick to point out the fuel efficiency of their
machines. The success of this message was,
however, short term in nature. Whereas a
whole new group of buyers was created in
the 1960s through the marketing of Honda
and others, the energy crisis buyers of the
1970s proved to be a fickle lot. They were
not buying motorcycles for the fun of it, rather,
they were seeking a cheap form of primary
transportation. Many of the new buyers had
never ridden a motorcycle before, yet they
started out by buying big, powerful models
that scared them away from cycling. Instead
of a "new generation" of buyers on which
future growth would be built, what the industry got was future decreases in sales.
Growth in the 1960s was based on both new
buyers and repeat first-time buyers who, having enjoyed their first purchase, moved up in
the market by buying new, more expensive
models. In the 1970s, however, there was no
second time for many first-timers.

Sales levels have never since reached
the 1.5 million level of 1973. The number of
motorcycles annually sold has hovered around
the 1 million mark since 1973. In 1984, 1.2
million bikes were sold. Motorcycle manufacturers have come to terms with the fact

that the boom of the sixties was an isolated
event and that the market for motorcycles
has matured (Table 3).

Why the Decline?

There are several reasons for the lagging sales
levels displayed by motorcycles since 1973.
As motorcycles grew bigger and more powerful, concerns over product safety and prac-
ticality arose. Fatality rates have continued
to rise and the fuel economy of big bikes is
comparable to that of small cars (Tables 4
and 5). Statistics showed that the fatality rate
for motorcycle riders was considerably higher
than that of automobiles. New buyers were
not starting out with 50 cc models as they had
before and thus exposed themselves to greater
danger than in the past. Motorcycle manufacturers were partially at fault because they
pushed big and expensive machines a lot
harder than the less lucrative small bikes. Also,
motorcycle makers failed to create new mar-

**TABLE 5 1985 Motorcycle Fuel Economy
Figures**

	ESTIMATED AVERAGE MILES PER GALLON*	
Engine Displacement	On-Highway Motorcycles	Dual Purpose Motorcycles
Under 125 cc	112	120
125–349 cc	82	98
350–449 cc	41	69
450–749 cc	50	60
Over 749 cc	41	—

*Derived from manufacturer exhaust emission test
results. The U.S. EPA requires manufacturers to certify exhaust emissions for all 50 cc and greater on-highway and
dual purpose motorcycles. The EPA does not require fuel
economy testing for motorcycles. However, fuel economy
figures can be derived from the exhaust emission test results. MPG figures were derived in this way from 69 1985
test vehicles representing over 80 models, produced by the
four leading manufacturers which represent about 95% of
the motorcycle sales nationwide.

kets for their products, relying too heavily on repeat buyers and seemingly forgetting the example of Honda in the 1960s. Finally, the potential for market creation was limited because the market itself had simply matured. Since the motorcycle is essentially a recreational vehicle, there are very definite limits as to available markets. Although the major motorcycle makers did pass up opportunities to expand their sales in the 1970s, it would have been unrealistic to expect growth rates similar to those of the previous decade.

New Product Lines and New Demographics

Motorcycle manufacturers have found ways to pad their sales figures by offering a wide range of stylish and pricy accessories. Heavy touring bikes feature engine guards, which protect the driver's legs, saddlebags, Plexiglas windshields, AM-FM stereo cassette players and a host of other appointments. Also offered are helmets, which can reach upwards of $300 (as one ad used to say, "You don't have a $19.95 head, so don't wear a $19.95 helmet."). It is also typical to see manufacturers offer a range of clothing such as leather jackets, pants, and gloves.

Perhaps the only product line that has enjoyed considerable growth in the 1980s is that of three- and four-wheel motorcycles. Sales of three-wheelers went from 100,000 in 1980 to 150,000 in 1981. The practical, low-slung vehicles can be used on a year-round basis and can even be written off as a business expense by groups such as farmers, who use them as they would a tractor. Once again, the leader in this new segment is Honda, which held 83 percent of the market as of 1981. To

TABLE 6 1984 Annual Operating and Ownership Costs Automobile vs. Motorcycle

	INTERMEDIATE AUTOMOBILE	MOTORCYCLE (500–650 cc STREET)
Operating Costs	$1,177	$257
Gasoline & oil	$ 873	$ 72
Repairs & maintenance	281	165
Tires	23	20
Ownership Costs	$2,370	$610
Depreciation	$1,489	$250
Insurance	732	350
Registration & titling	149	10
Total annual cost	$3,547	$867

Source for automotive costs (averaging 13,000 miles per year over 4 years): *Cost of Owning and Operating Automobiles and Vans 1984*, U.S. Department of Transportation, Federal Highway Administration.

Source for motorcycle costs (500–650 cc street motorcycle averaging 2,700 miles per year over 4 years): Gasoline: based on 52 MPG at $1.39 per gallon; Maintenance and Repairs: *1980 Survey of Motorcycle Ownership and Usage*, conducted for the Motorcycle Industry Council by Burke Marketing Research, Inc., Cincinnati, Ohio, April 1981. Tires: Based on the purchase of one tire at a cost of $80 over the four year period; Depreciation: *N.A.D.A. Motorcycle Appraisal Guide*, May–August 1984, National Automobile Dealers Assn.; Insurance based on a survey of a sample of companies. Includes coverage for comprehensive, collision and property damage and liability. Registration & Titling: *Polk's Motor Vehicle Registration Manual*, R. L. Polk & Co., Detroit, Michigan.

date, only Japanese manufacturers offer vehicles of this type.

None of this is to suggest that there is no future for the conventional motorcycle. For many, the vehicles remain an exciting and inexpensive mode of transport. While the demand for motorcycles has indeed matured, the machines are still considerably cheaper to operate than automobiles (Table 6). Furthermore, motorcycles are gaining in popularity among women, the well-educated and the affluent (Tables 7 and 8).

COMPETITION AS OF 1985

Global Competitors

Honda.   Today's Honda still prides itself on being the worldwide industry leader. Having judged the motorcycle market as mature, however, it has subtly diverted its attention to automobile production. Honda is still the industry leader in anticipating new markets for new products. It has played a major role in the growth of three- and four-wheel vehi-

TABLE 7   Motorcycle Owner Profile: Occupation, Income, Motorcycle Ownership

OCCUPATION OF OWNER	% OF TOTAL OWNERS* 1985	% OF TOTAL OWNERS* 1980	HOUSEHOLD INCOME FOR PRIOR YEAR	% of TOTAL OWNERS* 1985	% of TOTAL OWNERS* 1980
Laborer/Semi-Skilled	22.2%	20.7%	Under $10,000	11.9%	9.1%
Mechanic/Craftsman	16.4	23.3	$10,000–$14,999	9.4	13.0
Professional/Technical	15.8	18.8	$15,000–$19,999	12.5	13.9
Manager/Proprietor	7.4	8.6	$20,000–$24,999	8.2	12.9
Clerical/Sales	7.0	9.3	$25,000–$34,999	16.4	12.5
Service Worker	5.8	7.1	$35,000–$49,999	13.1	5.9
Farmer/Farm Laborer	5.6	4.6	$50,000 and over	6.4	2.4
Military	1.1	1.9	Don't Know	22.1	30.3
Other	9.1	0.0			
Not Stated	9.6	5.7	Median	$22,500	$17,500

YEARS REGULARLY RIDING MOTORCYCLES	% OF TOTAL OWNERS* 1985	% OF TOTAL OWNERS* 1980	TOTAL MOTORCYCLES EVER OWNED	% OF TOTAL OWNERS* 1985	% OF TOTAL OWNERS* 1980
1–2	12.5%	21.1%	1	22.3%	25.6%
3–5	24.1	27.6	2	20.6	21.4
6–10	26.8	29.8	3–4	27.9	26.5
Over 10	34.9	18.6	5–9	18.2	16.0
Not Stated	1.7	2.9	10 or more	9.8	7.6
			Not Stated	1.2	2.9
Median (yrs.)	8.0	6.0			
			Median (cycles)	3.0	3.0

*Owner defined as the primary rider.

Sources: *1980 Survey of Motorcycle Ownership and Usage,* conducted for the Motorcycle Industry Council by Burke Marketing Research, Inc., Cincinnati, Ohio, April 1981; *1985 Survey of Motorcycle Ownership and Usage,* Preliminary Six Months Results, conducted for the Motorcycle Industry Council by Burke Marketing Research, Inc., Cincinnati, Ohio, September 1985.

TABLE 8   Motorcycle Owner Profile: Number of Owners and Riders, Sex, Marital Status, Age, Education

6,492,000 Estimated Motorcycle Owners in 1984; 10,575,000 Estimated Motorcycle Riders in 1984

SEX	% OF TOTAL OWNERS*		MARITAL STATUS	% OF TOTAL OWNERS*	
	1985	1980		1985	1980
Male	89.8%	92.1%	Single	48.7%	51.7%
Female	10.2	7.9	Married	48.7	44.3
			Other/Not Stated	2.6	4.0

AGE	% OF TOTAL OWNERS*		HIGHEST LEVEL OF EDUCATION	% OF TOTAL OWNERS*	
	1985	1980		1985	1980
Under 18	16.2%	24.6%	Grade School	8.6%	13.5%
18–24	20.0	24.3	Attended High School	13.8	18.9
25–29	19.7	14.2	Graduated High School	37.7	34.6
30–34	12.3	10.2	Attended College	21.9	17.6
35–39	10.2	8.8	College Graduate	11.4	9.2
40–49	12.3	9.4	Post Graduate	4.4	3.1
50 and over	7.1	5.7	Not Stated	2.2	3.1
Not stated	2.2	2.8			
Mean Age	29.6 yrs.	26.9 yrs.			

*Owner defined as the primary rider.

Sources: *1980 Survey of Motorcycle Ownership and Usage,* conducted for the Motorcycle Industry Council by Burke Marketing Research, Inc., Cincinnati, Ohio, April 1981; *1985 Survey of Motorcycle Ownership and Usage,* Preliminary Six Months Results, conducted for the Motorcycle Industry Council by Burke Marketing Research, Inc., Cincinnati, Ohio, September 1985.

cles and, in 1984, it introduced two new scooters—Vocal and Eve—designed especially for the growing women's market. Honda remains committed to the development of products that appeal to the widest range of consumers possible. In 1983 alone, it introduced 41 new and redesigned models.

Yamaha. This company grew more rapidly than Honda since 1962 and now occupies second position in world production of motorcycles. Yamaha, however, improperly assessed motorcycle demand when, in 1979, it launched an all-out campaign to overtake Honda as the world's number one motorcycle maker. It sent production levels soaring to 2.9 million units in 1981, leaving it with a huge amount of unsold motorcycles. Its efforts to unload these inventories at bargain prices may have been partially responsible for the tariff relief program granted Harley-Davidson by the ITC in 1983. Yamaha was hit especially hard by this ruling because it does not have any U.S. based facilities. In spite of all its recent troubles, Yamaha remains firmly entrenched in the number two slot of the American market.

Kawasaki. This is the last of the big four Japanese manufacturers to enter the market. Kawasaki, a large concern that specializes in heavy industrial products, decided to compete in motorcycles at the global level after several years of difficulty as a strictly domestic producer. By stressing market share over profitability, Kawasaki was able to call itself a world class competitor by the mid-1970s. Kawasaki has always sought to produce performance bikes geared to the cycling enthusiast. In 1984, its *Ninja* line was introduced. Being lighter than some 750 cc bikes and more powerful than some 1100 cc models, the *Ninja* is the latest in a long line of swift and powerful Kawasakis. Their emphasis on large displacement engines and performance makes Kawasaki a formidable competitor in the big-bike sector.

Suzuki. Suzuki differs from Kawasaki in that it stresses comfort and solid design more than speed. Suzuki products, on the other hand, have always done well at racing competitions. Experts say that this is an indication of how easy to ride Suzukis generally are. The company has always prided itself on having the customers' interests at heart when designing their motorcycles. It does not concentrate on one sector of the market. In 1984, for example, it introduced bikes ranging from 250 cc to 1100 cc. It is perhaps for this reason that Suzuki has been able to overtake Kawasaki. Since 1982, Suzuki has maintained a solid hold on the number three position in market share.

Harley-Davidson. This is the sole remaining American motorcycle manufacturer. Harley has benefited from the previously mentioned ITC ruling but it has also made a concerted effort to reduce some of the enormous cost advantages enjoyed by the Japanese. The company has, ironically, instituted Japanese style production and inventory control methods in order to lower its unit costs. Its quest for survival remains limited, however, by its size (sales of 30,000–40,000 per year), its concentration on the highly competitive big-bike sector of the market and its inability to develop markets overseas.

BMW. This manufacturer concentrated on the 750 cc and up market sector. Since 95 percent of this company's sales revenue comes from automobiles, some might wonder why BMW remains in an already crowded area of the motorcycle market. BMW, however, is firmly committed to its tiny motorcycle division. Their bikes are considered to be technically solid. The recently introduced K100 model (1000 cc) is known as the quietest machine of its size. BMWs are extremely popular with racing enthusiasts and affluent pleasure seekers. It is similar in size to Harley-Davidson (production runs at about 30,000 per year), but it differs in that it realizes sales both in the United States, Europe and Asia. The BMW name also allows the firm to sell its motorcycles at relatively high prices. BMW's overall manufacturing strength and positive image make its prospects for the longer term seem brighter than Harley-Davidson.

11

COMPETITIVE ANALYSIS AND STRATEGY

It seems incredible, and yet it has happened a hundred times, that troops have been divided and separated merely through a mysterious feeling of conventional manner, without any clear perception of the reason.

Karl Von Clausewitz (1780–1831)
Vom Kriege (1832) Book III,
Chapter XI, "Assembly of
Forces in Space"

INTRODUCTION

The essence of marketing strategy is relating an organization to its environment. As the horizons of marketers have expanded from the domestic to global markets, so too have the horizons of competitors. Today, the global marketer can enjoy the fruits of serving global markets, but in life, everything has its price, and in this case the price is global competition. This chapter focuses on techniques of analyzing the competition and developing an effective global competitive strategy.

COMPETITION

An inevitable consequence of the expansion of international marketing activity is the growth of competition on a global basis. In industry after industry, international competition is a critical factor affecting success. In some industries, international companies have virtually excluded all other companies from their markets. An example of this phenomenon is the detergent industry where three companies—Colgate, Unilever, and Procter & Gamble—dominate an increasing number of detergent markets. Many companies can make a quality detergent, but the skills of packaging, pricing, distributing, merchandising, and advertising detergent products are so highly developed in a handful of large international companies that these factors have overwhelmed local competition in market after market. A good illustration of how they have done this is provided by the excellent series of cases on the competition in the detergent industry in the Central American Common Market.[1]

The automobile industry has also become increasingly competitive on an international basis. Part of the reason for the initial success of foreign cars in the United States was the reluctance of U.S. manufacturers to make a small and inexpensive product. The resistance of U.S. manufacturers was based on the economics of car production. The additional cost of a larger car is mainly in materials, not in fabrication. U.S. manufacturers had over the years established a pricing policy that linked price to size. The bigger the car, the higher the price. Under this formula, small cars meant smaller unit profits. Therefore U.S. manufacturers resisted the increasing preference in the U.S. market for smaller cars. Meanwhile, European and Japanese manufacturers' product lines have always been smaller than the U.S. line because of the different market conditions in Europe: less space, high taxes on engine displacement and on fuel, and a much greater market interest in functional design and engineering innovations (disc brakes, rack-and-pinion steering, five-speed gear boxes, small-displacement/high-performance engines, and so on). These manufacturers discovered that there was a growing demand for their product in the U.S. market. Sales of imports, predominantly of small cars, multiplied 20-fold between 1954 and 1959. The introduction of the American compacts in the early 1960s blunted the import penetration of the U.S. market, but as the U.S. compacts each year included an increase in size, power, and price, import sales more than doubled between 1962 and 1967 and then doubled again between 1967 and 1972. The share of market for foreign cars in the United States increased from less than 5 percent in the early 1960s to 17 percent in 1975 and to one-third of the market in 1987.

In many respects the U.S. market has gradually become quite similar to European and Japanese markets. In Europe, for example, taxes on engine displacement and gasoline have made economy a necessary feature in automotive products. Although the United States has not adopted this form of control, the U.S. industry committed itself to achieving voluntarily a 40 percent improvement in gasoline mileage by 1980. The U.S. government is aiming for a sales weighted average of 28 miles per gallon by 1985. Perhaps more important, the market has turned away from gas guzzlers.

The old relationship between price and size has eroded as Detroit has learned to promote the luxury compact with automatic transmissions, luxury-trim packages, air conditioning, and so forth. Meanwhile European and Japanese cars have, as a result of rising wages, become increasingly expensive. To hold share of market, European and Japanese manufacturers are being forced to establish manufacturing facilities in the United States. Volvo and Volkswagen were the first foreign companies to make this move; Honda of Japan was not far behind in making a similar commitment, followed by Nissan and Toyota.

The effect of international competition has been highly beneficial to consumers

---

[1] Available from Harvard Case Services, Boston, Massachusetts, 02163.

around the world. In the two examples cited—detergents in Central America and automobiles in the United States—consumers have benefited. In Central America, detergent prices have fallen as a result of international competition. In the United States, consumers have obtained from foreign companies the automobile products, performance, and price characteristics that they wanted. If the imported cars of the smaller size and price had not been available, it is unlikely that Detroit manufacturers would have provided a comparable product as quickly. What is true for automobiles in the United States is true for every product class around the world. International competition expands the choice available to consumers and increases the likelihood that consumers will get what they want.

The downside of international competition is its impact on the producers of goods and services. International competition creates value for consumers, but it also destroys jobs. When a company on the other side of the world offers the consumer a better product at a lower price, this company deprives a domestic supplier of a customer. Unless the domestic supplier can create new values and find new customers, the employees of the domestic supplier lose their jobs and their livelihood.

A country's trade policy is ultimately a function of its competitive strategy. A country that is successful in shifting resources including labor to higher and better uses is happy to give up even good paying manufacturing jobs. Welding, for example, is increasingly done in developing countries not only because wages are lower, but also because most developing countries do not have U.S. style OSHA,[2] regulations protecting the health and safety of workers.

INDUSTRY ANALYSIS

A useful way of gaining insight into competitors is through industry analysis. As a working definition, an industry can be defined as a group of firms that produce products that are close substitutes for each other. In any industry, competition works to drive down the rate of return on invested capital toward the rate that would be earned in the economist's "perfectly competitive" industry. Rates of return that are greater than this so-called "competitive" rate will stimulate an inflow of capital either from new entrants or from additional investment by existing competitors. Rates of return below this "competitive" rate will result in withdrawal from the industry and a decline in the levels of activity and competition.

Forces Influencing Competition

There are four forces influencing competition in an industry. These are shown in Figure 11–1. At the center is the rivalry and jockeying for position among current competitors. The four forces are the threat of new entrants, the threat of substitute

---

[2]OSHA is an acronym for Occupational Safety and Health Administration.

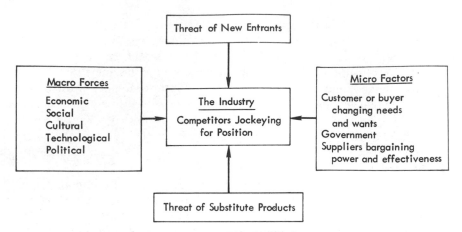

FIGURE 11–1 Forces Influencing Competition in an Industry

Source: Adapted from Michael E. Porter, *Competitive Strategy* (New York: The Free Press, 1980), p. 4.

products or services, and macro and micro forces. Let us look at each of these forces in turn.

THREAT OF NEW ENTRANTS.   New entrants to an industry bring new capacity, a desire to gain market share and position, and very often a new approach to serving customer needs. A decision to enter an industry as a new entrant is often accompanied by a major commitment of resources. As a result of new entry, prices may be pushed downward or costs may be increased, resulting in reduced profitability.

An example of a major entry move was the attempt by Fujitsu to enter the U.S. fiber optics market. Fujitsu turned in an undisputedly low bid to AT&T. The bid was thrown out by AT&T as a result of intensive pressure from the U.S. Congress and government officials who themselves had been lobbied by executives of U.S. companies who were bidding on the same contract.[3]

There are eight major sources of barriers to entry.[4] The first is economies of scale, which refer simply to the decline in unit costs of a product as the absolute volume per period increases. Scale economies occur in each business function, especially manufacturing, research and development, general administration, and marketing. Scale economies are often concentrated in one phase of a function. For example, in television manufacture, scale economies are more pronounced in tube production than in cabinet making or assembly. In marketing, they are more pronounced in advertising and field sales.

Product differentiation is a major entry barrier especially in consumer and service products where image becomes an important factor influencing the purchase decision. Often, this can be based on the simple fact of being the first entrant into

[3]"Japan Runs into America, Inc.," *Fortune,* March 22, 1982, pp. 56–61.
[4]Michael E. Porter, *Competitive Strategy* (New York: Free Press, 1980), pp. 7–33.

a product area. For example, Coke and Pepsi are the leading soft drinks worldwide. The main reason for their leading position is the fact they were first with the most. Being first is a strategy that can ensure a "share of mind" that followers can never attain. Who was the first person to fly solo across the Atlantic? Charles Lindbergh! Correct. Now, who was the second person? Tough to remember, isn't it?

A third entry barrier relates to capital requirements. Capital is required not only for manufacturing facilities but also for financing research and development, advertising, field sales and service, customer credit, and inventories. The enormous capital requirements in such industries as mainframe computers, chemicals, and mineral extraction, to mention only a few, present formidable entry barriers even to the largest corporation. In some cases, the cost of switching from one supplier to another is a formidable barrier. These one-time costs include employee retraining, new ancillary equipment, and the trauma of severing a relationship.

A fourth barrier to entry is the one time switching costs to the buyer of changing suppliers. These might include retraining, ancillary equipment costs, the cost of evaluating a new source, and so on.

A fifth barrier to entry is access to distribution channels. To the extent that channels are full, or unavailable, the cost of entry is substantially increased because a new entrant must create and establish new channels, which is always a costly exercise.

The success of Japanese and other foreign automobile companies in penetrating the U.S. market is in part due to their access to U.S. company dealer networks as

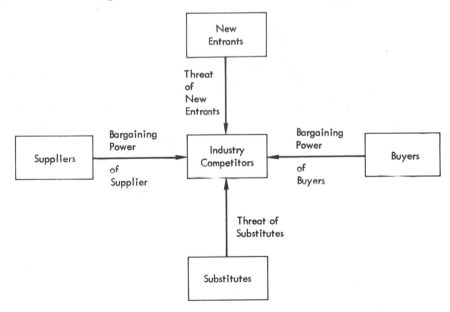

FIGURE 11–2 Elements of Industry Structure

Source: Adapted from Michael E. Porter, *Competitive Advantage* (New York: The Free Press, 1985), p. 6.

a result of antitrust legislation forbidding the establishment of exclusive dealership arrangements in the United States. Conversely, a significant barrier to the penetration of the Japanese automobile market for U.S. and other foreign companies is the fact that Japanese dealerships are exclusive and that this arrangement is permitted and allowed under Japanese law.[5]

There are cost disadvantages independent of scale. Established firms may have cost advantages that are quite independent of those associated with economies of scale. These might include favorable access to raw materials, favorable locations, government subsidies, and "learning" or the so-called "experience curve." It is important to distinguish between experience as a source of cost decline and scale. Experience results from working smarter and "learning" and is a function of accumulated volume. Experience-based cost declines are most significant in the early growth stage of product development. Economies of scale are dependent on volume per period, not on cumulative volume, and are very different from those associated with experience. In practice, it is extremely difficult to separate experience gains from those associated with economies of scale, but conceptually they are different, and it is important to identify this difference in analyzing the competition as well as in establishing the basis for a competitive strategy.

Government policy is frequently a major entry barrier. In some cases, the government will absolutely prohibit competitive entry. This is true in a number of industries, especially those outside the United States, that have been designated as "national" industries by their respective governments. It is notorious, for example, that in France, power generation companies will accept bids from foreign equipment suppliers but they always choose national suppliers. Japan's entire postwar industrialization strategy was based on a policy of reserving and protecting national industries in their development and growth phases.

Expected competitor response can be a major entry barrier. If new entrants expect existing competitors to respond strongly to entry, their expectations about the rewards of entry will certainly be affected. If a potential competitor believes that entry into an industry or market will be unpleasant, this may very well deter entry. One of the reasons Philips avoids the U.S. electric lamp market and GE avoids the European market is that each company does not wish to "invite" a competitive entrant to its "home" turf.

Bruce Henderson, former president of the Boston Consulting Group, used the term "brinksmanship" to describe an approach he recommended to creating a strong deterrent to competitive entry. Basically, brinksmanship involves convincing potential competitors that their moves will be countered with strong, vigorous, and unpleasant competitive responses.

---

[5] Whenever there is a significant disparity between conditions of competition in two national markets, it raises the issue of whether or not conditions should be "aligned." From a policy point of view, the U.S. auto industry has an overwhelmingly strong case for obtaining reciprocity of competitive positions. This could be obtained either by opening up Japanese channels of distribution or alternatively by closing U.S. channels. Of course, as this is written (1980), the horse is out of the barn so to speak. It is too late to close U.S. channels; therefore, the only feasible way of obtaining an alignment of competitive conditions would be to open up Japanese channels.

THREAT OF SUBSTITUTE PRODUCTS.   A second force influencing competition in an industry is the threat of substitute products. The key to evaluating the position of substitute products or of potential substitute products is to examine the substitute in relation to the market's needs and wants. The substitute is frequently an application of a new technology to an old task. The substitute may be unstoppable, for example, airplanes versus ships for long-distance travel. The only sensible response to such a major technological development is to reposition the industry product. Passenger ships went from serving all ocean travelers to serving the cruise market. Their product shifted from travel and recreation to recreation only.

MICRO FACTORS.   The micro factors in an industry are the customers or buyers, suppliers, and the government. The customer or buyer is the ultimate judge of the effectiveness of a competitive strategy. To succeed, the firm must have a competitive advantage—it must offer something that is better or more attractive than its competitor's offering.

Suppliers are an important element in the picture. They are part of the value chain, and their performance and effectiveness are key elements in determining the cost and quality of the product offering to customers. The availability, reliability, cost, and quality of suppliers are key elements in a manufacturing or service firm's competitive strategy. For new ventures, or for new directions in established businesses, proximity of suppliers is critical. As one executive put it, "When you shift from a cheap labor operation to a highly automated factory, you don't want to locate the factory halfway around the world from the brains that designed it." Holotek, Limited, the most advanced manufacturer of hologons (a combination of a holograph, a laser beam, and optics in a housing) believes that one of the company's distinctive competitive advantages is the fact that it is located in Rochester, New York, with ready access to one of the world's greatest collections of talent in optical science and technical know-how.

Government can help or hinder competitors. A government that is sensitive to the competitive environment in the world economy and the position of a global company's subsidiary can assist by supporting companies trying to improve their productivity and international competitiveness. In the view of many experts, this assistance need not be proactive in microeconomic domain. Jim Abegglen, author of *Kaisha,* has pointed out that the contribution of the Japanese government has been to not get in the way of fiercely competitive companies and let them decide themselves how to allocate resources.

Companies are best equipped to decide on company strategy: which target markets to serve, which technologies to employ, what strategies to adopt. Government should support companies by ensuring that monetary, fiscal, tax, and trade policies encourage investment and support high aggregate demand at home, open markets abroad, and exchange rates that maintain equilibrium in world trade. One of the sad facts of the Reagan administration in the United States is that its simple-minded adherence to "supply-side" policies has failed to provide this necessary *macroeconomic* support for American companies.

MACRO FORCES.   Macro forces, the broad economic, social, political, cultural, and technological trends and factors, impact every industry. Most of these forces evolve along predictable lines. For example, economic development follows foreseeable patterns. As the level of income rises, the birth rate declines and consumption patterns follow predictable paths. Consumers go from bare feet to shoes, to bicycles, to motorized two-wheel transportation to four-wheeled transportation. Washing machines replace hand washing and dryers replace the sun.

COMPETITOR ANALYSIS[6]

Have you ever heard of a successful athletic coach who was merely content to know the names and standings of teams in his league? Did you ever hear of a general who was merely content to know the size and location of the opposing army? Of course not. Coaches and commanders want to know as much as possible about how the opposing team or army operates. They want to know strengths and limitations and game plan and orders of battle. They try to anticipate the opponent's strategy and test their own game plans and strategies against what they think they will meet when they face their opponent. They use intelligence and scouting reports as a major input in developing their own plan.

Many business managers, however, fail to give more than a passing thought to competitive factors that will have a profound effect on the success or failure of their own plans. This section outlines the major ingredients of competitor evaluation by suggesting key questions to be answered and identifying some sources of information on competitors. To conduct an effective, strategically oriented competitor evaluation, you will need to determine the following about each major competitor.

1. How the competitor measures himself
2. His apparent strategy to date
3. His major strengths and weaknesses and any anticipated changes in strengths and weaknesses
4. His most likely future strategy

As you conduct your competitor analysis, always try to put yourself in the position of the competitor and, insofar as is possible, try to see the world as he sees the world. Although this is extremely difficult, it is absolutely vital to the success of competitor analysis. If your competitor is Japanese, you must learn something about the Japanese culture and general orientation to life to conduct a successful competitor analysis. If you fail to do this, you will unconsciously project your own values onto your competitor and inevitably fail to see the world as your Japanese competitor sees the world.

[6]This section draws heavily on Chapter 5, "Competitors: Getting to Know All (?) About Them," in William E. Rothschild, *Putting It All Together, A Guide to Strategic Thinking* (New York: AMACOM, 1976).

Phase 1: Mapping the Past

It is amazing how much one can learn about a competitor by simply reading the competitor's own statements as published in annual reports, quarterly reports, house organs, statements to security analysts, and interviews with the trade press. Business people, like all people, seem to need not only to explain what they have done but also to announce their intentions. By studying these public statements you can uncover priorities and value systems. If a competitor proceeds to do what it says it is going to do, at least you know what you are facing. If there are major deviations between actions and words, you have identified potential chinks in the competitor's armor that can be the basis for effective strategies vis-à-vis the competitor.

Phase 2: Identifying the Competitor's Strategy to Date

The next stage of competitor analysis is the identification of the competitor's game plan. Don't take the competitor's word for it, but actually reconstruct the strategy that is implicit in the competitor's actions to date. This is an important stage of competitor analysis because every company has a past and any future will inevitably reflect the major elements of the past. It is important to reconstruct actually the strategy because it is not uncommon to find companies talking about one thing and doing another. For example, in the 1960s, American Motors was talking about technological leadership as a key element in its strategy when in fact it was always a me-too competitor. Its so-called "leading technology" was in fact nothing more than product features like the ceramic-coated muffler. If anything, AMC was lagging in automobile technology, especially when it was compared with European companies.

Phase 3: Evaluating the Competitor's Resources

Research evaluation requires much more than simply listing the human, financial, and physical assets that a competitor possesses. The real question is how will these assets be used. The analysis of resources should focus on five key areas.

CONCEPTION AND DESIGN.   What is the competitor's ability to conceive, design, develop, engineer, and deliver products and services?

PRODUCTION.   How efficient and how flexible is the competitor in manufacturing its products and services? Here are some key questions: Does the company make the product itself and what are its costs and expansion possibilities in its present production locations? To what degree is the firm vertically integrated? Does the firm subcontract, establish joint ventures, or work with associates and partners?

There are many sources of data on cost at different locations, and these should all be used. In addition, suppliers who serve both you and your competitor can be a source of information. Finally, you should buy your competitor's products and completely analyze them to know as much as possible about your competitor's costs and capabilities.

MARKETING.   The key marketing factors in competitive analysis are the competitor's image and reputation, distribution channels, sales force, communication strategy, target markets, and the ability to perceive and identify customer values, to segment and target the marketing program, and to deliver competitive advantages in the marketplace.

MANAGEMENT.   The strengths, quality, and character of a company's management is a key aspect of the overall competitive strengths of the organization. Some companies have "bench strength" so that even if key players leave the team, there is ample replacement talent in the organization. Other companies are thinly staffed, and the departure of a key person or a handful of key executives will result in a substantial decline in the quality of management direction.

The more you know about the values of managers, the greater your potential insight is into how an organization will behave. What is the organization's vision? Or does the organization have a vision? The presence of a vision ("We intend to become the leading company in our industry . . . serving the health care industry worldwide") is a guide to action. The absence of a vision is also significant.

How are managers rewarded in the organization? If there is a payoff for short-run "bottom-line" results, managers will seek to attain these results. One of the reasons that many U.S. companies have been less than formidable competitors in recent years is that fact that managers have been handsomely rewarded for achieving short-run, bottom-line results. This fact of life is an extremely important item of competitive intelligence.

The final stage of competitor evaluation is to arrive at an assessment of competitor intentions. This might seem like the most difficult phase of competitive analysis, but because of the already mentioned need for people to talk about accomplishments and intentions, it often turns out to be remarkably easy to determine competitor intentions regarding major moves.

COMPETITOR SELECTION[7]

Competitors are most frequently viewed by firms as a threat. According to conventional thought, competitors are the enemy and must be eliminated. More market share is always better than less. In fact, the right competitors can *strengthen* rather than weaken a firm's competitive position. It is important to distinguish between good and bad competitors, identify the right competitors to attack and avoid battling competitors that are benefiting a company's position and industry structure.

The advantages or benefits of good competitors are numerous. A good competitor can

[7]This section is adapted from Michael E. Porter, *Competitive Advantage* (New York: The Free Press, 1985), pp. 201–228.

1. Increase competitive advantage by absorbing demand fluctuations
2. Enhance the ability of the firm to differentiate its product by serving as a standard of comparison
3. Serve unattractive segments
4. Provide a cost umbrella (For example, in the 1950s and 1960s American Motors served this function for General Motors, Ford, and Chrysler. The "big three" had a perfect excuse for not bringing down their prices. By keeping their prices above AMC's break-even cost they were insuring the survival of a competitor, which under U.S. anti-trust law was a noble act. The real beneficiaries of this pricing policy were the "big three" and not the consumer. Ironically, today the "big three" serve the same function for Japanese manufacturers: They create a price umbrella that allows Japanese companies to sell their cars in the United States for substantially more than they get for the same product in Japan.)
5. Improve the bargaining position with labor or regulators
6. Increase motivation

Good competitors can also benefit the overall industry structure by increasing industry demand; providing a second source (thereby reducing anxiety levels among customers about risks associated with a sole-source supplier), and reinforcing desirable elements of industry structure. For example, a competitor who stresses product quality and service can help reduce buyer sensitivity and mitigate price rivalry in an industry. Good competitors can also aid in developing a market for a new product by sharing costs of market development, reducing risk to buyers, and helping to standardize or legitimatize a new technology. Philips of The Netherlands, for example, is aggressively licensing its new home entertainment products, including laser discs and digital sound, to insure that the Philips' technology is adopted as an industry standard.

Competitors also play an important role in deterring other entrants by increasing the likelihood and intensity of retaliation, and by demonstrating the difficulty of successful entry into an industry. For example, the limited increase in market share and poor profitability of Procter & Gamble's Folgers coffee in the United States is a lesson in the costs of gaining share in the coffee industry. The enormous expenditures and limited market share that P&G obtained in the U.S. shampoo market with the introduction of Ivory shampoo ($70 million for approximately 4 percent of a $1.5 billion market or approximately $60 million in annual sales) testify to the difficulty of entering that business. Other entry deterrents are the blocking of logical entry avenues and the crowding of distribution channels.

Competitors are not equally attractive. A good competitor is one who performs the beneficial functions described above without representing a severe, long-term threat. The following characteristics describe a good competitor.

1. A good competitor is credible and viable. It must have enough resources to make retaliation a real threat to new entrants and it must be an acceptable alternative to buyers if they are going to forego looking for new sources.
2. A good competitor has clear weaknesses that are self-perceived and recognized. The ideal good competitor believes that its weaknesses will be difficult to change and lead

it to conclude that it is futile to attempt to gain relative position against a firm in the segments the firm is interested in.

3. A good competitor understands and plays by the rules of the competition and can recognize and read market symbols.
4. A good competitor is realistic about the industry and its relative position. It does not overestimate industry growth potential and therefore overbuild capacity and does not overrate its capabilities to the point of triggering a battle for market share.
5. A good competitor knows its costs and does not unwittingly cross-subsidize product lines or understate its overhead.

A good competitor also

1. Has a moderate strategic stake in the industry
2. Has a comparable return on investment target
3. Accepts its current profitability
4. Desires cash generation
5. Has a short time horizon
6. Is risk averse

It is interesting in looking at these characteristics of a *good* competitor that on many of the key items, U.S. and European companies are ideal competitors. The Japanese on the other hand are *terrible* competitors! They have long time horizons, they have major strategic stakes in expanding their position in an industry, they do not play by the rules, and they do not have clear self-perceived weaknesses. Indeed, they believe that they can achieve domination. One of the major problems facing advanced country competitors in global economy is that so few of the criteria that define a *good* competitor are met by aggressive firms in fast growing countries who are seeking to establish a strategic global position. Many American and European firms have unconsciously recognized that they are facing ''bad'' competitors and have decided to exit industries rather than face the challenge of competing with ''bad'' competitors.

Competitors are both a blessing and a curse. In the best of all worlds, a firm will compete only with ''good'' competitors, but in the real world a good competitor is hard to find. It is therefore necessary for a firm who wishes to succeed as a global competitor to prepare to compete with ''bad'' competitors.

COMPETITIVE STRATEGY

Competitive strategy must be adjusted to the industry environment, and the industry environment is itself a reflection of the characteristics of the different stages of the product life cycle. A strategy that makes sense in one type of industry environment, or at one stage of the product life cycle, may have no application at all in another industry environment or at a different stage of the product life cycle. The discussion that follows examines alternative competitive strategies.

The Value Chain and Three Strategic Roles of Global Marketing

The value chain (see Chapters 9 and 10) exposes three roles for marketing in a global competitive strategy. The first relates to the configuration of marketing. While many marketing activities must be performed in every country, advantage can be gained by concentrating some of the marketing activities in a single location. Service, for example, must be dispersed to every country. Training, however, might be at least partially concentrated in a single location for the world.

A second role for marketing is the coordination of marketing activities across countries to leverage a company's know-how. This integration can take many forms including the transfer of relevant experience across national boundaries (for example, global account management), and the use of similar approaches or methods (for example, marketing research and product positioning).

A third critical role of marketing is its role in tapping opportunities for upstream advantage in the value chain. The development of Canon's AE–1 camera is a case in point. Research provided the information on market requirements that enabled Canon to develop a "world" product. Upstream elements of the value chain benefited by this information and enabled Canon to develop a physically uniform product that required fewer parts, far less engineering, lower inventories, and longer production runs than they would have obtained if they had developed products that were adapted to the unique conditions in each national market.[8]

Competitive Strategy: Generic Approaches

There are three generic strategic approaches to outperforming other firms in an industry. They are (1) overall cost leadership, (2) differentiation, and (3) focus.[9] These strategies are illustrated in Figure 11–3.

OVERALL COST LEADERSHIP. This strategy has become increasingly popular in recent years as a result of the popularization of the experience curve concept. Basically, a firm seeking to base its competitive strategy on overall cost leadership must aggressively pursue a position of cost leadership by constructing the most efficient scale facilities and obtaining the largest share of market so that its cost per unit is the lowest in the industry. Cost leadership does not mean expenditure minimization. For example, the cost leader in an industry will probably be the largest advertiser, but because of its greater volume, its advertising cost per unit will be the lowest. Similarly, this ratio will apply to all aspects of the competitor's program, including selling costs, administrative costs, research and development, distribution, and servicing.

[8]See Michael Porter, *Competition in Global Industries* (Boston: Harvard Business School Press, 1986), Chapter 4, pp. 111–146.
[9]Michael Porter, *Competitive Advantage*, Ibid., p. 12.

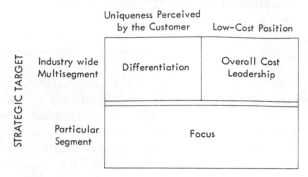

FIGURE 11–3 Generic Competitive Strategies
Source: Adapted from Michael E. Porter, *Competitive Strategy* (New York: Free Press, 1980), p. 39.

Cost leadership has been the cornerstone of highly successful strategies. In the United States, Briggs and Stratton in small-horsepower gasoline engines and Black and Decker in power tools stand out. In Japan, companies and suppliers in the 35mm camera, consumer electronics and entertainment equipment, motorcycle, and automobile industries have achieved leadership on a world basis.

Cost per Unit.   A critical aspect of industry competitiveness is production cost. The Boston Consulting Group and other researchers have demonstrated that for a wide variety of manufactured products, total cost per unit in constant dollars will decline characteristically by 20–30 percent each time accumulated production experience (the total amount ever produced) doubles. Although the precise reasons for this relationship are not entirely known, it appears to be a combination of learning by doing, management experience, working smarter, and scale economies in manufacturing as well as marketing and general management.

Given this relationship between cost and volume, a firm's cost position within an industry depends on its growth relative to the entire industry, that is, on its market share. Conversely, an industry's ability to lower prices for a given amount of production depends on the market shares of the individual producers or, put another way, on the industry's concentration. In the past a company's competitive strength was measured in a national framework. Today a company's competitive strength in an increasing number of industries must be measured on world scale.

The Case of Color Television.   Japanese television producers offer a pointed illustration of an industry that took advantage of greater accumulated experience to obtain a large cost-price advantage over U.S. competitors. Between 1962 and 1970, the Japanese producers accumulated experience at 170 percent per year whereas that of the U.S. producers was only 56 percent. This differential growth rate was inevitable because it was based on domestic market growth. Exports did not begin until Japanese domestic prices were below U.S. prices, and penetration of the U.S. market did not occur until the price differential was substantial and also until third-country export experience had been acquired in black-and-white sets.

The mistake of the U.S. manufacturers that had once had a leading position was in believing themselves to be solidly established in the U.S. market. This was an expensive illusion because, as they eventually learned, they were competing not in a national market but in a world market. The lower-cost position of the more concentrated higher-volume Japanese producers has been a continuing undermining threat to U.S. manufacturers. By the end of 1977 Japanese imports accounted for over 2 million of the roughly 9 million sets sold in the United States. Also in that same year, over 1 million Japanese sets were manufactured in production facilities in the United States. By ignoring the accumulation of experience in the Japanese domestic market, U.S. manufacturers permitted Japanese competitors to obtain the volume-cost position that has allowed them to make massive inroads into the U.S. market.

DIFFERENTIATION.   Differentiation, the second generic strategy, involves the creation of a product or service that is *perceived* as being unique. When achieved, this is an extremely effective strategy for defending market position and obtaining above-average returns. Examples of successful differentiation are Maytag in large home appliances, Caterpillar in construction equipment, Mercedes in luxury automobiles, and almost any successful branded consumer product. The strongest differentiation is on several dimensions. *position diff. prod. for diff. seg.*

FOCUS.   A third generic competitive strategy is focus, which is based on serving a particular market segment more effectively and efficiently than any other competitor. Again, as with overall cost leadership and differentiation, successful focusing will yield above-average returns.

The French have an expression, *Cherchez le creneau,* which means literally, "find the hole or niche." A *creneau* is a segment or a cluster of customers whose particular needs can be met better than anybody else by a company that is focused on this market segment. The key to the market niche strategy is to identify the segment basis for defining the niche.

Competition and the Product Life Cycle

The requirement for effective competitive strategy varies at different stages of the product life cycle (PLC). The indicated competitive strategies at different stages of the PLC are shown in Table 11–1. The global enterprise must address each of the stages of the PLC and decide whether to pursue them on a single- or multicountry basis. Consider innovative entry, for example, the indicated strategy for the infancy stage of the PLC. Should a company concentrate on a single- or multicountry entry strategy? To answer, it all depends on the company's resources. In general, a company should seek as many markets as possible as quickly as possible, consistent with its financial and human resources. It may be necessary to introduce a product in a subnational market to concentrate available resources, or for the very large, resource-rich company, it may be possible to introduce a new product in global

TABLE 11–1   Competitive Strategy and the Product Life Cycle

	STAGE 1	STAGE 2	STAGE 3	STAGE 4
Stage of PLC	Infancy	Growth	Approaching maturity	Maturity
Required Strategy	Innovative entry	Establishing new positions and defending old ones	Jostling for relative advantage	Slugging it out
Marketing Focus	Concept	Features	Features/price	Price

markets simultaneously. With sufficient resources, a company can target the global market for its product. The advantage of spreading the net as widely as possible is that it preempts the competition from establishing its own home base from which to venture out into the world. The disadvantage is that the task may exceed the resources of the enterprise, and the effectiveness of the global attack may be short of the requirements for market success.

For most companies, entry should take place in a single country. A maxim in global marketing holds that all success in global markets is based on a solid base in a single country or region. The solid base provides experience and resources to feed and support international growth.

The next stage of the PLC, growth, requires the establishment of new market positions and the defense of old ones. This is a delicate period in the competitive struggle. It is when the international contenders for global market leadership begin to meet each other in contested markets. This is the present stage of the development of the personal computer market. Both the United States and Japan have successful personal computer companies at home, and these companies are now attempting to defend their home market positions as well as establish new market positions. This is a time of testing in any industry, and many companies are eliminated.

When market offerings approach maturity, competitive strategies involve jostling for relative advantage. At this stage, the most common strategies in the struggle for share of market are product improvement, product line proliferation, sharper positioning of products with greater focus of the marketing effort on selected target segments, and cost reduction, which becomes the basis for offering a price advantage vis-à-vis competitors.

The next stage of the product life cycle, maturity, is one that is characterized by slugging it out. This may take the form of outright price competition, or it may continue to involve changing product features or slugging it out with advertising and promotion, or it may involve both as in the case of color television, where Matsushita, Toshiba, Hitachi, Sony, Zenith, RCA, Philips, and a host of other smaller competitors fight for market share. The survivors in this struggle will be the companies that manage to do a better job of strategic management. Clearly, the survivors will be positioned in the global market.

Strategies for Success

One of the most serious errors in mature, stagnant, or declining industry businesses is to attach pejorative labels to them. This may have a debilitating influence on the morale of management and an almost visible effect on the creative energy applied to the management of the business. The product portfolio model, which was quite popular in the 1970s and early 1980s, introduced the use of such terms as "cash cow" and "dog." As we have already pointed out, success in mature markets requires creative marketing and investments to improve quality, increase operating efficiency, and generate new products. These are aggressive and creative acts and are less likely to occur if the management and worker team in a company or division keep hearing themselves described as "dogs" or "cash cows" who are in place to be "milked."

Three strategies have proven highly successful in competing in stagnant industries.[10] Let us examine each in turn.

GROWTH SEGMENTS.   One of the ways of avoiding the limitation presented by a stagnant industry is to identify growth segments within the overall market addressed by the industry. For example, in the United States both the number of motion picture theaters and movie admissions as a percentage of recreational spending have been declining for the past 30 years. During this period of decline, one segment in the motion picture theater market—the shopping center theater—has been growing at an impressive rate. One company in this segment, General Cinema, has been able to maintain average earnings increases of over 20 percent and a return on equity of 20 percent during a period of general industry decline.

INNOVATION AND QUALITY.   Another characteristic of successful companies in stagnant industries is that they innovate and offer high-quality products. This is reflected in the results of the PIMS study (profit impact of marketing strategies), which suggests that the relationship between higher product quality and higher return on investments is most pronounced in stagnant markets and that high rates of R&D spending correlate with higher return on investment for businesses in stagnant markets. Companies that innovate and deliver quality avoid the profit destructive trap of competing on the basis of commodity or undifferentiated items. In short, innovation and quality are a key to successful competition in mature or stagnant markets.

Achieving the highest product/service/quality position relative to competition coupled with acceptable delivered cost is a winning strategy.

OPERATING EFFICIENCIES.   A third characteristic of successful competitors in mature industries is a concentration on cost reduction. It has been shown, for ex-

---

[10]This is adapted from Richard G. Hamermesh and Stephen B. Silk, "How to Compete in Stagnant Industries," *Harvard Business Review,* September–October 1979, pp. 161–168.

ample, that more than half the reduction in rayon costs at Dupont resulted from gradual improvements rather than from major investments and programs.[11] A company with the lowest delivered cost in an industry and acceptable quality has a winning combination.

In his study of survival strategies in a hostile environment, William K. Hall found that not only were companies surviving in hostile environments (i.e., mature markets) but that many companies were pursuing strategies that were resulting in outstanding success.[12]

Hall found that the leadership positions in mature markets were not being milked by any of the 16 competitors in his study, contrary to what some imply as the advice of the portfolio approach to asset management. Indeed, two of the managers in Hall's study laughed when they discussed the portfolio approach to asset management.

Of course, the best possible position is to combine these two approaches. Caterpillar is a company that has achieved spectacular success by combining lowest-cost manufacturing and an outstanding product with high-cost but truly outstanding distribution and aftermarket service and support.

Competitive Strategy in Fragmented Industries

The 1972 Census of Manufacturers in the United States lists over 100 four-digit (Standard Industrial Classification System or SIC code) industries in which the top four firms have less than the 40 percent share of the total market. The firms range from high to low technology, to radio and T.V. communication equipment, to burial caskets. The beginning of formulating a competitive strategy in a fragmented industry is to consider why an industry is fragmented in the first place. This occurs for a variety of reasons. The principal economic reasons are (1) low overall entry barriers, (2) not lending itself to economies of scale, (3) high transportation costs, (4) high inventory costs or erratic sales fluctuations, (5) no particular advantages of size in dealing with buyers and suppliers, (6) diseconomies of scale in some important aspects of the business, (7) heavy or important creative content in the final product, (8) fragmented or diverse marketing, (9) local regulation, and (10) government prohibitions.[13]

OVERCOMING FRAGMENTATION.   A significant opportunity is presented in any fragmented industry in overcoming fragmentation. The common approaches are the creation of economies of scale. This has been done in the beef cattle industry, with the development of feed lot operations and in the fast-food industry with the de-

---

[11] William J. Abernathy and James M. Utterback, "Patterns of Industrial Innovation," *Technology Review*, June–July 1978, p. 3 (quoted in Hamermesh and Silk, op. cit., p. 165.)

[12] William K. Hall, "Survival Strategies in a Hostile Environment," *Harvard Business Review*, September–October 1980, pp. 75–85.

[13] Porter, *Competitive Strategy*, pp. 196–214.

velopment of national brand names and standardized menus and production processes.

LIVING WITH FRAGMENTATION. In many industries, the fragmentation is inherent in the underlying characteristics of the industry and simply cannot be overcome. In such cases, competing in the industry and competitive strategy require strategic positioning. A few of the positioning possibilities are

1. *Tightly managed decentralization.* Using this approach, strategy makes no attempt to increase the scale of operations but rather focuses on keeping individual operations small and autonomous, stressing performance-oriented compensation for local managers.
2. *Specialization by product type or product segment.* This is a way of achieving above-average results. Ethan Allen has specialized in early American furniture and in the process has created a unique selling proposition, namely, what you can do with the product, not the product itself. This concentration has enabled Ethan Allen to charge up to a 20 percent premium for its products and to achieve above-average returns even though its share of total industry furniture sales is only about 3 percent.

Other specialization possibilities are customer type, order type, geographic area, and no frills, lowest price, to name just a few. The possibilities are endless, but the steps for formulating competitive strategies in fragmented industries are straightforward. They are shown in Table 11–2.

POSITIONING

Positioning is the act of locating a product in a market, in the channels of distribution, in relationship to other products, and ultimately in the mind of prospects or target customers. Positioning is essential in consumer marketing because density of appeals directed to consumers is so great that consumers protect their sanity by screening out most messages and appeals. In the United States, consumers are exposed to $200 worth of advertising per capita per year. To score in this jungle of communications, it is absolutely essential to concentrate on narrow targets. As a way of underlining the barrage of communications, try this little test. Aside from the governor of your state, do you know the name of the governor of any of the other 49

TABLE 11–2 Steps for Formulating Competitive Strategies in Fragmented Industries

Step 1	What is the structure of the industry and the position of the competitors?
Step 2	Why is the industry fragmented?
Step 3	Can this fragmentation be overcome? How?
Step 4	Would overcoming this fragmentation be profitable? How might we position ourselves to do this?
Step 5	If fragmentation is inevitable, what is the best alternative for coping with it?

Source: Michael E. Porter, *Competitive Strategy* (New York: Free Press, 1980), p. 213.

states? The average supermarket contains over 10,000 individual products or brands on display. How many of these do you even know about? The same thing is true in industrial products. There are 292 manufacturers of centrifugal pumps in the United States alone and 326 manufacturers of electronic controls, to mention just two categories.[14]

In any overcommunicated society, it is essential to get into the prospect's mind. One way of doing this is to be first. If you can't be number one, an alternative strategy is to be against number one. Avis exemplifies success based on relating to the leader. The company was not successful because it tried harder; it was successful because it related itself to Hertz. Establishing an "against" position is a classic positioning maneuver.

The basic rule of positioning is consistency; you must keep it year after year. Bermuda has positioned itself in the island vacation market as the place to go for unhurried, civilized fun. The copy and appeals have *not* changed for almost a decade. The competition, on the other hand, changes every year. The result has been an increasing share of market for Bermuda. The greatest enemy of consistency is what has been called the "FWMTS" trap ("forget what made them successful").

The importance of positioning can be illustrated by the adroit repositioning of Philip Morris' Marlboro brand.

> Before Marlboro cigarettes could become a global superstar, Philip Morris had to make an image change for the product from a feminine to a masculine cigarette, creating associations with a rugged cowboy in the old west ("Marlboro country"). They have been extraordinarily successful because they identified their product with an archetypal symbol of freedom and targeted their advertising on the urban consumer. Marlboro is a way of getting in touch with a powerful urge to be free and independent. Join that rugged, independent cowboy in the old west! The advertising succeeds because it is very well done and it fills a great, deep, and powerful need.[15]

The three basic positioning strategy alternatives are described in the following section.

Market Leadership

The market leader is usually the brand or company that established a leading position at the beginning of the product life cycle and has successfully defended its position of leadership. A typical industry position is a leader with twice the share of market as the number two brand and twice again as much as the number three company. A typical leader might have 40 percent of the market, with the number two company holding 20, number three 10, and all others 30 percent (Figure 11–4). Once a fragmented industry has been integrated, market leaders will appear. Indeed, market leadership is based on successfully integrating the threads of what was a fragmented

---

[14]Al Ries and Jack Trout, *Positioning: The Battle for Your Mind* (New York: McGraw-Hill, 1981).

[15]Jagdish N. Sheth, *Winning Back Your Market* (New York: John Wiley and Sons, 1985), p. 158.

All other companies 30% share of market	Company 3 10% share of market	Company 2 20% share of market	Company 1 40% share of market

FIGURE 11–4 Typical Industry Competitive Positions

industry. Examples are well-known multinationals such as IBM, Procter & Gamble, Caterpillar, Sony, and Boeing. The industry leader is always in a paradoxical position. In the short run, an industry leader really has very little to worry about. There is tremendous momentum in the dominant position. In the longer run, however, the industry leader must maintain constant vigilance or risk being displaced by an aggressive challenger. A visitor to the Caterpillar Tractor Company in Peoria, Illinois, several years ago would have found a sign reading, "Stay Number One in 1981." Even though Caterpillar has something over 50 percent of the world market for earth moving equipment, Komatsu is number one in its Japanese homeland and, with 15 percent of the world market, is pressing Caterpillar hard. Indeed, years ago Komatsu adopted the internal slogan *Maru-c* ("encircle Caterpillar"). Komatsu executives read the Peoria *Journal Star,* which is airmailed to Tokyo, to keep up with news of their rival. Each company flies aircraft over the other's testing ground. The success of Komatsu underscores what an aggressive and talented challenger can do to even a fine company such as Caterpillar. The first round of the competitive battle was in the Japanese market when Caterpillar entered into a 50:50 joint venture with two major Japanese companies in an effort to crush Komatsu, then the leading Japanese maker of earth moving equipment, but a much smaller company than it is today. They underestimated the *Maru-c* spirit at Komatsu, and as a result of its dedication, Komatsu has held its position in the market and today has 60 percent versus 30 percent for Caterpillar-Mitsubishi. Komatsu is continually improving its line and typically prices at least 10–15 percent below Caterpillar.

Caterpillar's response to this challenge included showing a film to employees that opened with footage of satisfied users of earth moving equipment, appearing in silhouette aboard their machines and voicing highly favorable comments such as, "I've worked 300 hours without a minute of trouble," and "This is the most productive tractor I've ever owned," and then on the screen, the lights come up and the viewers gasp as they see the users sitting on competitors' machines—Komatsu and others. An observer commented that when Cat employees saw this film, it was "as if they had been shot between the eyes." Excellent! One of the greatest dangers to the leader is complacency. Recognizing the strength of challengers is the first step in defeating this demon that can undermine the position of leadership.

QUICK RESPONSE. When a competitor makes a move, the complacent leader always takes the position, "Let's wait and see." This is the attitude that converts leaders into followers. Time is of the essence in blocking the encroachments of challengers.

STRATEGIES FOR MAINTAINING LEADERSHIP. A firm maintains leadership by following the von Clausewitz maxim:

> The best strategy is to be everywhere very strong—first generally, then at the decisive point.

In marketing terms, this means that a leader must be strong in its product position, its promotion, and its distribution. Companies vary on the particular elements of the marketing mix, which is the area not just of strength, but of exceptional strength or, in von Clausewitz's language, "the decisive point." Some companies have maintained leadership on the basis of their strong and consistently innovative product leadership. Polaroid in instant photography has relied on this strategy to maintain its number one position in that market. Other companies rely on price leadership (which is based on cost leadership) as the basis for their leadership position. A good example of such a strategy in integrated circuits is Texas Instruments, which has always priced aggressively for volume and managed volume to achieve the lowest cost position vis-à-vis global competitors. Revlon, the number one firm in cosmetics in the United States for many years under the leadership of Charles Revson, excelled in communicating the benefits of the company's products to its target markets.

Finally, some companies rely on place or distribution as the point of decisive advantage in the leadership position. Avon, in lower-priced cosmetics, has a unique worldwide direct sales organization that has enabled the company to hold its number one position in the market. Caterpillar, in earth moving equipment, is renowned for the strength of its dealer organization, which is perhaps the decisive edge in the Caterpillar strategy.

IBM is perhaps an archetypal example of a strong leadership company. A look at IBM's total strategy illustrates the fact that to be a leader, it is necessary to be strong in all areas, not just in one or two. IBM's leadership rests on the following policies:

1. *Customer knowledge.* No one knows the data processing customer better than IBM. The organization is customer-driven from the top to the bottom. One of the company's policies is that every member of management must spend at least 30 days a year with customers. It is well known that IBM's top management leadership from the very beginning has been forged in the anvil of the sales organization. Many observers have commented that IBM is not so much a technological leader or giant but rather a company that understands customer needs.

2. *Product innovation.* Although IBM does not have a reputation of being the number one product innovator, it is nevertheless a very strong company in terms of its product line. IBM may not be the first, but it is constantly innovating and developing new products to meet customer needs. The recent loss of market share to a competitor like Digital Equipment Corporation is a result of IBM's failure to maintain leadership in this area.

3. *Quality.* IBM products work. The company is committed to quality assurance and to delivery of quality, which means that the company backs up all its products with aftersales service.

4. *Competitive pricing.* When IBM was an absolute leader, it charged a premium price for its products, which reflected the fact that people were willing to pay more for the assurance of dealing with an obvious winner. As competitors have challenged IBM in different market segments, the company has responded by dramatic price reductions and has demonstrated that it recognizes that it does not occupy such a position of strength that it can ignore price challenges. IBM, in other words, is an intelligent pricer. It does not leave money on the table, but on the other hand, it does not sit back and allow competitors to take business off its table with a mere price advantage.

5. *Research and development.* IBM has an integrated worldwide R&D organization that is constantly working not only on basic research into technologies and fields of inquiry that relate to IBM's research effort but also on the development of new products. This program is a truly multinational effort, which adds great credence to IBM's claim of being a truly multinational company.

6. *Total communications program.* IBM is a heavy advertiser and at the same time has a commitment to developing the strongest possible field sales force. The combination of mass communications and highly trained direct selling is a reflection of the company's commitment to a communications strategy.

7. *Aftersales service.* IBM has long been renowned for the quality of its service organization. One of the impressive things about IBM is that the company has not been afraid to charge for service, because it is recognized from the outset that service is part of the product and that service is of value to the customer. IBM delivers service. The customer pays for highly qualified, well-trained, highly motivated, effective, service representatives.

8. *Global orientation.* From the very beginning, IBM sought to establish itself as a world-class company. One of the earliest mottos of IBM was "World Peace through World Trade," the banner for extending the company's marketing, research, and manufacturing activities around the world. IBM has never fallen into the trap of assuming that one or a handful of national markets were sufficient territory to establish a position of real leadership.

Procter & Gamble is another company that illustrates the principles of leadership. P&G's leadership is based on the following policies:

1. *Customer knowledge.* Again, as does IBM, P&G knows its customers, both the end users and the channels for distribution. To maintain its contact with customer needs and wants, the company recently introduced an 800 number, free-telephone-call program that enables end users to call P&G directly with any comments or feedback on company products.

2. *Product leadership.* P&G seeks to never enter a new market unless it has a real product benefit advantage. The company makes great efforts to maintain product benefit advantages in all the products in its line.

3. *Communications.* P&G spends over $500 million a year in advertising its branded products and follows up on this advertising with very aggressive selling to the channels for distribution and strong in-store point-of-sale promotion support for the products.

4. *Long-term outlook.* When P&G enters a market, it is never a hit-and-run affair. The company plans thoroughly, and when it makes a commitment to a market, it sticks with that commitment for the long haul. P&G never shirks from the investment required to establish a new product in a field or from the investment required to maintain a product position.

The Market Challenger

In some markets, there is a strong challenger who is seeking to displace the market leader. The challenger announces publicly its avowed intention of overtaking number one. There are a number of strategies available to the challenger seeking to displace the market leader. Let us examine each of these in turn.

1. *Price advantage.* The classic wedge for entering and eroding the leadership position in a market is to offer a product that is just as good or even better at a lower price. The Japanese have used price as an entry weapon in numerous markets. After they have established their position in the new market, they are able to bring their prices up to reflect fully the value of their product vis-à-vis the value of competitive offerings. One of the biggest mistakes that any leader can make is to assume that the price cue of a challenger is really speaking about the overall value of the challenger's offerings. The challenger must offer something to the customer to encourage him or her to switch, and price can be a factor that encourages a switch.
2. *Product innovation.* A leader can also be displaced by a challenger's being more innovative in developing new products or in the design of existing products.
3. *Promotion.* A leader may also be attacked by using creative and effective advertising and selling.

Market Follower

A market follower is a runner-up in an industry that consciously or unconsciously seeks to emulate the strategy of the market leader. This strategy works under one condition, and that is when either consciously or unconsciously the leader seeks to maintain an equilibrium in the industry. This can be accomplished by maintaining a price umbrella over the industry and not seeking to maximize market share. There are many reasons why a market leader would hold an umbrella over market followers, not the least of which is that either the government or, in the case of an industrial product company, the suppliers may insist on multiple suppliers or a number of competitors. Market followers exist either on the grace of the market leader who in turn may be responding to supplier requirements or government requirements or possibly even mere sentimentality. In any event, the market follower's strategy is potentially dangerous because if the leader decides to eliminate a follower, it is within its power to do so. This, of course, is assuming that the leader is a well-managed company and has been able to take advantage of its leadership position.

SUMMARY

In this chapter we focused on analyzing the competition and developing strategies for effectively competing in a variety of market and industry situations. The challenges of competing at the early stages of the product life cycle are dramatically different from those at the end of the life cycle. The secret to successful competitive strategy is to recognize the nature of the game and to formulate strategies that are appropriate to the situation. Today, more than ever before, competition is on a global scale. Competitive analysis, in order to be meaningful, must also be carried out on a global scale.

DISCUSSION QUESTIONS

1. What are the major forces influencing competition in an industry? How are these forces operating in the personal computer industry today?
2. What is the difference, if any, in the competitive approach of companies based in Japan, the United States, Sweden, and Korea? What are the similarities?
3. If you were the chief executive officer of Caterpillar, what if anything would you do about the competitive challenge of Komatsu?
4. If you were the chief executive officer of Komatsu, how would you approach competition with Caterpillar?
5. Identify four industries that are characterized by international competition and four that are not. Which, if any, of the four that are not might produce a global competitor within the next 10 years?

BIBLIOGRAPHY

Books

ABEGGLEN, JAMES C., AND GEORGE STALK, JR. *Kaisha: The Japanese Corporation.* New York: Basic Books, Inc., 1985.

CLIFFORD, DONALD K. JR., AND RICHARD E. CAVANAGH. *The Winning Performance.* New York: Bantam Books, 1985.

HALBERSTAM, DAVID. *The Reckoning.* New York: William Morrow and Company, Inc., 1986.

OHMAE, KENICHI. *Triad Power.* New York: The Free Press, 1985.

PORTER, MICHAEL E. *Competition in Global Industries.* Boston: Harvard Business School Press, 1986.

———. *Competitive Advantage.* New York: The Free Press, 1985.

———. *Competitive Strategy.* New York: The Free Press, 1980.

Articles

AHARONI, YAIR. "The State-Owned Enterprise as a Competitor in International Markets." *Columbia Journal of World Business,* Spring 1980, pp. 14–22.

AYAI, IGAL, AND JEHIEL ZIF. "Competitive Market Choice Strategies in Multinational Marketing." *Columbia Journal of World Business,* Fall 1978, pp. 72 ff.

DOUGLAS, SUSAN B., AND C. SAMUEL CRAIG. "Examining Performance of U.S. Multinationals in Foreign Markets." *Journal of International Business Studies,* Winter 1983, pp. 51–61.

JATUSRIPITAK, SOMKID, LIAM FAHEY, AND PHILIP KOTLER. "Strategic Global Marketing: Lessons from the Japanese." *Columbia Journal of World Business.* Spring 1985, pp. 47–53.

NEES, DANIELLE B. "Building an International Practice." *Sloan Management Review,* Winter 1986, pp. 15–26.

New York Stock Exchange. "U.S. International Competitiveness: Perception and Reality." New York Stock Exchange Office of Economic Research, August 1984.

RABINO, SAMUEL, AND ELVA ELLEN HUBBARD. "The Race of American and Japanese Personal Computer Manufacturers for Dominance of the U.S. Market." *Columbia Journal of World Business,* Fall 1984, pp. 18–30.

RAPP, WILLIAM V., "Strategy Formulation and International Competition." *Columbia Journal of World Business,* Summer 1973, pp. 98–112.

SMITH, KATHLEEN REICHERT. "Competing with AT&T." *Long Range Planning,* Vol. 18 (February 1985), pp. 1–6.

WHEELWRIGHT, STEVEN C. "Restoring the Competitive Edge in U.S. Manufacturing." *California Management Review,* Vol. 27, no. 3 (Spring, 1985), pp. 26–42.

HARLEY-DAVIDSON MOTOR CO., INC.: DEFENDING A PIECE OF THE DOMESTIC PIE [1]

INTRODUCTION

Throughout the twentieth century, motorcycles have been produced by a host of American companies. Names such as Indian, Yale, Pope, and Minnesota can be found in the graveyard of defunct American motorcycle producers. Today, only one company in the United States is a manufacturer of motorcycles—Harley-Davidson. Founded in 1903 by William S. Harley and a trio of Davidsons, Harley-Davidson was for many years the unchallenged leader in American motorcycle sales. The company's success was due to a combination of factors—innovative engineering and product design and a company image that inspired fierce loyalty on the part

[1]This case was prepared by Charles J. Anderer, research associate, under the supervision of Warren J. Keegan, Professor of International Business and Marketing, as part of the International Business Case Study Project, Center for International Business Studies, Pace University. This project was funded in part by a grant from the United States Department of Education. Copyright © 1986 by the Board of Trustees of Pace University.

of its customers. In fact, few American manufacturers have ever boasted a product as ingrained in the country's folklore as Harley-Davidson. Be it in movies such as *The Wild One* or *Easy Rider,* or in real life with motorcycle gangs like the Hell's Angels, the Harley-Davidson trademark has always evoked an image that is, for better or worse, distinctly American. Seen in this light, it is not so surprising that the first far-reaching piece of protectionist legislation of the Reagan presidency was granted in favor of none other than Harley-Davidson, the only remaining American manufacturer of motorcycles.

On April 1, 1983, the President heeded the recommendations of the International Trade Commission (ITC) that a five-year tariff relief program be accorded Harley-Davidson. The ruling culminated a six-year effort on the part of Harley for governmental help. Predictably, the company felt it had been vindicated by the Reagan administration. Vaughn Beals, chairman and CEO of Harley-Davidson had this to say: "The President's courageous action demonstrates his support for the concept that free trade must also be fair trade. The administration's decision, on the merits of the case, tells our trading partners that the U.S. fully supports the concept of free trade, but that does not mean that our government will tolerate unfair competition."

BACKGROUND TO THE TARIFF RULING

In the 1950s, Harley-Davidson possessed a share of the American market of anywhere from 60 percent to 70 percent. It produced powerful, uniquely styled motorcycles that inspired an unusually high degree of brand loyalty. It was in this decade that other American motorcycle makers ceased to exist. Harley was totally unprepared for what it would call the "Japanese invasion" of the 1960s. The Japanese were able to produce quality merchandise for cheaper prices because of their size and efficient production techniques. These companies were also willing to spend huge amounts on advertising and they successfully introduced millions of Americans (and Europeans) to the joys of motorcycling.

Harley-Davidson, for its part, was bogged down with an image problem that was largely of its own making. For years it had catered to the rough hewn biker because he was, after all, Harley's most loyal customer. This strategy did not at all mesh with the spirit of the 1960s most typified by Honda's, "You meet the nicest people on a Honda" campaign. Unable to capitalize on this huge new market for motorcycles (sales increased by 35 percent in 1962 and by an average of 18 percent for ten years afterward), Harley watched its market share drop precipitously.

In 1970, it claimed a mere 5 percent of the American market (see Table 1 for current data).

AMF-Harley-Davidson

In 1969, Harley-Davidson was bought by AMF, a recreational equipment conglomerate. AMF proceeded to manage the company in a way that "only portfolio theory can embrace," (*Business Marketing* 8/84). Product lines that were deemed unprofitable were dropped instead of improved and very little money was directed to shore up Harley's position. By 1976, the company offered only four models to consumers, whereas the four big Japanese producers routinely offered 20 to 25 models. Harley's only remaining strength was in large bikes (700 cc and up), and here too they would lose a huge amount of market share. In 1972, Harley-Davidson sold 99.6 percent of the heavy bikes purchased in America. By 1975, this figure was down to 44.4 percent (see Table 2 for current data).

The company's initial reaction to these results was to accuse the Japanese of "dumping" their products at unfairly low prices and of copying some of the Harley-Davidson big bike models. A petition for some form of protection was unsuccessfully submitted to the government in 1977. At the same time, Harley did very little to extricate itself from its poor market position. The company experienced a gradual decline both in terms of share and product performance. "Quality went to hell and labor relations went to pot," CEO Beals would later say. Harley continued to emphasize the emotional appeal of its machines rather than stress their performance features: "No other motorcycle arouses the same pride, passion, even fanaticism," proclaimed one ad, (*Business Week* 8/21/83). Later, they would direct much of their energies toward the Japanese, giving their seal

TABLE 1 New Motorcycle Registrations 10 Leading Brands by Market Share, 1979–1984

Make	1984 Rank	1984 Mrkt. Share	1983 Rank	1983 Mrkt. Share	1982 Rank	1982 Mrkt. Share	1981 Rank	1981 Mrkt. Share	1980 Rank	1980 Mrkt. Share	1979 Rank	1979 Mrkt. Share
Honda	1	57.7%	1	54.8%	1	45.1%	1	39.1%	1	39.5%	1	39.7%
Yamaha	2	18.6	2	19.0	2	22.2	2	24.9	2	23.5	2	23.0
Suzuki	3	10.0	3	11.8	3	14.2	4	13.6	4	14.9	4	13.3
Kawasaki	4	8.9	4	9.8	4	12.7	3	15.7	3	15.4	3	14.7
Harley-Davidson	5	3.7	5	3.3	5	4.5	5	5.0	5	4.7	5	6.1
BMW	6	0.6	6	0.6	6	0.5	7	0.4	7	0.4	6	0.7
Husqvama	7	0.2	7	0.3	8	0.2	9	0.2	9	0.2	10	0.3
Moto Guzzi	8	0.1	9	0.1	10	0.1	—	—	—	—	—	—
Can Am	9	*	—	—	9	0.1	10	0.1	10	0.1	—	—
Vespa	10	*	8	0.1	7	0.3	6	0.5	6	0.8	7	0.7
Triumph	—	—	10	*	—	—	8	0.2	8	0.3	8	0.6
Hodaka	—	—	—	—	—	—	—	—	—	—	9	0.3

*Less than 0.05%.

R. L. Polk new registrations include the three most current model years. Some off-highway motorcycle and all-terrain vehicle new registrations are included.

California new off-highway motorcycle and ATV registrations have been added to 1983 and prior year new registrations, so that comparisons can be made with 1984 and subsequent years which include California off-highway registrations.

New York new registrations were not available from October 1983 through December 1984.

Oklahoma new registrations are not available.

Source: *New Motorcycle Registrations*, R. L. Polk & Co., Detroit, Michigan.

TABLE 2   New Registrations of 700+ cc Motorcycles and Market Share Breakdown

	REGISTRATIONS		% Change	Market Share		% Change
	1984	1983		1984	1983	
Harley-Davidson						
700+ cc	28,354	25,342	+11.9	15.5	12.3	+3.2
Honda						
700+ cc	79,337	103,794	−23.6	43.2	50.6	−7.4
Kawasaki						
700+ cc	24,262	23,398	+3.7	13.2	11.4	+1.8
Suzuki						
700+ cc	15.797	17.179	−8.1	8.6	8.4	+0.2
Yamaha						
700+ cc	31,420	31,159	+0.8	17.1	15.2	+1.9
BMW						
700+ cc	3,617	3,257	+11.1	2.0	1.6	+0.4
Other						
700+ cc	668	1,018	−34.4	0.4	0.5	−0.1
Grand Total						
700+ cc	183,455	205,147	−10.6	100.0	100.0	—

(Data includes 699 cc "Tariff Busters")
Source: R. L. Polk.

of approval to T-shirts bearing the message "I'd rather eat worms than ride a Honda," (*Fortune* 5/16/83).

Leveraged Buyout (1981)

Perhaps the most important development of the past decade was the leveraged buyout of Harley-Davidson in 1981 led by Vaughn Beals himself. Beals has since established himself as a charismatic and dedicated manager. In fact, company literature describes him as providing the perfect blend of technical expertise and management skill required to spearhead the "new" Harley-Davidson's aggressive revitalization programs. The most important feature of the buyout, beyond putting Mr. Beals in charge, was that it got the company away from the short term mentality that characterized the AMF years. Freed from the duty to annually present its performance

to a group of dividend hungry shareholders, management has been able to concentrate on spending the necessary funds to put Harley on its feet again.

The Tariff Ruling (1983)

Essential to the rebirth of Harley-Davidson, argued Beals, was a tariff program that would allow time for its program to prove successful. Particularly annoying to Beals was the way in which each Japanese company would slash its prices whenever its inventories built up due to faulty demand assessments or a general economic slowdown. This practice irked Harley to no end because its products were more expensive to begin with. The recession years of 1981–1982 were very bad for Harley. The company, teetering near the edge of bankruptcy, decided to once again petition for help from Washington. This time, it got some.

The five-year tariff, which went into effect April 15, 1983, provided an additional 45 percent tariff (on top of the existing 4.4 percent) on motorcycles having an engine displacement of 700 cc or more, in the first year, with reductions to 35, 20, 15, and 10 percent respectively, in the four succeeding years. European imports are effectively excluded from the surcharge, through tariff-rate quotas which provide that only motorcycle exporters of significant size (i.e., X number of units exported) have to absorb the surcharge cost.

Without getting involved in a debate on the merits of free trade versus protectionism, two basic arguments on this ruling have been advanced. First, free trade purists would argue that the tariff is unfair because it protects an inefficient producer of motorcycles. Harley-Davidson is inefficient, they would say, because it has shown itself incapable of offering the consumer anything but overpriced bikes of second-rate quality. The proof of this lies in the vote of the customers in the marketplace. On the other hand, Harley-Davidson argues that the ruling is necessary because the government has a duty to protect its only remaining producer of motorcycles, who, in addition to competing in an unfair environment, has showed itself to be more than willing to make the financial commitment to improve, but needs time to do so.

THE "NEW" HARLEY-DAVIDSON (1981–1985)

Operational Improvements

The most remarkable aspect of Harley's new approach is how heavily it borrows from the Japanese. Today, the company stresses employee involvement, uses "Just-In-Time" inventory and manufacturing principles and manages all of its processes statistically. This, from a company that had said the Japanese owed their success to unfair practices and the copying of Harley's own models. Intelligently, Harley-Davidson has admitted that there might be something to the Japanese approach after all. Says Thomas A. Gelb, Vice President/Operations: "Initially, our management attributed the price and quality differences of Japanese motorcycles to culture, wage rates, and illegal trade practices such as dumping. Only after extensive research did it become apparent that a large part of the competitive edge they enjoyed was achieved through a truly different manufacturing approach, using improved and more efficient manufacturing techniques.

"One of the first examples of Harley-Davidson's willingness to adopt innovative manufacturing techniques is in the employee involvement area. Harley-Davidson was the second U.S. manufacturing company to implement Quality Circles—back in 1978. At this point, over half of the company's employees in Wisconsin are active participants in this program. This employee involvement and participation program permits employees to contribute their ideas, do hands-on problem solving, and improve the efficiency and quality of their work. Doors that were previously closed to employees are now being opened. For example, company policy now requires that employees be consulted in the planning of any changes to an employees's workplace or layout, or where equipment or process changes are being considered. Rapport and morale are up. Grievances have been cut in half; absenteeism has been reduced by 44 percent, and a job security committee (with representatives of both labor and senior management) meets regularly.

"The second area of Harley-Davidson leadership is the "Just-In-Time" manufacturing program. Since J.I.T. is based on large numbers of small parts runs, it is critical that machine set-up times be held to an absolute minimum. This was one of the first hurdles that was attacked. Set-up reduction is being approached aggressively and, to date, has resulted in an average of 75 percent reduction in the set-up times of the machines to which the process has been applied. These reductions have not been achieved through major capital investments, but rather, through team efforts. Usage of J.I.T. has also helped reduce floor space requirements by 40 percent, required movement through the complete production process by 62 percent.

"In the Statistical Process Control (SPC) area, Harley-Davidson is proving daily the premise that a continual improvement in quality reduces overall operating costs. Essentially, SPC uses statistics to identify variations in a 'process' (be it in the office, shop, or field) and thus pinpoints items that need tighter controls and improvement.

"These three areas—Statistical Process Control, Just-In-Time manufacturing, and Employee Involvement—are producing dramatic quality and efficiency results, such as:

50 percent reduction in reject rates;

40 percent reduction in warranty costs;

300 percent increase in defect-free vehicles received by dealers since 1982;

Consumers rating quality and reliability as 'excellent' increased by 25 percent from 1982 to 1984 (Diagnostic Research Inc. study);

Increasing inventory turns from 4.5 turns in 1982 to 16 turns in 1984;

Improving productivity by 19.8 percent per employee, from 1982 to 1984."

Development of a Quality Product Line

Harley-Davidson has increased the number of models it offers to the consumer to 12 from the lowpoint of 4 in 1976 (see Table 3). More importantly, the new Harleys have been praised more for their performance than for their trademark. Since the buyout in 1981, Harley-Davidson has spent two and a half times the national average for manufacturing companies on research and development, resulting in numerous product improvements. The single most notable achievement has been the introduction of the Evolution engine, the product of five years of intensive engineering development. The Evolution engine features all new major components using the latest design techniques and advanced materials. The result is an engine that produces 15 percent more usable torque and 10 percent more horsepower, while using 10 percent less fuel. The engine is designed for high reliability and durability with a minimum of scheduled maintenance, making it simpler and less expensive to operate and maintain.

Product Innovations

Harley-Davidson has also succeeded in introducing a host of product innovations:

1. 1984 introduction of a patent-pending "anti-dive" air suspension system that keeps the front end of the motorcycle stable during a hard stop to increase braking efficiency and safety for the rider.

2. Application of elastomer-isolated engines to reduce the vibration previously associated with Harley-Davidson engines.

TABLE 3 Harley-Davidson 1986 Model Year Price List

MODEL CODE	MODEL NAME	RETAIL PRICE	
FLHTC Lib.	Electra Glide Lib.	$10,474.00	
FLHTC	Electra Glide Classic	10,224.00	
FLHT	Electra Glide	9,624.00	
FXRD	Grand Touring Sport Glide	9,474.00	
FXRT	Sport Glide		8,749.00
FXST-C	Softail Custom	9,499.00	
FXST	Softail	8,949.00	
FXWG	Wide Glide	8,899.00	
FXRS Lib.	Low Rider Lib.		8,849.00
FXRS	Low Rider	8,499.00	
FXRS	Low Rider Special	8,649.00	
FXR	Super Glide		7,549.00
XLH Lib.	Sportster 1100 Lib.	5,699.00	
XLH	Sportster 1100	5,399.00	
XLH	Sportster	4,545.00	
XLH	Sportster 883		4,195.00

Note: All Harley-Davidsons have an engine displacement of 1340 cc with the exception of the XLH models which range from 883 cc to 1100 cc.

3. Introduction of a new-design, smooth shifting 5-speed transmission.
4. The first application in the motorcycle industry of solid-state electronic ignition (in 1979) to improve performance and reliability, followed by the first computer-controlled ignition system in 1983.
5. Changes in chassis design and steering geometries to improve handling and increase rider comfort and safety, including introduction of computer-designed frames in 1981.

These improvements have not gone unnoticed by longtime Harley customers. Motorcycle gangs and police forces alike have returned to buying Harleys. Michael O'Farrell, president of the Oakland Hell's Angel chapter remarked in a recent article in *The New York Times:* "It's amazing, the difference. (The motorcycles) don't beat you to death any more and your kidneys are still intact."

Development of a New Harley Image

Management has strived to make a break with the past by changing the company's image. Rather than continuing to cultivate the impression that Harley-Davidson represents quality because it is the motorcycle of choice for lawbreaker and lawman alike, the company now portrays doctors, lawyers, craftsmen, and foremen as being the "real" Harley riders. In an attempt to differentiate itself from others in the crowded big bike sector (which remains Harley's meal ticket), the company cites market research data which indicates that the Harley rider is generally more educated, has a higher income and a more responsible job than Japanese motorcycle owners:

44 percent of Harley purchasers have attended college, versus 34 percent to 39 percent for the owners of Japanese imports.

Only 11 percent of Harley owners *do not* have a high school diploma, versus 18 percent for Honda and 30 percent for Kawasaki owners.

Harley purchasers have significantly higher incomes than the owners of Japanese machines. A full 28 percent of Harley purchasers earn more than $35,000, compared with 11 percent of Honda owners and only 5 percent of Kawasaki owners. At incomes from $25,000 to $35,000, the contrast is even sharper—35 percent of Harley purchasers earn in this range, with only 12 percent to 14 percent of the owners of Japanese motorcycles earning at this level.

Reactions from Harley Dealers and Riders

Harley-Davidson's efforts to improve their product have not at all been in vain, those familiar with the company will tell you. In Harley's New York City showroom a dealer points to a handful of bikes and says that this is all that is left from the 1985 stock. In general, the mood is upbeat concerning Harley-Davidson: "Here in New York City, at least, management's commitment to quality is showing up both in sales figures and performance. Vaughn Beals is the Lee Iacocca of the motorcycle industry."

In suburban White Plains, 42-year-old Richie Pierce, a long-time cycling enthusiast, sells both Harley-Davidsons and Suzukis. Pierce fully acknowledges all that Harley has done to improve itself, yet he says that Harleys and Suzukis, or any other Japanese bike for that matter, should never be compared.

"The Harley is, and always has been, an image bike. Japanese bikes are performance bikes. Even with the tariff Harleys sell at a premium. This is because Harley-Davidsons are prestige bikes. As for performance, Harleys just don't match up. The Japanese can easily outspend them and it shows up in the type of motorcycles they produce."

Even though there is a significant difference in performance, Pierce feels there will always be a market for Harleys: "I own three bikes and one of them is a Harley. There is something about Harley-Davidson that sets them apart from other bikes. The Japanese have tried to copy the Harley look but it just doesn't work. That's why it is so much easier to resell a Harley than a Japanese bike. If you're going to buy performance, why buy used performance? Harleys have an inimitable style and that's what keeps them going. Besides, the government would never let the only American motorcycle company left go down the tubes."

Harley-Davidsons do indeed seem to have that special something that other bikes lack. When asked to review one of Harleys large touring bikes, the FLTC, for the magazine *Cycle Guide,* Marc Cook came back with these remarks: "The Harley makes me giggle. Out on the highway, with little else to do but watch the white line, the FLTC makes me laugh out loud inside my helmet. And I'm not entirely sure why. Perhaps it's the seductive rhythm of the engine pulses, or the way that massive vee-twin never seems to run out of torque. Or it could be the uncanny directional stability of the big 'Hog.' Maybe it's the response of the young ladies at the local Haagen-Dazs. But, really, I don't think any of these is the answer. The truth is, the Harley flat surprises me. It works so well on the open road—in spite of its rough edges and idiosyncrasies—that I have a hard time *not* watching the scenery."

TABLE 4   New Motorcycle Wholesale Sales by Major Brands, 1980–1984

| | Wholesale $ Volume ($000's) | Est. Retail $ Volume ($000's) | Total Units | MODEL TYPE | | | ENGINE TYPE | | UNITS | | DISPLACEMENT SIZE (cc) | | |
				On-Highway	Off-Highway	Dual Purpose	Two Stroke	Four Stroke	Under 125 cc	125–349 cc	350–449 cc	450–749 cc	750 cc & Up
1980	$1,702,130	$2,136,866	1,156,843	711,295	332,753	112,795	314,854	841,989	322,294	263,336	133,069	182,202	255,942
(% of Total Units)			(100.0%)	(61.4%)	(28.9%)	(9.7%)	(27.2%)	(72.8%)	(27.9%)	(22.8%)	(11.5%)	(15.7%)	(22.1%)
1981	$1,861,821	$2,326,790	1,137,918	669,062	391,599	77,257	271,633	866,285	270,743	301,357	78,476	225,589	261,753
(% of Total Units)			(100.0%)	(58.8%)	(34.4%)	(6.8%)	(23.9%)	(76.1%)	(23.8%)	(26.5%)	(6.9%)	(19.8%)	(23.0%)
1982	$1,600,070	$1,993,127	1,018,840	495,521	476,419	46,900	286,529	732,311	307,713	342,283	28,223	117,519	223,102
(% of Total Units)			(100.0%)	(48.6%)	(46.8%)	(4.6%)	(28.1%)	(71.9%)	(30.2%)	(33.6%)	(2.7%)	(11.6%)	(21.9%)
1983	$1,985,979	$2,468,186	1,241,808	539,040	641,758	61,010	294,256	947,552	294,711	507,960	25,873	215,026	198,238
(% of Total Units)			(100.0%)	(43.4%)	(51.7%)	(4.9%)	(23.7%)	(76.3%)	(23.7%)	(40.9%)	(2.1%)	(17.3%)	(16.0%)
1984	$2,270,332	$2,816,370	1,310,240	446,968	802,530	60,742	220,833	1,089,407	251,365	634,403	37,280	227,286	159,906
(% of Total Units)			(100.0%)	(34.1%)	(61.3%)	(4.6%)	(16.9%)	(83.1%)	(19.2%)	(48.4%)	(2.8%)	(17.4%)	(12.2%)

Model Type Definition: *On-Highway* motorcycles are those certified by the manufacturer as being in compliance with the Federal Motor Vehicle Safety Standards, and designed primarily for use on public roads. Includes scooters. Excludes mopeds and nopeds (limited speed motor-driven cycles under 50 cc which are not generally defined by state law as mopeds). *Off-Highway* motorcycles are those which are not certified by the manufacturer as being in compliance with the Federal Motor Vehicle Safety Standards. Includes three- and four-wheeled all-terrain vehicles (ATV's) and off-highway competition motorcycles. *Dual Purpose* motorcycles are certified by the manufacturer as being in compliance with the Federal Motor Vehicle Safety Standards, and designed with the capability for use on public roads as well as off-highway recreational use.

Source: *Manufacturers Shipment Reporting System, Annual Statistical Report,* 1980–1984 Motorcycle Industry Council, Inc., Costa Mesa, California. Includes wholesale shipments to dealers by Harley-Davidson, Honda, Kawasaki, Suzuki, and Yamaha.

TABLE 5 U.S. Motorcycle Imports by Country 1978–1984

	1978	1979	1980	1981	1982	1983	1984
Japan							
Units	882,038	848,959	1,072,856	1,032,520	897,861	522,573	417,825
$ Value	$741,232,155	$825,909,951	$1,091,699,966	$1,270,949,357	$1,079,362,753	$666,284,854	$482,238,238
European Countries							
Units	50,623*	33,824*	40,455*	22,112*	16,100*	13,597*	17,397*
$ Value	$ 54,297,847	$ 40,121,247	$ 44,199,496	$ 39,213,065	$ 27,977,592	$ 29,266,634	$ 38,296,805
All Others							
Units	2,825*	3,969*	6,905*	2,081*	3,242*	4,043*	6,198*
$ Value	$ 1,737,985	$ 4,258,537	$ 6,036,560	$ 3,624,403	$ 2,827,574	$ 1,633,326	$ 2,851,599
Total							
Units	935,486*	886,752*	1,120,216*	1,056,713*	917,203*	540,213*	441,420*
$ Value	$797,267,987	$870,289,735	$1,141,936,022	$1,313,786,825	$1,110,167,919	$697,184,814	$523,386,642

Dollar Value = Dutiable value for 1978–1979 and C.I.F. value for 1980 and subsequent years. All-terrain vehicles not included.

*Excludes estimated imports of mopeds (motorized bicycles) as follows:

1978—350,027 units, $90,470,166	1981—66,779 units, $23,097,891
1979—129,663 units, $36,775,715	1982—18,145 units, $ 4,384,230
1980—182,037 units, $61,714,528	1983—21,645 units, $ 5,471,009
	1984—32,889 units, $ 8,900,146

Source: U.S. Dept. of Commerce, Domestic and International Business Administration; *U.S. Motorcycle Imports*, Werner C. Single, Foreign Trade Services, West New York, New Jersey.

TABLE 6   U.S. Motorcycle Imports by Engine Displacement 1978–1984

	1978	1979	1980	1981	1982	1983	1984
Under 191 cc							
Units	410,260*	390,900*	418,829*	313,944*	312,891*	175,212*	191,856*
$ Value	$163,144,748	$173,583,756	$189,667,483	$154,771,771	$152,019,038	$94,634,569	$97,761,171
191–490 cc							
Units	203,659	166,768	316,596	249,586	182,948	75,321	67,792
$ Value	$173,111,295	$167,195,874	$307,104,651	$259,816,032	$198,421,920	$82,609,575	$78,049,993
491–790 cc							
Units	226,584	224,984	240,604	369,142	298,182	215,975	141,716
$ Value	$301,554,886	$326,914,082	$372,062,671	$639,025,333	$532,150,656	$362,771,480	$256,491,632
Over 790 cc							
Units	76,182	93,222	127,518	120,224	119,625	65,093	34,828
$ Value	$153,575,906	$198,020,881	$266,590,704	$258,903,692	$226,188,672	$153,545,173	$88,441,983
Unspecified							
Units	18,801	10,878	16,669	3,817	3,557	8,612	5,228
$ Value	$5,881,152	$4,575,142	$6,510,513	$1,269,997	$1,387,633	$3,624,017	$2,641,863
Total							
Units	935,486*	886,752*	1,120,216*	1,056,713*	917,203*	540,213*	441,420*
$ Value	$797,267,987	$870,289,735	$1,141,936,022	$1,313,786,825	$1,110,167,919	$697,184,814	$523,386,642

Dollar Value = Dutiable value for 1978–1979 and C.I.F. value for 1980–1984. All-terrain vehicles not included.

*Excludes estimated imports of mopeds (motorized bicycles) as follows:

1978—350,027 units, $90,470,166	1981—66,779 units, $23,097,891
1979—129,663 units, $36,775,715	1982—18,145 units, $ 4,384,230
1980—182,037 units, $61,714,528	1983—21,645 units, $ 5,471,009
	1984—32,889 units, $ 8,900,146

Source: U.S. Dept. of Commerce, Domestic and International Business Administration; *U.S. Motorcycle Imports*, Werner C. Single, Foreign Trade Services, West New York, New Jersey.

HARLEY'S POST-TARIFF PERFORMANCE

In spite of the above improvements, Harley-Davidson has yet to return to profitability. The company is certainly in better shape compared to 1981–1982 and yet management doesn't forsee any substantial profits before 1987. Demand for motorcycles has yet to bounce back from the recessionary levels of 1982. A glimpse at new motorcycle wholesale sales data reveals that sales in the big bike segment have declined sharply since 1981 (see Table 4). As for Harley, its sales have actually decreased since the pre-tariff era. There have, however, been gains made in terms of market share. In 1984, Harley's share of the big bike segment increased 3.2 percent, from 12.3 percent to 15.5 percent. Harley-Davidson has also succeeded in reducing the gap between itself and Honda, the leader in the heavyweight segment. On the other hand, Harley-Davidson's overall share of the American market has actually decreased since 1981, from 5 percent to 3.7 percent.

The impact of the tariff on the Japanese has been offset, in part, by Honda and Kawasaki, who both have production facilities in the United States. According to Beals, this has enabled the Japanese to sidestep the tariff: "The Japanese have managed to duck the tariff on about two-thirds of the vehicles that should have been subject to it, by stepping up their U.S. final assembly operations and through the introduction of 699 cc motorcycles which fall just below the 700 cc tariff limit." On the other hand, statistics show dramatic decreases both in the number of Japanese-produced motorcycles entering the United States since 1982 and in the number of Japanese-produced motorcycles with an engine displacement larger than 790 cc (see Tables 5 and 6).

International Sales/Global Strategy

Harley-Davidson, while it has made some key changes in the areas of operations, design, and product image, has chosen to remain an essentially domestic company. This point is underscored by the fact that, in 1984, Japanese motorcycle manufacturers exported 660,484 units to the United States, while a mere 1,046 Harleys made their way to Japan. European export figures are similarly low. Is the passion American Harley owners feel for their machines exportable? Alfred E. Eckes, chairman of the ITC, hopes as much. Eckes wrote in his tariff ruling that "as exports become more competitive with the depreciation of the dollar, it is reasonable to think that Harley . . . will participate again in export sales."

The difference in size between Harley-Davidson and the four Japanese companies means that it will continue to operate with severe technological and cost disadvantages in relation to its competitors. Tariff or no tariff, the Japanese were able to produce 4,026,307 motorcycles in 1984, or one hundred times as many units as Harley-Davidson produced. The only other surviving small motorcycle maker is BMW and it does so with the benefit of the technological and production experience gained through its large automobile division.

When the tariff on large displacement motorcycles expires in 1988, Harley-Davidson's fate will be determined by the marketplace. What remains to be seen is if its reputation and history, combined with some noticeable improvements over the last five years, will enable it to survive on its own in the face of stiff competition from companies much larger than itself.

(NOTE: See Appendix for the reaction of Mr. Vaughn Beals, Chief Executive Officer of Harley-Davidson Motor Company, to the above case study.)

Appendix: Letter to Warren J. Keegan from Vaughn L. Beals, Jr., Chairman of the Board and Chief Executive Officer, Concerning the Harley-Davidson, Inc., Case Study, dated December 13, 1985

AMF-Harley-Davidson

Contrary to your statement, AMF was most generous in their investment in Harley-Davidson. In the period from '69 to '75 (prior to my association), they invested very heavily in facility expansion and in new product development. Most, if not all, the new product development effort was wasted.

From the period of '75 to '81, they also met the vast majority of our capital needs. That is not to say it wasn't a subject of annual debate, but there was only one major capital program that they refused (and in hind-sight that wasn't a bad decision).

The Japanese copying of Harley styling did not commence until after we filed the dumping suit in 1977 and received the decision in 1978. It was in the late 1970's that the Japanese started to copy our styling (Yamaha first), and it took them until early in 1981 for them to copy our V-engine format (again Yamaha). In fact, the time from the ITC decision to copying correlates almost perfectly with the time to modify their products.

Rest assured, we have not given our seal of approval to nasty t-shirts. To the contrary, we undertook a trademark licensing program three or four years ago. While this was partially motivated by a need to protect our trademarks by vigorously defending them, it also served the key purpose of cleaning up the offensive t-shirts, etc. which were emblazoned with Harley trademarks. We didn't believe then, and we don't believe now, that insulting the rider of a competitive product is a good way to convince him to switch to your product. Unfortunately, there are still a large number of offensive t-shirts out there, but far less of them are now displayed at our dealers and only rarely do they use our logo and then illegally.

As part of our program to combat this, we have seized merchandise under court order where trademark violations are involved.

Leveraged Buyout (1981)

Your statement, "putting Mr. Beals in charge," etc. is misleading. I was Deputy Group Executive (No. 2 responsible for the Motorcycle Group) from 1975 through 1977. From 1977 to 1981, I was Group Executive with full responsibility for the Motorcycle Group and became CEO in June of 1981. Basically, I have directed the organization since November, 1977.

The Tariff Ruling (1983)

You referenced "faulty demand assessments" by the Japanese as a cause for price reductions. Unquestionably from time to time they, like Harley, misjudged the market. The facts surrounding our complaint in September, 1982 were that the Japanese had *increased* production substantially (if I recall correctly, it was like 20%) at a time when the world market for motorcycles had been depressed for the better part of two years.

Published Japanese production data only shows the segment from above 250cc's. However, because of the dominance of the U.S. in the world market for these larger displacement motorcycles, it isn't a great leap of logic to correlate this with increases in the heavyweight (700cc and up) category.

Harley's Post Tariff Performance

Harley returned to profitability in 1983 and has remained so since. The company was profitable in every year from the depression through 1980. In fact, 1979 and 1980 were years of record profit for the Motor Company. While these years were records for Harley, they were not outstandingly high in an absolute sense for a couple of reasons. During the late 1970's we were making extraordinarily heavy investments in new product development which was reducing earnings; secondly, our basic cost structure prevented us from being high earners in competition against the Japanese who were steadily driving their prices down.

In 1981 and 1982 we had record losses, but by downsizing, we were able to return the total corporation to profitability in 1983 and improve that a bit in 1984. Through October, 1985, we were a bit ahead of last year.

Our contract business, which is wholly performed at the York plant, has grown significantly since 1982 in both revenue and profit. This has been a vital contributor to the profitability of the company. In the future, the benefits of an extensive cost reduction program plus manufacturing productivity improvements will bring us pretty close to cost parity with the Japanese on our basic motorcycle business. Even despite record losses in 1982, we generated a small positive cash flow as a result of our downsizing of the company and our very tight control of raw material and work-in-process. We have maintained a positive operating cash flow (prior to principal repayment) in 1983, 1984 and 1985.

You indicated in the same paragraph that "Harley sales have actually decreased since the pre-tariff era." In discussing sales it is important to distinquish between retail and wholesale sales. Since retail inventories vary from time to time, the focus should be on *retail* sales. We measure these by daily reports from our dealers whom we audit several times per year. Occasionally, there are discrepancies between our estimated retail sales and reported registrations. In most cases, we believe our data is more reliable than that published by Polk.

In this context, our U.S. retail sales were as follows:

	(OOO) UNITS		
1981	*1982*	*1983*	*1984*
41.0	31.2	26.3	31.5

You commented on the decrease of Harley's market share in the total market. That is correct, but the data is grossly distorted by the tremendous growth of three and four wheeler (balloon tire) off-road bikes plus scooters. We recently extracted this information from registration data with the following results:

Total Motorcycle* Registrations Nine Months Total U.S. (OOO) Units

1978	*1979*	*1980*	*1981*	*1982*	*1983*	*1984*	*1985*
671	722	699	667	536	534	458	366
			Harley Volume (OOO Units)				
44.7	48.0	35.6	37.5	28.6	23.7	25.2	25.6
			H-D Market Share (OOO) Units				
6.7%	6.6%	5.1%	5.6%	5.3%	4.4%	5.5%	7.0%

*This includes all displacements, but excludes three and four wheel all-terrain vehicles as well as scooters.

Let me reemphasize the above data is for the first nine months of each of those years. This study was just completed and that happened to be our frame of interest.

As you can see, there has been a significant drop in the total motorcycle market. In this environment, Harley's share has been increasing significantly. I believe this reflects the greater committment of Harley riders to the sport, as well as the fact that the destruction of used motorcycle values by Japanese pricing practices in the last three or four years has removed many of them from the market. We expect the demographics (which are very favorable to motorcycling and Harley-Davidson), combined with a firming up of Japanese prices when they liquidate their excess inventories, to reverse this downward trend in two-wheelers. When that happens, I would not expect Harley's market share to hold the current levels. In short, we believe our share improves in a shrinking market and worsens in an expanding market.

International Sales—Global Strategy

I don't believe that Harley is operating with severe technological disadvantages versus our competitors today. This is verified by the fact that we have been first to market with many innovations (belt drive, computer ignition, true anti-dive suspension, vibration isolation, etc). Except for the last year, we have also been able to dominate dirt track racing. We temporarily lost first position in 1984 and 1985 as a result of a massive investment by Honda (probably 10 times Harley's investment). By the end of the 1985 season, we showed the ability to beat them on many occasions. With some updating to our race engine, we expect to be fully competitive in 1986 or 1987 at the latest.

While the above may represent the claims of a proud CEO, I believe a quick reading of the last couple years of motorcycle press reviews of our product will provide third party judgement as to our technical ability.

We clearly are at a cost disadvantage versus our competitors. Our entire manufacturing strategy, and more recently our cost reduction strategy, has been aimed at eliminating this disadvantage. Our objective is to attain cost parity, which we think is achievable.

It is interesting to observe, when you look at market share, that Honda is clearly our only competitor of significance. Now all of Honda's heavyweights are assembled in the United States. We believe that Honda's labor rates in their chassis plant are now higher than those in our chassis plant. With the opening of a new motorcycle engine plant in Ohio, we expect to see increasing U.S. content in Honda's heavyweight motorcycles. Thus, relatively soon we will both be using U.S. employees and paying comparable rates to manufacture the bulk of our products. Thus, the game with our critical competitor degenerates to who can manage best. Today, we would acknowledge their lead, but we don't believe it is necessary or appropriate to concede them the race in the long run.

The premise for your third paragraph is that the tariffs have helped Harley in the marketplace. I would strongly argue that. All the tariffs have done is to force the Japanese to finally liquidate their excess inventories in the U.S. They are still way in excess of current needs, despite the fact that they have been substantially discounting the old product. In a recent analysis I conducted, I picked one heavyweight model of each of our four competitors and contrasted the original suggested retail price (in 1981 or 1982) to the current price of the same *new* motorcycle of the same model year. (A quick check will confirm that you can still buy three- and four-year-old new motorcycles at Japanese stores.) This showed a range from 48% to 52% price reduction—in itself, an interesting consistency in pricing practices.

Harley's share increase in its heavyweight market and the entire two-wheel market (as shown above) has been accomplished in an environment of heavy discounting. Our large displacement motorcycles (FX designation), which represent the largest of our three generic product lines and also the most profitable, are priced two to three times above comparable competitive models. Despite this, our unit volume and share from this segment of our business is slowly but steadily increasing. (Effectively, we're selling Mercedes versus Fords.)

Additionally, the Japanese have succeeded in evading virtually all tariff payments. All Honda and Kawasaki heavyweight motorcycles are now *assembled* in the U.S.; previously Kawasaki was virtually out of U.S. assembly. Nearly all 750cc displacements (half of the heavyweight volume prior to the tariffs) have been downsized to 695 to 699cc's to evade the tariff. Thus, as a practical matter, only Suzuki and Yamaha, who do not have U.S. assembly facilities, have been paying tariff and then only on their motorcycles of 1000cc displacement and above. Since the special tariff provides for a few thousand (7,000 to 8,000, if I recall correctly) of tariff free imports, my guess is that this has covered the vast majority of imported Yamahas and Suzukis.

A final comment–an International Trade Commission report on the first year after the tariffs reported a 2% *reduction* in the average retail price of heavyweight motorcycles despite the 45% tariff increase. Realize, when reading that number, that this included the period during which Kawasaki, in particular, and Honda to a lesser extent, were moving assembly on-shore.

That finishes the comments on your specific draft. All in all, I thought it was a very good effort. I hope the above will clarify a few points.

To the above let me add the following—some thoughts I had while reading your case study:

1. *Lightweights:* Harley was not asleep at the switch on lightweights. If you go back in time, Harley has been in the scooter business (in the 1960's), mopeds, lightweights, etc. The company bought a 50% interest in Aermacchi, an Italian lightweight motorcycle manufacturer, many years ago and purchased the balance of that interest in the mid to late 1960's. They made a good motorcycle, but basically could not remain competitive with the Japanese. Market scale was the difference. We had a plant in Italy making 25,000 motorcycles with 500 people as contrasted to a Honda plant making 985,000 motorcycles with 1400 people.

Undoubtedly, we were too late in discovering that difference or we would have taken action earlier. However, the capital investment in tooling up for that large Honda scale production plus the investment in developing the distribution system to sell that many products was orders of magnitude beyond the ability of Harley-Davidson as a private company, and I suspect would not have been even possible under AMF ownership. Frankly, I think that's an area where the industrial/banking relationships in Japan make high risk taking possible. A book published a couple of years ago on Honda reported on the tremendous increases in investment and the resultant volume increases during some of those periods. Frankly, I don't believe that is possible in the United States in today's capital markets.

2. *Product Quality:* I think it would be helpful to elaborate on Harley's quality/ product situation in the early 70's.

From 1969 to approximately 1973, the first four years of AMF ownership, the company's unit volume increased by three to four times and revenues quadrupled. At the beginning of that period you had a small manufacturing company in which each functional head was a family member who had run that function for literally decades. Systems were appropriate to a closely held family company that had a fairly stable volume history. Manufacturing was characterized by craftsman knowing what to do without reference to drawings.

The tremendous growth imposed upon the company in that state in the early 70's caused utter chaos. They converted from a craftsman to a production line environment, and the systems utterly failed to keep the company under control. The ultimate result was terrible quality and worse labor relations. The whole thing came unglued in 1974 with a 100-day plus strike. As a result, management was changed and the rebuilding process which is still going on was initiated.

A new group executive was brought in in early 1974. (I'm not sure whether this was before or during the strike.) His first effort was to quickly get manufacturing under control. He then started a major effort in 1975 to expand the Engineering Department staff and facilities and to totally redesign the product line. As a practical matter, the last major piece of that program was completed in June of 1985 when we introduced our last new engine.

When those efforts were well underway in the late 70's, we then turned our attention to improving quality and then productivity. Briefly then the 1975 to 1980 period could be defined as "getting the product line modernized" and the 1980 to 1985 period getting manufacturing pointed in the right direction.

As I noted above, the catch-up game in product development is behind us. The manufacturing improvements now have their own momentum and require little input from senior management. The current focus in the last year has been on strengthening the dealer network. We are already starting with a network that we believe is the most effective and most profitable (albeit the smallest).

With our catch-up work well along in the engineering and manufacturing area, we deemed it appropriate about a year ago to really kick off a major effort to further strengthen our dealer network. This is aimed at making them better businessmen and improving their ability to close on sales. As a result, we expanded the sales force by about 50% and have started to invest more heavily in their training and later in dealer training.

3. *Contract Business:* There has been a legacy of contract business at the York plant for some years. This represented only 2 to 3% of sales in 1982, but now it is between 15 and 17%. This provides a source of profit, but more importantly a source of jobs to absorb people freed up by productivity improvements in the motorcycle business. We are aggressively trying to expand that business at York and to develop a similar ability to successfully perform contract business in our Wisconsin operations. It is our expectation that this business will represent a quarter to a third of our business in three or four years, thus, also giving us some degree of internal diversification.

By adopting various Japanese manufacturing methods in our motorcycle business, we are improving our position relative to the Japanese, but we are not there yet. However, when these methods are applied in domestic markets (which all of our contract business represents), they give us an extremely great competitive advantage which has been directly responsible for our rapid growth in this area.

4. *Parts & Accessories:* The company has had a successful parts and accessories business for many years. In late 1976, we established this as a separate division, ultimately giving it it's own president, administrative staff, etc. As a result it grew

very rapidly in the late 1970's. Shortly after buying the company, in an effort to reduce our overhead, we consolidated it back into the Marketing organization. As a result of that and having to "cherry pick" some of our best people out of that area, we lost ground. About a year ago, we again spun it off as a separate entity to give it greater senior management focus.

As in most companies, the parts business is extremely profitable. Because of the stability of Harley's designs as opposed to the Japanese and also because of the very large population of older Harleys in the field (most of the Japanese motorcycles don't last beyond three or four years due to high repair costs in the context of a decreasing new price), Harley represents a prime target for aftermarket competitors. A couple of years ago, we introduced a second tier product line (Eagle Iron) to combat this. These products are sourced in the orient (as are our aftermarket competitors' parts) rather than the U.S. as are most of our OEM parts. This new product line is growing rapidly, and we expect it to recapture a significant part of the lost parts business today.

We also have tried to become the "the" motorcyle store for rider apparel, helmets, etc. as a way of developing floor traffic. Large numbers of our dealers have set up apparel boutiques which are achieving this purpose as well as generating considerable profitability for the individual dealerships.

5. *Recreational vs. Transportation Vehicles:* In viewing Harley-Davidson's position in the motorcycle industry, it is important to distinquish between a motorcycle as a recreational vehicle and a transportation device. In the U.S. motorcycles are toys. While they are occasionally used for transportation, it is rare indeed to find someone who's sole means of transport is a motorcycle.

By contrast, in many less developed countries, a motorcycle is the first step above a bicycle. Classically, motorcycle sales drop as the economy strengthens and people move into small automobiles. Only after they satisfy their need for four wheel transportation do they then come back to motorcycles as toys.

As you know, Harley's displacement range until last June started from 1000cc's and up; today, we start at 883cc's and go up. In the 60's and 70's, we offered a wide variety of smaller displacement motorcycles from 50cc's to 350cc's. As noted above, we could not remain cost competitive in that area. Frankly, we never expect to be able to reenter that market.

We do believe, however, that we can go down in displacement range successfully to about 500cc's. Our Nova project was conceived to produce a V-4 that would be competitive with 750cc's (the bottom half of the heavyweight market which is defined as 700cc's plus) and a two cylinder version would give us a 400 or 500cc motorcycle. Fortunately, the volumes in these larger displacement ranges (500cc's and above) are such that we do not feel we will be at a great disadvantage with the Japanese. Their giant production numbers all relate to their small displacement vehicles sold in developing countries. Otherwise, our manufacturing scale is about the same.

QUESTIONS FOR DISCUSSION

1. Do you consider Harley-Davidson to be the victim of unfair competitive practices or of its own lack of strategic vision?
2. How does the size difference between Harley-Davidson and its Japanese competitors affect H-D's ability to compete?
3. What are the basic strategic alternatives for Harley-Davidson? What do you recommend? Why?

12

PRODUCT DECISIONS

The prospects for American car manufacturers in Europe would appear to be good if they will meet the conditions and requirements of these various countries but to attempt to do so on the lines on which business is done in America would make it a fruitless task.

Statement by James Couzens, 1907,
officer of the Ford Motor Company

INTRODUCTION

The focus of this chapter is the product, probably the most crucial element of a marketing program. To a very important degree, a company's products define its business. Pricing, communication, and distribution policies must fit the product. A firm's customers and competitors are determined by the products it offers. Its research and development requirements will depend upon the technologies of its products. Indeed, every aspect of the enterprise is heavily influenced by the firm's product offering.

In the past, product decisions in global marketing have been neglected by managers who have fallen into two types of errors, often simultaneously. One error has been to ignore product decisions taken by subsidiary or affiliate managers and in effect abandon any effort to influence or control product policy outside the home country market. The other error has been to impose product policy upon all affiliate companies on the assumption that what is right for customers in the home market must also be right for customers everywhere. In most cases neither of these extreme positions can be justified by profit-maximization criteria. The challenge facing a company with global horizons is to develop a product policy and strategy that is sensitive to market needs, competition, and company resources on a global scale. This requires a product policy that strikes a balance between the need and payoff for adapting to local market preferences and the competitive advantages that come from concentrating company resources on a limited number of products.

This chapter examines the major dimensions of global product decisions. First, basic concepts are explored. The diversity of preferences and needs in international markets is then underlined by an examination of product saturation levels. Product design criteria are identified and attitudes toward foreign products are explored. The next section outlines strategic alternatives available to international marketers, and the chapter concludes with an examination of new products in international marketing.

BASIC CONCEPTS

As an introduction to international product decisions it is worthwhile to begin by briefly reviewing basic marketing concepts of a product. In addition to these concepts which have full application to international marketing, there are also product concepts that apply specifically to international marketing.

Definition of a Product

What is a product? At first glance this is a simple question. A product is defined by its physical attributes—weight, dimensions, and material. Thus an automobile could be defined as 3,000 lb of metal, mainly iron, and as 190″ long, 75″ wide, and 59″ high. This description could be expanded to include color, texture, density, shape, contour, and so on, but any description that is limited to physical attributes will remain inadequate as a full description because it says nothing about the needs a product fills. The automobile, for example, is a product that fulfills many needs. The most obvious is transportation, but the marketer cannot ignore the important recreation, status, and power needs satisfied by this product. Indeed, major segments of the automobile market are developed around these consumer desires.

The most basic contribution of marketing thought in the product decision area has been to shift the emphasis from the product itself to the needs and desires of the customer. This shift in emphasis applies with equal weight to consumer and industrial products. This new concept of marketing is still lost on many marketers more than 25 years after it was brilliantly expounded by J. B. McKitterick[1] and then expanded by Theodore H. Levitt in his article, "Marketing Myopia."[2] We shall define a product, then, as a collection of physical, service, and symbolic attributes which yield satisfaction, or benefits, to a user or buyer. Product management is

---

[1]"What Is the Marketing Management Concept?" speech given to the American Marketing Association, Philadelphia, December 27, 1957. Reprinted by Intercollegiate Case Clearinghouse, ICHDCIM 64.

[2]*Harvard Business Review,* July–August 1960.

concerned with the decisions that affect the customer's perception of the firm's product offering.

Product Characteristics

Products have been characterized in a number of ways. The oldest classification has been the consumer industrial goods distinction among users. Consumer goods have been distinguished on the basis of how they are purchased (convenience, shopping, and specialty goods) and according to their life span (durable and nondurable). These and other classification frameworks developed for domestic marketing are fully applicable to international marketing.

LOCAL VERSUS INTERNATIONAL VERSUS MULTINATIONAL VERSUS GLOBAL PRODUCTS. By a process of both acquisition and expansion of existing businesses, many multinational companies have products that they offer in a single national market. A typical example of this situation is the case of General Foods, when it was in the chewing gum business in France, the ice cream business in Brazil, and the pasta business in Italy. While each of these unrelated businesses in isolation was quite profitable, the scale of each was too small to justify international headquarters marketing, production, financial management, or heavy expenditures on R&D. Indeed, if such headquarters systems were developed, it would in the case of a single-country business amount to one-over-one management.

An important question regarding any product is whether it has the potential for expansion into other markets. The answer to this question will depend upon the company's goals and objectives and upon perceptions of opportunity. The four product categories that companies choose from are:

1. *Local products:* In the context of a particular company, products that are perceived as having potential only in a single national market.
2. *International products:* Products that are perceived as having potential for extension into a number of national markets.
3. *Multinational products:* Products that are adapted to the perceived unique characteristics of national markets.
4. *Global products:* Products that are designed to meet the needs of a global market segment.

The local product may be quite profitable, but the existence of a single national business does not provide an opportunity to develop international leverage from headquarters services in such areas as marketing, R&D, and production and from the transfer and application of experience gained in one market to other markets. One of the major tools available to the multicountry marketer is comparative analysis, which is unavailable to the single-country marketer. Another shortcoming of a single-country product business is the lack of transferability of managerial expertise acquired in the single-product area. A manager who gains experience in this single-product area can utilize his or her product experience in the company only in the single market where the product is sold. Similarly, any manager coming from outside the market area where the single product is sold will not have had any experience in the single-product business. Therefore, while attractive profit opportunities in unrelated product areas may present themselves from time to time to the international company, there is a substantial opportunity cost of moving into the single-product area.

It is critically important for the international company to evaluate proposed new products in terms of their local-international-multinational-global potential. All other things being equal, the product with profitable international-global potential is more attractive than the product whose potential for any reason is basically local or multinational. In general, a company should not add a purely local or multinational product to its line when an attractive international-global product addition is available.

Another way of looking at a product is to consider its characteristics. John Fayerweather suggests five important characteristics that are relevant to international marketing consideration: primary functional purpose, secondary purpose, durability and quality, method of operation, and maintenance.

Primary function is illustrated by the example of the refrigerator as used in the industrialized high-income countries. The primary function of the refrigerator in these countries is (1) to store frozen foods for a week or more, (2) to preserve perishable food (vegetables, milk, and meat) between car trips to the supermarket, (3) to store products such as margarine not requiring refrigeration, and (4) to keep bottled drinks cold for short-notice consumption.

In lower-income countries, frozen foods are not widely used. Housewives shop on a daily basis rather than a weekly basis, and because of lower incomes people are reluctant to pay for the third and fourth industrialized country uses of the refrigerator. These are luxury uses that require high-income levels to support. The function of the refrigerator in a lower-income country is merely (1) to store small quantities of perishable food for one day and (2) to store leftovers for slightly longer periods. Because the needs fulfilled by the refrigerators are limited in these countries as compared with advanced countries a much smaller refrigerator is quite adequate.

In some developing countries, refrigerators have an important secondary purpose. They fulfill a need for prestige. In these countries, there is demand for the largest models, which are prominently displayed in the living room rather than hidden in the kitchen.

Durability and quality are important product characteristics that must be appropriate for the proposed market. The durability and quality of an appliance, for example, must be suited to the availability of service within a market. In lower-income markets, appliances are more likely to be repairable (a repairable appliance is a quality product in these markets) than in advanced countries, where the cost of labor makes it prohibitively expensive to repair appliances costing under $40. In advanced countries appliances are constructed without the additional "quality" that would allow a repairperson to take the appliance apart and repair it. Since the availability of repair is either nonexistent or prohibitively expensive, to build repairability into appliances would add nothing of value for the consumer. However, the high-income product in a low-income market may be a lower-quality product because of its lack of repairability.

Two other important characteristics are method of operation and maintenance. For example, the voltage and cycle requirements for an electrical appliance or the driving conditions for an automobile are important method-of-operation considerations in determining the product design and characteristics. The same principle is true of maintenance. Standards and conditions of use vary considerably, and the level of maintenance available is highly variable; this should be incorporated into considering the appropriate characteristics of a product for a market.

WORLD BRANDS. A world brand is defined by the following characteristics:

Same Strategic Principles. A world brand is guided by the same strategic principles in every market in the world. Take for example a brand like Marlboro. Marlboro is an urban brand which appeals to the universal human desire for freedom and space, which is missed especially by urban dwellers who typically lack freedom and physical space. Marlboro is positioned around the world as an urban brand and its Marlboro man symbolizes freedom and space.

Same Positioning. A world brand is positioned the same way in every market. If the brand is a premium priced brand, it will be premium priced around the world. If it is positioned vis-à-vis an age segment of the market, the positioning will be the same in every market. For example, Benetton's has positioned its main Benetton's line vis-à-vis the 16- to 24-year-old youth market around the world.

Same Marketing, Except. A world brand is marketed the same way in every market in the world except—the marketing mix can vary to meet local consumer and competitive requirements. For example, Coke and Pepsi both increased the sweetness of their beverages in the Middle East where customers prefer a sweeter drink. Only an ideologue would insist that a product cannot be adapted to meet local preferences and certainly no company building a world brand needs to limit itself to absolute product uniformity. The issue is not exact uniformity, but rather, are we offering essentially the same product? Other elements of the marketing mix, such as price promotion, appeal, media, distribution channels, and tactics may also vary.

The essential characteristic of a world brand is not an absolutely uniform marketing mix or execution. A world brand is guided by the same strategic principles, is positioned the same in every market, and follows the same marketing approach in every market with the caveat that the marketing mix may vary.

Coke is an example of a world brand. It is positioned and marketed the same in all countries. Although the product itself may vary to suit local tastes, the price may vary to suit local competitive conditions, and the channels of distribution may differ, the basic, the underlying strategic principles that guide the management of the brand are the same worldwide. Coke projects a global image of fun, good times, and enjoyment.

A world brand, like a national or regional brand, is a set of consumer beliefs or perceptions about a product. A product is not a brand—it is an objective, physical entity or service. A brand is a perception created in the mind of consumers who ascribe beliefs and values to the product. World brands then do not exist in nature: they must be created by marketers. They are an option that should be considered and assessed systematically by global marketers large and small. The effort required to create a world brand is different from the effort required to create multiple national brands: the up front creative vision necessary to create a great world brand is greater than that required for a national brand. On the other hand, the ongoing effort to maintain brand awareness is less for a great world brand than it is for a collection of national brands.

How and on what basis can or should marketers decide whether or not to establish world brands? One expert has argued that "world branding must, in the final analysis, be an option to be determined by bottom-up consumer driven considerations, not by top-down manufacturer driven business convenience."[3] In practice, what this means is that if you attempt to create a world brand, you must closely monitor the success of the effort. A major variable in determining success will be whether or not you are starting with a blank slate so to speak, or, whether you have existing brands in national markets that must be repositioned and even renamed. Obviously the former task is vastly easier than the latter, which may range from the challenging but clearly feasible to the impossible. Examples of major companies that have succeeded in replacing national with world brands are Exxon for various Standard Oil brands and Nissan for Datsun outside Japan. Today there are thousands of world brands, and every day the list grows longer. Global marketers should be alert to the advantages and possibilities of world brands.

PRODUCT SATURATION LEVELS IN INTERNATIONAL MARKETS

Many factors determine market potential. Income is clearly a necessary enabling factor, but availability, price levels, need, and custom all act as important codetermining influences.

Complementarity can be an important determinant of demand that will not be revealed by examination of income and general cultural data. The differences within Europe in saturation levels for electric vacuum cleaners is due to the type of floor coverings used in the different countries. Virtually all the homes in The Netherlands

---

[3] A. E. Pitcher, "The Role of Branding in International Advertising," *International Journal of Advertising*, #4, 1985, p. 244.

have rugs on the floor, whereas French and Italian homes tend not to have rugs as floor covering. Thus, in addition to attitudes toward cleanliness, the complementarity factor operates very significantly for electric vacuum cleaners. If the French had more carpets covering their floors, the saturation level for vacuum cleaners would be higher.

The existence of wide disparities in the demand for a product from one market to the next is an indication of the possible potential for that product in the low-saturation-level market. For example, a major new product category in the United States in the early 1980s was "mousse," a hair grooming product for women that is more flexible than stiff, dry hair spray. This product, known as a gel in France, had been available in France and Europe for 25 years prior to its introduction in the United States. The success of the product in Europe was a clear signal of market potential. Indeed, it is more than likely that this opportunity could have been tapped earlier. Every company should have an active global scanning system to identify potential market opportunities based on demand disparities.

PRODUCT DESIGN

Product design is a key factor determining success in international marketing. Should a company adapt product design or offer a single design in international markets? It depends upon (1) the extent to which a design change will increase sales and (2) the cost of changing a product's design and testing it in the market. The impact of design upon sales will depend largely upon the factors discussed in the paragraphs that follow.

PREFERENCES.   There are marked and important differences in preferences around the world for factors such as color and taste. The marketer who ignores preferences does so at her own peril. In the 1960s the Olivetti Corporation discovered that its award-winning modern consumer typewriter designs (Olivetti typewriters have been placed on display at the Museum of Modern Art in New York City) were quite successful in Europe, but not successful in the United States. The U.S. consumer wanted a heavy bulky typewriter that was "ugly" by modern European design standards. Bulk and weight were considered prima facie evidence of quality by American consumers, and Olivetti was therefore forced to adapt its award winning design in the United States.

More recently, Ford Motor Company decided to introduce U.S. cars with a European aerodynamic design. The dramatically different look, popular in Europe, was an immediate success in the United States and was credited with contributing to the company's huge success in 1986 when Ford profits exceeded those of GM for the first time since 1923.

COST.   When product design is determined, cost factors must be considered broadly. The cost of the product will place a floor under pricing alternatives. The cost of associated inputs must also be considered. The cost of labor, for example, varies quite substantially around the world. One example of how labor cost affected product design in a high-technology area is the approach to design of aircraft by the British and the Americans. The British approach, which resulted in the Comet, was to place the engines inside the wing. This produced an aircraft that had lower wind resistance and therefore greater fuel economy, with the disadvantage of an engine that was less accessible than an externally mounted engine and therefore more time consuming to maintain and repair. The American approach to this question of engine location was to hang the engine from the wings at the expense of efficiency and fuel economy to gain a more accessible engine and, therefore, to reduce the amount of time required for engine maintenance and repair. Both approaches to engine location were rational. The British approach took into account the relatively lower cost of the labor required for engine repair, and the American approach took into account the relatively high cost of labor for engine repair in the United States.

LAWS AND REGULATIONS.   Laws and regulations have a major impact on product design in international marketing. For example, in the health care field, government regulations determine the rate of reimbursement for various medical procedures. The market for any medical product or procedure will depend upon the rate of reimbursement for a procedure. In the United States the dollar rate of reimbursement for a CAT (computer-aided tomography) scan is, for example, over 5 times that in Japan. For any given number of CAT scans in the U.S., the total revenue to a U.S. hospital is 5 times that of a Japanese hospital. Clearly, the U.S. market is more attractive given the high level of government support.

Taxes on automobiles based upon engine displacement are another good example. The engine displacement tax, which is found in almost every country in the world outside the United States and Canada, makes the car equipped with a large engine more expensive to buy abroad than in the United States. Taxes on gasoline are much higher abroad than in the United States. The higher taxes make the larger engine more expensive to operate.

Nontariff Barriers

An important factor for the marketer sourcing across national boundaries is the so-called "nontariff barriers" (NTBs) to trade. These barriers are assorted requirements and rulings that may purport to be impartial regulations but that in fact serve only to restrict or eliminate foreign competition. Florida tomato growers, for example, succeeded in persuading the U.S. Department of Agriculture to issue regulations establishing a minimum size for tomatoes marketed in the United States. The effect of this regulation was to eliminate the large Mexican tomato industry, which raised a tomato that just happened to fall below the minimum size specified.

In other cases, NTBs are quite blatant. In France, any company can bid on a contract to supply CAT scanning equipment to hospitals. All hospital purchases must be approved by the Ministry of Health. If the purchase order is for the equipment made by a French company, it is immediately approved. If it is for equipment made by a foreign company, it will be delayed in the Ministry of Health for at least a year and a half.

It is critically important for a company to determine if it is facing a nontariff barrier or indeed, if it is facing a legitimate national condition that is nondiscriminatory. The real test here is whether or not there is discrimination, not whether or not the national conditions are "reasonable." No foreigner has the right to tell a sovereign what is or is not reasonable. However, if it is determined that the government actions are discriminatory, they are then ipso facto nontariff barriers and the strongest possible action should be taken on the part of any serious competitor.

Indeed, if you face discrimination in a target market and competitors from that market have access to your home market, any alert competitor should absolutely insist on comparable treatment. Failing to receive comparable treatment, the serious competitor should take every conceivable action to retaliate by imposing similar discriminatory restrictions on the foreign competitor in the home market. Anything less than a full and vigorous response is an invitation to disaster. To allow a competitor to operate in a protected home-country market is analogous to fighting a war where your enemy has a completely free and protected home base from which to operate while your home base is open and vulnerable to attack by the enemy.

Other prescriptions levied may be labeled as nontariff barriers when they are in fact quite legitimate efforts to promote the public welfare. Automobile safety regulations have, for example, been objected to by some foreign manufacturers as a trade barrier. The intention behind the prescription is important. If a country has a prescription that is designed to reduce or eliminate foreign competition, any effort to comply with the prescription would probably be met with additional legislation or rulings that eliminated foreign competitors. A good test of a country's intention when prescriptions affect a product is to determine whether the prescription affects all companies or just foreign companies. If the effect of the prescription is universal, this is a priori evidence that they were not motivated by an effort to restrict foreign-based competition.

COMPATIBILITY.   A product must be compatible with the environment in which it is used. Power systems must be compatible with their environment, particularly electrical power, which varies in voltage and cycles around the world. Proper size must be compatible with the country standard, and so on.

T.V. manufacturers face three different T.V. broadcast systems in the world today: the U.S. NTSC system, the French SECAM system, and the German PAL system. Companies that are targeting global markets design sets that will operate on each of the systems by simply throwing a switch. Companies that are not aiming for the global market design a set that will operate in only one of the systems.

Climate is an environmental characteristic that often demands compatibility.

Many products require tropicalization to withstand humidity, whereas other products must withstand extreme cold. Many European automobiles are not suited to extremely cold conditions of parts of North America, particularly those cars coming from Britain and Italy, two countries that do not have extreme winters.

Measuring systems do not demand compatibility, but the absence of compatibility in measuring systems can create product resistance. The lack of compatibility is a particular danger for the United States, which is the only nonmetric country in the world. Products calibrated in inches and pounds are at a competitive disadvantage in metric markets. When companies integrate their worldwide manufacturing and design activity, the metric-English measuring system conflict requires expensive conversion and harmonization efforts.

ATTITUDES TOWARD FOREIGN PRODUCTS

One of the factors in international marketing that must be faced is the existence of stereotyped attitudes toward foreign products. Stereotyped attitudes may either favor or hinder the marketer's efforts. No country has a monopoly on a favorable foreign reputation for its products or a universally inferior reputation. There are marked differences in general country attitudes toward foreign products. One new enterprise in Brazil, which supplied a sensitive scientific instrument to the oil-drilling industry, discovered the impact of attitudes toward foreign products when it attempted to market its product to an oil-drilling company in Mexico and found that its Mexican customers would not accept scientific instruments manufactured in Brazil. To overcome the prejudice in Mexico against instruments from Brazil, the company was forced to export the components for its instruments to Switzerland where they were assembled and the finished product stamped ''Made in Switzerland.'' The company then obtained a very satisfactory sales result for its product in Mexico.

The reputation of a country as a manufacturer of products varies from country to country. Indeed the attitudes of countries toward foreign products vary quite considerably around the world. For example, the Germans have a very high regard for products manufactured in Germany. In a survey of the reputation of nine countries as manufacturers, Germans rated their own products for quality with an index number of 54 as compared with 30 for British, 24 for Dutch, 16 for French, 8 for Belgian, and 2 for Italian products. The Italians, on the other hand, rated German products with an index number of 37, Dutch products 25, British 10, Italian 24, French − 1, and Belgian − 2.[4]

Nagashima measured business managers' perceptions of products made in the United States, Japan, Germany, France, and England. In a replication of his 1970 study published in 1977, he reported that the ''Made in U.S.A.'' image has lost

[4]The European Common Market in Britain, ''Basic Report, A Market Survey,'' sponsored by *Readers' Digest*, Copyright 1963, Table 52.

ground rather dramatically as compared with the "Made in Japan" image.[5,6] Narayana found in his study that U.S. products are perceived by U.S. consumers to be of generally higher quality than Japanese-made products. Japanese consumers, on the other hand, believe that Japanese products are of higher quality.[7]

In a study of the overall quality image of "Made in" labels from different countries among industrial product buyers in the middle west of the United States, American buyers indicated a preference for German and Japanese products. Sweden was rated third and The Netherlands much lower.[8]

An experimental study by Curtis C. Reierson tests various communications to determine their impact on attitudes toward foreign products.[9] Reierson found that if prejudice toward foreign products is not too intense, consumer attitudes may be improved by exposure to communication and promotion devices. However, if there are strong unfavorable attitudes toward a nation's products, such attitudes cannot be changed without substantial efforts. If a marketer is willing to engage in substantial and sustained communications efforts, then even a nation with strong unfavorable attitudes can expect a cumulative effect of communications efforts to change attitudes toward its products.

A very interesting finding of the Reierson study is that association with a prestige retailer is beneficial to the image of a nation's products. Thus an international marketer should consider as an alternative to mass communications to improve its product image the strategy of obtaining distribution through a prestige retailer. When the budget for a marketing effort is limited, the latter strategy may be the only economically feasible method open to the international marketer.

In some market segments, foreign products have a substantial advantage over their domestic counterparts simply because they are foreign. For example, this appears to be the case with beer in the United States. In one study, subjects were asked to indicate preference ratings for domestic and foreign beer in a blind test. Subjects indicated a preference for the domestic beers. The same subjects were asked to indicate preference ratings for beers in an open test with labels attached. In this test, the subjects preferred imported beer.[10]

When foreign origin has a positive influence on perceptions of quality, this is

[5]A. Nagashima, "A Comparison of Japanese and U.S. Attitudes Toward Foreign Products," *Journal of Marketing,* January 1970, pp. 68–74.

[6]A. Nagashima, "A Comparative 'Made-In' Product Image Survey Among Japanese Businessmen," *Journal of Marketing,* July 1977, pp. 95–100.

[7]Chem L. Narayana, "Aggregrate Images of American and Japanese Products: Implications on International Marketing," *Columbia Journal of World Business,* Summer 1981, pp. 31–35.

[8]Private communication, Mr. Tord Carmel, president, Swedish Industrial Development Corporation, Greenwich, Connecticut.

[9]Curtis C. Reierson, "Attitude Changes Toward Foreign Products," *Journal of Marketing Research,* November 1967.

[10]David T. Meinertz, Michael Nadelberg, William Pelicot, and Michael R. Sullivan, "The 'Imported' Label and Consumer Choice," unpublished Columbia Business School student report, January 8, 1968.

a happy situation for the international marketer. One way to reinforce foreign preference is by charging a premium price for the foreign product to take advantage of the widespread tendency to associate price and quality.[11] Such a doubly reinforced quality image can put a product in a commanding position in the so-called quality segment of the market. Certainly imported beer in the U.S. premium-priced beer market is an excellent example of this segmentation strategy.

There are numerous examples of a negative association between perception of quality and foreign origin. The perception varies from product group to product group and from source and market country to source and market country. When a product is found to have a negative quality association because of its foreign source, the international marketer has two alternatives. One is to attempt to hide or disguise the foreign origin of the product. Package and product design can minimize evidence of foreign sourcing. A brand policy of using local names or of using well-known local brand names will contribute to a domestic identity. The other alternative is to continue the foreign identification of the product and attempt to change consumer or customer attitudes toward the product.

Some countries have a very poor image that is not based on product experience. Chasin and Jaffe did a study of American industrial product buyers of whom less than 30 percent had had business dealings of any sort over the previous 10 years with one or more of the East European countries. They found that the images of the East European countries were quite poor as compared with the United States.[12] This means that anyone seeking to market a "Made in East Europe" industrial product has an image problem. Each of the four P's can be used to attack this problem: product quality can be offered, price can be lower, promotion can build an image, and place (distribution) can support the overall image campaign with information and evidence.

More recent studies of the impact of country of origin on product evaluation suggest that country-of-origin effects may be less significant than has generally been believed and they may occur predominantly in relation to a valuation of specific attributes rather than overall product. Johansson, Douglas, and Nonaka conclude that there is little support for the hypothesis that the country of origin is used as a surrogate variable to evaluate the product when a respondent has limited experience or knowledge about the product.[13] nevertheless, even if this conclusion is valid, country stereotyping can certainly at times represent a considerable price disadvantage to a competitor in a market. Because of this, global marketers should consider shifting production locations to exploit country-specific advantages. This strategy is

---

[11]The positive correlation between price and perception of quality is well documented in the marketing literature. See, for example, J. Douglas McConnell, "The Price-Quality Relationship in an Experimental Setting," *Journal of Marketing Research,* August 1968.

[12]Joseph B. Chasin and Eugene D. Jaffe, "Industrial Buyer Attitudes Toward Goods Made in Eastern Europe," *Columbia Journal of World Business,* Summer 1979, pp. 74–81.

[13]Johnny K. Johansson, Susan Douglas, and Ikujiro Nonaka, "Assessing the Impact of Country of Origin on Product Evaluations: A New Methodological Prospective," *Journal of Marketing Research,* Vol. 12, November 1985, p. 395.

more attractive to a competitor who does not have an established brand name. One of the advantages of an established brand name is the ability to avoid the country-of-origin effect.[14]

GEOGRAPHIC EXPANSION—STRATEGIC ALTERNATIVES

International companies can grow in three different ways.[15] The traditional methods of market expansion—further penetration of existing markets to increase market share and extension of the product line into new product market areas in a single national market—are both available. In addition the international company can expand by extending its existing operations into new countries and areas of the world. The latter method, geographical expansion, is one of the major opportunities of international marketing. To pursue geographic expansion effectively, a framework for considering alternatives is required. Given any geographic product market base within a multicountry system, five strategic alternatives are available to the company seeking to extend this base into other geographic markets.

STRATEGY 1: PRODUCT-COMMUNICATIONS EXTENSION. In extending their operations internationally many companies employ product extension, which is the easiest and in many cases the most profitable marketing strategy. In every country in which they operate, these companies sell exactly the same product with the same advertising and promotional themes and appeals they use in the United States. One of the leading practitioners of this approach is Pepsico, whose outstanding international performance is a persuasive justification of this practice.

Unfortunately, Pepsico's approach does not work for all products. When Campbell Soup tried to sell its U.S. tomato soup formulation to the British, it discovered after considerable losses that the English prefer a more bitter taste. Another U.S. company spent several million dollars in an unsuccessful effort to capture the British cake mix market. It offered U.S.-style, fancy frosting-covered cake mixes only to discover that the British consume their cake at teatime and that the cake they prefer is dry, spongy, and suitable for being picked up with the left hand while the right manages a cup of tea. Another U.S. company, which turned to a panel of housewives and asked them to bake their favorite cake, discovered this about the British and has since acquired a major share of the British market with a dry, spongy cake mix.

Closer to home, Philip Morris attempted to take advantage of U.S. television

---

[14]For further discussion, see Johnny K. Johansson and Hans B. Thorelli, "International Product Positioning," *Journal of International Business Studies*, Fall 1985, pp. 57–76.

[15]This section is adapted from Warren J. Keegan, "Multinational Product Planning: Strategic Alternatives," *Journal of Marketing*, January 1969.

advertising campaigns that have a sizable Canadian audience in border areas. The Canadian cigarette market is a Virginia or straight tobacco market in contrast to the U.S. market, which is a blended tobacco market. Philip Morris officials decided that they would ignore market research evidence, which indicated that Canadians would not accept a blended cigarette, and go ahead with programs that would achieve retail distribution of U.S. blended brands in the Canadian border areas served by U.S. television. Unfortunately, the Canadian preference for the straight cigarette remained unchanged. American-style cigarettes sold right up to the border but no farther. Philip Morris had to withdraw its U.S. brands.

CPC International attempted to popularize Knorr dry soups in the United States. Dry soups dominate the soup market in Europe and Corn Products tried to transfer some of this success to the United States. However, a faulty marketing research design led to erroneous conclusions concerning market potential for this product. CPC International based its decision to push ahead with Knorr on reports of taste panel comparisons of Knorr dry soups with popular wet soups. The results of these panel tests strongly favored the Knorr product. Unfortunately, these taste panel tests did not simulate the actual market environment for soup, which includes not only eating but also preparation. Dry soups require 15 to 20 minutes cooking time, whereas wet soups are ready to serve as soon as heated. The preparation difference is apparently a critical factor in influencing the kind of soup purchased, and it resulted in another failure of the extension strategy.

The product-communications extension strategy has an enormous appeal to global companies because of the cost savings that are associated with this approach. Two sources of savings, manufacturing economies of scale and elimination of duplicate product R&D costs, are well known and understood. Less well-known but still important sources of savings are the substantial economies associated with standardization of marketing communications. For a company with worldwide operations, the cost of preparing separate print and T.V.-cinema films for each market would be enormous. Although these cost savings are important, they should not distract executives from the more important objective of maximum profit performance, which may require the use of an adjustment or invention strategy. As we have seen, product extension in spite of its immediate cost savings may in fact prove to be a financially disastrous undertaking.

STRATEGY 2: PRODUCT EXTENSION-COMMUNICATIONS ADAPTATION.

When a product fills a different need or serves a different function under use conditions that are the same or similar to those in the domestic market, the only adjustment required is in marketing communications. Bicycles and motor scooters are illustrations of products that often fit this approach. They satisfy needs mainly for recreation in the United States and for basic transportation in many foreign countries. Outboard motors are usually sold to a recreation market in the United States, whereas the same motors in many foreign countries are sold mainly to fishing and transportation fleets.

When the approach to products fulfilling different needs is pursued (or, as is often the case, when it is stumbled upon by accident), a product transformation occurs. The same physical product ends up serving a different function or use than that for which it was originally designed. An example of a very successful transformation is provided by the U.S. farm machinery company that decided to market its U.S. line of suburban lawn and garden power equipment in less developed countries as agricultural implements. The company's line of garden equipment was ideally suited to the farming task in many less developed countries, and most important, it was priced at almost a third less than competing equipment offered by various foreign manufacturers and especially designed for small-acreage farming.

There are many examples of food product transformation. Many dry soup powders, for example, are sold mainly as soups in Europe and as sauces or cocktail dips in the United States. The products are identical; the only change is in marketing communications. In the soup case the main communications adjustment is in the labeling of the powder. In Europe the label illustrates and describes how to make soup out of the powder. In the United States the label illustrates and describes how to make sauce and dip as well as soup.

The appeal of the product extension-communications adaptation strategy is its relatively low cost of implementation. Since the product in this strategy is unchanged, R&D, tooling, manufacturing setup, and inventory costs associated with additions to the product line are avoided. The only costs of this approach are in identifying different product functions and reformulating marketing communications (advertising, sales promotion, point-of-sale material, etc.) around the newly identified function.

STRATEGY 3: PRODUCT ADAPTATION-COMMUNICATIONS EXTENSION.   A third approach to international product planning is to extend without change the basic communications strategy developed for the United States or home market and to adapt the United States or home product to local use conditions. The product adaptation-communications extension strategy assumes that the product will serve the same function in foreign markets under different use conditions.

Exxon (then Esso) followed this approach when it adapted its gasoline formulations to meet the weather conditions prevailing in market areas and employed without change its basic communications appeal, "Put a Tiger in Your Tank." There are many other examples of products that have been adjusted to perform the same function internationally under different environmental conditions. International soap and detergent manufacturers have adjusted their product formulations to meet local water conditions and the characteristics of washing equipment with no change in their basic communications approach. Agricultural chemicals have been adjusted to meet different soil conditions and different types and levels of insect resistance. Household appliances have been scaled to sizes appropriate to different use environments, and clothing has been adapted to meet fashion criteria.

STRATEGY 4: DUAL ADAPTATION.   Market conditions indicate a strategy of adaptation of both the product and communications when there are differences in environmental conditions of use and in the function that a product serves. In essence, this is a combination of the market conditions of strategies 2 and 3. U.S. greeting card manufacturers have faced this set of circumstances in Europe, where the function of a greeting card is to provide a space for the sender to write an individual message in contrast to the U.S. card, which contains a prepared message, or what is known in the greeting card industry as "sentiment." The conditions under which greeting cards are purchased in Europe are also different from those in the United States. Cards are handled frequently by customers, a practice that makes it necessary to package the greeting card in European markets in cellophane. American manufacturers pursuing an adjustment strategy have changed both their product and their marketing communications in response to this set of environmental differences.

STRATEGY 5: PRODUCT INVENTION.   Adaptation and adjustment strategies are effective approaches to international and multinational marketing, but they may not respond to global market opportunities, and they do not respond to the situation in markets where customers do not have the purchasing power to buy the existing or adapted product. The latter situation applies to the less developed parts of the world, which include roughly three-quarters of the world's population.

To reach a global market, it is often necessary to plan and design for the global market. An example is the rechargeable battery market. Around the world, electrical power available to users ranges from 50 to 230 volts and from 50 to 60 cycles. Anton/Bauer, a small Connecticut company, offers a portable power system (batteries and chargers) that will operate anywhere in the world without adjustments by the user. The charger "knows" or reads the type of power that it is plugged into and adjusts accordingly. The Anton/Bauer approach is to design for the global market: they manufacture one product instead of many and thereby keep their costs down. The product's portability is a bonus to customers. This design feature enables Anton/Bauer to manufacture one chassis instead of three, which in turn enables them to achieve greater economies of scale and greater experience. Scale and experience mean lower costs, and lower costs and higher quality are the names of the game in serving global markets. The winners are the companies that can come up with the design that creates the greatest value, which is often defined in the equation value = performance/price ($V = P/P$). The greater the performance, the lower the price, and the greater the value.

There are other global markets where value is not defined in the $V = P/P$ equation but rather value = perception of the customer. An example of this type of value is an expensive perfume or champagne or an inexpensive soft drink such as Coke or Pepsi. Product quality is essential, but it is also necessary to support the product quality with creative value creating advertising and communications. This can be done with a global advertising campaign. Most industry experts believe that

breakthrough prod.

a global appeal and a global campaign are more effective in creating the perception of value than is a series of separate national campaigns.

When potential customers cannot afford a product, the strategy indicated is invention, or the development of an entirely new product designed to satisfy the need or want at a price that is within the reach of the potential customer. This is demanding, but, if product development costs are not excessive, it is potentially a rewarding product strategy for the mass markets in the middle and less developed countries of the world.

Although potential opportunities for the utilization of the invention strategy in international marketing are legion, the number of instances in which companies have responded is small. For example, an estimated 600 million women in the world still scrub their clothes by hand. These women have been served by multinational soap and detergent companies for decades, yet until recently not one of these companies had attempted to develop an inexpensive manual washing device.

How to Choose a Strategy

Most companies seek a product strategy that optimizes company profits over the long term, or more precisely one that maximizes the present value of cash flows associated with business operations. Which strategy for international markets best achieves this goal? There is, unfortunately, no general answer to this question. Rather the answer depends upon the specific product-market-company mix.

Some products demand adaptation, others lend themselves to adaptation, and still others are best left unchanged. The same is true of markets. Some are so closely similar to those in the United States as to require little adaptation, others are moderately different and lend themselves to adaptation, and still others are so different as to require adaptation of the majority of products. Finally, companies differ not only in their manufacturing costs but also in their capability to identify and produce profitable product adaptions.

PRODUCT-MARKET ANALYSIS.   The first step in formulating international product policy is to identify the product-market relationship of each product in question. Who uses the product, when is it used, for what, and how is it used? Does it require power sources, linkage to other systems, maintenance, preparation, style matching, and so on? Examples of almost mandatory adaptation situations are products designed for 60-cycle power going into 50-cycle markets; products calibrated in inches going to metric markets; products that require maintenance going into markets where maintenance standards and practices differ from those of the original design market; and products that might be used under different conditions than those for which they were originally designed. Renault discovered this last factor too late with the ill-fated Dauphine, which acquired a notorious reputation for breakdown frequency in the United States. Renault executives attributed the frequent mechanical failure of the Dauphine to the high-speed turnpike driving and relatively infrequent U.S. maintenance. The driving and maintenance turned out to be critical differences for a product that was designed for the roads of France and the almost daily maintenance that French people lavish upon their cars.

Even more difficult are the product adaptations that are clearly not mandatory but are of critical importance in determining whether the product will appeal to a narrow market segment rather than a broad mass market. The most frequent offender in this category is price. Too often, U.S. companies believe that they have adequately adapted their international product offering when they make mandatory adaptations to the physical features of a product (for example, converting 120 volts to 220 volts) but extend its U.S. price. The effect of such practice in markets where average incomes are lower than those in the United States is to put the U.S. product in a specialty market for the relatively wealthy consumers rather than in the mass market. When price constraints are considered in international marketing, the result can change from margin reduction and feature elimination to an "inventing backwards" approach that starts with price and specifications and works back to a product. Gillette's success in developing markets can be partially attributed to distribution of smaller, cheaper packages abroad than in the United States. These smaller quantities of personal care products are more affordable by Third World consumers.

Even if product-market analysis indicates an adaption opportunity, each company must examine its own product/communication development and manufacturing costs. Clearly any product or communication adaption strategy must survive the test of profit effectiveness. The often-repeated exhortation that in international marketing a company should always adapt its products, advertising, and promotion is clearly superficial because it does not take into account the cost of adjusting or adapting products and communications programs.

Adaptation costs fall under two broad categories: development and production. Development costs will vary depending on the cost effectiveness of product-communications development groups within the company. The range in costs from company to company and product to product is great. Frequently the company with international product development facilities has a strategic cost advantage. The vice president of a leading U.S. machinery company has offered an example of this kind of advantage:

> We have a machinery development group both here in the States and also in Europe. I tried to get our U.S. group to develop a machine for making the elliptical cigars that dominate the European market. At first they said "who would want an elliptical cigar machine?" Then they grudgingly admitted that they could produce such a machine for $500,000. I went to our Italian product development group with the same proposal and they developed the machine I wanted for $50,000. The differences were partly relative wage costs but very importantly they were psychological. The Europeans see elliptical cigars every day, and they do not find the elliptical cigar unusual. Our American engineers were negative on elliptical cigars at the outset and I think this affected their overall response.[16]

---

[16] Interview with a vice president of a large U.S. manufacturing company.

TABLE 12–1 Multinational Product-Communications Mix: Strategic Alternatives

STRATEGY	PRODUCT FUNCTION OR NEED SATISFIED	CONDITIONS OF PRODUCT USE	ABILITY TO BUY PRODUCT	RECOMMENDED PRODUCT STRATEGY	RECOMMENDED COMMUNICATIONS STRATEGY	RELATIVE COST OF ADJUSTMENTS	PRODUCT EXAMPLES
1	Same	Same	Yes	Extension	Extension	1	Soft drinks
2	Different	Same	Yes	Extension	Adaptation	2	Bicycles, motor scooters
3	Same	Different	Yes	Adaptation	Extension	3	Gasoline, detergents
4	Different	Different	Yes	Adaptation	Adaptation	4	Clothing, greeting cards
5	Same	—	No	Invention	Develop new communications	5	Hand-powered washing machine

1 = Full Extension

2 = Product Extension/Communications Adaptation

3 = Product Adaptation/Communications Extension

4 = Full Adaptation

5 = Invention

Analysis of a company's manufacturing costs is essentially a matter of identifying potential opportunity losses. If a company is reaping economies of scale from large-scale production of a single product, then any shift to variations of the single product will raise manufacturing costs. In general, the more decentralized a company's manufacturing setup, the smaller the manufacturing cost of producing different versions of the basic product. In the company with local manufacturing facilities for each international market, the addition to marginal manufacturing cost of producing an adapted product for each market is relatively low.

A more fundamental form of company analysis occurs when a firm is considering whether or not to pursue explicitly a strategy of product adaptation. At this level, analysis must focus not only on the manufacturing cost structure of the firm but also on the basic capability of the firm to identify product adaptation opportunities and to convert these perceptions into profitable products. The ability to identify preferences will depend to an important degree on the creativity of people in the organization and the effectiveness of information systems in the organization. The existence of sales people, for example, who are creative in identifying profitable product adaption opportunities is no assurance that their ideas will be translated into reality by the organization. Information in the form of their ideas and perceptions must move through the organization to those who are involved in the product development decision-making process, and this movement is not automatic.

To sum up, the choice of product and communications strategy in international marketing is a function of three key factors: (1) the product itself defined in terms of the function or need it serves; (2) the market defined in terms of the conditions under which the product is used, the preferences of potential customers, and the ability to buy the products in question; and (3) the costs of adaptation and manufacture to the company considering these product-communications approaches. Only after analysis of the product-market fit and of company capabilities and costs can executives choose the most profitable international strategy. The alternatives are outlined in Table 12–1.

NEW PRODUCTS IN GLOBAL MARKETING

Managers in dynamic economies are realizing that the key to growth and survival is the continuous development and introduction of new products. In spite of the major efforts behind new product management in the United States, where it is a highly developed activity, the failure rate of new products introduced in the United States is extremely high. Estimates of this rate vary from a Booz, Allen & Hamilton estimate of 33 percent to a 90 percent estimate by a New York industrial design firm. Unfortunately, a study of the international new product failure rate does not exist, but the large number of known failures of international new products suggests that the rate is very high.

New products create many strategic advantages for companies. Some benefits to market pioneers are:

1. Long-term marketing mix advantages (relative direct costs held constant)
2. Direct cost savings relative to competition
3. Consumer information advantages from familiarity or experience
4. Early access to best channel/distribution *and* market segment
5. Some trial and error advantages over latecomers. Undoubtably "order of entry is a major determinant of market share . . ."[17]

What is a new product? There are many degrees of newness. A product may be an entirely new invention or innovation, or it may be a slight to major modification of an existing product. Newness may be organizational, which is the case when an existing product is new to a company. Finally, an existing product that is not new to a company may be new to a particular market. Table 12–2 illustrates these four degrees of product newness.

Any of the degrees of newness in Table 12–2 may apply to an international new product, but the most characteristic type of newness is category IV, an existing product already marketed by a company that is introduced for the first time to a particular national market. When this type of new product is introduced, the performance of the product in one or more markets is known, and an important question facing the international marketer is the extent to which the record of the product in existing markets is relevant to the proposed new international market.

Timing is a critical factor in appraising the relevance of previous market experience. Typically, entirely new products are first introduced in high-income markets. The extension of such products to less affluent markets must often wait until the general development of the economies in these markets has progressed enough to create income and sociocultural conditions that create a demand for the product.

 There are degrees of difficulty in new product introduction. The most difficult situation in which a company can become involved occurs when it attempts to market an entirely new product in a market where the company has little experience. This situation should be avoided by all companies. A variation on this situation is assigning a manager without experience in the product or the country to manage a market development program. GE once did this when it assigned a steam turbine generator manager from the United States to manage its computer business in France. The results were less than satisfactory, in part because the manager was hit with a double dose of learning: culture/country/market and product/technology. This is too much for the individual and the organization to cope with, and it should not be attempted.

Another difficult situation occurs when a company takes on an existing product that is new to the company and the market. This also should be avoided. A third degree of difficulty occurs when a company takes a product, which is new to the company, and introduces it into an existing market. An example of this kind of introduction is CPC International's attempt to extend the success of Knorr soup

[17]William T. Robinson and Claes Fornell, "Sources of Market Pioneer Advantages in Consumer Goods Industries," *Journal of Marketing Research,* August 1985, pp. 305–317.

TABLE 12–2   Degrees of Product Newness

	V	IV	III
Degree of newness	New products, new markets	New products, existing markets	Existing products, new to company but not to market

	II	I
	Existing products, not new to company, that is, new to a national market	Existing products, new to company and market

products acquisition from Europe to the United States. The marketing plan for Knorr soups was based on the assumption that there would be a substantial increase in the market share of dry soups at the expense of wet soups. Unfortunately, Corn Products' inexperience in dry soups in the United States led to an underestimation of the difficulty of converting the U.S. wet soup user to the dry soup product.

Identifying New Product Ideas

The starting point for an effective worldwide new product program is an information system that seeks new product ideas from all potentially useful sources and channels these ideas to relevant screening and decision centers within the organization. The major sources of new product ideas are customers, suppliers, competitors, company sales people, distributors and agents, subsidiary executives, headquarter's executives, documentary sources such as information service reports and publications, and, finally, the actual observation of the physical market environment. A good example of the last means of getting information was the observation by a Pan American airline pilot that over 90 percent of Japanese homes used an efficient, safe, and economical kerosene heater. He reasoned that there was a market for such a heater in the United States and quit his job as an airline pilot to form the Kerosun company, which distributes Kerosun heaters in the United States. This very successful company established a market for kerosene heaters in the United States and today has a leading position in a fast-growing kerosene heater market.

The International New Product Department

Davidson and Harrigan found a relationship between organization structure and speed of introduction of new products abroad. In functionally organized firms, 40 percent of the innovations from firms with international divisions went abroad in two years or less as compared with 6 percent of innovations that went abroad in functionally organized firms without international divisions. For firms organized along product lines, the analogous figures are 33 percent and 18 percent, respectively. For globally integrated organizations, 80 percent of all products introduced in such organizations go abroad in two years or less, and *every* innovation in their sample was introduced abroad in five years or less.[18]

One approach to dealing with the problem of the high volume of information flow required to scan adequately new product opportunities and subsequently to screen these opportunities to identify candidates for investigation is a headquarters new product department.[19] In the multiproduct, multicountry company, the enormous number of possibilities for new product extension combined with the massive potential flow of information dealing with new product ideas requires that a full-time organizational unit be established to oversee this whole area. The function of such a department would be fourfold: (1) to ensure that all relevant information sources are continuously tapped for new product ideas; (2) to screen these ideas to identify candidates for investigation; (3) to investigate and analyze selected new product ideas; and (4) to ensure that the organization commits resources to the most likely new product candidate and is continuously involved on a worldwide basis in an orderly program of new product introduction and development.

With the enormous number of possible new products, most companies establish screening grids in order to focus on those ideas that are most appropriate for investigation. The following questions are relevant to this task: (1) How big is the market for this product at various prices? (2) What are the likely competitive moves in response to our activity with this product? (3) Can we market the product through our existing structure? If not, what changes and what costs will be required to make the changes? (4) Given estimates of potential demand for this product at specified prices with estimated levels of competition, can we source the product at a cost that will yield an adequate profit? (5) Does this product fit our strategic development plan? (a) Is the product consistent with our overall goals and objectives? (b) Is the product consistent with our available resources? (c) Is the product consistent with our management structure? (d) Does the product have adequate international potential?

---

[18] William H. Davidson and Richard Harrigan, ''Key Decisions in International Marketing: Introducing New Products Abroad,'' *Columbia Journal of World Business,* Winter 1977, p. 22.

[19] See, for example, ''Introducing a New Product in a Foreign Market,'' Management Monograph No. 33 (New York: Business International 1966), p. 7.

Introducing New Products in National Markets

The major lesson of new product introduction in foreign markets has been that whenever a product interacts with human, mechanical, or chemical elements, there is the potential for a surprising and unexpected incompatibility. Since every product is involved with one or more of these interactions, it is important whenever any significant investment of money or personnel is involved to test a product under actual market conditions before proceeding with full-scale introduction. A test does not necessarily involve a full-scale test-marketing effort. It may simply involve the actual use of the product in the proposed market. A typical example of the kind of problem that can emerge if this is not done is the case of the Singer sewing machine sold in African markets. This machine, which was manufactured in Scotland by Singer, was slightly redesigned by Scottish engineers. A small bolt was relocated at the base of the machine, which had no effect on the functional performance of the machine but did save a few pennies per machine in manufacturing costs. Unfortunately, when the modified machine reached African markets, it was discovered that this small change was disastrous for product sales. The Scottish engineers had not realized that in Africa the Singer sewing machine was transported on the heads of women, and their relocated bolt was placed at the exact point where women were accustomed to setting the machines on their heads!

Comparative Analysis

One of the most useful techniques for aiding the new product decision in international marketing is comparative analysis. Comparative analysis is always possible when an experience record for a product exists in one or more markets at the time of introduction of the product into a new market. The secret to effective comparative analysis is finding market comparability. There are two ways to obtain comparability. One is to find an example of a market that is basically similar in terms of economic and social structural development to that of the target market and to compare the position of the product under study in the two markets. If such comparability exists, for example, in Colombia and Mexico, one can take the experience in one market, Colombia, and make estimates of performance for another market, Mexico, on the experience accumulated in the first market.

Another means of achieving comparability is to displace time periods and find points of comparability at different time periods for markets that are not comparable in the same time period. If, for example, one seeks to apply the experience gained on a product in the United States to a marketing problem in Mexico, it is clear that in most cases U.S. experience will not be applicable to current Mexican circumstances. However, it is possible that U.S. experience in 1948–1958 would be applicable in certain situations to the current marketing situation in Mexico.

If this analogy exists, the time displacement device can be an effective instrument for obtaining comparability. An interesting example of the time displacement device is the history of efforts to market Kleenex facial tissues in Germany. The first effort to market this product in Germany centered on a program that promoted Kleenex as a substitute for handkerchiefs. The result of this effort was unsuccessful because Germany had a four-ply heavy paper towel that was stronger than Kleenex and in the German consumer's judgment a better substitute for a handkerchief. When this effort failed, Kleenex turned to a second advertising problem, which promoted Kleenex as an all-purpose tissue. Again the effort achieved no success. German consumers were confused by the multiple uses identified in this promotion and concluded that Kleenex had no purposes. A third effort promoted the tissue as a woman's facial tissue. This promotion proved to be very successful. Interestingly, the third approach to marketing the Kleenex tissue was identical to the approach utilized to introduce it to the U.S. markets in the 1930s.[20]

SUMMARY

The product is the most important element of a marketing program. At any point in time a company is largely defined by the products it offers. Global marketers face the challenge of formulating a coherent global product strategy for their companies. Product strategy requires an evaluation of the basic needs and conditions of use in the company's existing and proposed markets, together with an evaluation and appraisal of the company's basic strengths and weaknesses. Full recognition must be given to the importance of establishing a viable and economic headquarters organization that can develop leverage (that is, the application of useful experience developed in one market to the formulation of a program for another market and the ability to avoid repeating mistakes within the multinational system). To develop leverage, the organization must have at the supranational level an organization that can accumulate and transfer knowledge concerning successful and unsuccessful practices. Another important dimension of the supranational organization's activity is the application of comparative analysis between comparable national markets to further enhance the effectiveness of marketing planning and marketing programs within the global system.

DISCUSSION QUESTIONS

1. What is the difference between a product and a brand?
2. What are the differences among a local, an international, and a global product or brand? Cite examples.
3. What does the trade cycle model predict will happen to the location of production of a new product? Why does the location of production change at different stages of the product life cycle?

---

[20]This example is taken from Richard Alymer, "Marketing Decisions in the Multinational Firm," unpublished doctoral dissertation, Harvard Business School, 1968.

4. What are the conditions and reasons for extending elements of the marketing program internationally?

5. When should a marketing program be adapted to a target market instead of extended from an existing market?

BIBLIOGRAPHY

Book

LEROY, GEORGES P. *Multinational Product Strategies: A Typology for Analysis of Worldwide Product Innovation Diffusion.* New York: Praeger, 1976.

Articles

ALYMER, RICHARD. "Marketing Decisions in the Multinational Firm." Unpublished doctoral dissertation, Graduate School of Business Administration, Harvard University, 1968.

AYERS, ROBERT U., AND WILBUR A. STEGER. "Rejuvenating the Life Cycle Concept." *The Journal of Business Strategy,* Vol. 6, no. 1 (Summer 1985), pp. 66–76.

BUZZELL, ROBERT D. "Can You Standardize Multinational Marketing?" *Harvard Business Review,* November–December 1968.

DAVIDSON, WILLIAM H., AND RICHARD HARRIGAN. "Key Decisions in International Marketing: Introducing New Products Abroad." *Columbia Journal of World Business,* Winter 1977, pp. 15–23.

HACKETT, DONALD W. "The International Expansion of U.S. Franchise Systems." In *Multinational Product Management,* Warren J. Keegan, and Charles S. Mayer, eds. Chicago: American Marketing Association, 1977, pp. 61–82.

JOHANSSON, JOHNNY K., SUSAN P. DOUGLAS, AND IKUJIRO NONAKA. "Assessing the Impact of Country of Origin on Product Evaluations: A New Methodological Prospective." *Journal of Marketing Research,* Vol. 12 (November 1985), pp. 388–396.

———, AND HANS B. THORELLI. "International Product Positioning." *Journal of International Business Studies,* Fall 1985, pp. 57–74.

KEEGAN, WARREN J. "Multinational Product Planning: Strategic Alternatives." *Journal of Marketing,* January 1969, pp. 58–62.

———, AND CHARLES S. MAYER. *Multinational Product Management.* Chicago: American Marketing Association, 1977.

NAGASHIMA, A. "A Comparative 'Made-In' Product Image Survey Among Japanese Businessmen." *Journal of Marketing,* July 1977, pp. 95–100.

———. "A Comparison of Japanese and U.S. Attitudes Toward Foreign Products." *Journal of Marketing,* January 1970, pp. 68–74.

NARAYANA, CHEM L. "Aggregate Images of American and Japanese Products: Implications on International Marketing," *Columbia Journal of World Business.* Summer 1981, pp. 31–35.

ONKVISIT, SAK, AND JOHN J. SHAW. "An Examination of the International Product Life Cycle and Its Applications within Marketing." *Columbia Journal of World Business,* Fall 1983, pp. 73–79.

PITCHER, A. E. "The Role of Branding in International Advertising." *International Journal of Advertising,* Vol. 4 (1985), pp. 241–246.

RONKAINEN, ILKKA A. "Product-Development Processes in the Multinational Firm." *International Marketing Review,* Winter 1983, pp. 57–64.

VENKATESH, ALLADI, AND DAVID WILEMON. "American and European Product Managers: A Comparison." *Columbia Journal of World Business,* Fall 1980, pp. 67–74.

VERNON, RAYMOND. "Gone are the Cash Cows of Yesteryear," *Harvard Business Review,* November–December, 1980.

———. "International Investment and International Trade in the Product Cycle." *Quarterly Journal of Economics,* May 1966, pp. 190–207.

———. "The Product Cycle Hypothesis in a New International Environment," *Oxford Bulletin,* November, 1980.

WELLS LOUIS T., JR., ED. *The Product Life Cycle and International Trade.* Boston: Division of Research, Graduate School of Business Administration, Harvard University, 1972.

GLOBAL MARKETING STRATEGY:
A CEO'S PERSPECTIVE[1]
An Interview with J. Tylee Wilson, Chairman and Chief Executive Officer RJR Nabisco, Incorporated

WJK[2] As you know, RJR Nabisco, Incorporated[3] was selected by a Delphi panel of experts as one of the top global marketing strategy companies. As the CEO of an advanced practice company, you have a unique perspective on global marketing strategy.

Thank you for agreeing to share your experience and insight in this interview.

TW[4] I'm delighted to have this opportunity to share my views and experience.

WJK Great. My first question is: How do you define global marketing?

TW I could probably look in a strategic plan book and give you the exact words, but without doing that, let's put it this way. Reynolds is a combination of an international marketer and a global marketer. We are an international marketer but we have global brands

---

[1] This case was prepared by the author.

[2] Dr. Warren J. Keegan, Professor of Business and International Marketing, Director, Center for International Business, Pace University, Pace Plaza, New York, New York 10038.

[3] Principal Divisions of RJR Nabisco, Incorporated are: Del Monte Corporation, Heublein Inc., Kentucky Fried Chicken Corporation, Nabisco Brands, Inc., R. J. Reynolds Tobacco Company, R. J. Reynolds Tobacco International, Inc.

[4] J. Tylee Wilson, Chairman and Chief Executive Officer, RJR Nabisco, Incorporated.

and therefore those brands, when marketed anywhere in the world, are marketed the same no matter what the market is, no matter what the continent is. They are fundamentally positioned the same; the underlying strategic principles that guide the management of the business are basically the same. The product can vary to suit local tastes if in fact local tastes are important as it relates to product acceptance. That's particularly true with tobacco products.

In Brazil, you do have to formulate your products differently than you would for a Western European market. So—we are an international marketer with global brands because not all of our brands are marketed the same in every country in the world. But some are.

Let me give you an idea of our global brands. Camel cigarettes is our global brand for tobacco. Smirnoff Vodka is our global brand for spirits. Canada Dry Ginger Ale is our global brand for soft drinks. (That's emerging. That was not true when we acquired it, but it will be true by the end of 1986.) These are the three best examples that I can name.

Del Monte is now in the process of going global with fruit products under the positioning of "The man from Del Monte," and you can understand how this could stand for pears or peaches or pineapples or whatever because the "man from Del Monte" stands for the highest quality, fresh picked, etc., etc.

Nabisco is clearly an international marketer. They do not have one product that can truly be called global. While you'll find Premium saltines and Ritz crackers in most of the major markets, they are not, at this moment in time, in my view, global.

Brands that are driven by image—tobacco, soft drinks, and spirits—are, in my view, better product categories to do global marketing with than others. I can't talk about

the electronics industry because I don't know anything about it.

WJK There are two categories that are high potential for global. High tech and high marketing.

TW As it relates to Camel, we have growth rates on Camel cigarettes—the fastest growing cigarette in the world—ranging from 13 percent to 25 percent depending on the year. Those kinds of growth rates started when we went global. We simply told the managers around the world: This is the brand positioning; this is the copy strategy; these are the executions that you are going to use. You can change the words and build your product to suit the market, but this is the way it is going to be. That's what Marlboro did years ago. There is only one market in the world where Marlboro is not positioned as a cowboy and that's because from a social acceptability position, it doesn't work because the cowboy is downscale (Latin America).

WJK I have seen one of the Camel campaigns that broke through the Japanese barrier.

TW There are no exceptions—even in Brazil. It is a marketing phenomenon. Other brands like Winston, we treat regionally. They position it as best they can. In Spain, where it is the number one brand, it is marketed differently than in Puerto Rico where it is the number one brand as well.

Salem is the product that the international people are viewing as their next global brand. There is a growing interest around the world in menthol. Whether it can be accomplished or not remains to be seen.

WJK What is it that causes you to select a brand to designate as a global brand?

TW It would depend on whether the product is established or not established. Take Smirnoff Vodka—very much established in every market in the world—with the exception of the Scandinavian countries, the number one selling vodka. Vodka does not account for a large percentage of alcoholic beverage consumption outside the United States, but it is generally available in most markets of the world. Smirnoff was marketed country by country, so we had a presence everywhere in the world where vodka could be sold. We decided to experiment and see if through commonality of strategies and all the synergies that come out of that, we can make this into a truly global *power* brand. It was experimental, because we were already in these markets.

In the case of Camel, we were not there. We started in Germany and then went Pan-European, then came to the United States, then to other parts of the world—new markets where Camel did not have a franchise. It evolved through experimentation.

We tried it with Winston under a number of different positionings and it didn't work. Probably because of the heritage of the brands in those particular markets. If you started out with an Americana positioning—"Number One in the U.S.A."—as in Spain, that is what built the brand and they aren't going to buy anything else. It's still got an American positioning, but it cannot be called Number One in the world. Had they started way back when, as Pepsi did, and said this is our positioning for international expansion, it would have happened that way.

With Canada Dry, we simply said, "Look, you are everywhere in the world with this ginger ale; why do we sell it fifteen different ways?"

WJK   That's a big difference—when you are already started and when you are creating a category. Coke is a $7 billion company; McDonald's is a $10 billion company. McDonalds have been around for 15 years as opposed to Coke's 100 years.

TW   Take Kentucky Fried Chicken, which has more stores outside the United States than McDonalds or Burger King. Kentucky Fried Chicken, again, is evolving into a global strategy. The stores and operating procedures are the same all around the world. What they have found out is that in an entry market, you must go with a different strategy than in an established market. In an entry market, it will largely depend upon the existing eating habits of people as it relates to which strategy you choose. Fast food QSR concepts in Europe are very tough to get off the ground and make successful because the culture of those countries is not one that lends itself to "drive through" or "take home." They don't know what take home means. It is very different in the Far East. So Kentucky Fried Chicken is evolving into global marketing, but they are already positioned globally from an operations point of view.

WJK   In a Times' CBS poll today, they asked Japanese people what American products they would want to buy. They did not want very many, but they did list IBM computers and Kentucky Fried Chicken.

TW   There are 512 Kentucky Fried Chicken stores in Japan and we are increasing this to 800.

WK   Do you believe that one of your company's major objectives is to be an effective worldwide marketer by following a global strategy?

TW   On certain products. We are a consumer products and services company so what we do globally will depend upon the product and the ability to make that product global.

WJK   How long have you been following a global strategy?

TW   In tobacco, since 1978; in other brands, more recently.

WJK   Do you have any formal written statements that provide direction in this area?

TW   Yes. The strategic plan documents. There is a worldwide plan for Smirnoff Vodka, but I can only speak globally about one product. How we implement that strategy country by country other than on Smirnoff, may in fact be different.

Let me give you an example of the United States in terms of vodka. The worldwide vodka strategy is to segment the market because there is a difference in vodka. In terms of benefit and price, we have shut everybody else out. We have five brands in vodka in the United States now, and we may soon have a sixth. Our premium brand is Smirnoff and priced under that is Popov and under that is Relska. That gives us a 32 percent share to start with. On top of that, we have super-priced Finlandia, imported because there is a product benefit difference there. Imported vodkas can have additives in them, U.S. can't. So there is a little taste differential. A recently introduced product called Vicenfiord, less than super premium priced, is going in. By 1986, we will have a major viable entry in every segment. We segment the market in consumer terms. That is the worldwide vodka strategy.

WJK   There is only one global brand. The flanking brands could vary in other markets.

TW   It's a worldwide strategy led by one world brand. In tobacco, it's Camel. The global strategy says we are going to segment markets as follows: We are going to have markets established on the basis of priorities and those market priorities will be certain things for mature markets and another set of things in a developing market and another set in an emerging market. You husband your resources in one place and you let it go full speed ahead in another and that can change year to year according to economic plan or political circumstances.

WJK   That is another element that's an essence of a global strategy—the willingness to take resources from one area and put them in another area.

TW   We manage the resources internationally, centrally. We allocate. The Strategic Business Unit heads know how their country will be treated as it relates to priority. Mature, established, developing, emerging. They develop plans along these lines and if we think there is not enough money, we'll allocate resources from somebody else to that area. Same for Del Monte. Nabisco is too new to talk about. The worldwide strategy for Kentucky Fried Chicken clearly is growth. But, again, in 1986, it's going to be on a priority basis, and I would judge the top priority will be the Pacific Basin. Latin America and the United Kingdom will be lower on the list, i.e., limited new investment. It's a brand development index approach. Country by country.

WJK   You've been acting with a global strategy since 1978?

TW   Yes. On certain brands within the portfolio.

WJK   How do you assess market opportunities?

TW   The consumer has a lot to say about that. Assume that consumer research presents you with information that you have an opportunity or you don't. In some countries, you have to overcome other barriers. In the soft drink industry, you have to find the right partner—the bottler. You have to look at the category, consumption, buying habits, product preferences. We have a lot going on corporately in China and we're going to continue with highest priority, because it is the biggest country in the world in terms of people. We think that we have products that will fulfill emerging as well as existing needs. So we have a joint venture in cigarettes, canned foods, and soon, Kentucky Fried Chicken. Nabisco has signed a cookie and cracker arrangement and that's going to be top priority. We make money in China.

WJK   How do you position yourself vis-à-vis global competitors?

TW   We do in tobacco. There is no other

international chicken chain. Vodka—Russian, Polish. Too early for Nabisco. We monitor all of them. In tobacco, Marlboro and Rothman are the competitors. In the soft drink business, it's obvious who's global. We're in a niche business in soft drinks—global is the mixer, the refreshing beverage.

Global brands are managed centrally and executed locally. As for global manufacturing, you have bottling networks in the soft drink business. In the tobacco business, it depends on the country. In some countries we license the brand. In some countries we source from our own plants; our sourcing could be the United States, Latin America, or Asia. It depends on the market and what restrictions are present as relates to local sourcing. You are also dependent on the cost of inside vs. outside sourcing. The EEC is sourced out of four factories in Germany, Belgium and the Canary Islands. There are no exports in Europe that are sourced from both the United States and Germany. Canada is Canada. Asia we source out of the United States, Malaysia, etc.

Access to markets, the political climate and the economic climate are factors. There is a point at which it pays to have a local production facility. Some places you just want to license.

WJK   How would you describe your organizational structure?

TW   It varies from operating company to operating company. There is no organization structure at Reynolds Industries. Each company is a freestanding operation, fully integrated. We do very few things centrally for any operating company. We do manage cash centrally and have the right of override in any area; we do manage legal questions centrally. Otherwise, day-to-day management is done by each operating company which has its own structure. We're kind of a holding company with seven operating companies reporting to the parent. When I speak of struc-

ture, I have to speak of it company by company. It's a little different from a lot of the companies you are talking to.

WJK   Would you call the companies worldwide product divisions?

TW   In the case of tobacco, it's a company called Reynolds Tobacco International. Reporting into headquarters are nine strategic business units, two of which are single countries—Germany and Canada. The rest of which are regional vice presidents with multicountry responsibility and they report into headquarters. If the country has a factory in it, the regional vice president is responsible for that country. We don't run the factories out of here.

Del Monte has an international division. That is organized into the classic four area concept—Asia, Canada, Latin America, and Europe/Africa/Middle East.

Heublein has a head of international, but because all of the markets outside the United States are licensed markets that require very little staffing—a couple of guys in Asia, a couple of guys in London who look after Europe/Africa/Middle East, so there is a very, very small staff and no infrastructure. Corporate does all the accounting. The licensees manufacture the product and execute the marketing, but we decide what the marketing will be. We control the product, the marketing, the investment. The same is true for cigarettes. Even in Yugoslavia we control the product, the advertising, the investment. But we don't make much money.

Kentucky Fried Chicken has an international division headquartered in Louisville. It has a head, an accounting department—all the traditional things. And it, too, has areas.

Nabisco is the largest food company in Canada, so it is a free-standing company called Nabisco, Ltd. and it reports directly to headquarters. Nabisco International has a couple of divisions—the United Kingdom,

Europe/Africa/Middle East, South America, and the Far East—all as direct reports. Classic. It has a small staff of 57 people at International Headquarters. International Headquarters in tobacco has about 75 people. You might wonder with all this staff in international whether we ought to have an R. J. Reynolds International some day. That is something we want to look at.

WJK   What would cause you to have such an operation?

TW   Money. Synergy. Each SBU has its own international structure. There is an amount of duplication of staffing. Should we have the operating companies with their own international divisions plus the freestanding Tobacco International or should we have an R. J. Reynolds International responsible for all product lines? It has to be looked at. Of course Nabisco has motivated all of this for us. It weren't for Nabisco, we would have left it the way it was.

WJK   What organizational form best describes your present structure? International Division, Area Organization, Worldwide Product, Matrix/Grid, or Other?

TW   We're a very complex company. We are not a one product company. We're "other."

WJK   Based on your experience, what do you feel are the most critical issues which need to be resolved to make a global marketing strategy highly effective?

TW   Again, we are talking about a global marketing strategy for certain products. In order to make that effective, you have to have exceptionally good relationships and good will between your senior management at headquarters level and your field executive. The biggest problem in the international marketplace in consumer products is here. We were fortunate enough to have a spirit of cooperation on one hand, and also fortunate enough to have a success model that we couldn't deny

at least trying. We used Germany and then went Pan-American with Camel.

When I came into the picture in the U.S. tobacco business, I simply said, "I'm sorry, but you have to research this. If it proves that it is not viable in the United States, I will accept that, but you have to research it."

WJK   In other words, you can't do it from theory, you really have to do it case by case.

TW   What happens today in Reynolds opposed to what happened 10 years ago is if the United States is going with a new product, every step of the way international is involved so they can do some concurrent research; clearly, we wrap up the trademarks. Fifteen years ago we didn't do that, so we can sell more internationally. We cannot sell Salem in many markets, but we have the Ritz name sewed up in every country in the world where we can get in. What was researched in the United States has been researched in many other markets outside the United States, and when it was successful in the United States on a national basis, they were ready to roll. Could Ritz be a global brand? Yes. But maybe it won't work in a lot of countries. We're ready to find out. That's the difference.

WJK   As a precondition, exceptional relationships and good will. If you don't have that NIH (Not Invented Here) will take over.

TW   Senior management must have perspective in terms of global perspective. The problem with too many companies in the United States is that their international divisions are treated as secondary sources of opportunity and therefore they often end up with less than the best people. You need to put your best talent there. It's a very complex world out there. More than half of the people who serve in a senior capacity in the line in this company have had international experience. It's not a precondition to be promoted, but we sure like it when someone has had the experience.

WJK The next question is, "If you were advising someone as to the *one most critical factor* for success as a marketer following a global strategy, what would that factor be?"

TW In the world of consumer package goods, you have to have advertising agency partners in your marketing strategy. So a critical factor is that your partners in this endeavor must think globally as well. And that is why, as it relates to international brand assignments, agencies which do not have the capacity to implement global campaigns, do not get our business. Advertising agencies with no international capability are not in a position to think globally. We have six major advertising agencies working with Reynolds (excluding Nabisco) who control about 96 percent of our billings worldwide. Four of those agencies have major international presence. Also, if you develop a global strategy, you have to be willing to execute it, invest in it and adjust it.

WJK I see. You must have vision and commitment, but you can't be inflexible and rigid about it. Are products developed with any specific world view?

TW Every product in the new brand context does not necessarily have to be developed for global purposes. It is good to begin there, but it doesn't mean that you mandate what is going to be global or not global. Let me see if I can give you an example of that. We call it the savings segment in the cigarette industry. In the U.S., the brands are Century and Doral—two entirely different propositions. Doral is priced at generic price levels and Century is priced at regular levels, but its value for the money is five extra cigarettes.

There is a worldwide strategy in place for value brands in every market, but we've not implemented it in every market because we would only implement it if we saw a need to become defensive. If the market is going to move toward price positioning, we must

be ready. Everybody has a brand ready on the shelf, but it could be very, very different country to country. The name could be different and the proposition could be different.

WJK In other words, there's a world wide strategy on cigarette segments.

TW You start out saying, can I do this globally? There is a strategy for value, menthol, etc., although it might be a different brand in a different location. Some things that sell in the United States do not work globally. Like Vantage cigarettes.

In my business, I can establish packaging, but pricing and product is going to have to be relevant to the market—at least in tobacco.

WJK Out of your total existing products and brands, what percentage would you say are global, multinational, and local?

TW We do business in 160 countries from quick service restaurants to canned foods, fresh fruit, spirits, to cookies and crackers. I'd have to put a team of researchers on to answer that question. A large percentage of our unit volume growth (Ex-Nabisco) is being fueled by global brands. That is true in spirits, tobacco, and Del Monte. Of course, Kentucky Fried Chicken is something on its own, but it's true of Canada Dry. The international growth is coming out of Ginger Ale.

WJK Is there an effort to increase the emphasis on any of the categories of global, multinational, or local or are they going to remain in the same relationship?

TW The emphasis will continue on global, but that's not to obviate the opportunity for international or even local brands.

Let me tell you about our three market priorities. This is how they break down:

Established markets: Priority (1) Where we have major presences. Priority (2) Markets like Belgium, Holland, Ecuador, Hong Kong—we're going to continue to invest to maintain market share, but if an opportunity came up in Canada, it would get priority over Holland. Priority (3) Scandinavia, Portugal, etc. Each of these has a guideline for the investment that has to be made.

Development Markets: These are the markets where you are going to put in investment capital. That does not necessarily mean in assets; it may mean manpower, marketing, etc. Priority (1) This is where we are just going to pour it to them (France, Greece, Italy, Japan, China). Priority (2) We are going to manage them for the purpose intended (Iraq, Turkey, The U.K. and the Philippines).

Access Markets: Places where you aim, generally because of government—where you want to be (Korea, Taiwan).

WJK Which statement comes closest to the company's policy on new product development?

A. New products are developed for the U.S. market and the successful products might later be sold internationally.

B. New products are developed both in the United States and by our foreign subsidiaries to be marketed in their own home country. If successful, these products might be later expanded internationally.

C. New products are developed up front as "global" so that global considerations are built into the brand from the beginning. New products would usually be tested and introduced in more than one country from the start. The new product would not be introduced unless it appeared to have viable sales potential *globally*.

TW I would choose the second one.

WJK Do you have a worldwide advertising policy for global brands?

TW Yes.

WJK For a global brand, how do you determine advertising objectives, strategy, and specific appeals in a given country?

TW It is determined in conjunction with worldwide local management. Take Camel and

Smirnoff. Once a year, there is a worldwide marketing seminar on Camel and Smirnoff attended by all the principal players from around the world dealing with those brands to show them where we are going, if we have new executions, a new pool of ads, etc. Everybody has a chance to participate.

WJK How do you define a global advertising campaign?

TW One in which the imagery and the fundamental consumer benefit is expressed the same.

WJK How many global campaigns have been created?

TW Two. With two more coming right behind it. Camel and Smirnoff were the first two; Del Monte will be next and we are working on one for Canada Dry.

WJK Has global advertising worked for R. J. Reynolds? How do you measure its success?

TW It has worked for us. Agencies play a major role because they are considered partners. We use a lot of agencies, but four have the bulk of our billings—J. Walter Thompson, Young & Rubicam, McCann Erickson, and one other. We are consolidating and it has paid off. The final decision for agencies is made here for everything having to do with advertising strategy. The operating company cannot make this decision. We monitor and guide the market research from headquarters for each operating company, but research is done locally by those accountable.

WJK Has there been any attempt to standardize research techniques and make certain the data is comparable country by country?

TW Yes. There has been an attempt to standardize research techniques country by country.

WJK Does your company use outside research services that specialize in international research? Do you use different services in each country or is there an attempt to consolidate this function?

TW   International research is contracted for locally. It's very, very important when you have brand franchises that, on the basis of consumer research, you can market the brand comparably around the world. I think it has a future, and I think that more and more companies are going to be doing it because it's more efficient. If you want to consider the world as a truly global village, and if you're dealing with categories and products within those categories that are part of lifestyles in most countries of the world, it is far better for your brand to be positioned and advertised and presented the same everywhere in the world. It's more effective, more efficient, and if you consider that a large percentage of this world's population moves around a lot and you're presenting a product in terms of its advertising and its package the same in every part of the world, people are going to have confidence in it and buy it there as well. This is particularly true of pleasure products and we're in the pleasure product business. Where you have universal distribution and universal acceptance of the pleasure, I would like to see our products in every corner of the world.

WJK   Years ago, people used to resist this. They said efficiency isn't important, what is important is adapting in each market.

TW   You can't believe the money that is saved by a global advertising campaign as opposed to having the same campaign developed and managed locally in a hundred different countries. Savings on production costs are 10 percent of the advertising budget. Our advertising budget is a billion dollars. Also, the client is in a far better position to negotiate fees with his agency because the agency is only doing it one time as opposed to 15 percent commission in every country.

There is a lot of synergy that comes from this as well.

WJK   This has been an exceptional interview, Tylee. You have crystallized and focused some of the essential elements of what it takes to really succeed with a global marketing strategy. I'm really impressed with your vision. Thank you again for sharing your experience and insight.

TW   I'm not suggesting that every consumer package good has a global possibility. I'm sure that many of the well known brands couldn't. We found that the name Del Monte was recognized throughout the world for standing for highest possible quality. You can't throw your money behind one product and expect that to have a synergistic effect down the line on everything else. In developing the global strategy for Del Monte, which currently is just in the international arena, (it hasn't hit the United States yet—the U.S. positioning for Del Monte is "good for your body"), the positioning is "The Man From Del Monte." What we have come up with instead of a brand per se is an umbrella for a line of products under the same name. You can throw in any product you want. It's taken us three years to develop this idea.

WJK   In Japan, where U.S. companies are not performing very well in terms of getting their fair share, are you satisfied with the availability of market to Reynolds?

TW   No. We have made progress, but the issue in Japan is access to the market. We have presence in Japan, but not the kind of access we want. It is legal for imported cigarettes to be sold in 250,000 outlets in Japan. We have about 15,000. We push the Japanese government, the Japanese monopoly, the U.S. government, and they say, "Well, it's all in the system . . ." Tobacco in Japan is a state-run business. It's run by the government. The government is obligated to buy every pound of leaf tobacco that the Japanese farmer makes. It is very poor quality, but the law says that they have to buy it all. They do not want to give us a big piece of the market. We lobby all the time and we're making a little progress. We have good joint venture partners over there to help us on that side—in spirits, cigarettes and food. We also have 500 Kentucky Fried Chicken stores, and that's a joint venture, too. But that business was established ten years ago and it wasn't a takeaway. But these other businesses are take aways from local Japanese industry.

WJK   Do you have a written statement concerning global brands?

TW   Yes. This is the essence of it.

Our key objective is achievement of long term business growth. The objective is to concentrate limited resources on priority markets and brands, recognizing new growth opportunities and insuring a superior competitive focus.

Our policy is to:

1. Manage on a global priority of markets basis, concentrating resources on high priority markets.

2. Manage individual markets according to local brand priorities concentrating resources against one or two brands.

3. Continue to develop Camel as a global power brand while recognizing the importance of Winston.

4. Optimize Winston's volume and earnings in line with business potential.

5. Monitor competitive strategies and actions to insure that our programs are competitively superior.

Development opportunity strategies for maximizing:

1. In attractive markets where we have a small share and momentum for extraordinary growth, invest significantly ahead of current volume and share.

2. In large established markets where we have a substantial business base and a sound new brand concept capable of breakthrough growth, invest in new brands.

3. In opportunistic markets where we have no current earnings base, build volume aggressively without significant out of pocket costs.

4. Lead the industry in removing barriers to attractive closed markets.

Those are our marching orders.

WJK   Thank you, Tylee, for sharing your wisdom and experience on this vital topic.

_13_

PRICING DECISIONS

The real price of everything is the toil and trouble of acquiring it.

Adam Smith, Wealth of Nations, *1776*

INTRODUCTION

In any single market three basic factors determine the boundaries of the pricing decision. The *price floor,* or minimum price, is bounded by product cost. The *price ceiling,* or maximum price, is bounded by competitive prices for comparable products and the ability of customers to pay. Between the floor and ceiling for every product there is an *optimum price,* which is a function of the demand for the product and the cost of supplying the product. The global executive must develop a pricing system and pricing policies that address these fundamental factors in each of the national markets in which his or her company operates in a world of fluctuating exchange rates which may bear only limited relationship to underlying costs. If exchange rates were directly linked to domestic prices as is posited in the purchasing power parity (PPP) theory outlined in Chapter 7, fluctuating exchange rates would not present serious problems for the global marketer. A rise or decline in the home country currency would be offset by an opposite rise or decline in domestic price levels.

For example, if U.S. prices rose 10 percent in a year as compared to nil for the U.S. trading partners, according to PPP the U.S. dollar would decline 10 percent in foreign exchange markets to offset the rise in domestic prices. A widget that cost $1.00 would increase to $1.10. Assume that the DM/U.S.$ exchange rate starts at

DM 2.00 = U.S.$ 1.00. At this exchange rate, the widget would cost DM 2.00. If the U.S. export price was raised to $1.10, this would increase the DM price at the old exchange rate to DM 2.2 ($US 1.10 × DM 2.00 = DM 2.2). However, according to PPP, the exchange rate under the above assumptions would adjust to DM 1.8181 = $US 1.00 (DM 2 ÷ 1.1 = 1.8181) and at this new exchange rate the U.S. price of $1.10 widget remains DM 2.00 (US$ 1.10 × DM 1.8181 = DM 2.00).

In the real world, exchange rates do not move in lock step with inflation so that global marketers are faced with difficult decisions about how to deal with exchange rate windfalls and exchange rate adversity.

The system must also be consistent with a number of uniquely global constraints. In addition to the diversity of national markets in all three basic dimensions—cost, competition, and demand—the international executive is also confronted by conflicting governmental tax policies and claims as well as governmental controls such as dumping legislation, resale price maintenance legislation, price ceilings, and general review of price levels. Other factors affecting global pricing decisions are the often surprisingly high international transportation costs, middlemen in elongated international channels of distribution, and global accounts demanding equal price treatment regardless of location.

Pricing decisions have a major impact on a number of societal groups or stakeholders: consumers, customers, employees, stockholders, the public interest, and, of course, the competition. These interest groups are affected by pricing decisions, which in turn constrain the international executive. For example, IBM, in response to U.S. antitrust pressure, offered its equipment on a purchase as well as a lease basis. In the process of developing the purchase price schedule, the company raised its lease prices. The British government calculated that this price increase would cost Britain several million dollars per annum and that this cost exceeded the government's price guidelines. The company was forced to roll back its price increase for the U.K. market, but it was successful in obtaining the increase in most other markets.

A widespread effect of international business is to lower prices. Indeed, one of the major arguments favoring international business is the favorable impact of foreign competition upon national price levels and upon a country's rate of inflation. The reason for this effect will be discussed later in this chapter.

Within the corporation there are many interest groups and frequently conflicting price objectives. The divisional vice president is concerned about profitability at the divisional level. Regional executives are concerned about profitability at the regional level, and country managers are concerned about profitability at the country level. The direction of international marketing seeks competitive prices in world markets. The controller and financial vice president are concerned about profits. The manufacturing vice president seeks long runs for maximum manufacturing efficiency. The tax manager is concerned about compliance with government transfer pricing legislation. And company counsel is concerned about the antitrust implications of international pricing practices.

With such a large number of divergent and often conflicting interests combined with the limitations of our existing measures of demand, it is premature to expect that we should be able to determine "optimal" prices in international marketing. A more feasible objective for the international executive is to formulate international pricing strategy and policy that will contribute rather than detract from company sales and profit objectives worldwide. To manage the pricing function in international marketing effectively, the international executive needs a knowledge of the factors affecting the pricing decision and a framework for approaching the pricing decision. The purpose of this chapter is to provide the knowledge and the framework required.

EXPORT PRICING

Cost-Plus Pricing

Cost-plus pricing is one of the most frequently used export pricing policies, especially by companies that are just getting started in global marketing. There are two cost-plus pricing methods: The older is the historical accounting cost method which defines cost as the sum of all direct and indirect manufacturing and overhead costs. A more recent method is the so-called *estimated future cost method*.

Cost-plus pricing based upon *historical* accounting costs has a number of serious disadvantages. First it completely ignores demand and competitive conditions in target markets. Because it ignores these factors, historical accounting cost-plus prices will always be either too high or too low in the light of market and competitive conditions. If historical accounting cost-plus prices are right, it is only by chance. Nothing in the historical accounting cost-plus formula directly addresses the competitive and the customer value issues that must be considered in a rational pricing strategy. The only thing that can be said in favor of this method is that it is cheap, easy, and convenient to use (if the accounting costs are already available).

The alternative to the historical cost-plus formula method is the view that pricing is a major strategic variable that can help achieve marketing and business objectives. In this approach, the relevant price is not historical accounting costs, but, rather, expected future costs at the volumes that are forecast. Estimated costs are based upon assumptions about production volume. Since production volume will depend upon sales volume, and sales volume will depend upon prices, pricing decisions will be a factor determining costs.

For example, when Sony developed the digital tape unit, the cost for the unit at initial sales volumes was over $600. As this was a "no go" in the company's target markets, Mr. Morita instructed management to price the unit in the $200-range so the company would reach the target markets that it wanted to serve. The volume in these markets would enable the company to get its costs down. In this example, historical costs were ignored and the relevant cost for the pricing decision was the expected cost.

Costs are important, but an effective export pricing strategy must recognize competitive prices as a second constraint on the pricing decision. Competitive prices can be determined only by examining the price levels of competitive and substitute products in the target market locations. Once these price levels have been established, the base price, or price that the buyer will pay for the product, can be determined. Three steps are involved in determining a base price.

1. Estimate the relevant demand schedules (quantities that would be purchased at various prices) over the planning period.
2. Estimate incremental and full manufacturing and marketing costs to achieve projected sales volumes.
3. Select the price that offers the highest profit contribution, that is, sales revenue net of all costs.

The final determination of a base price for a product can be made only after other elements of the marketing mix have been established. These include the distribution strategy and product strategy. The nature and length of channels utilized in the marketing program will affect margins, thus the final price of the product, and product adaptation costs will affect the cost base for a marketing program.

The three steps outlined may sound simple, but they are in fact so difficult that it is not really possible to reach definitive and precise answers to the questions posed. Estimating demand, for example, must take into account product appeal if a product is differentiated from competitive products. Product appeal can be measured in experimental settings and in test markets, but these measures are costly and are subject to error. In many export markets, the size of the potential market is often too small to justify even minimum expenditures on formal market research involving testing and data collection from potential consumers or customers. Under these circumstances, potential demand estimates must be based upon judgmental estimates of company and trade executives. One way of improving the potential demand estimates, if a company has experience with a product in markets, is to extrapolate potential demand for target markets from actual sales in markets judged to be similar to target markets in terms of the basic factors affecting demand.

Estimates of full manufacturing costs are normally available in any company that has installed a cost accounting system. Incremental costs, however, are normally not available in standard management reports. To identify incremental costs, it is necessary to separate fixed and variable costs. If production can be expanded without expanding fixed costs, the only additional cost of obtaining additional output is variable cost.

Pricing Objectives

Clearly, selection of the profit-maximizing price depends upon the time period for which the profit estimates are based. If the time horizon extends beyond the short term, then the pricing decision must be based upon all costs that will be incurred over the planning period. The pricing decision must also recognize the competitive and governmental responses that might be encountered. In practice, the complexity of these variables leads companies to pursue secondary objectives rather than the ultimate optimum profit-maximization goal. Three of the most frequently encountered objectives are market penetration, market skimming, and market holding.

PENETRATION PRICING.   Penetration pricing is the use of low prices to stimulate market growth and obtain share of market from competitors. Penetration pricing uses price as a competitive weapon to gain market position. The most frequent practitioners of this type of pricing in international marketing today are the Japanese, Koreans, and Taiwanese, who have used penetration pricing all over the world to move from minor to major position in a host of markets. An example of penetration pricing was the Japanese entry into the 4K RAM (random access memory) market in the United States. Before entry by three Japanese companies, American suppliers were selling this device at an average price of $18.00 to $20.00. Three Japanese companies entered the market with an identical product in almost all respects (it even had the same "pin-out" or interface configuration as the American product) at a price of $10.00. The price shocked the American producers because this device was being sold on allocation (i.e., demand exceeds production capacity). The goal of this kind of pricing is aggressive penetration of the market.

MARKET SKIMMING.   The market skimming pricing strategy is a deliberate attempt to reach a segment of the market that is willing to pay a premium price for a product because the product has high value to them. This pricing strategy is often used when production capacity is limited. By setting a deliberately high price, demand is limited to those who are willing and able to pay the price. One goal of this pricing strategy is to maximize revenue on limited volume and to match demand to available supply. Another goal of market skimming pricing is to cue customers to perceive high product value. When this is done, the price is part of the total product positioning strategy.

MARKET HOLDING.   Market holding is a pricing strategy of pricing to hold a company's share of market. This strategy is frequently adopted by companies that have a market position they want to maintain. Many American companies used this strategy in the 1980s when the dollar appreciated against all other currencies. If American companies continued to translate U.S. prices into foreign currencies, they would have priced themselves out of many target markets. To avoid this, companies set prices based not on the U.S. price translated at the current exchange rate, but rather on the competitive situation in each market and the ability of the market to pay.

Price Escalation

Price escalation is the frequently remarkable increase in a foreign-sourced product's price as transportation, duty, and distributor margins are added to the product's former factory price. Table 13–1 is a typical example of the kind of price escalation that can occur. The reader will note that a shipment, in this case ordinary household chemicals such as insecticides and cleaners, that cost $10,090 in Kansas City ends up having a total retail price of $21,390 in Encarnación, Paraguay. This is double the F.O.B. (free on board, or delivered to the ship, aircraft, or truck at a specific location) Kansas City price.

Let us examine this shipment to see what happened. First, there is the total shipping charge of $2,862, which is 28 percent of the F.O.B. Kansas City price. The principal component of this shipping charge is the $1,897 freight charge for ocean freight from New Orleans to Buenos Aires, Argentina, and a river boat from Buenos Aires to Encarnación. In addition there is a $434 "port charge" and an insurance charge of $383, which is necessitated by the heavy pilferage and breakage that occurs in ocean shipping. Many observers feel that the freight and other charges involved in ocean shipments are completely out of line with what charges might be if the whole ocean freight industry were organized more efficiently. At this point, the

TABLE 13–1 Price Escalation in International Marketing: A Shipment of 1,908 Cases of Assorted Household Chemicals (weight 35,000 lb., 40 ft)*

ITEM			AS A PERCENTAGE OF F.O.B. PRICE
F.O.B. Kansas City		$10,090	100%
Freight to New Orleans	$ 110		
Freight to Encarnación, Paraguay	1,897		
Counselor Invoices	21		
Port toulaye	6		
Forwarding fee	8		
Insurance ($19,000 value)	383		
Port charge	434		
Documentation	3		
Total shipping charges		2,862	28
C.I.F. value		$12,952	
Duty (20% on C.I.F. value)		2,590	26
Distributor markup (10%)		1,553	15
Dealer markup (25%)		4,295	43
Total retail price		$21,390	212%

*This shipment was sent by truck to New Orleans, by ocean freighter to Buenos Aires, Argentina, and by river steamer to Encarnación, Paraguay. Total transit time for Kansas City to distributor is 6 to 10 weeks.

international marketer can only appraise the extent and nature of these charges and either factor them into the pricing equation or seek alternative methods of transportation, such as air freight. For the future, the modernization of the ocean freight industry and the introduction of jumbo jets, together with developments in the containerization and materials-handling areas, should substantially reduce existing transportation charges. This will make it possible to consider a number of heretofore excluded sourcing alternatives in international marketing.

The duty on the household chemical shipment in Table 13–1 is 20 percent of the C.I.F. (cost + insurance + freight) value ($2,590), which is 26 percent of the F.O.B. Kansas City price, because the duty is levied not only on the F.O.B. price but on the insurance and freight charges as well. A distributor markup of 10 percent ($1,553) is 15 percent of the F.O.B. Kansas City price, again because it is a markup not only on the F.O.B. price but on freight and duty as well. Finally, a dealer markup of 25 percent, which is quite low in percentage terms, adds up to $4,295, or 43 percent of the F.O.B. Kansas City price, again because it is added on to everything else. The net effect of this add-on accumulating process is a total retail price in Paraguay of $21,390, or 212 percent of the F.O.B. Kansas City price. This is price escalation.

This example is by no means an extreme case. Indeed, if longer distribution channels or channels that required a higher operating margin were utilized, and they typically are in export marketing, the markups in Paraguay could easily exceed 50 percent of the C.I.F. value.

The international marketer has two options in addressing the problem of price escalation. One option is to search the international manufacturing system of the company to identify a potential lower-cost source of merchandise. This source could include local manufacture but, alternatively, could involve sourcing at other points in the world to take advantage of lower freight and duty charges. The second weapon available is a thorough audit of the distribution structure in the target markets. In some cases distribution channels include intermediaries who perform no real function or make no contribution to the total marketing program and who therefore unnecessarily add to the price of the product in the marketplace. When this situation exists, a rationalization of the distribution structure by selecting new intermediaries, assigning new responsibilities to old intermediaries, or by establishing direct marketing operations can substantially reduce the total markups required to accomplish distribution programs in the target market.

International Dumping Regulations

Each country has its own policies and procedures for protecting national companies from dumping. The U.S. antidumping act of 1921, which is enforced by the U.S. Treasury, did not define dumping specifically but instead referred to unfair competition. However, the Congress has defined *dumping* as "unfair trade practices—unfair price cutting having for its objective the injury, destruction, or prevention of the establishment of American industry." Under this definition, dumping in the United States embraces every form of price differential resulting from sales of imports on the U.S. market at prices either below those of comparable domestic goods or below those prevailing in the producing country.[1] The General Agreement on Tariffs and Trade (GATT), on the other hand, defines *dumping* as the difference between the normal domestic price and the price at which a product leaves the exporting country. The GATT definition is more constrained than the U.S. definition because it refers only to prices that differ from those in the producing country.

Dumping legislation may be either a legitimate device to protect local enterprise from predatory pricing practices by foreign companies or a device for limiting foreign competition in a market. The rationale for dumping legislation is that "dumping" is harmful to the orderly development of enterprise within an economy. Few economists would object to long-run or continuous dumping. If this were done, it would be an opportunity for a country to take advantage of a low-cost source of a particular good and to specialize in other areas. However, continuous dumping only rarely occurs (the sale of agricultural products at international prices with farmers receiving subsidized higher prices is an example of continuous "dumping"). The common type of dumping practiced by companies is a sporadic variety that is unpredictable and does not provide a reliable basis for national economic planning but may result in injury and harm to domestic enterprise.

Several different approaches to solutions of the dumping issue have been taken. When, for example, the Japanese share of the color T.V. market in the United States jumped from 11 percent to 29 percent in the first six months of 1976, U.S. manufacturers filed complaints with the International Trade Commission (formerly the Tariff Commission) and brought suit against the Japanese companies for dumping and illegal price fixing. U.S. labor unions formed committees to petition the commission for T.V. tariffs and quotas.

In 1976 the U.S. Treasury Department, after an investigation of foreign car pricing practices, concluded that 23 out of 28 foreign automakers had been dumping cars in the United States and demanded an increase in prices by 1977. Volkswagen, for example, was forced to raise its 1977 car prices an average of 2.5 percent. In a similar case that same year, the International Trade Commission ruled that Japanese steelmakers were engaged in unfair competition, ordered them to stop "predatory" pricing of their estimated $20 million steel exports to the United States, and forced the steel companies to provide detailed production and pricing figures. Citing the 1974 Trade Act provision that calls for the establishment of reference prices below which importers will be charged with dumping, the Treasury Department then set minimum steel import price levels.

[1] *Columbia Law Review*, February 1965, pp. 185–231.

For a positive finding of dumping to occur in the United States, both price discrimination and injury must be present. The existence of either one without the other is an insufficient condition to constitute dumping. Companies that are concerned with running afoul of antidumping legislation have developed a number of approaches for avoiding the dumping laws. One approach is to differentiate the product sold from that in the home market. An example of this is an auto accessory that one company packaged with a wrench and an instruction book, changing the "accessory" in the process to a "tool." The tariff rate in the foreign market happened to be lower on tools, and the company also acquired immunity from antidumping laws because the package was not comparable to competing goods in the target market. Another approach is to make nonprice competitive adjustments in arrangements with affiliates and distributors. For example, credit can be extended and, to a point, have the same effect as a price reduction.

Devaluation and Revaluation

Devaluation is the reduction and *revaluation* an increase in the value of one currency vis-à-vis other currencies. Under the floating exchange rate system, devaluation and revaluation take place when currency values adjust in the foreign exchange markets in response to supply and demand pressure.

If a devaluing country's domestic prices were unaffected by a currency devaluation, the prices of all goods to the foreigner would decline by the amount of the devaluation. In practice the rise in the cost of imported goods as a result of devaluation raises costs and prices in the devaluing country, so that part of the price reduction resulting from a devaluation is taken up by devaluation-induced cost increases. Any price adjustments subsequent to devaluation should anticipate this source of price inflation, which is related to the size of the import component of a country's total national product.

In practice the business executive exporting or sourcing from a country that has devalued its currency must evaluate his basic marketing and competitive position. If the competitive position is strong and demand is price inelastic, prices can be maintained in the target market. If this is not the case, it may be necessary to reduce prices in target markets.

Revaluation is an increase in the value of a currency vis-à-vis other currencies. The effect of revaluation on an exporter or a marketer sourcing in a revaluing country is the opposite of devaluation. If export prices are maintained in local currency, the price of goods in foreign currencies will go up by the amount of revaluation. The international marketer must decide whether to (1) pass the price increase on to its customers, (2) absorb the price increase and reduce operating or marketing expenses in an effort to maintain profit levels, or (3) absorb the price increase by reducing the price in the home country currently.

When the underlying reason for a country's surplus has been a more attractive national product, a slight revaluation has little effect upon export performance. In many cases price increases are passed on to foreign customers by individual firms with no significant effect upon volume. In more competitive market situations, companies in the revaluing country will often absorb the price increase by maintaining foreign market prices at pre-revaluation levels.

PRICING IN AN INFLATIONARY ENVIRONMENT

Inflation, or a persistent upward change in price levels, is a worldwide phenomenon. Thus the existence of inflation is not a unique variable facing the international marketer. The unique international aspects of inflation are the differential rates of inflation that are encountered in the world today.

Obviously, inflation requires periodic price adjustments. These adjustments are necessitated by rising costs that must be covered by increased selling prices. An essential requirement of pricing in an inflationary environment is the maintenance of operating profit margins. Regardless of cost accounting practices, if a company maintains its margins, it has effectively protected itself from the effects of inflation. It is not within the scope of this text to examine the many issues and conventions employed in accounting to deal with price adjustments. However, it is worth noting that the traditional FIFO (first-in, first-out) costing method is hardly appropriate for an inflationary situation. A more appropriate accounting practice under conditions of rising prices is the LIFO (last-in, first-out) method, which takes the most recent raw material acquisition price and uses it as the basis for costing the finished product. For very rapidly inflating environments, perhaps the most appropriate costing method is NIFO (next-in, first-out). This method involves an estimate of the price that will be paid for raw and component materials and the use of these prices to arrive at a costing of final product or finished product.

Regardless of the accounting methods used, an essential requirement under inflationary conditions of any costing system is that it maintain gross and operating profit margins. Managerial actions can maintain these margins subject to the following constraints.

Government Controls

If government action limits the freedom of management to adjust prices, the maintenance of margins is definitely compromised. Under certain conditions, government action is a real threat to the profitability of a subsidiary operation. A country that is undergoing severe financial difficulties and is in the midst of a financial crisis (for example, a foreign exchange shortage caused in part by runaway inflation) is under pressure to take some type of action. In some cases, governments, rather than getting at the underlying causes of inflation and foreign exchange shortages, will take expedient steps, such as the wholesale use of price controls or, more likely, selective use of price controls. When selective controls are imposed, foreign companies are more vulnerable to control than is a local enterprise, particularly if the former lack the political influence over government decision making possessed by local managers.

Competitive Behavior

A second constraint on the flexibility of management to maintain its gross and operating profit margins is the behavior of competition. If competition, both local and international, does not adjust its prices in response to rising costs, a management with a sophisticated awareness of the effect of rising costs on its operating margins will be severely constrained in its ability to reflect that awareness in price adjustments. Clearly, as in all pricing situations, decisions are bounded not only by cost but also by demand and competitive action.

Market Demand

A final constraint on the ability of a manufacturer to adjust prices is the market itself. A company should be alert to the effect of price adjustments upon demand for its products. The objective of a business is not merely to maintain any specific gross or operating margin but to survive and operate as profitably as possible. In some situations, a reduction in margins can lead to more profitable results than the maintenance of margins. Management should be alert to this possibility.

TRANSFER PRICING

As companies have expanded by creating decentralized operations, the concept of the corporate profit center has become increasingly popular. Ideally, the decentralized profit center is a device for measuring and evaluating performance and motivating divisional management to achieve corporate goals. To achieve these goals, a rational system of transfer pricing is required. In domestic operations the aim in developing transfer pricing systems has been to devise methods that would simultaneously (1) motivate divisional management to achieve subsystem goals, (2) provide sufficient flexibility to enable divisional management to achieve goals, and (3) at the same time further corporate profit goals. When a company with such a transfer pricing system extends its operations across national boundaries, new and complicating dimensions to the transfer pricing problem are added.

Taxes, particularly income, duties, and tariffs, have received much attention in discussions of transfer pricing in international operations. In addition, however, a number of other environmental factors must be considered, including market conditions, the ability of potential customers to pay for a company's product, the competitive circumstances of different markets' profit transfer rules, the sometimes conflicting objectives of international partners in joint ventures, and government requirements such as deposit requirements on foreign imports.

There are at least four major alternative approaches to transfer pricing. Each approach has advantages and disadvantages, which vary with the nature of the firm, products, markets, and the historical circumstances of each case. The alternatives are (1) transfer at direct cost, (2) transfer at direct cost plus overhead and margin, (3) transfer at a price derived from end market prices, and (4) transfer at an "arm's-length" price, or the price that unrelated parties would have reached on the same transaction.

A few companies employ the transfer-at-cost pricing method, recognizing that sales of foreign affiliates contribute to corporate profitability by generating scale economies in domestic manufacturing operations. Many companies follow the cost-plus pricing method, however, taking the position that foreign affiliate sales must earn a profit at every stage of their movement through the corporate system. This approach may result in a price that is completely unrelated to competition and the ability to buy in foreign markets, and is not recommended as a pricing policy.

A market-based transfer price is derived from the price required to be competitive in the foreign market. The constraint on this price is cost. However, there is a considerable degree of variation in how costs are defined, and since costs generally decline with volume, there is a question as to whether to price on the basis of current or planned volume levels.

One overlooked and potentially valuable strategy is to use market-based transfer prices and foreign sourcing as a device to enter a new market that is too small to support local manufacturing. This enables a company to establish its name or franchise in the market and to develop a cadre of people with experience. With its own experienced people, a company is in a much better position to appraise the potential of the market and to develop and implement effective strategies.

A fourth approach to transfer pricing is to adopt a system that attempts to set transfer prices at the "arm's-length" (the price that would have been reached by unrelated parties in a similar transaction) level. The problem with this approach is the extreme difficulty in identifying a point "arm's-length" price for all but the commodity type of products, and since few companies are dealing in commodities, this is a very real limitation. The "arm's-length" price can be a useful target if it is viewed not as a point but rather as a range of prices. The important thing to remember is that pricing at "arm's length" in differentiated products results not in predeterminable specific prices but in prices that fall within a predeterminable range.

In a world characterized by differential rates of income taxation, there is an incentive for a multicountry organization to seek to maximize system income in the lowest tax environments and to minimize income in high tax environments. Governments, naturally, have been aware of the possibilities of tax minimization efforts on the part of international companies. During recent years, there has been a considerable effort on the part of a number of governments to maximize their tax revenues by examining company returns and reallocating income and expenses.

Section 482

As governments pursue their tax maximization objectives, it is becoming increasingly necessary for companies to comply with government prescriptions in this area. Since the U.S. Treasury transfer price review program is perhaps the most advanced in the world today, it is valuable to examine the nature of this program and its implications for management.

Treasury review of transfer pricing includes the sale of tangible property ranging all the way from raw materials to intermediate and finished goods; the pricing of money (loans) and services (research and development, consulting, managerial assistance); the use of tangible property (equipment, buildings); and the transfer or use of intangible property (patents, copyrights, trademarks, procedures, forecasts, estimates, customer lists). In addition to the normal internal control problems posed by such transfers in a domestic environment, when a corporation spans national boundaries and tax jurisdictions, such transfers are subject to review and must be accepted by frequently inscrutable national tax authorities. Interest in the transfer and approaches to taxation are potentially in conflict. When the transfer involves tangible property, for example, the customs authorities must accept the transfer price. Their interest in a high import price to maximize duties is in direct conflict with the income tax authority's interest in a low price, which raises local company income and thereby raises income tax revenues.

For the U.S.-based global corporation, Section 482 is one of the most important single provisions of the U.S. tax law affecting international pricing practice.

According to Section 482, Internal Revenue Code, 1954,

> In any case of two or more organizations, trades, or businesses (whether or not incorporated, whether or not organized in the United States, and whether or not affiliated) owned or controlled directly or indirectly by the same interests, the Secretary or his delegate may distribute, apportion, or allocate gross income, deductions, credits, or allowances between or among such organizations, trades, or businesses, if he determines that such distribution, apportionment or allocation is necessary in order to prevent evasion of taxes or clearly to reflect the income of any of such organizations, trades, or businesses.

The question facing international marketers and their advisers is, "What can a company do in the international pricing area in the light of current tax law?" The U.S. Treasury promulgated regulations that spell out approaches to international pricing in considerable detail.[2] The IRS is bound to follow these approaches in its enforcement efforts. It is important to note, however, that Treasury regulations do not have the weight of law until they are accepted by the courts. Thus it is important to examine the regulations carefully, not because they are the tax law but because they guide the IRS review of transactions between related business organizations.

Sales of Tangible Property

Section 482 of the Treasury regulations is of particular interest to international marketers because it deals with controlled intracompany transfers (for example, transfer pricing) of raw materials and finished and intermediate goods. The general

---

[2]"Allocation of Income and Reduction Among Taxpayers: Determination of Source Income" (Section 482, Internal Revenue Code), *Federal Register,* April 16, 1968.

rule that applies to sales of tangible property is again the "arm's-length" formula. Three methods are spelled out in the regulations for establishing its existence. They are, in order of preference, the "comparable uncontrolled price method," the "resale price method," and the "cost-plus method."

COMPARABLE UNCONTROLLED PRICE METHOD. Uncontrolled (where buyer and seller are unrelated) sales are considered comparable to controlled sales (sales between related parties) if the physical property and circumstances involved are identical or nearly identical to the physical property and circumstances of controlled sales. The precision of this method is impressive, but unfortunately in practice it will have little applicability except in cases of companies dealing in such standard items as number 2 winter grade wheat or number 16 nails.

RESALE PRICE METHOD. Of the other two methods the resale price method is given preference in the regulations. It provides that an arm's-length price can be established by reducing the applicable resale price by an appropriate markup and making adjustments to reflect any differences between uncontrolled sales used as the basis for establishing the appropriate markup percentage and the resale of property involved in the controlled sale. The applicable resale price is the price at which property purchased in a controlled sale is resold by the buyer in an uncontrolled sale. This method must be used if all the following circumstances exist: there are no comparable uncontrolled sales, an applicable resale price is available, and the buyer has not added more than an insubstantial amount of the value of the property.

What is an appropriate markup? According to the regulations, it is the gross profit as a percentage of sales earned by the reseller or another party on the resale of property that is both purchased and resold in an uncontrolled transaction most similar to the resale of property involved in the controlled sale. The regulations permit markup percentages to be obtained from resales by other resellers in the foreign market if these are available, and then markup percentages earned by U.S. resellers performing comparable functions may be used. Market —

COST-PLUS METHOD. The third and lowest priority method of establishing the existence of an arm's-length price is the cost-plus method. Note that this method is easily the most relied upon method currently in use by U.S. corporations to establish transfer prices.

The regulations specify that cost must be determined by following standard accounting practices that neither favor nor burden controlled sales as compared with similar uncontrolled sales. The allowable gross profit percentage is the figure that is equal to the gross profit earned by the seller on uncontrolled sales that are most similar to the controlled sale in question. The regulations specify that, wherever possible, gross profit percentages should be derived from uncontrolled sales made by the seller involved in the controlled sale and that, in the absence of such sales, evidence may be obtained either from uncontrolled sales of other sellers that perform a similar function or, failing this, from the prevailing gross profit percentages in the particular industry involved. Since the comparable uncontrolled price and the resale price are likely to find little application in practice, the "cost-plus" method could eventually be the most applicable section of the regulations dealing with tangible property.

Competitive Pricing

A businessperson examining the Section 482 regulations might wonder, with all the emphasis on an arm's-length price, whether it is possible under the spirit of these regulations to continue to price with regard to market and competitive factors. Clearly, if only the arm's-length standard is applied, it does not necessarily permit a company to respond to competitive factors that exist in every market, domestic and foreign. Fortunately, the regulations may provide an opening for the company that seeks to be price competitive or to price aggressively in its international marketing of U.S.-sourced products. It appears that drafters of the Treasury regulations intended to leave a wide opening for companies that wish to respond to competitive factors or any other price factors that may exist in foreign markets. The applicable passage in Section 482 reads

> One of the circumstances which may affect the price of property is the fact that the seller may desire to make sales at less than a normal profit for the primary purpose of establishing or maintaining a market for his products. Thus, a seller may be willing to reduce the price of his product, for a time, in order to introduce his product into an area or in order to meet competition. However, controlled sales may be priced in such a manner only if such price would have been charged in an uncontrolled sale under comparable circumstances. Such fact may be demonstrated by showing that the buyer in the controlled sale made corresponding reduction in the resale price to uncontrolled purchasers, or that such buyer engaged in substantially greater sales-promotion activities with respect to the product involved in the controlled sale than with respect to other products.

The key provision in this section is the third sentence citing "comparable circumstances." This term could be interpreted as a nullification of what is an essential provision in the regulations. A company may properly reduce prices and increase marketing expenditures in a market through a controlled affiliate when it would not do so through an independent distributor. This would be the case when a company lowered its prices to gain a market position. The market position is, in effect, an investment and an asset. A company would invest in such an asset only if it controlled the reseller. If the third sentence applies, there is extremely limited endorsement of competitive or marginal cost pricing. If the last sentence applies, and it should, the regulations will permit a company to lower its transfer price for the purpose of entering a new market or meeting competition in an existing market either by price reductions or by increased marketing efforts in the target markets. Companies must have and use this latitude in making price decisions if they are to achieve any success in foreign markets with U.S.-sourced goods.

Importance of Section 482 Regulations

Whatever the pricing rationale, it is important that executives involved in the pricing policy decisions of multinational companies familiarize themselves with the Section 482 regulations and that the pricing rationale utilized by the company conform with the intention of these regulations. In practice this will not result in a massive adoption of the Treasury's arm's-length pricing standard, but companies should be prepared to demonstrate that their pricing methods were not the result of oversight but of informed choice. There is ample evidence that regardless of the sometimes perplexing inscrutability of Treasury regulations and IRS enforcement policy, there is no intention on the part of the government to do anything other than seek to prevent tax avoidance and to ensure that the income from the operations of multinational companies is fairly distributed. The company that makes a conscientious effort to comply with the new regulations and documents this effort should have no difficulty with IRS deficiencies. In the event that there are deficiencies, it should be able to make a strong case for its decisions in court.

Other Constraints on International Pricing

COMPANY CONTROLS.   Transfer pricing to minimize tax liabilities can lead to unexpected and undesired distortions. One interesting case of distortion occurred in a major U.S. company a few years ago. The company, a decentralized profit-centered organization, had promoted and given substantial salary increases as frequently as twice a year to its divisional manager in Switzerland. The reason for the manager's rapid rise was his outstanding profit performance record, which was picked up by the company's performance appraisal control system, which in turn triggered the salary and promotion actions. The problem in this very large company was that the control system, which rewarded managers for profit performance, had not been adjusted to recognize that in this company a Swiss "tax haven" profit center had been created and that the manager's "profits" were simply the result of artificially low transfer pricing into the tax haven operations and artificially high transfer pricing out of the Swiss tax haven to operating subsidiaries. It took a team of outside consultants to discover the situation. In this case the company's profit and loss records were a gross distortion of true operating results. The company had to adapt its control system to evaluate realistically tax haven manager performance.

DUTY AND TARIFF CONSTRAINTS.   Corporate costs and profits are also affected by the rates of import duty applied by a country. The higher the duty rate, the more desirable a lower transfer price. A country's customs duties and tax rates do not always create the same pressure on transfer prices. For example, consider a country with a high import duty and a low income tax rate. The high duty creates an incentive to reduce transfer prices to minimize the customs duty. The low income tax rate, however, creates a pressure to raise the transfer price to locate income in the low tax environment. These two factors are of course pulling in the opposite direction. Notwithstanding the importance of tax and duty considerations, many companies tend to minimize the influence of taxes on pricing policies or ignore them altogether. There are a number of reasons for such approaches. Some companies consider tax savings to be trivial in comparison with the earnings that can be obtained by concentrating on effective systems of motivation and corporate resource allocation. Other companies consider any effort at systematic tax minimization to be morally improper. Other companies argue that a simple, consistent, and straightforward pricing policy minimizes the tax investigation problems that can develop if sharper pricing policies are pursued and that the savings in executive time and the costs of outside counsel compensate for any additional taxes that might be paid by such an approach. Other companies have analyzed the worldwide trend toward harmonization of tax rates and have concluded that any set of policies appropriate to a world characterized by wide differentials in tax rates would soon become obsolete, and they have therefore concentrated on developing pricing policies that are appropriate for a world that is very rapidly evolving toward relatively similar tax rates, at least in the major industrial countries.

GOVERNMENT CONTROLS. A number of government requirements can influence the pricing decision. One of these is the frequently encountered cash deposit requirement imposed on importers. This is a requirement that a company has to tie up funds in the form of a noninterest-bearing deposit for a specified period of time, frequently six months or more, if it wishes to import foreign products. Where such requirements exist, there is clearly an incentive to minimize the price of the imported product. Other government requirements that affect the pricing decision are profit transfer rules that restrict the conditions under which profits can be transferred out of a country. Under such rules the transfer price paid for imported goods by an affiliated company can be a device for transferring profits out of a country.

Other government controls go directly to market pricing in a country. The British Monopolies and Mergers Commission, for example, forced the Swiss-based F. Hoffman–La Roche & Company to reduce the price of Librium by 60 percent and Valium by 75 percent and to refund $27.5 million for overcharging. In a nutshell, the government's case was based on the argument that the company was spending too much on research.

Joint Ventures

Joint ventures present an incentive to transfer price goods at a higher rate than one that would have been used in transfer pricing goods to their own wholly owned affiliates because a company's share of the joint venture earnings is less than 100 percent. Any profits that occur in the joint venture must be shared, whereas profits taken in wholly owned subs or at headquarters are not shared. Because of this potential conflict, it is important for companies with joint ventures to work out in advance a pricing agreement that is acceptable. The increasing frequency of tax authority audits is an important reason for working out an agreement that will also be acceptable to the tax authorities. The tax authorities' criteria of "arm's-length" prices is probably most appropriate for most joint ventures.

GLOBAL PRICING—THREE POLICY ALTERNATIVES

What pricing policy should a global company pursue? Viewed broadly, there are three alternative positions a company can take toward worldwide pricing.

Extension/Ethnocentric

The first can be called an *extension/ethnocentric* pricing policy. This policy requires that the price of an item be the same around the world and that the customer absorb freight and import duties. This approach has the advantage of extreme simplicity because no information on competitive or market conditions is required for implementation. The disadvantage of this approach is obvious. It does not respond to the competitive and market conditions of each national market and therefore does not maximize the company's profits in each national market.

Adaptation/Polycentric -decentralized.

The second pricing policy can be termed *adaptation/polycentric*. This is a policy of permitting subsidiary or affiliate companies to establish whatever price they feel is most desirable in their circumstances. Under such an approach, there is no control or fixed requirement that prices be in any way coordinated from one country to the next. The only constraint on this approach is in setting transfer prices within the corporate system. Such an approach is sensitive to local conditions, but it does present problems of product arbitrage opportunities in cases where disparities in local market prices exceed the transportation and duty cost separating markets. When such a condition exists, there is an opportunity for the enterprising business manager to take advantage of these price disparities by buying in the lower price market and selling in the more expensive market. There is also the problem that under such a policy, valuable knowledge and experience within the corporate system concerning effective pricing strategies is not applied to each local pricing problem. The strategies are not applied because the local managers are free to price in the way they feel is most desirable, and they may not be fully informed about company experience when they make their decision.

Invention/Geocentric – interdependent.

The third approach to international pricing can be termed *invention/geocentric*. Using this approach a company neither fixes a single price worldwide nor remains aloof from subsidiary pricing decisions, but instead strikes an intermediate position. A company pursuing this approach works on the assumption that there are unique local market factors that should be recognized in arriving at a pricing decision. These factors are principally local costs, income levels, competition, and the local marketing strategy. Local costs plus a return on invested capital and personnel fix the price floor for the long term. However, for the short term, a company might decide to pursue a market penetration objective and price at less than the cost-plus return figure using export sourcing to establish a market. Another short-term objective might be to estimate the size of a market at a price that would be profitable given local sourcing and a certain scale of output. Instead of building facilities, first supply the target market from existing higher-cost external supply sources. If the price and product are accepted by the market, the company can then build a local manufacturing facility to exploit the identified market profitably. If the market does not materialize, the company can experiment with the product at other prices because it is not committed by existing local manufacturing facilities to a fixed sales volume.

Selecting a price that recognizes local competition is essential. Many international market efforts have floundered on this point. A major U.S. appliance manufacturer introduced its line of household appliances in West Germany and, using U.S. sourcing, set price by simply marking up every item in its line by 28.5 percent. The result of this pricing method was a line that contained a mixture of underpriced and overpriced products. The overpriced products did not sell because better values were offered by local companies. The underpriced products sold very well, but they would have yielded greater profits at higher prices. What was needed was product *line* pricing, which took lower than normal margins in some products and higher margins in others to maximize the profitability of the full line.

For consumer products, local income levels are critical in the pricing decision. If the product is normally priced well above full manufacturing costs, the international marketer has the latitude to price below prevailing levels in higher-income markets and, as a result, reduce the gross margin on the product. While no business manager enjoys reducing margins, they are merely a guide to the ultimate objective, which is profitability, and in some markets income conditions may dictate that the maximum profitability will be obtained by sacrificing "normal" margins. The important point here is that in international marketing there is no such thing as a "normal" margin.

The final factor bearing on the price decision is the local marketing strategy and mix. Price must fit the other elements of the marketing program. For example, when it is decided to pursue a "pull" strategy that uses mass-media advertising and intensive distribution, the price selected must be consistent not only with income levels and competition but also with the costs and heavy advertising programs.

In addition to these local factors, the geocentric approach recognizes that headquarters price coordination is necessary in dealing with international accounts and product arbitrage. Finally, the geocentric approach consciously and systematically seeks to ensure that accumulated national pricing experience is applied wherever relevant.

Of the three methods, only the geocentric approach lends itself to global competitive strategy. A global competitor will take into account global markets and global competitors in establishing prices. Prices will support global strategy objectives rather than the objective of maximizing performance in a single country.

SUMMARY

Pricing decisions are a critical element of the marketing mix. The general rule of pricing is that over the long-run, prices must exceed costs and that prices may never exceed those of the competition. There is no absolute maximum price, but for any customer, price must correspond to the customer's perceived value of the product. The aim of most marketing strategies is to set a price that corresponds to the customer's perception of value in the product and at the same time does not leave money on the table, so to speak. In other words, the objective is to charge what a product is worth to the customer and to cover all costs and provide a margin for profit in the process.

International pricing is complicated by the fact that an international business must conform to different rule-making bodies and to different competitive situations in each country. Both the countries and the competition are constraints on pricing decisions. Each company must examine the market, the competition, and its own costs and objectives and local and regional regulations and laws in setting prices that are consistent with the overall marketing strategy.

DISCUSSION QUESTIONS

1. What is a transfer price? What is the difference, if any, between a transfer price and a "regular" price?
2. What are the three alternative approaches to global pricing? Which one would you recommend to a company that has global market aspirations?
3. If you were responsible for marketing CAT scanners worldwide (average price, $1,200,000) and the country of manufacture was experiencing a strong and appreciating currency against almost all other currencies, would you adjust your prices to take into account the strong currency situation? Why? Why not?

BIBLIOGRAPHY

Articles

BARRETT, M. EDGAR. "Case of the Tangled Transfer Price." *Harvard Business Review,* May–June 1977, pp. 20–39.

COHEN, STEPHEN S., AND JOHN ZYSMAN. "Countertrade, Offsets, Barter and Buyouts." *California Management Review,* Vol. 28, no. 2 (Winter 1986), pp. 41–55.

GERSTNER, EITAN. "Do Higher Prices Signal Higher Quality?" *Journal of Marketing Research,* Vol. 22 (May 1985), pp. 209–215.

HOWARD, FRED. "Overview of International Taxation." *Columbia Journal of World Business,* Summer 1975, pp. 5–11.

KEEGAN, WARREN J. "How Far Is Arm's Length?" *Columbia Journal of World Business,* May–June 1969, pp. 57–66.

KIM, SEUNG H., AND STEPHEN W. MILLER. "Constituents of the International Transfer Pricing Decision." *Columbia Journal of World Business,* Spring 1979, pp. 69–77.

LEFF, NATHANIEL H. "Multinational Corporate Pricing Policy in the Developing Countries." *Journal of International Business Studies,* Fall 1975, pp. 55–64.

SCHUSTER, FALKO. "Barter Arrangements with Money: The Modern Form of Compensation Trading." *Columbia Journal of World Business,* Fall 1980, pp. 61–66.

SHULMAN, JAMES. "When the Price Is Wrong—By Design." *Columbia Journal of World Business,* May–June 1967, pp. 69–76.

MINOLTA CAMERA CO. LTD.[1,2]

"We have got to fix this problem," said Mr. Katsusaburo Nakamura as he read the letter he had just received from one of his company's European retailers. (See Figure 1.) It was July 1971. Mr. Nakamura was the manager of the International Division of the Minolta Camera Co. Ltd., a leading manufacturer of cameras and camera accessories, headquartered in Osaka, Japan. The letter he was reading came from Mr. Wilfried Reuter, president of a large camera dealership in Germany with stores in Cologne, Düsseldorf, and Essen. Mr. Reuter, who had recently visited the Minolta headquarters in Osaka, complained about the fact that sizable quantities of Minolta cameras moved through unofficial channels from Hong Kong to Germany, where they were sold at prices substantially below Minolta's official suggested retail prices.

Mr. Reuter's letter was not the first of its kind that Mr. Nakamura had received. A

[1]This case was prepared by Ulrich Wiechmann as the basis for class discussion rather than to illustrate either effective or ineffective handling of an administrative situation. Copyright © 1976 by the President and Fellows of Harvard College. Used with permission.

[2]Certain names, places, and financial data have been disguised.

Dear Mr. Nakamura,

After having safely returned to Cologne, I would like to thank you again for the kind welcome extended to me at the occasion of my visit to Japan. It was certainly a pleasure to see you and have the opportunity to exchange thoughts and discuss various matters with you.

On my way home I spent one day in Hong Kong, where I had to notice the very low prices at which the Minolta cameras and particularly the lenses are offered. For a German photo dealer, it is still very much worthwhile to purchase the products in Hong Kong direct. This situation should really urgently be changed. We would like to point out again that this price difference makes business very difficult and has repeatedly been the subject for unpleasant discussions with some of our customers.

We are convinced that you, as International Manager, can appreciate our difficulties, and we suggest that you exchange your position with the Manager of your Domestic Department for a while, which would most certainly make him understand our problems much better afterwards!

We sincerely hope that the "problem Hong Kong" can soon be solved. Meanwhile, we remain, with best regards,

Yours very truly

REUTER PHOTO AG

Wilfried Reuter
President

FIGURE 1 Letter of a Camera Retailer in Germany

number of other authorized dealers in Europe and in the United States had voiced similar complaints about unfair price competition because of an inflow of Minolta cameras through irregular channels. In virtually all these cases, the source of the problem seemed to be that merchants in Hong Kong bypassed Minolta's regular distribution system by exporting directly to camera retailers abroad. The basis of these export transactions was the significant price difference for Minolta cameras that existed between Hong Kong and Japan, on the one hand, and Europe and the United States, on the other.

Mr. Nakamura estimated that these "gray exports," as he called the movement of Minolta cameras through irregular channels, accounted for less than 10 percent of Minolta's total camera sales. A disturbing fact, however, was that the magnitude of these transactions, while hard to measure, seemed to be increasing rather than decreasing. Just a few days ago Mr. Nakamura had received a letter from one of Minolta's exclusive dis-

Dear Sirs,

Understanding that you are important photographic dealers, we address this letter with the hope of establishing business relations with your esteemed firm.

By way of introduction, we are a Japanese firm with head office in Tokyo. We specialize in the photo line trade.

From the free port of Hong Kong, we are in position to supply you with all Japanese brands of cameras and accessories at low Hong Kong prices. We are in position to supply ASAHI PENTAX, CANON, FUJICA, KONICA, KOWA, MAMIYA, MINOLTA, MIRANDA, YASHICA, OLYMPUS, and NIKON and also all brands of accessories.

Please specify the brand name you are particularly interested in. Offers will be promptly submitted for your perusal and consideration.

We are also in position to supply Hong Kong–made transistor radios.

Very truly yours,

*INTER EXPORT ENTERPRISES
HONG KONG B.C.C.*

FIGURE 2   Direct-Mail Promotion of an Export Firm Sent to European Camera Outlets

tributors in Europe. The distributor was very concerned that in trying to sell Minolta cameras to the retail accounts in his country he frequently found himself competing against unauthorized exporters in Hong Kong. Attached to the letter was a piece of direct-mail promotion that one of these exporters, Inter Export Enterprises, had sent to major camera retailers in the distributor's country. (See Figure 2.) The distributor commented:

I wish to emphasize that similar direct mail is regularly coming into our market from firms in Hong Kong offering photographic equipment at exceptionally low prices. We are obviously concerned at these overseas firms selling in our market as the recent increase in such selling by overseas outlets causes great discounting to take place in our market and also reduces our market possibilities. There is nothing illegal whatsoever in companies, such

as Inter Export, exporting to our country but, like other official photographic equipment distributors, we are being heavily affected because of this unreasonable practice.

COMPANY BACKGROUND

Minolta Camera Co. Ltd. was one of the leading Japanese manufacturers of still and movie cameras, lenses, and camera accessories. Founded in 1928, the company reached a 1970 sales volume of ¥22.8 billion.[3] Sales of cameras, lenses, and accessories accounted for 82 percent of this volume. The remaining 18 percent were predominantly sales of electrostatic office copiers; a small fraction of total

[3] 1 U.S.$ = ¥360 in 1970.

company sales was contributed by a diverse line of products, such as light-sensing devices, planetaria, hand calculators, and specialized optical instruments. Minolta's sales had shown a rapid growth over the past five years. (See Table 1.) For 1971, management expected to reach a sales volume of ¥24.5 billion.

Minolta's line of cameras covered almost the whole spectrum from modestly priced simple cameras for the beginner or occasional photographer to premium-priced sophisticated equipment for the serious amateur or the professional photographer. Throughout its history, the company had been a pioneer in the development of advanced Japanese camera equipment. The Auto-Minolta, introduced in 1935, was the first rangefinder press camera in Japan when it was marketed in 1937. The Minolta SR-7, introduced in 1962, was the world's first single-lens reflex camera with a built-in CdS exposure meter. While manufacturing and marketing a full line of still and movie cameras, Minolta's sales volume and marketing efforts concentrated on sophisticated 35mm single-lens reflex still cameras and a range of interchangeable lenses for these cameras. With these products Minolta competed against other well-known Japanese brands, such as Nikon, Canon, and Asahi

Pentax, as well as foreign brands such as Leica. All manufacturers offered essentially similar camera features and equipment. Furthermore, with the exception of the premium-priced Leica, all brands sold at more or less comparable prices.

All Minolta's products were manufactured in Japan. The company operated four plants for the manufacturing of cameras and lenses and two plants for the business machines and other products. In spite of the rapid sales growth over the past years, Minolta, as were other Japanese camera manufacturers in 1970, was finding it difficult to fill the production capacity in its camera and lens factories. "The whole industry is characterized by a discrepancy between supply and demand and, consequently, intense competition," Mr. Nakamura observed.

INTERNATIONAL ACTIVITIES

As did most Japanese camera manufacturers, Minolta depended heavily on sales outside of Japan. In 1970, Minolta's camera products were sold in about 100 countries. Exports contributed roughly 60 percent to the company's total sales of cameras and equipment; for 1971, management expected this figure to

TABLE 1   Consolidated Sales, 1965–1971

YEAR	TOTAL SALES (BILLION ¥)	SALES OF CAMERAS, LENSES, AND ACCESSORIES AS A PERCENTAGE OF TOTAL
1965	¥ 8.4	95%
1966	9.0	92
1967	12.1	84
1968	14.7	82
1969	18.5	79
1970	22.8	82
1971 (est.)	24.5	86

Source: Company records.

rise to 65 percent. Moreover, export sales were considerably more profitable than were domestic sales in Japan. (See Table 2.)

Of the various export markets, the United States and Europe were the most important geographical areas for Minolta. The United States accounted for 45 percent and Europe for 35 percent of Minolta's export sales of photographic products.

In the United States and in Germany, Minolta had established wholly owned sales subsidiaries. In all other foreign countries, the company worked through exclusive distributors for the sale and servicing of its products. It was company policy to appoint only one distributor per country. "We want foreign operations to run as orderly as possible," Mr. Nakamura explained. Usually, these exclusive distributors carried only Minolta cameras and equipment. Exceptions were made in some of the smaller countries where the distributors had to carry competing camera brands to reach a viable sales volume.

As did most marketers of expensive photographic equipment, Minolta and its distributor attempted to be selective in choosing retail outlets for Minolta cameras. Worldwide, Minolta cameras were sold through ap-proximately 25,000 retail stores, most of which could be classified as camera specialty stores or camera specialty departments of large department stores.

In most countries the retailer played a very important role in the consumer purchasing process. Consumer studies Minolta had obtained from several major European countries had shown that most consumers relied heavily on the advice and information of the retailer in deciding what type and brand of camera to buy. Moreover, these studies indicated that less than one-fourth of all prospective buyers entered a retail store with a clear idea about the brand of camera they wanted to buy. Even then, consumers often would not insist on that particular brand if the dealer argued strongly in favor of another brand.

The marketing of Minolta cameras was fairly standardized from country to country, due to the fact that many of the important dimensions of the marketing activities in each country were determined in Osaka.

The products, model names, and packaging were identical in all markets. Occasionally in the past, a distributor had suggested changes in either the packaging or the

TABLE 2   Profit and Loss Statement for Sales of Camera Products, October 1970—March 1971 and April 1971—September 1971 (in millions of yen)

	OCTOBER 1970— MARCH 1971		APRIL 1971— SEPTEMBER 1971 (est.)	
	Domestic	Export	Domestic	Export
Sales	¥3,684	¥5,869	¥3,510	¥7,036
Cost of goods sold	2,382	4,105	2,304	5,011
Gross profit	1,302	1,764	1,206	2,025
Selling and administrative expense	1,092	902	1,133	1,045
Operating profit	210	862	73	980

Source: Company records.

model design for his or her country. So far, such suggestions had never been followed; the headquarters management in Japan feared that even slight deviations from a uniform product policy would create serious problems in production scheduling and incur additional costs. It was already not easy to provide the brochures, instruction booklets for the cameras, and dealer manuals in many different languages. Accurate forecasting of demand in each country was a major problem.

Aside from the uniform product policy, the advertising for Minolta cameras was also highly standardized on a worldwide basis. Print media campaigns and posters were mostly prepared in Japan and then sent to the foreign distributors and subsidiaries for placement in local media.

Minolta also granted a uniform worldwide warranty for its products. Within the warranty period of one year, a customer could get free service in case of defective workmanship or materials from any of the authorized Minolta service representatives in the world. Management had always considered free worldwide warranty service, coupled with a uniform worldwide advertising approach, as a mark of quality and prestige in the field of high-priced consumer products. It was the accepted practice not only of most major camera manufacturers but also, for example, of famous watchmakers.

While Minolta's marketing approach showed great similarity from country to country in terms of product, advertising, service, and distribution policy, it varied considerably in terms of price. In 1970, all export prices for Minolta products were quoted in U.S. dollars. Wide differences in retail prices existed between one export market and another and also between certain export markets and the Japanese domestic market. The reason for these price differences was primarily fierce competitive conditions in some markets, which forced prices down to a very low level. Hong Kong, Singapore, and also Japan were these low-price markets.

Table 3 gives an example for the price

TABLE 3 **Price Schedule for a Minolta Single-Lens Reflex Camera with Case in Japan, Hong Kong, Germany, and the United States, First Quarter 1971*,†**

	Japan	*Hong Kong*	*Germany*	*United States*‡
		(*IN U.S. DOLLARS*)		
Production cost	$ 62	$ 62	$ 62	$ 58
Price net to wholesalers	108	—	—	—
Export price F.O.B. Japan	—	98	94	99
Landed cost to distributors	—	121	130	123
Price net to dealers	136	148	189	205
Retail list price	170	174	270	342
Approximate actual retail price	160	165	248–271	260–280

*Disguised data.

†Exchange rates in early 1971 were U.S.$1 = ¥360 = H.K.$6.06 = DM3.66. In mid-1971 there were strong signs that significant changes in the exchange rates would take place. The position of the U.S. dollar had weakened. The German mark had begun to float. Market observers predicted a devaluation of the U.S. dollar by 5 to 10 percent before the end of 1971.

‡Case not included.

Source: Company records.

differences that existed in Japan, Hong Kong, the United States, and Germany for a popular Minolta single-lens reflex camera. For many items in the Minolta product line, the price differences were even more drastic. In several instances, the price net to dealers in Japan was similar to the landed cost of distributors in Europe and in the United States. "Generally, the retail prices in Europe and in the United States are between 50 percent and 200 percent higher than in Hong Kong or Japan; 200 percent is more typical," said Mr. Nakamura. "Prices in Hong Kong and Japan are very close; usually Hong Kong is only about 5 percent above retail prices in Japan. Our low prices in Hong Kong and in Japan are dictated by the tough competitive situation and the overhang of supply and demand. Our distributors in Hong Kong and Japan buy from us at prices that are close to our F.O.B. prices for Europe and the United States. The margins for the distributors and the retailers in Japan and Hong Kong are relatively low; in Hong Kong, in particular, a retailer often takes only a 2–3 percent markup. Distributors and dealers in Europe and in the United States insist on much higher margins. These high margins have largely historical reasons. When Japanese camera manufacturers first started to enter the Western markets after the war, high margins were absolutely necessary to gain distribution. We have thought of reducing these margins in Europe and in the United States, but we can't do a thing as long as our competitors keep their margins high."

HONG KONG AND THE "GRAY EXPORT" PROBLEM

In Hong Kong, Minolta had been represented for more than 10 years by Goddard & Co. Ltd. as its exclusive distributor. Goddard was one of the many medium-sized specialist camera distributors that operated in Hong Kong. The company carried only Minolta camera products.

Goddard & Co. Ltd. was founded by Mr. George Ho, a Chinese businessman, well connected in business and government circles in Hong Kong. Aside from being a camera distributor, Mr. Ho was associated with other businesses in Hong Kong, the most prominent of which were in T.V. and radio broadcasting. Through his association with Minolta, Mr. Ho had become a personal friend of Mr. Kazuo Tashima, the founder and president of Minolta.

"Through his connections, Mr. Ho is very valuable to us," Mr. Nakamura observed. "Mr. Ho comes from an old family with excellent connections to Chinese merchants, banks, and the Hong Kong government. He has a lot of information that we couldn't get alone."

Goddard & Co. Ltd. sold to roughly 80 regular retail accounts. Many of these retailers carried very little inventory. "When a customer comes into his store and the retailer doesn't have a particular item, he orders it from Goddard for same-day delivery," explained Mr. Nakamura. "Goddard has messenger boys making daily deliveries to retail stores."

Goddard employed two salesmen for sales to retailers. The salesmen were paid a commission and a small fixed salary. The salary amounted to roughly 30–35 percent of the salesmen's total compensation.

While Goddard served about 80 regular Minolta accounts, there was no effective control of who the salesmen visited and to whom they sold. Mr. Nakamura suspected that they occasionally sold to dealers who reexported Minolta cameras to other parts of the world. "It is hard for Goddard and their salesmen to turn down an order," Mr. Nakamura commented. "Goddard has done a good selling job for us over the past 10 years, and we have a very nice relationship with them. But they don't control distribution. They don't care about 'gray exports,' who they sell to and where the merchandise goes after they have sold it. Of course, distribution control is very hard to do. The people who reexport to Europe and to the United States are not easily identified; the frequency and quantity of their purchases may be an indication."

Minolta's export sales to Hong Kong had increased rapidly in the past and in 1970 had accounted for almost 4 percent of the company's total export sales. This figure was, however, only a fraction of the total volume of Minolta cameras moving from Japan to Hong Kong. Mr. Nakamura explained:

"Most of the gray exports to Europe and to the United States are organized by traders in Hong Kong. But the Hong Kong market has to be seen together with the Japanese market. The gray exporters in Hong Kong, we call them 'smugglers' although there is nothing illegal about their operations, actually get most of their merchandise from regular camera retailers in Japan. It works like this: Every day a lot of Hong Kong ships and a lot of Chinese sailors come into Japanese ports. Many of these sailors 'work' for the 'smuggler' in Hong Kong. On his order they each buy one camera tax free[4] in a regular camera store, take it back to Hong Kong, deliver it to the 'smuggler,' get reimbursed for whatever they paid, and receive a commission. Since they buy only one camera and some lenses at a time as personal property, there is no export or import documentation necessary.

"I don't know how many cameras move this way to Hong Kong. The retail price level

[4]Under Japanese law, foreign visitors were allowed tax exemption on cameras and several other products—a saving of from 10 to 20 percent.

and the supply and demand situation in Japan are decisive factors. If the market in Japan is weak, and it frequently is with so many camera makers around, a lot of merchandise flows into Hong Kong.

"What I do know is that this is a regular, organized business. Sometimes the "smugglers" also "employ" airline stewardesses and pilots. The annoying thing is that all this happens strictly within the boundaries of the law; so from that angle there is nothing we can do to stop it.

"The individual deliveries that reach Hong Kong from Japan in this manner are then pooled and perhaps combined with purchases the "smuggler" makes in the Hong Kong market to form large shipments to Europe and the United States. Again, this whole export operation is perfectly legal. At the moment, most of the cameras go to Europe, West Germany in particular. The buyers at the other end are typically large department stores, discount-type operations, specialty camera retailers, and sometimes even our authorized Minolta dealers.

"The Hong Kong exporter can offer very low prices to these outlets. First, he buys the merchandise cheaply in Hong Kong or in Japan. He takes only a small markup, usually less than 5 percent. The price difference between the Far East markets and the markets in Europe and the United States is large enough to pay for shipping expenses and still offer an attractive price to the Western dealers. For example, for a shipment from Hong Kong to West Germany, we figure that an exporter would have to pay roughly 20.5 percent of the F.O.B. Hong Kong value for freight, insurance, and import duty.

"Sometimes the shipments from Hong Kong don't go directly to retailers but to somebody who specializes in 'gray imports' from Hong Kong. We have identified a number of these firms in Germany, France, Belgium, and Switzerland. The 'gray importer' usually takes another 7 percent of the F.O.B. Hong Kong price.

"This is pretty much all we know about the situation and probably all we are ever going to know. We certainly also know that these 'gray exports' are a danger to our idea of orderly marketing. Just recently 3,000 SR-Ts[5] emerged through the Hong Kong system in the United States. Our regular dealers screamed like hell.[6] In Germany, a department store just offered 600 SR-Ts at 'drastically reduced prices.' The problem is that these 'gray exports' create a lot of attention; the retailers who buy them in Europe or in the United States, of course, heavily advertise that they have a special deal 'as long as supply lasts.'"

TACKLING THE PROBLEM

"We have got to fix this problem," said Mr. Nakamura. He had called a meeting with key executives of the International Division. The meeting was attended by Mr. Isao Izuhara, manager of the Export Department, Mr. Akio Miyabayashi, general manager of Minolta Camera Handelsgessellschaft G.m.b.H. in Hamburg, Germany, Mr. Sadahei Kusumoto, president of Minolta Corporation in New York, and Mr. Koji Kusumoto, who had previously been the general manager of Minolta's Hamburg subsidiary and was now working in the Export Department.

"I agree," said Mr. Koji Kusumoto. "I got into some very uncomfortable situations with our regular dealers when I was over in

Germany. At the last Photokina[7] a number of our dealers cornered my sales manager and me; they wanted to know what Minolta is going to do about it. But I am not sure whether there is anything we can do unless we eliminate the current differences in price that exist between the Far East and the Western markets. Water will flow from high points to low points, and cameras will flow from low-price markets to high-price markets."

"Well, our dealers don't see it quite that way," replied Mr. Miyabayashi. "They think that what we should do, first, is have better control of our distribution. They keep arguing that other companies, prestigious watchmakers like Omega, in particular, which have similar price differences, don't seem to have our problem. Of course, what the dealers don't say is that wristwatch distribution is much more selective, almost exclusive, than ours; I don't think that would be feasible for our products."

"Still, distribution control and stock control is something we can do and we should do better," said Mr. Izuhara. "Goddard in Hong Kong just isn't doing a good job in this respect. We have discussed the matter with them several times. They don't care where our products go. I think we should control the Hong Kong operation ourselves. I have had some very preliminary discussions with George Ho about this. I think there may be a chance of talking him into changing Goddard into a 50:50 joint venture with us. We have made some rough calculations; for a 50:50 joint venture we might need a capital expenditure of roughly HK$600,000."

"But, certainly, we would want more than an equity participation," said Mr. Nakamura. "If we do it, we would have to insist

---

[5] Model designation for one of Minolta's single-lens reflex cameras.

[6] Minolta's total export sales of the SR-T model to the United States in 1970 had amounted to about 51,000 units.

[7] Important trade exhibition of photographic products in Cologne, Germany.

on Japanese management of the joint venture. I wonder whether George Ho would go along with that.''

"If he doesn't, I believe that we should terminate our agreement with Goddard and establish a wholly owned subsidiary in Hong Kong,'' Mr. Izuhara replied.

"These are all very drastic steps,'' commented Mr. Sadahei Kusumoto from New York. "I think there are a number of tactical changes we can make to improve the situation. I believe that if we sold our cameras under different model names in the Far East and in the West we would reduce the inflow of 'gray exports' from Hong Kong significantly. Consumers in the United States would be reluctant to buy the Hong Kong imports if the imports carried a model designation that is different from the models we show in our advertising. They would feel that they would get an inferior model if they bought the lower-priced Hong Kong imports.''

"Furthermore, we could change our current warranty policy under which we service any camera free of charge during the warranty period, irrespective of where the camera was bought. Why not impose a handling charge, say, $25.00, for any camera we receive for service that was not imported through the Minolta Corporation in New York? We could make similar arrangements in Europe. Since each of our cameras and lenses carries a number, it's easy to determine whether we imported a specific camera or whether it reached the U.S. in some other way.''

"These are all very interesting ideas,'' said Mr. Nakamura. "I wish we had more information about the 'gray export' problem. But I am sure we won't get much more. We have got to make some decisions on the basis of what we know now. The fluctuation in currency exchange rates we are experiencing at the moment certainly doesn't make this job easier.''

DISCUSSION QUESTIONS

1. What alternatives are available to Minolta in this situation?
2. What would you do if you were Mr. Nakamura? Why?

14

CHANNEL DECISIONS

Wherever the Roman conquers, there he dwells.

> *Lucius Annaeus Seneca, 8 B.C.–A.D. 65,* Moral Essays to Helvia on Consolation

INTRODUCTION

According to marketing definitions of the American Marketing Association, a *channel of distribution* is "the structure of intracompany organization units and extracompany agents and dealers, wholesale and retail, through which a commodity, product, or service is marketed."[1] This definition of the channel of distribution purposely includes both the internal company marketing organization and the external independent organization because the marketing manager must combine these systems to achieve product distribution. Distribution is the physical flow of goods through channels, and channels are the internal and external organizational units that perform functions that add utility to a product or service. The major sources of utility created by channels are place, or the availability of a product or service in a location that is convenient to a potential customer; time, or the availability of a product or service at a time that fills a customer need; and information that answers questions and communicates useful product and applications knowledge to potential customers. Since these main utilities are a basic source of competitive advantage and "product" value, one of the key policy decisions marketing management must make at the policy level is what channel strategy to adopt.

[1] *Marketing Definitions: A Glossary of Marketing Terms* (Chicago: American Marketing Association, 1960), p. 10.

The distribution channels in markets around the world are among the most highly differentiated aspects of national marketing systems. For this reason, channel strategy is one of the most challenging and difficult components of an international marketing program. Smaller companies are often blocked by their inability to establish effective channel arrangements. In larger multinational companies, operating via country subsidiaries, channel strategy is the element of the marketing mix that is least understood and controlled by headquarters. To a large extent, channels are an aspect of the marketing program that is left to the control and discretion of the local marketing management group. Nevertheless, it is important for managers concerned with world marketing programs to understand the nature of international distribution channels. Distribution is an integral part of the total marketing program and must either fit or be fitted to product design, price, and communications aspects of the total marketing program. Another important reason for placing channel decisions on the agenda of international marketing managers is that channel decisions typically involve outside agents and organizations and long-term legal commitments and obligations to other firms and individuals, which are often extremely expensive to terminate or change. Even in cases where there is no legal obligation, commitments may be backed by good faith and feelings of obligation, which are equally difficult and painful to adjust.

From the viewpoint of the marketer concerned with a single-country program, international channel arrangements are a valuable source of information and insight into possible new approaches to more effective channel strategies. For example, self-service discount pricing of food and hard and soft goods in the United States was studied by retailers from Europe and Asia who then introduced the self-service concept in their own countries. The Japanese trading company has been examined with great interest by governments and business executives all over the world who are anxious to learn from the success of these Japanese organizations.

This chapter will examine international channel systems by focusing on (1) what the multinational marketer should know about channels in order to contribute to channel planning and control and (2) what the marketer concerned with a single country should know to exploit channel innovations that have been tried in other countries.

CHANNEL OBJECTIVES AND CONSTRAINTS

The starting point in selecting the most effective channel arrangement is a clear determination of the market target for the company's marketing effort and a determination of the needs and preferences of the target market. Where are the potential customers located? What are their information requirements? What are their preferences for service? How sensitive are they to price? Each of the dimensions of customer preference must be carefully determined because there is as much danger to the success of a marketing program in giving too much service, credit, and so forth, as there is in giving too little. Moreover, each market must be analyzed to determine the cost of providing service. What is appropriate in one country may not be effective in another.

An example of giving too much service is the case of the international manufacturer of construction products who emphasized the speedy service provided by his sales force in radio-equipped station wagons. The company prided itself on the fact that the maximum elapsed time between the receipt of an on-site customer order and the actual delivery by a salesperson was under two hours. While its service record was outstanding, the company discovered that in the United States the cost of this service, which was included in the price the company charged for its products, placed it at a serious competitive price disadvantage vis-à-vis its major competition. Customers had praised the company for its service, but their preference in terms of actual buying behavior was for the offering of the competitor whose costs were much lower because it did not offer the immediate delivery service and passed on these cost savings to customers in the form of lower prices. This finding for the United States did not apply to European markets, where competition and custom made delivery necessary.

Channel strategy in a global marketing program must fit the company's competitive position and overall marketing objectives in each national market. If a company wants to enter a competitive market, it must either provide incentives to independent channel agents, which will induce them to promote the company's product, or it must establish company-owned or franchised outlets. The process of shaping international channels to fit overall company objectives is constrained by the following factors, each of which will be discussed briefly.

Customer Characteristics

The characteristics of customers are an important influence on channel design. Their number, geographical distribution, income, shopping habits, and reaction to different selling methods all vary from country to country and therefore require different channel approaches.

In general, the larger the number of customers, the greater the need for channel agents regardless of the stage of market development. For example, if there are only 10 customers for an industrial product in each national market, these 10 customers must be directly contacted by either the manufacturer or an agent. If a product is sold to millions of customers, retail distribution outlets or mail-order distribution is required. If there is a large number of low-volume retailers, it is usually cheaper to reach them via wholesalers. For large-volume retailers, it may be more cost effective to sell direct. These generalizations apply to all countries, regardless of stage of development.

Product Characteristics

Certain product attributes such as degree of standardization, perishability, bulk, service requirements, and unit price have an important influence on channel design.

Products with high unit price, for example, are often sold through a direct company sales force because the selling cost of this "expensive" distribution method is a small part of the total sale price. Moreover, the high cost of such products is usually associated with complexity or with product features that must be explained in some detail, and this can be done most effectively by a controlled sales force. A good example of this type of product is a computer, which is expensive and complicated and requires both explanation and applications analysis focused on the customer's needs. A controlled and trained salesperson or "sales engineer" is tailor made for this task.

Some products require margins to cover the costs of expensive sales engineering. Others require margins to provide a large monetary incentive to a direct sales force. Encyclopedias are an excellent example of this latter type of product. The function of the encyclopedia sales representative is to call on potential customers and to create an awareness of the value of an encyclopedia and to evoke in the customer a feeling of need for this value. The sales activity must be paid for. Companies using direct distribution for consumer products rely upon wide gross selling margins to generate the necessary compensation revenue for sales people.

Perishable products usually require more direct marketing to ensure that the condition of products in channels is satisfactory for purchase by the ultimate customer. In developed countries, vegetables, bread, dairy products, and many perishable food products are distributed by controlled sales forces, and stock is checked by these sales distributor organizations to ensure that it is fresh and ready for distribution. In less developed countries, producers typically sell these products in public marketplaces. Bulky products usually require channel arrangements that minimize the shipping distances and the number of times products are turned over in the channels before they reach the ultimate customer. Soft drinks and beer are examples of bulky products whose widespread availability is an important aspect of an effective marketing strategy and that are typically handled by a bottler or brewer sales distribution organization whenever a bottler or brewer is large enough to support direct distribution.

Middleman Characteristics

Channel strategy must recognize the characteristics of existing middlemen. Middlemen are in business to maximize their own profit and not that of the manufacturer. They are notorious for their "cherry picking," that is, the practice of taking orders for products, brands, and manufacturers that are in demand and avoiding any real selling effort for a manufacturer's products that may require "push." This is a rational response by the middleman, but it can present a serious obstacle to the manufacturer attempting to break into a market with a new product. The "cherry picker" is not interested in building a market for a new product. This is a problem for the expanding international company. Frequently, this practice forces a manufacturer with a new product or a product with a limited market share to set up some arrangement for bypassing the "cherry picking" segment of the channel. In some cases manufacturers will set up an expensive direct distribution organization to obtain a share of the market. When they finally obtain a share of the target market, they may abandon the direct distribution system for a more cost-effective intermediary system. The move does not mean that intermediaries are "better" than direct distribution. It is simply a response by a manufacturer to the altered attractiveness of his or her product to independent distributors.

Another method of dealing with the "cherry picking" problem without setting up an expensive direct sales force is to subsidize the entire cost of sales representatives who are assigned by a distributor to the products of the subsidizing company. The advantage of this method is that it eliminates the cost of sales management and physical distribution by tying the missionary and support selling in with the distributor's sales management and physical distribution. Using this method it is possible to place managed direct selling support and distribution support behind a product at the expense of only one salesperson per selling area. The distributor's incentive for cooperating in this kind of arrangement is that he or she obtains a "free" sales representative for a new product that promises to be a profitable addition to his or her line. This cooperative arrangement is ideally suited to getting a new export-sourced product into distribution in a market.

SELECTION AND CARE OF DISTRIBUTORS AND AGENTS.   The selection of distributors and agents in a target market is a critically important task. A good commission agent or stocking distributor can make the difference between realizing zero performance and performance that exceeds 200 percent of what is expected. At any point in time, some of any company's agents and distributors will be excellent, others will be satisfactory, and still others will be unsatisfactory and in need of replacement.

To find a good distributor, a firm can begin with a list provided by the U.S. Department of Commerce or the equivalent ministry or department of other countries. The local chamber of commerce in a country can also provide lists, as can local trade associations. Do not waste time trying to screen the list by mail. Go to the country and talk to end users of the products that you are selling and find out which distributors they prefer and why. If the product is a consumer product, go to the retail outlets and find out where they are buying products similar to your own and why. Two or three names will keep coming up. Go to these two or three and see which of them would be available to sign. Before signing, make sure that there is someone in the organization who will be the key person for your product. The key person is someone who will make it a personal objective to make your product a success in that country.

This is the critical difference between the successful distributor and the worthless distributor. There must be a personal, individual commitment to the product. The second and related requirement for successful distributors or agents is that they must be successful with the product. Success means that they can sell the product and make money on it. In any case, the product must be designed and priced to be competitive in the target market. The distributor can assist in this process by providing information about customer wants and the competition and by promoting the product he or she represents.

The RF Division of Harris Corporation achieved great success in international markets with its short-wave radios. One of the reasons for its success was the quality of agents in key markets and their commitment to the Harris product. They were attracted to Harris because the company made a product that was as good as or better than any other product on the market and Harris offered commissions of 33 percent on all sales. This commission rate was at least 15 percent higher than that offered by any other competitor and was certainly one of the single most important factors in ensuring Harris' success. The generous commission gave the agents a compelling reason to sell Harris products and the financial resources to support a strong marketing effort.

The only way to keep a good distributor is to work closely with him or her to ensure that he or she is making money on the product. Any distributor who does not make money on a line will drop it. It is really quite simple. If a distributor is not working out, in general, it is wise to terminate the agreement and find another one. Few companies are large enough to convert a mediocre distributor or agent into an effective business representative. Therefore, the most important clause in the distributor contract is the cancellation clause. Make sure that it is written in a way that will make it easy to terminate the agreement. There is a myth that it is expensive or even impossible to terminate distributor and agent agreements. Some of the most successful international marketers have terminated hundreds of agreements and know that their success is based on their willingness to terminate if a distributor or agent does not perform. The key factor is performance: If a distributor does not perform, you must either improve his performance or replace him.

Environmental Characteristics

The general characteristics of the total environment are a major consideration in channel design. Because of the enormous variety of economic, social, and political environments internationally, there is a need to delegate a large degree of independence to local operating managements or agents. A comparison of food distribution in countries at different stages of development illustrates how channels reflect and respond to underlying market conditions in a country. In the United States high incomes, high wages, large-capacity refrigerators with large freezer units, intensive automobile ownership (two persons per car), convenience food acceptance, and availability and attitudes toward food preparation combine to make the supermarket or the self-service one-stop food store the basic food retailing unit. The American householder wants to purchase in one trip enough food to last for a week. The consumer has the money, the refrigerated storage capacity, and the hauling capacity of the car to move this large quantity of food from the store to the home. The supermarket, because it is efficient, can fill the food shoppers' needs at lower prices than that of traditional service food stores. Additionally, supermarkets can offer

TABLE 14–1 Number of Grocery Shops
per 1,000 Inhabitants in
Different Countries

COUNTRY	1970	1979	1983
Australia	1.2	.7	.7
United States	1.1	.8	.8
South Africa	1.3	1.0	.8
The Netherlands	1.3	1.0	.8
Sweden	1.6	1.1	1.0
Canada	1.7	1.3	1.3
Great Britain	2.1	1.3	1.0
New Zealand	1.7	1.4	1.3
Switzerland	2.4	1.5	1.4
Germany, Fed. Rep	2.8	1.6	1.4
France	2.7	1.8	1.5
Austria	2.7	1.9	1.6
Brazil	1.9	2.0	2.0
Belgium	3.6	2.1	1.7
Japan	1.4	2.2	2.1
Ireland	5.9	2.6	2.4
Mexico	3.2	3.1	2.5
Spain	3.9	3.2	3.1
Portugal	5.7	4.5	4.3

Source: *The Grocery Marketing Scene,* Nielsen Marketing Research, No. 8, 1984, p. 9.

more variety and a greater selection of merchandise than can smaller food stores, which is appealing to higher-income-level consumers.

The 1970s saw a severe drop in grocery outlet density in nearly all countries. Six countries—Australia, the United States, South Africa, The Netherlands, Great Britain and Sweden—now have one outlet or less per thousand head of population. A number of other countries—Ireland, Belgium, Germany—have experienced reduction in outlet density by more than half.

The trend continues even in countries with a low density of stores already, for example, in the United States, where 8,000 stores have disappeared in the past two years, and The Netherlands, where 1,400 stores closed in the 1982–84 period. Industry observers expect this trend of fewer grocery stores to continue at varying rates in different countries in the future. Stabilization may come at or before the U.S. level, or at an artificially elevated level, due (for example) to worker-protective legislation limiting the opening of large supermarkets, as in the past in Italy.

There are seven countries in Table 14–1 which have more than three grocery stores per thousand inhabitants, namely Italy, South Korea, Spain, Argentina, Portugal, Greece and Colombia. One store in these countries serves about 300 inhabitants, or less than 100 families.[2]

[2]*The Grocery Marketing Scene,* Nielsen Marketing Research, no. 8, 1984, p. 8.

CHANNEL TERMINOLOGY[3]

Nielsen adopted the following definitions to classify three categories of large grocery stores according to their selling areas:

1. Hypermarkets: stores with selling areas exceeding 2,500 m² (25,000 square feet)
2. Supermarkets: stores with selling areas between 400–2,500 m² (4,000 to 25,000 square feet)
3. Superettes: stores with selling areas between 100–1,000 m² (1,000 to 4,000 square feet)

In practice, these types of stores have many different names in different countries and the selling area definitions also vary. Lower limits of 1,000 m² or 1,500 m² are quite frequently adopted, and the names of very large stores include hyper-

TABLE 14–2 Share of Total Trade Accounted for by Superettes, Supermarkets, and Hypermarkets

	% NUMBER	% TURNOVER	
	1.1.83	1976	1982
United States	67.6	96.2	97.0
Canada	42.2		95.9
The Netherlands	41.9	78.5	88.3
France	14.7	76.3	87.1
Norway	57.7		86.3
Belgium	19.1	75.8	84.6
Germany	30.2	70.6	79.8
Switzerland	29.1	72.6	79.0
Austria	39.5	64.9	78.8
Brazil	6.0	58.4	69.3
New Zealand	33.7		68.4
Japan	9.5	55.8	62.1
Mexico	1.8	22.6	56.3
Spain	4.0	20.1	48.8
Colombia	.9		47.0
Italy	5.6	23.7	39.0
Argentina	2.7		30.7
Greece	1.6		
Portugal		18.7	
Sweden		70.2	
South Africa	30.6		

Source: *The Grocery Marketing Scene,* Nielsen Marketing Research, No. 8 (1984), p. 18.

[3]This section draws heavily on *The Grocery Marketing Scene,* A. C. Nielsen Company, various issues.

markets, mass merchandisers, discounters, consumer markets, superstores, and so on. The proportion of grocery stores which fall in this classification ranges from 1.5 percent in Greece to 67.6 percent in the United States.

In general, countries where the proportion of store numbers is low in relation to their share of turnover, such as France, Belgium, Spain, Brazil and Colombia, are those which joined the supermarket revolution many years after it began and thus started with large, modern, and highly efficient units.

Italy is slowly implementing a network of large surface stores, despite adverse laws affecting such openings (49 percent share today versus 24 percent six years ago).

In other countries, where supermarkets have existed for more than two decades, some of the smaller units have been closed down and the new, very large stores are, in a sense, replacements rather than innovations. Of the 19 countries listed for 1982, 12 had more than two-thirds of their volume concentrated in large stores.

The share of total trade accounted for by these three categories is shown in Table 14–2.

CHANNEL STRUCTURE

Consumer Products

Figure 14–1 summarizes channel structure alternatives for consumer products. A consumer products manufacturer can sell directly to his customer either by a door-to-door sales force, through mail-order selling using a catalog or other printed description of offerings, or through manufacturer-owned stores. Of the three direct alternatives, the mail-order business is the most thriving. Indeed, some observers predict that this form of distribution will grow in importance as time, one of the scarcest of modern resources, becomes increasingly scarce as consumers trade off the time cost of in-store shopping versus the demands upon time of leisure activity.

Door-to-door selling, which is an expensive form of distribution that requires high gross margins and results in higher prices to the customer, is a form of selling that is not growing in importance and is possibly declining. Certain items continue to be sold in this manner—namely, encyclopedias, brushes, vacuum cleaners, and cosmetics. A variation on the door-to-door selling method is the consumer party selling arrangement where a representative of a manufacturer arranges an informal semisocial gathering in the home of a cooperating consumer in order to describe and demonstrate the goods he is selling. This "house party" form of selling has been particularly effective for manufacturers of cosmetics and kitchenware. Although the house party method originated in the United States, its viability has been demonstrated in Europe and Asia by successful applications of the method.

Another variant of the door-to-door selling method, which has achieved some success in Europe, is the consignment sale of merchandise to part-time sales people who take orders for the company's product from a circle of acquaintances and friends.

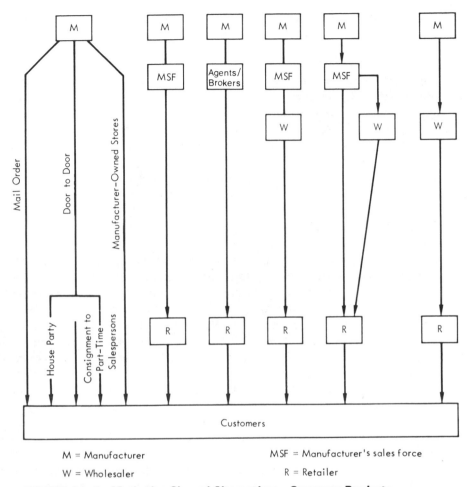

M = Manufacturer   MSF = Manufacturer's sales force

W = Wholesaler   R = Retailer

FIGURE 14–1   Marketing Channel Alternatives—Consumer Products

A French company established a major market position in the liquid household cleaner market in France by using this distribution method.

A third direct selling alternative is the manufacturer-owned store. Although in some industries manufacturer-owned stores are a major channel of distribution, most companies avoid this alternative. They choose instead to establish one or two retail outlets for obtaining marketing intelligence rather than as a distribution strategy. In those areas where a manufacturer's product line is sufficient to support a viable retail outlet, the possibilities for this form of distribution are much more attractive. The shoe store, for example, is a viable retail unit, and shoe manufacturers typically have established their own direct outlets as a major weapon in their distribution strategy. One of the first successful U.S. international companies, Singer, established a worldwide chain of company-owned and -operated outlets to sell and service sewing machines.

The other alternatives for consumer products channel structure are various combinations of a manufacturer's sales force and wholesalers calling upon retail outlets, which in turn sell to customers.

These alternatives usually produce patterns that are characteristic of a product class in a country at a particular time. In Japan, for example, several layers of small wholesalers play an important role in the distribution of food. Attempts to bypass these apparently unnecessary units in the channel have failed because the cost to a manufacturer of providing their service (frequent small deliveries to small grocery outlets) is greater than the margin they require. Channel patterns that appear to be inefficient *may* reflect rational adjustment to costs and preferences in a market, or they may present an opportunity to the innovative international marketer to obtain a competitive advantage by introducing more effective channel arrangements.

Global Retailing

Global retailing is retailing activity that spans national boundaries. There is a growing interest among successful retailers today to expand globally. This is not a new phenomenon. For centuries, venturesome merchants have gone abroad both to obtain merchandise and ideas and to operate retail establishments. In 1929 the spread of foreign-owned jewelry shops in New York City led the *New Yorker* to speak of "the invasion of Rue de la Paix houses."[4] The development of trading company operations in Africa and Asia by British, French, Dutch, Belgian, and German retailing organizations progressed extensively during the nineteenth and early twentieth centuries. International trading and retail store operation was one of the economic pillars of the colonial system of the nineteenth and early twentieth centuries. The big change taking place in international retailing today involves the gradual dissolution of the colonial retailing structure and, in its place, the creation of international retailing organizations, which operate in the industrialized countries.

The large number of unsuccessful international retailing ventures suggests that anyone contemplating a move into international retailing should do so with a great deal of caution. The critical question, which the would-be international retailer must answer, is, "What advantages do we have relative to local competition?" The answer to this question, when local laws governing retailing practice are taken into account, in many cases will be "Nothing." In such cases there is no reason to expect highly profitable operations to develop from a venture into international retailing. On the other hand, the answer may indicate positive points. Basically, a retailer has two things to offer the public. One is the selection of goods at a price, and the second is the overall manner in which the goods are offered in the store setting. This includes the store site, parking facilities, in-store setting, customer service, and so on. An excellent example of an international retailer with an advantage over local competition is Benetton's, which combines a superb logistics and information system that

[4]"On and Off the Avenue," November 23, 1929, p. 95, quoted in Stanley C. Hollander, "The International Storekeepers," *MSU Business Topics,* Spring 1969.

insures that all outlets carry colors and styles customers want with a fresh approach to store location and in-store display. The Benetton's formula is so successful that the company as of 1987 had opened a new Benetton's every day somewhere in the world since 1985. This is a new record and demonstrates the potential that can be tapped.

Industrial Products

Figure 14–2 summarizes marketing channel alternatives for the industrial product company. Three basic elements are involved: the manufacturer's sales force, distributors or agents, and wholesalers. A manufacturer can reach customers with his or her own sales force, or a sales force that calls on wholesalers who sell to customers, or a combination of these two arrangements. A manufacturer can sell directly to wholesalers without using a sales force, and wholesalers in turn can supply customers. Finally, a distributor or agent can call on wholesalers or customers for a manufacturer.

Patterns vary from country to country. To decide which pattern to use and

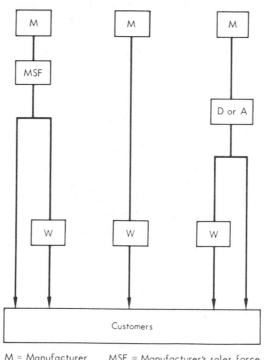

M = Manufacturer   MSF = Manufacturer's sales force

W = Wholesaler   D or A = Distributor or Agent

**FIGURE 14–2   Marketing Channel Alternatives—
Industrial Products**

which wholesalers and agents to select, each country must be studied individually. The larger the market, the more feasible the manufacturer's sales force alternative.

CHANNELS IN LESS DEVELOPED COUNTRIES

One of the conspicuous features of channels in less developed countries is the remarkable number of people engaged in selling merchandise, usually in very small quantities. The number and variety of intermediaries in the channel have been criticized by official and unofficial observers. B. P. Bauer comments on these criticisms as follows:

> These criticisms rest on a misunderstanding. The system (in LDCs) is a logical adaptation to certain fundamental factors in the West African economies which will persist for many years to come. So far from being wasteful, it is highly economic in saving and salvaging those resources which are particularly scarce in West Africa (above all, real capital) by using the resources which are largely redundant and for which there is very little demand: and thus it is productive by any rational economic criteria.[5]

Another way of looking at the channel arrangements in less developed countries is to examine the costs of these arrangements to consumers. A study of East Africa revealed that the small *dukas* (a small store typically carrying under 100 items and occupying no more than 50 to 75 sq ft of space) indicated that they were operating on average gross margins of approximately 12 percent. This fact the reader will recall is to be compared with the average gross margin in the typical U.S. supermarket of roughly 22 percent. Clearly, by the measure of markup the small East African *duka* is a lower-cost form of distribution.

Since these *dukas* operate at lower costs, does it mean that they are more efficient than the supermarket? If a measure of efficiency is the ratio of productivity or output per worker-hour, and if in retail trade the measure of productivity is the physical volume or monetary volume of sales per person, the East African *duka* is a highly inefficient form of distribution compared with the U.S. supermarket. The sales per person in the *duka* are a fraction of sales per person in the U.S. supermarket. *Duka* prices and margins are lower because the total income or salary of the *duka* operator is a fraction of that of even the lowest-level employee of a large American supermarket. By using overabundant resources that are in surplus (labor), the *duka* employs resources that would otherwise be unemployed and does so at a cost to the consuming public market that is only slightly more than half the cost of U.S. supermarket retailing.

In the early 1960s the Tanganyika government decided that it would contribute to the general welfare of the nation by opening government-managed supermarkets or food distribution outlets that would compete with the small *duka*. At the time, it was mistakenly alleged by the government, and perhaps believed by some of the population, that *duka* operators were overcharging the public. The government, after

[5]B. P. Bauer, *West African Trade* (Cambridge: Cambridge University Press), p. 22.

establishing its own food distribution outlets, discovered that it was impossible to compete in price with the *dukas*. The government discovered that the operators of the *dukas,* or *dukawallas* as they are known, were earning modest incomes and that, in terms of cost to the consumer, the private retail system of East Africa was a lower-cost arrangement than the government-run stores. The main reason for this was that the *dukawalla* was willing to work from dawn to dusk for the same or less return than the government employee who worked from 9:00 A.M. to 5:00 P.M. with two hours off for lunch.

INTERNATIONAL CHANNEL INNOVATION

The nature of channels in markets around the world is highly differentiated. At first glance there is little to explain the nature of this differentiation other than culture and the income level that exists in the market. Upon further study, however, four postulates have been formulated that explain the incidence and rate of innovation in channels at the retail level:

1. Innovation takes place only in the most highly developed systems. Channel agents in less developed systems in general will adapt developments already tried and tested in more highly developed systems.
2. The ability of a system to successfully adapt innovations is directly related to its level of economic development. Certain minimum levels of economic development are necessary to support anything beyond the most simple retailing methods.
3. When the economic environment is favorable to change, the process of adaptation may be either hindered or helped by local demographic-geographic factors, social mores, government action, and competitive pressures.
4. The process of adaptation can be greatly accelerated by the actions of aggressive individual firms.[6]

Self-service, or the provision for customers to handle and select merchandise themselves in a retail channel without supervision, is a major channel innovation of the twentieth century. It provides an excellent illustration of the propositions just outlined. Self-service was first introduced in the United States. The spread of self-service to other countries supports the hypothesis that the ability of a system to accept innovations is directly related to the level of economic development in the system. Self-service was first introduced internationally into the most highly developed systems. It has spread to the countries at middle and lower stages of development but serves very small segments of the total market in these countries.

If a marketing system has reached a stage of development that will support a channel innovation, it is clear that the action of well managed firms can contribute considerably to the diffusion of the channel innovation. The rapid growth of Benetton's and McDonald's is a testament to the skill and competence of these firms as well as to the appeal of their product.

[6]Adapted from Edward W. Cundiff, "Concepts in Comparative Retailing," *Journal of Marketing,* January 1965, pp. 59–63.

CHANNEL STRATEGY FOR NEW MARKET ENTRY

A global company expanding across national boundaries often finds itself in the position of entering a new market. A major obstacle to establishing a position in a new market can be obtaining distribution. This obstacle is particularly true in the case of entering a competitive market with established brands and supply relationships. There is little immediate incentive for an independent channel agent to take on a new product when established names are accepted in the market and are satisfying current demands. The global company seeking to enter the market must provide some incentive to channel agents or establish its own direct distribution. Each of these alternatives has its disadvantages. If a company decides to provide special incentives to independent channel agents, these incentives can be extremely expensive. They might involve outright payments for sales performance, either a direct cash bonus or some contest award. Another incentive could be the guarantee of a gross margin in highly priced competitive markets. Both incentive payments and margin guarantees are expensive. The incentive payments are directly expensive; the margin guarantees can be indirectly expensive because they affect the price to the consumer and the price competitiveness of a manufacturer's product.

The alternative of establishing direct distribution in a new market has the disadvantage of being expensive. Sales representatives and sales management must be hired and trained. The sales organization will inevitably be a heavy loser in its early stage of operation because in a new market it will not have sufficient volume to cover its overhead costs. Therefore any company contemplating the establishment of a direct sales force, even one assigned to distributors, should be prepared to underwrite losses for this sales force for a reasonable period of time.

The expense of a direct sales force acts as a deterrent to establishing direct distribution in a new market. Nevertheless, it is often the most effective method. Indeed, in many instances the only feasible way that a new company can establish itself in a market is via direct distribution. With a sales force the manufacturer can ensure aggressive sales activity and attention to his or her products. With sufficient resource commitment in sales activity, backed up by appropriate communications programs including advertising, in time a manufacturer with competitive products and prices can expect to obtain a reasonable share of market. When the market share has been obtained, the manufacturer is in a position to consider the abandonment of the direct sales force and shift to reliance upon independent intermediaries. This shift becomes a possibility when market share and its corollary, market recognition, makes the manufacturer's brand interesting to independent intermediaries.

CASE EXAMPLE: JAPAN

Japan has presented an especially difficult distribution challenge.[7] Distribution in Japan has often been described as complex because of the many fragmented retail

[7]This section is adapted from "Planning for Distribution in Japan," Japan External Trade Organization (JETRO) Marketing Series No. 4, rev. 1978.

outlets and the number of intermediaries needed to service these outlets. Perhaps a more apt description of Japanese distribution would be a highly developed system that has evolved to satisfy the needs of the Japanese consumer.

The categories of wholesalers and retailers in Japan are very finely divided. For example, meat stores in Japan do about 80 percent of their business in meat items. Similar concentrations exist in other speciality stores as well. This kind of concentration is also true at the wholesale level. This very high degree of specialization in Japan is made possible by the clustering of various types of stores at major street intersections or stops along commuter rail lines.

There are, of course, many instances in which overseas firms have entered the Japanese market and have been able to overcome difficulties presented by the distribution system. Unfortunately, problems in coping with and adapting to Japanese distribution have also prevented a number of firms from achieving the success they might have had. Foreign marketers in Japan make two basic mistakes. The first is their attitude that distribution problems can be solved the same way they would be in the West, that is, by going as directly as possible to the customer and thus cutting out the middleman. In Japan, because of the very fragmented nature of retailing, it is simply not cost effective to go direct.

The second mistake often made is in treating the Japanese market at arm's length by selling to a trading company that in turn sells to a very limited segment of the market, such as the luxury segment at low volumes. With limited volume, there is usually limited interest on the part of the trading company and the end result is disappointing to everybody involved.

Successful distribution in Japan (and in any other market) requires adaptation to the realities of the marketplace. In the Japanese case, this means adaptation to the reality of fragmented distribution. Second, it requires research into the market itself: customer needs, competitive products, and then the development of an overall marketing strategy that positions the product vis-à-vis market segment identified according to need, price, and so forth, and that positions the product against competitors and lays out a marketing plan including a distribution plan for achieving volume and share-of-market objectives.

Six Steps to a Japanese Distribution Strategy

Shimaguchi and Rosenberg recommend six steps for mastering a distribution strategy for Japan[8]:

1. Find a Japanese partner. As long as the trade practices and thinking of Japanese business managers remain mysterious, it is wise to find a partner who can navigate the strange water. The most common partners are import agents ranging from small local distributors to the giant *sogo-shosha* (general trading companies).
2. Seek a distinctive market position. The best bet in Japan is better quality or a lower price or a distinctive positioning as a foreign product.

[8]Mitsuaki Shimaguchi and Larry J. Rosenberg, "Demystifying Japanese Distribution," *Columbia Journal of World Business,* Spring 1979, pp. 38–41.

3. Identify available alternative distribution routes. Also consider alternatives to present channels. Philips, for example, has devised a way of marketing its shavers and coffee makers in both large and small outlets. S. C. Johnson Son linked up with the wholesalers who reach 300,000 individually operated retailers with 60 percent of the market and terminated all direct dealings with large retailers. This strategy achieved a very high penetration because the wholesalers sold to the large retailers as well.

4. Focus your distribution resources. The market is too big for a shotgun approach.

5. Prepare for a long-term effort and modest returns. Nothing happens quickly in Japanese distribution. Be patient.

6. Cultivate personal relationships in distribution. Remember, loyalty and trust are important.

SUMMARY

Channel decisions are difficult to manage globally because of the variety of channel structure from country to country. Nevertheless, certain patterns of change associated with market development offer the global marketer who recognizes this pattern the opportunity to innovate and gain a competitive advantage in the channels.

In retail channels, there is a substitution of capital for labor in developed countries in the self-service store, which offers a wide range of articles at relatively low gross margins. Less developed countries with abundant labor disguise their unemployment in "inefficient" retail and wholesale channels that are suited to the needs of consumers and operate gross margins that are often 50 percent lower than those in more efficient self-service stores in developed countries. A global marketer must either tailor his marketing program to these different types of channels or he must introduce a new retail concept that creates value for customers.

BIBLIOGRAPHY

Books

BARTELS, ROBERT. *Comparative Marketing: Wholesaling in Fifteen Countries*. Homewood, Ill.: Richard D. Irwin, 1963.

BAUER, P. T. *West African Trade*. Cambridge: Cambridge University Press, 1954.

FIELDS, GEORGE. *From Bonsai to Levi's: An Insider's Surprising Account of How the Japanese Live*. New York: Macmillan, 1983.

GUNNAR, BEETH. *International Management Practice, An Insider's View*. New York: AMACOM, 1973.

HARVEY, MICHAEL G., AND ROBERT F. LUSCH, eds. *Marketing Channels: Domestic and International Perspectives*. Norman, Okla.: Center for Economic & Management Research, 1982.

STERN, LOUIS W., AND ADEL L. EL-ANSARY. *Marketing Channels,* 3rd ed. Englewood Cliffs, N.J.: Prentice-Hall, 1988.

WALDMAN, CHARLES. *Strategies of International Mass Retailers.* New York: Praeger Publishers, 1978.

Articles

SHIMAGUCHI, MITSUAKI, AND LARRY J. ROSENBERG. "Demystifying Japanese Distribution." *Columbia Journal of World Business,* Spring 1979, pp. 32–41.

SORENSON, RALPH Z., II. "U.S. Marketers Can Learn from European Innovators." *Harvard Business Review,* September–October 1972.

WARNER-LAMBERT JAPAN LTD., SCHICK PRODUCTS DIVISION[1]

In May 1976, Mr. Stewart H. Burnett,[2] representative director, and Mr. H. Hirao, general manager of the Schick Products Division of Warner-Lambert Japan, met with managers of K. Hattori & Co., Ltd., Warner-Lambert's sole distributor in Japan for Schick shaving products. The purpose of the meeting was a preliminary discussion of the 1977 marketing plan for Warner-Lambert's line of razors and razor blades. The company's advertising agency, Dai-Ichi Compton, Inc., had recommended an increase in the 1977 media budget from ¥350 million in 1976 to ¥600 million,[3] to be allocated in equal parts to the Schick Division's major product, the Schick Injector, and the newest product, the Schick Super II.

While an increased media budget would not present any cash flow problems, Mr. Burnett was not sure whether such an increase was really necessary to meet the division's marketing objectives. Moreover, he wondered what should be the division's overall marketing strategy for 1977 and beyond.

COMPANY BACKGROUND

Warner-Lambert Company, headquartered in Morris Plains, New Jersey, was one of the largest pharmaceutical companies in the United States. The company had grown rapidly since the early 1960s, mainly through acquisitions. Two major acquisitions in recent years were American Optical Co. and the pharmaceutical firm Parke-Davis & Co.

Total company sales in 1975 amounted to roughly $2.2 billion, generating net profits of $164 million. Approximately 56 percent of total sales and 60 percent of total profits came from the U.S. market. Foreign sales were becoming increasingly important; in 1975 they had grown by 16 percent over the preceding year's figure. International operations were the fastest-growing segment of the company's business. Table 1 shows the development of total corporate and international sales from 1971 to 1975.

Warner-Lambert products were sold in

---

[1] This case was prepared as the basis for class discussion rather than to illustrate either effective or ineffective handling of an administrative situation. Copyright © 1979 by the President and Fellows of Harvard College. Used with permission.

[2] Some names have been disguised.

[3] Exchange rate in 1976: $1 = ¥290.

TABLE 1 Development of Sales and Profits of Warner-Lambert Company and Warner-Lambert International, 1971–1975 (in millions of dollars)

| | WARNER-LAMBERT COMPANY | | | WARNER-LAMBERT INTERNATIONAL | |
| | | Total Corporate Profit | | | Profit as a Percentage of Total Corporate Pretax Profit |
Year	Total Corporate Sales	Pretax	After-Tax	Sales	
1971	$1,346	$205	$108	$498	28%
1972	1,472	228	124	556	30
1973	1,665	256	146	692	39
1974	1,911	263	148	821	40
1975	2,172	289	164	954	38

Source: Warner-Lambert *1975 Annual Report.*

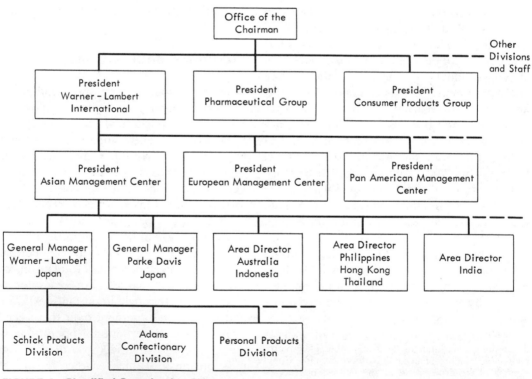

FIGURE 1 Simplified Organization Chart

Source: Company records.

more than 140 countries; the company's most important foreign markets were Germany, France, the United Kingdom, Japan, Canada, and Mexico. Razors and blades were manufactured in Canada, Sweden, The Netherlands, Hong Kong, and Venezuela, aside from the United States. All foreign operations were controlled by the international division, Warner-Lambert International. Figure 1 shows a simplified organization chart for the company's international operations and, in particular, the operations in the Far East.

Warner-Lambert's products could be grouped into four major categories:

1. *Pharmaceutical products.* Included in this category were ethical pharmaceuticals such as cardiovascular drugs and antibiotics; biologicals, such as vaccines; and diagnostics, such as reagents. In 1975 this product category contributed 38 percent to worldwide sales.

2. *Scientific instruments and ophthalmic products.* Products in this category included testing and diagnostic instruments for hospitals and dental clinics as well as all types of eyeglass lenses and frames. The contribution of this product category to 1975 worldwide sales was 15 percent.

3. *Proprietaries and shaving products.* This product category included health care specialties sold over the counter, such as denture cleanser tablets, antiseptics, and convenience drugs. In addition this product group included all types of razors and blades sold under the Schick label. In 1975 this product category contributed ' 18 percent to Warner-Lambert's worldwide sales.

4. *Chewing gum and confectionaries.* Warner-Lambert was one of the leading producers of chewing gum (principal brands: Chiclets, Dentyne) and also marketed confectionaries and mints. Together, these products contributed 22 percent to 1975 worldwide sales.

In addition to these four major product categories, Warner-Lambert marketed a range of less important products that together accounted for the remaining 7 percent of corporate sales.

ORGANIZATION FOR MARKETING IN JAPAN

The Schick Products Division of Warner-Lambert Japan was responsible for marketing the company's line of razors and blades in Japan. The Japanese division accounted for a sizable portion of Warner-Lambert's Schick sales.

Sales of Schick razors and blades in Japan had started during the American occupation following World War II. A small number of the Schick razors imported into Japan for military personnel could be found in the civilian market. They attracted the attention of managers of K. Hattori & Co. Ltd. Hattori was originally a trading company and import house. The company later started manufacturing watches and became one of the world's leading watch manufacturers, selling its products under the Seiko brand name.

For several years, Hattori imported Schick razors and blades into Japan without having a formal agreement with Schick. The imported products were simply bought from one of Schick's U.S. distributors on the West Coast. Around 1955 management of Schick became interested in Japan as a potential market for overseas expansion. Much to its surprise, it discovered that its products were already represented in Japan through the import initiative of Hattori. A formal contract was concluded by which Hattori became officially the sole distributor of Schick products in Japan.

This arrangement proved satisfactory to both parties and still existed in 1976. Under the terms of this arrangement, Hattori had primary responsibility for distribution. The overall marketing plan for the Schick line of products was, however, a matter of discussion and negotiation between both the managements of the Schick Products Division of Warner-Lambert Japan and the Sundry Goods Department of K. Hattori & Co. Typically, but not exclusively, management of the Schick Products Division provided the major inputs into decisions about new products, pricing, and advertising, whereas Hattori's influence concentrated on the distribution and sales promotion decisions.

The total marketing plan, and in particular proposals for new products and advertising campaigns, developed through the joint work of Hattori and the Schick Products Division, required approval by the U.S. headquarters of Warner-Lambert International. In the view of Mr. Burnett of Warner-Lambert Japan, headquarters allowed local management a great deal of autonomy for marketing decision making. He commented on the relationship with Hattori:

We have an excellent association with Hattori. I think we have been very fortunate to be tied up with such a good and successful Japanese company. We also had the good fortune to listen to the advice of our Japanese partner. Schick was not the world leader in shaving products when they started in Japan.

Management of Hattori was equally pleased with its association with Schick. As one senior Hattori executive said,

It has been a long and mutually rewarding marriage. Our only worry is, can Schick keep up the technology pace? Fortunately, Schick was very fast in following Gillette with the twin-blade system. Otherwise, we would have lost. All our excellent distribution is not worth much if we don't get the right products.

The Schick Products Division acted merely as a marketing unit. There was no manufacturing of Schick products in Japan; all goods were imported.

Hattori bought the goods from Shick as a wholesaler, and resold them at a certain margin[4] to five primary wholesalers. The primary wholesalers sold roughly 80 percent of total volume at a margin of approximately 15 percent over cost to 680 secondary wholesalers and about 20 percent of total volume at a margin of roughly 32 percent over cost directly to retailers. The 680 secondary wholesalers in turn sold the products to retailers at a margin of about 15 percent over cost. In total, there were about 100,000–110,000 retail outlets carrying Schick products. Table 2 gives a breakdown of Schick's sales volume by type of retail outlet. Retailers typically sold the products at a margin of 33 percent over cost to final consumers. The margins given for wholesalers and retailers were typical for the industry.

THE RAZOR AND BLADE MARKET IN JAPAN

It was customary in the industry to describe market size, sales volume, and market shares in terms of the volume of blades sold. Sales of replacement blades rather than blade holders or razors determined the fortunes of any company competing in this industry.

---

[4]Confidential figure.

TABLE 2   Breakdown of Total Sales of the Schick Products Division by Type of Retail Outlet, 1975

TYPE OF RETAIL OUTLET	AS A PERCENTAGE OF SALES
Drugstores*	28%
Cosmetic stores	21
Supermarkets*	21
Barber shops	16
Variety stores	5
Department stores	3
Hardware stores	2
Miscellaneous	4
Total	100%

*Outlet type of increasing importance.

Source: Industry statistics.

The total Japanese market for razor blades was usually segmented in two ways: (1) by the type of steel used for the blades and (2) by the type of shaving system for which the blades were used.[5]

With respect to the type of steel used, a carbon steel and a stainless steel market could be distinguished. Until the early 1960s, all blade manufacturers made only carbon steel blades. Beginning in 1961 in Great Britain and in 1964 in Japan, a conversion to stainless steel swept the industry. As a result, in 1976 all major contenders in the Japanese market for refill blades marketed essentially only stainless steel blades. The same situation existed in other industrialized nations.

The stainless steel segment of the blade market could be subsegmented by type of shaving system. There were three major systems competing against each other; for each

one of these three systems, there existed minor variations. The three systems were (1) the double-edge system, (2) the single-edge system, and (3) the twin-blade system.

The term *double-edge* system referred to the traditional razor blade with a cutting edge on each side. The principal variation of this conventional system was a blade holder that allowed an adjustment of the cutting angle of the blade for beards of different strengths.

The term *single-edge* system described the injector system pioneered by Schick, the "Techmatic" system introduced by Gillette, and the "Bonded" cartridge of Wilkinson. All these variations of the single-edge system had in common that there was only one cutting edge on the blade. The injector system consisted of a slim holder into which the blades were "injected" from the side of a blade magazine. The "Techmatic" system featured a continuous band of steel in a cartridge instead of individual blades. The band was transported by a lever when the cutting edge became dull. The "Bonded" system was essentially a single-edge blade housed in a replaceable cartridge for convenience and safety. Except for the "Bonded" system, all major manufacturers had introduced their own versions of these single-edge systems. Furthermore, adjustable versions of these systems were available.

The *twin-blade* system was developed by Gillette and was introduced in the United States in 1971. Its principal feature was that two blades were placed above each other in a cartridge. By using two blades rather than one for shaving, a cleaner shave could be obtained.

More recently hybrid forms of the three principal shaving systems had appeared on the market. Schick had introduced a twin-blade injector and a twin-blade double-edge

[5] As explained later, there was a third way of segmenting the market that was almost synonymous with the first: refillable versus disposable razors.

system.[6] Both introductions were attempts to transfer the superior shaving performance of the twin-blade system to the older injector and double-edge systems. Industry observers considered the injector twin-blade as moderately successful in terms of sales but felt that the double-edge twin-blade produced unattractive sales and profit results.

Despite the fact that the multinational razor blade firms in Japan concentrated exclusively on the stainless steel segment, there still existed a fairly stable carbon steel segment. In 1975 it accounted for more than 40 percent of the total yen market and more than 75 percent of the unit market for razor blades.

This was a peculiarity of the Japanese market. The carbon steel blades were mostly sold set in cheap disposable razors. These disposable razors, called *keiben* in Japan, were highly popular. They were provided, free of charge, to guests in most hotels and at low cost in public bath houses.

Keiben (disposable razor) users represented 25 percent of the total shaving population in Japan, equivalent to 9 million shavers. Exclusive *keiben* users represented 13 percent of the total shaving population in 1975. The major reasons for using *keiben* stated by a sample of consumers were "easy to use," "convenience," and "right price." Also, while the *keiben* did not reach the shaving performance of, say, a stainless steel twin-blade system, it was quite satisfactory for the generally softer beards of the Japanese male population as compared with other ethnic groups.

In 1975, 27 manufacturers competed in the *keiben* segment; among them one local company, Kai-Mark, was estimated to have more than a 60 percent share of the 1975 market. The carbon *keiben* typically sold to con-

sumers at a price of ¥10 per razor. Consumer research in 1975 had shown that on the average, each razor was used 2.3 times, 42 percent of *keiben* users discarded it after one shave.

More recently, Kai-Mark had introduced more expensive disposable razors fitted with a stainless steel blade and even stainless steel twin blades. These razors sold for about ¥40–50 to consumers. This move signaled that the *keiben* market, which still was largely synonymous with the carbon steel market, was developing into a segmented market comprising both a low-priced (carbon) segment and a higher-priced (stainless steel) segment. The industry had therefore started another classification of the market: disposable razors (comprising both carbon and stainless steel blades) versus refillable razors.

Some industry observers predicted a significant revitalization of the disposable razor market. In addition to Kai-Mark, two multinational firms had entered the higher-priced disposable razor segment in June 1975. Bic, the French company reputed for its worldwide success in the fields of disposable writing instruments and lighters, was offering a stainless steel disposable razor selling for ¥50. Gillette had introduced a stainless steel twin-blade razor for ¥90. Both Bic and Gillette had also introduced their disposable products in the United States and Europe. Schick had not yet entered the disposable razor market anywhere in the world.

Figure 2 and Table 3 show the quantitative composition and development of the Japanese razor blade market by market segment. The following principal conclusions may be drawn from these data:

1. The total razor blade market was constantly decreasing in units, while the market size in value was slightly expanding. Industry analysts attributed this

---

[6] Because of these hybrid forms, the original twin-blade system that used a replaceable cartridge was commonly referred to as "twin-blade cartridge system."

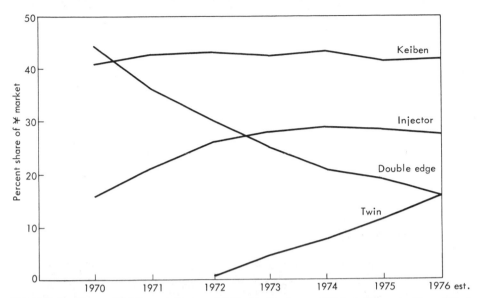

FIGURE 2 **Share of Different Types of Shaving Systems of Total Japanese Razor Blade Market, 1970–1976 (in ¥ at manufacturers prices)**

Source: Industry statistics.

market shrinkage in units to the fact that economy-minded consumers tried to achieve more shaves per blade and that many consumers shifted to electric razors.

2. The carbon steel refillable segment was decreasing rapidly in units. The *keiben* segment (more than 95 percent carbon steel) was also decreasing, but less dramatically.

3. In the stainless refillable category, the twin-blade segment was growing most rapidly, both in terms of units and value.

4. The double-edge system showed the characteristics of a declining product: losses in units, value, and market share.

5. The single-edge segment remained fairly stable with slight increases in market share. Industry analysts maintained that the reason for this stability was not that single-edge had hard-core users but that

single-edge gained about an equal number of new users from double-edge and *keiben* as it lost users to twin-blade systems.

THE JAPANESE MARKET FOR ELECTRIC SHAVERS

The "wet" shaving system described so far faced increasing competition from "dry" (electric) razors. A survey conducted in 1975 revealed the following percentages for the ownership of wet and dry systems among consumers in the area around Tokyo: wet system only, 36 percent of shaving population; dry system only, 25 percent; both systems, 39 percent.

The firms competing in the electric razor market were mostly large electrical goods manufacturers with high brand awareness and high public recognition. The leading brand

TABLE 3 Composition and Development of the Japanese Razor Blade Market, 1973–1977 (manufacturers' sales in thousands of blades and millions of yen)

Unit Sales (000 blades)	1973 Sales	1973 % Total Market	1974 Sales	1974 % Total Market	1975 Sales	1975 % Total Market	1976* Sales	1976* % Total Market	1977 Sales	1977 % Total Market
Refillable razor total	275,160	20.3%	269,581	24.1%	247,540	24.7%	242,700	25.9%	243,595	27.3%
Stainless steel total	208,616	15.4	220,516	19.7	214,848	21.4	219,718	23.4	230,806	25.9
Single-edge total	93,336	6.9	99,425	8.8	86,193	8.6	85,874	9.2	86,480	9.6
Single-edge injector	84,322	6.2	91,607	8.1	81,115	8.1	82,460	8.8	84,415	9.4
Techmatic and cartridge	9,014	.7	7,818	.7	5,078	.5	3,414	.4	2,065	.2
Double-edge total	106,039	7.8	95,821	8.6	85,392	8.5	80,236	8.5	74,745	8.4
Single-blade double-edge	106,039		95,821	8.6	84,780	8.4	79,287	8.4	73,348	8.3
Twin-blade double-edge	—		—		612	.1	949	.1	1,397	.1
Twin-blade total	9,241	.7	25,270	2.3	43,223	4.3	53,608	5.7	69,581	7.8
Twin-blade injector	—		5,288	.5	11,988	1.2	16,003	1.7	22,113	2.5
Twin-blade cartridge	9,241	.7	19,982	1.8	31,235	3.1	37,605	4.0	47,468	5.3
Carbon steel total	66,544	4.9	49,065	4.4	32,692	3.3	22,982	2.5	12,789	1.4
Disposable (keiben) razor total	1,080,029	79.7	850,396	75.9	753,770	75.3	692,817	74.1	647,120	72.7
All razor blades total	1,355,189	100.0%	1,119,977	100.0%	1,001,310	100.0%	935,517	100.0%	890,715	100.0%
Yen (millions)										
Refillable razor total	8,096	47.5%	9,132	50.4%	10,345	53.7%	11,969	56.7%	14,461	59.3%
Stainless steel total	7,394	43.4	8,549	47.2	9,921	51.5	11,621	55.1	14,200	58.2
Single-edge total	3,940	23.1	4,207	23.2	4,218	21.9	4,570	21.7	5,221	21.4
Single-edge injector	3,457	20.3	3,788	20.9	3,923	20.4	4,360	20.7	5,143	21.1
Techmatic and cartridge	483	2.8	419	2.3	295	1.5	210	1.0	78	.3
Double-edge total	2,952	17.3	2,835	15.7	2,782	14.4	2,823	13.4	2,975	12.2
Single-blade double-edge	2,952	17.3	2,835	15.7	2,745	14.2	2,766	13.1	2,883	11.8
Twin-blade double-edge	—		—		37	.2	57	.3	92	.4
Twin-blade total†	502	3.0	1,507	8.3	2,921	15.2	4,228	20.0	6,004	24.6
Twin-blade injector	—		295	1.6	708	3.7	894	4.2	1,377	5.6
Twin-blade cartridge	502	3.0	1,212	6.7	2,213	11.5	3,334	15.8	4,627	19.0
Carbon steel total	702	4.1	583	3.2	424	2.2	348	1.6	261	1.1
Disposable (keiben) razor total	8,949	52.5	9,002	49.6	8,912	46.3	9,129	43.3	9,938	40.7
All razor blades total	17,045	100.0%	18,134	100.0%	19,257	100.0%	21,098	100.0%	24,399	100.0%

*Estimates of Schick management.

†Does not include hybrid types (e.g., double-edge twin blades).

Source: Industry statistics.

was National, with a market share of approximately 40 percent. It was followed by Seiko (13 percent); Hitachi, Toshiba, and Sanyo (about 10 percent each); Braun, a subsidiary of Gillette (about 8 percent); and Philips (about 3 percent). Seiko was the brand of K. Hattori & Co., which also distributed the Schick wet shaving products in Japan. Marketing of the Schick and Seiko shavers was, however, handled by different departments within the Hattori organization.

The electric razor industry spent heavily on advertising. Total industry media expenditures in 1975 were estimated at ¥1.5 billion; expenditures in 1976 were expected to reach ¥1.6 billion.

THE POSITION OF SCHICK IN THE JAPANESE RAZOR BLADE MARKET

Schick was the market leader in the stainless steel segment of the Japanese market. Although Schick had started as a newcomer in the early 1960s against established positions of Feather, a local firm, and Gillette, its multinational rival, by 1976 the Schick brand enjoyed an overall share of roughly 60 percent of the stainless steel refillable razor market. Executives at Warner-Lambert realized that it would be difficult to increase this market share further. There was, consequently, considerable concern about alternative product-market areas for growth.

The spectacular rise of Schick in the Japanese market was attributed by management mainly to the fact that in Japan, Schick had always managed to be at the forefront of product innovations and that it had maintained an excellent distribution system. Schick emphasized the single-edge and twin-blade injector razors when competing companies were still concentrating their efforts on the traditional double-edge system. Schick also was more aggressive in opening new channels of distribution for razor blades, such as barber shops and Pachinko halls.[7] More than Gillette, for example, Schick also relied on a vast number of primary and secondary wholesalers for the distribution of its products. Management admitted that as the retail industry became more concentrated, a smaller number of secondary wholesalers and a greater emphasis on direct sales to retail chains would be feasible.

The injector razor and blades had been the basis of Schick's early success. When the injector system was brought to Japan by Hattori in 1955, it had been a different and innovative product. In 1976, although copied by major competitors, it continued to be the mainstay of Schick's business. The company made big efforts to continuously revitalize the injector system. That was why, in 1974, after the twin-blade cartridge had turned out to be a solid market success, Schick introduced a twin-blade injector system.

While Gillette and Bic had started to enter the disposable razor (*keiben*) segment in several countries around the world, including Japan, Schick so far had not moved into this market. Some members of Schick's management argued that entry into the disposable razor segment might only cannibalize injector sales and not generate additional volume.

Tables 4 through 7 show the developments of sales, market shares, distribution, and advertising expenditures from 1973 through 1975 for Schick and its principal competitors. The following are some of the conclusions that can be drawn from these exhibits:

[7] Pachinko halls were a uniquely Japanese institution. Pachinko was a very popular leisure game played on slot machines.

TABLE 4 Sales and Shares of Total Japanese Razor Blade Market of Schick and Competitors, 1973–1975

(THOUSANDS OF BLADES AND MILLIONS OF YEN)

Firm and Product Category	1973				1974				1975			
	Sales (in 000 blades)	% of Total Market	Sales (in mil. ¥)	% of Total Market	Sales (in 000 blades)	% of Total Market	Sales (in mil. ¥)	% of Total Market	Sales (in 000 blades)	% of Total Market	Sales (in mil. ¥)	% of Total Market
Schick total	96,607	7.1%	¥ 3,937	23.1%	116,037	10.4%	¥ 4,952	27.4%	120,502	12.0%	¥ 6,326	32.9%
Single-edge	76,074	5.6	3,189	18.7	85,839	7.7	3,640	20.1	83,372	8.3	4,211	21.9
Double-edge	15,911	1.2	506	3.0	16,442	1.5	505	2.8	15,940	1.5	553	2.9
Twin-blade (cartridge)	4,622	.3	242	1.4	13,756	1.2	807	4.5	22,190	2.2	1,562	8.1
Gillette total	27,354	2.0	1,199	7.0	26,902	2.4	1,261	7.0	26,477	2.6	1,407	7.3
Single-edge	7,293	.6	385	2.2	6,563	.6	346	1.9	5,273	.5	305	1.6
Double-edge	15,442	1.1	554	3.3	14,113	1.3	509	2.8	12,319	1.2	460	2.4
Twin-blade (cartridge)	4,619	.3	260	1.5	6,226	.5	406	2.3	8,885	.9	642	3.3
Feather total	60,316	4.5	1,356	8.0	53,381	4.8	1,383	7.6	47,766	4.8	1,333	6.9
Single-edge	8,057	.6	258	1.5	9,046	.8	330	1.8	7,271	.8	280	1.4
Double-edge	52,259	3.9	1,098	6.5	44,335	4.0	1,053	5.8	40,335	4.0	1,043	5.4
Twin-blade (cartridge)	—	—	—	—	—	—	—	—	160	.0	10	.1
Wilkinson total	21,850	1.6	831	4.9	22,614	2.0	911	5.0	19,437	1.9	837	4.3
Single-edge ("Bonded")	1,722	.1	98	.6	3,153	.3	181	1.0	2,257	.2	128	.6
Double-edge	20,128	1.5	733	4.3	19,461	1.7	730	4.0	17,180	1.7	709	3.7
All other total Refillable (safety)	2,489	.2	71	.4	1,582	.1	42	.2	666	.1	18	.1
Razor total	208,616	15.4	7,394	43.4	220,516	19.7	8,549	47.2	214,848	21.4	9,921	51.5
All razor blades total	1,355,189	100.0%	¥17,045	100.0%	1,119,977	100.0%	¥18,134	100.0%	1,001,310	100.0%	¥19,257	100.0%

Source: A. C. Nielsen Co.

TABLE 5 **Market Shares of Schick and Major Competitors of the Stainless Steel Refillable (Safety) Market Segment and Subsegments, 1973–1975**

	VOLUME (BLADES)			VALUE (¥)		
	1973 (%)	1974 (%)	1975 (%)	1973 (%)	1974 (%)	1975 (%)
Schick	46.3%	52.6%	56.1%	53.2%	57.9%	63.8%
Single-edge	81.5	82.0	84.9	81.0	80.9	85.5
Double-edge	15.0	17.2	17.5	17.1	17.8	19.9
Twin-blade cartridge	50.0	68.8	71.1	48.3	66.5	70.5
Gillette	13.1	12.2	12.3	16.2	14.7	14.2
Single-edge	7.8	6.3	5.4	9.8	7.7	6.2
Double-edge	14.6	14.7	14.4	18.8	18.0	16.5
Twin-blade cartridge	50.0	31.2	28.4	51.7	33.5	29.0
Feather	28.9	24.2	22.2	18.3	16.2	13.4
Single-edge	8.6	8.6	7.4	6.5	7.3	5.7
Double-edge	49.3	46.3	47.3	37.2	37.1	37.5
Twin-blade cartridge	—	—	.5	—	—	.5
Wilkinson	10.5	10.3	9.1	11.3	10.7	8.4
All others	1.2	.7	.3	1.0	.5	.2

Source: A. C. Nielsen Co.

1. Schick was the only brand that had managed consistently to increase its *overall share* of the stainless steel refillable razor market.

2. In the *single-edge* segment, Schick gained sales in yen but in 1975 experienced a loss of sales in units. Other brands, however, suffered heavier losses in 1975. This was the first time that Schick saw a unit sales decrease for its single-edge line. While the reasons for this decrease were far from clear, some executives felt that insufficient advertising support for the injector in 1975 resulted in losing injector users to other advanced wet shaving systems or to electric shaving. Dai-Ichi Compton, the company's advertising agency, reported that "Communication of [the] technological and psychological value of injector shaving could not effectively be sustained to consumers in 1975 due to [the] drastic cut of injector media support."

3. In the *double-edge* segment, Schick, as did all other brands, showed a unit sales decrease but a slight increase in sales in yen.

4. In the *twin-blade* cartridge segment, Schick, by 1975, had acquired the leading market position; in 1973, the innovator Gillette and Schick had had roughly identical market shares. Still, in 1975, Gillette occupied about 30 percent of the twin-blade cartridge segment.

5. Sales of *injector holders* were shrinking rapidly between 1974 and 1975. Management of Schick viewed this development with concern. Maintaining and expand-

TABLE 6 Media Expenditure by Brand, 1973–1977

	1973 ¥ (millions)	1973 %	1974 ¥ (millions)	1974 %	1975 (¥ millions) TV	Radio	Print	Total	%	1976 (¥ millions) First Half	Second Half	Total	%
Schick	¥397	43.4%	¥500	50.3%	¥164	¥ 47	¥105	¥316	70.0%	¥187	¥163	¥350	71.4%
Injector	263		362		59	12	29	100		41	49	90	
Twin-blade cartridge	132		138		105	35	68	208		127	103	230	
Double-edge	2		—		—	—	8	8		—	—	—	
Promotions	—		—		—	—	—	—		19	11	30	
Gillette	139	15.2	144	14.5	77	—	23	100	22.2	43	77	120	24.5
Single-edge	3		—		—	—	—	—		—	—	—	
Twin-blade cartridge	130		144		77	—	23	100		43	77	120	
Double-edge	6		—		—	—	—	—		—	—	•	
Feather	257	28.1	210	21.2	2	—	26	28	6.2	10	10	20	4.1
Single-edge	243		210		2	—	18	20		4	4	8	
Twin-blade cartridge	—		—		—	—	4	4		3	3	6	
Double-edge	14		—		—	—	4	4		3	3	6	
Wilkinson	121	13.2	140	14.0	1	—	6	7	1.6	—	—	—	
Total	¥914	100.0%	¥944	100.0%	¥244	¥ 47	¥160	¥451	100.0%	¥240	¥250	¥490	100.0%

Source: Company records.

TABLE 7 Store Coverage (Weighted Distribution) by Type of Retail Store, March–April 1976

Brand	TYPE OF RETAIL STORE	
	Drug/Cosmetics	Food
Any *Schick* product	99%	95%
Any *Gillette* product	85	75
Any *Wilkinson* product	66	68
Any *Feather* product	81	90

Source: Nielsen Drug/Food Index, March–April 1976.

ing the ownership of injector holders obviously influenced the level of repurchases of injector blades. Some managers felt that the numbers reflected inadequate advertising support for the injector. For this reason, it was argued, new users were not becoming injector users, and current injector users were replacing worn-out razors with alternative systems.

6. Although some executives thought that *advertising* in 1975 might have been too low, Schick had continuously outspent its competitors. (See Table 6.)

7. Schick also had more intensive *distribution* than its competitors. (See Table 7.) However, distribution was much less developed for Schick's twin-blade cartridges than for its injector products.

Background Data on Competitors

GILLETTE. The Gillette Company, headquartered in Boston, was the world's largest manufacturer and marketer of shaving products. The company enjoyed a worldwide reputation as a leader and innovator in shaving technology and as a manufacturer of products of the highest quality.

The company had started manufacturing and expanding abroad as early as 1909. In 1975, Gillette's share of most of the world's blade and razor markets exceeded 50 percent. Table 8 shows the market shares of Gillette and Schick in selected countries.

Gillette's total company sales in 1975 amounted to roughly $1.4 billion, giving an after-tax net profit of about $80 million. Blades and razors accounted for 30 percent of total sales and 73 percent of total profits. Aside from blades and razors, the company manufactured and marketed a wide range of other consumer products, such as toiletries and grooming aids, writing instruments, gas lighters, and, through its German subsidiary Braun AG, electric shavers, small appliances, and radio and photographic products. Sales of the company had shown a rapid growth in recent years, as shown in Table 9.

Sales outside the United States and Canada accounted for more than half of total

TABLE 8 Shares of Gillette and Schick of the Stainless Steel Razor Blade Market in Selected Countries, 1975

Country	SHARE OF MARKET	
	Gillette	Schick
United States	58.0%	22.4%
Canada	51.0	25.9
Venezuela	61.7	35.0
Belgium	65.5	29.4
France	62.2	27.1
Germany	40.0	6.5
Holland	59.9	33.2
Sweden	53.7	46.1
Japan	14.2	63.8

Source: A. C. Nielsen Co.

TABLE 9   The Gillette Company: Development of Sales and Profits, 1971–1975

	(IN MILLIONS OF DOLLARS)					
	TOTAL COMPANY		BLADES AND RAZORS		FOREIGN OPERATIONS*	
Year	Sales	Net Profit	Sales	Net Profit	Sales	Net Profit
1971	$ 730	$62	$270	$41	$327	N.A.
1972	871	75	287	46	382	N.A.
1973	1,064	91	330	58	520	N.A.
1974	1,246	85	374	59	629	48
1975	1,407	80	521	58	721	48

N.A.—not available.

*Not including Canada.

Source: The Gillette Company, annual reports.

corporate sales. Gillette products were sold in more than 200 countries. The company had manufacturing operations in 21 foreign countries and 21 sales subsidiaries in 21 others. In the remaining areas, agents and distributors sold Gillette products. Foreign operations (excluding Canada) accounted for roughly 60 percent of Gillette's 1975 net assets; about 72 percent of foreign net assets were tied up in Western Europe, 21 percent in Latin America, and the remaining 7 percent in Africa, Asia, and Oceania.

Until the mid 1960s Gillette had relied mainly on internal growth. This growth was based on technological innovation in the company's traditional product category: razors and blades. Only rarely in the company's history had technological leadership been won by a competitor. The most significant of these rare events came in 1961. A British firm, Wilkinson, introduced the stainless steel razor blade, "which caught Gillette flat-footed and helped to slash the company's American market share from 72 percent to 50 percent. Since then, the blade business had seen more innovations than it had since the turn of the century."[8] In rapid succession, Gillette in-

[8]Bro Uttal, "Gillette Swings a Mighty Blade Abroad," *Fortune*, November 1974.

troduced first its own version of the stainless razor blade (1963), then the single-edge band cartridge razor, "Techmatic" (1968), the twin-blade cartridge razor "Trac II" (1971), the adjustable twin-blade razor (1974), and a lady's twin-blade razor "Daisy" (1975). In 1975, Gillette also introduced a disposable version of the twin-blade razor.

In its U.S. home market, Gillette had typically had about one year's lead over competition with its technological innovations. This was not always true, however, for the company's overseas markets. In Japan, for example, Gillette's twin-blade "Trac II" cartridge was not introduced before August 1972 (U.S., October 1971). Schick, in contrast, introduced its own twin-blade cartridge in the United States in July 1972, and in Japan as early as August 1972. Table 10 gives the introduction dates for the twin-blade shaving systems of Schick and Gillette in selected countries.

In the view of one industry observer, Gillette for a long time failed to realize the full potential of its foreign subsidiaries:

Until the mid-1960s they were treated as little more than blade mills, and they received new shaving products only after the U.S. market had been satisfied. . . . Gillette's problems went beyond ne-

TABLE 10 Introduction Dates of Twin-Blade Cartridge Shaving Systems of Schick and Gillette in Selected Countries

	INTRODUCTION DATE	
Country	Schick	Gillette
United States	July 1972	October 1971
Canada	May 1975	June 1972
Venezuela	April 1973	April 1973
Belgium	November 1973	January 1973
France	June 1974	November 1972
Germany	June 1974	May 1972
Holland	June 1974	September 1972
Sweden	August 1972	August 1972
Australia	September 1972	September 1972
Japan	August 1972	August 1972

Source: Company records.

glect. The company had adopted some formal policies that were as rigid and distant as a colonial emperor's. Boston decreed that all foreign subsidiaries would be wholly owned by Gillette, that all new products would be sold throughout the United States before being offered abroad, and that no subsidiary would sell any product that Gillette did not manufacture itself.[9]

The same industry observer noted, however, that Gillette's strategy had changed significantly in the mid-1960s. One of the first changes was to speed up new product introductions overseas. At the same time the company moved to an increased development of new products exclusively for overseas markets. As Gillette's President Colman M. Mockler stated,

More and more we're looking at things from a worldwide perspective. We're constructing new worldwide product lines with products generated both here and abroad. At the same time, overseas companies sell separate product lines adapted to their own local markets. We take advantage of resources *wherever* they exist.[10]

Reflecting on a recent event where Gillette strove for simultaneous new product introduction abroad even at the risk of creating domestic shortages, Mockler said

The choice was to take a limited number of machines and commit them all to the U.S., or to take a part of our resources and fan them out to give each market a limited supply. We decided to do the latter. If we had diverted our resources to the U.S., then Schick would have leap-frogged us and gained an advantage.[11]

As a result of the change in Gillette's strategic outlook, the relationship between headquarters and subsidiaries seemed to have undergone modifications. A former Gillette marketing manager described the involvement of headquarters in local marketing decisions before the mid-1960s with the following words:

Gillette assumed that new product ideas could only be generated in South Boston [company headquarters]. Changes in advertising campaigns needed approval from headquarters. In those days, all

[9]Ibid.
[10]Ibid.

[11]Ibid.

campaigns, all packages, all products were developed in Boston.

Talking about Gillette's new approach to managing foreign operations, Peter Mohrfeld, the international marketing director, mentioned

We take great pains to avoid cramming new products down local managers' throats. I was a local manager in Spain, and I know what it's like to have some jerk in Boston telling me what he thinks I should introduce, when I know more about my own market.[12]

In Japan, Gillette had started selling its shaving products prior to World War II. Industry observers stated that up to the early 1960s Gillette commanded a market share of about 20 percent; the remaining market share was held by local brands, dominant among them the brand Feather. By 1975 Gillette's share of the total Japanese blade market in yen had dropped to less than 8 percent.

Gillette's distribution system differed from that of Schick in several respects. Unlike Schick, Gillette had not associated with an exclusive distributor. Instead, Gillette Japan, the local subsidiary, sold to 31 primary wholesalers. Roughly 80 percent of Gillette's volume went through these primary wholesalers directly to retailers. The remaining 20 percent went from the 31 primary wholesalers via 100 secondary wholesalers to retailers. Prior to arriving at this distribution setup, Gillette had experimented with several other arrangements. Moreover, the composition of the 31 primary wholesalers had changed several times.

Despite these differences in the distribution systems of Schick and Gillette, both companies' products were sold through similar types of retail stores—drug/cosmetic stores

and food stores being the most important types. Moreover, both companies had accomplished very intensive store coverage. (See Table 7.)

Gillette offered the company's full line of razors and stainless steel blades in Japan: double-edge; injector systems; band ("Techmatic") systems; twin-blade systems; and, since June 1975, disposable razors.

For several years, Gillette had concentrated its marketing and advertising effort on the twin-blade cartridge system. As a result, the company's other products, which were not heavily advertised, suffered losses in market share. In 1975, Gillette spent a total of about ¥100 million on media advertising, all of which was allocated to its twin-blade products. For 1976 and 1977 management of Schick expected Gillette's media advertising budget to increase to ¥120 million and ¥150 million, respectively. Management also thought that Gillette would concentrate its advertising effort exclusively on the densely populated areas of Japan and emphasize television as a medium.

WILKINSON. Wilkinson Match Limited was a diversified multinational company headquartered in the United Kingdom. The company manufactured and marketed a range of consumer products and fire protection equipment and had interests in printing, packaging, engineering, wood chipboard, and lumber and plywood. The principal consumer products were matches, razors and razor blades, writing instruments, lighters, and garden tools.

Total company sales in 1975 amounted to £145.2 million[13]; profits after taxes were £4.1 million. Razors and blades accounted for roughly 19 percent of corporate sales and 24 percent of the company's total operating profit of £11.1 million. The most important product

---

[12]Ibid.

[13]Exchange rate in 1975: £1 = U.S.$2.40.

group in the company's broad product line was matches; they contributed about 37 percent to total corporate sales and roughly 48 percent to total operating profit.

Table 11 shows the development of Wilkinson's sales and profits for the years 1971 through 1975. In 1975 more than 60 percent of total company sales and almost 70 percent of Wilkinson's operating profit came from outside the United Kingdom. The Pacific area (including Japan) accounted for about 11 percent of 1975 corporate sales and roughly 13 percent of total operating profit.

Wilkinson had the leading share of the total U.K. razor and blade market. Outside of the United Kingdom, however, Wilkinson typically trailed Gillette and Schick in market share. Wilkinson razors and blades were sold worldwide through a network of subsidiaries, distributors, and agents. Manufacturing plants were located in England, Germany, Kenya, Spain, the United States, South Africa, and Australia.

Wilkinson had a product line that was different from and narrower as compared with either Schick or Gillette. The company's shaving products business owed its growth to the 1961 introduction of the double-edge stainless steel blade. With a superior product and a two-year lead time over competitors, Wilkinson's market share in the United Kingdom skyrocketed from 7 percent to 45 percent and made similar gains in other countries. Much of this increase in market share was subsequently lost when the Gillette and Schick companies introduced their own stainless steel products and, more important, when they brought out new competitive shaving systems.

Up to 1975 Wilkinson sold neither an injector nor a twin-blade system. In addition to the traditional double-edge blade, the company had introduced, in 1971, its own single-edge shaving system called the Wilkinson "Bonded" razor. In the opinion of many industry observers, the "Bonded" razor was an obsolete product: it did not offer advantages over the single-edge injector system and was inferior to the twin-blade systems of competitors. Moreover, Wilkinson's "Bonded" blades could only be used in Wilkinson razors; the replacement blades of both Schick and Gillette also fitted competitors', a fact that was widely advertised.

TABLE 11 Wilkinson Match Limited: Development of Sales and Profits, 1971–1975 (in millions of pounds sterling)

	TOTAL COMPANY		After-Tax Net Profit	RAZORS AND BLADES		FOREIGN OPERATIONS*	
Year	Sales	Operating Profit		Sales	Operating Profit	Sales	Operating Profit
1971	£ 75.3	£ 5.9	£3.4	N.A.	N.A.	N.A.	N.A.
1972	71.7	6.2	3.3	N.A.	N.A.	N.A.	N.A.
1973	76.8	8.6	4.8	N.A.	N.A.	N.A.	N.A.
1974	131.9	13.1	6.2	£23.4	£3.2	£75.6	£9.3
1975	145.2	11.1	4.2	27.2	3.3	89.0	7.6

N.A.—Not available.

*Outside the United Kingdom.

Source: Wilkinson Match Limited, annual reports.

In 1976, Wilkinson had just started to introduce in Europe an adjustable twin-blade cartridge system. It was virtually identical to the twin-blade systems of Schick and Gillette. As usual, Wilkinson advertised not only the quality of its blade but also the fact that its replacement cartridges fitted any twin-blade razor. It was expected that over the next few years, Wilkinson would concentrate its worldwide marketing efforts on its new twin-blade products.

In Japan, Wilkinson had started operating in 1963. It had entered the market through an importer/sole distributor. This arrangement did not prove to be satisfactory. So, in 1965, Wilkinson appointed The Lion Dentifrice Co. Ltd. as its sole distributor. Lion was the leading Japanese manufacturer and marketer of toothpaste. While exact figures were difficult to obtain, industry analysts indicated that Lion commanded a 75 percent share of the Japanese toothpaste market, that it spent in excess of ¥10 billion annually on media advertising for toothpaste, and that the company's profits depended quite predominantly on the toothpaste business. Because of this heavy dependence on one type of product, diversification seemed to be of major interest to the management of Lion. Some observers speculated that Lion might be willing to incur big losses for some time to buy market share in nontoothpaste product categories. Wilkinson shaving products was one area of diversification; Lion was also the joint venture partner of Bristol-Myers, a U.S. producer of toiletries and proprietary drugs.

With Lion as its sole distributor in Japan, Wilkinson participated in the tremendous reputation of Lion and its strong distribution system in drug/cosmetic outlets and supermarkets. Wilkinson products moved through 117 Lion wholesalers to drug and food outlets. Most of Wilkinson's sales occurred in drug outlets.

Despite the association with the very powerful Lion Dentifrice Company, market performance of Wilkinson in Japan had been disappointing. The major reason was that Wilkinson had stayed too long with two essentially obsolete products, double-edge and "Bonded" blades, while the market favored first injector and then twin-blade systems. Wilkinson's market share had declined steadily. In 1975 it had 8.4 percent of the stainless steel blade market measured in yen (see Table 5); its weighted distribution in drug/cosmetic and food outlets was 66 percent and 68 percent, respectively. (See Table 7.)

Wilkinson's media advertising effort in the past few years had been ¥121 in 1973, ¥140 in 1974, and just ¥7 in 1975. As of mid-1976, Wilkinson had done virtually no media advertising for the year. The opinions of industry observers varied widely as to why Wilkinson had cut advertising almost completely in 1975 and in early 1976 and as to what marketing and advertising effort the company might launch in 1977. On the one hand, it was argued that Wilkinson had realized that it was fighting a senseless battle and had started to "milk" the Japanese business in an effort to maximize cash flow. On the other hand, it was said that Wilkinson might be preparing for a major attack on the twin-blade segment with its adjustable twin-blade system that it had recently introduced in Europe. So far, neither Schick nor Gillette had given much emphasis to its adjustable version of the twin-blade system in its advertising.

FEATHER. Feather was the only Japanese manufacturer of any significance competing against Schick, Gillette, and Wilkinson in the stainless steel blade market. Until the mid 1960s, Feather had been the major market force in Japan, holding about an 80 percent share of the market. With the arrival of Schick and Wilkinson and the increasing aggressiveness of Gillette, Feather's market share had continuously gone down. In 1975, the company had a share of 6.9 percent of the total razor blade market (in yen) and 13.4 percent of the stainless steel segment, but it dominated the double-edge segment. (See Table 4.)

Feather offered a full line of products: double-edge, injector, band, and twin-blade. While not an innovator in shaving technology, the company was usually quite fast in imitating new technological developments of its multinational competitors.

To distribute its products, the company used a complicated channel: 8 primary wholesalers sold to 324 secondary wholesalers. Of these secondary wholesalers, 24 sold directly to retailers; the remaining 300 moved the products through roughly 3,000 tertiary wholesalers to the retail trade. The system was further complicated by the fact that some of Feather's primary wholesalers also supplied tertiary wholesalers and retailers.

Feather's advertising expenditures had recently been drastically cut. While the company in 1974 spent ¥210 million on media advertising, the budget for 1975 was only ¥28 million and was expected to reach ¥20 million and ¥30 million in 1976 and 1977, respectively. In 1975 and 1976 virtually all media advertising featured the twin-blade system that Feather had introduced in April 1975.

The 1977 Marketing Plan

It was against this background that Mr. Burnett and Mr. Hirao together with managers from Hattori & Co. tried to work out the advertising and general marketing strategy for 1977.

Schick's advertising agency, Dai-Ichi Compton, had proposed the following advertising objectives as part of the 1977 marketing plan:

1. *Overall:* to build up an overall product image of Schick as an international, reliable, and high-quality product and to establish strong brand-name identification for Schick as the champion of total shaving.

2. *For the twin-blade cartridge:* to maximize Schick brand awareness and project product merit to accelerate farther the growing trend of twin-cartridge sales and to confine Gillette to a minimum.

3. *For the injector products:* (a) to make injector a major weapon with a revitalized mission to capture noninjector, electric, *keiben* users, and newcomers; (b) to strongly promote "In-Set" sales to maintain and expand injector franchises; and (c) to give continuous assurance to current injector users.

To attain these objectives, the agency had proposed a total of ¥600 million as Schick's media budget for 1977. This represented roughly an increase of 70 percent over the 1976 spending level.

The agency's proposal for the budget allocation was as follows:

Injector	¥300 million
	(+233% over 1976)
Twin-blade cartridge	¥300 million
	(+30% over 1976)

The agency felt that for the injector, in particular, a larger investment was imperative since Schick had to face two enemy fronts: the electric razor system and Gillette. Since Gillette would try to gain new Gillette twin cartridge users from the Schick injector, increased injector advertising was necessary as an effective defense and counterattack.

The primary target group defined for the injector campaign were newcomers, ages 16 to 20, and all young noninjector users, ages 18 to 34, with emphasis on the 18- to 24-year-old bracket. For the twin-blade cartridge product, all male shavers, but especially those in the 18- to 24-year-old age bracket were named as the target group.

Among the managers of Schick and Hattori there existed considerable difference of opinion about the direction and emphasis of the 1977 advertising plan.

One executive questioned the overall size of the advertising budget and the wisdom of increasing it so dramatically over 1976. He said

The market share patterns are such that a gain in market share from competitors can only be accomplished at a tremendous cost. We can safely assume that those consumers who have not yet switched from Gillette or Feather to Schick are "hard-core" users, not likely to switch easily to us. Besides, Schick's share of both injector and twin-blade has now reached such a high percentage that there would be a high possibility of cannibalizing each other among Schick brands instead of increasing Schick's business in total. All we should aim for is to maintain what we have now and that doesn't need such a high budget.

Those managers who supported this view added that Schick had already a superior image among consumers. (The Appendix gives excerpts from a consumer survey conducted in 1975.)

Several other executives were less concerned with the absolute size of the proposed budget than with its allocation to Schick's two major product categories. A wide range of opinions was mentioned for the most sensible split of the total budget between injector and twin cartridge. Some executives favored an allocation of 80 percent of the budget to the injector; others argued in favor of an 80 percent allocation to the twin cartridge; still others found numbers in between these extremes most sensible, including the agency's 50:50 proposal.

The product manager for the Schick injector argued for the greater part of any budget to be allocated to the injector. He stated

We must keep in mind that the injector is the basis of our company. This basis must be strengthened. The injector still has great opportunities. We face no strong competition in this segment, we dominate it. Consequently, if advertising stimulates injector sales, it will stimulate our own sales. On the other hand, if we emphasize the twin cartridge in our advertising, we will also stimulate Gillette's sales.

This product manager found support from several of his colleagues. One manager observed

I feel that putting so much emphasis on twin cartridges in 1976 and 1975 was a mistake. We neglected our core business that gives us distinctiveness. Moreover, it was expensive. We shouldn't exceed an advertising-to-sales ratio that makes economic sense. The smaller sales volume of the twin cartridge cannot carry as large an advertising budget as the injector business, and certainly not one that is larger. We should keep an eye on our profit margins for each product in making these decisions.

Those executives who favored a heavy concentration of the budget on the twin-blade cartridge pointed to the much higher growth rate of the twin-blade segment. Mr. Minoru Nakajima, the product manager for Schick's twin-blade cartridge system, said

This is where all the market growth takes place. It is the market of the future, where we also face the strongest competitive threat. Both the market opportunities and the threats dictate that we put our advertising emphasis on the twin-blade system.

Mr. Burnett could see a lot of merit for either side of the arguments. "Maybe the agency's proposal for an even split of the budget really gives us the best of all worlds,'' he pondered. He observed with interest that more of the Hattori managers than of the Schick managers leaned toward a greater allocation of the budget to the twin-blade cartridge.

While the budget allocation was an important issue, Mr. Burnett knew that Warner-Lambert headquarters in the United States would ask in particular for a justification of the budget size and its drastic increase over the 1976 figure. True, the razor and blade business generated more than enough cash flow to allow the budget increase, but Mr. Burnett had an obligation to think beyond the razor and blade business about alternative investment opportunities for Warner-Lambert Japan. He commented

Around the world Warner-Lambert International is raising questions about the total scope of our business. In Japan we are a little bit in the position Gillette used to face in Europe and in the U.S.: we are too successful and, therefore, preoccupied with razor blades. In what direction should we take our company in the future is a big question to us. That's why we look at other product areas.

APPENDIX I: Selecting Agents and Distributors[1]

Both new and experienced sales managers face the same problem when it comes to agents and distributors: finding the few good ones. It's hard. There's always a shortage and competition is fierce.

Even if you've been doing a good job, your roster at any point in time will most likely include only a few excellent distributors, a majority of mediocre ones, and some real duds. It's inevitable, since there just aren't enough technically capable, growth-oriented distributors to go around. (We use the word ''distributors'' to also include agents.)

The scarcity of good distributors is a fact of life every sales manager recognizes. Naturally, some learn to deal with the problem better than others, and those who do gain a significant advantage. That's what you're after—the kind of techniques and practices that increase your chances of signing up the most promising distributors.

Consultants? Forget It!

Sure, there are consultants who want to locate distributors for you. After all, it's easy to find just any distributor, but locating one that can knock off the orders is quite a different matter. One group of independent consultants, calling itself the World Trade Group, charges $2,500–5,000 for merely providing written evidence of

---

[1]*The Export Advisor,* May 1982. Used with permission.

a distributor's interest in your company and a bit of background information. The distributor's not necessarily good—he's simply expressed an interest.

That's expensive, not only in dollars, but most of all in the information you lose by not being involved in the search yourself. If you don't know *all* your options in the marketplace, you'll be limited in negotiations, and you may be hesitant to change distributors should that become necessary later on.

Besides, you've got to become self-reliant in tracking down the top distributors—there's no better way. Evaluation is such an industry—and market-specific matter that you're really the only one capable of rejecting or selecting. Experience shows that your success is directly related to your degree of involvement.

Your Game Plan

Distributors are continually adding, dropping, and changing emphasis of their various product lines, and new distributors are constantly starting up. How do you take advantage of these situations?

Even for experienced sales managers who specialize in one territory, keeping tabs on distributor availability is an ongoing effort—taking time, visits, contacts. Open up a new territory or take charge of a new product line in an established one and you have no old-boy network to touch for leads, no current status to go on. Where to begin?

First, you need to use as many sources of information as you can. Fortunately, the front-end costs of locating good distributors yourself can be done on a minibudget.

Locating Distributor Leads

COMPETITORS' DISTRIBUTORS.   The experienced sales manager looks here first. You never can tell, some excellent ones may want to jump ship for perfectly valid reasons. These are prospects too valuable to overlook. After all, they're already familiar with similar products, they have the right organization in place, and they call on the right accounts. You get a running start—saving valuable time and effort. Since they'll usually pull some accounts to you right off, you also slip up a competitor in the bargain.

How do you get a list of your competitors' distributors? Many companies make them available for the asking. Some even list them in industrial directories or sales brochures right along with their domestic representatives.

Sometimes the list of a company's distributors isn't readily obtainable. To get it, some sales managers use friends in other companies or even bogus companies as decoys to pry it out.

Once you get the list, how do you approach a competitor's distributor when you think he's a good prospect? With a direct proposition: "Drop his line and take mine." Don't be coy.

The best way is to contact the managing director personally when you're in the country. But circumstances may only permit you to reveal your proposal by letter. That's second best, but suitable, too.

Even if you're rejected, you can use the occasion to gather leads. Ask for his recommendations. More likely than not, he'll try to put you on the wrong track and give you bum advice—you are an adversary, remember. Naturally, you suspect his referrals, but even misinformation can be valuable. After several such tries, a relative standing among the qualified distributors emerges.

There's a danger, however, in this game. Your competitor's distributor may accept your line simply to take it out of the running, making certain no one else gets it. This happens. To guard against it, make sure the competitive line is dropped when yours is taken on.

Distributors of compatible products are also invaluable prospects. Here again, you're looking at an organization already in motion with the account coverage and technical proficiency you need.

AGENT/DISTRIBUTOR SERVICE (ADS). This is a customized service of the Department of Commerce to help businesses locate overseas representatives. A U.S. government employee at the foreign post (usually a national of that country) contacts prospects and reports their level of interest in your line.

This service works well for many companies. But it has limitations: It can be used only when entering a new territory or after having served notice to a present distributor. If you want to use the master distributor technique, you will lose the element of surprise, because even nonexclusive distributors must be informed before the government will undertake an ADS search. Obviously they don't want to get caught in the cross-fire between you and an unhappy distributor. In fact, the government wants written assurance (a copy of the letter informing your present distributor) before a search can begin.

Lead times for processing ADS applications are currently running from 60 to 90 days. (Last year it was oversubscribed and backed up to 120 days.) For this reason, some planning is needed. One way you can get around the delay is to inform ADS that you'll be visiting the target country shortly and need priority service. They will cable the information on your application to start the paperwork moving overseas. You should be able to collect the results abroad personally about 30 days after submitting your application.

You can expect anywhere from zero to six leads, three being the norm. Quality of the leads varies with the preparer (some being more conscientious than others). By all means specify that you want the names of those distributors contacted who didn't show interest as well as those who did. In this way you can eliminate names duplicated in other sources.

Sometimes ADS is used to nudge a prospect who has been procrastinating. A call by a government official indicates your seriousness and the urgency of the decision. The cost is $90 per report.

BANKS.   If you're into your banker for enough, he might help you. Naturally, there's got to be something in it for the bank if you expect any leads from this source. That means that you must have a track record or a new product that's sure to turn into documentary business.

Usually the smaller banks, hungry to establish new accounts, will make the effort to help you locate distributors. They'll contact their correspondents overseas for assistance. But don't put all your eggs in this one basket; the method locates leads only about half the time.

DIRECTORIES.   Nearly every country has industrial directories, and quite often they list distributors, too. The negative side here is that the lists are often incomplete, general, and two to three years out of date. For many high-tech fields, that's ancient history.

Some specialized directories (electronics, computers, etc.) are available for European countries and certain other advanced areas. Don't expect to find them elsewhere. Even the best directories won't list many of the new distributors, and the small ones are frequently omitted altogether.

Directories are usually too expensive to purchase for only occasional use. They're soon outdated. Better to go to the business section of a good library to use them.

TRADE SHOWS.   Obviously, a lot of planning is needed, but it's a good way to get market exposure while at the same time looking for distributors. You'll be approached on the spot by distributors who would like your line. Often many have exhibits at the show, too, so you can meet a large number of salespeople and product specialists all at one time. Besides, you can get an idea of how sharp they are and how well they promote by seeing them in action. (Sell enough off the floor and you pay for the trip, too.)

MAIL SOLICITATION.   Do this through personal business correspondence not by a form letter, of course. Since you may not always know the name of the managing director, you may be forced to send to a title, but that's okay.

Count on back and forth mail transit times amounting to two weeks and another two weeks for normal procrastination/decision delays—that eats up a full month. (A telex reminder will hasten the response.)

You may compile the most important item—the mailing lists—from your searches through directories and competitor/compatible company rosters. Or you may mail out to a distributor list extracted from the Department of Commerce's Foreign Traders Index (FTI). Its Export Mailing List Service allows a computerized search through hefty FTI, which is constantly growing (well over 100,000 foreign businesses). You can pull distributors with certain characteristics from this file. The most important: country, SIC code (two-, three-, or four-digit selection), and recency of data entry (last four years is normally used). Request that the list be printed on gummed mailing labels and you'll save some work. Delivery is 21–30 days ARO.

The cost is $15 (setup charge) plus 12 cents per name. (You'll receive an estimate of the number of names before the final printing to prevent computer-sized errors.)

MISCELLANEOUS

1. The executive director of the local American Chamber of Commerce usually has spent a long time in the country and can put you on to good leads and perhaps steer you clear of disaster. Of course, some are more helpful than others. It pays to ask. Write for information or visit when you're there.

2. Like the executive director, the U.S. commercial officers at the embassies see lots of action. A visit when you're in the country may pay off, but be sure to handle it in the proper way. It may be your government, but it's their system. They listen to their own, so ask the director of the Department of Commerce's local district office to write a letter before your visit. You'll get that extra measure of effort.

3. What to do about over-the-transom requests? Some sales managers we know qualify them by having the prospect fill out a distributor's application form—pertinent information as to the company's needs. This is a good way to keep from wasting your time with off-the-wall inquiries. Yet it's a good idea to file the applications away. They might come in handy someday.

Checking Up on Them

Information is always spotty when doing a desk search on foreign firms. Run one or two business and credit reports to help flesh out the picture. (FCIA requires two such reports for insuring a new distributor on your roster.)

WORLD TRADERS DATA REPORTS (WTDRs). This isn't a credit report but a business report—it gives financial/trade information and references. In addition, it gives a bottom-line recommendation by the U.S. Government official compiling the data (e.g., 50 percent of WTDRs coming out of Nigeria now recommend *not* to do business). A WTDR is current—within last 12 months—and the official is supposed to double-check the information against other sources.

The biggest complaint about WTDRs is lead time: 30 to 45 days if the report must be brought up-to-date. Otherwise 5 to 10 days. If a WTDR is already on file, you can get the information read to you over the phone (202-377-4203) free of charge. It's quick and easy. All you need is the name and address of the distributor.

If you're running an ADS, it's important to submit a request at the same time for WTDRs on the leads produced. WTDRs should run 5 to 10 days later than the ADS report. The cost is $40 per written report.

CREDIT REPORTS. International credit reporting isn't nearly as detailed as in the United States. Few European and Latin American firms will voluntarily reveal their financial situation (not even sales volume), so don't expect much here. Some D&Bs can be substantial, others skinny—it's inconsistent. Remember, too, these reports are unaudited.

The ubiquitous recommendation, "Good for normal business engagement," is too ambiguous. What does that mean, anyway? The most important questions you need answers to are "Does he pay sight or time drafts on time?" If not, "Under what circumstances are they late?" and "How late?" Ask your bank to use its branch or correspondent to get these answers. Banks know who pays and who doesn't. The cost is $60–120 per D&B (banks charge for telexes).

Narrowing the List

Gathering leads and paper reports on distributors isn't enough. For a clearer picture, you must also collect the kind of information that's not written down.

HOW DO THE DISTRIBUTOR'S PRINCIPALS RATE HIM? Getting evaluations from references isn't hard, not in the United States anyway. (Try to coax the same information out of sales managers in Europe and you soon learn the difference.) It's surprising how much Americans will reveal over the phone to a total stranger.

Seek out the sales manager of a compatible product manufacturer. It's easy to establish rapport by discussing your mutual problems in locating capable distributors. But don't go on to make the common mistake of asking for blunt, outright recommendations or evaluations right off. These put him on the spot. (He may have terminated the distributor just last week, but doesn't want to ruin the guy's future chances, so he leaves you with a favorable impression.) Common sense tells you to be a little subtle in probing.

For example, if you're interested in, say, his distributor in France, start off by talking European problems: Who performs best? How do they stack up to the company's domestic counterparts? Is the company's market share in France comparable to that in other markets? How does the capability of the French distributor compare with the German one? A picture begins to emerge.

If he's been obliging to this point, you can ask more direct questions, for example, the distributor's practices on prices? service? cooperation? advertising? payment? You may not get answers to all these questions, but you can usually compress the essence of another's experiences into a 20-minute conversation. Some of these may well be ones you'd much rather hear about than have.

SEE THE OPERATIONS UP CLOSE. If you can't make a personal visit to evaluate the distributor yourself, then hold off the selection until you can. That's the best way and the only way we feel comfortable recommending.

How do you go about getting the most out of a visit? Obviously you sell most where you know customers best. Since you normally know less about foreign customers than those in the United States, you should use the opportunity of interviewing distributors to gain customer contacts too. Let your distributor prospects do the footwork. Ask them to arrange three or four sales calls with potential buyers. They'll gladly do this for you.

There are several benefits in doing this: (1) You gather market and customer intelligence firsthand; (2) You see how the distributor handles sales calls and whether the correct accounts have been chosen; (3) You gain customer contacts to use later on for checking up on the distributor.

Of course, the distributor will make every effort to impress you and will take you to his best accounts only. But even with this advantage, you can size up his performance and capability.

Watch for the little things that say a lot: If you're both kept waiting an hour, and then given only five minutes, you know this guy's a zero. If your prospect takes you to his uncle who happens to be the managing director of a large potential user of your products, well, that's something else.

It doesn't matter that you can't understand the language; the other communication gives it all away.

PERSONALITY TYPE.   It can help or hurt you. As with people, distributor organizations have personalities, too. If you were to classify distributors as to the relationship they have with their principals, you'd find them spread across a wide spectrum. At one end of the scale would be the capitulators, at the other the initiators.

The capitulator is cooperative and accedes readily to your demands but needs excessive support and direction from you. At first you might think this is a perfect partner—cooperative and eager to follow your advice. In execution, however, the capitulator stumbles badly. He's not especially aggressive or imaginative—he has trouble helping himself, much less you. The capitulator can sap your time and efforts and still not show much improvement on the bottom line. A few of these on your company's roster and the drain on your time, effort, and money investment will be crippling.

The initiator is just the opposite: independent and difficult to deal with. This firm wants to do things its own way and knows exactly where it's going—up! Whether large or small, this distributor is confident, self-reliant, growth oriented, just the sort to knock off big numbers any way it can. The initiator is bankable. Your company happens to fit in with its plans. Your job is to make this firm tow the line in your own best interests. Clearly, the initiator can help you far more than the capitulator can.

APPENDIX II: Guidelines for Terminating Agents and Distributors[1]

Cancellation or nonrenewal of foreign agent and distributor contracts is serious business—not to be taken lightly. Unlike in the United States, where all provisions of a contract are binding on the parties signing it, your foreign agent or distributor

---

[1] *The Export Advisor,* November 1981. Used with permission.

may not be held to the termination provisions he signed. Why? Because many countries view termination as not just a private matter between two parties, but as something of national concern. Your company can become the target of a host of protective laws—often biased and punitive—that can grant the distributor a big chunk of your checkbook.

It's well known that many smaller companies lose their export shirts by jumping into situations they're legally unprepared for. Today, with the trend toward tougher laws and more litigious agents and distributors, the situation is worsening. (Bad news came earlier this year when Belgium refused to ratify the Benelux Commercial Agency Treaty. And petty bickering still continues in Europe over the EEC Council's directive on agencies.)

What can be done? First, know what you're getting into. Don't walk into a hostile legal environment unprepared. Many U.S. managers, unfortunately, simply assume that the rest of the world uses the same system of *common law* used here. Wrong! A number of countries in Europe, Latin America, and elsewhere use *civil law,* which is entirely different—and harsher—with respect to agency/principal relationships.

If a foreign termination were only a legal matter, it would be relatively straightforward. However, there are other problems that are not so neatly defined that call for practical experience and judgment. *The Export Advisor* spells out guidelines for you to follow.

The Export Advisor Approach: Termination as Strategy

There are a good many reasons for termination: going direct with a branch office or subsidiary, changes in corporate policy, and company mergers or acquisitions. But by far the most common is an agent's or distributor's poor performance. Not meeting reasonable sales quotas, insolvency, lack of effectiveness, inadequate market penetration, sudden drop-off in sales, incapacity to grow financially, wrong market approach, technical incompetence, won't/can't learn proper sales techniques—we're sure you know the list. Some of these probably describe not a few of your own agents and distributors. (It's clumsy to say "agent and distributor." We'll simply use "agent" as a generic term from here on unless a clear difference exists.)

It's important to realize that these problems describe the *normal* state of affairs. If your company sells through agents, it will have to live with the first rule of export: *the limitation in international sales is the shortage of good agents.* You will never have all really top people. If you've been managing sales like most, you'll have a few good agents, many mediocre ones, and some rotten apples. Keep in mind, too, that the smaller company cannot turn bad agents into adequate ones. Even very large companies try and fail. You'll only squander time, energy, and money trying. It's amazing how many experienced sales managers have failed to learn this basic lesson.

Fortunately, this situation is not as hopeless as it first sounds. To boost sales above the norm, you must play the same game successful agents do. They're continually searching for better principals. It stands to reason that you, too, should always be on the lookout for more productive, go-getter agents. Their ranks and product lines are ever changing. You should use this situation to improve your distribution team, too. The sophistication of the marketplace will govern how frequently the opportunities present themselves. To play the game, too, you have to understand the legal, economic, and cultural constraints, or as we call them "the headwinds of international flight."

To know where and when this approach can be used, and to what extent, is part of the fine art of international sales. After all, this is where a careful reading of foreign business practices, and cultural differences come into play. The world's a big place—there's no such thing as an international market, there's not a European market, there's not a Far Eastern market, but rather, many markets, each with its own peculiarities. Failing to recognize such differences is a serious error that will end up red on your bottom line.

Here's a simple example to illustrate what we mean by "headwinds." Suppose that you have recently terminated—with just cause—your old agents in Germany, France, and Japan. You discuss your line with several promising agents. They seem receptive, but what are they really thinking? (We'll generalize hugely because life is short.)

> Hans thinks, "Yes, this manufacturer knows how to run his business. He is taking determined measures to better sales. I'd better take his line."
> Henri thinks, "His old agent didn't know how to approach the market. Since the cancellation doesn't come due for 6 weeks, I can stall negotiations and get a better price."
> Hiroshi thinks, "Another American company that cannot live up to its commitments. I'll call the old agent to find out just how bad this company's reputation is."

One of the well-known "headwinds" here: A termination in Japan, unlike European countries, is not a normal business occurrence. The practice is looked upon with suspicion. Changing agents in Japan more than three or four times in 10 years will get your company blacklisted.

Being able to terminate bad agents quickly, cleanly, and economically is vital. But never practice it ignorantly.

Confusion over Terms

It's not surprising how much confusion surrounds the terms "sales agent" and "sales representative." In the United States, the terms are interchangeable. However, many foreign legal and tax jurisdictions separate the two clearly.

The difference lies in how much control your representative has over your business. The *agent* has the power of attorney, meaning that he can legally bind you to a contract and expose you, but not himself, to legal and economic risk. From a foreign tax standpoint, the kind of decision-making power invested in the agent often makes him a "permanent establishment"—obligating you to the government treasury in the form of corporate taxes, registration fees, and so on. Because of this and the fact that termination indemnities for an agent are more severe than for reps, *The Export Advisor* advises clients to stay away from agency agreements. As an extra precaution, you should state in your contract that your sales rep or distributor is *not* an agent and that he does *not* have the authority to consummate contracts. Then you have written proof in the event he alleges he had the powers of an agent and so is entitled to a bigger settlement upon termination.

The sales *representative* arrangement is safer both legally and economically. You get decreased liability and tax exposure. He cannot sign on your behalf and must pass all legal documents to you for final approval. The rep simply sells and supports your products under contract. He does not take title—as a distributor does—but receives a commission from you on each sale in his territory.

With the term "distributor" there is some confusion, too. He is an independent businessperson and buys your products to *resell*. In the United States, the distributor is actually more independent in that he may stock several competitive products for his customers. This works well here because many hi-tech/industrial companies— especially electronics companies—use both an exclusive rep and a distributor to sell and stock in each territory.

Such an arrangement is seldom used abroad. Your foreign distributor must not only stock for the local market, he must also *represent* you. Functionally, he's both distributor and exclusive sales rep. This means that he must not carry competing products. In return, he expects some kind of exclusivity (territorial? product? market?). (It's interesting to note that for those companies using both reps and distributors, this dual function of the foreign distributor gives a lower cost per sale for international than for U.S. sales.)

Play by Their Rules or Don't Play at All

Since agent contract law in the United States is rather simple, you might assume it's the same elsewhere. Not necessarily so. The traditional *common law* that prevails in the United States gives you and the agent the independence to decide upon any contract clauses—including termination clauses—and to make these binding. Simple enough. (Of course, if one of the parties violates the contract, he can be hauled into court. This is just as true in the rest of the world as it is in the United States.) Fortunately, the United States is not the only country to allow freedom in drawing up agent contracts. Other enlightened ones are Canada, the United Kingdom, Australia, New Zealand, South Africa, Israel, Hong Kong, the Bahamas, and Singapore. But many just make life difficult.

They do so in numerous ways. Typically, there are special laws that come down particularly hard on the principal. In the absence of such special laws, the civil and commercial codes strengthen the position of the agent, compensating him for past efforts that were not directly covered by the commissions he received. Still other traps include some labor laws that treat the agent's employees that work on your business as if they were *your* employees and entitle them to generous compensation—at your expense, of course.

Originally, these protective laws were intended to ensure fair treatment for agents. However, many of them have turned into a form of nationalism. Some countries are downright abusive to foreign principals yet at the same time treat their own with kid gloves. Another injustice of such statutes is that they are based on false economic conceptions of the agent as the weaker party. With many hi-tech/industrial products, the huge costs of distribution, technical and field support, and service are fast approaching that of the product itself. In practice, we find that the laws often serve to protect only bad agents and actually contribute to poor performance in no small way.

Common Ground Rules

As you would expect, termination laws differ from country to country. And, as with laws everywhere, they can be vague, confusing, and open to interpretation. A survey of the laws of many different countries shows that certain negative aspects recur over and over. As such they should be kept in mind anytime you enter new contracts or renew old ones.

1. The applicable legal jurisdiction is national law, not U.S. law or that of a third country.
2. The employees of the agent are protected by local labor laws that determine compensation for dismissal. The agent's liability flows through to you.
3. The agent must be given sufficient notice prior to cancellation of the contract (three months meets most requirements).
4. The indemnity increases with the length of the relationship. Indefinite-term contracts carry stiffer indemnities than do definite-term contracts.
5. Laws granting the agent compensation and other rights may not be waived by contract.
6. The agent is compensated for the increased value of the market he has created for the principal (usually the equivalent of one year's commissions—payable in lump sum— for a multiple-year relationship).
7. "Just cause" is defined by existing law or the terms of the contract. The law specifies such generalities as negligence, incompetence, serious decrease in sales on the part of the agent, disloyalty to the principal, and so on. Proving these vis-à-vis the agent's denials is another matter. It's best to define breach of contract with razor-sharp precision. For example, "Agent agrees to sell a minimum of 100 gizmos every quarter" or "Distributor agrees to buy a set of spare parts for every five systems installed in his territory."
8. The agent may call for arbitration upon notice of termination to determine whether the principal has "just cause."
9. Unless "just cause" is shown, *renewal* of the contract may be mandatory.
10. Even if "just cause" is proved, the agent may be compensated if the principal benefits from the relationship after termination.

Birds of a Feather

When viewed from an historical perspective, it's not so surprising that the different countries of the world tend to cluster together when it comes to protective laws for agents.

The most blatantly biased and punitive laws are in the Central American countries, where nationalism has done its best to poison the business environment. (For example, in Honduras an indemnity can run up to *five times* annual gross profits *plus* the value of the agent's investment *plus* all kinds of additional payments, even for short-term contracts.) South American countries check in with a maze of laws that must surely have been drawn up as a lawyer's employment act.

> MEXICO. The labor law allows an agent who has been terminated without "just cause" the same right to compensation as a dismissed employee. For a fixed-term contract, the agent receives 6 months' compensation plus 20 days' compensation for every year of service after the first year.

Puerto Rico is a territory of the United States, but its laws pertaining to agents are more like those of Latin America. As more U.S. companies move their manufacturing operations there (the purchasing function usually follows), many suppliers find they need local reps. But often Puerto Rico is part of a company's domestic sales territory. It is of particular importance to make sure that Puerto Rico receives the same consideration as foreign countries when it comes to contracts, as many once naïve national sales managers have learned to their regret.

> PUERTO RICO. Terminating an agent without "just cause" entitles him to claim an amount equal to his profit for the previous *five years*. Or, if the agency existed for fewer years, *five times* the average annual profit. Additional compensation may include the value of the agent's expenses in setting up and running the business, the value of his inventory, the loss of his profits, and the value of his goodwill.

Special care must be taken in Latin America. Although some may view this marketplace as one of secondary importance, an export management company should not be casually assigned to take charge of business there. If it's signing up agents in your company's name, you might as well add a new entry to your ledger: *Indemnities Payable!*

The Middle Eastern and North African countries have a growing number of laws for protecting agents. Compensation is by statute in many countries. And reliance on the Shari'a, or Islamic law, for resolving conflicts is prevalent. In this region, too, there are rules requiring agents to be of national origin. Such restrictions present special problems for smaller companies that are unable to support individual agents in small markets and whose products will not allow sufficient profits for two-tier distribution.

The Far Eastern countries are comparatively free of these one-sided laws. By and large, the parties may agree to the terms of the agency contract as they see fit. Common law principles are widely used. Japan specifies only a termination notice of two months. Same for Korea. India, Thailand, and Malaysia all provide compensation for termination without just cause.

African countries are relatively free of such penalizing laws. There is compensation for termination without just cause in Ethiopia and Tanzania.

Europe has a maze of national protective laws. Here you have to be especially careful. Laws are weighted in the agent's favor, and this is compounded by the fact that Europeans are prone to litigate anyway.

In 1976 the EEC Commission proposed a directive to harmonize the laws governing agency contracts. It predicted passage in 1978 but today it is still years away. (Can you believe 1989 for even a common electrical plug!) Besides, even when a common law is finally adopted, it will most likely be severe. We see it as closely following the current agency law in The Netherlands.

Highlights of some European laws:

BELGIUM (often used as a prime example of overprotective European law). Terminal compensation for agents and distributors includes the value of any increase in goodwill, plus expenses incurred in developing the business, plus the amount of compensation claimed by discharged employees who worked on your account. Minimum notice is three months. Definite-term contract may become indefinite-term after two extensions. Only Belgian law is applicable.

DENMARK. Local Chamber of Commerce decides whether termination is just. It is customary to give agent one year's commissions. Minimum notice is three months.

FRANCE (most protective law in Europe for agents). Terminal compensation is usually no more than one year's commission. A special feature of French law is that the agent does not have to prove he has gained any clients for the principal or that there were any clients at all. The fact that the agent has lost the right to represent the principal may entitle him to compensation. If parties agree to a "trial" contract of a specified duration, the principal is not obliged to pay compensation if he does not renew. No laws have been enacted for regulation of distributors.

GERMANY. Terminal compensation of one year's commission is customary. An unusual feature of German law is that the agent may die or decide to retire and still be entitled to terminal compensation. Minimum notice is three weeks for contracts up to three years' duration, otherwise three months. Choice of law is allowed, but agent may not waive his right to compensation.

ITALY. Agents are entitled to damage compensation and social security charges. Principal is liable for "clientele's indemnity" when the agent is terminated without just cause. This amounts to 3 percent of all commissions received by the agent while the contract was in force. No laws have been enacted for regulation of distributors.

THE NETHERLANDS. Whether a just or unjust termination, the agent is entitled to up to one year's commission as goodwill compensation (a full year is usually awarded). Minimum notice is one month if specified, otherwise four months. Choice of law is allowed, but agent may not waive any of his rights. No laws have been enacted for regulation of distributors as yet.

SWITZERLAND. Agents are entitled to a maximum of one year's net profit from new clients gained for the principal. Minimum notice is one month. Only Swiss law is applicable.

Get Your Ammunition on Paper

We know some companies that don't use written agent contracts. They feel secure in the belief that it is safer not to have anything on paper. And another company has a contract that is so thick, unreadable, and one-sided that agents refuse to sign it. In such situations we can visualize the agent in the local court pleading for "justice." He will wave a fistful of sales receipts in the judge's face to prove his loss and demand the full weight of the law. A written—and signed—contract always gives you more rights, not fewer.

The two most important parts of the agent contract are (1) What constitutes a breach of contract? and (2) How to deal with a breach of contract? Precisely! There cannot be any misunderstandings here or they will surely be at your expense.

A clause in the contract should stipulate transfer of your legitimate property upon termination. The trademark, patent, and company name registrations and commercial permits should all be surrendered. (A devious trick by some agents is to register them, yes, but in their own name!) Of course, all signs, logos, or other evidence of your relationship should be removed from his place of business. And of special importance to your ongoing business is the return and confidentiality of the agent's lists of customers and contacts for your account (an item he'll be reluctant to surrender, so have a clause to strengthen your position and negotiate for it early in the notification period). Your new agent will need these to make a fast start out the gate.

International Boilerplate

Naturally, contracts have a lot of boilerplate clauses. International contracts are no different and have a few more that are of special importance to termination.

NOTICE. This clause gives the agent time to adjust before the termination is final. Many countries have legal minimums, which if broken entitle the agent to compensation. To ensure that the other party receives notification, the contract should specify certified conveyances like registered mail, confirmed cable, or telex. Also, the method of acknowledging receipt should be included.

CHOICE OF LAW. This is of crucial importance. As a rule, the more commercially sophisticated countries will allow choice of law and forum clauses. Many countries recognize the law of the place where the contract is consummated. Since U.S. law is obviously preferable, make sure your contract signing is completed in the United States. (Don't make the mistake—as we've so often seen—of an overseas signing ceremony.) When U.S. law is not acceptable to the other party, compromise on a widely understood—and advantageous—body of law, such as that of a country with a common law system (Canada or United Kingdom).

CHOICE OF FORUM. Where will the dispute be heard? Some countries require cases to be tried in local courts. But most will allow commercial arbitration. The International Chamber of Commerce says that 20 percent of its arbitration cases concern agency/principal disputes. Arbitration avoids the hazards of foreign litigation and is normally less expensive. The arbitration clause has the effect of excluding jurisdiction in the law courts and the arbitral judgment is binding and can be enforced. However, make sure the country in which the agent resides has ratified the United Nations Convention on the Recognition and Enforcement of Arbitral Awards (most major countries have).

Although less expensive than litigation, arbitration is still not cheap. Arbitrators (normally one or three) receive about $150–$200 a day. The arbitration organization (International Chamber of Commerce, Inter-American Commercial Arbitration Commission, American Arbitration Assn., etc.) will also want a fee based on the amount in dispute. Customarily it's paid by both parties, but sometimes by the losing party alone. Cost? The ICC fee is about $5,000 for a $100,000 dispute.

LANGUAGE. As a courtesy, you may have a contract translated for the agent but require the English version to be binding. English should be specified as the language for all communications.

Legal Brains—Necessary and Expensive

You can do your homework and you can ask the right questions, but you cannot hope to know all the tricks and quirks of local law. It's constantly changing. The standard contract that you draw up may be omitting special protection, or an invalid clause may subject you to the whims of local statutes. Therefore, it is important to have foreign counsel review your contract before using it in that country.

We prefer a good foreign lawyer to a branch of a U.S. international law firm for the simple reason of competence. Local practitioners are usually more savvy. They understand the ins and outs better. The U.S. commercial officer in the country can put you in touch with the good ones. Another point we have found useful in selection is a telex machine—not all lawyers have them. Should you need further clarification later on, it's a major convenience.

It seems lawyers have the same voracious appetite the world over. So be careful! U.S. international law firms are usually more expensive. If you use a foreign lawyer, make sure he charges on an hourly or per diem basis—not a percentage of the deal, which is often customary. As a rule, for legal review of your agent contract expect to pay about $400 in the less developed countries and no more than $800 elsewhere.

Annulment Beats Divorce

We favor the definite-term contract over the indefinite-term and a six-month trial contract, if you can get it. However, under few circumstances would a contract longer than one year work to your advantage. Six to nine months is generally sufficient time to judge an agent's motivation, competence, solvency, and sales performance. As mentioned before, foreign laws carry greater indemnities as the duration of the relationship extends. If the marriage has been short, little indemnity should flow.

Naturally a written record of your evaluation of an agent's performance would serve a legal purpose as well as a business one. One manufacturer we know sends each new distributor, in addition to regular day-to-day correspondence, a formal evaluation by registered letter every quarter. The distributor should have completed training, installed demo centers, and stocked inventory three months after the contract signing—or else the letter expresses concern over delays: What's the matter? How can we help? At the end of six months, concern turns to worry: Why aren't you measuring up? Account for this formally! The letter includes a checklist that details corrections to be made by the distributor. If improvement in three more months is still not to the manufacturer's satisfaction, a termination notice of three months is then served. The manufacturer is, of course, called ruthless by the distributor. But the distributor is not unprepared for such a decision and disputes are settled by negotiation—seldom by arbitration or litigation. After one or sometimes two of these trial periods, an adequate distributor is found. Not surprisingly, international sales for this resolute firm are large—55 percent of total company sales.

The Human Side

The legal aspects are not the whole story of termination. A termination is not as cool and clinical as it might first appear. Emotions tend to run deeper in dealings with foreign agents—more so than with those in the United States, almost to the point where it resembles a personal friendship. This can be good, but too often it interferes with the prime goal—increasing sales. Not infrequently the sales manager is so concerned about friendships or behaving as a goodwill American ambassador that sales stagnate—or worse.

In many less developed countries, the agent's image in the community is closely tied to the lines he represents. Handling your company gives him status. It doesn't matter how much legitimate "just cause" you find against him; even a bad agent will take your termination as a personal insult. So be prepared to handle the matter gently and prudently. It's most important to keep an eye on retaining your reputation and goodwill—expensive intangibles—in the local market. Make every effort to sever the relationship cleanly and within the notification period. To get the agent to shut-up and not bad-mouth your company may take generous use of your checkbook—buying back some of his inventory, compensating him in part for back orders, reimbursing him for selected expenses. Reasonable measures like these should help stop the flow of bad blood and help you stay out of court.

Insist that your customers receive a jointly issued statement of your "amicable" separation. Foreign customers are usually suspect about the commitment of American suppliers to their market, anyway. Therefore, your major customers should receive special attention. This could be a letter or even a personal visit to explain the separation and your determined commitment to their market and needs. The disruption in sales and technical support will not be taken lightly by customers, so you must maintain continuity by signing up a new agent immediately. You should always have in mind at least *two* replacements before serving notice.

A Skill That Pays

Your ability to terminate agents cleanly, completely, and economically has a big influence on your bottom line. With reasonable care and planning, you should feel almost as comfortable moving out of foreign business relationships as going into them. Termination may at times seem difficult, but it is the only way to keep sales momentum moving in the right direction.

APPENDIX III: Excerpts from the Results of a Survey Conducted by Inra Among 1,010 Consumers in the Tokyo and Osaka Areas in 1975

UNAIDED AWARENESS FOR EACH TYPE OF WET SHAVING SYSTEM.   The level of awareness was highest for *disposable* with 62 percent, followed by *double-edge* with 49 percent, *injector* with 37 percent, *barber's razor* with 25 percent, and *twin blade* with 22 percent.

UNAIDED BRAND AWARENESS OF RECALLED WET SHAVING TYPE.   Among the respondents who recalled the Injector ($N = 373$), 59 percent gave Schick, 23 percent Gillette, 21 percent Feather, and 6 percent Wilkinson. Among those respondents who recalled the double-edge ($N = 496$), 53 percent gave Feather, 21 percent Gillette, 18 percent Schick, and 12 percent Wilkinson. For the twin blade ($N = 222$), 40 percent gave Schick, 37 percent Gillette, 16 percent Feather, and 8 percent Wilkinson.

ATTITUDES TOWARD DIFFERENT BRANDS.   All respondents ($N = 1,010$) were asked to rank the four brands—Schick, Gillette, Wilkinson, and Feather—on a number of attributes. The main results are as follows:

1. *Quality*. Schick, Gillette, and Wilkinson rate about equally with rather favorable ratings, with Feather slightly behind.
2. *Price*. None of the brands received favorable ratings on this attribute, but Feather, with the highest average and lower "Don't Know" response, can be considered to have the best image on this attribute among the four brands.
3. *Reliability*. There is no difference among the four brands on this point, with all brands receiving slightly above-average ratings.

4. *Package design*. None of the brands received a favorable rating on this attribute, but Schick, with the highest average and lower "Don't Know" response, can be considered to have the best image on this attribute.

5. *Shaving quality*. Schick, with the highest rating and a lower "Don't Know," is the leader with a rather favorable image, followed with somewhat above-average ratings by Gillette, Wilkinson, and Feather in that order.

6. *Shaver's design*. All brands received only average ratings on this point, with Schick and Gillette about equal, followed by Wilkinson and then Feather.

ADVERTISING RECALL.   All respondents ($N = 1,010$) were shown a show card listing the names of four manufacturers—Schick, Gillette, Wilkinson, and Feather— and were asked had they seen any advertising recently for any of these manufacturers. Thirty-seven percent had seen advertising for Schick, 36 percent for Feather, 26 percent for Gillette, and 21 percent for Wilkinson.

All respondents ($N = 1,010$) were shown four photographs and were asked to identify which brands were being identified. The order of showing the photographs was rotated to avoid bias. There was a high "Don't Know" rate for all advertisements. Of those able to give a response to this question, Feather had the highest correct identification rate with 28 percent, Schick Super II with 18 percent, Gillette II with 11 percent, and Schick Injector with 8 percent.

All respondents ($N = 1,010$) were asked which of the four advertisements is the most impressive. Schick Super II was considered the most impressive advertisement by 29 percent, followed by Gillette G-II with 19 percent, Feather with 18 percent, and the Schick Injector with 9 percent. Twenty-five percent of the respondents thought that none of the advertisements was impressive.

RATING ATTRIBUTES OF SAFETY RAZOR BRANDS
All respondents (N = 1,010) were asked to rate the brands of safety razor on certain attributes.

	SCHICK	GILLETTE	WILKINSON	FEATHER	KAI-JIRUSHI	NONE FIT	DON'T KNOW
World leader/best in world	7%	11%	14%	7%	1%	9%	52%
Long tradition/oldest established	4	10	16	19	7	4	41
Largest share of Japan market	8	4	1	32	5	3	48
See its products in shop front very often/well displayed	19	7	1	25	8	4	37
Most innovative	14	7	2	10	1	6	60
Most expensive	3	7	16	2	.2	3	68
High-class product	4	9	22	2	—	4	59

15

PROMOTION DECISIONS

Doing business without advertising is like winking at a girl in the dark. You know what you are doing, but nobody else does.

Steuart Henderson Britt

INTRODUCTION

Promotion is a critical tool in the marketing mix. As used in this book, promotion refers to all forms of communications that seek to influence buying behavior of existing and potential customers. The principal means of marketing promotion are advertising, personal selling, direct mail, point-of-sale displays and literature, publicity, and word-of-mouth communications. Promotion's role in the marketing mix is to tell existing and potential customers about the benefits and values that a product offers. This chapter surveys the major characteristics of the international promotion environment and then reviews different approaches to this element of the marketing mix.

ADVERTISING

Advertising, one of the major promotion tools in the marketing mix, is more important for consumer than industrial products. In general, the fewer the number of purchasers of a product, the less important advertising is as an element of the promotion mix. A frequently purchased low-cost product can be sold by advertising, whereas an infrequently purchased expensive and technically complex product can be sold only by a highly trained direct sales force. Even for the latter type of product, however, advertising has a role in setting the stage for the work of the sales force. A good advertising campaign can make it significantly easier for a salesperson to get in the door and, once in, can make it easier to make the sale.

Advertising and Stages of Economic Development

Until recently per capita GNP and advertising as a percentage of GNP were directly correlated; that is, the higher the per capita GNP, the higher the advertising as a percentage of GNP. As a country's income rises, countervailing forces emerge. On one hand, rising incomes create an even larger potential market for goods and services and thus create a greater incentive to engage in advertising. On the other hand, this increasing level of advertising in response to the growing potential and size of the market results in higher intensity of communications messages, which are directed toward customers and reduce the effectiveness of any particular message. Another major factor is the availability of media, television, in particular. In many countries, advertising on television is severely restricted or even totally prohibited.

Table 15–1 illustrates the relationship of these variables. The sales/awareness impact of any particular advertising message (A) is a function of the effectiveness of the advertising message and media combination (B), the potential market size (C), and the receptiveness of audiences to additional advertising messages (D). This principle can be written $A = (B)(C)(D)$. As incomes rise, C becomes larger, and D, because of the increasing intensity of advertising in the economy, becomes smaller. Therefore, C and D work in opposite directions as a country moves from lower to higher incomes.

An intriguing question for global marketers that has not yet been empirically studied is the marginal efficiency of advertising expenditures in countries at different stages of economic development. Is a marginal dollar of advertising in Argentina, where the potential market size is smaller than that in the United States but where the receptiveness to additional advertising message is presumably higher than in the United States, greater than the marginal expenditure of a dollar of advertising in the United States? From the point of view of the global advertising manager attempting to optimize his or her global expenditure of advertising revenues, this is an important question.

TABLE 15–1 Advertising Payoff: The Major Variables

A	B	C	D
Sales/awareness impact of advertising message	Advertising message/media effectiveness	Potential number of customers	Receptiveness of audiences to additional advertising

A global company needs to determine the optimum total level of worldwide advertising expenditure as well as the optimum allocation of expenditure among countries. Under optimum allocation conditions the marginal payoff (sales/awareness impact) of country advertising expenditures is equal. This can be expressed as follows.

Let

$$A = \text{advertising sales/awareness effect}$$
$$C = \text{country markets, } 1 \ldots n\text{th}$$
$$M = \text{marginal advertising expenditure}$$

At the optimum allocation point,

$$A = M_1 = M_2 = M_3 = M \ldots n\text{th}$$

WORLD ADVERTISING EXPENDITURES[1]

In 1985, world advertising expenditures exceeded $146 billion. The United States with expenditures of almost $95 billion spent more than twice as much on advertising as the next 10 countries combined. Table 15–2 shows total advertising expenditures

TABLE 15–2 Total Advertising Expenditures— Top 13 Countries, 1985

COUNTRY	TOTAL REPORTED 1985 ADVERTISING EXPENDITURES (IN MILLIONS OF U.S. $)
United States	$ 94,750.0
Japan	12,809.3
United Kingdom	5,843.4
Germany, Fed. Rep.	5,430.2
Canada	4,465.0
France	3,292.4
Brazil	2,452.7
Australia	2,317.6
Italy	1,950.5
Spain	1,671.0
Switzerland	1,485.7
Sweden	1,134.2
Finland	1,121.7
Total	138,723.7
World Total (46 countries)	$146,000.0

[1]This section is excerpted from *World Advertising Expenditures,* 1985 edition, sponsored by Starch INRA Hooper Inc., in cooperation with International Advertising Association. Copyright © 1986, by Starch INRA Hooper, used with permission.

for the top 13 advertising countries in the world in 1985. Japan held second place with expenditures of $12.8 billion and the United Kingdom was in third place with expenditures of $5.8 billion. The total advertising expenditures of the top thirteen countries accounted for 95 percent of the 1985 world total.

Per Capita Advertising Expenditures

The largest per capita advertising expenditures occurred, for the most part, in the more highly developed countries of the world. The lowest per capita expenditures were in the less developed countries.

Per capita advertising expenditures in 1985 averaged $66.38 for the 46 countries covered, and a total of 16 countries spent more than $50 per capita on media advertising. Four of these, the United States, Switzerland, Finland, and the United Arab Emirates, spent over $200 per capita and 7 other countries each exceeded $100 per capita.

Details on per capita expenditures for all countries for which this information is available are shown in Table 15–3.

Advertising Expenditures as a Percent of Gross National Product

The United States and Finland spent more than two percent of their gross national product on advertising in 1984 and 13 other countries reported percentages in excess

TABLE 15–3 Per Capita Advertising Expenditures, 1985

COUNTRY	PER CAPITA ADVERTISING EXPENDITURES IN 1985 (IN U.S. $)
United States	$397.11
Switzerland	232.14
Finland	228.91
United Arab Emirates	214.25
Norway	186.43
Canada	175.79
Qatar	148.81
Australia	148.56
Sweden	136.65
Japan	106.13
United Kingdom	103.61
Germany, Fed. Rep.	89.02
France	59.86
Belgium	53.93
Singapore	52.05
Israel	50.29

TABLE 15—4 Advertising Expenditures as a Percentage of Gross National Product

COUNTRY	1984
United States	2.39%
Finland	2.03
Australia	1.47
Netherlands	1.47
Taiwan	1.45
Switzerland	1.39
New Zealand	1.34
Canada	1.34
United Kingdom	1.26
South Africa	1.23
Norway	1.22
Colombia	1.18
Sweden	1.13
Venezuela	1.03
Korea, So.	1.02

of one percent. GNP statistics were not available from a central source for 1985, so these ratios have all been calculated using 1984 data.

The countries in which the proportion of gross national product allocated to advertising was the lowest were the less developed countries of Africa and Asia, and some of the oil rich countries of the Middle East. Table 15–4 shows those countries, in rank order, with advertising expenditures exceeding one percent of their gross national product.

Print Advertising

Print advertising (see Table 15–5) continues to be the number one advertising vehicle in most countries. In 1985, the United States spent close to $30 billion in print and six others surpassed $1 billion.

TABLE 15—5 Advertising Expenditures In Print Media (In Millions of U.S. Dollars)

COUNTRY	1985
United States	$30,325.0
Japan	4,515.4
United Kingdom	3,685.5
Germany, Fed. Rep.	3,538.5
Canada	1,710.9
France	1,352.1
Australia	1,125.0

TABLE 15–6 Per Capita Print Expenditures (In U.S. Dollars)

COUNTRY	1985
Finland	$157.2
United States	127.1
Norway	118.7
Switzerland	117.9
United Arab Emirates	104.6
Sweden	80.5
Australia	72.1

Per capita print expenditures (see Table 15–6) were highest in Finland, the United States, and Norway.

In countries where commercial television or commercial radio are unavailable or of limited use, the proportion of measured media[2] advertising funds allocated to print is extremely high. The countries in Table 15–7 each expended over 80 percent of their 1985 measured media expenditures in print.

Television Advertising

The United States and Japan continued to be the two leaders in television advertising during 1985. Their combined expenditure was over $25 billion and accounted for most of the world's expenditures in this medium (see Table 15–8).

On a per capita basis, advertisers in the United Arab Emirates and Qatar were the foremost users of television, both with per capita expenditures of over $90.00. As can be seen in Table 15–9, six other countries spent over $20.00 per capita.

The importance of television in Latin America is clearly evident. Five of the 15 countries which allocated more than 40 percent of their measured media expenditures to television were Latin American (see Table 15–10).

TABLE 15–7 Percent of Measured Media Advertising Expenditures Allocated to Print Media

COUNTRY	1985
Saudi Arabia	100.0%
Norway	96.8
Sweden	95.7
Finland	87.6
India	84.2
Switzerland	80.8

[2]Print, television, radio, cinema, outdoor, and transportation.

TABLE 15—8 Advertising Expenditures in Television Media (In Millions of U.S. Dollars)

COUNTRY	1985
United States	$20,770.0
Japan	4,510.2
United Kingdom	1,810.5
Brazil	1,438.6
Italy	959.5
Australia	788.9
Canada	765.7
France	562.5
Germany, Fed. Rep.	510.8

TABLE 15—9 Per Capita Television Expenditures (In U.S. Dollars)

COUNTRY	1985
United Arab Emirates	$110.0
Qatar	94.0
United States	87.0
Australia	50.6
Japan	37.4
United Kingdom	32.1
Canada	30.1
Hong Kong	21.6

TABLE 15—10 Percent of Measured Media Advertising Expenditures Allocated to Television Media

COUNTRY	1985
Peru	86.3%
Venezuela	66.8
Bahrain	66.7
Qatar	63.2
Brazil	59.2
Cyprus	58.3
Guatemala	56.1
Portugal	55.8
Turkey	52.5
Hong Kong	52.0
Greece	52.0
Colombia	51.9
United Arab Emirates	51.3
Thailand	51.0
Philippines	50.4

TABLE 15–11 Advertising Expenditures in Radio Media (In Millions of U.S. Dollars)

COUNTRY	1985
United States	$6,490.0
Japan	669.0
Canada	417.5
France	300.5
Australia	213.1
Germany, Fed. Rep.	184.2

Radio Advertising

Radio continues to be less important than print and television. As shown in Table 15–11, five countries reported radio expenditures of more than $200 million, and only one other reported a radio budget of $180 million or over.

Per capita radio expenditures in 1985 were above $10 in three countries and above $5 in three others (see Table 15–12).

As a proportion of total measured media advertising expenditures, radio trailed considerably behind both print and television. Radio accounted for more than 20 percent of the total measured media in three countries and exceeded 15 percent in only three others (see Table 15–13).

ADVERTISING STRATEGY—FORMULATING OBJECTIVES

A cardinal rule of advertising is that it should be undertaken only for specific purposes and that these purposes should be translatable into objectives that can be measured and assessed. Ultimately, the only reason to advertise is to increase sales and earnings. However, for a company entering a market for the first time, the first step to

TABLE 15–12 Per Capita Radio Expenditures (In U.S. Dollars)

COUNTRY	1985
United States	$27.2
Canada	16.4
Australia	13.7
France	5.5
Japan	5.5
Austria	5.4

TABLE 15—13 **Percent of Measured Media Advertising Expenditures Allocated to Radio Media**

COUNTRY	1985
Nepal	37.2%
Colombia	27.2
Guatemala	21.6
Philippines	19.7
Thailand	19.0
Portugal	17.2
Australia	14.3
Canada	13.2
Spain	11.7
Austria	11.6
France	11.2
United States	11.1

increasing sales and earnings may be the creation of a favorable image or, if the product is new, creation of product awareness.

A second major objective of advertising is to develop interest and to stimulate an evaluation of the company's products that will lead to their sale. Advertising must communicate appeals that are effective in the target market environment. Because products are frequently at different stages in their life cycle in various national markets, and because of the basic cultural, social, and economic differences that exist in markets, the most effective appeal for a product will vary from market to market. Therefore, it is essential to consider what advertising is intended to accomplish in the particular stage of the marketing plan and in the circumstances of the target market.

For example, the same product may be at entirely different stages of the life cycle in different national markets. In some markets, awareness of the product may be low—advertising should focus on creating awareness and interest in a new product. In other markets, the same product may be mature—in these markets advertising should focus on mature market selling appeals, such as price. The danger for the international advertiser is that the advertising approach in major markets will be followed or imposed worldwide. This is very often done in a way that ignores the real communications need in target markets that are very different from major markets.

Extend, Adapt, or Create?

The global advertiser must decide whether to extend, adapt, or create appeals, illustrations, and copy in each national market. The basic differences of economic, social, and cultural dimensions in markets around the world provide the framework for this decision.

The requirements of effective communication and persuasion are fixed and do not vary from country to country. The specific advertising message and media strategy must often be changed from region to region and must frequently be adapted from country to country to correspond with the requirements for effective communication and persuasion in the particular region or country. An advertiser should locate his or her market segments as precisely as possible and study the backgrounds and motivational influences that operate in the target market before preparing an advertising campaign.

During the 1950s the widespread opinion of advertising professionals was that effective international advertising required delegating the preparation of the campaign to a local agency. In the early 1960s this idea of local delegation was repeatedly challenged, most effectively by Eric Elinder, head of a Swedish advertising agency, who wrote, "Why should three artists in three different countries sit drawing the same electric iron and three copywriters write about what after all is largely the same copy for the same iron?"[3] Elinder argued that consumer differences between countries were diminishing and that he would more effectively serve a client's interest by putting top specialists to work devising a strong international campaign. The campaign would then be presented with insignificant modifications that were mainly directed toward translating the advertisement into idiomatic local language.

To the extent that markets are similar, Elinder's point of view has great merit. Within Europe, for example, there is a growing similarity among markets, and the application of his approach is increasingly effective. On the other hand, it is clear that across the world there are still major cultural, social, and economic differences that, for many products, demand more than superficial adaptations to advertising strategy.

There is a difference between the basic appeal (or benefit or selling proposition) of a product and the creative execution of the appeal. For example, the basic appeal of the S. C. Johnson's shaving cream product, Edge, is the smoothness of the shave the user gets by using this product. To demonstrate this advantage or benefit, the creative execution in the United States is a credit card test: A man takes a credit card and scrapes it on each side of his face. The side shaved using Edge is smoother than the side using another brand of shaving cream. The appeal, a smooth shave, can be extended to global markets, but in many cultures, the absence of credit cards would make the credit card test less than effective as a demonstration.

For industrial advertising, the possibilities of extension and scale economies in advertising are much greater than in consumer products. Industrial products are bought and used in the same way and for the same reasons in every country. The more sophisticated and technically complicated a product is, the truer this statement is. When this is the case, there is no point in letting national agencies duplicate each other's efforts. By avoiding the duplication of effort, it is possible to increase the effectiveness of the advertising budget or to reduce the size of the budget.

[3] Eric Elinder, "International Advertisers Must Devise Universal Ads, Dump Separate National Ones, Swedish Ad Man Avers," *Advertising Age,* November 27, 1961, p. 91.

Certain consumer products also lend themselves to advertising extension. If a product appeals to the same need around the world, there is a possibility of extending the appeal to that need. The basic issue is whether or not there is in fact a global market for the product—if the market is global, appeals can be standardized and extended. Examples of global markets are soft drinks such as Coke and Pepsi, Scotch whiskey, expensive Swiss watches, and Italian designer clothing.

Some marketing experts maintain that consumer products in general and food in particular are so culturally linked that it is impossible to extend any element of the marketing mix for these types of products. In fact, experience suggests otherwise.

Pierre Liotard-Vogt, former chief executive officer of Nestlé, one of the world's largest global food companies, commented on Nestlé's experience:

> *Advertising Age:* Are food tastes and preferences different in each of the countries in which you do business?
>
> *Liotard-Vogt:* The two countries where we are selling perhaps the most instant coffee are England and Japan. Before the war they didn't drink coffee in those countries, and I heard people say that it wasn't any use to try to sell instant coffee to the English because they drink only tea and still less to the Japanese because they drink green tea and they're not interested in anything else.
>
> When I was very young, I lived in England and at that time, if you spoke to an Englishman about eating spaghetti or pizza or anything like that, he would just look at you and think that the stuff was perhaps food for Italians. Now on the corner of every road in London you find pizzerias and spaghetti houses.
>
> So I do not believe [preconceptions] about "national tastes." They are "habits," and they're not the same. If you bring the public a different food, even if it is unknown initially, when they get used to it, they will enjoy it too.
>
> To a certain extent we know that in the north they like a coffee milder and a bit acid and less roasted; in the south, they like it very dark. So I can't say that taste differences don't exist. But to believe that those tastes are set and can't be changed is a mistake.[4]

While markets are becoming increasingly similar in industrial countries, media situations still vary to a great extent. For example, consider the case of television advertising in Europe: It does not exist in Denmark, Sweden, or Norway. The time allowed for advertising each day varies from 12 minutes in Finland to 80 in Italy, with 18 minutes allowed in France, and 20 in Switzerland, Germany, and Austria. Regulations concerning content of commercials vary, and there are waiting periods of up to two years in several countries before an advertiser can obtain broadcast time. Indeed, a media director of a large Paris-based agency concluded after surveying the European media situation,

> The media situations differ so much from one country to the next that the same problem may be solved in a different way in each country. . . . Continental Europe is comprised of 15 nations whose differences are greater than their similarities.[5]

---

[4]"A Conversation with Nestlé's Pierre Liotard-Vogt," *Advertising Age,* June 30, 1980, p. 31.

[5]Philippe Chopin, "International Media Planning: The Europe Jigsaw," *International Advertiser,* (Vol. 13, no. 2) pp. 10–11.

Three major difficulties can emerge in attempting to communicate internationally:

1. The message may not get through to the intended recipient. This difficulty could be a result of an advertiser's lack of knowledge about media that are appropriate for reaching certain types of audiences. For example, the effectiveness of television as a medium for reaching mass audiences will vary proportionately with the extent to which television viewing occurs within a country.

2. The message may reach the target audience but may not be understood or may be misunderstood. This can be the result of an inadequate understanding of the target audience's level of sophistication.

3. The message may reach the target audience and may be understood but still may not induce the recipient to take action desired by the sender. This could result from a lack of cultural knowledge about a target audience.

Appeals

Advertising appeals should be consistent with tastes, wants, and attitudes in a market. The trade literature of marketing is filled with anecdotal conclusions about the basic differences that exist in markets, which make adaptation of appeals necessary. In Belgium, it is said, fashion models would not enhance a product's appeal because they are scarce and their trade is hardly considered honorable. In France the appeal of an effective toothpaste is less cogent than in the United States because the French are not as inclined as Americans are to be concerned about the number of cavities in their teeth. Nigerian men are openly physique conscious, and products, especially in food and drink areas, can be sold using this approach.

> A stockbroker in Manchester, New Hampshire, might well have more in common with a stockbroker in Boston, East Anglia, than with, say, a car worker in Detroit, particularly in terms of life style, products they desire, education, etc., but in terms of what psychologists would call symbolic references (e.g., cultural norms, idioms, myths, history, humor, etc.) they are quite far apart. These "symbolic references" or cues are critical to advertising.[6]

In the face of all these cautionary conclusions, many international marketers are searching for and finding universal appeals for their products. Coke and Pepsi have both discovered that slogans have universal appeal.

Perhaps the best known universal campaign was the Esso "Put a tiger in your tank" campaign, which, after considerable success in the United States, was tested in Europe and Asia. Modifications in wording were made in certain countries. For example, in France the word "tank" is *reservoir,* which in the context of the phrase could have been risqué so the word *moteur* was substituted. In Thailand the campaign was modified because the tiger is not a symbol of strength and therefore was misunderstood.

[6]Greg Harris, "The Globalization of Advertising," *International Journal of Advertising,* no. 3, (1984).

Illustrations and Layouts

Some forms of artwork are universally understood. Revlon, for example, has used a French producer to develop television commercials in English and Spanish for use in international markets. These commercials, which are filmed in Parisian settings, communicate the appeals and advantages of Revlon products in international markets. In France Revlon obtains effective television commercials at a much lower price than it would have to pay for similar-length commercials made in the United States.

Pepsico has used four basic commercials to communicate its advertising themes. The basic setting of young people having fun at a party or on a beach has been adapted to reflect the general physical environment and racial characteristics of North America, South America, Europe, Africa, and Asia. The music in these commercials has also been adapted to these five regions: rock for North America, bossa nova for Latin America, high life for Africa, and so on.

Pepsi has been so successful in its adaptations that consumers often mistake it for a local product:

> The phenomenon of Pepsi-Cola being mistaken for a "native" drink is not unusual. Most of the time, it is happenstance rather than by design.
>
> For example, Mexico is a very important market for Pepsi-Cola. We make no effort to position Pepsi as a Mexican drink, frequently using American television commercials for our advertising (dubbed in Spanish) as well as our usual red, white, and blue logo. It is not unusual for Mexicans visiting the U.S. to comment that they were quite surprised that we also have Pepsi-Cola here.
>
> In the case of countries in the Eastern bloc, we have an unusual situation. While our overall international policy is to present Pepsi using "one sight, one sound, one sell," we do have to vary somewhat in the commercials used in Eastern countries. For example, you will note in the U.S. commercials that there is a sense of freedom, of casual living, of enjoyment of life, etc. For many people in the Eastern countries, such as Romania, this is too much of a contrast with the kind of life that they lead. In other words, in some countries people cannot relate to the lifestyles which we use in most of our U.S. commercials. Under those circumstances, we often re-shoot the same type of commercial, but modified to fit into a Romanian or similar background. Thus, it is not really unusual, especially in places where we have made these special arrangements, for people to assume that Pepsi-Cola is a local product.[7]

The international advertiser must make sure that advertisements are not inappropriately extended into markets. An example of such an inappropriate extension would be the advertisement for cheese alongside a foaming glass of beer in France. Such an ad would be perfectly consistent with German eating habits, but in France a more appropriate combination would be cheese and wine.

> Transplanted American creative people always want to photograph European men kissing women's hands. But they seldom know that the nose must never touch the hand or

[7]Private communication from Morten M. Lenrow, director, Marketing Information, Pepsico International.

that this rite is reserved solely for married women. And how do you know that the woman in the photograph is married? By the ring on her left hand, of course. Well, in Spain, Denmark, Holland, and Germany, Catholic women wear the wedding ring on the right hand.

When photographing a couple entering a restaurant or theater, you show the woman preceding the man, correct? No. Not in Germany and France. And this would be laughable in Japan. Having someone in a commercial hold up his hand with the back of it to you, the viewer, and the fingers moving toward him should communicate "come here." In Italy it means "good-bye."[8]

Copy

Translating copy, or the written text of an advertisement, has been the subject of great debate in advertising circles. There is some agreement that effective translation requires (1) good literary knowledge and command of the technical terminology of both the original and the translated language, (2) a good understanding of technical aspects of the products and any special appeals of the products, and (3) copywriting ability, which can recreate the persuasive tone of the original copy. In effect, there is a need for effective creative translation and not just literary translation. This need is not different from the requirement for literary translation. There is ample evidence that translations can be exceedingly effective when accomplished by a creative individual. For example, some bilingual German-English speakers have concluded that the German translation of Shakespeare is more powerful than the English original.

Inept translations can detract from the intended message. There are hundreds of examples of translation bloopers, including the Japanese translation of "As smooth as a baby's bottom" to "As smooth as a baby's ass." The all time classic error was not in translation per se but in the selection of a brand name that was not tested to determine its meaning in world languages. This was Chevrolet's Nova, which in Spanish means "no go" or, "it doesn't run!" One expert on international advertising makes the following suggestion:

> Before deciding whether to prepare new copy for a foreign market, or simply to translate the English copy, an advertiser must consider whether the message as translated can be received and comprehended by the foreign audience to which it is directed. Anyone with a knowledge of foreign languages realizes that it is usually necessary to be able to think in that language in order to communicate accurately. One must understand the connotations of words, phrases, and sentence structures, as well as their translated meaning, in order to be fully aware of whether or not his message will be received and how it will be understood. The same principle applies to advertising—perhaps to an even greater degree. Difficulty of communication in advertising is compounded, because it is essentially one-way communication, with no provision for immediate feedback. The most effective appeals, organization of ideas, and the specific language, especially colloquialisms and idioms, are those developed by a copywriter who thinks in the language and understands the consumer to whom the advertisement is directed. Thinking

[8]John O'Toole, *The Trouble with Advertising* (New York: Chelsea House, 1981), pp. 209–210.

in a foreign language involves thinking in terms of the foreigner's habits, tastes, abilities, and prejudices: One must assimilate not only words but customs and beliefs.

People the world over have the same needs—such as food, safety, and love. But people differ in the ways in which they satisfy their needs. Just as it is important to provide physical variations in products to meet the varying demands of diverse market segments, it is also important to tailor advertisements to meet the requirements of each market segment. But it is the demands of the market segments which are diverse, not the approach to planning and preparing marketing programs. The principles underlying communication by advertising are the same in all nations. It is only the specific methods, techniques, and symbols which sometimes must be varied to take account of diverse environmental conditions. Therefore U.S. advertisers may be well advised to export their approach to planning and preparing international advertising; but before making final decisions on copy or media they should be sure to consult personnel who know the foreign market intimately.[9]

An example of an international marketing problem was the situation faced by Levi Straus in Japan.[10] While Levi Straus was busy managing its expansion in Europe, several Japanese manufacturers had positioned their products as real American jeans, giving them brand names such as Big John and using Western models, music, and themes in their advertising. With lots of innovative hard work, Levi's got its product into the distribution channels but, in spite of trade recognition, market share (3 percent), brand awareness (6 percent), and ad recall (2 percent) were low.

The solution that Levi's agency developed capitalized on the Japanese propensity to hero worship by using famous movie stars to "endorse" the Levi's product. This tied into the Japanese fascination with U.S. television and film stars. There were, however, problems. One was the company's long-standing policy not to use celebrity endorsements. The other was cost. Still, it was a good idea, and the creative head of Levi's agency, Drew Fagen, was not one to let a good idea slip away. After a brainstorming session with some colleagues, he came up with the idea of using deceased film stars. The choices were easy: John Wayne, Marilyn Monroe, James Dean, all of whom ranked among the top favorite film stars in the 15- to 20-year-old market age group. Rights were obtained, and after 3½ years, there were indications that the campaign had been a solid success: brand awareness soared to 75 percent and advertising awareness to 65 percent.

GLOBAL ADVERTISING AND WORLD BRANDS

Global advertising is the transfer of advertising appeals, messages, art, copy, photographs, stories, and video and film segments (or spots) from one country to another. Everyone recognizes the importance of the advertising element of the communica-

[9]Gordon E. Miracle, "Management of International Advertising," Michigan International Business Studies Number 5, University of Michigan, 1966, p. 12.

[10]Richard D. Arroyo, "Levi Conquers Japan with Hero Worship," *Advertising Age*, December 13, 1982, p. M-24.

tions mix. The cost of an ineffective campaign is usually just as great as an effective campaign, but there is no comparison in the sales results achieved. Therefore, the ability to transfer a successful campaign worldwide is a critical advantage to a multinational or global company.

In spite of the obvious advantages of a global campaign, there are failures in the annals of global campaigns. For example, a leading producer of farm equipment developed a very successful campaign in North America around the testimonials of small farmers. The campaign was introduced to Europe and withdrawn within two weeks of launch. The dealers found the campaign insulting. Most European farms are small, and the emphasis on smallness made the European customers think that the company was using peasants, not real farmers.

It is important to distinguish between the buying proposal or the selling proposition and the creative presentation. The buying proposal is what one says, and the creative presentation is how one says it. For example, the buying proposal for many products is fun or pleasure, and the creative presentation shows people having fun with the product.

In one survey, experienced advertising executives felt that strong buying propositions can be transferred more than 50 percent of the time. An example of a buying proposal that transfers well is "top quality." The promise of low price or of value for money regularly surmounts national barriers. In the same survey, most executives indicated that they did not believe that creative presentations traveled well. The obstacles are cultural barriers, communications barriers, legislative problems (for example, children cannot be used in France to merchandise products), competitive positions (the advertising strategy for a leading brand or product is normally quite different from that for a minor brand), and execution problems.

These are real barriers, but there are powerful reasons to try to create an effective international campaign. To develop an international campaign means that the company is forced to discover the global market for its product. The first company to find a global market for any product is always at an advantage over those who discover this later. The search for an international campaign can be the spearhead of the search for a coherent global strategy. To do this, it is advisable to bring together all the people who are involved with the product and let them share information and experience. This creation of a common data base can be the foundation for the development of a truly global campaign, and the global campaign can be the conceptual glue that pulls together a truly global strategy.

Green, Cunningham, and Cunningham did a cross-cultural study to determine the extent to which consumers of different nationalities use the same criteria to evaluate two common consumer products, soft drinks and toothpaste. Their subjects were college students from the United States, France, India, and Brazil. In relation to France and India, the U.S. sample placed more emphasis on the subjective and less functional product attributes, and the Brazilian sample appeared more concerned with the subjective attributes than did the U.S. sample. The authors concluded that advertising messages should not use the same appeal for these countries if the advertiser is concerned with communicating the most important attributes of his or her product in each market.[11]

The decision of whether or not to use a global or standardized appeal is in the end a trade-off that must recognize the substantial benefits of cost savings and increased control as well as the potential creative leverage of a global appeal versus the benefits and advantages of appeals that zero in on the most important attributes of a product in each culture.

Another issue which the global company must face is whether to invite advertising agencies to serve product accounts on a multi-country or even global basis. There is a growing tendency for clients to designate global agencies for product accounts in order to support the integration of the marketing and advertising function. Agencies have seen this trend and are themselves engaged in a major program of international acquisition and joint venturing to extend their international reach and their ability to serve clients on a global account basis.

A recent study[12] indicates that consumer goods companies are taking globalization seriously—particularly non-food companies where 61 percent said they were working toward a global strategy on existing brands. The findings of this study also indicated that there are two stages of globalization: phase 1, the globalization of existing products, and phase 2, the development of *global* new products. Global new products were defined as those which are "developed up-front as global so that global considerations are built into the brand from the beginning. The new product would usually be tested and introduced in more than one country from the start. It would not be introduced unless it appeared to have viable sales potential globally."

Six major consumer goods companies stated they were already involved in phase 2, global new product development. Fourteen major companies said they would not proceed with a new product unless it had potential beyond the United States. The geographic area used as criteria for these companies ranged from the United States plus one other major foreign country to several foreign countries to worldwide potential. As an interim stage in the possible future move to global new product development, 80 percent of the companies now look to *both* foreign divisions and subsidiaries as well as the United States for successful local new products which may have international potential.

When asked their opinion of global new product development for the future, about two-thirds of the executives believed that more and more companies would eventually adopt the global new product development concept. About half of the executives were convinced that global new product development was feasible and practical for their product categories.

As a group the major holdouts against globalization of either existing or new products were the food companies. Out of 22 major food companies, only one stated

[11]Robert T. Green, William H. Cunningham, and Isabella C. M. Cunningham, "The Effectiveness of Standardized Global Advertising," *Journal of Advertising,* Summer 1975, pp. 25–30.

[12]Dean van Nest, "Global Marketing Strategy: A Study of U.S. Consumer Goods Companies," unpublished dissertation, Pace University, 1985.

it had adopted a globalization strategy. This generally negative response was apparently due to the perception that wide cultural differences exist in local foods and food tastes. On the other hand, when food company executives were asked if they thought global new product development was practical and feasible, about half of them agreed. When asked whether they felt globalization of new products was a concept more and more companies would pursue, about half of the food executives said yes.

SUMMARY

Promotion is a critical element of the marketing mix. It presents opportunities for global extension and requirements for local adaptation. Some countries are much more advertising intensive than others: The United States for example accounts for less than 25 percent of gross world product but over 60 percent of world advertising expenditures. In Japan, expenditures on advertising are second to those of the United States, but they are only one-eighth of U.S. expenditures and amount to only 1 percent of GNP as compared with the United States where advertising expenditures account for 2.39 percent of GNP. The availability of media varies considerably from country to country. Television is the leading medium in many markets and is unavailable in others.

In spite of the many failures, there are powerful reasons to try to create a global campaign: The exercise of creating a global campaign forces a company to identify a global market for its product, and this is the beginning of the development of a global marketing strategy. In addition, the identification of global appeals and benefits forces a company to probe deeply to identify basic as opposed to superficial needs and buying motives. The success of Coke, Pepsi, Marlboro, and Sony is a testament to the payoff of a successful global brand strategy.

DISCUSSION QUESTIONS

1. What is the role of advertising in the promotion mix? What is the role of promotion in the marketing mix? How do these roles differ for industrial and consumer products?
2. Does the role of promotion in the marketing mix vary from one country to the next for the same product?
3. Which elements of the promotion mix can be extended?
4. Which elements of the promotion mix must be adapted or invented?
5. What percentage of the world's advertising expenditure is made in the United States?
6. Is the United States "under-" or "over"-advertised as compared with other countries?
7. Is a global appeal a possibility? Cite examples to support your answer.

BIBLIOGRAPHY

Books

NEELANKAVIL, JAMES P., AND ALBERT B. STRIDSBERG. *Advertising Self-regulation: A Global Perspective*. New York: Hastings House, 1980.

PEEBLES, DEAN M., AND JOHN K. RYANS, JR. *Management of International Advertising: A Marketing Approach*. Allyn and Bacon, Inc., Newton, Mass.: 1984.

Articles

BLACK, GEORGE. "Ten Commandments for International Industrial Advertiser." *Industrial Marketing*, February 1981, p. 60.

BODDEWYN, J. J. "The Global Spread of Advertising Regulations." *MSU Business Topics*, Spring 1981, pp. 6–13.

BRITT, STEUART HENDERSON. "Standardizing Advertising for the International Market." *Columbia Journal of World Business*, Vol. 9, no. 4 (Winter 1974), pp. 39–45.

COLVIN, MICHAEL, ROGER HEELER, AND JIM THORPE. "Developing International Advertising Strategy." *Journal of Marketing*, Vol. 44 (Fall 1980), pp. 73–79.

ELINDER, ERIK. "How International Can European Advertising Be?" *Journal of Marketing*, April 1965, pp. 7–11.

FATT, ARTHUR C., "The Danger of 'Local' International Advertising." *Journal of Marketing*, January 1967, pp. 60–62.

GREEN, ROBERT T., WILLIAM H. CUNNINGHAM, AND ISABELLA C. M. CUNNINGHAM. "The Effectiveness of Standardized Global Advertising." *Journal of Advertising*, Summer 1975, pp. 25–30.

HARRIS, GREG. "The Globalization of Advertising." *International Journal of Advertising*, no. 3 (1984), pp. 223–234.

KILLOUGH, JAMES. "Improved Payoffs from Transnational Advertising." *Harvard Business Review*, July–August 1979, pp. 102–110.

KLIPPEL, R. EUGENE, AND ROBERT J. BOEWADT. "Attitude Measurement as a Strategy Determinant for Standardization of Multinational Advertising." *Journal of International Business Studies*, Spring 1974, pp. 39–50.

LEVITT, THEODORE. "The Globalization of Markets." *Harvard Business Review*, May–June 1983, pp. 92–102.

LILIEN, GARY L., AND DAVID WEINSTEIN. "An International Comparison of the Determinants of Industrial Marketing Expenditures." *Journal of Marketing*, Vol. 48 (Winter 1984), pp. 46–53.

LIOTARD-VOGT, PIERRE. "Nestlé—At Home and Abroad." *Harvard Business Review*, November–December 1976, pp. 80–88.

MIRACLE, GORDON E. "International Advertising: Principles and Strategies." *MSU Business Topics*, Autumn 1968, pp. 29–36.

PEEBLES, DEAN M., JOHN K. RYANS, JR., AND IVAN R. VERNON. "Coordinating International Advertising." *Journal of Marketing*, 1978, pp. 28–34.

QUELCH, JOHN A., AND EDWARD J. HOFF. "Customizing Global Marketing." *Harvard Business Review,* May–June 1986, pp. 59–68.

RYANS, JOHN K. "Is It Too Soon to Put a Tiger in Every Tank?" *Columbia Journal of World Business,* March–April 1969, pp. 69–75.

RYANS, JOHN K., JR., AND JAMES H. DONNELLY. "Standardized Global Advertising, A Call as Yet Unanswered." *Journal of Marketing,* April 1969, pp. 57–60.

SORENSON, RALPH Z., AND ULRICH F. WEICHMANN. "How Multinationals View Marketing Standardization." *Harvard Business Review,* May–June 1975, pp. 38–56.

STARCH INRA HOOPER, INC. "Twentieth Survey of World Advertising Expenditures: A Survey of World Advertising Expenditures in 1985." Mamaroneck, New York: 1985.

WEICHMANN, ULRICH E. "Intercultural Communication and the MNC Executive." *Columbia Journal of World Business,* Vol. 9, no. 4 (Winter 1974), pp. 23–28.

WEINSTEIN, ARNOLD K. "Foreign Investments by Service Firms: The Case of the Multinational Advertising Agency." *Journal of International Business Studies,* Spring–Summer 1977, pp. 83–92.

SWATCH WATCH U.S.A.: CREATIVE MARKETING STRATEGY[1]

"Vision is the art of seeing things invisible."

Jonathan Swift

INTRODUCTION

As speaker after speaker paid tribute to the extraordinary skills that had earned him the award of "Marketing Executive of the Year," Max Imgruth, President of Swatch Watch U.S.A. grew more and more uneasy. Fully confident that the product that changed the watch industry forever, the Swatch watch, would enjoy continued success, Imgruth nonetheless felt the need to change gears. The competition, which was at first slow to react, had begun to implement strategies that stood to erode Swatch's position. Gazing from his privileged place on the dais, Imgruth saw an audience that was content to rehash past successes for a night, which was nice, but not at all his style.

Imgruth had recently guided his company through a fast paced and, some would say, controversial diversification program. Having already achieved spectacular success with the Swatch watch, Imgruth spearheaded a plan to establish Swatch as a total fashion enterprise. This move was accompanied by a good deal of skepticism from colleague and competitor alike. His next objective was to make sure that this year's #1 marketing ex-

[1] This case was prepared by Charles Anderer, case writer and research associate, under the supervision of Warren J. Keegan, Professor of International Business and Marketing, as part of the Leading Edge Case Study Project, Center for International Business Studies, Pace University. This project was funded in part from a grant from the United States Department of Education. Copyright © 1986, Pace University.

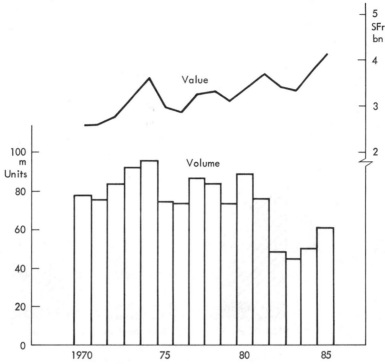

FIGURE 1 **It's All in the Price Swiss Watch Production***

*Including unassembled movements

Source: Federation of the Swiss Watch Industry.

ecutive did not become one of the decade's more memorable disappointments.[2]

BACKGROUND—THE SWISS WATCH INDUSTRY

1985 was a good year for the Swiss watch industry. The number of finished watches shipped abroad rose 41% to 25.1 million and the value of watch exports increased by 12.2%.

[2]This situation is fictional. Its purpose is to highlight the issues faced by the company described herein.

Luxury watches still comprised the backbone of the Swiss watch trade, accounting for only 2.1% of total shipments but 41.8% of total earnings. In 1985, the Swiss raised their share of the world market to 10% by volume (number of units sold) and 45% by value (Figures 1–3). For the first time in 15 years, an increase in employment was registered as 1,000 new jobs were created. The industry's good performance in 1985, combined with a strong year in 1984, gave every indication that the Swiss watch industry was back on its feet after struggling for much of the previous decade.

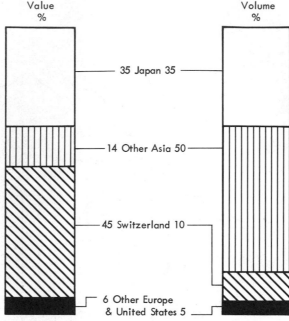

FIGURE 2   World Watch Production, 1985, by Country (estimates)

Source: Federation of the Swiss Watch Industry.

The comeback had been led by the success of Swatch (a blend of Swiss and watch). Over 10 million of its brightly colored, plastic wristwatches were sold worldwide in 1984–85. Success had been most notable in the United States, where Swatch's latest move was the launching of a diversification program aimed at making the company a total fashion enterprise.

Whether or not this expansion of the Swatch product line proved successful remained to be seen. What was certain, on the other hand, is that the Swatch watch had given new life (and increased market share) to an industry that was recently engaged in a very difficult struggle with Asian competitors. What was also clear is that Swatch's willingness to break with convention, especially in the area of marketing strategy, gave it a head start in

what had become a vast new market—the low-priced watch as a fashion accessory.

Some might say that the Swatch watch was just another in a long line of Swiss successes. In the 1950s, few other industries enjoyed the domination known by the Swiss watch industry. In that decade, the Swiss possessed an estimated 80% share of the (non-Communist) world watch market. Production was centered in the Jura region where snowed-in farming families, doubling as skilled watchmakers, supplemented their incomes by assembling mechanical watch parts during the winter months. At the industry's peak in 1956, there were 2,332 such *maisons*. Two large watchmaking groups, Allgemeine Schweitzer Uhren AG (Asuag) and Societe Suisse pour l'Industrie Horlogere (SSIH), controlled most of the Swiss brands at this time.

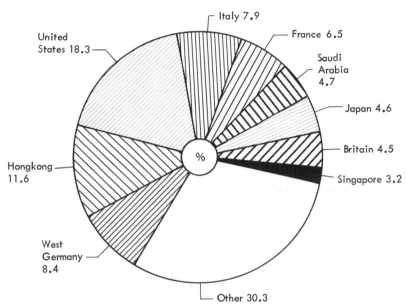

Total: SFr 4.3 bn

Italy 7.9
United States 18.3
France 6.5
Saudi Arabia 4.7
Japan 4.6
Hongkong 11.6
Britain 4.5
%
Singapore 3.2
West Germany 8.4
Other 30.3

FIGURE 3   Swiss Watch Exports,* 1985, by Destination

Source: Federation of the Swiss Watch Industry.

*Including unassembled movements

The Swiss remained industry leaders until the mid-1970s when the mass production of electronic watches changed the watch industry forever. The most important difference between an electronic watch and a mechanical watch is that the former is much easier to manufacture. A mechanical watch is an intricate piece of machinery whose assembly necessitates a highly skilled work force. The electronic watch is typically composed of microchips and printed units and lends itself well to mass production and automated processes. After having ruled supreme over the watch industry for decades, the Swiss suddenly found themselves faced with strong competition from Japan and such low wage producers as Hong Kong, Singapore, Taiwan and South Korea. These newcomers produced inexpensive watches with digital faces that were more accurate than mechanical watches.

Even though it was the Swiss who introduced the first electronic quartz watch in 1968, they were slow to accept the importance of the new technology. Hindsight suggests that small and fragmented producers had a vested interest in keeping things as they were—the new technology was still unproven in the marketplace and the Swiss position was secure. In any event, the Swiss were late and reluctant entrants into a new market whose rules were different. In the 1970s, for example, watches were introduced to mass outlets such as department stores and supermarkets. This was nothing short of blasphemous to the proud Swiss who required their watches to be sold in approved watch and jewelry stores. The Swiss continued to produce watches whose styles were no longer in touch with consumer demands, and they displayed a noticeable lack of marketing creativity. In reality, the Swiss had ceased to be leaders in the watch industry. The Swiss luxury watch market was still healthy, but they had lost a huge amount of market share at the lower end of the market. In 1974 Swiss watch exports still accounted for 60% of the world's total. By 1979, the Swiss represented about a third of the world's watch exports. Economic recession and a sharp rise in the value of the Swiss franc played a part in the industry's problems. Most observers, however, now attribute the decline of the Swiss watch industry to too many years of unqualified success that gave it an aura of invincibility. As one watch executive put it:

Just imagine the situation in the early post-war years when the Swiss were the only people making and selling watches; the industry had a waiting list of months; and selling prices were set to enable even inefficient firms to survive. The more efficient ones were making enormous profits. Why would any manager in his senses want to change things? (*Management Today, 12/80*)

As Switzerland entered the 1980s, the structure of its watchmaking industry, which had more or less retained its form since the late eighteenth century, finally began to adapt to the electronic age. This meant rationalization of production, automation, concentration and the corollary of fewer jobs. Between 1980 and 1983, production of watches dropped by 50%. By 1983, only 686 *maisons* remained and overall employment stood at about 40,000 jobs, down from 90,000 in the early 1970s.

THE MERGER OF ASUAG-SSIH

The merger of Asuag, whose flagship brand is Longines, and SSIH, whose best known brand is now Swatch but also boasts Omega and Tissot, was Switzerland's first response to the Asian challenge. The new group was granted a financial package worth $310 million, representing the largest rescue scheme in the history of Swiss banking. Heavy reorganization took place in both groups, especially SSIH which had lost $77 million in the year ending March 31, 1981. Most of SSIH's management was sacked and control of the watch division was transferred to Ernst Thomke, a rank outsider to the industry, who possessed both a medical doctor's degree and an advanced degree in chemistry.

The merger, as it turns out, was a sensible move because Asuag was far better technologically equipped to face the 1980s than SSIH, having already made a substantial commitment to the research and development of electronic watches. SSIH, for its part, possessed the better known brand names. (In the summer of 1985, Asuag-SSIH was renamed the Swiss Corporation for Microelectronics and Watchmaking Industries, SMH in short.)

Dr. Thomke made two important, tradition-breaking decisions in his first year. The first was to sell Swiss watch movements all over the world instead of restricting such sales to Switzerland, a move that allowed Asuag-SSIH to improve its technological base through increased production. The second was to recapture the lower end of the watch market by developing a product that was inexpensive to manufacture, low-priced, durable, technically advanced and stylish. The result was the Swatch watch, which was especially successful in the United States, with total retail sales increasing from $3 million in 1983 to $150 million in 1985.

PRODUCT DESCRIPTION

The Swatch is a lightweight ($\frac{3}{4}$ ounce), shock proof, water resistant (up to 100 feet), electronic watch with a plastic band that uses a quartz analog (with dial and hands) movement. It is manufactured by robots and sealed by lasers in a state of the art factory in Switzerland. The watch is comprised of only 51 components (the average is 91), which lends itself well to the thin look that is currently in vogue, and is manufactured off a single assembly line (the Japanese use three). What most distinguishes the product is its design and its departure from convention. A wide variety of faces have been used and even glow in the dark and scented bands (banana, raspberry and mint) have been tried. Battery life is estimated to be three years, and the watch retails from $30 to $35, which represents a substantial mark-up on cost.

THE SWATCH MARKETING STRATEGY

Central to the marketing strategy of the Swatch watch is the notion of the watch as a fashion accessory. This is a novel approach in that it is typically used as a selling point for gold and diamond-studded watches at the higher end of the market. Watches in the $30–$35 range normally compete on the basis of price, performance or, in the case of digitals in the late 1970s and early 1980s, on accessory features such as a stopwatch and/or calculator. Swatch, on the other hand, describes its target market as "fashion-oriented 12-to-24 year olds."

One trend that worked in Swatch's favor from the start is that, during the period 1976–1986, more and more people bought watches. No longer was the watch primarily a gift item and no longer was it only the rich who owned more than one. In 1976, 240 watches per 1,000 inhabitants were sold in America. Ten years later the figure was 425 watches per 1,000 inhabitants. About 90% of sales were composed of inexpensive electronic watches of various styles and brands. (*The Economist,* 5/17/86)

Of course, Swatch never would have been able to take advantage of this trend without a sound marketing strategy. According to Imgruth, his company's strategy is divided into three elements: design, distribution and production.

1. *Design.* An essential feature of the fashion oriented approach is a constant variety of product lines whose designs suit seasonal fashions. According to Imgruth, the company has "a clear product concept based on four directions: young and trendy; active and sporty; cool and clean high style; and classic. These four lines are available at all times. There are 12 small-faced models, and 12 larger ones. Every face is only out a restricted amount of time, sometimes only three months, sometimes 12 months, depending on the design concept of the watch." Each line is given a distinct theme such as the "Cosmic Western" group which was described as a combination of Buck Rodgers and the Wild, Wild West. New models are introduced four times a year, the seasons being spring/summer/fall/holiday (see Figure 4). In addition, special versions of the Swatch Watch such as the $100 diamond-studded Limelight and limited edition art watches are added periodically. Generally speaking, the trendier the design, the shorter it will remain available; the more classic the design, the longer it will remain on the market. Says Imgruth: "This is done on purpose, to create collecting and spur multiple ownership." (*Marketing and Media Decisions,* Spring/1985) Advertising media are chosen based on the product concept. There are four campaigns running si-

FIGURE 4

Source: Company records.

multaneously, each geared to a specific element of the four-tiered product mix.

2. *Distribution*. Distribution was originally limited to fashion outlets and now includes upscale department stores such as Bloomingdale's, Saks Fifth Avenue, Macy's, etc. Such stores never used to handle Swiss watches and still only account for 10% of all watches sold. Imgruth scrupulously avoids distributing through drugstores and mass merchandisers such as Sears and J.C. Penney, even though these are the usual paths for watches priced under $100. Distribution is limited to 5,000 locations in the United States, although Imgruth claims that 5,000 more would love to sell his products. As one Swatch executive puts it: "You have to control distribution and not flood the market, or people lose their hunger for the product." (*Sales and Marketing Management*, 3/11/85)

3. *Production*. The production process described above makes the design strategy possible. The flexibility that Swatch enjoys is unknown elsewhere in the industry. Design changes for other watchmakers typically require a substantial capital investment whereas Swatch can make changes without adding cost. Such flexibility is absolutely essential because of Swatch's product strategy. Without it, design runs of three months would be out of the question.

SWATCH MARKETING STRATEGY IN ACTION

In view of the fact that Swatch's strategy is unorthodox, it is not at all surprising that its marketing executives would look out of place in most corporate boardrooms. All advertising, marketing and promotion activities are handled by 27 year-old Steve Rechtschaffner, vp/marketing, and Nancy Kadner, director of advertising, 31. Rechtschaffner, a former member of the U.S. Ski Team and self-

described workaholic who recently overcame a bout with thyroid cancer, has no formal business education. He began his career by forming his own sports promotion business. As for Kadner, prior to her work at Swatch she spent over 4 years in the marketing department at MTV.

Rechtschaffner and Kadner are the creative forces behind Swatch's novel marketing strategy. Before Swatch entered the market, watches priced under $50 competed on the basis of price or performance. To gain an appreciation of just how different the Swatch strategy is, a glance at a typical advertisement for a low-priced watch would suffice. Normally, the watch is placed against a background in the hope that the right message is communicated. Timex developed one of the more creative performance-oriented campaigns in the early 1980s when it strapped a watch to an auto tire and proclaimed that the product "Takes a lickin' and keeps on tickin'." Others have not been so imaginative. For example, it is not uncommon to see digital watch advertisements where product features are simply listed next to a black and white photograph of the watch.

Swatch, for its part, has taken roads previously untraveled by watch producers. It employs the use of colorful (and often humorous) print ads, multi-page advertising inserts in magazines such as *Vogue* and *Rolling Stone,* concert and event sponsorship, and the use of music videos and MTV.

A good example of the Swatch strategy in action is its use of a rap music group and a graffiti artist to promote and develop its products. In September, 1984, Swatch sponsored the World Breakdancing Championships. One of the participating rap music groups, the Fat Boys, was hired to do a commercial on MTV on which its lead singer, the Human Beat Box, incessantly chants "BrrrSWATCHUM ha ha ha SWATCHUM." In addition, Swatch wanted an artist to help promote the breakdancing championships so it hired Keith Haring, New York's best known graffiti artist. The result was a four-watch-series called the Keith Haring Swatch.

The Haring watches were promoted under the banner of "Great Modern Art That Tells Time." Swatch produced 9,999 of each edition. Each watch is numbered and, in Imgruth's words, is "a collectible piece of art, a distinctive fashion accessory, and a sturdy timepiece." The watches were introduced in separate months, the first being released in December, followed by new editions in April, May and June.

THE COMPETITION

The under $50 watch segment is the most competitive in the watch industry in terms of the number of companies involved. Based on 1984 watch sales, this segment of the watch market also was responsible for the large majority of all U.S. watch sales:

1984 Watch Sales By Price

Under $10	29%
$10–$50	52
Over $50	19

Source: Timex

Because the Swatch watch was such a novelty at its introduction, the company had free reign over the plastic fashion watch market (some have called it "cheap chic") for well over a year. The picture has now changed considerably as strong competitors in the under $50 segment such as Casio, Timex, Lorus, Armitron and Parker Watch have entered the fray. In addition to imitating some of the very styling and advertising techniques that Swatch employs (Figure 5), the new competition has targeted drug stores and mass retail outlets, the very areas Swatch has shied away from, as their primary points of distribution.

While it remained to be seen if the new entries could match Swatch's creativity and design flexibility (one Swatch insider said that technology-conscious Casio's bid to enter the fashion watch market was "like John Deere getting into sportscars"), the new array of low-cost watches was certain to exert downward pressure on retail prices. Lorus' initial line of plastic watches sold for $19.95 at full mark-up, Timex's Fun Timers sold for $17.95 and Casio's ColorBurst line started at $19.95. Most drug retailers feel prices will eventually fall to the $12–$14 range. (*Drug Store News*, 5/27/85)

Swatch has also had to concern itself with the sale of phony Swatch watches and unlicensed sales. In October, 1985, 5,000 fakes were uncovered by U.S. Customs and Asuag-SSIH quickly sued three Swiss imitators. There is also a thriving "gray market" in which unlicensed traders exploit price differences between the United States and Europe (the watch sells at a lower price in Europe). Swatch elected to buy up all such watches in 1985, spending an estimated $500,000 in order to maximize control over the sale of its products.

THE NEXT STEP: SWATCH AS A TOTAL FASHION ENTERPRISE

It was perhaps with an eye to an increasingly competitive environment that Swatch embarked on a fast-paced diversification program in late 1985. The company created over 470 "Swatch Shops" within major department stores nationwide selling, in addition to watches, a new ready-to-wear line called "Funwear" and an accessories line called "Fungear" (See Figure 6).

Swatch will continue to employ the same

FIGURE 5

SWATCH FUNWEAR & FUNGEAR

The **NEFERTITI COLLECTION** is out there. In Watches, Shirts, Shorts, Sweaters and Sweats.

In Swim Suits, Sarongs and Beach Towels. It's all over the map. In Leather Knapsacks. Even

Sun Shields. See how it fits. See how it feels. It's all **SWATCH** and **IT'S REALLY OUT THERE!**

 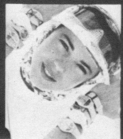

swatch +

Design © 1986 SWATCH WATCH U.S.A., Inc.
608 Fifth Avenue, New York, N.Y. 10020

bloomingdale's

FIGURE 6

516

strategies that it uses to sell its watches. The new product groups are aimed at the same fashion-oriented 12-to-24 year olds who are the target market for Swatch. Funwear is described as "a bright and whimsical line of unisex casual wear including shorts, T-shirts, tank tops, slip-on-pants, big shirts, and beachwear." Each collection has a theme that ties in with a Swatch watch theme. Swatch's own marketing and design people will introduce new collections every eight weeks, and prices range between $10 and $50. Fungear is a collection of leather and rubber knapsacks, belts, bags, and the jacketpack, which is a backpack containing a windbreaker and a hood. Prices range from $10 to $65.

Swatch offers more than just the above two product lines. There are Swatch Shields, which are described as high-fashion sunglasses; Swatch Guards, small, colorful devices that cover watch faces; Swatch Chums, which are eyeglass holders, and umbrellas and sweats that feature current watch designs. Swatch also imports and markets pens, notebooks, address books, key rings and safety razors.

The Swatch drive to open shops within major department stores is based on management's conviction that products should be sold in a total Swatch environment—an environment that has the Swatch "personality." The company president, Max Imgruth has predicted that ready-to-wear and accessories will represent from 30% to 40% of total 1986 sales. In the long term, he expects the new product lines to account for the majority of Swatch sales.

on the success of its first product by using its brand name on other, not necessarily related products. One of the more infamous examples is that of Bill Blass, who put his name on chocolates only to see the idea fail miserably. Another example of failure is that of Nike, which unsuccessfully expanded its collection of footwear to runningwear and leisurewear. A Nike spokesman looking back at that experience notes: "When you're tremendously successful in one area, there's a tendency to develop an arrogance about your ability to transfer the value of a brand name." (*Forbes*, 1/27/86)

On the other side of the coin, there was the example of Conran's, which successfully expanded from a producer of home furnishings to a retailer of everything from towels to desk lamps. Like Swatch, Conran's started out catering to the needs of young people and, when expansion took place, stayed with the same target market. Another point in Swatch's favor was its Swatch Shops, which spared the company from having its new product lines being placed on shelves next to competitors who had the advantage of an established image as quality producers of ready-to-wear. In order to keep its shops and continue to avoid head to head competition with more established companies, Swatch had to remain a trend setting, creative company. In this way they could avoid the fate of Bill Blass chocolates, which were sometimes found placed next to boxes of Godiva chocolates, leaving the consumer with what might be called a choice easily made.

OTHER EXAMPLES
OF BRAND TRANSFER

There are several examples of companies that have attempted, for better or worse, to build

DISCUSSION QUESTIONS

1. Swatch is a unique success story. Why has the company been so successful? Was it important that the Swiss watch industry recap-

ture the lower end of the market? Why? Why not?

2. Do you see any parallels between the decline of the Swiss watch industry and other Western industries?

3. Evaluate the cultural dimension of the Swatch story, taking into account such practices as the willingness to bring in people from other industries, to delegate authority to younger executives, and to employ new media such as rock concerts and music videos.

4. Swatch created a new market—can they continue to expand that market? What must they do to defend their position in this market?

5. What do you think of Swatch's chances for success as a total fashion enterprise? Do you agree with management's extension of the Swatch brand name to other products? Why? Why not?

6. Swatch is a classic example of marketing success through creativity. What lessons can be learned from their experience?

Appendix: Prometheus Unbound[1]

In Greek mythology Prometheus was considered a savior because he brought fire to mankind. For that, unfortunately, he was chained to the top of a mountain and left to die.

Clearly the invention—if one can call it that—of the use of fire represented a major turning point in the development of mankind. The number of other major events, mythical or otherwise, contributing to mankind's development are few when one takes a long view of history: block printing in Japan, followed by Gutenberg's printing press, Eli Whitney's cotton gin, Marconi's wireless telegraph, Edison's electric light bulb, and the Bell System's transistor.

But from a socio-economic standpoint, the invention of the cotton gin, which transformed a largely agrarian, extractive economy to a new industrial one, was unprecedented in the impact it had on the modern-day world.

Today we are riding the crest of another major wave of change brought about by the invention, innovation, and pervasive use of microelectronics which, like fire unbounded, is spreading into every nook and cranny of our existence, pushing us headlong into the long-heralded post-industrial information society and an economy not based on farming or the production of goods or even services so much as on the production, use, and dissemination of knowledge.

The broadcasting business, which lives at the core of this information-age phenomenon, is likely to be further transformed as the impact of microelectronics pervades every aspect of production, distribution, and reception of programming. The first wave of change is already evident in the U.S.

Fifteen years ago, there were three commercial national networks, 73 independent stations, 128 public television stations, and 5.4 million homes using cable. Average viewing was 5.9 hours per day.

[1]Tokyo Broadcasting Lecture, Tokyo, Japan, September 12, 1985. Reproduced by permission of John M. Eger, Attorney at Law and President, Worldwide Media Group, Suite 700, 331 Madison Avenue, NY, NY 10017.

Today we still have the three national networks, but we now have 214 independent stations, 312 public television stations, and 38 million homes using cable television; we also have 46 cable networks including eight so-called superstations, 25 pay television systems, and 15 million videocassette recorders. There are plans for 11 DBS systems and 336 low-power stations. Average viewing is 7.8 hours per day.

What the next 15 years will bring—to the year 2000—is anybody's guess. However, the prospects for technological abundance are clear.

But this is just the first wave—a technological wave mostly reflecting the advances in television distribution and reception. What will happen when VCR capability is built into every television set or, as it is now being called, the television monitor? And when every rooftop has its own two-foot earth station, capable of receiving hundreds of signals from everywhere around the world? And more importantly, perhaps, what will the world be watching? How and where will all the programming be produced to fill all the channels of distribution and who will pay for it?

Candor requires acknowledgment on my part that I don't have all the answers to these questions. No one does. But as both a lifelong student of the information revolution and a practitioner of the art and the business of television, my visceral instincts tell me that inherent in the answer or answers is a second major wave of change—a wave so awesome we can only begin to see the outlines of the changed media and market landscape.

For here is the technology that knows no barriers, no national boundaries, and does not of itself recognize any of the essential artificial divisions between the different people and places of the world. Here is a technology that does not recognize color, creed, race, or nationality, but rather is supranational, acultural, and alingual. Here is a technology of sight and sound in binary data bits that can indeed saturate the world.

It is a technology that creates simply by providing the means—a flow of information and ideas, a force throughout the world that simply will not be stopped however we may resist its flow. What we are dealing with is a technology that involves social change, something technology has always done, but on a scale and a speed never before experienced by human beings or their institutions. And we find ourselves immersed in an age of truly vast and revolutionary change, propelled by our technology toward an acceptance of the concept that we are indeed one people on this planet Earth, one family living in one home, a family with common problems, concerns, and interests.

A fundamental question is whether we are ready for this. Are we human beings and our political institutions ready to think of ourselves as one family, to address common problems, and to work for common global goals? Or, as some have less optimistically suggested, are we so inexorably, so tightly bundled in national, economic, cultural, and racial security blankets that we cannot reach out and communicate with the freedom our technology offers?

Already our technology is providing the means for a vast flow of information, data and new ideas throughout the world—from the evening television news and the international electronic fund transfer of payment systems to the almost-routine exchange of data between computers in the United States drawing airline reservation information or, in the universities, drawing scientific or economic data to and from a terminal in Tokyo, London or Kampala.

This flow is increasing at an exponential rate and is forming an enormous wave that is spilling over cultural lines and national boundaries and, inevitably, changing people's views, altering attitudes, awakening ancient hopes and, it is also true, rousing ancient fears around the world.

Already, there are those holding up their hands to hold back or tell the wave of that enormous change to stop. There are men and women building little boxes into which all the breadth and force of that roaring wave is supposed to come washing in, to be spoiled, broken up, and compartmentalized into numbered sections of statutes, regulations, rules, court decisions, customs and precedents to impede the free flow of information and the accompanying goods and services.

There is a growing patchwork of economic and cultural protectionism that at one time may have been simply an annoyance but now has reached crisis proportions. A convergence of developments has heightened the impact of these barriers for all of us in the programming business. For one thing, program production costs seem to have no reasonable ceiling in the United States. They keep going up. This means that ancillary uses of programs, including foreign markets, are more important than ever as the point of profit becomes even more distant.

For another thing, the worldwide new media explosion, particularly communication satellites, cable systems, and videocassette recorders, is creating a much larger market for all types of programming. Trade barriers only clog the pipeline, hampering the program seller and program buyer alike, hampering everyone's ability to create, produce, develop, and distribute, using whatever technology makes the most sense. And these barriers hamper the public's right to receive.

I am basically an optimist and have no doubt that in the long run the development of technology and the desire of people all over the world for program diversity will erode those barriers to the free flow of information. But for the short term, in the here and now, the barriers are many, complex, and often rooted as much in emotion as in law. Beating back shortsighted protectionism will require tireless effort and patient negotiation, but the benefits truly will be worldwide.

Thomas H. Wyman, Chairman, President, and Chief Executive Officer of CBS Inc., issued a report last September on trade barriers, based on his work as chairman of a subcommittee advising the Office of the United States Trade Representative in its preparation for the next General Agreement on Tariffs and Trade. In his words, "The subcommittee assignment was to report on the major problems the motion picture and television, prerecorded entertainment, publishing, and advertising industries incurred in exporting their products and services."

After interviewing scores of businessmen, Mr. Wyman reported, "We found that U.S. communications executives saw copyright infringement as the overwhelming trade problem, followed in varying degrees by cultural restrictions, foreign exchange problems, and competition with government-owned firms."

The Wyman Committee found that every U.S. executive interviewed identified copyright infringement as a trade barrier. Unlicensed use of copyrighted material on videocassettes, audiotapes, and records is a severe problem in many nations of the world. Likewise, the vast majority of those interviewed cited cultural restrictions as barriers, including quantitative restrictions on programming, restrictions on broadcast advertising, and restrictions on the use of foreign-produced commercials. Almost all of the executives found foreign exchange remittance restrictions a trade barrier. And more than half were hampered by competition with government-owned or subsidized distribution or production systems.

Other trade barriers included foreign ownership restrictions, transborder data flow restrictions, quantitative restrictions on import of products through quotas or licensing arrangements, restrictions on earnings, discriminatory taxation or limitation on rental terms and royalties, discriminatory customs valuation practices, local work and local content requirements, and hiring and immigration restrictions.

Everyone with a stake in the communications industry, indeed anyone with a stake in creativity and freedom, should take a position against these barriers. Information and ideas will flow, will permeate the world. They must, say those of us who believe in the freedom of ideas, information, and speech. We know that there are other peoples in the world who do not share our belief in freedom. We admit that there are people who fear that we can exercise our freedom only at their expense. And this is the heart of the problem.

It is the problem of finding a way to make the maximum use of our communications while convincing our detractors that the global unity of man can be achieved without destroying man's diversity, that our technology will advance and not retard the fortunes of mankind. Indeed our own history in the United States is a striking example of the fact that technology can unite a disparate people without destroying individuality.

Arthur C. Clarke, who foresaw the synchronous satellite and some of its uses almost 40 years ago, rightly observed that without the invention of the railroad and the telegraph there could have been no United States, and that with those inventions the United States became inevitable. In turn, the telephone and automobile, radio and airplane, tied us even closer together into a continental community than could the telegraph and railroad alone.

Yet we have never been homogenized. The idea of America as a melting pot has long given way to the recognition that we have become the most pluralistic and individualized society the world has ever seen, rooted in almost every cultural and national strain, and still committed to freedom and equality for all. And this is not simply rhetoric. It is a fact of our daily life.

Perhaps it is time not simply to remind but to convince the doubting nations of the world that this is so, and that Clarke and others are right in their conviction that the spread of microelectronics offers mankind an opportunity to create not a United States of the world but a global community of diverse and individualized people living together, perhaps not without contention, but not without a fundamental harmony now, and always until now, lacking in the world.

I, for one, do not foresee cultural genocide as *Dallas* engulfs the world in melodrama. Obviously we have no desire to obliterate or even to compromise a different culture. And how can a healty culture be wiped out by *Leave It To Beaver* or *Kojak* any more than the U.S. be crippled by the fact that half of our restaurant menus are in some form of French?

To the contrary, I think we are headed toward a world in which U.S. programming benefits from the ideas of other countries and program diversity becomes more apparent, not less. I believe there will be an increasing number of television programs devised, not imposed, on various countries to meet program needs that are ascertained through consultation and cooperation. Such successful U.S. television series as *All In The Family* and *Sanford And Son* were Americanized versions of British comedy hits, even as *Dynasty* is being emulated abroad.

International co-production has been around a long time but given the number of outlets for distribution developing in every nation in the world, the variety and volume of coproductions will grow dramatically in the next several years. And, of course, it must. By one estimate of the European Economic Commission, if all the channels proposed or in planning stages were to come to fruition, they would require 500,000 hours of fresh programming a year.

One result of this demand for programming is the need for someone to pay for it, and thus increasing reliance on national, international, and global advertising. I should acknowledge at this point that I am Chairman of the International Advertising Association's Global Media Commission, so my prejudices may be showing, but I think that more and more advertisers will design worldwide campaigns for worldwide products.

Global marketing can and will provide important new revenues for commercial broadcasters around the world. It can also stimulate a variety of barter arrangements whereby broadcasters are supplied with high-quality programs free of charge. Commercial announcements will be part of the package, along with positions for local commercials—a win/win situation for the broadcaster. For the global companies, it means the opportunity to sell the same products with highly unified marketing techniques in all the nations of the world. Increasingly, products and their marketing support systems will be truly global.

Most importantly, it must be remembered that global marketing is a public communications endeavor which relies on attracting television viewers competitively. A threshold requirement is public appeal, public entertainment, public satisfaction. More television choices are coming to the peoples of the world; their attention must be earned. In the broader sense, it is the public who will benefit because:

- There will be a greater diversity of viewing alternatives.
- There will be much greater consumer information dispensed through the medium of competitive commercials.
- There will be a greater flow of information generally; advertising will pay for the maintenance of media that also broadcast news.

- There will be a greater availability of high-quality, inexpensive, reliable world-class consumer goods.
- There will be vastly stimulated, increasingly interdependent national economies—a political benefit even to those in public life who might be most chary of the implications of global marketing.

Global marketing and global media will benefit virtually everyone. Those who do not benefit will be those who refuse to see the future or who see but do not believe in it and will not participate in making it work.

The public interest and the private interest are not mutually exclusive. Nations which fail to recognize this may cut themselves off from the mainstream of economic development.

Last October, the Chinese Communist Party's First Secretary Deng Xiaoping said, "No country can now develop by closing its door. We suffered from this and our forefathers suffered from this. Isolation landed China in poverty, backwardness, and ignorance." It is no secret why the expansion of television in China is one of the major goals of modernization.

I believe that it is isolation and the closing of doors that we must strive against.

16

EXPORTING
AND IMPORTING

No nation was ever ruined by trade.

Benjamin Franklin, 1706–1790
Thoughts on Commercial Subjects

INTRODUCTION

Exporting and importing are two sides of the same coin. Exporting supplies customers with products manufactured in another country. Importing does exactly the same thing.

It is important to distinguish between *export selling* and *export marketing*. Export selling is analogous to the old concept of marketing with its focus on the product and emphasis on selling. Key elements of the marketing mix are fixed: product, price, and promotion are the same as in the home market. Only place or distribution is adjusted in export selling.

Export marketing focuses on the customer in context and the total environment and on strategic management. The export marketer does not take the product as given and "sell" it to foreign markets. To the export marketer, the product offered in the home market is a starting point. It is modified as needed to meet the preferences of target markets. Similarly, the export marketer sets prices to fit the marketing strategy and does not merely extend the home country prices to the target market. Of course, the export marketer also adjusts the communications strategy and plan and the place strategy and plan to fit the market and competitive situation and the overall strategic design.

Export marketing is global marketing using a foreign source of product supply. The essence of export marketing is the sourcing plan or design: Product manufactured in one country is supplied to another country. The location of production facilities in a global company should be a function of factor costs; transportation charges; tariff and duty charges; entry barriers, including nontariff barriers; supply or delivery considerations; and management's ability to manage the production process in different locations. This is a *sourcing* decision. Regardless of the outcome of this decision, each company must decide whether or not it wants to make a selling effort or a marketing effort in target markets. Needless to say, if this issue is consciously addressed, the choice will always be to make a marketing effort because this is more profitable and more enjoyable.

World exports have been growing at an annual compound rate in excess of 15 percent. Exports now account for over 15 percent of global GNP. The unmistakable fact is that exporting is becoming increasingly important in the world economy as national economies become more involved in supplying and servicing markets located outside their national boundaries. Virtually every large corporation, in particular every corporation referred to as global because of the scope and extent of its international involvement, is an active exporter. One percent of U.S. companies, the big multinationals, account for 85 percent of all U.S. exports.[1] The involvement of smaller U.S. enterprises in export activities is much less pronounced. Eugene Lang, president of REFAC corporation of New York City, has estimated that there are 250,000 U.S. manufacturers in the small-business category that are not exporting and have no export objectives or programs for developing overseas markets. For many of these firms, exporting is a major untapped market opportunity. For the U.S. government or any other government concerned with its balance of payments, the export potential of uninvolved firms could be a major factor contributing to the elimination of a balance-of-payments deficit.

Export marketing is the integrated marketing of goods and services that are produced in a foreign country. Export marketing requires

1. An understanding of the target market environment;
2. The application of all the tools of marketing, specifically
   a. The use of marketing research and the identification of market potential
   b. The product design decision, pricing decisions, distribution and channel decisions, and advertising and promotion decisions
   c. Organization, planning, and control

Each of these major topics is dealt with in a specialized chapter in this book. The purpose of this chapter is to focus specifically on some unique problems and aspects of export marketing.

EXPORT BEHAVIOR OF FIRMS

Bilkey reviewed 43 studies on the export behavior of firms and reached three major conclusions.[2] The first is that exporting is essentially a developmental process. This

---

[1] "The Reluctant Exporter," *Business Week*, April 10, 1978. p. 56.

[2] This section relies heavily on Warren J. Bilkey, "Attempted Integration of the Literature of the Export Behavior of Firms," *Journal of International Business Studies*, Vol. 9 (Spring–Summer 1977), pp. 33–46.

process can be divided into distinct stages derived from Rogers' stages of the adoption process.[3] The stages are as follows:

1. The firm is unwilling to export; it will not even fill an unsolicited export order. This is due to apathy, prejudice ("too busy to fill the order"), or whatever reason the company may come up with.
2. The firm fills unsolicited export orders but does not explore the feasibility of exporting.
3. The firm explores the feasibility of exporting (this stage may bypass stage 2).
4. The firm exports experimentally to one or more markets.
5. The firm is an experienced exporter to one or more markets.
6. The firm evaluates global market potential and screens the "best" target markets for inclusion in its marketing strategy and plan. This screening is open equally to domestic and foreign markets.

The second conclusion is that the probability of a firm going from one stage to the next depends on different factors. The probability of a firm going from stage 2 to 3 depends upon the firm's international orientation (i.e., management's attitude toward the attractiveness of exporting and management's confidence in the firm's ability to compete abroad). The probability that the firm will go to stage 4 is a function of whether or not the firm receives unsolicited export orders and the quality and dynamism of management. Stage 5 follows from stage 4 if there is success. Stage 6 is the mature, geocentric company that is relating global resources to global opportunity. This stage is never reached without the vision and commitment of management to be this kind of company.

A third conclusion is that export profiles can be formulated. Cavusgil[4] found, for example, that 96 percent of the firms with the following characteristics exported:

1. They had very favorable expectations regarding the effect of exporting on the firm's profitability and growth.
2. They planned for exporting.
3. They had sales of more than $1 million (1975 dollars).
4. They had favorable expectations regarding the effects of exporting on the firm's market development.

COMPANY POLICIES TOWARD EXPORTS

The theory of international trade looks for country comparative advantage as a basis for explaining trade and for determining national policy toward trade. Unfortunately, in services and manufacturers, this theory is absolutely useless as a guide to action. What is true is that companies with new and innovative products have a better than average chance of succeeding in export markets. However, the most significant

[3] Everett M. Rogers, *Diffusion of Innovations*, New York, Free Press, 1962.
[4] S. T. Cavusgil, "Organizational Determinants of Firms' Export Behavior: An Empirical Analysis," Ph.D. dissertation. The University of Wisconsin (Madison), 1976.

factors affecting export performance are not product characteristics but, rather, firm characteristics. In a study of the influence of factors on exports, McGuinness and Little found that two firm characteristics—"restrained from exporting" and "high technology"—had such a powerful effect on exports and their influence overwhelmed the influence of product characteristics in regression analysis.

The implications of these findings are clear. New product advantages such as relative improvement are definitely a plus in influencing export performance. However, an emphasis on product improvement is not enough. The attitude and commitment of the firm to exporting is of critical importance. Put another way, the single most important factor in determining export success is company attitude and commitment.[5]

NATIONAL POLICIES TOWARD EXPORTS

National policies toward exports can be summarized by a single term: schizophrenic. The nation-states of the world have for centuries combined two opposing policy attitudes toward the movement of goods across national boundaries. Nations take steps to encourage exports by outright subsidy and by indirect measures, such as tax rebates and extensive government support programs in the area of promotion and producer education. The flow of goods in the other direction, imports, is generally restricted by national policy. Measures such as tariffs, import control, and a host of nontariff barriers are employed by nation-states to limit the inward flow of goods. Thus the international situation is a combination of measures designed to encourage exports and restrict imports. The combination of policy measures is offsetting to some extent.

GOVERNMENT PROGRAMS SUPPORTING EXPORTS

There are three major governmental activities designed to support export activities of national firms. Tax incentives treat earnings from export activities preferentially either by applying a lower rate to earnings from these activities or by providing for a refund of taxes already paid where income is associated with exporting. Outright subsidies are used to reward export performance. And the third support area is governmental assistance to exporters, particularly in providing information concerning the location of markets and credit risks and in promotion, including assistance in the establishment of trade fairs and other exhibits designed to promote sales to foreign customers.

The tax benefits of export-conscious governments include varying degrees of tax exemption or tax deferral on export income, accelerated depreciation of export-

[5]Norman W. McGuinness and Blair Little, "The Influence of Product Characteristics on the Export Performance of New Industrial Products," *Journal of Marketing*, Spring 1981, pp. 110–122.

related assets, and generous tax treatment of overseas market development activities. Naturally, in many cases, the actual treatment of export-related income is even more favorable than tax statutes would imply. Far Eastern, Latin American, and European trading nations have been particularly generous in providing these kinds of special aids to exporting companies.

GOVERNMENT EXPORT EXPANSION PROGRAMS— THE U.S. EXAMPLE

The United States is a classic example of a country with an export expansion problem. American business managers lack export consciousness. Less than 10 percent of the approximately 350,000 U.S. manufacturers export at all, and most of these export only marginally. Major competing nations export up to 20 percent of their total production, whereas the United States exports only 9 percent. These percentages reflect the fact that the United States is a massive continental market accounting for one-quarter of global national income. The American business manager's foreign counterpart in the typical industrialized country abroad has exhausted his or her home market long before his or her U.S. counterpart has. As a result, when the foreign company is forced by the smaller size of the home market to search internationally for expansion opportunities, his or her U.S. counterpart is still profitably expanding within the U.S. market. It is simply not true that all U.S. companies that are not exporting are missing an opportunity. Many of these companies are in fact devoting their efforts to the most profitable and feasible potential market for them— the U.S. market.

Nevertheless, the enormous size of the U.S. market has created a relative insularity and lack of export awareness that is increasingly a problem both from a private and from a public policy perspective. For companies, the export myopia creates dangerous competitive threats by giving up market position and volume to manufacturers in other parts of the world, who inevitably will decide to enter and compete in the U.S. market. From a public policy perspective, weak export performance creates balance-of-payments and currency pressures that are politically undesirable. The root cause of the poor U.S. export performance is a lack of will or determination to export. The Department of Commerce has estimated that there are 20,000 U.S. companies that could successfully sell in foreign markets but are not doing so. The resulting asymmetry between the United States and the rest of the world is typified by the U.S. auto industry, which designs U.S.-manufactured cars for the U.S. market and exports almost none of its U.S. production. Figure 16–1 shows the export ratios of selected auto producing countries.

Government Regulations of Exports— The U.S. Case

The U.S. government controls the exportation of U.S. goods to all countries except Canada. Control and licensing, which are exercised by the Department of Commerce,

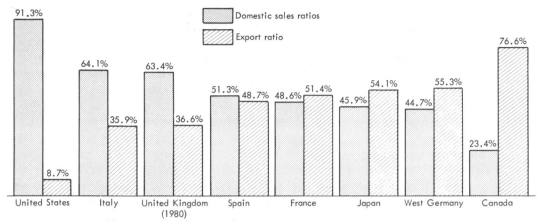

FIGURE 16–1 1981 Automobile Sales Ratios by Country

Source: *Honda: A Statistical View*, Overseas Public Relations Department of Honda Motor Co. Ltd., Tokyo, Japan.

with few exceptions are based on the commodity to be exported and the country of destination. Two types of licenses are issued: general and validated. A *general license* is a privilege permitting exportation within limits without requiring that an application be filed or that a license document be issued. A *validated license*, a document authorizing exportation within the specific limitations it sets forth, is issued only upon formal application. Most goods can move from the United States to a free world country under a general license. A validated license is required when shipments involve certain strategic goods regardless of destination and when shipping most goods to Soviet bloc countries in Eastern Europe. Details of U.S. export control regulations can be obtained from the U.S. Department of Commerce.

TERMS OF ACCESS

The phrase *terms of access* refers to all the conditions that apply to the importation of goods manufactured in a foreign country. The major instruments covered by this phrase include import duties, import restrictions or quotas, foreign exchange regulations, and preference arrangements.

Tariff Systems

Tariff systems provide either a single rate of duty for each item applicable to all countries, or two or more rates, applicable to different countries or groups of countries. Tariffs are usually grouped into two classifications.

SINGLE-COLUMN TARIFF. The single-column tariff is the simplest type of tariff and consists of a schedule of duties in which the rate applies to imports from all countries on the same basis.

TWO-COLUMN TARIFF.   Under the two-column tariff, the initial single column of duties is supplemented by a second column of "conventional" duties, which shows reduced rates agreed through tariff negotiations with other countries. The conventional rates, for example, those agreed upon by "convention," are supplied to all countries enjoying MFN (most favored nation) treatment within the framework of GATT (General Agreement on Tariffs and Trade). Under GATT, nations agree to apply their most favorable tariff or lowest tariff rate to all nations who are signatories to GATT, with some substantial exceptions.

Preferential Tariff

A preferential tariff is a reduced tariff rate applied to imports from certain countries. GATT prohibits the use of preferential tariffs with the major exceptions of historical preference schemes, such as the British Commonwealth preferences and similar arrangements that existed before the GATT convention; preference schemes that are part of a formal economic integration treaty, such as free trade areas or common markets; and the granting of preferential access to industrial country markets to companies based in less developed countries.

Types of Duties

Customs duties are of two different types. They are calculated either as a percentage of the value of the goods or ad valorem, or as a specific amount per unit or specific duty, or as a combination of both of these methods.

AD VALOREM DUTIES.   This duty is expressed as a percentage of the value of goods. The definition of *customs value* varies from country to country. Therefore, an exporter is well advised to secure information about the valuation practices applied to his or her product in the country of destination. A uniform basis for the valuation of goods for customs purposes was elaborated by the Customs Cooperation Council in Brussels and was adopted in 1953. In countries adhering to the Brussels convention on customs valuation, the customs value is landed C.I.F. cost at the port of entry. This cost should reflect the arm's-length price of the goods at the time the duty becomes payable.

The United States is now a signatory to the GATT Customs Valuation Code. The U.S. customs value law was amended in 1980 to conform to the GATT valuation standards. Under the new GATT valuation code, the primary basis of customs valuation is known as "transaction value." As the name implies, transaction value is defined as the actual individual transaction price paid by the buyer to the seller of the goods being valued.

In those cases in which the buyer and seller are related parties, as in the case of most multinational corporate sales, the customs authorities have the right to scrutinize the transfer price to make sure that this price is a fair reflection of market value. If there is no proper "transaction value" for the goods, alternative methods are used to compute the customs value, sometimes resulting in increased values and, consequently, increased duties.

SPECIFIC DUTIES. These duties are expressed as a specific amount of currency per unit of weight, volume, length, or number of other units of measurement, for example, 50 U.S. cents per pound, $1.00 per pair, or 25 cents per square yard. Specific duties are usually expressed in the currency of the importing country, but there are exceptions, particularly in countries that have experienced sustained inflation. In the Chilean tariff, rates are given in gold pesos and, therefore, must be multiplied by an established conversion factor to obtain the corresponding amount of escudos.

ALTERNATIVE DUTIES. In this case both ad valorem and specific duties are set out in the custom tariff for a given product. Normally, the applicable rate is the one that yields the higher amount of duty, although there are cases where the lower is specified.

COMPOUND OR MIXED DUTIES. These duties provide for specific plus ad valorem rates to be levied on the same articles.

ANTIDUMPING DUTIES. The term *dumping* refers to the sale of a product at a price lower than that normally charged in a domestic market or country of origin. To offset the impact of dumping, most countries have introduced legislation providing for the imposition of antidumping duties if injury is caused to domestic producers. Such duties take the form of special additional import charges designed to cover the difference between the export price and the ''normal'' price, which usually refers to the price paid by consumers in the exporting countries. Antidumping duties are almost invariably applied to articles that are produced in the importing country.

COUNTERVAILING DUTIES. Countervailing duties are additional duties levied to offset subsidies granted in the exporting country. In the United States, countervailing duty legislation and procedures are very similar to the antidumping format. The U.S. Commerce Department and U.S. International Trade Commission jointly administer both the countervailing duty and antidumping laws.

Other Import Charges

VARIABLE IMPORT LEVIES. Several countries, including Sweden and those that are part of the European Economic Community, apply a system of variable import levies to their imports of various agricultural products. The objective of these levies is to raise the price of imported products to the domestic price level.

TEMPORARY IMPORT SURCHARGES. Temporary surcharges have been introduced from time to time by certain countries, such as the United Kingdom and the

United States, to provide additional protection for local industry and, in particular, in response to balance-of-payments deficits.

COMPENSATORY IMPORT TAXES. In theory these taxes correspond with various internal taxes, such as value added taxes and sales taxes. Such "border tax adjustments" must not, according to GATT, amount to additional protection for domestic producers or to a subsidy for exports. In practice, one of the major tax inequities today is the fact that manufacturers in value added tax (VAT) countries do not pay a value added tax on sales to non-VAT countries such as the United States, whereas U.S. manufacturers that pay income taxes in the United States must also pay VAT taxes on sales in VAT countries.

TRADE NEGOTIATIONS. A major development of the 1960s was agreements negotiated in the 1963–1967 period, popularly known as the Kennedy Round. During these negotiations, tariff concessions on nonagricultural products by the four largest industrial participants—the United States, the United Kingdom, Japan, and the European Economic Community—averaged slightly more than 35 percent and covered about $20 billion of trade. On agricultural products, excluding grains, the average reduction by the major industrial countries amounted to about 20 percent and affected about one-half of the dutiable imports. Tariff reductions under the agreement took place in five equal installments. The first was concluded on January 1, 1968, and the last on January 1, 1972. Over 60,000 items were involved, representing approximately $40 billion in world trade annually.

At the conclusion of the Kennedy Round negotiations, tariffs on dutiable nonagricultural products averaged 9.9 percent in the United States, 8.6 percent in the European Economic Community, 10.8 percent in the United Kingdom, and 10.7 percent in Japan.[6]

A second Tokyo Round of trade negotiations was undertaken by the 92-nation General Agreement on Tariffs and Trade in the 1970s. The target in these negotiations was to achieve another 35 percent tariff reduction. This was achieved and the reduction in tariff rates was scheduled to be completed in 1987.

Nontariff Barriers

With the success of the Kennedy Round tariff negotiations, attention has naturally turned to the remaining nontariff obstacles to trade. A *nontariff trade barrier* is defined by economists as any measure, public or private, that causes internationally traded goods and services to be allocated in such a way as to reduce protential real-world income. Potential real-world income is the attainable level when resources are allocated in the most economically efficient manner. To the business manager, a nontariff barrier is any measure, other than tariffs, that provides a barrier or

[6]Robert E. Baldwin, *Non-Tariff Distortion of International Trade* (Washington, D.C.: Brookings Institution), p. 1.

obstacle to the sale of his or her products in a foreign market. The major nontariff trade barriers are as follows:

QUOTAS AND TRADE CONTROL.   These are specific limits and controls. The trade distortion of a quota is even more severe than a tariff because once the quota has been filled, the price mechanism is not allowed to operate. The good is simply unavailable at any price. *State trading* refers to the practice of monopolizing trade in certain commodities. In Communist countries all commodities are monopolized, but there are many examples of non-Communist government monopolies: the Swedish government, for example, controls the import of all alcoholic beverages and tobacco products and the French government controls all imports of coal.

DISCRIMINATORY GOVERNMENT AND PRIVATE PROCUREMENT POLICIES.   These are the rules and regulations that discriminate against foreign suppliers and are commonly referred to as "Buy British" or "Buy American" policies.

RESTRICTIVE CUSTOMS PROCEDURES.   The rules and regulations for classifying and valuing commodities as a basis for levying import duties can be administered in a way that makes compliance difficult and expensive.

SELECTIVE MONETARY CONTROLS AND DISCRIMINATORY EXCHANGE RATE POLICIES.   Discriminatory exchange rate policies distort trade in much the same way as selective import duties and export subsidies. Selective monetary policies are definite barriers to trade. For example, many countries from time to time require importers to place on deposit at no interest an amount equal to the value of imported goods. These regulations in effect raise the price of foreign goods by the cost of money for the term of the required deposit.

RESTRICTIVE ADMINISTRATIVE AND TECHNICAL REGULATIONS.   These include antidumping regulations, size regulations, and safety and health regulations. Some of these regulations are intended to keep out foreign goods, while others are directed toward legitimate domestic objectives. For example, the safety and pollution regulations being developed in the United States for automobiles are motivated almost entirely by legitimate concerns about highway safety and pollution. However, an effect of these regulations, particularly on smaller foreign manufacturers, has been to make it so expensive to comply with U.S. safety requirements that they have withdrawn from the market.

One GATT report listing nontariff barriers to trade included such obscure items as an Italian sanitary tax on foreign snake poison. Another example was the California wine industry's proposal that all wine sold in the U.S. market be bottled in the standard U.S.-sized wine bottle, which was slightly different in size and shape from the standard European bottle.

Germany requires that imports of meal used to feed poultry and swine contain only 5 percent fat. Wellens & Company, a Minneapolis-based firm, produces a meal that contains about 10 percent fat, and, according to the company president, "We simply don't sell any to the Germans. To change the meal's fat content would involve special machinery which would greatly increase production costs; it simply wouldn't be worth it." Wellens expects several other Western European countries to adopt the 5 percent regulation, which the company claims does nothing for the animal's health.

Stanley Works of New Britain, Connecticut, was exporting thousands of electric drills to Mexico. Then the Mexican government banned the import of drills with handles that measured a half inch in diameter or less. The move effectively shut off drill imports because the only significant market in Mexico was for the smaller-size drills.

Packaging regulations often erect a hurdle for exports. Brazil, for example, requires that tires be removed from certain types of vehicles imported from the United States. This regulation adds approximately 5 percent to the cost of U.S.-made vehicles, principally because additional labor is needed to remove the tires before vehicles are shipped to Brazil.

Tariff Classification

Before World War II specific duties were widely used and the tariffs of many countries, particularly those in Europe and Latin America, were extremely complex. Since the war the trend has been toward the conversion to ad valorem duties. Tariff administration has been simplified by the adoption by a large number of countries of the Brussels nomenclature (BTN). This nomenclature was worked out by an international committee of experts under the sponsorship of the Customs Cooperation Council, which in 1955 produced a convention that entered into force in 1959. The rules of this convention are now being applied by most GATT countries.

The BTN groups articles mainly according to the material from which they are made. For less developed countries, it is both easy to use and applicable to the goods they produce. An additional advantage of the BTN is its widespread use. A common basis for the classification of goods facilitates comparison of duties applied by different countries and simplifies international tariff negotiations.

In spite of the progress made in simplifying tariff procedures, the task of administrating a tariff presents an enormous problem. Even a tariff schedule of several thousand items cannot clearly describe every product that enters into international trade. The constant flow of new products and new materials used in manufacturing processes introduces new problems. Often, two or more alternative classifications must be considered in assessing the rate on a particular article depending upon how it is used or its component material. The classification of a product can make a substantial difference in the duty applied. There are two important implications of this fact for export marketers. The first is that exporters should seek the most favorable classification for their products to minimize the duty levied in the importing country. The second is that the difficulties of classification raise serious questions about the accuracy of data on international trade patterns. When using international trade data, it is important to bear in mind the enormous problems posed by classi-fication and recognize that the numbers in trade reports may often reflect hasty and arbitrary classifications that distort the true picture of the trade flows. Evidence of the inaccuracy of trade classification practices is provided by frequent failure of import and export figures of the same commodity to reconcile between two countries.

THE DECISION TO INVESTIGATE EXPORT MARKETS

A company committeed to growth has four basic expansion alternatives. *Vertical integration* involves moving from a finished product back to basic materials, or vice versa. For a steel manufacturer, this would involve moving forward from the man-ufacture of steel to the fabrication of metal products. For the metal fabricator, vertical integration would involve moving back to the manufacture of steel. A second ex-pansion alternative is *horizontal expansion* of the product line. This involves moving to configurations and adaptations in the product that are variations on the company's basic line. For example, a sled manufacturer might introduce a low-priced utility model and a high-priced luxury model, thus expanding his sled line from one basic medium-priced sled to three. A third and more venturesome expansion alternative is *product diversification*. This involves moving into an entirely new product tech-nology area via acquisition. A fourth expansion alternative is geographical diversi-fication, or the extension of existing products to new geographic markets. If the move into foreign markets involves the use of goods manufactured in the home or domestic market, the fourth expansion alternative is export marketing or export selling depending on the degree of involvement in foreign markets.

When should a company investigate export markets? This question must be answered by comparing the business opportunity in export markets with that in domestic markets. For each market, determine the export opportunity as shown:

M = potential market size in market X_1
C = competitive offering
P_1 = product
P_2 = price (sum of manufacturing cost plus transportation, insurance, taxes, duty, and trade margins)
P_3 = product distribution or availability
P_4 = advertising and promotion
TR = total revenue in market
cost = manufacturing, marketing, tariff, and overhead costs
TR = $f(M, C, P_1, P_2, P_3, P_4)$

then

$$\text{export opportunity} = TR - \text{cost}$$

Export opportunities should be compared with each other and with domestic opportunities to determine investigation priorities.

CHOOSING EXPORT MARKETS

Creating a Product-Market Profile

The first step in choosing export markets is to establish the key factors influencing sales and profitability of the product in question. If a company is getting started for the first time in exporting, its product market profile will have to be based upon its experience in its home market. The basic questions to be answered can be summarized as the nine W's:

1. Who buys our product?
2. Who does not buy our product?
3. What need or function does our product serve?
4. What problem does our product solve?
5. What are customers currently buying to satisfy the need and/or solve the problem for which our product is targeted?
6. How much are they paying for the products they are currently buying?
7. When is our product purchased?
8. Where is our product purchased?
9. Why is our product purchased?

This profile will provide answers to critical questions that any company must answer if it is going to be successful in export markets. Each of the questions when answered provides an input into decisions about each of the four P's. The general rule for export markets is that if you want to penetrate an existing market, you must have an advantage that can be perceived and accepted. Usually, this is gained by offering equivalent quality or better with equivalent features or better with a lower price. The customers will discount the quality claims and the feature advantages, and most will even discount or not respond to the price advantage, but enough will respond to an overwhelming advantage to obtain a foothold. From this point on, if the company has a superior product, success is assured. Indeed, it is only a matter of time before the market begins to respond to the better offering.

Market Selection

Given the product-market profile for the company's product, the next step in choosing an export market is to appraise possible markets. To do this, six basic elements of information are required.

MARKET POTENTIAL. What is the basic market potential for the product in foreign markets? The best place to start in getting an answer to this question is at your desk or library table. What are major factors determining demand for your company's product? Using some of the tools and techniques described in Chapter 9, it is possible with statistical analysis and published data to come up with a rough estimate of total potential demand for your company's product in particular markets. At this stage in the analysis, accuracy is unnecessary and irrelevant to the decision task. For a large number of products, gross national product will be a sufficient statistic for obtaining a sufficiently accurate estimate of total demand for the product. For many other products, additional statistical measures will considerably sharpen the estimate of total demand. For example, if you are interested in the demand for automobile tires, information on the total number of cars registered in any country in the world is easily obtained. This could be combined with information on gasoline consumption to come up with an estimate of the total mileage driven in the target market. When this figure is combined with tire life predictions, demand estimates are easily obtained.

Many products will defy such accurate estimation from published statistics. Frequently, the most useful statistical analysis for products for which specific data are unavailable is estimation by analogy. When the researcher has information on consumption or use of the product in a single market, if there is any basis for assuming that demand conditions for the product are similar in other markets, the method of estimation by analogy described in Chapter 8 can be applied.

TERMS OF ACCESS.   This phrase covers the entire set of national controls that applies to important merchandise. It includes such items as import duties, import restrictions or quotas, foreign exchange regulations, and preference arrangements.

SHIPPING COST.   Ask the shipping companies to give you some idea of shipping charges to various potential markets or consult a freight forwarding firm. Investigate the alternative ways of shipping, such as sea, air, or even parcel post if the product is very small.

APPRAISING THE LEVEL AND QUALITY OF COMPETITION IN THE POTENTIAL MARKET.   Interviews with exporters, bankers, and other industry executives are extremely useful at this stage. Using a country's commercial representatives abroad can also be valuable. When contacting country representatives abroad, it is important to provide as much specific information as possible. If a manufacturer simply writes and says, "I make lawn mowers. Is there a market for them in your territory?" the representative cannot provide much helpful information. On the other hand, if the manufacturer would write providing the following information: (1) sizes of lawn mowers manufactured, (2) descriptive brochures indicating features and advantages, and (3) estimated C.I.F. and retail price in the target market, the commercial representative could provide a very useful report based upon a comparison of the company's product with market needs and offerings.

PRODUCT FIT.   With information on market potential, cost of access to the market, and local competition, the next step is to decide how well your company's product

TABLE 16–1 Market Selection Framework

MARKET	MARKET SIZE	COMPETITIVE ADVANTAGE		MARKET POTENTIAL	TERMS OF ACCESS	EXPORT MARKET POTENTIAL
A	100	0	=	0	100	0
B	50	.10	=	5	.60	3.0
C	20	.20	=	4	.90	3.6

fits the market in question. In general, a product fits a market if it satisfies the following criteria: (1) The product is likely to appeal to customers in the potential market; (2) the product will not require more adaptation than is economically justifiable by the volume expected in the potential market; (3) import restrictions and/or high tariffs do not exclude or make the product so expensive in the target market as to effectively eliminate demand; (4) shipping costs to the target market are in line with the requirements for competitive price; and (5) the cost of assembling sales literature, catalogs, and technical bulletins is not out of line with the market potential. (This factor is particularly important in selling high technical products.)

SERVICE.   If service is required for the product, can it be delivered at a cost that is consistent with the size of the market?

Table 16–1 presents a market selection framework that incorporates the information elements just discussed. Three countries, A, B, and C, are arranged in order of declining size of market. The competitive advantage of a hypothetical firm is zero in market A, 10 percent in market B, and 20 percent in market C. The product of the market size and competitive advantage index yields a market potential of 5 in market B and 4 in C.

The next stage in our analysis requires an assessment of the "terms of access" to the market. This phrase covers all the conditions affecting the entry of a foreign manufactured good through a market: import duties, import restrictions and quotas, foreign exchange regulations, nontariff barriers, and transportation costs. In Table 16–1, all these conditions or terms reduced to an index number, which is 60 percent for market B and 90 percent for market C. In other words, the "terms of access" are greater to market C than to B. As a result of the multiplication of the market's potential and the "terms of access" index, we now find that market C has become a market of greater potential than B. In this example, a company with limited resources would want to begin its export marketing program in market C because this country (all things considered) offers the largest export market potential of the countries examined.

Visiting the Potential Market

After a desk research has zeroed in on potential markets, there is no substitute for a field visit to conclude research and begin the development of an actual export marketing program. There are four major functions of a market visit. The first is to confirm assumptions that were made during the desk appraisal. All the information concerning terms of access, competition, and even the size of the market is based on secondary sources and may require adjustment or revision on the basis of firsthand data obtained in the market.

A second major purpose is to gather additional data necessary to reach the final decision about whether to go ahead with an export marketing program. There are certain kinds of information that simply cannot be obtained from secondary sources. For example, a manufacturer may have a list of potential distributors provided by the U.S. Department of Commerce. He or she may correspond with distributors on the list and have achieved some tentative idea of their availability. It is difficult, however, to complete an effective arrangement with foreign distributors without actually meeting face to face to allow both sides of the contract to appraise the capabilities and character of the other party.

A third reason for a visit to the export market is to develop, in cooperation with the local agent or distributor, a marketing plan. Agreement should be reached on necessary product modifications, pricing, advertising and promotion expenditures, and a distribution plan. If the plan calls for investment, agreement on the allocation of costs must also be reached.

A fourth important justification for a visit to a market is that it provides an opportunity to engage in direct selling. One excellent way to test a market is to exhibit in trade fairs. At a trade fair exhibitors can study the reactions to their product compared with their competitors'. Exhibitors can also make contact with possible agents or customers.

A foreign manufacturer of athletic footwear makes most of his contacts and does nearly all of his selling in the United States, his main market, by partaking each winter in the national sporting goods show in Chicago. At the show he meets buyers from U.S. department stores and finds that he needs no other outlets. Specialized or "vertical" trade fairs are particularly useful in selling technical products because they offer an exhibitor an excellent demonstration ground and a group of potential buyers who talk his or her language. In addition, vertical fairs are attended by people in the trade who are potential agents or distributors, whereas the horizontal fair, which attracts all types of products and the general public, is usually not visited by special buying agents.

Developing an Export Program

After an export market has been selected, the export program must be developed. The best checklist for insuring a complete program is the four P's: Product (P_1), Price (P_2), Place (P_3), and Promotion (P_4). The export program issue for each P is whether to extend, adapt, or invent. For example, can the product be exported as is (extended) or is adaptation necessary?

TRADE TERMS

A number of terms covering the conditions of the delivery are commonly used in international trade. Many of these terms have through long use acquired precise meanings. Every commercial transaction is based upon a contract of sale, and the trade terms used in that contract have the important function of naming the exact point at which the ownership of merchandise is transferred from the seller to the buyer.

The simplest type of sale "as is, where is." Under this type of contract in export, the seller must guarantee the buyer that the buyer will receive an export permit but the buyer's responsibility ends there. At the other extreme, the easiest terms of sale for the buyer are "Franco Delivered" including duty and local transportation to his or her warehouse. Under this contract, the buyer's only responsibility is to obtain an import permit if one is needed and to pass the customs entry at the seller's expense. Between these two terms there are many expenses that accrue to the goods as they move from the place of manufacture to the buyer's warehouse. Following are some of the steps involved in moving goods from a factory to a buyer's warehouse:

1. Obtaining an export permit if required (in the United States, nonstrategic goods are exported under a general license that requires no specific permit)
2. Obtaining a currency permit if required
3. Packing the goods for export
4. Transporting the goods to the place of departure (this would normally involve transport by truck or rail to a sea or airport)
5. Preparing a bill of lading
6. Completing necessary customs export papers
7. Preparing customs or consular invoices as required in the country of destination
8. Arranging for ocean freight and preparation
9. Obtaining marine insurance and certificate of the policy

Who carries out these steps? This depends on the terms of the sale. In the following paragraphs some of the major terms are defined.

EX-FACTORY (OR EX-WORKS, EX-MILL, EX-PLANTATION, EX-WARE-HOUSE). In this contract, the seller places goods at the disposal of the buyer at the time specified in the contract. The buyer takes delivery at the premises of the seller and bears all risks and expenses from that point on.

F.A.S. (FREE ALONGSIDE SHIP) NAMED PORT OF SHIPMENT. Under this contract, the seller must place goods alongside the vessel or other mode of transportation and pay all charges up to that point. The seller's legal responsibility ends once he or she has obtained a clean wharfage receipt.

F.O.B. (FREE ON BOARD).   In an F.O.B. contract, the responsibility and liability of the seller does not end until the goods have actually been placed aboard a ship. Terms should preferably be "F.O.B. ship (name port)." In an F.O.B. contract the seller must

1. Deliver the goods on board the vessel named by the buyer at the port of shipment on the date specified in the contract
2. Bear all cost payable on or for the goods until they have effectively been placed aboard the ship or other mode of transportation
3. Suitably pack the goods for the mode of transportation specified
4. Provide documentation indicating proof of delivery of goods aboard the mode of transportation

In turn, with an F.O.B. contract the buyer must

1. Arrange for transportation specifying the mode of transportation to the port of departure
2. Bear all cost and risk from the time the goods have been placed on board the mode of transportation

C.I.F. (COST, INSURANCE, FREIGHT) NAMED PORT OF DESTINATION.   Under this contract, as in the F.O.B. contract, the risk of loss or damage to goods is transferred to the buyer once the goods have been loaded on board ship, freight car, or airplane. But the seller has to pay the expense of transportation for the goods up to the port of destination, including the expense of insurance.

DELIVERED DUTY PAID.   Under this contract the seller undertakes to deliver the goods to the buyer at the place he or she names in the country of import with all costs, including duties, paid. The seller is responsible under this contract for getting the import license if one is required.

EXPORT ORGANIZATION—MANUFACTURER'S COUNTRY

Manufacturers interested in export marketing have two broad alternatives organizationally. They can negotiate a representation agreement with one of the many external independent organizations that typically concentrate in a product area and sometimes in a geographic area. Alternatively, they can create their own inhouse export department that will deal directly with foreign markets.

External Independent Export Organizations

The terms used to describe various types of export firms, "export merchant," "export broker," "combination export manager," "manufacturer's export representative or commission agent," and "export distributor," have never been used precisely to describe the services performed by an export organization. The definitions in Table 16–2 are suggested as reasonable approximations of current usage in the industry. Because of the variations in usage of these terms, the reader is warned to check and confirm the services performed by an independent export organization.

WEBB-POMERENE ASSOCIATIONS.   The Webb-Pomerene Act of 1918 authorized the creation of associations of U.S. exporters to engage in export trade. The purpose of the act was to increase the competitive effectiveness of U.S. exporters, particularly those in competition with large European cartels. The act permits the exporters who combine to share costs of export operations to reap common rewards. The legislation further exempts companies in a Webb-Pomerene association from the normal strictures of antitrust legislation and enforcement.

Well over 200 Webb-Pomerene associations have been formed since the legislation was passed in 1918, but most have been disbanded for various reasons, including changing market conditions and a decision by members to handle their own exports independently.

TABLE 16–2   Export Agents and Organizations—Definition

A. NO ASSIGNMENT OF RESPONSIBILITY FROM CLIENT

Purchasing Agent

Foreign purchasing agents are variously referred to as "buyer for export," "export commission house" or "export confirming house." They operate on behalf of, and are remunerated by, an overseas customer. They generally seek out the U.S. manufacturer whose price and quality match the demands of their overseas principals.

Foreign purchasing agents often represent large users of materials abroad—governments, utilities, and railroads, for example. They do not offer the U.S. manufacturer stable volume except when long-term supply contracts are agreed upon. Purchases may be completed as domestic transactions with the purchasing agent handling all export packing and shipping details, or the agent may rely on the manufacturer to handle the shipping arrangements.

Export Broker

The export broker receives a fee for bringing together the U.S. seller and the overseas buyer. The fee is usually paid by the seller, but sometimes the buyer pays it. The broker takes no title to the goods and assumes no financial responsibility. A broker usually specializes in a specific commodity, such as grain or cotton, and is less frequently involved in the export of manufactured goods.

Export Merchant

Export merchants are sometimes referred to as "jobbers." They seek out needs in foreign markets and make purchases in the United States to fill these needs. Conversely, they often complement this activity by importing to fill needs in the United States. Export merchants often handle staple, openly traded products, for which brand names or manufacturers' identifications are not important.

Export Merchant

Compensation is in the form of a markup the merchant bases on market conditions. Manufacturers sell to the export merchant in an ordinary domestic transaction. The merchant generally purchases from the lowbidding manufacturer or middleman. Many merchant houses, to stabilize their businesses, also operate as export distributors or export commission representatives.

TABLE 16–2 *continued*

B. ASSIGNMENT OF RESPONSIBILITY FROM CLIENT

Export Management Companies

Export Management Company (EMC) is the term used to designate an independent export firm that acts as the export department for more than one manufacturer. The EMC usually operates in the name of a manufacturer-client for export markets but it may operate in its own name. It may act as an independent distributor, purchasing and reselling goods at an established price or profit margin, or as a commission representative taking no title and bearing no financial risks in the sale.

Manufacturer's Export Representative

Combination export management firms often refer to themselves as manufacturer's export representatives whether they act as export distributors or export commission representatives.

Export Distributor

The export distributor assumes financial risk. The firm usually has exclusive right to sell a manufacturer's products in all or some markets outside the United States. The distributor pays for goods in the United States in a domestic transaction and handles all financial risks in the foreign sale. The firm ordinarily sells at manufacturer's list price abroad, receiving an agreed percentage of list price as remuneration. The distributor may operate in its own name or in the manufacturer's. It handles all shipping details. The export distributor usually represents several manufacturers and hence is a combination export manager.

Export Commission Representative

The export commission representative assumes no financial risk and is sometimes termed an "agent," although this term is generally avoided because of the legal connotations of the term. The commission representative is assigned all or some foreign markets by the manufacturer. The manufacturer carries all accounts, although the representative often provides credit checks and arranges financing. The representative may operate in its own name or in the manufacturer's. Generally, export commission representatives handle several accounts and hence are combination export managers.

Cooperative Exporter

The cooperative exporter, sometimes called a "mother hen," a "piggyback" exporter, or an "export vendor," is an export organization of a manufacturing company retained by other independent manufacturers to sell their products in some or all foreign markets. Cooperative exporters usually operate as export distributors for other manufacturers, but they operate in special cases as commission representatives. They are regarded as a form of export management company.

Webb-Pomerene Association

Webb-Pomerene associations are organizations jointly owned, maintained, or supported by competing U.S. manufacturers especially and exclusively for export trade. Special legislation gives them qualified exemption from antitrust laws. They may provide informational services to their members, as well as buy and sell abroad, and may engage in other activities such as setting prices and allocating orders.

Foreign Freight Forwarder

Foreign freight forwarders are licensed by the Federal Maritime Commission and are considered an integral part of the American merchant marine. They are highly specialized in traffic operations, overseas import regulations, customs clearances, and shipping rates and schedules. They assist manufacturers or combination export managers in determining and paying freight, fees, and insurance charges. Forwarders may also do export packing. For a fee paid by the overseas customer, they usually handle goods from port of exit to overseas port of entry. They may also move inland freight from factory to port and, through affiliates abroad, handle freight from foreign port to customer.

A licensed forwarder may receive brokerage or rebates from shipping companies for booked space. Some companies and manufacturers engage in freight forwarding or some phase of it on their own, but they may not, under law, receive brokerage from shipping lines.

Source: NICB (National Industrial Conference Board), *Organizing for Exporting, Studies in Business Policy No. 126* (New York: NICB, 1968); adapted by author.

The Export Trading Company Act of 1982

In 1982, the Congress of the United States completed action on the Export Trading Company Act of 1982, a measure designed to spur the development of export trading companies.[7] The act is divided into four titles. Title I contains the finding of congressional investigations and the declaration of purpose. In brief, Title I notes that exports are responsible for creating one out of every nine manufacturing jobs in the United States and for generating $1 out of every $7 of total U.S. goods produced. Export trade services are fragmented into a multitude of separate functions, and companies attempting to offer export trade services lack financial leverage to reach potential exporters. The act notes the need for export trading companies that can draw on the expertise, knowledge, and resources of the U.S. banking system. The purpose of the act is to increase U.S. exports by encouraging more efficient provision of export trade services and by permitting bank holding companies, bankers' banks, and Edge Act corporations and agreement corporations that are subsidiaries of bank holding companies to invest in export trading companies; by reducing restrictions on trade financing provided by financial institutions; and by modifying the application of the antitrust laws to certain export trade.

Title II is the "Bank Export Services Act" and provides for bank participation in trading companies. Title III is "Export Trade Certificates of Review." The certificates confer protection from criminal and civil action under the U.S. antitrust laws. Title IV is known as "Foreign Trade Antitrust Improvements Act of 1982" and amends the Sherman Act and the Federal Trade Commission Act to protect trading company operations from prosecution under these acts.

The trading company legislation has already accomplished one of its purposes by drawing attention to exports and by making it possible for large companies such as Sears and General Electric to establish trading companies to draw on their extensive experience and overseas representation. As of this writing, it remains to be seen whether or not banks will take advantage of the opportunity to invest in trading companies. Certainly old obstacles have been removed.

In-House Export Organization

Most larger companies handle export operations in their own organization. There is a rule of thumb that when a company's export sales exceed $400,000 to $1,000,000 a year, volume is sufficient to justify the establishment of an internal organization. The possible arrangements for handling exports are manyfold:

1. As a part-time activity by domestic employees
2. Through an export partner that is part of the domestic marketing structure
3. Through an export department that is independent of the domestic marketing structure
4. Through an export department within an international division
5. For multidivisional companies, each of the foregoing possibilities exists within each division

[7] For the full text of the act, see *Congressional Record*, Vol. 128, no. 134, October 1, 1982.

For the company that considers its export business sufficiently interesting to establish an in-house organization, the question of how to organize effectively depends on the company's appraisal of the opportunities in export marketing and on its strategy for allocating its resources to markets on a global basis. It is entirely possible that a company would arrive at an optimal position by allocating export responsibility on a part-time basis to domestic employees. The advantages of this arrangement are twofold. First, it is a very-low-cost arrangement requiring no additional specialized personnel, and second, the domestic employees assigned to the task can be thoroughly competent in terms of their product and customer knowledge, which although developed in the domestic market may be applicable to the target foreign markets. A key variable in the equation leading to the internal structure is the extent to which the target export market is different from the domestic market. If customer circumstances and characteristics are similar, the requirements for specialized regional knowledge are of course lessened.

EXPORT ORGANIZATION—MARKET COUNTRY

The export organization, regardless of whether it is located within the manufacturing company or in an external independent export organization, must make arrangements to distribute the product in the market country. The basic decision that every exporting organization faces is the extent to which it will rely upon direct market representation as opposed to representation by independent intermediaries.

Direct Market Representation

There are two major advantages to direct representation in a market. The first is *control;* the second is *communications*. Control is an important feature of direct representation. When a marketer wishes to develop a particular program, commit resources to some activity such as advertising, change price, or make any of a host of moves, direct representation allows these moves to be made without the need to negotiate and achieve consent of an independent party. When a product is not yet established in a market, special efforts are necessary to achieve sales. The advantage of direct representation is that these special efforts can be obtained as part of the marketer's investment. With indirect or independent representation, such an investment is often not forthcoming. This is in no way a criticism of independent representation. Because they acquire no contractual claim on the value of the market position developed, independent representatives in many cases would be foolish to invest significant time and money in a product. The other great advantage to direct representation is that the possibilities for feedback and information from the market are much greater. This information can vastly improve export marketing decisions concerning product, price, communications, and distribution.

Direct representation does not mean that the exporter is selling directly to the consumer or customer. In most cases direct representation involves selling to wholesalers or retailers. For example, the major automobile exporters in West Germany and Japan rely upon direct representation in the U.S. market in the form of their distributing agencies, which are owned and controlled by the manufacturing organization. The distributing agencies sell products to franchised dealers.

Independent Representation

In smaller markets, it is usually not feasible to establish direct representation because the volume of sales does not justify the cost that would be involved. A small manufacturer usually lacks adequate sales volume to justify the cost of direct representation even in the larger markets. Whenever sales volume is small, use of an independent distributor is an effective method of sales distribution. Finding "good" distributors can be the key to export success.

Piggyback Marketing

"Piggyback marketing" or the use of a "mother hen" sales force is an innovation in international distribution that has received much attention in recent years. This is an arrangement whereby one manufacturer obtains distribution of products through another's distribution channels. The motivation for this arrangement exists on both sides of the contract. The active distribution partner obtains a fuller utilization of its distribution system and thereby increases the revenues generated by the system. The manufacturer using the piggyback arrangement does so at a cost that is much lower than that required for any direct arrangement. Successful piggyback marketing requires that the combined product lines be complementary. They must appeal to the same customer, and they must not be competitive with each other. If these requirements are met, the piggyback arrangement can be a very effective way of fully utilizing an international channel system to the advantage of both parties.

EXPORT PROMOTION

Each year hundreds of fairs are held in major markets. U.S. trade centers alone, for example, hold 60 product shows annually in major cities abroad. At these fairs, which are usually organized around a product, a group of products, or activity, manufacturers can exhibit their products and meet potentially interested customers.

EXPORT FINANCING[8]

Sales of merchandise by exporters to buyers abroad are generally made on the basis of one of the following forms of finance.

[8] From *Export and Import Procedures*, Morgan Guaranty Trust Company of New York, 1968.

Export Letters of Credit

Except for cash in advance, export letters of credit as a means of obtaining payment afford the highest degree of protection to the exporter. Particularly in the case of the irrevocable letter of credit, the credit risk of the buyer is eliminated and replaced by that of the bank opening the letter of credit. If the credit is confirmed by a bank in the exporting country, the exportee is protected from foreign exchange restrictions in the country of destination. If a letter of credit is obtained, the exporter ordinarily receives dollars at the time of presentation of shipping documents to the bank holding the credit. In the case of irrevocable credits, the possibility of cancellation of the order prior to payment is eliminated.

Dollar (or Foreign Currency) Drafts Covering Exports

The draft may be on a sight basis for immediate payment, or it may be drawn to be accepted for payment 30, 60, or 90 days after sight or date and at times for longer periods. Drafts directed to a bank for collection usually are accompanied by shipping documents consisting of a full set of bills of lading in negotiable form, airways bills of lading, or parcel post receipt, together with insurance certificates, commercial invoices, consular invoices, and any other documents that may be required in the country of destination.

Sales Against Cash Deposit in Advance

When credit risks abroad are doubtful, when exchange restrictions within the country of destination are such that the return of funds from abroad may be delayed for an unreasonable period, or when the exporter for any other reason may be unwilling to sell on credit terms, the exporter may request payment in whole or in part in cash in advance of shipment. Because of competition and restrictions against cash payment in many countries, the volume of business handled on a cash-in-advance basis is small.

Sales on Open Account

Open account terms generally prevail in areas where exchange controls are minimal and exporters have had long-standing relations with good buyers in nearby or long-established markets. Open account terms also prevail when sales are made to branches or subsidiaries of the exporter. The main objection to open account sales is the absence of a tangible obligation. Normally, if a time draft is drawn and is dishonored after acceptance, it can be used as a basis of legal action, whereas in the case of a dishonored open account transaction, the legal procedure may be more complicated.

Sales on a Consignment Basis

As in the case of sales on open account, no tangible obligation is created by consignment sales. In countries with free ports or free trade zones, it can be arranged to have consigned merchandise placed under bonded warehouse control in the name of a foreign bank. Sales can then be arranged by the selling agent and arrangements made to release partial lots out of the consigned stock against regular payment terms. The merchandise is not cleared through customs until after the sale has been completed.

Although there is much concern regarding credit on the part of those companies that have never exported, the experience of Felix Norman, president of Hart-Carter International, is not unusual. During a four-year period, Hart-Carter exported $9 million worth of agricultural machinery to over 105 countries and never had a single default:

> With new export customers we utilize a letter of credit form of payment, whereby we merely present proof of shipment to a U.S. bank in which our foreign customer has established a credit. That way we get paid the day we ship.
>   Later, as we gain experience with these customers, we reduce our credit requirements—even placing many on an open account basis.
>   Almost without exception, we find these open accounts pay within thirty days of delivery and many pay sooner.[9]

BARTER AND COUNTERTRADE[10]

In recent years, barter and countertrade have become increasingly important means of exchange in international trade. These methods of completing international transactions are an alternative to trade that is completed by the exchange of money for goods or services. Unconfirmed estimates of the barter and countertrade share of world trade volume put it as high as 25–30 percent. For East-West trade, the share is estimated to be even higher.

Huszagh and Barksdale developed a typology of barter and countertrade to clarify the differences among the various approaches to what is potentially a very confusing mixture of trade and financing. Their work is summarized in Table 16–3 and in the discussion that follows.

Barter

SIMPLE BARTER.   Also termed straight, classical, or pure barter, this term describes the least complex and oldest form of bilateral, nonmonetized trade. Simple

[9]U.S. Department of Commerce, Bureau of International Commerce, "Export Awareness, an Advertising Test," July 1970.

[10]This section is adapted from the paper "Barter and Countertrade: A 'New' Approach to International Marketing," by Sandra M. Huszagh and Hiram C. Barksdale, College of Business Administration, University of Georgia (Athens), no date.

TABLE 16–3 Types of International Transactions*

CONVENTIONAL	BARTER	COUNTERTRADE
Exporting	Simple	Counterpurchase
Importing	Closed-end barter	Offset
Licensing	Clearing account barter	Compensation trading
Management contract	Indirect barter	Cooperation agreements
Overseas sales office or marketing subsidiary†	Switch trading	Switch trading
Overseas Production†		
Assembly operations		
Complete manufacturing		
Operations		

*It is possible that any of the forms given can be combined, for example, licensing with a cooperation agreement joined to classical barter.

†Ownership and control may be shared in a joint venture or be wholly owned by the investing firm.

Source: Adapted from Sandra M. Huszagh and Hiram C. Barksdale, "Barter and Countertrade: A 'New' Approach to International Marketing," College of Business Administration, University of Georgia (Athens), no date.

barter is a direct exchange of goods or services between two parties. Although no money is involved, both partners construct an approximate shadow price for products flowing in each direction. Generally distribution is direct between trading partners with no middlemen included. One contract formalizes simple barter transactions, which are generally less than one year to avoid problems in price fluctuations. However, for some transactions, the exchange may span months or years, with contract provisions allowing adjustments in the exchange ratio to handle fluctuations in world prices.

CLOSED-END BARTER. This type of transaction modifies simple barter in that a buyer is found for goods taken in barter before the contract is signed by the two trading parties. Obviously, risk related to product quality is significantly reduced in closed-end barter arrangements. Again, no money is involved in the exchange.

CLEARING ACCOUNT BARTER. Also termed clearing agreements, clearing arrangements, bilateral clearing accounts, or simply bilateral clearing, the principle is for the trades to balance without either party having to acquire hard currency. In this form of barter, each party agrees in a single contract to purchase a specified and usually equal value of goods and services. The duration of these transactions is commonly one year, although occasionally they may extend over a longer time period. The contract's value is expressed in nonconvertible, clearing account units (also termed clearing dollars) that effectively represent a line of credit in the central bank of that country with no money involved. Clearing account units are universally accepted for the accounting of trade between countries and parties whose commercial relationships are based on bilateral agreements.

The contract sets forth the goods to be exchanged, the ratio of exchange, and the length of time for completing the transaction. Limited export or import surpluses may be accumulated by either party for short periods. Generally after one year's time, imbalances are settled by one of the following approaches: credit against the following year, acceptance of unwanted goods, payment of a previously specified penalty, or payment of the difference in hard currency. Trading specialists also have initiated the practice of buying clearing dollars at a discount for the purpose of using them to purchase salable products. In turn, the trader may forfeit a portion of the discount to sell these products for hard currency on the international market. Compared with simple barter, clearing accounts offer greater flexibilities in length of time for drawdown on the lines of credit and the types of products exchanged.

Countertrade

Countertrade is a generic term incorporating a real distinction from barter, since money or credit is involved in the transaction. Countertrade broadly defines an arrangement in which firms both sell to and buy from their overseas customers. If market conditions are volatile, the duration of the transaction may be short. For other transactions, arrangements may extend over months, or even years, with contract provisions allowing adjustments in the exchange ratio as market prices change. According to the U.S. International Trade Commission, countertrade generally means that Western products or technology are paid for in full or partially by products produced in the importing countries. Two conditions determine the probability that importing nations will demand countertrade: (1) the priority attached to the Western import and (2) the value of the transaction. Overall, the advantages to nonmarket and developing economies are access to Western marketing expertise and technology in the short term and creation of hard currency export markets in the long term.

COUNTERPURCHASE.   This form of countertrade, also termed parallel trading or parallel barter, is distinguished from other forms in that each delivery is paid for in cash. Generally, products offered by the foreign principal are not related to the Western firm's exports and thus cannot be used directly by the firm. In most counterpurchase transactions, two separate contracts are signed, one in which the supplier sells products for a cash settlement (the original sales contract), the other in which the supplier agrees to purchase and market unrelated products from the buyer (a separate, parallel contract). The dollar amount that the supplier agrees to market is generally a set percentage or may even be the full value of the products sold to the foreign principal. When the Western company sells these goods, the trading cycle is complete.

OFFSET.   Another variety of countertrade, offset, is easily confused with counterpurchase arrangements, since both entail the supplier's commitment to assist the foreign buyer in marketing his or her products overseas. On occasion, offset may involve cooperation in manufacturing in addition to product marketing. For example, a foreign principal may include requirements to place subcontracts locally and/or to arrange local assembly or manufacturing equal to a certain percentage of the contract value. The commitment to local assembly or manufacturing under the supplier's specifications is commonly termed a coproduction agreement, which is tied to the offset but in itself does not represent a type of countertrade. This type of countertrade has emerged from foreign purchases of machinery and equipment for large-scale industrial projects, commercial and military aircraft, and defense-related products and services. Countries practicing offset include some highly developed nations such as Canada, Switzerland, and Australia. The major distinction between offset and other forms of countertrade is that the agreement is not contractual but reflects a memorandum of understanding that sets out the dollar value of products to be offset and the time period for completing the transaction. In addition, there is no penalty on the supplier for nonperformance. Typically, requests range from 20 to 50 percent of the value of the supplier's product, with highly competitive sales requiring over 100 percent.

The major advantage to the foreign principal is access to new markets in the process of purchasing essential capital goods. There are significant disadvantages to Western firms, including the commitment of resources to market products that cannot be used directly by the firm. High marketing expenditures may also be incurred in selling the products.

COMPENSATION TRADING. This form of countertrade is also called buyback, and involves two separate, and parallel, contracts. In one contract, the supplier agrees to build a plant or provide plant equipment; patents or licenses; or technical, managerial, or distribution expertise for a hard currency down payment at the time of delivery. In the other contract, the supplier agrees to purchase in cash a portion of the plant's output equal to his or her investment (minus interest) for a period up to as many as 20 years. Essentially, the transaction rests on the willingness of each firm to be both a buyer and a seller.

In general, the terms are set so that the value of goods taken back and the costs of the Western firm's offering are balanced over the life of the agreement. Financing may include Western banks as well as lending institutions in the host country. The cash-to-goods ratio in East-West compensation contracts generally averages 20 percent cash to 80 percent goods—the inverse of the situation in the mid-1970s.

COOPERATION AGREEMENTS. Cooperation agreements meet the needs of Western firms doing business with nonmarket economies, which are reluctant to link selling and buying. What distinguishes these arrangements from other types of countertrade is the specialization of each Western firm for either buying or selling, not both. Each of the three forms of cooperation agreements represents an increasingly complex accommodation to the needs of trading partners. They include cooperation and simple barter (triangular deals); cooperation and counterpurchase; and cooperation, counterpurchase, and credit by a bank. As an example of cooperation and simple barter, the parties to the transaction might be two unrelated Western firms with a U.S. firm specialized as a seller, a Western European firm as a buyer, and an Eastern European FTO. The U.S. firm may perform the selling function by delivering goods to the Eastern European FTO. In payment for the goods, the FTO might deliver raw materials to the Western European firm, which carries out the buying function. The Western European firm then pays the U.S. firm for the raw materials—an amount equivalent to the value of goods originally sent to the Eastern FTO. The advantage to the U.S. firm offering goods is in removing the obligation to buy and, for the Western European firm receiving raw materials, a considerable reduction in transport costs. Problems associated with these arrangements include finding two Western firms with the appropriate supply-demand fit and the flexibilities to handle time delays in receipt of payment or in delivery of goods.

HYBRID COUNTERTRADE ARRANGEMENTS.   Hybrid forms of countertrade are becoming more prevalent in trading arrangements. For example, the investment performance contract in Third World markets is an additional condition of offset arrangements. Countries such as Brazil, Mexico, and even Canada now condition official approval of investment proposals to commitments by the investors to export. As a second example, "project accompaniment" typifies an arrangement in which a Western supplier is encouraged to buy a greater volume and/or wider range of products, compared with the countertrade commitment. Project accompaniment has surfaced as a condition to the exchange of industrial goods by the West for oil from Middle Eastern producers.

SWITCH TRADING.   Also called triangular trade and swap, switch trading is a mechanism that can be applied to barter or countertrade. In this arrangement, a professional switch trader, switch trading house, or bank steps into a simple barter arrangement, clearing agreement, or a countertrade arrangement when one of the parties is not willing to accept all the goods or the clearing credits received in a transaction. The switching mechanism provides a "secondary market" for counter-traded or bartered goods and credits and reduces the inflexibilities inherent in barter and countertrade. Fees charged by switch traders range from 5 percent of market value for commodities to 30 percent for high-technology items. Switch traders develop their own networks of firms and personal contacts and are generally head-quartered in Vienna, Amsterdam, Hamburg, and London. If a party anticipates that the products he or she receives will be sold eventually at discount by a switch trade, the common practice is to price products higher or build in "special charges" for port storage or consulting or require shipment by the national carrier.

The advantages of switching are that (1) its multilateral character offers a greater degree of economic efficiency in pricing and in increasing trade, (2) discounted prices can open new markets more rapidly, and (3) Western firms can shed the responsibilities of marketing goods received in countertrade. Disadvantages include (1) disruptions of producers' established markets, when switch dealers offer their products at discount to such markets; (2) products that may be in oversupply or difficult to sell on the world market; (3) the foreign principal assessing the Western firm as uncommitted to a long-term trade relationship, particularly if the foreigner's established markets are threatened by discounted products; and (4) the complex and cumbersome nature of switching transactions. Switch trading's complexity relates to the mechanics of the transaction; in a typical transaction, the switch trader sells a commodity for soft currency, uses the soft currency to purchase another commodity, and repeats the process until he or she can purchase a commodity that can be sold for hard currency.

EXPORT DOCUMENTATION AND CONTROL

Every country requires documentation of export activity. Some countries, the United States included, also control the type of exporting that is carried out by domestic firms.

A major difference between trade in one's own country and trade with a foreign customer is documentation requirements. Documents must accompany every export shipment. If they are not correct, expensive delays and, in some cases, fines can result.

Some business managers avoid exports because they feel that they could not handle the documentation. Although documentation is difficult, it is something that can be learned and there are many experts to help. The ministry or department of commerce in almost every country has staff specialists to help in this area, as do many chamber of commerce and trade associations. There are excellent reference books kept up to date by regular supplements.

Finally, a good freight forwarder includes obtaining and filling out documents in the many services that he offers to exporters.

TRADE AND ECONOMIC DEVELOPMENT

The impact of foreign trade on economic growth is multiple and complex, but recent experience clearly demonstrates that strong export performance is associated with rapid internal growth and a relatively efficient price system. The correlation coefficient between export and GNP growth rates exceeds 0.9.

The link between export and GNP growth rates reflects the fact that ability to compete in export markets requires attention to market needs, competition, relative costs of production, and avoidance of investment in noncompetitive industries. Trade creates incentives for better utilization of available resources and therefore affects productivity and overall growth. In addition, export success generates foreign exchange, which is available to finance imports of needed components and finished goods that are in demand. Adequate foreign exchange eliminates the possibility of a foreign exchange bottleneck that could limit growth.

SUMMARY

Exports and imports are growing faster than domestic shipments as the world becomes increasingly specialized and integrated. The essence of successful exporting is to apply the marketing concept to the task. This means that it is essential to focus on the customer to take long enough to learn about his needs and wants. Without this focus, there is always the danger of lapsing into export selling, which is increasingly not a successful approach to world markets.

DISCUSSION QUESTIONS

1. What are the major findings of the research on the behavior of exporting firms? Is one company more likely to export than another, and if so, what are the characteristics of the exporting company?
2. Why is exporting from the United States dominated by large companies? What, if anything, could be done to increase exports from smaller companies?
3. What is the difference between barter and countertrade? Why do companies barter?
4. What does it take to be a successful exporter?

BIBLIOGRAPHY

Books

CZINKOTA, MICHAEL R. *Export Development Strategies: U.S. Promotion Strategy.* New York: Praeger, 1982.

———, AND GEORGE TESAR. *Export Policy: A Global Assessment.* New York: Praeger, 1982.

———, AND GEORGE TESAR. *Export Management: An International Context.* New York: Praeger, 1982.

DAVIDSON, WILLIAM H. *Global Strategic Management.* New York: John Wiley, 1982.

U.S. Department of Commerce, International Trade Administration. *15 Ways the U.S. Dept. of Commerce Can Help Make Your Business More Profitable Through Exports.* Washington D.C.: Government Printing Office, January 1981.

———. *A Basic Guide to Exporting.* Washington, D.C.: Government Printing Office, November 1981.

———. *A Guide to Financing Exports.* Washington D.C.: Government Printing Office, 1981.

Articles

Analysis of Recent Trends in U.S. Countertrade. USITC Publication 1237, March 1982.

AYAL, IGAL. "Industry Export Performance: Assessment and Prediction." *Journal of Marketing,* Summer 1982, pp. 54–61.

BELLO, DANIEL C., AND NICHOLAS C. WILLIAMSON. "The American Export Trading Company: Designing A New International Marketing Institution." *Journal of Marketing,* Fall 1985, Vol. 49, pp. 60–69.

————, AND NICHOLAS C. WILLIAMSON. "Contractual Arrangement and Marketing Practices in the Indirect Export Channel." *Journal of International Business Studies*, Summer 1985, pp. 65–81.

BILKEY, WARREN J. "Attempted Integration of the Literature—The Export Behavior of Firms." *Journal of International Business Studies*, Spring–Summer 1977, pp. 33–46.

————. "A University Experience with the MBA Export Expansion Program." *Journal of International Business Studies*, Spring 1973, pp. 15–29.

————. "Variables Associated with Export Profitability." *Journal of International Business Studies*, Fall 1982, pp. 39–55.

————, AND GEORGE TESAR. "The Export Behavior of Smaller-Sized Wisconsin Manufacturing Firms." *Journal of International Business Studies*, Spring 1977, pp. 93–98.

BRASCH, JOHN J. "Using Export Specialists to Develop Overseas Sales." *Harvard Business Review*, May-June 1981, pp. 6–8.

CZINKOTA, MICHAEL R., AND DAVID A. RICKS. "Export Assistance: Are We Supporting the Best Programs?" *Columbia Journal of World Business*, Summer 1981, pp. 73–78.

DAVIES, G. J. "The Role of Exporter and Freight Forwarder in The United Kingdom." *Journal of International Business Studies*, Winter 1981, pp. 99–108.

DE LA TORRE, JOSE R., JEFFREY S. ARPAN, MICHAEL JAY JEDEL, ERNEST W. OGRAM, JR., AND BRIAN TOYNE. "Corporate Adjustments and Import Competition in the U.S. Apparel Industry." *Journal of International Business Studies*, Spring–Summer 1977, pp. 5–22.

GREEN, ROBERT T., AND ARTHUR W. ALLAWAY. "Identification of Export Opportunities: A Shift-Share Approach." *Journal of Marketing*, Vol. 49 (Winter 1985), pp. 83–88.

————, AND JAMES LUTZ. "Of High-Technology Exports." *Columbia Journal of World Business*, Spring 1980, pp. 52–60.

HUSZAGH, SANDRA McRAE. "Exporter Perceptions of the U.S. Regulatory Environment." *Columbia Journal of World Business*, Fall 1981, pp. 22–31.

JOHANSSON, JOHNY K., AND IKUJIRO NONAKA. "Japanese Export Marketing: Structures, Strategies, Counterstrategies." *International Management Review*, Winter 1983, pp. 12–25.

KING, AUDREY MARSH. "How to Find a Distributor." *International Trade Forum*, August 1968, pp. 28–30.

LEE, WOO-YOUNG, AND JOHN J. BRASCH. "The Adoption of Export as an Innovative Strategy." *Journal of International Business Studies*, Spring–Summer 1978, pp. 85–93.

McGUINNESS, NORMAN W., AND BLAIR LITTLE. "The Influence of Product Characteristics on the Export Performance of New Industrial Products." *Journal of Marketing*, Spring 1981, pp. 110–122.

RABINO, SAMUEL. "Barriers to Exporting by Small Business." *Management International Review*, January 1980, pp. 67–73.

————. "An Attitudinal Evaluation of an Export Incentive Program: The Case of DISC." *Columbia Journal of World Business*, Spring 1980, pp. 61–65.

————. "Tax Incentive to Exports: Some Implications for Policy Makers." *Journal of International Business Studies*, Spring–Summer 1980, pp. 74–86.

REID, STANLEY. "The Decision-Maker and Export Entry and Expansion." *Journal of International Business Studies*, Fall 1981, pp. 101–112.

WORTZEL, LAWRENCE H., AND HEIDI VERNON WORTZEL. "Export Marketing Strategies for NIC and LDC-Based Firms." *Columbia Journal of World Business*, Spring 1981, pp. 51–60.

RICHARDSON MANUFACTURING COMPANY, INC.

A DOMESTIC COMPANY CONSIDERS INTERNATIONAL MARKETING OPPORTUNITIES

In 1893 Emmit D. Richardson, father of Bob and Ray Richardson, began serving agriculture in Glen Elder, Kansas. In February 1908 he purchased a blacksmith shop in Cawker City, Kansas, a farming community in the North Central part of the state, which at that time had a population of 1,064. By 1978 the population of Cawker City had declined to 686, but net sales of the successor to Richardson's original blacksmith shop, the Richardson Manufacturing Company, Inc., were $865,000 and net profit was $79,000. Richardson's 1974–1978 profit and loss statement and balance sheet are shown in Tables 1 and 2.

The Richardson brothers, both of whom were graduates of Kansas State University, divided between them responsibilities for company operations. Bob, with the title of president, concentrated upon the financial side of the company, and Ray took responsibility for design, engineering, and manufacturing. As sales of the company expanded, the two brothers decided to expand the executive staff of the company by hiring a director of sales. The man selected for this position was George "Jiggs" Taylor. Before coming to Richardson, Jiggs had been for 15 years the personal pilot to E. C. Riley, Cawker City's most famous entrepreneur whose widespread operations included a 5,000-acre Mexican cotton ranch, apartment buildings and office buildings in widely scattered locations, distributorships for farm implements, domestic and foreign automobiles, cattle feed lots, and,

finally, a construction company whose operations consumed the liquid funds of Mr. Riley's operations and forced him into bankruptcy.

PRODUCTS AND U.S. MARKETS

Richardson 1978 sales were accounted for by three principal products:

Products 40 and 45, the Richardson AD-Flex Treader and Mulch Treader, 45 Percent of Sales ($407,000)

This implement, which had been invented by James Van Sickle, a son-in-law of E. D. Richardson, was priced at $100 per foot at retail and sold mainly in 11- to 15-foot lengths. It was designed for the ground tillage and follows the initial ground breaking either by the traditional moldboard plow or by one of the more recent approaches to ground breaking, such as the undercutter plow.[1] The treader enabled a farmer to practice what was known as stubble mulch farming, a

system of farming including harvesting, tillage, and planting operations that maintains much of the crop residue anchored on the soil surface. The main purpose of this system of farming is to keep enough residue on the surface to protect both the soil and the young crop from damage by water and wind erosion.[2]

---

[1] The moldboard plow was a device that cut a furrow into the earth and with a curved board or metal plate turned over the earth from the furrow. The undercutter plow simply cuts under the earth to form a furrow without turning over the earth.

[2] "Use of Stubble Mulch Tillage Tools" by Walter E. Selby, Extension Agricultural Engineer (duplicated) (no date).

TABLE 1 Profit and Loss Statement, 1974–1978

	1974	1975	1976	1977	1978
Sales	$601,308.73	$613,528.77	$733,735.98	$848,040.50	$910,162.12
Less: Cash discount given	30,054.88	29,829.60	38,901.82	44,417.43	45,407.80
Net sales	$571,253.85	$583,699.17	$694,834.16	$803,623.07	$864,754.36
Beginning inventory	59,597.50	78,160.88	78,381.88	65,631.88	70,138.98
Purchases	283,752.40	276,521.23	296,756.00	339,669.59	311,380.88
Direct mfg labor	59,080.44	56,092.19	69,375.55	78,665.32	81,572.08
Subtotal	402,430.34	410,774.30	444,516.43	483,966.72	463,091.94
Ending inventory	78,160.88	78,384.88	65,631.81	70,138.98	50,369.42
Cost of goods sold	$324,269.46	$332,389.42	$378,884.62	$413,827.74	$412,722.52
Gross profit (loss) on manufacturing	$246,984.39	$251,309.75	$315,949.54	$389,795.33	$452,031.84
Indirect manufacturing expense	62,432.37	61,053.73	81,430.11	93,475.87	102,944.17
Production control expense	2,219.11	1,502.22	3,406.17	2,839.90	3,675.96
Engineering expense	13,600.11	17,398.53	17,238.60	22,647.37	22,018.95
Sales expense	86,016.63	85,228.51	105,226.88	143,836.93	154,232.74
Advertising expense	24,779.01	27,946.61	26,897.99	31,824.46	33,314.75
Administrative and office expense	46,760.19	46,781.88	61,873.96	74,766.84	79,658.91
Net profit (loss) on manufacturing	$ 11,176.97	$ 11,398.27	$ 19,875.83	$ 20,403.96	$ 56,186.36
Other income					
Sales tax collections	374.51	467.66	279.17	317.95	352.06
Parcel post charged tax	11,951.62	13,472.15	16,075.18	15,519.49	16,521.55
Interest income	1,339.86	1,502.68	2,144.44	1,359.87	1,274.14
Rental income	956.00	1,333.42	1,113.00	942.00	912.00
Cash discount on purchases	2,055.75	2,359.38	1,676.98	2,711.96	2,925.52
Salvage scrap sales	1,177.76	287.63	758.82	4,500.13	757.04
CO-OP patronage dividend	166.02	175.57	126.20	144.09	143.46
Other expenses					
Rental expenses	547.90	978.74	923.56	4,533.96	536.18
Net profit (loss) on operations	$ 28,650.59	$ 29,958.04	$ 41,146.06	$ 41,365.49	$ 78,535.95

557

TABLE 2 Balance Sheet, 1974–1978

	1974	1975	1976	1977	1978
Current assets					
Cash in register	$ 150.00	$ 150.00	$ 150.00	$ 150.00	$ 150.00
Farmers & Merchants State Bank	(18,088.93)	(18,569.52)	(23,128.10)	(24,781.39)	(27,295.83)
Exchange Nat'l Bank	1,000.00	1,159.40	1,306.93	995.89	1,003.29
Accounts receivable	18,635.13	14,299.90	24,486.80	15,511.05	38,858.60
Investments					
Treasury bills		25,000.00	25,000.00		
Note participation	25,319.25	25,000.00			
Saving and loan	20,971.76	22,267.63	25,970.20	25,636.00	25,100.00
Stamps	61.61	59.43	2.66	2.66	
Inventory	78,160.88	78,384.88	65,631.81	70,138.98	50,369.42
Total current assets	$126,209.70	$122,751.72	$119,520.30	$ 87,653.19	$ 88,185.48
Fixed assets					
Depreciable assets cost less accumulated depreciation	54,785.70	57,019.66	66,644.48	70,774.82	67,871.04
Investment in Cawker City Clinic	80.00				
Deposits	166.91	239.65	365.85	381.10	451.68
Land special assessment improvements	7,216.93	7,665.74	9,284.58	9,433.39	9,582.20
Total fixed assets	62,249.54	64,925.05	76,294.91	80,589.31	77,904.92
Total assets	$188,459.24	$187,676.77	$195,815.21	$168,242.50	$166,090.40
Current liabilities					
Accounts payable	2,223.32	4,392.05	14,331.73	4,242.50	2,090.40
Accrued property taxes					
Notes payable					
Cash with order	2,486.86	947.30			
Total current liabilities	$ 4,710.18	$ 5,339.35	$ 14,331.73	$ 4,242.50	$ 2,090.40
Net worth					
Capital	164,000.00	164,000.00	164,000.00	164,000.00	164,000.00
Paid-in surplus	1,098.47	1,098.47	1,098.47	1,098.47	
Shareholders undistributed taxable income	10,043.50	10,043.50	10,043.50	10,043.50	
Net income (loss) year to date	28,650.59	29,958.04	41,146.06	58,848.97	78,535.95
Net income paid to shareholders	20,043.50	29,958.04			
Total net worth	183,749.06	$182,337.42	181,483.48	164,000.00	164,000.00
Total liabilities and net worth	$188,459.24	$187,676.77	$195,815.21	$168,242.50	$166,090.40

558

Product 46, the Richardson AD-Flex Stubble Mulch Plow, 40 Percent of Sales ($364,000)

This plow, which was pulled by a tractor, was priced at $100 per foot of length, retail. The average length sold was 15 feet. It was especially designed to prepare a seed in ground that received limited annual rainfall. It was an undercutter plow that literally cut a straight furrow under the soil instead of turning the soil over as the traditional plow did.

Richardson's principal markets for this plow were wheat farmers in the three-state area of Kansas, Colorado, and Nebraska. The total potential U.S. market for this type of plow was estimated by Bob Richardson to be $15–25 million.

The competition in the undercutter plow market was described by Mr. Taylor as "extreme." There were five major competitors, all of them small specialized manufacturers like Richardson. Deere and Oliver, two full-line implement manufacturers, had entered this market and withdrawn according to Mr. Taylor apparently due to production problems and the small size of the market. Richardson's success in this market was attributed by Mr. Taylor to "our dealer organization, service, a good product, and top performance." The main competitive weakness, in Mr. Taylor's view, was the relatively high average price of the Richardson product.

The AD-Flex Picker Treader and the Mulch Treader were identical in performance and were both tractor-drawn farm implements. The only difference between them was in construction. The AD-Flex Picker Treader was a modular design and was used in tandem with the AD-Flex Stubble mulch plow. The only direct competitor in this product line was by the Williston Co. of Albany, Georgia, who began production of a product in 1977. The treader was a substitute for the spring tooth harrow, a traditional farm implement with large steel teeth, that was used to break up the soil after plowing.

The advantage of a mulch treader was best realized in geographical areas that were semiarid where the soil was subject to erosion by wind and water. The treader inverted the soil, thus conserving moisture while the spring tooth harrow broke the soil up and exposed moisture in the soil to the air which resulted in evaporation and moisture loss. The retail price of a mulch treader was $100 per foot, and sold mainly in 11- to 15-foot lengths. This was approximately double the retail price of a quality spring tooth harrow. Richardson estimated that the 1978 market for spring tooth harrows was about $20 million.

The Richardson brothers considered the treaders, shown in Figure 1, to be the main hope for the company's continued expansion. They held patents on the treaders and were encouraged by their growth in popularity. The treader was first used in 1969 by Kansas wheat farmers and then spread to wheat farmers in Nebraska and Colorado. More recently, its use had spread to corn, soybean, and alfalfa growers in Illinois, Southern Louisiana, Indiana, Utah, California, and to Canada as well.

Product 442, the Richardson Flexo Guard, 15 Percent of Sales ($110,000)

The Flexo Guard was an attachment for combines that extended ahead of the cutting sickle to retrieve and deliver grain heads that would otherwise fall back onto the ground. This device was sold at retail for $45 to $50 all over the Middle West, in California and Arizona, and to a limited extent in the East. Richardson faced one competitor in the Flexo Guard market, another small company located in Clay Center, Kansas, a town of 4,613 people only

THREE-POINT MODELS—

These models are available to the farmer whose operation permits him to enjoy the convenience of 3-point tools. They provide the same quality construction and superior tillage and seedbed preparation as the wheel-type Mulch Treader. Consult your dealer or write for additional information concerning the one for your tractor.

SPECIFICATIONS:	MT 32-116	MT 32-96	MT 31-96	MT 31-76	MT 31-66
Working Width	11'6"	9'6"	8'6"	7'6"	6'6"
Max. Overall Width	12'6"	10'6"	9'6"	8'6"	7'6"
Total No. of Wheels—Front	24	20	18	16	14
Rear	26	22	20	18	16
Shipping Wt.	1650	1485	1232	1150	1068
Three-Point Category	II	II	I	I	I

BIG FARMING IS EASY WITH DUAL HITCH —

The Richardson Dual Hitch pairs two Mulch Treaders for fast, easy tillage of large acreages. Ideal, too, for harrows, hoes, drills, etc. Large caster wheels, box beam construction and heavy-duty Timken bearings give it the brawn for the big jobs. Put it to work in your operation.

The Low-Draft Leader in Stubble Mulch Country —

The Richardson ADflex Plow and AD-flex Treader provide a big 25% power-savings bonus, and matchless performance when close work is required. A demonstration will show you why it's the low-draft leader.

RICHARDSON MANUFACTURING CO., Inc. ° Cawker City, Kansas 67430

210.09 8-1-67

Printed in U.S.A.

FIGURE 1

560

The Seedbed Comes First...

Give
It
Top
Priority
Treatment
with -

RICHARDSON

Mulch Treader

FIGURE 1 *continued*

Perfect size clods and well distributed residue prevent wind and water
erosion in this field.

The pattern of action — no continuous tracks, to provide better sub-
surface drilling conditions.

RICHARDSON

Mul
Tre

U.S. Pat. No. 3107737 and other patents pending —
Can. Pat. No. 717,296

Seeding Goes Better — Yields Go Higher With Mulch Treader

No other seedbed tool lends itself to so many farming
methods. In summer fallow — continuous crop — dryland
or irrigation — moldboard or stubble mulch — its unique
ability to eliminate weeds and leave the soil firm and seed-
ready eliminates those extra trips over the field. Crop
residues in stubble mulch operations are evenly distributed
and firmly anchored to make hoe or disc furrow opener
drills work troublefree. You get better stands and the
young crop benefits right from the start from the extra
moisture you've conserved by this more profitable way to
farm. Since no ridges are found nor furrows left in its
wake, the Mulch Treader may be used without regard to
contours of the field.

Get your crops off to a Mulch Treader start with the perfect seedbed and in soil that has retained more of the
available moisture.

Weeds are controlled easily in summer fallow or continuous crop practices. Cloddy condition prevents
blowing and slicking over by show-
ery activity.

Leveling action of treader is demonstrated in irrigated corn ground. The
roots are turned up to make subsequent tillage easier and more effective.

❶ Two heavy 4"x1½" Steel Channel, electric welded into one piece form heavy-
duty carrier frame to provide solid support for the tillage gangs. This assures
even distribution of weight and soil
penetration of the tillage wheels.

❷ Each tillage gang is supported on three
self-aligning ball bearings triple sealed
and grease packed. The bearings are
bolted to heavy bearing brackets secure-
ly clamped to the rugged 4"x3⅛" gang
beam.

❸ Bearings are triple sealed ball bearings
especially built for this kind of service.
They are pre-lubricated and require no
greasing. A specially designed bearing
shield protects the bearing seals from
outside damage, insuring long life to
the bearing.

❹ Perfect alignment and spacing of the
tillage wheel gang bearings is assured
by the use of adjustable bearing brackets. Each bracket is clamped to the
gang beam by four steel bolts.

❺ Once the tillage depth of the
mined, the depth control adjust
depth. Each time the Treader
pre-determined depth without th
cylinder. This is standard equip

FIGURE 1 *continued*

562

with EXCLUSIVE
Magic Mulch
TOOTH DESIGN

'ch ader

Special high-carbon steel teeth are specially stress relieved to insure long life and ductility. The cross section of the tooth is a half oval. The outer ends are beveled at 45° making a sharp point. Each tooth is curved and twisted. This shape permits easy soil penetration to go in deep and break out a solid clod. At the same time, the side motion of the tooth rips out weeds and leaves them roots-up on the surface.

⑤ The Mulch Treader is mounted on fourteen-inch drop center wheels for easier transporting from one field to another, across hard-surfaced roads, grass waterways and other areas. These wheels are mounted on Timken tapered roller bearings on a removable stub axle which facilitates switching single wheels from inside to outside position, or for easy addition of duals. See SPECIFICATIONS for tread widths obtainable by switching wheel positions.

⑥ A parking stand is built into the Treader to aid in parking and hitching.

⑦ All models of the Mulch Treader are equipped to use the standard 8-inch hydraulic lift cylinder. The "parallelogram" lift mechanism automatically maintains the level of the Treader in all positions in or out of the ground. This assures even penetration of all tillage wheels and saves time when changing the working depth of the Treader. The Treader may be raised to clear the ground 8 inches and lowered to work 8 inches below the surface.

...arming operation has been determent is set to accommodate this ...is lowered it will return to this ...e use of a stroke control hydraulic ...ment.

The wheels are 18 inches in diameter spaced on six-inch centers on the gang bolt. Wheels and teeth are replaceable.

Zero angle adjustment of rear gangs.

Built for Your Job and Built to Do It for Years to Come

Heavy-duty construction throughout, and quick, positive adjustments, combine to make the Richardson Mulch Treader a tool that will meet your seedbed preparation requirements for years to come. An almost limitless variety of soil treatment is possible with adjusting depth, angle, and speed of travel. No other tool in a single pass can promise • a soil surface protected from run-off and blowing • the perfect seedbed — firm with fine soil below — clods at top • trouble-free seeding and best possible germination • a more desirable young plant environment.

Specifications

	MTA-83	MTA-93	MTA-103	MTA-113	MTB-123	MTB-133	MTB-143	MTB-153
Working Width	8'3"	9'3"	10'3"	11'3"	12'3"	13'3"	14'3"	15'3"
Number of Tillage Wheels	37	41	45	49	53	57	61	65
Transport Wheels Tread Width (C to C)								
Wheels In	80"	80"	80"	80"	101"	101"	101"	101"
Wheels Out	106"	106"	106"	106"	127"	127"	127"	127"
Weight (Less Tires)	2076	2186	2271	2351	2534	2619	2699	2779

ACRES TREADED PER HOUR AT GIVEN SPEEDS

Treader Width	5 mph	6 mph	7 mph	8 mph
8'	4.84	5.81	6.78	7.74
10'	6.05	7.26	8.47	9.68
12'	7.26	8.71	10.16	11.62
14'	8.47	10.16	11.86	13.55

Strippers are available for operating in extremely wet-trashy conditions.

Optional middle buster will work the soil left undisturbed by certain angle settings.

FIGURE 1 *continued*

FIGURE 1 *continued*

77 miles east of Cawker City. Richardson, which had manufactured the Flexo Guard for almost 15 years, had a majority of the available market.

The complete 1978 product line and the sales of each product are shown in Table 3.

CUSTOMERS

What kind of farmer bought the Richardson Stubble Mulch Plow and Mulch Treader? According to Mr. Taylor,

the farmer who buys our product is interested in change as a means of increasing his profitability. The person who will switch from the traditional implement to our new design is a farmer who is aggressive and who understands costs and performance. We can make a strong impression on this kind of farmer. We offer 25 percent less power consumption when our tools are used, and our method leaves the seedbed in much better condition for retaining moisture and therefore in much better condition to produce high crop yields. We're selling lower-cost ground preparation, better crop yields, and a soil erosion prevention method of farming.

TABLE 3   Product Sales, 1978

PRODUCT	PRODUCT DESCRIPTION	1978 JAN–DEC.	1978 PERCENTAGE
40	Ad-flex Treader	$294,914.06	32.4%
41	Dual Hitch	263.48	
42	Flexo Guard	110,179.54	12.1
43	Simflex	2,271.80	.2
44	Sta-Kleen	3,061.48	.3
45	Mulch Treader	112,264.09	12.3
46	Ad-flex Plow	363,555.87	39.9
47	Furrow Opener Wire Winder	17,754.14	2.0
48	Cylinder and Concave Rasp		
49	Miscellaneous	7,507.98	.8

Source: Company records.

U.S. Channels of Distribution

Richardson employed a two-phase distribution program. Roughly 75 percent of the company's sales were realized by 88 contract dealers located in the company's three principal territories: Kansas, 38 dealers; Oklahoma and the Texas Panhandle, 32 dealers; and Colorado and Nebraska, 18 dealers. A sales representative was assigned to each of these territories and called upon the dealers in the territory. Each of the contract dealers was located in a geographical trading area, and almost all the dealers were contract dealers for one of the major implement manufacturers such as John Deere or International Harvestor.

The remaining 25 percent of the company's sales were through seven distributors, located in Kansas City, Missouri; Dallas and Amarillo, Texas; Evansville, Indiana; Fargo, North Dakota; Raleigh, North Carolina; and Stockton, California. The geographical distribution of Richardson sales is shown in Table 4.

The discount schedule was 40 percent

TABLE 4   Geographical Distribution of Richardson's Sales, 1977–1978

	NO. OF FARMS GROWING WHEAT	ACRES OF WHEAT HARVESTED 1977	ANNUAL RAINFALL	RICHARDSON'S 1978 SALES
Kansas	84,171	11,081,000	19–35″	$295,722
North Dakota	N.A.	7,962,000	14–18″	0
Oklahoma	31,200	5,217,000	18–37″	387,797
Montana	15,513	4,734,000	12–18″	0
Texas	29,172	3,326,000	18–33″	48,454
Nebraska	39,712	3,325,000	16–29″	47,948
Colorado	9,600	1,961,000	10–14″	0
Washington	8,755	2,922,000	9–20″	0
Other U.S. and Canadian	—	—	—	130,241
Total U.S.	366,598	59,004,000		$910,162

N.A.—Not available.

Source: Company records.

off list for distributors, and for dealers, 20 percent plus 5 percent 10 days, net 30 days.[3] In addition, dealers could earn up to an additional 7 percent of list through volume discounts which were paid in the form of rebates at the end of the year.

U.S. Advertising and Promotion

Richardson spent $33,314 on advertising in 1978, or roughly 3.75 percent of sales. The entire program was print, and magazines were the principal media, with newspapers and mailed circulars filling out the program. A partial list of the farm trade magazines used was as follows:

> *Colorado Rancher & Farmer*
>
> *Dakota Farmer*
>
> *Farmer Stockman* (Oklahoma, Kansas, Texas)
>
> *Farm Journal* (Montana, Wyoming, North and South Dakota and other midwest states)
>
> *High Plain Journal* (Colorado, Kansas)
>
> *Irrigation Age* (Montana, Wyoming, South Dakota, Nebraska, Kansas, Colorado).
>
> *Kansas Farmer*
>
> *Nebraska Farmer*
>
> *Western Farm Life*

Typical advertisements are shown in Figure 1. The production and placement of company advertising was handled by the George Eschbaugh Agency in Wilson, Kansas, a town 64 miles south of Cawker City.

In addition to print advertising, Richardson also supported a promotional program at a cost of about $4,000 to $5,000 per year.

---

[3]That is, 25 percent off list if the bill was paid in 10 days, net about (20 percent off list) due in 20 days.

This program, which was implemented by the three territory managers responsible for direct sales to dealers and for distributors in their areas, consisted mainly of facilitating and arranging demonstrations and making necessary arrangements to rent space and transport equipment to fairs in the area. Mr. Taylor thought that field demonstrations arranged by county agricultural agents were particularly effective because they attracted, as he put it, "people who are really interested, not just the curiosity viewers that you get at the fairs."

EXPORTS

In the late 1960s Richardson had shipped a small order to a company in South America that had seen an advertisement for a Richardson product and placed an order. Since then, Richardson had not made any efforts to achieve foreign sales, and none had materialized. Finally, on June 8, 1977, Richardson received an unsolicited letter from Napier Bros. Limited, an Australian manufacturer and distributor of agricultural implements requesting "your best price C.I.F. Port of Brisbane for the supply of a Mulch Treader equipped with Zero Angle Attachment and 15″ Dual Wheels less tyres and tubes and less hydraulics." (See Figure 2.) With the press of business, Richardson did not get around to answering the letter immediately, and on the first of July, it received a second letter from Napier requesting a reply to the first letter. Meanwhile, Mr. Taylor had requested a freight forwarder in Kansas City to provide him with a quotation on charges for ocean shipment of equipment to Australia. He received a quotation on July 20 and discovered, to his surprise, that an implement that sold for $945.84 in Cawker City would incur shipping and insurance costs of $642.50 just to

NAPIER BROS. LIMITED
(INCORPORATED IN QUEENSLAND)
Manufacturers of Agricultural Implements and General
Engineers.
Registered Office: Bunya Street, Dalby, Queensland.

1370/02   5th June, 1977.

Request for Price Quotation
Richardson Manufacturing Co., Inc.
Cawker City,
KANSAS. . . . . .U.S.A.

Dear Sir,

          We refer to correspondence which we had with you some two years
ago in regard to the possibility of importation of one of your Mulch Treaders. At that
time, we were unable to raise sufficient interest in the machine to warrant its
importation but we have now received very definite enquiries and we would
appreciate your quoting us your best price C.I.F. Port of Brisbane for the supply of a
Mulch Treader equipped with Zero Angle Attachment and 15″ Dual Wheels less
tyres and tubes and less hydraulics in the following sizes -

                              10′ 3″
                              12′ 3″
                              14′ 3″
                              15′ 3″

          With your quotation, which we would appreciate in seven copies for
customs purposes, we shall be obliged if you could also forward us twenty copies of
your descriptive leaflets.

          We would appreciate your forwarding the above information as early
as possible and at the same time would you please advise the best delivery available
from time of receipt of order.

                         Yours faithfully,

                         NAPIER BROS. LIMITED

                         (N. Coldham-Fussell)

                         SECRETARY

FIGURE 2

May 27, 1978

Napier Brothers Limited
Bunya Street
Dalby,
Queensland, Australia
Attention: N. Coldham-Fussel

Dear Sir:

We thank you for putting one of our Mulch Treaders to work in your country. We have not to date received any word of its success, therefore we are very interested to know many things such as: types of soil the machine was used in, when and where it was used, what crops used on, annual rainfall amounts, whether it satisfied your expectations and any other pertinent information regarding the machine you have available.

Assuming the answers are favorable, can you suggest a preferred way to introduce this tool into general use? Do you distribute your own agricultural implements or work through other distributors? Also do you feel we have a market for our Mulch Treader in your country?

May we hear from you by return airmail.

If we may be of any assistance at any time, please do not hesitate to call on us.

Sincerely yours,

RICHARDSON MANUFACTURING CO., INC.

George A. Taylor
Director of Sales

GAT/mm

FIGURE 3

the port of Brisbane, for a total C.I.F. price of $1,587.34. This did not, of course, include inland transportation in Australia, or the 27 percent F.O.B. ad valorum Australian duty on imported implements.[4] He was somewhat taken aback by the cost of shipping abroad, particularly as he recalled having just made a shipment weighing 3,000 lb (the same weight as the Australian quotation) to Fresno, California, by truck at a cost of $254.00.

The realization that the Richardson Mulch Treader would cost roughly twice as much in Australia as it did in Kansas dampened considerably Mr. Taylor's hopes that an Australian market for the treader might be opened up. Nevertheless, he forwarded the quotation to Napier Bros. To his surprise, a month later he received an order for the MTBCD-153L (Dual Wheel Unit) Mulch Treader with a C.I.F. Port of Brisbane price of $1,832.55.

By October 5, the Mulch Treader for Napier Bros. was crated and ready to be shipped. Everything seemed to be in order until October 17 when Richardson learned from its forwarding agent in Kansas City that it would be unable to get the Mulch Treader on an ocean vessel until November. As a result, Richardson wrote to Napier Bros. requesting an extension on the letter of credit and also an adjustment on price as the ocean freight turned out to be $30.00 higher than was anticipated. Napier increased and extended its letter of credit as requested and also expressed concern that the delay in shipment might make it impossible to test the Mulch Treader on stubble after the conclusion of the 1977 wheat harvest in mid- to late

[4]This duty could be reduced to 7.5 percent if it was shown that no Australian manufacturer was offering for sale a "suitably equivalent good." If neither an Australian nor a U.K. company were supplying the item, the duty could be eliminated.

December. When Mr. Taylor learned that the shipment would arrive in Brisbane on December 19, he was hopeful that this would enable Napier to arrange for a test following the December 1977 harvest. If this were not done, the next harvest was a year away, and Richardson would lose an entire year in its effort to penetrate the Australian market.

In the ensuing months, Taylor heard nothing from Napier. In May 1978, at the suggestion of Ray Richardson, he attended a regional export expansion conference sponsored jointly by Drake University and Iowa export expansion council. Attending the conference reminded Mr. Taylor again of the potential of export markets, and he resolved to follow up the Richardson lead as soon as he returned to Cawker City. The letter he wrote is reproduced in Figure 3.

Mr. Taylor received an immediate reply from Napier. (See Figure 4.) Six weeks later he received another letter that enclosed the results of a field test of the Richardson treader by an Australian government agricultural extension agent by the name of Tod. The following are excerpts from the agent's report, dated June 6, 1978:

In general this machine has exceeded our expectations in its ability to handle heavy straw and weeds, and to prepare soil for conventional planting equipment and we are very pleased with its performance.

It would be a tremendous help in saving our soil from erosion, which in this state is a problem of some magnitude. Most of the 5 million acres of cultivated land in this state has a subtropical summer rainfall, most of which falls in high density rainstorms, which, allied with the winter cropping programme, makes it imperative that crop residues be kept standing as long as possible, to help conserve this rain and prevent soil erosion. Most of our machinery is designed for the gentle winter rainfall areas of the southern states, where this type of erosion is not a problem. Therefore it is unsuitable for our conditions.

Napier Bros. Limited
Bunya Street
Dalby
Queensland, Australia

31st May, 1978

Richardson Mfg. Co. Inc.
P.O. Box 5
Cawker City
Kansas, 64730, U.S.A.

Attention: Mr. G. A. Taylor, Director of Sales

Dear Sir:

We thank you for your letter of the 27th May, 1978.

In connection with the second paragraph of your letter, I have asked our Design Staff to prepare for you a report to answer the matters which you raised in the second paragraph of your letter. As soon as this is in hand we will forward it to you. We are also endeavoring to obtain a report from the Government Department of Primary Industries who have been particularly interested in this project and we will also forward this to you.

We advise that our Company manufactures and distributes a wide range of agricultural tillage and general purpose equipment. The company has its own subsidiary marketing organisation, i.e., Napier Machinery Sales Pty. Limited which markets through distributors and dealers in the Eastern States of Australia. In addition we manufacture equipment for tractor companies and number amongst our clients, Ford, Fiat, Case, Massey-Ferguson and Chamberlain. In addition we have a substantial export operation working mainly in South America, South-East Asia and East Africa.

As the Mulch Treader only arrived towards the end of the mulching season, it was not possible for a complete testing to be carried out and we had it in mind to wait for the results after this year's harvest in approximately October/December before taking the matter up further with you. If there is sufficient interest in this item we feel that there may be an opportunity to develop substantial business by the following steps:

(a) Initially importing the units,
(b) As volume grows, entering into part manufacture of the implements, and
(c) When volume is sufficient enter into some arrangement to manufacture the units under license.

FIGURE 4

We would appreciate your thoughts on these types of arrangements and will forward you the reports on the operations of the machine as soon as they come to hand.

Yours faithfully,

NAPIER BROS. LIMITED (N. Coldham-Fussell, Export Manager)

FIGURE 4 *continued*

To sum up, your mulch treader could solve one of our two main problems in the search for suitable stubble mulching machinery, that is, preparing a standing stubble quickly for planting. However, our other pressing need is for a more efficient sub-surface tillage implement, with enough tyres to give soil disturbance for weed killing. Neither the present scarifier nor the chisel plough have enough clearance for heavy stubble, and the latter is not an efficient weed killer. We would be interested to hear if your company makes an implement of this type.

We would also be grateful for more information on the adjustment of the treader to get a level surface when using the machine as a cultivator only.

> H. H. Tod, Agricultural
> Extension Agent
> Growers Representative
> Soil Conservation Committee

Mr. Taylor replied to the two letters and report from Australia. (See Figure 5.)

After signing this letter, Mr. Taylor wondered if Richardson was following the right approach to international marketing. One possibility he considered was to sign on with an export merchant. He had recently attended an export expansion conference in Iowa where he had been approached by a Kansas City export manager who offered to take on the Richardson line of equipment for export markets if Richardson would give him the distributor discount of 40 percent plus an additional "export bonus" of 15 percent off list. The problem with this offer, according to Mr. Richardson, was that 55 percent off list cut too deeply into Richardson's operating margin. (See Table 5 for company operating ratios.) Also, he wondered how much push an export merchant would give to the Richardson line.

Tables 6, 7, and 8 and Figures 6 and 7 contain data Mr. Taylor kept in a file labeled "International Markets." As he opened this file his thoughts were focused on the question of whether Richardson should take the plunge and go international. It seemed clear that there was a market overseas for Richardson's products, but the question in Taylor's mind was how to approach these markets. Also, he wondered how much attention and effort he should give to international as opposed to domestic markets.

NEGOTIATION ASSIGNMENT

Richardson teams: Negotiate an agreement with Napier for penetrating the Australian market with Richardson products.

Napier teams: Negotiate an agreement with Richardson for penetrating the Australian market.

Issues (partial list)

Sourcing: location and responsibility
Marketing: responsibility, plans, budgets
Product adaptation
Pricing

July 22, 1978

Napier Brothers Limited
Bunya Street
Dalby
Queensland, Australia 4405
Attention: Mr. N. Coldham-Fussel

Dear Sir:

We have read with much interest your letter and Mr. Tod's report regarding the use of the Mulch Treader. We are enclosing some literature on our AD-Flex Plow which is a highly successful implement for undercutting stubble and the AD-Flex Picker Treader may be attached for a more effective weed kill.

The undercutting plow is made in five foot sections and may be used by itself leaving the stubble standing or by adding the Picker Treader which somewhat mixes the stubble and mulches the soil, also tearing out the growing vegetation. It would appear to be a highly suitable implement for your stubble mulching program with the Mulch Treader following up to do a more complete job of chopping up the straw and finishing up the seed bed.

We do have a new model plow but the literature and instruction books are not available as yet, although the picker treader is shown mounted on the new model plow.

In Mr. Tod's report, he asked for more information on adjusting the treader so we are enclosing an operators manual which explains adjustments under the heading of OPERATING INSTRUCTIONS.

The middle buster tyne sells for $20.41. This included bracket, bolts and curved shank. A chisel point or small shovel may be attached. We cannot furnish this point.

The steps you outlined in your letter of May 31st certainly look feasible in regards to the distribution of our implements.

I certainly wish it were possible to visit with you personally regarding the operations of the plows and to see the conditions you are confronted with as the farmers in the arid and semi-arid regions of this country have and are adopting these practices and implements. Their farming expenses are being reduced approximately one-third and are conserving more moisture along with eliminating soil erosion by water and wind and many are claiming higher yields per acre over previous practices.

In Mr. Tod's report, he mentions a slasher which we are not sure of. Possibly what we call a stalk cutter or rotary mower. Perhaps you could enlighten us more on this implement.

I presume you will pass along this information to Mr. Tod and if we can be of further assistance, please do not hesitate to let us know.

FIGURE 5

Twenty sheets of mulch treader literature will be forwarded under separate cover.

Sincerely,

RICHARDSON MANUFACTURING CO., INC.

George A. Taylor
Director of Sales

GAT/mm

Enc.   210.09 81-1-77 Mulch Treader
       210.6 5M/6-1-77 AD-Flex Plow
       410.09 6-10-77 Instruction Booklet

FIGURE 5 *continued*

TABLE 5   True Operating Ratios, 1978

	1978	
Adjustments necessary to reflect true operating ratios		
(1) Cost of goods sold	412,722.52	
Less: Salvage scrap sales	757.04 Cr	
Cash discount on purchases	2,925.96 Cr	
	409.039.52	
(2) 500's engineering expenses	22,018.95	
Add: 50% Ray's salary from 602	12,500.00	
	34,518.95	
(3) 600's sales expenses	154,232.74	
Less: 50% Ray's salary to 500's	12,500.00 Cr	
Parcel post and freight charged for	16,521.55 Cr	
patronage dividend	143.46 Cr	
Add: Out freight from 800's (parcel post)	2,670.40	
	127,738.13	
(4) 800's administrative and office expenses	79,658.91	
Less: Out freight to 600's	2,670.40 Cr	
Sales tax collections	352.06 Cr	
Interest income	1,274.14 Cr	
	75,362.31	

True Operating Ratios for	*1978*	*1977*
Cash discount/total sales	4.99%	5.23%
Cost of goods sold/total sales	44.95	47.94
Indirect manufacturing expense and production control expense/total sales	11.71	11.82
Engineering expense/total sales	3.79	4.14
Selling expense/total sales	14.00	13.64
Advertising expense/total sales	3.66	3.75
Administrative and office expense/total sales	8.28	8.62
Net profit on operations/total sales	8.62	4.86
	100.00%	100.00%

TABLE 6   Acres of Wheat Harvested in Selected Geographical Areas

AREA	ACRES HARVESTED (in millions)	YIELD PER ACRE (in bushels)
European Economic Community	48.2	33.9
United States	49.9	26.3
Canada	29.7	27.9
Mexico	1.7	35.0
Argentina	12.9	17.8
India	31.3	12.2
Australia	20.3	23.0

TABLE 7   Wheat Farm Investments

	U.S.*	AUSTRALIA†	CANADA‡	ARGENTINA§
No. of Farms	366,593	51,000	77,395	
Farm value				
Land			$20,358–41,679	
Buildings	$66,397	$76,000– 93,000	16,774–26,360	
Livestock			2,799– 4,560	
Total	$66,397	$76,000–$93,000	$39.931–72,599	
No. of acres/farm	456	1,800	802–1,434	
Value/acres	$122	$42–52	$50–51	
No. of tractors/farm	2.1	1.62	1.48	.29
Annual rainfall	17–30″	11–20″	20–30″	12–22″

*U.S. farm is average one in Kansas in 1964. (*Source:* 1964 U.S. Census of Agriculture.)

†Australia farm is a "typical" one in Victoria in 1964 (medium and large). The larger acreage is due to the need for grazing area for sheep. (*Source:* Department of Primary Industry, Agriculture Production Branch).

‡Canadian farm is average of medium and medium-large, in 1958. (*Source:* Handbook of Agriculture Statistics by Canadian Bureau of Statistics.)

§In the wheat belt of Argentina, which includes the provinces of Buenos Aires, Cordoba, La Pampa, and Santa Fe, there are about 12,500 farms of 400 acres or larger. It is not known how many grow wheat.

Source: Argentine Commercial Attaché in New York.

TABLE 8

File Note: Canada

The climate in the Canadian wheat belt in the province of Saskatchewan is similar to that here in Kansas. All farm implements and equipment manufactured in the United States can be imported into Canada duty free.

File Note: Argentina

The taxes in Argentina are 90 percent ad valorem on C.I.F. value, a 5 percent statistics tax on C.I.F. value and a charge of 20 Argentine pesos per gross kilo. Also, there is a 10 percent sales tax on retail value in Argentina levied at the time of importation.

File Note: Australia

Australia's wheat belt follows the eastern coast, plus a small section in the west. The particular states and their 1966–67 acreages are

New South Wales	7,135*	15,300†
Victoria	3,138	6,400
Queensland	1,227	3,400
South Australia	2,960	5,100
Western Australia	6,347	8,100
Total Australia	20,823	31,900
Total U.S.	159,000	145,600

The wheat belt is typified by a 10–20" rainfall, somewhat less than the 17–30" annual rainfall in the United States. The Department of the Interior mentioned in its April 1967 publication, "The Northern New South Wales and Queensland wheats rely heavily on the conservation of summer rain moisture in the soil, while spring rains are important for the growth of wheat in Victoria." The Bulletin states more explicitly later that rains in all the regions are very unreliable and that the threat of a serious drought is omnipresent. The soil is also less rich than in the United States and Canada and is particularly deficient in nitrogen and phosphate.

It is difficult to draw conclusions based on the number of farms. In the United States there are 3,400,000 farms, but they differ from the 252,000 Australian farms; many of the Australian farms are devoted to sheep grazing, making the average acres per farm considerably higher than in the United States, which considers livestock farms a separate category. Over 51,000 farms grow wheat in Australia, but few grow solely this crop.

The tractor sales in 1964 were a record 25,000 units, whereas the U.S. sales were 143,000 units. Tillage implements sold about 9,000–11,000 units in Australia, 83,000 units in the United States. Nearly 87 percent of all tractors owned in Australia belong to farmers in the wheat belt states named above.

The farmer has a supported pricing structure for export wheat. The wholesale wheat price in 1966–67 was $1.75 compared with $1.41 in the United States. The government offers the wheat farmer rural credits and preferential interest rates and guarantees to marketing groups for prepayments. Favorable depreciation allowances plus investment credits aid the farmer. Also, farm items that are not available in the country may be imported duty free.

Australia has a climate and soil that are suitable to stubble mulch farming. Both the mulch treader and the AD-Flex Plow could be used to advantage here. It appears from the tractor sales figures that the Australian farmer does tend to be a capital-expenditure-oriented businessmanager. Figure 6 substantiates this by demonstrating a consistently high, for the size of the country, tractor sales pattern.

*Acres of wheat, in thousands.

†Acres of total grains, in thousands.

Source: Commonwealth Bureau of Statistics, Canberra.

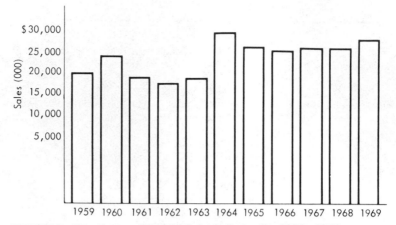

FIGURE 6   New Tractor (Wheels) Sales in Australia, 1959–1969

FIGURE 7   Map of Australia

Distribution

Selling, advertising, promotion

Service

Design: export licensing, joint venture, split ownership

Timing

Plan

Key assumptions

QUESTIONS

1. Identify the strengths and weaknesses of Richardson in the North American market.
2. Should Richardson go international? Why? Why not?
3. If Richardson decides to go international, what alternative strategies should it consider?
4. Recommend a strategy for Richardson. Identify objectives and develop a marketing, sourcing, staffing, and financial plan for years 1 and 5.

APPENDIX I: Trading Companies: An Executive Briefing[1]

Definition of Terms: Trade, Traders, and Trading Companies

TRADE.   The dictionary definition of "trade" is:

> The buying and selling or exchanging of commodities either by whole or by retail *within* a country or *between* countries, i.e., *domestic* trade or *foreign* trade.

I have emphasized domestic trade, because there are those who overlook the importance of domestic trade in constructing trading companies. While it may be appropriate for certain specialized trading companies to avoid domestic trade, the larger trading companies of the world have strong roots in domestic market.

TRADER.   While there may be some misunderstandings about what is meant by "trade," there are enormous differences in people's perceptions about what a "trader" is. The following is my own definition:

> A trader is one who knows enough about the business infrastructure of a commodity or product to:
> Locate suppliers then buy the products
> Locate customers and sell the merchandise
> Coordinate all the activities required to move the goods from supplier to customer

[1]This section has been condensed and edited from a longer report on the subject by Myron H. Miller, managing director, Global Trade Services, Ltd., The Army and Navy Club Building, 1627 Eye Street N.W., Suite 610, Washington, D.C. 20006.

Find the money to support the transaction

Negotiate with shipping companies, insurance companies and any others involved in providing trade services

Judge the creditworthiness of customers

A trader may trade in a variety of commodities or merchandise, but they will differ greatly in their dexterity in handling different goods.

While this definition can stand on its own, it is well to qualify the latter aspect of this definition, then proceed to describe some of the characteristics of a trader.

Traders differ greatly in their degree of dexterity in handling a variety of goods. Some traders confine themselves to a narrow product line. Others branch out into related commodities or similar semifinished goods. Still others deal in any goods, services, or technology they think will be profitable.

There are no hard and fast rules as to how far a trader can diversify. Generally, traders in bulk commodities move into other bulk commodities before trying intermediate and finished goods (from cotton into greige goods then into textiles, for example).

Traders in finished goods are constrained by the complexity of the products they propose to buy and sell. The more complex the product, the harder it will be to compete with traders who specialize in that complex product, and the harder it will be to compete with manufacturers of the product who sell the product directly.

CHARACTERISTICS OF TRADERS. The following are important to understand about traders:

They understand very well the risks and rewards associated with their trading

A really good trader knows the worldwide business infrastructure of his business

A trader knows where his commodities or merchandise are produced, processed or grown, and knows the costs to produce the goods and to land those in the key markets of the world

A trader knows the world trade flows for his products

A trader knows the customer's needs, key markets and channels of distribution

A trader personally has developed sources of supply for the products and personally has marketed to and sold his products. The better traders have a stable of long time loyal customers who will follow him wherever he goes.

A trader knows important competitors throughout the world sufficiently well that he can anticipate many of their moves

A trader knows what factors affect the future of his business and monitors those very carefully

The trader knows the principal information sources for his business, and also has an informal "early warning system" to alert him to significant developments

A trader has a network of people who help to generate leads for him, and to provide support in getting deals accomplished

A trader often is involved in a variety of ventures, because he likes to get involved in what he anticipates may be profitable deals, and because he is free to become involved

A good trader can size up business opportunities very quickly, and can also size up people very quickly. That ability is vital to a trader's success. He may be involved in putting together three miniventures in the same day.

A trader is not likely to be constrained by the rules and pay structures of corporations. This is one of the major problems in trying to put some traders into a corporate structure. A good trader is probably making several hundred thousand dollars and thinks he can make a million—and occasionally does. He always wants to feel he can make a million with the right deal, and doesn't want to think some corporation might prevent him from making the "big deal of his life."

These are the characteristics of individual, entrepreneurial traders. We shall see that there are relatively few real traders in a trading company, even though there is a trading mentality.

A trading company performs essentially two tasks:

One is acting as a trade intermediary, working between someone who wants a product and someone who can supply it, providing trading services to facilitate the movement of the product.

The second is to develop trade flows by engaging in various activities which increase the supply of products and create additional demand.

Most of the other activities of trading companies which are frequently mentioned, such as financing, risk absorption, resource development, organizing, investment and provision of information, are undertaken particularly for the purpose of facilitating or creating new flows of trade.

Trading companies serve (1) as intermediaries between buyers and sellers, as well as (2) being active creators of trade flows. They are not primarily oriented toward users (customers) or manufacturers, but instead are supply/demand oriented, always seeking new opportunities to meet market demands, and to capitalize on new sources of supply.

Trading companies do not invest in manufacturing companies unless that is necessary to maintain or enhance its position in trading, usually by gaining exclusive distribution rights for having made an investment (usually a minority holding).

SOME CHARACTERISTICS OF TRADING COMPANIES. The basic concept behind a trading company is the *selling of efficiency,* that is, providing a series of trading services more efficiently than its customers can provide for themselves, particularly in the costs of transactions, the costs of marketing and the costs of finance.

This characteristic of the selling of efficiency is the prime reason for the existence of trading companies. Unless trading companies can prove that they can perform services more efficiently than their customers, they will have no reason for being.

Quite a few companies perform trading services, but that is not the most important thing they do. Therefore, for a company to be considered a trading company, it should have more than 50 percent of its revenues from trading services, and over 50 percent of its revenues should come from foreign trade.

Why—and How—A Firm Should Use a Trading Company

Before examining the functions and services of various types of trading companies, it is necessary to determine why individual firms would want to use a trading company, either as a trade intermediary or to help it capitalize on new opportunities.

Individual companies are made up of a value-adding chain of activities all of which are required (1) to bring materials into the company, (2) to convert those materials into some finished product, (3) to ship those goods to some ultimate destination, (4) market and sell the products, (5) provide after-sales service, (6) design and develop the products, and (7) provide the support structure for all the other activities.

A firm could try to be totally integrated and perform all those value-adding activities itself, or it can do those it thinks it can do most economically and in effect subcontract those activities that others can do most economically. The following examples are meant to illustrate this point (but are not meant to represent scientifically derived percentages). These examples show two companies in the consumer durables business, one which has chosen to do almost everything itself, and the other represents a company which has retained only those activities it can do best, and has contracted out many activities it thinks others can do more economically.

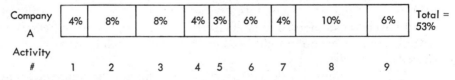

Gross margin earned by highly integrated consumer durables co.

Company A	4%	8%	8%	4%	3%	6%	4%	10%	6%	Total = 53%
Activity #	1	2	3	4	5	6	7	8	9	

Activity description:

1. Sourcing of raw materials and other components
2. Research and development
3. Manufacturing and/or sourcing finished products
4. Information and communications
5. Shipping and other cargo management functions
6. Taking title to inventory and warehousing
7. Finance and insurance
8. Marketing and sales
9. After-sales service

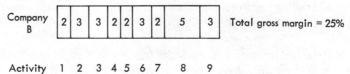

Company B	2	3	3	2	2	3	2	5	3	Total gross margin = 25%
Activity	1	2	3	4	5	6	7	8	9	

Company A is highly integrated: It owns its own forest reserves, manufactures everything that went into its end products, sells through its own retail stores, and finally, handles all of its after-sales service.

While such a company can earn very high margins by performing every activity itself, there are tremendous costs and investments required to support each activity. Also, there is a very high likelihood that other companies can provide some of those services much more economically than Company A can provide for itself. Not only is there the high risks associated with investing to support all those activities, but there are the inefficiencies of doing things that others can do much better.

Company B represents another consumer durables company which has chosen to have other firms perform many of its functions, and doing only those where they have unique value-adding capabilities and which they can perform economically.

As any company examines its value chain of activities to determine what it should do and what it should have others do, particularly in its international business, it will often find that a trading company has many of the capabilities needed to be most efficient in total. Trading companies are ideally equipped to perform a number of value-adding activities in international business for manufacturing and service companies.

Even a trading company will not do everything itself. Because the orientation of a trading company is toward the "principle of comparative advantage," it will perform only the functions it does most economically and subcontract to other firms those functions which others perform more efficiently.

Given this analytical background on why firms can use the services of trading companies to their advantage in their global business, let's look at some of the principal reasons firms turn to trading companies for help, and which activities are most importantly handled by trading companies.

COMPANIES NEEDING HELP IN EXPORTING.   A number of surveys have been made of why firms need the help of trading companies in exporting. The following is a prioritized listing of what is most important to firms which need the help of an export trading company:

1. Assistance in selecting competent distributors.
2. Financing, or arranging for financing, of trade transactions.
3. Assistance in developing marketing strategies and marketing plans in foreign countries.
4. Understanding and assistance in export documentation.
5. Understanding of foreign competitive conditions.
6. Know international transportation practices.
7. Provide after-sales service.
8. Handle countertrade requirements.
9. Evaluation of credit risk associated with foreign buyers.
10. Assumption of responsibility for physical delivery of product to foreign buyer.
11. Personal contact with foreign buyers.

12. Arrange for C.I.F. quotes in response to inquiries from abroad.
13. Ability to pioneer new foreign markets for supplier's products.
14. Sales personnel calling on foreign customers in person.
15. Ability to correspond in the necessary foreign languages.
16. Advising on, or arranging for, all export packaging and marking.
17. Preparation of advertising and sales literature for use in foreign markets.
18. Ability to inform supplier on impending import controls, tariff increases, etc.
19. Promotion of supplier's products at foreign trade shows.
20. Ability to train and instruct foreign sales network in product.

Companies That Need Assistance in Sourcing

1. Locate good suppliers.
2. Provide quality control services.
3. Insure prompt, reliable deliveries from overseas sources.
4. Establish a forecasting/feedback system so the overseas supplier receives a rolling one-year production forecast, the first few months of which are frozen for production planning purposes.
5. Finance imported products.
6. Handle all logistical aspects of delivering the products from foreign sources.
7. Provide for all business infrastructure support in the supplying country.

Companies Which Want to Invest Overseas for Market Entry, Sourcing, or Manufacturing

1. Locate suitable joint venture partners or acquisitions.
2. Negotiate for the joint venture or acquisition.
3. Manufacturing site selection, negotiation for purchase of real estate, equipment, financing and support services.
4. Handle all local government arrangements regarding the investment.

The above are only a sampling of the reasons why firms involved in international business turn to trading companies to get services that the firm cannot do nearly as efficiently.

Functions of Trading Companies

TRADITIONAL FUNCTIONS OF TRADING COMPANIES. To look at the broadest array of traditional trading functions, it is best to look at the Japanese general trading companies, for they represent a model by which to understand all other trading companies around the world. The following are the functions that those companies have performed for many years:

- Exporting and importing.
- Domestic wholesale and OEM sales.
- Marketing and selling/distributing—includes market research, credit investigations, product planning and development, advertising and public relations.
- Inventory management—Hold buffer stocks, so manufacturers can enjoy the efficiencies of large production runs.
- Logistical services (including transportation and distribution)—large sales volumes from multiple manufacturers lower the cost of goods shipped internationally.
- Market intelligence—trading companies acquire, process and transmit information among its world-wide branches.
- Financing—the trading company provides capital for purchases, production, and exports.
- Assumption of risks.

Starting in the 1960s, the Japanese broadened their role to include certain activities generally not performed by other trading companies throughout the world. These activities have drawn much attention, but it must be remembered that these new activities were done with the intent of supporting their traditional trade intermediary role and to create new trade flows.

THE NEWER FUNCTIONS OF TRADING COMPANIES

Resource development ventures—the purpose of which is to secure supply sources through overseas investment.

Overseas manufacturing ventures—this involves the procurement of plants, capital equipment and machinery; supply of raw materials and intermediate products; in return for which the trading company often gets the output of such a manufacturing venture or exclusive rights to the distribution of the products. This investment is a means of "capturing" trade opportunities with minimal investment.

Intermediation in Technology Transfer—Japanese trading companies identify new technologies and then negotiate license agreements to bring technology to Japan.
The float glass process, developed by Pilkington in the U.K., was brought into Japan by Mitsui.
The nylon technology from DuPont was brought to Japan by Mitsui.
The hydraulic shovel technology developed by Poclain (France) was taken to Japan by Marubeni.

Project organizers—because of their vast network of offices throughout the world and their great variety of capabilities, the Japanese have been in a good position to organize vast projects in the areas of engineering and construction.

Plant exporting ventures—the Japanese trading companies are able to handle the export of entire factories and power stations throughout the world.

Leasing—having been involved in exporting factories, they have gone further and are leasing such facilities. Initially, they had gotten experience in leasing of aircraft, ships and computers.

Quasi-banking activities—this involves the provision of direct loans, credit guarantees, and supply credit and prepayments for merchandise to their affiliated ventures.

Needless to say, the scope of these activities is beyond what most trading companies do in other parts of the world, but it does illustrate the fullest range of activities that a trading company can perform to serve as a trade intermediary and to create new trade flows.

Services Provided by Trading Companies

In the previous section we examined the functions that trading companies perform. How do trading companies package these functions into services they provide to their customers? The following is a "menu" of trade services that a trading company can choose from in constructing their particular portfolio. Every trading company is a composite of some or all of these services.

TRADE SERVICE	GROSS MARGINS*	RESOURCES/COSTS TO SUPPORT THE SERVICE	INVESTMENT REQUIRED TO PERFORM SERVICE
Broker	1%–3%	Low	Low
Agent	5%–6%	Low	Low
Distributor	15%–22%	Medium	Medium
Manufacturer/Distributor	25%–35%	High	High
Sourcing	6%–10%	Medium	Medium
Trade Finance	$\frac{1}{4}$%–1% + fees	Medium	High
Logistics/Freight Forwarding	2%–5%	Medium	Medium
Countertrade	4%–5% + fees	Medium	Medium
Trade & Investment Consulting	Avg. daily rate approx. $800	Low	Low
Develop New Int'l. Business	• Consulting fee • Equity position • Distr. rights	Medium	Medium
Commodity Trading	8%–10%	High	High
Project Finance	Moderate	Medium	High
Venture Capitalist	25%–40% (annual return)	Medium	High
Project Manager	Moderate	High	High

*Note: The margins shown above and the indications of cost and investment are approximations only.

This listing is not complete, but serves to illustrate the variety of services that a trading company can elect to provide. Considerable care should be taken to put together a unique portfolio, for your estimates of revenues and associated costs and investment will be based on this selection of services to provide. Many trading companies are started without this analysis and planning, somehow hoping that if they provide some minimal staffing then just take advantage of all the opportunities that will occur, that somehow everything will turn out alright.

Not only must this portfolio be planned carefully at the beginning of establishing a trading company, but the portfolio must be managed and adjusted constantly to achieve maximum profitability and to ensure that you have the capabilities available to perform what is expected by your customers.

Profile of a Representative Trading Company

The figure illustrates only one example of how a trading company might be formulated. In the example below, the company has determined what portfolio of services

Profile of a Representative Trading Company

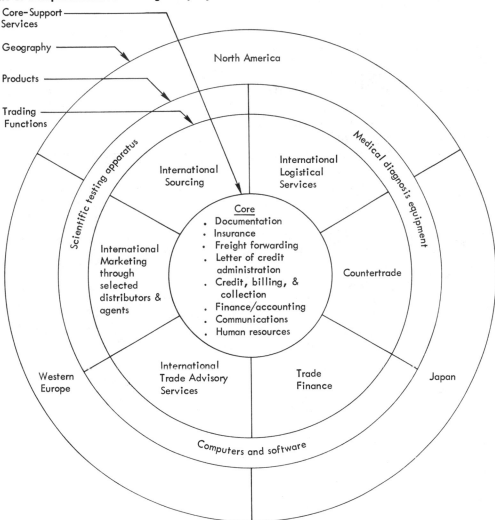

it was capable of providing, then constructed a trading company encompassing those services.

In this illustration, the total revenues are shown as equally divided among the six service categories. In fact, the share of revenues of each of the services would be unequal, and would depend on the relative importance the company wants to place on each service.

The point to be made here is that when a company decides to establish a trading company, it can construct one that particularly suits its needs and capabilities.

Survey of Various Types of Trading Companies

This section describes how actual trading companies throughout the world have put together their portfolio of services.

JAPANESE TRADING COMPANIES. Because they are so dominant in the trading world, the Japanese trading companies are often looked at as the model of what a trading company should be. That is a great mistake, and often frightens companies away from establishing a trading company or even using a trading company. Nevertheless, they are well worth analyzing because they do include just about every kind of trade service imaginable.

Although people tend to think primarily about the largest Japanese trading companies, there are over 6,000 trading companies in Japan, and most are very small. The top nine trading companies are gigantic "general" trading companies and are called the "sogo shosha." The vastness of these companies is illustrated by the number of offices they have throughout the world.

Trading Company	NUMBER OF OFFICES		
	Domestic	Foreign	Total
Mitsubishi	46	128	184
Mitsui	51	145	196
Marubeni	49	132	181
C. Itoh	41	111	152
Sumitomo	41	123	164
Nissho-Iwai	46	118	164
Toyo Menka	34	80	114
Kanematsu-Gosho	22	64	86
Nichimen	28	65	93

The following are the characteristics of a "sogo shosha" which set them apart from other trading companies:

- They must be engaged in both importing and exporting.
- They must have offices in various parts of the world.
- They must wield considerable power in the spheres of marketing and finance.
- They must be engaged in "offshore" trade, i.e., trading where none of the trading involves Japan.
- They must undertake various activities (such as warehousing, transportation, resource development, manufacturing, etc.) to complement its trading activities.
- They must play a leadership role in industrialization, most particularly in the developing countries.
- They must account for a large share of the foreign trade of the country of domicile.

The major sources of revenue for the sogo shosha are:

- Exports of plants and machinery, and iron and steel
- Imports of fuels (petroleum, gas—such as LPG and LNG and other alternative energy such as coal and uranium ore)
- Imports of raw materials including ore of ferrous and non-ferrous metals
- Import of foodstuffs

Because the sogo shosha have relied on these basic businesses, they have become vulnerable as those businesses have matured. Later, we will determine what these companies have done to expand their activities into newer, high growth areas. Some of the newer functions were indicated earlier.

LARGE GENERAL TRADING COMPANIES.   General trading companies have their roots in the beginnings of major trade between the major European countries and their colonies, and therefore go back several hundred years. Trading companies often began in the smaller countries, which needed such mechanisms for their economic survival. You will note that there is only one American trading company listed, and that is because it is the only one large enough to note.

COMPANY	HEADQUARTERS	ANNUAL SALES	PRINCIPAL BUSINESSES
Getz	San Francisco	$500 million	(1) International marketing and distribution of consumer goods, technical products & industrial products; (2) transportation, sales agents, and services;

COMPANY	HEADQUARTERS	ANNUAL SALES	PRINCIPAL BUSINESSES
			(3) manufacturing, trade management and logistical services.
Hagemeyer	The Netherlands	$850 million	(1) Consumer goods trading, 45%; coffee trading, 45%; (3) manufacturing, 10%.
SHV Holdings	The Netherlands	Several billion	(1) Consumer goods distribution, primarily retailing (Makro stores); (2) coal and oil trading; (3) trading, transport and services.
East Asiatic	Denmark	$1.7 billion	(1) Consumer products, mostly processed foods 27%; (2) Commodities 20%; (3) graphic arts 17%; (4) shipping 18%; (5) synthetics, chemicals, metals 9%; (6) technical equipment 2%.
Inchcape	London	$2.4 billion	(1) Distributor or general export agent 42%; (2) motor vehicle assembly and distribution 42%; (3) Finance and insurance 7%; (4) Commodities/plantations 4%; (5) shipping 2%; (6) manufacturing 2%; (7) engineering 1%.
Ceteco	The Netherlands	$410 million	(1) Consumer—wholesale trade and agency representation, and export buying services; (2) industrial distribution; (3) manufacturing.
Diethelm	Zurich	Several billion	Major agencies for pharmaceuticals, consumer goods, chemicals, technical products, foodstuffs
Jardine Matheson	Hong Kong	$1.6 billion	(1) Property and hotels 45%; (2) marketing and distribution 16%; (3) financial services 14%; (4) transportation and services 14%; (5) natural resources 7%; (6) engineering and construction 4%.

There are a number of other trading companies in Europe and the Far East. Several major trading companies are headquartered in Switzerland however, they are privately held and it is more difficult to get information on those companies.

KOREAN TRADING COMPANIES.   Inspired by the success of the Japanese sogo shosha, the Koreans have copied the concept with a fair amount of success. The

Korean trading companies include:

Samsung
Daewoo
Hyundai
Kukje
Bando
Koryo
Sunkyung
Hyosung
Ssango ng

Though founded relatively recently, these trading companies have grown dramatically in recent years and are becoming a major force in the world trade. In many cases, they are more aggressive than the Japanese trading companies.

U.S. EXPORT TRADING COMPANIES.   The United States has not been a major exporting nation relative to its size. As recently as 1960, exports were only 6 percent of Gross National Product, and it was still 6 percent in 1970. By 1980, however, exports increased to 13 percent, and by 1985 to 15 percent of our GNP.

There are several thousand export trading companies in the United States, most of them very small.

- 50 percent have sales less than $2 million.
- 67 percent have less than 10 employees.
- 37 percent have four employees or less.
- 12 percent employ more than 25 people.
- 90 percent have single or majority interest ownership.
- 82 percent have only one office in the United States.
- The largest have sales slightly over $50 million.
- They average 15–25 supplier relationships, but the top 5 suppliers usually represent about 80 percent of their business.
- Unlike the sogo shosha, the U.S. companies predominantly export—87 percent list exporting as their major business.

Unlike the Japanese trading companies, the U.S. export trading companies seldom get involved in importing. The importing business in the U.S. is very separate.

The Export Trading Company Act was passed in 1982 for the purpose of stimulating the creation of new trading companies to export by permitting banks to establish trading companies and by providing some protection from anti-trust laws for those who wanted to work with others to obtain overseas business, but there is little evidence to suggest that that legislation has had a significant effect on U.S. exports.

The following are some of the principal services provided by U.S. export trading companies:

SERVICE	ALWAYS	SOMETIME
Locating distributors, agents, and buyers	82%	14%
Setting or recommending prices	62	31
Foreign language assistance	56	35
Credit analysis	55	33
Market research	50	42
Participate in trade shows	39	50

Conclusion

There will always be a place for a trading company which starts with some unique, cost-effective capabilities to provide certain trade services, and which can reach outside to bundle other required trade services for a customer that is striving to be as cost-competitive as possible.

APPENDIX II: The 10 Most Common Mistakes of Potential Exporters[1]

In exporting, as in so many things, there is no substitute for experience. As you put into practice the export techniques examined in preceding chapters, they will become more familiar, more comfortable, and easier to use in an effective way. Your confidence, too, should grow proportionally with your exporting proficiency. However, since experience also includes knowledge gained from mistakes, the following items are identified by experienced trade specialists of the U.S. Department of Commerce as the 10 most common mistakes and pitfalls to be avoided by new exporters.

1. FAILURE TO OBTAIN QUALIFIED EXPORT COUNSELING AND TO DE-VELOP A MASTER INTERNATIONAL MARKETING PLAN BEFORE STARTING AN EXPORT BUSINESS.   To be successful, you must first clearly define your goals, objectives, and the problems you face. Second, you must develop a definitive plan to accomplish your objectives despite the problems involved. Unless you are for-

---

[1]U.S. Department of Commerce, International Trade Administration, Washington, D.C. *A Guide to Exporting*, Washington, D.C.: U.S. Government Printing Office, November 1981, pp. 84–85.

tunate enough to possess a staff with considerable export expertise, you will not be able to take this crucial first step without qualified outside guidance.

2. INSUFFICIENT COMMITMENT BY TOP MANAGEMENT TO OVERCOME THE INITIAL DIFFICULTIES AND FINANCIAL REQUIREMENTS OF EXPORTING. It may take more time and effort to estabish yourself in a foreign market than in domestic ones. Although the early delays and costs involved in exporting may seem difficult to justify when compared to your established domestic trade, you should take a long-range view of this process and shepherd your international marketing efforts through these early difficulties. If you have laid a good foundation for your export business, the benefits derived should eventually outweigh your investment. (Remember: Getting started in the U.S. market can also be difficult at first!)

3. INSUFFICIENT CARE IN SELECTING OVERSEAS DISTRIBUTORS. The selection of each foreign distributor is crucial. The complications involved in overseas communications and transportation require international distributors to act with greater independence than their domestic counterparts. Also, since a new exporter's history, trademarks, and reputation are usually unknown in the foreign market, your foreign customers will buy on the strength of your distributor's reputation. You should therefore conduct a personal evaluation of the personnel handling your account, the distributor's facilities, and the management methods employed.

4. CHASING ORDERS FROM AROUND THE WORLD INSTEAD OF ESTABLISHING A BASIS FOR PROFITABLE OPERATIONS AND ORDERLY GROWTH. If you expect distributors to promote your account actively they must be trained and assisted, and their performance must be continually monitored. This requires a company marketing executive permanently located in the distributor's geographical region. Therefore, new exporters should concentrate their efforts in one or two geographical areas until there is sufficient business to support a company representative. Then, while this initial core area is expanded, the exporter can move into the next selected geographical area.

5. NEGLECTING EXPORT BUSINESS WHEN THE U.S. MARKET BOOMS. Too many companies turn to exporting when business falls off in the United States. When domestic business starts to boom again they neglect their export trade or relegate it to a secondary place. Such neglect can seriously harm the business and motivation of their overseas representatives, strangling their own export trade and leaving them without recourse when domestic business falls off once more. Even if domestic business remains strong, they may eventually realize that they have only succeeded in shutting off a valuable source of additional profits.

6. FAILURE TO TREAT INTERNATIONAL DISTRIBUTORS ON AN EQUAL BASIS WITH DOMESTIC COUNTERPARTS.   Often, companies carry out institutional advertising campaigns, special discount offers, sales incentive programs, special credit term programs, warranty offers, and so on in the U.S. market but fail to make similar assistance available to their international distributors. This is a mistake that can destroy the vitality of your overseas marketing efforts. (They don't change gross margin requirements either.)

7. UNWILLINGNESS TO MODIFY PRODUCTS TO MEET REGULATIONS OR CULTURAL PREFERENCES OF OTHER COUNTRIES.   Local safety and security codes, as well as import restrictions, cannot be ignored by foreign distributors. If necessary modifications are not made at the factory, the distributor must do them—usually at greater cost and, perhaps, not as well. It should also be noted that the resulting smaller profit margin makes the account less attractive.

8. FAILURE TO PRINT SERVICES, SALES, AND WARRANTY MESSAGES IN LOCALLY UNDERSTOOD LANGUAGES.   Although your distributor's top management may speak English, it is unlikely that all sales personnel (let alone service personnel) will have this capability. Without a clear understanding of sales messages or service instructions, these personnel will be less effective in performing their functions.

9. FAILURE TO CONSIDER USE OF AN EXPORT MANAGEMENT COMPANY. If a firm decides it cannot afford its own export department (or has tried one unsuccessfully), it should consider the possibility of appointing an appropriate export management company (EMC).

10. FAILURE TO CONSIDER LICENSING OR JOINT VENTURE AGREEMENTS. Import restrictions in some countries, insufficient personnel/financial resources, or a too limited product line cause many companies to dismiss international marketing as simply not feasible. Yet nearly any product that can compete on a national basis in the United States can be successfully marketed in most markets of the world. A licensing or joint venture arrangement may be the simple, profitable answer to your reservations. In general, all that is needed for success is flexibility in using the proper combination of marketing techniques.

17

GLOBAL MARKETING PLANNING

One does not plan and then try to make circumstances fit these plans. One tries to make plans fit the circumstances.

General George Patton

INTRODUCTION

This chapter focuses on the integration of each element of the marketing mix into a total plan that responds to expected opportunities and threats in the global marketing environment. In the global firm, marketing planning must be conducted not only at the national level but also at one or more headquarters levels. The challenge is the integration of national and regional plans into an overall plan that best utilizes organizational resources to exploit global opportunities.

GLOBAL STRATEGY—A CONCEPTUAL FRAMEWORK

A strategic plan is based on an assessment of the environment, the organization, and the values of organization stakeholders. By pulling together information from all sources, the planners must identify key assumptions about major trends, customers, competitors, and governments. This analysis and identification of facts and key assumptions leads to an assessment of opportunities, threats, and trends. The fact that this is the way it should be done does not mean that it is always done this way. For example, Juan Trippe, the former chief executive officer of Pan American, was famous for not conducting market studies before making company decisions about equipment purchases. According to one observer, Trippe "would not have looked at market analysis. There was no planning department in Pan Am. Trippe sat in his corner office, made plans, and then made them come true.''[1]

Unfortunately, Trippe's fateful decisions to purchase Boeing 747s were made at a time when the industry's growth based on market share captured from steamship lines and railroads had come to an end and possibilities for further growth were limited. Without environmental analysis, Trippe and the industry did not know this. Intuition, luck, and feeling are invaluable tools for marketing planners, but they must not be used in isolation. It is essential to also look at the facts and at the analysis of the facts to make sure that *they* also support a direction or course of action.

The next stage of the global planning process is the analysis of the organization and the values and aspirations of organization stakeholders. As outlined in Table 2–1, this analysis leads to a determination of what is desired based on a selection of a course of action from a list of what is possible. When the decision about what is desired has been reached, the next step is to make it happen by developing creative, effective, integrated plans.

WHAT KIND OF GLOBAL PLAN?

Standardized

A standardized global marketing plan offers a number of advantages. First, there are significant cost savings if standardization is practiced. A company that limits the number of models and variants of its product can achieve longer production runs and greater economies of scale. This is elementary and has been demonstrated in actual practice thousands of times over. Henry Ford was probably the first industrialist to demonstrate the potential of mass production for achieving scale economies and creating a national market. Similarly, the Italian appliance industry during the 1960s achieved remarkable cost reduction through standardization and long production runs and in the process took a leadership position in Europe. Of course, cost savings can be achieved not only in production but also in packaging, in distribution, and in the creation of advertising materials.

There are other benefits of standardization. In an increasingly mobile world a standardized product is the same in every national market and is therefore uniform for increasing numbers of customers who travel across national boundaries. There are pressures today to standardize products so that the customer can develop standardized programs in its operations. Another benefit of standardization is that it extends successful products and good ideas into all markets.

There are, however, a number of obstacles to standardization. Market characteristics may be so different in so many major ways that it is impossible to offer a standardized product. There was, for example, simply no significant market in Europe (or Japan and many other countries) for the 3,500–4,000-lb, 120″ wheel-base U.S. automobile. It was too big to fit in the streets, it consumed too much gasoline,

[1]John Newhouse, *The Sporting Game* (New York: Knopf, 1982), p. 114.

it cost too much to license, and it did not appeal to the European sense of style. American automobile manufacturers who wish to compete in more than a very minor segment of the European market must adapt their product or develop entirely new products to suit overseas market preferences.

In cases where the same product can be sold, other elements of the marketing mix can be obstacles to standardization because of environmental differences in company position. For example, consider the company whose market share position is quite different from market to market. Although other characteristics in markets may be relatively similar, different market share positions make standardization of promotional and pricing decisions extremely difficult. Where the local position is commanding, an advertising message that expands the total market for the product category will benefit the dominant company. But the same company may have a minor position in an adjoining market where its advertising strategy should be to obtain a share of the market for its particular product.

Decentralized

Many companies have followed a decentralized planning approach either because of poor results using the standardized approach or after noting the many differences from country to country in market environments. This approach has received perhaps more support in marketing than any other functional area. An executive of a major international company expressed what is probably a representative view: "Marketing is conspicuous by its absence from the functions which can be planned at the corporate headquarters level. It is in this phase of overseas business activity that the variations in social patterns and the subtlety of local conditions have the most pronounced effect on basic business strategy and tactics. For this reason, the responsibility for marketing planning must be carried out by those overseas executives who are most familiar with the local environment."[2]

A common feature of both the standardized and the decentralized approaches is the absence of responsibility for analysis and planning at the headquarters level for multicountry marketing programs. In the standardized case such activities are assumed to be unnecessary. Once the marketing problem is solved for the United States, or the home country, it is solved for the world. In the decentralized company the need for analysis and planning to respond to local conditions is recognized, but it is assumed that knowledgeable efforts can only be attempted at the country level and that there is no opportunity for effective supranational participation in these activities.

Interactive

A third approach to formulating a global marketing plan is the interactive, or integrated, approach. This is superior to either the standardized or the local plan because

---

[2]Millard H. Pryor, "Planning in a Worldwide Business," *Harvard Business Review*, January–February 1965.

it draws on the strengths of each of these approaches in planning to formulate a synthesis. Under the interactive marketing planning approach, subsidiaries are responsible for identifying the unique characteristics of their market and ensuring that the marketing plan responds to local characteristics.

Headquarters, both global and regional, is responsible for establishing a broad strategic framework for planning in such matters as deciding on major goals and objectives and on where to allocate resources. In addition, headquarters must coordinate and rationalize the product design, advertising, pricing, and distribution activities of each subsidiary operation. Headquarters must constantly be alert to the trade-offs of concentrating staff activities at headquarters locations in an attempt to achieve a high level of performance versus the advantages of decentralizing staff activities and assigning people directly to subsidiaries.

Each decision must stand on its own merit, but there are significant opportunities for the improvement of performance and cost saving by concentrating certain activities at one location. For example, many companies have successfully centralized the preparation of advertising appeals at world or regional headquarters. Another activity that can be done in one location is product design. Information and design criteria need to come from the world, but the design itself can be done by one design team in a single location.

Current Planning Practices

Sorenson and Weichmann, in a survey of 100 senior executives in 27 leading multinationals in consumer package goods industries, found that on their index, 63 percent of the total marketing programs were judged to be highly standardized.[3] The idea of standardization for the other elements of the marketing mix in the Sorenson and Weichmann study is shown in Figure 17–1. The highest degree of standardization observed was in product physical characteristics, brand names, and packaging. In addition to advantages of longer production runs, executives mentioned the advantages of better international legal and trademark protection and the intangible advantages of having a worldwide as opposed to a merely national brand franchise. This is increasingly valuable as consumers become more mobile.

In contrast to product decisions, pricing decisions are much less standardized. Manufacturing costs, competitors' prices, taxes, company market position, tariffs and duties, and so on, vary from country to country, making it extremely difficult to standardize prices.

In advertising and promotion, Sorenson and Weichmann found that almost three-quarters of the advertising messages had been highly standardized but that the frequency of standardization for media allocation was much lower. The explanation for this difference is the fact that advertising media availability varies considerably among countries.

---

[3]Ralph Z. Sorenson and Ulrich Weichmann, "How Multinationals View Marketing Standardization," *Harvard Business Review,* May–June 1975, pp. 38 ff.

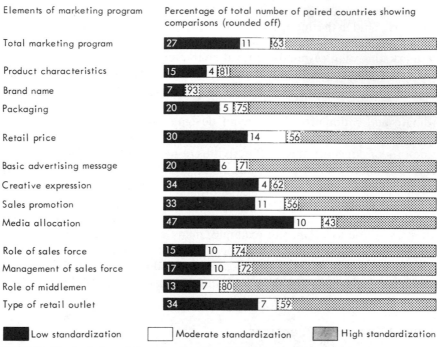

Elements of marketing program   Percentage of total number of paired countries showing
                                       comparisons (rounded off)

Total marketing program   27   11   63

Product characteristics   15   4 81
Brand name   7   93
Packaging   20   5 75

Retail price   30   14   56

Basic advertising message   20   6 71
Creative expression   34   4 62
Sales promotion   33   11   56
Media allocation   47   10   43

Role of sales force   15   10   74
Management of sales force   17   10   72
Role of middlemen   13   7 80
Type of retail outlet   34   7   59

■ Low standardization   □ Moderate standardization   ▨ High standardization

**FIGURE 17–1   Index of Standardization of Marketing Decisions Among European
Subsidiaries of Selected Multinational Enterprises**

SOURCE: Ralph Z. Sorenson and Ulrich Weichmann, "How Multinationals View Marketing
Standardization," *Harvard Business Review,* May–June 1975, p. 39.

The major finding, however, of the Sorenson-Weichmann study is that the real
competitive advantage of the multinational company comes not from the extent to
which it is able to standardize marketing programs but rather the extent to which it
is able to standardize the marketing process. To the successful multinational, it is
not really important whether marketing programs are internationally standardized
or differentiated; what is important is that the process by which these programs are
developed is standardized. A standardized process provides a disciplined framework
for analyzing marketing problems and opportunities. It also provides a framework
for the cross-pollination of experience, ideas, and judgments from one market to
another. Sorenson and Weichmann quote a headquarters executive:

> A total standardization of all the elements of the marketing mix is hardly thinkable. On
> the other hand, the intellectual method used for approaching a marketing problem, for
> analyzing that problem, and for synthesizing information in order to arrive at a decision,
> can absolutely be standardized on an international basis.
>   It is desirable that marketing decisions be as decentralized as possible toward the
> field of economic battle. Nevertheless, if decision-making is done in each country ac-
> cording to the same intellectual process, it can be more easily understood by head-
> quarters management: a standard process eliminating guesses in the subjective side of

marketing permits one to arrive more easily at the standardization of certain elements of the marketing mix.[4]

CUSTOMIZING GLOBAL MARKETING[5]

Clearly, global marketing has pitfalls but it can also yield impressive advantages. The standardization of marketing mix elements and effective coordination and transfer of experience can exploit the company's products and ideas, minimize cost, and maximize the quality of the company's total offering.

It is a fundamental mistake to view global marketing as an either/or proposition. To apply the concept of global marketing and make it work, flexibility is absolutely essential. Managers must tailor their approach to fit their own products and markets and make their plan work.

Quelch and Hoff identified four dimensions of global marketing: business functions, products, marketing mix elements, and countries. They then compared the approach of Nestlé and Coke in adaptation versus standardization in each of these dimensions. Their findings are shown in Figures 17–2 and 17–3.

It is clear from these findings that Coke has proceeded much farther toward standardization than Nestlé. To conclude, however, that Coke is a global marketer and that Nestlé is not would be simplistic and would miss the point that each company must address its own unique product, market, and organizational circumstances in determining the extent and degree to which it can proceed along the path of standardization.

Figure 17–3 shows a global marketing planning matrix which is a framework for guiding a company in getting from where it is to where it would like to be. It is important to recognize that even in the case of Coca Cola which directs most of the elements of the marketing mix from its Atlanta headquarters, there is great emphasis on the role and importance of country marketing management to insure that critical elements of the marketing program are adapted to local market and competitive conditions. A pro-active headquarters organization and a pro-active global strategy do not guarantee success. To succeed a company must have a strong country marketing team.

PLANNING IN THE GLOBAL ENTERPRISE[6]

Hulbert and Brandt found that the annual operating plan (AOP) was the keystone for virtually all multinational firms. The exception was several Japanese companies that relied on a six-month planning cycle. Most companies combine their AOP with

[4]Ibid., p. 54.

[5]Adapted from John A. Queloh and Edward J. Hoff, "Customizing Global Marketing," *Harvard Business Review,* May–June 1986, pp. 59–68.

[6]This section draws heavily on James M. Hulbert and William K. Brandt, *Managing the Multinational Subsidiary* (New York: Holt, Rinehart and Winston, 1980), pp. 35–64.

Business functions		Adaptation		Standardization	
		Full	Partial	Partial	Full
Business functions	Research and development			Nestle	Coca-Cola
	Finance and accounting			Nestle	Coca-Cola
	Manufacturing		Nestle	Coca-Cola	
	Procurement	Nestle		Coca-Cola	
	Marketing		Nestle		Coca-Cola
Products	Low cultural grounding / Low economies or efficiencies				Nestle
	Low cultural grounding / High economies or efficiencies				
	High cultural grounding / Low economies or efficiencies		Nestle		
	High cultural grounding / High economies or efficiencies				
Marketing mix elements	Product design			Nestle	Coca-Cola
	Brand name			Nestle	Coca-Cola
	Product positioning		Nestle		Coca-Cola
	Packaging			Coca-Cola	
	Advertising theme		Nestle		Coca-Cola
	Pricing		Nestle	Coca-Cola	
	Advertising copy	Nestle			Coca-Cola
	Distribution	Nestle	Coca-Cola		
	Sales promotion	Nestle	Coca-Cola		
	Customer service	Nestle	Coca-Cola		
Countries Region 1	Country A			Nestle	Coca-Cola
	Country B			Nestle	Coca-Cola
Region 2	Country C		Nestle		Coca-Cola
	Country D		Nestle		Coca-Cola
	Country E	Nestle			Coca-Cola

■ Coca-Cola   ▨ Nestle

FIGURE 17–2 Global Marketing Planning Matrix: How Far To Go

SOURCE: John A. Quelch and Edward J. Hoff, "Customizing Global Marketing," *Harvard Business Review*, May–June 1986, p. 61.

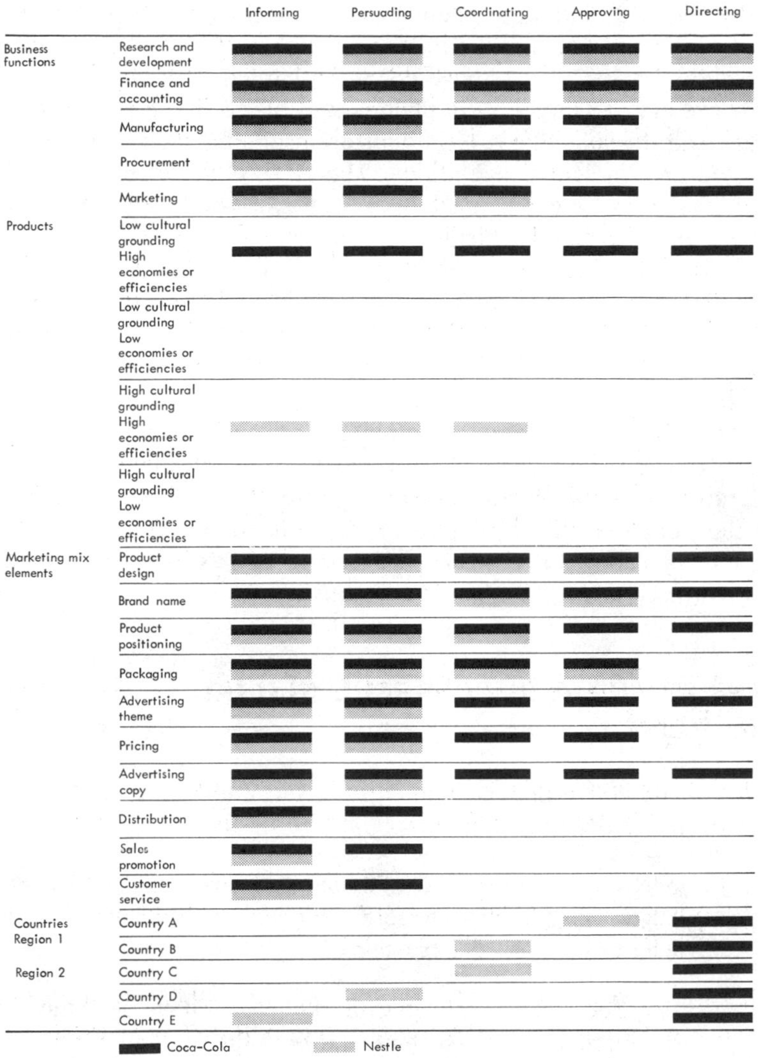

	Informing	Persuading	Coordinating	Approving	Directing
Business functions					
Research and development	▮	▮	▮	▮	▮
Finance and accounting	▮	▮	▮	▮	▮
Manufacturing	▮	▮	▮	▮	
Procurement	▮		▮	▮	
Marketing	▮	▮	▮	▮	▮
Products					
Low cultural grounding / High economies or efficiencies	▮	▮	▮	▮	▮
Low cultural grounding / Low economies or efficiencies					
High cultural grounding / High economies or efficiencies	▨	▨	▨		
High cultural grounding / Low economies or efficiencies					
Marketing mix elements					
Product design	▮	▮	▮	▮	▮
Brand name	▮	▮	▮	▮	▮
Product positioning	▮	▮	▮	▮	▮
Packaging	▮	▮	▮	▮	
Advertising theme	▮	▮	▮	▮	▮
Pricing	▮	▮	▮	▮	
Advertising copy	▮	▮	▮		▮
Distribution	▮	▮			
Sales promotion	▮	▮			
Customer service	▮	▮			
Countries					
Region 1					
Country A				▨	▮
Country B			▨		▮
Region 2					
Country C			▨		▮
Country D		▨			▮
Country E	▨				▮

▮ Coca-Cola   ▨ Nestle

FIGURE 17–3 Global Marketing Planning Matrix: How To Get There

SOURCE: Quelch and Hoff, "Customizing Global Marketing," p. 64.

601

a rolling forward planning system that covers a five-year period. Many companies did not appear to know the difference between a budget and a plan. As a result, their "plans" were 2- to 15-page documents filled with numbers and little else.

There are two locations of planning problems in the global company: the headquarters and the subsidiary. Headquarters problems include poor definition of planning roles and unclear expectations. The AOP is a cooperative effort, and a clear definition of roles and responsibilities is necessary to ensure that it is done well. Another headquarters problem is a short-run perspective and an insensitivity to foreign conditions. The subsidiary problems with planning include a cultural bias against planning in some countries, a local market myopia that arises when subsidiary management dedicates itself to furthering the growth and profit of the subsidiary at the expense of the broader interests of the worldwide company.

The purpose of planning is to create a design for action. It should be a major force for increasing the degree of integration and coordination in the global company. Hulbert and Brandt concluded that most of the problems with planning lie with people and not with planning systems. Effective global planning is possible only when the people in the subsidiaries and the headquarters recognize that each must play a part in a cooperative exercise that must be based on information and decisions inputs from the headquarters and the subsidiary.

REQUIREMENTS FOR A SUCCESSFUL GLOBAL MARKETING PLAN

The successful global plan is an integrated set of effective national marketing plans. Each national marketing plan must be based upon three types of information:

1. Knowledge of the market—especially of customers, competitors, and the government
2. Knowledge of the product—the formal product, its technology, and its core benefit
3. Knowledge of the marketing function

Information or knowledge about the market in itself must come from people who are assigned to that market. Normally, this is the staff of the local operating subsidiary. Product knowledge is closely associated with engineers and production managers. For most industrial products, knowledge becomes a very important part of the advertising and selling program for the product. For many consumer products, technical information is not important to the buyer and therefore need not necessarily be combined or associated with advertising and selling activities. The third major input of a successful marketing plan is knowledge of the marketing function, including the analytic and conceptual tools of marketing.

A global company must decide how it will obtain these three key types of knowledge on a global basis. It must also decide how it will assign responsibility for formulating a marketing plan. If plan formulation is assigned to national subsidiaries, the global headquarters must ensure that the subsidiary planners are fully informed on the technical and engineering characteristics of the product as well as being up to date in their functional skills. One of the ways of doing this is to involve head-quarters marketing staff specialists in the planning process so that they can ensure that the highest standard of product and functional knowledge is associated with the local marketing staff's market knowledge.

Thus the global plan is neither the product of the subsidiary nor the product of headquarters. It is neither "top-down" nor "bottom-up" but rather an interactive product that combines inputs from both the global and the local perspective. This balance is essential if the plan is to approximate the objective of global optimization as opposed to national suboptimization.

The global plan should be initiated by a global overview that attempts to assess the broad nature of opportunity and threat on a global basis and attempts to break down this assessment on a country-by-country basis with an indication of sales and earnings expectations for each country. These expectations are proposed by head-quarters as guidance to each country subsidiary for the formulation of country plans. Guidance, when properly utilized, should be nothing more than guidance. If a sub-sidiary concludes that headquarters guidance is unrealistic, it should openly challenge headquarters, and the challenge should produce a dialogue that searches for the realistic target.

After receiving guidance from headquarters, subsidiaries need to search for programs that in the context of the company's areas of operation will achieve the targets specified by the guidance. After preparing their plans, headquarters and subsidiaries come together to negotiate an agreement. Headquarters is seeking top performance from each subsidiary *and* the integration of its global plan. If a subsidiary is a supplier for home and third-country markets, production schedules and transfer prices must be agreed upon. If a subsidiary is to market a product produced elsewhere in the company, the sales and delivery plans must be coordinated. The subsidiary is seeking approval of a plan that it feels it can attain.

GROUPING WORLD MARKETS FOR PRODUCT PLANNING

The large number of countries in the world demands a simplified grouping of markets for planning purposes. Numerous approaches to grouping world markets have been undertaken, including grouping based on selected criteria. The most common group-ings using this method are geographic and linguistic (for example, Europe, the Amer-icas, Asia, and Africa or English-speaking countries that group the United States, the United Kingdom, Canada, Australia, South Africa, and so on in the same set). Another method of grouping is the use of analytical methods such as cluster and factor analysis that employ sophisticated statistical and computer techniques to form sets that maximize within-group similarities and between-group distances on multiple descriptor scales.[7]

[7]See, for example, Eugene D. Jaffe, *Grouping: A Strategy for International Marketing* (New York: American Management Association, 1974); and S. Prakash Sethi, "Comparative Cluster Analysis for World Markets," *Journal of Marketing Research*, Vol. 8 (August 1971), pp. 348–354.

Each company needs to come up with its own grouping for planning and operating purposes. Company-specific grouping needs to take into account not only the market characteristics but also the company characteristics. For General Electric, for example, there are several countries with multiproduct manufacturing affiliates. These countries are different from all other countries for GE because of these affiliates, and therefore they must be taken into account in both planning and operations. They do not exist in any other company and therefore cannot be part of a general approach to clustering.

The general criteria that should be a part of every company's grouping are market size, market accessibility, stage of market development, present and future prospects for growth (some companies are anxious to position themselves in growing markets and are willing to sacrifice immediate returns to be well positioned in growth markets), economic risk (a key question is whether or not the country will be in a position to permit companies to repatriate earnings and transfer funds; if a country is going to be in a permanent financial crisis, this condition will be a negative factor in the country's evaluation), and political risk.

Some companies have formed separate groups for planning and operating purposes. A geographic grouping makes sense for operating purposes because it cuts down on travel time for company executives. However, for planning purposes it may be desirable to group countries based on a criterion such as stage of economic development which may or may not have a relationship to geography.

Table 17–1 is a typology based on five criteria: market size, market accessibility (i.e., market vs. command economies), stage of market development, prospects for growth, and promise for future growth and development. The use of this table requires the categorization of countries according to their market accessibility and expected rate of future growth. Each company should define the terms "large," "medium," and "small," and the criteria for coding a country as promising vs. unpromising less developed. An example of a clearly unpromising country for most companies is Uganda: The political and economic chaos there is so great that it is virtually impossible to conduct a normal business. On the other hand, a country like Tanzania might be "unpromising" for some companies and "promising" for others.

PLANNING CONCEPTS

Competence Centers

A competence center is an organizational unit that is designated the lead business unit in the corporation for the guidance of the development of a new product, market, or technology or, in short, a new business. The mission of a competence center is to formulate and implement a global business strategy for a new business. A competence may be located anywhere in the world, and anywhere in the organization. The concept of a competence center is to identify the organization unit which is

TABLE 17–1 World Markets for Product Planning (in thousands of U.S. dollars)

Typology Category	LARGE-SCALE ECONOMIES		MEDIUM-SCALE ECONOMIES		SMALL-SCALE ECONOMIES		TOTAL		
	GNP	No.	GNP	No.	GNP	No.	GNP	No.	% of Total
1. Industrial countries									
a. Western market economies									
b. Eastern bloc planned economies									
2. Industrializing countries									
a. OPEC countries									
b. Other industrializing countries									
3. Promising less developed countries									
4. Unpromising less developed countries									
Total									

most *competent* to lead a company into a new area, as opposed to selection of a leadership group based upon a formula such as the rule that all new business direction should come from the home country management group.

An example of the application of this concept is the case of a U.S. based global auto parts company which decided to enter the auto tune-up service business with a franchise business model. This idea originated in a regional headquarters of the company, and was tested in a major Latin American country. The business was a big success in Latin America. After reviewing this success, top management of the company decided that the market for tune-up service represented a major opportunity for the company and designated the company's Latin American regional headquarters as the worldwide competence center for the business.

As the most advanced location in the company for the new business, the competence center assumes the role of worldwide product division for the new business. At some point in time and experience, this business group may be organizationally and physically relocated to strengthen its ability to lead and coordinate the business worldwide. Initially, however, the competence center is an existing team of experts in a country or region that understands a business and takes on responsibility for the globalization of the business from its existing location.

The basic concept underlying the competence center is that competence in a global company is globally dispersed. It can be a part of a global plan to develop product X in country Y and then to transfer country Y's experience directly to other markets without channeling it through a headquarter's intermediary.

Orientation and Global Marketing Planning

The basic orientation of management toward international business is an important influence on planning.[8] A management group that assumes that all markets are alike and that its major source of competence and ability is in the home market is going to pursue a basically ethnocentric approach to multinational marketing because its assumptions will lead it to this approach. Conversely, a management that assumes that each national market is unique and therefore unrelated to any other national market is going to pursue a polycentric approach to international marketing planning because its assumptions demand such an approach. We have argued that neither the ethnocentric nor the polycentric assumptions are applicable to today's global market environment and that the effective manager will pursue a synthesis of the approaches, which can be termed geocentric. The geocentric assumption is that there are major differences and important similarities among markets, and these similarities and differences must be recognized to develop an effective integrated and coordinated global marketing plan that maximizes the profitability of a worldwide marketing effort.

[8]Howard V. Perlmutter, "The Tortuous Evolution of the Multinational Corporation," *Columbia Journal of World Business*, January–February 1969, pp. 9–18.

SUMMARY

The global marketing plan integrates each element of the marketing mix into a program that focuses on target market opportunities. The development of an effective marketing plan requires inputs at every level of the organization from customers in each country to the overview of the staff at world headquarters. As companies evolve, they develop from plans based on a top down approach or plans based on a bottoms up approach to interactive plans that incorporate both the country and the headquarters perception of opportunity and threat.

DISCUSSION QUESTIONS

1. What kind of planning problems develop in the headquarters of a global company?
2. What are the problems in planning at the country or subsidiary level in a global company?
3. How would you advise a company manufacturing a line of construction equipment to group its market for planning purposes?

BIBLIOGRAPHY

Books

HULBERT, JAMES M., AND WILLIAM K. BRANDT. *Managing the Multinational Subsidiary.* New York: Holt, Rinehart and Winston, 1980.

PORTER, MICHAEL E. *Competition in Global Industries,* Boston: Harvard Business School Press, 1986.

PRAHALAD, C. K., AND YVES C. DOZ. *The Multinational Mission.* New York: The Free Press, 1987.

Articles

AYLMER, R. J. "Who Makes Marketing Decisions in the Multinational Firm?" *Journal of Marketing,* October 1970.

BERG, NORMAN. "Strategic Planning in Conglomerate Companies." *Harvard Business Review,* May–June 1965.

BRANDT, W. K., AND J. M. HULBERT. "Patterns of Communications in Multinational Corporations: An Empirical Study." *Journal of International Business Studies,* Spring 1976, pp. 57–64.

———, AND J. M. HULBERT. "Headquarters Guidance in Marketing Strategy in the Multinational Subsidiary." *Columbia Journal of World Business,* Winter 1977, pp. 7–14.

———, AND J. M. HULBERT. "Marketing Planning in the Multinational Subsidiary: Practices and Problems." *Journal of Marketing,* Summer 1980, pp. 7–15.

BUZZELL, ROBERT D. "Can You Standardize Multinational Marketing?" *Harvard Business Review,* November–December 1968.

CAIN, W. W. "International Planning: Mission Impossible?" *Columbia Journal of World Business,* July–August 1970.

CHAKRAVARTHY, BALAJI S., AND HOWARD V. PERLMUTTER. "Strategic Planning for a Global Business." *Columbia Journal of World Business,* Summer 1985, pp. 3–10.

FRANKO, LAWRENCE G. "Who Manages Multinational Enterprise?" *Columbia Journal of World Business,* Vol. 8 (Spring 1973), pp. 30–42.

GLUCK, FREDERICK W. "Strategic Planning in a New Key." *The McKinsey Quarterly,* Winter 1986, pp. 18–41.

HARRELL, G. D., AND R. O. KIEFER. "Multinational Strategic Market Portfolios." *MSU Business Topics,* Winter 1981, pp. 6–15.

KATZ, ABRAHAM. "Planning in the IBM Corporation." *Long-Range Planning,* June 1978, pp. 2–7.

KEEGAN, WARREN J. "Multinational Marketing: The Headquarters Role." *Columbia Journal of World Business,* January–February 1971.

———. "Strategic Market Planning: The Japanese Approach." *International Marketing Review,* Autumn 1983, pp. 5–15.

KOGUT, BRUCE. "Designing Global Strategies: Comparative and Competitive Value-Added Chains." *Sloan Management Review,* Summer 1985, pp. 15–28.

PERLMUTTER, HOWARD V. "The Tortuous Evolution of the Multinational Corporation." *Columbia Journal of World Business,* January–February 1969.

PRYOR, MILLARD H. "Planning in a Worldwide Business." *Harvard Business Review,* January–February 1965.

QUELCH, JOHN A. AND EDWARD J. HOFF. "Customizing Global Marketing." *Harvard Business Review,* May–June 1986, pp. 59–68.

SORENSON, RALPH Z., AND ULRICH E. WEICHMANN. "How Multinationals View Marketing Standardization." *Harvard Business Review,* May–June 1975, pp. 38–56.

WEICHMANN, ULRICH L. "Integrating Multinational Marketing Activities." *Columbia Journal of World Business,* Winter 1974, pp. 7–16.

POLAROID FRANCE, S.A.[1]

In July 1967, M. Jacques Dumon, general manager of Polaroid France, S.A., was preparing a preliminary marketing plan for 1968. M. Dumon was scheduled to present his proposals to the marketing executives at the headquarters office of the American parent firm, Polaroid Corporation, in September. Following this review, a final version of the plan would be adopted as a basis for Polaroid's operations in France during the forthcoming year.

In preparing his recommendations for 1968, M. Dumon was especially concerned with problems of pricing and promotion for the Model 20 "Swinger" camera. The Swinger had been introduced in France during the fall of 1966 and was the first Polaroid Land Camera available to French consumers at a retail price under NF 300.[2] Sales of the Swinger

[1]This case was written with the cooperation of Polaroid Corporation and Polaroid France (S.A.), by Professor Robert D. Buzzel of the Harvard Business School with the assistance of M. Jean-Louis Lecocq of the Institut Europeen d'Administration des Affaires (INSEAD). Copyright © 1968 jointly by the President and Fellows of Harvard College and the Institut Europeen d'Administration des Affaires (INSEAD). Used with permission.

[2]New franc = U.S.$.20 (approx.) in 1967.

during 1966 and early 1967 had not reached expected levels, and M. Dumon was aware that the basic attitude of headquarters management toward overseas operations in 1968 was cautious, because Polaroid's unconsolidated foreign subsidiaries had incurred a combined loss of $907,000 in 1966. He recognized, therefore, that all proposals for 1968 would be subject to extremely careful scrutiny.

COMPANY BACKGROUND

Polaroid Corporation, with headquarters in Cambridge, Massachusetts, produced a wide line of photographic equipment, polarizing products, and X-ray products. Total 1966 sales in the United States amounted to $316.5 million, more than three times the amount of business done in 1962. Worldwide sales in 1966, including Polaroid's 13 subsidiaries, totaled $363 million. A summary of sales and profits for the period 1950–1966 is given in Table 1.

The company was founded in 1937 by Dr. Edwin H. Land to produce polarizing products, including sunglasses, photographic filters, and glare-free lamps. By 1941, sales had reached $1 million. Following World War II, Dr. Land developed a new method for developing and printing photographs. The Polaroid Land Camera was announced in 1947, and the first models were sold in November 1948. The Polaroid Land Camera utilized a "one-step" process, in contrast with the "three-step" process required for conventional photography. In conventional still photography, the sequence involved in producing a black-and-white picture is as follows:

TABLE 1 Sales and Net Earnings of Polaroid Corporation in the United States and Canada, 1950–1966 (in thousands of dollars)

Year	SALES United States Only	SALES United States and Canada	NET EARNINGS United States Only	NET EARNINGS United States and Canada
1950	N.A.	$ 6,390	N.A.	$ 726
1951	N.A.	9,259	N.A.	512
1952	N.A.	13,393	N.A.	597
1953	N.A.	26,034	N.A.	1,415
1954	N.A.	23,500	N.A.	1,153
1955	N.A.	26,421	N.A.	2,402
1956	N.A.	34,464	N.A.	3,667
1957	N.A.	48,043	N.A.	5,355
1958	N.A.	65,271	N.A.	7,211
1959	$ 89,487	89,919	$10,750	10,743
1960	98,734	99,446	8,838	8,813
1961	100,562	101,478	8,008	8,111
1962	102,589	103,738	9,872	9,965
1963	122,333	123,459	11,078	11,218
1964	138,077	139,351	18,105	18,323
1965	202,228	204,003	28,872	29,114
1966	316,551	322,399	47,594	47,963

N.A.—Not available.

Source: Company annual reports.

1. A photosensitive material ("film") is exposed to light. The light converts grains of silver bromide into specks of silver, the amount of silver deposited in a given area depending on the amount of light reaching that area.

2. The film is developed by immersing it in a chemical solution that converts the exposed grains into black silver. The unexposed grains are then dissolved with a second solution and washed away. This yields a finished "negative" in which all of the natural tones are reversed (i.e., black appears as white, and vice versa).

3. The negative is placed in contact with a sheet of light-sensitive paper and exposed to light. The developing process is then repeated to produce a finished "positive" print.

The second and third steps of conventional photography require that exposed film be processed in a commercial laboratory or in a home "darkroom." For the vast majority of amateur photographers, this means a delay of several days between taking a picture and receiving a finished print of it.

The technique developed by Dr. Land yielded finished prints from the *camera itself,* with no delay for processing. Basic discoveries in photographic chemistry, and new materials based on these discoveries, permitted the entire process to be completed in 60 seconds (later, in 10 seconds) with no equipment other than the camera and film.

The Polaroid Land Camera was commercially successful almost from the beginning. In 1949, sales of cameras and film amounted to over $5 million.

PRODUCT LINE

Between 1949 and 1964, research and development activities at Polaroid provided the basis for a continuous improvement and diversification of Polaroid's camera product line.

The earliest versions of the Polaroid Land Camera produced sepia-colored prints of a quality inferior to that of conventional films. Subsequent improvements in the film permitted clear, black-and-white photographs and, beginning in 1963, color pictures as well. Another major innovation in 1963 was the introduction of the Automatic 100 Land Camera. The Model 100 utilized a film "pack" rather than the film roll that had been used in all earlier Polaroid cameras. With a film pack, the camera could be loaded more easily and quickly, since it was not necessary to wind the film around a series of rollers. Instead, the user simply opened the camera, inserted the pack, and closed the camera. In addition to the pack-loading feature, the Model 100 incorporated several other improvements over the earlier models. It weighed less than earlier models and had a better exposure control.

Following the introduction of the Model 100, Polaroid introduced three lower-priced pack cameras: the Model 101 in 1964 and Models 103 and 104 in 1965. In early 1967, a redesigned line of five pack cameras was introduced. Thus, in mid-1967, the models offered and their suggested retail prices in the United States were as follows:

Model 250	$159.95
Model 240	124.95
Model 230	94.95
Model 220	69.95
Model 210	49.95

All these cameras produced both black-and-white and color photographs in $3\frac{1}{4}'' \times 4\frac{1}{4}''$ format, and all had electric eye mechanisms for automatic exposure control. The main differences among the various models were in lens qualities and in materials. For example, the Model 250 features a Zeiss rangefinderviewfinder, a three-piece precision lens, an all-metal body, and a leather carrying strap. The Model 210 had a plastic body, a nylon strap, a less expensive focusing system, and a two-piece lens and was not designed to accommodate the accessories (such as a portrait lens) that could be employed with the higher-priced models.

In late 1965, Polaroid introduced the Model 20 "Swinger" Land Camera in the United States.[3] The Swinger was a roll-film camera, capable of taking black-and-white photos only, in a $2\frac{1}{4}'' \times 3\frac{1}{4}''$ format and with a 15-second development time. It was made of white plastic; the suggested retail price, which was emphasized in national advertising, was $19.95. The introduction of the Swinger enabled Polaroid to compete for the first time in the large-volume market for inexpensive cameras; around three-fourths of all still cameras purchased each year sold for less than $50 at retail. Thus, the launching of the Swinger was a major contributing factor in the dramatic growth of the company's sales during 1965 and 1966. (See Table 1.) According to company reports, by "sometime in 1967" over 5 million Swinger cameras had been sold by Polaroid.

All Polaroid's cameras were produced for the company by outside contractors. The company itself manufactured black-and-white and color film rolls (for pre-1963 cameras), film packs for pack cameras, and film rolls for the Swinger.

In addition to amateur cameras and film, Polaroid produced one camera (the Model 180) for professional photographers and highly skilled amateurs, as well as several different types of industrial photographic equipment and supplies. Special-purpose industrial products included a system for producing identification cards and badges, X-ray equipment and film, and the MP-3 Industrial View Land Camera, designed for such applications as photomicrography.

Polaroid Corporation did not publish sales figures for individual products. According to the company's annual reports, photographic products accounted for between 93 and 97 percent of sales during the 1950s and 1960s. The remaining 3 to 7 percent of total volume was derived from sunglasses, polarizers, and other nonphotographic products. Trade sources estimated that cameras represented about 55 to 60 percent of Polaroid's sales volume in the mid-1950s and around 40 percent in the mid-1960s.

THE U.S. CAMERA MARKET

The market for still cameras in the United States expanded dramatically during the early 1960s. According to trade estimates, some 14 million still cameras were sold in 1966, three times as many as in 1960. Estimates of total industry sales and of Polaroid's market share (in units) were as shown in Table 2.[4]

According to trade estimates, Polaroid camera sales in 1966 represented approximately 50 percent of the total *dollar value* of U.S. retail camera sales.

---

[3]The name "Swinger" was chosen so as to emphasize the appeal of the new camera to teenagers and young adults. The word "Swinger," in American slang, designated a youthful and exciting person. Presumably this usage was related to the much older word "swing," a popular type of jazz music in the 1930s and 1940s. Because of the worldwide popularity of this kind of music, the word "swing" had essentially the same meaning (and pronunciation) through Western Europe as in the United States. The term "Swinger" was, however, strictly American.

[4]Industry sales estimates published in annual statistical reports, prepared by Augustus Wolfman of *Modern Photography* and *Photo Dealer* magazines; Polaroid market share estimates from various trade sources; for 1964, from Duncan M. Payne, *The European Operations of the Eastman Kodak Company,* Institut d'Etudes Européenes de Geneve, 1967, p. 28.

TABLE 2 Total Industry Still Camera Sales and Polaroid's Market Share, Selected Years 1954–1966

YEAR	INDUSTRY SALES (millions of units)	POLAROID MARKET SHARE (%)
1954	4.5	4–5%
1959	4.9	—
1960	4.6	8
1962	5.3	—
1964	8.4	11
1965	11.0	—
1966	14.0	30–35

The rapid growth of the camera market was due, in the opinion of industry observers, to rising levels of consumer income and to the introduction of new products by Polaroid and by the Eastman Kodak Company. As described in the preceding section, Polaroid had introduced a series of new models in 1963, 1964, and 1965 at progressively lower prices and with various improvements in operating features.

In 1963, Kodak had introduced its new line of "Instamatic" cameras. Instamatic cameras, like Polaroid's pack film used rolls in earlier models. Instamatic cameras were designed to use 35mm film that was enclosed in a special cartridge produced only by Kodak. Thus, although Kodak licensed other companies to manufacture cameras using Instamatic film, it was the only source of film for all such cameras.

Kodak's own line of Instamatic cameras included simple, fixed-focus models selling at retail for around $12 and more sophisticated models priced as high as $100. Thus, Instamatics competed in virtually all price segments of the camera market, except the under-$10 category. According to trade estimates, Instamatics accounted for around a third of all still cameras sold in the United States in 1964 and 1965.

Still cameras were purchased primarily by "amateur" users for personal recreational use. In 1966, 70 to 75 percent of all U.S. households owned one or more still cameras. Some cameras, and a significant proportion of all film, were bought by business, institutional, and governmental users for use in research, sales promotion, record keeping, and so on. The principal objective of Polaroid's marketing programs was, however, the sale of Polaroid Land Cameras to household consumers.

Household consumers used several different types of cameras, ranging from very simple, inexpensive "box" cameras up to very complex 35mm instruments. According to Polaroid estimates, 35mm cameras (exclusive of Instamatics) represented only about 5 to 7 percent of total camera purchases in 1965. In terms of retail price categories, around 15 percent of all cameras were sold at retail prices under $10, between 60 and 65 percent were priced between $10 and $49, and 20 percent to 25 percent cost $50 or more. Nearly half of all cameras were for the purchasers' own use, over 40 percent were purchased as gifts, and almost 10 percent were obtained as prizes, premiums, or in return for trading stamps.

Because of the importance of gift-giving, camera sales were highly seasonal. November and December accounted for over 50 percent of total annual retail sales. The second most important selling season, May–July, accounted for nearly one-fourth of annual sales.

Up to 1963, the dominant type of customer for still cameras costing over $10 was the relatively affluent family with small children. The introduction of the Instamatics, the Swinger, and the relatively inexpensive Models 104 and 210 pack cameras resulted in a substantial broadening of the household market. The estimated distribution of purchasers by income groups and age groups in 1965–1966 was as shown in Table 3.

TABLE 3   Estimated Distribution of Camera Purchasers by Age Group, 1965–1966

Income Group	PURCHASERS OF			
	All Still Cameras	Polaroid Pack Cameras	Polaroid Swingers	All U.S. Households
Under $3,000	4%	1%	3%	17%
$ 3,000–$4,999	11	9	20	18
5,000– 6,999	21	16	—	20
7,000– 9,999	31	31	38	26
10,000 or more	34	43	39	19
Age of Principal User				All U.S. Individuals
19 or younger	30%	23%	26%	22%
20–49 years	53	63	65	50
50 years or more	16	14	9	28

POLAROID MARKETING IN THE U.S.A.

Polaroid had no direct competition in the instant photography field. Although the patents on the original version of the Polaroid Land Camera had expired in 1965, Polaroid still held some 750 unexpired patents on various improvements in film chemistry and camera design that had been developed during the 1950s and 1960s. The company's products were, however, in active competition with many conventional types of cameras and films.

POLAROID ADVERTISING

At the time of its introduction in 1948, the first Polaroid Land Camera was a radical product innovation in photography. According to *Fortune* magazine,[5]

Land's revolution was at first derided by all the experts . . . [including] virtually every camera

[5]Francis Bello, "The Magic That Made Polaroid," *Fortune*, April 1959.

dealer in the country, every "advanced" amateur photographer, and nearly everyone on Wall Street.

To overcome the skepticism of consumers and dealers, Polaroid placed considerable emphasis on national advertising. According to trade estimates, the company's advertising expenditures increased during the 1950s and 1960s as shown in Table 4.[6]

Especially during the introductory phases of Polaroid marketing, the Land Camera lent itself ideally to the medium of television, where the method of operation and its results could be demonstrated. The company was among the first major sponsors of "big-time" network television programs in the 1950s, such as the Garry Moore and Perry Como music-variety shows. Advertising trade publications estimated that around 45 percent of Polaroid's total advertising budget was devoted to network television in the mid-1960s, about 30 percent to magazines, and less than 5 percent to newspapers.

[6]Estimates by *Advertising Age* and other trade sources.

TABLE 4 Polaroid's Advertising Expenditures, Selected Years 1954–1966

YEAR	ESTIMATED ADVERTISING EXPENDITURES	
1954	$ 1,700,000	
1957	3,000,000	
1958	4,000,000	
1960	7,500,000	
1963	8,000,000 ⎱	(color film and pack
1964	8,500,000 ⎰	cameras introduced)
1965	12,000,000	(Swinger introduced)
1966	18,000,000	

Early Polaroid advertising in the United States was designed to acquaint consumers with the basic idea of instant photography. An illustrative advertisement from the mid-1950s is shown in Figure 1. Later, after the great majority of prospective buyers were familiar with the concept of "a picture in a minute," the company's advertising efforts were devoted to announcements of successive changes in product features, such as color film and pack-loading cameras, and to publicizing the availability of lower-priced cameras. An example of a 1966 Swinger advertisement is given in Figure 2.

DISTRIBUTION AND PRICING

In the United States, Polaroid sold its cameras and film directly to around 15,000 retailers. Pack cameras were sold primarily by specialty photographic stores, department stores, and general merchandise "discount" stores. Swinger cameras and Polaroid films were carried by a greater number and variety of outlets, including many drugstores. Sales were made to many of the smaller outlets via wholesalers, but the bulk of Polaroid sales was made directly to stores and to buying offices of chain and mail-order firms.

Polaroid Corporation established "suggested" retail prices for cameras and film, but there were no legal or other restrictions on the freedom of dealers to set their own resale prices. The suggested retail prices provided gross margins for the retailers of around $33\frac{1}{3}$ percent on the Model 250, 28 percent on the Model 210, $33\frac{1}{3}$ percent on the Swinger, and $33\frac{1}{3}$ percent on pack films. Because Polaroid Land Cameras were regarded by the larger retailers as attractive products to feature in "discount" promotions, the prevailing retail prices were often well below suggested levels. In mid-1967, consumers in large metropolitan areas could buy the Model 250 at a discount of around $129.95, the Model 210 for around $39.95, and the Swinger for as little as $14.00. The smaller "conventional" photographic stores sold Polaroid cameras and films at lesser discounts and, often, at full list price. Polaroid films were also often sold at prices significantly below the suggested or list figures. (See Table 5.)

Discounting by retailers was also common in the sale of competing cameras. Some of the larger and more aggressive discount stores sold cameras at prices very slightly above cost, and the smaller conventional stores found it very difficult to compete with such outlets. Partly for this reason, a substantial

How to take a picture 1 minute and see it the next! Today's Polaroid Land Camera is a magnificent photographic instrument that not only takes beautiful pictures — but develops and prints them as well. With this camera in your hands, you are a magician, who can produce a finished print in 60 seconds. You are a professional photographer, fully equipped to produce expert pictures — clear, sharp, lasting black and white prints — on the spot. Whether you own several cameras or have never even owned one, you will have to own a Polaroid Land Camera. Ask your dealer to show you this remarkable instrument. There are three to choose from, including a new smaller, lower-priced model. *the amazing* **POLAROID** *Land* **CAMERA**

FIGURE 1 **Magazine Advertisement for Polaroid Land Camera—United States, Mid-1950s**

proportion of total retail camera sales were made by a relatively small number of dealers. For example, 40 percent of Polaroid's total sales were accounted for by 10 percent of its total number of sales accounts, and 60 per-cent of total sales by 20 percent of the accounts.

Sales were made to dealers by Polaroid's field sales force of some 55 sales representatives. The sales reps were responsible

FIGURE 2   Magazine Advertisement for Swinger Camera—United States, 1966

for calling on dealers periodically, setting up displays in the stores, training retail salespersons, assisting dealers in planning retail advertising of Polaroid products, and introducing new products. From time to time, the sales representatives conducted special promotional campaigns, such as used camera trade-in campaigns. For these programs, Polaroid would provide display and advertising materials to the dealers and the salespeople would assist them in promoting the sale of new Polaroid cameras via special trade-in allowances on used Polaroid cameras.

The frequency of sales calls depended

TABLE 5   Retail versus Discounted Polaroid Film Prices, Mid-1967

		RETAIL PRICE	
	Film Type	Suggested	Discount Price
Type 107	Black-and-white pack	$2.85	$1.99–2.49
Type 108	Color pack	5.39	3.99–4.99
Type 20	Black-and-white Swinger	2.10	1.49–1.79

on a dealer's size and location. Small dealers located in remote areas were visited only once every four to six months. Large dealers located in major metropolitan areas were visited weekly. Dealers' orders were almost always placed by telephone or mailed to one of Polaroid's six regional warehouses.

Polaroid salespeople were compensated on a salary basis. A typical sales territory included about 300 regular dealers, along with wholesalers and other types of accounts.

POLAROID OVERSEAS OPERATIONS

Up to 1964, Polaroid's sales outside the United States and Canada were relatively small. Cameras and film were exported from the United States and were subject to the high tariffs that most countries imposed on photographic products. As a result, prices of Polaroid products were so high as to make them virtually luxury items.

Beginning in 1965, Polaroid undertook a more aggressive program of developing international markets. Mr. Stanford Calderwood, marketing vice president of Polaroid, commented on this development at an international distributors' meeting in September 1966:

In 1965, things began to change somewhat and the international curve began perking up as we introduced the Models 103 and 104. . . . In 1966, international sales began to climb very sharply be-cause of the introduction of the Swinger. It is our goal—and we think it is an achievable goal—that in the next decade we can make the international business grow so it will be equal in size to the U.S.A. total.[7]

According to the company's annual reports, sales to dealers by Polaroid's overseas subsidiaries in 1966 amounted to $36 million, compared with $18.2 million in 1965. Beginning in 1965, the company had adopted a policy of pricing cameras and film "as if they were being made behind the Common Market and Commonwealth tariff barriers." Also in 1965, Polaroid established manufacturing facilities for Swinger film at Enschede, The Netherlands, and at the Vale of Leven, Scotland. Swinger camera production in the United Kingdom commenced in late 1965 at a plant set up by one of Polaroid's American camera suppliers.

Along with the establishment of manufacturing facilities, Polaroid embarked on a program designed to stimulate increased demand for its products overseas. Margins were adjusted downward to bring prices to the foreign consumer more in line with those to U.S. consumers. . . . Greatly expanded magazine and newspaper advertising, as well as commercial television where available, carried the Polaroid instant-picture message in many languages.[8]

[7]*Intercom,* Polaroid International Communique, October 1966.

[8]Polaroid *1966 Annual Report,* p. 13.

The costs of the expanded marketing program, coupled with delays in providing Swinger cameras from the new overseas factory, contributed to an operating loss of $907,000 by Polaroid's unconsolidated subsidiaries (excluding Canada) in 1966.

A portion of Polaroid's organization for international marketing, showing the activities affecting operations in Europe, is depicted in Figure 3. As shown, the general managers of the European subsidiary companies reported to a European coordinator, located at the Polaroid international headquarters in Amsterdam, who in turn reported to Polaroid's vice president of sales, Mr. Thomas Wyman. Mr. Wyman and his assistant manager for international sales also had frequent contact with the subsidiary managers by mail and through periodic visits.

Advertising policies were established by the company's vice president of advertising, Mr. Peter Wensberg, in consultation with representatives of Doyle Dane Bernbach, the company's advertising agency. The agency was also charged with directing the work of its subsidiary and affiliate agencies in other countries. Thus, advertising campaigns for European markets were developed by the overseas agencies within broad guidelines established by Mr. Wyman and by DDB-New York. Mr. Wensberg stated that "we are great believers in the power of advertising," and that "much of the success of our advertising efforts over the years has been due to the fact that we have what we feel is the world's best advertising agency—Doyle Dane Bernbach, in New York."

INTERNATIONAL PLANNING AND CONTROL

During 1965, Polaroid's marketing executives had developed a new planning and control system for overseas marketing operations. This system included a standardized format

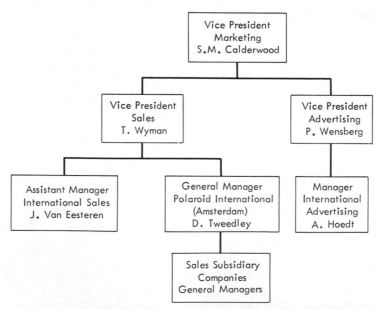

FIGURE 3 Partial Organization Chart—European Marketing Activities, 1967

for financial accounting, standardized monthly performance reports, and annual operating plans for each subsidiary company. The system required that an annual operating plan be developed and submitted to Cambridge each fall, covering proposed operations during the next calendar year. The format of the plan called for

1. A review of market conditions, including trends in total industry sales, competitive developments, distribution, and changes in consumer buying habits
2. A statement of objectives for the year, expressed in concrete terms (e.g., "increase distribution by adding at least 20 more department stores and 100 more photographic stores")
3. A summary of planned marketing activities, including
   a. Sales force
   b. Advertising budget and media
   c. Publicity
   d. Market research
   e. Customer service
4. Estimated operating results for the year, including monthly sales forecasts for each major product, operating expenses, estimated profits, and cash flow.

Monthly reports to Cambridge indicated actual results in comparison with the plan, and significant discrepancies were explained via accompanying correspondence.

POLAROID FRANCE, S.A.

Polaroid France, S.A., was established in November 1961 as a wholly owned subsidiary of Polaroid Corporation. Up to 1964, sales in France were relatively small. With the introduction of the Models 103 and 104 cameras

in 1964 and 1965, followed by the Swinger in late 1966, sales of Polaroid France increased rapidly.

M. Dumon became general manager of Polaroid France early in 1966. During 1966, he was responsible for making preparations for the introduction of the Swinger, which took place in September. The addition of the Swinger involved a significant expansion of sales volume, advertising and promotional efforts, and retail distribution for Polaroid France. Consequently, M. Dumon had devoted most of his efforts during 1966 to discussions with the major advertising media, hiring additional personnel, and working with retailers to obtain distribution and promotional support for the new camera.

In mid-1967, Polaroid France employed 86 persons. The company's headquarters office and warehouse were located at Colombes, a suburb of Paris. Reporting to M. Dumon were the sales manager, the advertising manager, and the manager of administration. An organization chart is given in Figure 4.

THE FRENCH CAMERA MARKET

The market for still cameras in France was about one-tenth as large as that in the United States. According to estimates by Polaroid's marketing research department, total camera sales to household and business users in France had increased slowly since 1963, as shown in Table 6.

In comparison with the U.S. market, cameras selling for less than NF50 ($10) comprised a larger proportion of total camera sales—around one-third. These inexpensive cameras were primarily simple, fixed-focus "box" cameras, many of which were imported. In France and elsewhere in Europe, Kodak offered less expensive models in the

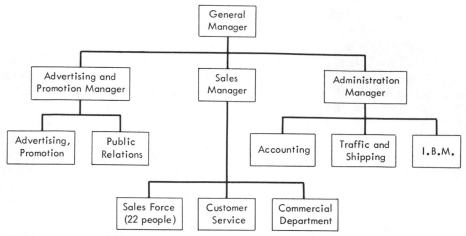

FIGURE 4   Organization Chart, 1967

Instamatic line than those available in the U.S. According to one source, Kodak sales represented about half of the French camera market in 1965 and 1966.

Altogether, there were some 11,000 retail outlets for cameras in France.[9] Specialty photographic stores sold around three-fourths of all still cameras bought by French household consumers. Other important types of outlets included department stores (5 percent to 10 percent of total sales), supermarkets (5 percent), and opticians (2 percent). There were fewer general merchandise discount retailers in France than in the United States, and this type of outlet sold only 1 to 2 percent of all still cameras.[10] Some of the larger photo retailers were aggressive discounters, however, especially in the Paris metropolitan area. The large department stores, such as Galeries Lafayette and Au Printemps, also sold cameras at substantial discounts from suggested

[9]Payne, *European Operations of the Eastman Kodak Company*, p. 98.

[10]Some French "supermarkets" carried diversified lines of general merchandise in addition to food, however, and were essentially combinations of U.S. food supermarket and discount-department store types of outlets.

retail prices. Outside Paris, smaller conventional photo stores dominated the retailing scene. These smaller stores typically had markups on photographic products of 25 percent to 30 percent, while the larger stores operated on margins of around 20 percent. As in the United States, the dealers earned their highest margins on film processing (35 to 40 percent).

Market studies by Polaroid indicated that about one-third of total camera sales were made in Paris, although only 17 percent of the population lived in the region. An additional 15 percent of camera sales were accounted for by other major cities (population over 100,000).

TABLE 6   Still Camera Sales in France, 1963–1966 (in thousands of units)

YEAR	TOTAL	OVER $50	UNDER $10
1963	1,200	210	390
1964	1,350	220	390
1965	1,300	220	400
1966	1,350	230	420

In France, about a third of all still cameras were purchased to be given as gifts. This compared with a gift proportion of nearly half in the United States. Because gift-giving played a lesser role in the market, Christmas season sales naturally represented a smaller percentage of annual industry volume than in the United States. The peak selling season in France was during the spring and summer: May, June, and July accounted for more than half of annual camera sales, and November–December represented less than 15 percent.

According to Polaroid estimates, sales of Kodak Instamatic cameras amounted to over a fourth of the French market; 35mm cameras, including the Agfa "Rapid" line manufactured in West Germany and designed to compete with Instamatics, had a market share of over 20 percent.

Camera purchases were relatively concentrated in the higher income groups. (See Table 7.) About two-thirds of all French camera users were men. Among both men and women, persons under 24 years of age accounted for 34 percent of all camera users.

Among Polaroid Swinger buyers, nearly 20 percent were under 21 years of age, and another 20 percent were between 21 and 30. The corresponding figures for all cameras selling for less than NF100 were 30 percent and 35 percent.

POLAROID MARKETING IN FRANCE

Prior to the introduction of the Models 103 and 104 pack cameras, Polaroid products were distributed in France on a limited scale. In 1963, only around 400 outlets carried Polaroid cameras. During 1965 and 1966, the marketing program had undergone a complete transformation. A broadened product line, lower prices, increased distribution, and more aggressive promotion all contributed to the company's growth.

DISTRIBUTION AND SALES FORCE

The number of outlets handling Polaroid products increased steadily from 1,300 in 1964, to 1,600 in 1965, and 3,400 in 1967. By mid-1967, M. Dumon estimated that Polaroid accounts represented around two-thirds of total retail camera sales among all photographic specialty stores and 60 percent in the department store category. The largest 15 percent of Polaroid's accounts represented about 80 percent of the company's total sales.

Polaroid's sales force, which consisted of 10 people in mid-1966, had grown to 22 by July 1967. On average, each salesperson made eight calls per day. The salespeople were compensated on a straight salary basis. They

TABLE 7 Distribution of Camera Purchases by Income Group

Income Group	All Still Camera Buyers	All French Individuals Over 15 Years	POLAROID BUYERS	
			Pack	Swinger
Under NF6,000	3%	17%	1%	1%
NF 6,001–8,400	15	17		
8,401–12,000	31	26	1	1
12,001–24,000	38	30	4	9
Over 24,000	19	11	94	89

called on the dealers, took orders, arranged for in-store promotions of Polaroid cameras and handled dealer problems relating to camera repairs, deliveries, and so on.

PRICING

While Polaroid Corporation did not release cost figures for individual products, Polaroid France's gross margin on total sales (cameras and film) was approximately 30 percent. (See Table 8.)

According to industry sources, Polaroid France's gross margin on the Swinger was probably slightly less than that earned on other cameras. These sources also indicated that gross margins on cameras were typically about twice what they were on film. If Polaroid was typical of the French camera industry, these sources added, it probably sold about 8 rolls of film for each camera during the first year in the user's hands.

Experience with other cameras suggested that the Swinger would probably have a useful life of five to six years.

Because cameras were easily shipped from one country to another, Polaroid felt that it was essential to coordinate prices on an international level. Consequently, all selling prices for Polaroid France were prescribed within narrow limits by management in Cambridge. Following the changes in Polaroid's marketing policies in 1965, prices to dealers were reduced substantially. The price paid by a dealer depended on quantities ordered. On the average, dealer costs of Polaroid pack cameras and film provided gross profits for the retailer of about 33 percent if they were resold at full list price. Typical retail selling prices for Polaroid cameras and film and for major competing products in the United States and France are shown in Table 9. These prices were from 15 to 20 percent below suggested retail prices.

When the Swinger was introduced, it was believed that small dealers would be reluctant to handle it, unless there were some kind of guarantee of obtaining adequate margins. Resale price maintenance was permitted in France only when specifically authorized. Polaroid applied for, and received, permission to establish a retail price of NF99 ($19.90) for the Swinger; under French law, dealers were permitted to deviate from this price by up to 5 percent, and the prevailing

TABLE 8 Condensed Operating Statement and Unit Sales of Cameras, 1966–1967 (in thousands of dollars)

	1966 ACTUAL	1967 ORIGINAL PLAN	1967 REVISED ESTIMATE
Net sales	$ 5,640	$ 8,800	$ 7,300
Cost of goods sold	3,950	6,170	5,150
Gross margin	$ 1,690	$ 2,630	$ 2,150
Advertising and promotion costs	800	750	630
Selling costs	150	370	370
General and administrative costs	1,000	850	750
Operating profit	($ 260)	$ 660	$ 400
Unit Sales			
Pack cameras	25,000	30,000	25,000
Swinger cameras	85,000	115,000	95,000

TABLE 9 Retail Prices of Polaroid Cameras and Film of Major Competing Products in the United States and France, 1967

Camera Model or Film Type	UNITED STATES Typical Prices	FRANCE* Typical Prices	FRANCE* Lowest Discount Prices
Cameras			
Polaroid Swinger	$17.00	—	$19.08
Polaroid Model 104	40.00	$70.04	67.40
Kodak Instamatic 104	13.50	15.00	—
Films			
Polaroid Type 20	1.77	2.01	—
Pack film—color	4.49	5.03	—
Pack film—black and white	2.09	2.48	—
Kodak Instamatic Color film			
Per pack (12 prints)	1.24	.97	—
Per finished print	.44	.45	—

*French prices include taxes on "value added" of approximately 20 percent of retail price.

price in larger retail outlets was quickly established at NF94. The price paid by the dealer to Polaroid was NF84.

ADVERTISING AND PROMOTION

During 1966, Polaroid France spent some $600,000 on advertising, of which slightly over half was devoted to the introduction of the Swinger. The budget for 1967 was somewhat lower at around $550,000. About 40 percent of the total was devoted to magazines, 50 percent to newspapers, and 10 percent to cinema advertising.[11]

Because Polaroid cameras were much less well known in France than in the United States, a major objective of Polaroid advertising was to increase consumers' awareness and understanding of the "instant picture" idea. According to studies by the company's marketing research department, in early 1966

[11]Total advertising expenditures by all photographic manufacturers in France were estimated at $1.8 million in 1965.

fewer than 5 percent of French consumers demonstrated "proved awareness" of Polaroid Land Cameras, and the level of awareness had increased only slightly by early 1967. A consumer was classified as having "proved awareness" if he or she (1) indicated knowledge of the Polaroid brand name *and* (2) knew of the instant picture feature. The French level of awareness compared with an estimated 85 percent in the United States, 70 percent in Canada, 15 percent in Germany, and 26 percent in the United Kingdom. An illustrative Swinger advertisement from the 1966 introductory campaign is shown in Figure 5.

A major obstacle to increasing awareness of Polaroid was the fact that commercial television was not available in France. Polaroid marketing executives believed that television had been a major factor in the growth of Polaroid sales in the United States, and in other countries where commercial television was available—such as West Germany and the United Kingdom—it was used extensively.

FIGURE 5 Advertisement for the Polaroid Swinger (*Tele 7 Jours* magazine, September 1966)

To demonstrate the concept of instant photography to French consumers, Polaroid placed considerable reliance on in-store sales demonstrations. The company encouraged dealers to perform demonstrations by offering a free roll or pack of film (8 exposures) for each 14 demonstration photos taken by the dealer. To qualify for this partial reimbursement, the retailer had to send the negative portions of 14 film exposures to the company.

In-store sales demonstrations were also conducted by Polaroid demonstrators. These demonstrators, who were paid NF35 per day, visited retail stores on prearranged schedules to conduct demonstrations of Polaroid cameras before groups of potential customers. Polaroid France provided the films for the demonstrations, provided that the dealer ordered cameras in advance. For example, if the dealer ordered 15 pack cameras, the company provided 6 packs of black-and-white film and 3 packs of color film for use in the demonstrations.

Total expenditures for promotion in 1966 amounted to $200,000, and approximately the same amount was budgeted for 1967. Polaroid marketing executives were not satisfied with the dealers' participation in the promotion program. Mr. Wyman, vice president of sales of Polaroid Corporation, wrote to M. Dumon in May 1967, stating that

it appears that the dealer is not demonstrating cameras frequently and as skillfully as we should like.

1966–1967 RESULTS AND 1968 PROSPECTS

Sales and profits of Polaroid France during 1966 and the first half of 1967 had not lived up to expectations. As shown in Table 8, a net loss was incurred in 1966. Moreover, by July it was apparent to M. Dumon and to the Polaroid headquarters marketing staff that the goals set for 1967 would not be attained. Hence, a revised plan was prepared calling for lower sales volume and lower levels of expenditure.

Polaroid's other European subsidiaries were also below the levels planned for 1967, but not to the same degree as in France. In several countries, including Italy, Switzerland, and Belgium, Polaroid's estimated share of the camera market was significantly higher than in France. Polaroid's market penetration was about the same in France, West Germany, and the United Kingdom, however, despite much higher levels of consumer awareness in the latter countries. In some other countries, the company's advertising expenditures were proportionately higher than in France; with the French 1966 expenditure per camera sold set as 100, indexes of cost per unit for West Germany, the United Kingdom, and Italy were 112, 133, and 120, respectively.

For 1968, it was anticipated that the French camera market would grow very slightly, if at all. No major competitive new product introductions were in the United States around midyear, but production would probably not be adequate to meet worldwide demand until the end of the year. Consequently, M. Dumon's plans for 1968 were to be based on the same basic product line as in 1967.

In considering his marketing program for 1968, M. Dumon was especially concerned with the problems of pricing and promoting the Swinger. With regard to pricing, he wondered whether he should recommend that the company apply for a one-year continuance of government approval for resale price maintenance. The current approval was due to expire on August 1, 1967, and M. Dumon felt that there might be some advantages in allowing completely free pricing after that date. On the other hand, he did not want to lose any of the distribution that had been so carefully built up during the preceding year, on account of "cutthroat" price competition by the discount stores.

The problem of promotion was a chronic one for Polaroid. Awareness of the Polaroid name and instant picture feature had increased only slightly between early 1966 and early 1967, and even Polaroid camera owners displayed a lack of full understanding of some important features. For example, among a group of 100 Swinger owners interviewed in June 1967, nearly half did not realize that it was possible to obtain duplicates of Polaroid pictures from the company's print copy service.

Although the need for further consumer education about Polaroid photography seemed great, it was also clear that advertising had played a very important role in building demand during 1966 and 1967. Among a sample of Swinger owners interviewed in November 1966, 53 percent mentioned advertising as their original source of information about the camera, 5 percent mentioned conversations with photo dealers, and 5 percent in-store demonstrations.

M. Dumon wanted to recommend a program that would contribute to the company's longer-term marketing goals in France. At the same time, he was aware of the need to improve current operating results. He had recently received a letter from Mr. Wyman, indicating that

we must be in a position, with a prepared advance plan, to reduce expenditures and limit our activities to insure that we are producing a profit for the year.

QUESTIONS

1. Describe and evaluate Polaroid's U.S. marketing strategy. What factors account for Polaroid's success in the United States?
2. How does the French market differ from the U.S. market? Describe and evaluate Polaroid's strategy and marketing program in France.
3. What should Polaroid have done in France regarding market strategy? Regarding 1968 marketing plan and budget?

18

ORGANIZATION FOR GLOBAL MARKETING

A prince should therefore have no other aim or thought, nor take up any other thing for his study, but war and its organization and discipline, for that is the only art that is necessary to one who commands.

Niccolo Machiavelli, 1469–1527
The Prince

INTRODUCTION

Organization is a subject of major importance to any company that has decided to market globally. When a domestic company decides to expand internationally, the issue of how to organize arises immediately. Who should be responsible for this expansion? Should product divisions operate directly or should an international division be established? Should individual country subsidiaries report directly to the company president or should a special corporate officer be appointed to take full-time responsibility for international activities? Once the first decision of how to organize initial international operations has been reached, a growing company is faced with a number of reappraisal points during the development of its international business activities. Should a company abandon its international division and, if so, what alternative structure should be adopted? Should an area or regional head-quarters be formed? What should be the relationship of staff executives at corporate, regional, and subsidiary offices? Specifically, how should the marketing function be organized? To what extent should regional and corporate marketing executives become involved in subsidiary marketing management?

The goal in organizing for international marketing is to find a structure that enables the company to respond to relevant differences in international market environments and at the same time enables the company to extend valuable corporate knowledge, experience, and know-how from national markets to the entire corporate system. It is this pull between the value of centralized knowledge and coordination and the need for individualized response to the local situation that creates a constant tension in the international marketing organization.

At the outset it is important to recognize that there is no single correct organizational structure for international marketing. Geographical diversity is a consequence of a strategy of international expansion. The effect of operations in different countries and areas is to present a major new dimension of required response to the organization. A geographically dispersed company in addition to its knowledge of product, function, and the home territory, must acquire knowledge of the complex set of social, political, economic, and institutional arrangements that exist within each international market. Most companies, after initial ad hoc arrangements (all foreign subsidiaries reporting to a designated vice president or to the president, for example), establish an international division to manage their geographically dispersed new business. It is clear, however, that the international division in the multiproduct company is an unstable organizational arrangement and that as a company grows, this initial organizational structure gives way to various alternative structures.[1]

PATTERNS OF INTERNATIONAL ORGANIZATIONAL DEVELOPMENT

The conflicting pressures of the need for (1) product and technical knowledge, (2) functional expertise in marketing, finance, planning, and so on, and (3) area and country knowledge make it difficult to achieve performance and balance in organizations that typically have country operations that range over a long spectrum of size, potential, and local management competence. Because the matrix of pressures that shape organizations are never exactly the same, no two organizations pass through organizational stages in exactly the same way, nor do they arrive at precisely the same organizational pattern. Nevertheless, some general patterns have developed.

Most companies undertake initial foreign expansion with an organization similar to that in Figures 18–1 and 18–2. When a company is organized on this basis, foreign subsidiaries report directly to the company president or other designated company officer, who carries out his or her responsibilities without assistance from a headquarters staff group. This is a typical initial arrangement for companies getting started in international marketing operations.

---

[1]John M. Stopford and Louis T. Wells, Jr., *Managing the Multinational Enterprise* (New York: Basic Books, 1972). The interested reader will find in this book a complete exposition of research examining the organizational structure used by 170 U.S. manufacturing firms for their international operations. Stopford and Wells's research demonstrated that the international division is merely the first of a series of organizational structures utilized by companies to accomplish their international objectives.

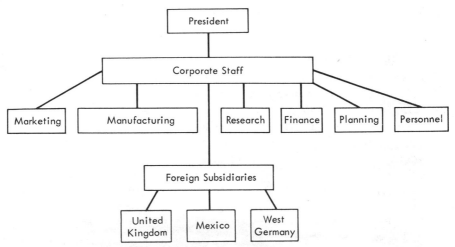

FIGURE 18–1 Functional Corporate Structure, Domestic Corporate Staff Orientation, Preinternational Division

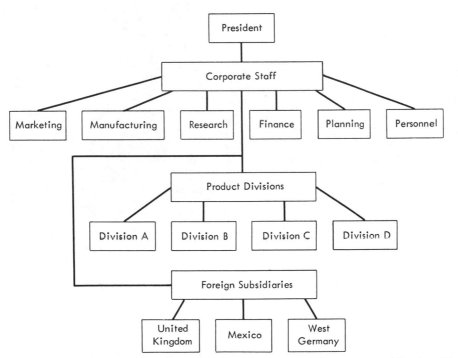

FIGURE 18–2 Divisional Corporate Structure, Domestically Oriented Product Division Staff, Preinternational Division

International Division Structure

As a company's international business grows, the complexity of coordinating and directing this activity extends beyond the scope of a single person. Pressure is created to assemble a staff group that will take responsibility for coordination and direction of the growing international activities of the organization. Eventually, this pressure leads to the creation of the international division, as illustrated in Figures 18–3 and 18–4. The corporate staff may or may not be involved in the management of international marketing activities at this point. If the international division is fully developed in terms of staff appointments, there is a tendency for it to operate autonomously and independently of corporate staff. On the other hand, if the international division staff is small and limited, there is a tendency for a service such as marketing research to be supplied by the corporate staff organization.

The international division structure occurs in both the functional and the divisional organization. It allows an organization to concentrate in one headquarters location all its expertise in dealing with foreign markets. In companies that have the bulk of their sales in a domestic market, this arrangement assures that an organizational location in the corporation gives its full attention to international markets.

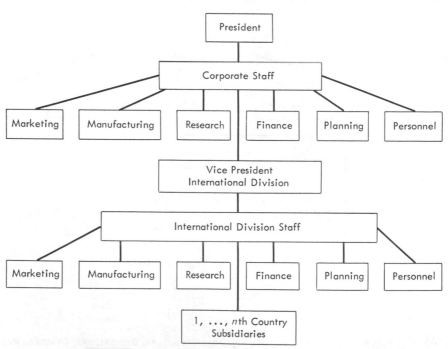

FIGURE 18–3   Functional Corporate Structure, Domestic Corporate Staff Orientation, International Division

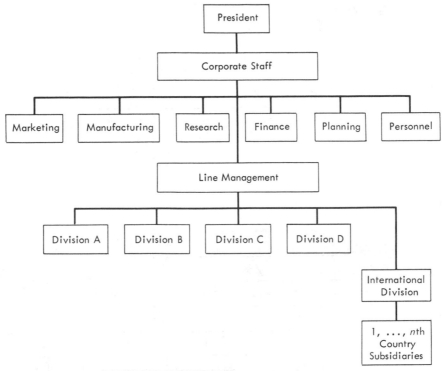

FIGURE 18–4   Divisional Corporate Structure, Domestically Oriented Corporate Staff, Domestically Oriented Product Divisions, International Division

Regional Management Centers

The next stage of organizational evolution is the emergence of an area or regional headquarters as a level of management between the country organization and the international division headquarters. This division is illustrated in Figures 18–5 and 18–6. When business is conducted in a single region that is characterized by certain similarities in economic, social, geographical, and political conditions, after it reaches a certain size, there is both justification and need for a management center. The center would coordinate interdependent decisions on such matters as pricing and sourcing and would participate in the planning and control of each country's operations with an eye toward applying company knowledge on a regional basis and also toward regional optimization of the application of corporate resources.

The arguments in favor of regional management have been stated as follows:

> the majority of regional managers agree that there is no better solution at the present time than an on-the-scene regional management unit, at least where there is a real need for coordinated, Europewide decision-making. Coordinated European planning and control is becoming necessary as the national subsidiary continues to lose its relevance as

Pro's
local input strong

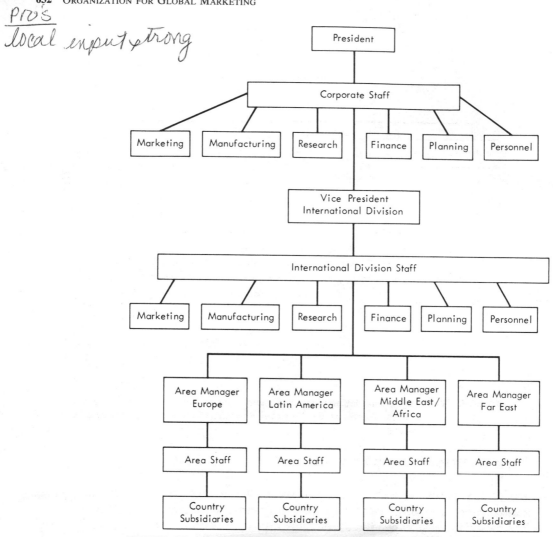

**FIGURE 18–5 Functional Corporate Structure, Domestic Corporate Staff
Orientation, International Division, Area Divisions**

an independent operating unit. Regional management can probably achieve the best balance of geographical, product, and functional considerations required to implement corporate objectives effectively and to maximize profitability of the European area.[2]

The pressure for the creation of a regional headquarters comes from two sources. One is the scale and complexity of a company's operations within a region. Size generates revenues that can cover the cost of a regional headquarters, and complexity creates a pressure to respond at the regional level. A second important source of

[2]Charles R. Williams, "Regional Management Overseas," *Harvard Business Review,* January–February 1967, p. 91.

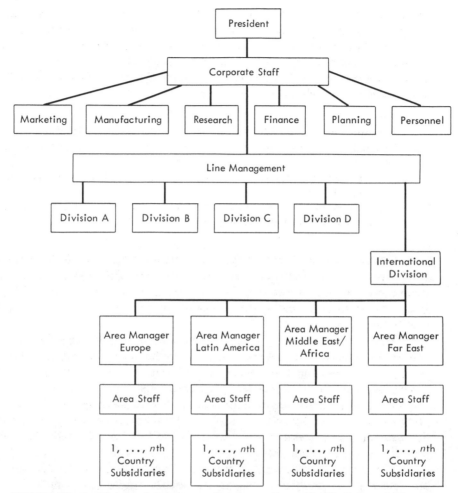

FIGURE 18–6   Divisional Corporate Structure, Domestically Oriented Corporate Staff, International Division, Area Subdivisions

pressure is the nature of regions. A geographical region is by definition a group of countries related to each other by geographic proximity. When a region is additionally unified by tariff reduction applying within the regional boundaries, by interregional communication media, by the development of interregional transportation systems, by various regional moves toward economic, social, and political cooperation, and by basic economic and cultural similarities, then the development of the region itself generates a pressure for the creation of a regional headquarters that will guide corporate activities in a way that will take advantage of the economic, social, and political integration that exists within the region.

One of the best examples of the combination of economic, social, and political integration with geographic proximity and relatively large-scale operations has occurred in the European Community. In the EC, the progress toward economic, social, and political integration during the past two decades has created preconditions for the integration of business activities in EC countries. However, these pressures in themselves are not sufficient to make it desirable for every company to create a regional headquarters. The company situation itself must be considered. Companies in a region can be placed in four categories:[3]

1. Initial operations, small annual sales in a handful of countries
2. Regional operations dominated by one or two sizable national subsidiaries, each of which has its own substantial management staff
3. Regional operations comprised of several large, strong, historically independent national operating subsidiaries
4. Regional operations of companies of national subsidiaries that have been closely integrated according to a worldwide plan

Categories 1 and 2 are the type of operations that have little need for a regional headquarters. The principal subsidiaries are so large that they can effectively function as operating units and in many cases are multicountry companies in their own right. In any event, there is really little coordination between companies of vastly different size to be pursued.

Whenever a company's operations become sizable and are scattered over a number of subsidiaries, the pressure for regional integration grows. This pressure is perhaps the greatest in the category 3 situation, where large unintegrated subsidiary companies are operating relatively autonomously and have therefore avoided the cost savings and rationalization moves that an overall direction would provide. Most companies today feel that the category 4 situation merits a regional headquarters in an area such as Europe where the opportunities for rationalization and areawide coordination are significant.

The major disadvantage of a regional center is its cost. Whenever operations are under profit pressure, these costs become quite apparent and have in many companies been responsible for the abandonment of a regional headquarters. Extra compensation for living abroad and the cost of replacing incompetent employees can run up an enormous bill simply for transportation. Overhead cost for office space is expensive. Thus, creating an organizational unit adds personnel, transportation, and communication costs that must be justified by the unit's contribution to organizational effectiveness. Even a two-person office could cost in excess of $500,000 per year. The scale of regional management must be in line with scale of operations in a region. A regional headquarters is premature whenever the size of the operations it manages is inadequate to cover the costs of the additional layer of management. Thus the basic issue with regard to the regional headquarters is, "Does it contribute enough to organizational effectiveness to justify its cost?"

---

[3]The following material is drawn from ibid.

Beyond the International Division

As companies develop their capability to operate in foreign markets with an international division, they usually find that the growing size and complexity of their international operation demands organizational modifications that fully apply organizational capabilities to market opportunities. In the functional single-product company, or product group, one modification involves the creation of geographical structure. In the multidivisional company, this involves the creation of the worldwide product division.

Geographical Structure

The geographical structure involves the assignment of operational responsibility for geographic areas of the world to line managers. The corporate headquarters retains responsibility for worldwide planning and control, and each area of the world— including the "home" or base market—is organizationally equal. For the company with U.S. origins, the United States is simply another geographic market under this organizational arrangement. The most common appearance of this structure is in companies with closely related product lines that are sold in similar end-use markets around the world. For example, the major international oil companies utilize the geographical structure, which is illustrated in Figure 18–7.

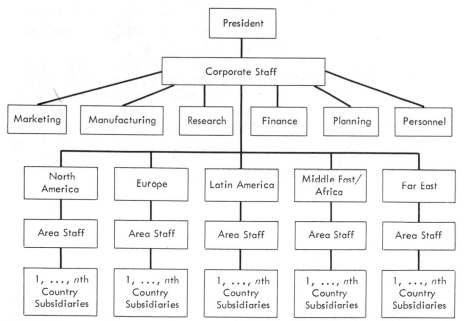

FIGURE 18–7   Geographic Corporate Structure, World Corporate Staff Orientation, Area Divisions Worldwide

Worldwide Product Division Structure

When an organization assigns worldwide product responsibility to its product divisions, the product divisions must decide whether to rely upon an international division, thereby dividing their world into domestic and foreign, or to rely upon an area structure with each region of the world organizationally treated on an equal basis. In most cases when a divisional company shifts from a corporate international division to worldwide product divisions, there are two stages in the internationalization of the product divisions. The first stage occurs when international responsibility is shifted from a corporate international division to the product division international departments. The second occurs when the product divisions themselves shift international responsibility from international departments within the divisions to the total divisional organization. In effect, this shift is the utilization of a geographical structure within each product division. The worldwide product division with an international department is illustrated in Figure 18–8.

Strategic Business Units

One of the important organizational expressions of the growing importance of strategy is the strategic business unit (SBU). This term, first used at General Electric, refers to the organizational unit that is responsible for preparing the business plan. The SBU may or may not correspond to the divisions, groups, or other organizational units in the company. The criterion for the definition of an SBU is that it be a group of products and technologies that serves an identified market and competes with identified competitors—in other words, a business.

The growing importance of global competition has made it necessary for the SBUs to address global markets and global competition in developing their business strategy, even if their operations do not extend beyond the home country. A business that has not targeted global markets is not immune from global competition.

In many cases, the SBUs are not part of the formal structure of the company but, rather, represent a process or system overlay for the purpose of developing a business strategy. The implementation of the strategy may be carried out by divisions or groups that are organized along traditional lines.

The Matrix Structure

The most sophisticated organizational arrangement brings to bear four basic competences on a worldwide basis. These competences are as follows:

1. *Geographic knowledge.* An understanding of the basic economic, social, cultural, political, and governmental market and competitive dimensions of a country is essential. The country subsidiary is the major structural device employed today to enable the corporation to acquire geographic knowledge.

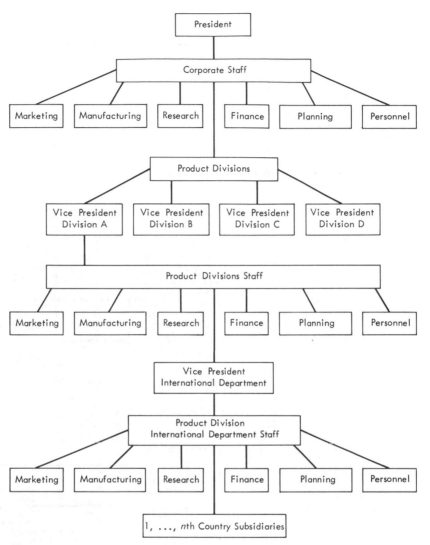

FIGURE 18–8 **Divisional Corporate Structure, International Product Division with an International Department in the International Product Division**

2. *Product knowledge and know-how.* Product managers with a worldwide responsibility can achieve this level of competence on a global basis. Another way of achieving global product competence is simply to duplicate product management organizations in domestic and international divisions, achieving high competence in both organizational units.

3. *Functional competence in such fields as finance, production, and especially marketing.* Corporate functional staff with worldwide responsibility contributes toward the development of functional competence on a global basis. In a handful of companies, the

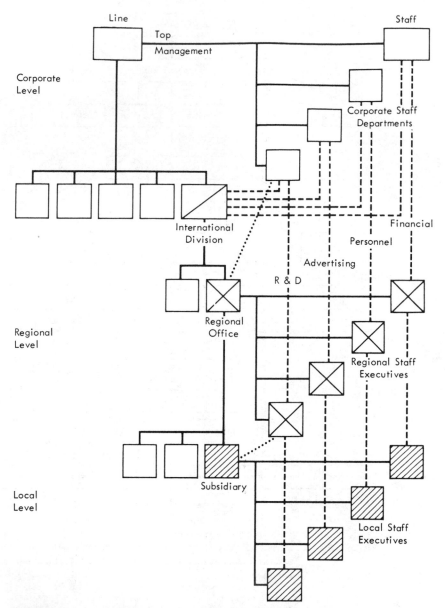

Line
Staff
Top
Management
Corporate
Level
Corporate Staff
Departments
International
Division
Financial
Personnel
Advertising
R & D
Regional
Office
Regional
Level
Regional Staff
Executives
Subsidiary
Local
Level
Local Staff
Executives

FIGURE 18–9 Organization Chart Showing Relationships Between Staff Executives in Corporate Departments, Regional Office, and Subsidiary

appointment of country subsidiary functional managers is reviewed by the corporate functional manager who is responsible for the development of her functional activity in the organization on a global basis. What has emerged in a growing number of multinational companies is a dotted-line relationship among corporate, regional, and country staff. These relationships are illustrated in Figure 18–9. The dotted-line relationship ranges from nothing more than advice offered by corporate or regional staff to regional country staff to a much "heavier" line relationship where staff activities of a lower organizational level are directed and approved by higher-level staff. The relationship of staff organizations can become a source of tension and conflict in an organization if top management does not create a climate that encourages organizational integration. Headquarters staff wants to extend its control or influence over the activities of lower-level staff.

For example, in marketing research, unless there is coordination of research design and activity, the international headquarters is unable to compare one market with another. If line management instead of recognizing the potential contribution of an integrated worldwide staff wishes to operate as autonomously as possible, the influence of corporate staff is perceived as undesirable. In such a situation the "stronger" party wins. This can be avoided if the level of management to which both line and staff report creates a climate and structure that expects and requires the cooperation of line and staff, and recognizes that each has responsibility for important aspects of the management of international markets.

4. *A knowledge of the customer or industry and its needs.* In certain large and very sophisticated international companies, staff with a responsibility for serving industries on a global basis exists to assist the line managers in the country organizations in their efforts to penetrate specific customer markets.

In the fully developed large-scale international company, product, function, area, and customer know-how are simultaneously focused on the organization's worldwide marketing objectives. This type of total competence is a matrix organization. In the matrix organization the task of management is to achieve an organizational balance that brings together different perspectives and skills to accomplish the organization's objectives. Under this arrangement, instead of designating national organizations or product divisions as profit centers, both are responsible for profitability: the national organization for country profits, and the product divisions for national and worldwide product profitability. Figure 18–10 illustrates the matrix organization. This organization chart starts with a bottom section that represents a single-country responsibility level, moves to representing the area or international level, and finally moves to representing global responsibility from the product divisions to the corporate staff, to the chief executive at the top of the structure.

The key to successful matrix management is the extent to which managers in the organization are able to resolve conflicts and achieve integration of organization programs and plans. Thus the mere adoption of a matrix design or structure does not create a matrix organization. The matrix organization requires a fundamental change in management behavior, organizational culture, and technical systems. In a matrix, influence is based on technical competence and interpersonal sensitivity, not on formal authority. In a matrix culture, managers recognize the absolute need to resolve issues and choices at the lowest possible level and do not rely upon higher authority. A sure sign that managers do not understand matrix organizations is when

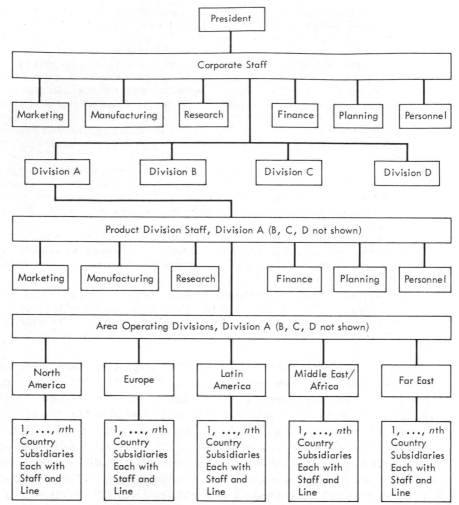

FIGURE 18–10 **Divisional Corporate Structure, Globally Oriented Corporate Staff, Global Product Division (globally oriented product division staff with area subdivisions)**

issues and problems are regularly pushed to the chief executive officer for resolution. Matrix organizations develop because companies refuse to accept the trade-offs of alternative traditional structures. For example, in traditional hierarchical structures, there is a choice between country or national organization and worldwide product divisions as the profit center or accountability location for strategic business management. Which is more important—in-depth knowledge of language, customs, laws, and customers, or in-depth knowledge of technology, products, and markets? In the traditional design, organizations must choose. In the matrix, *both* locations are responsible for profits. Traditional structures minimize conflict, whereas matrix structures are acknowledged generators of conflict. The potential conflict in a matrix is accepted as inherent in the structure rather than as the consequence of poor management. Finally, a matrix requires a substantial investment in control systems—dual accounting, transfer pricing, corporate budgets, and so on.

MATRIX VARIATIONS. The divisional company that disbands its international division in favor of assigning direct responsibility for international operations to its product divisions is seeking an organizational structure that is much more capable of directing the organization's product-market competence toward opportunities in international markets. Unfortunately, a company utilizing this structural arrangement will have multiple division organizational units operating simultaneously and independently in many countries where the market is not large enough to employ fully the resources committed. The major areas of duplication are in administrative and financial services. Another shortcoming of this arrangement is a lack of coordination of product division activities that could be centralized. For example, divisions may work entirely independently of each other in advertising to establish a corporate image. Another shortcoming is that the separation blocks the exchange of valuable information.

A matrix solution to this problem might involve the creation of so-called "umbrella companies" in each country that are responsible for specified pooled activities such as administering reporting requirements to national authorities and coordinating corporate image-building activities, cash management, and pooled services such as office management and transportation. Product divisions would have responsibility for country strategies and programs and would directly employ their own staff. They would have profit and loss accountability, and the umbrella organization would be a cost center whose costs would be allocated to each of the product divisions on the basis of a formula. This would be a matrix with heavy emphasis on product division responsibility and is illustrated in Figure 18–11. Another matrix could shift major emphasis for profit and loss to the country or national organization. Still another matrix variation would be the attempt to divide responsibility equally between product and national organization.

Relationship Among Structure, Foreign Product Diversification, and Size

John Stopford and Louis Wells, Jr., have hypothesized the relationship among structure, foreign product diversification (defined as sales of a firm outside its major product line expressed as a percentage of the total sales), and size. This formulation posits that when size abroad grows, the emergence of an area division develops so that whenever size abroad is 50 percent of total size or more, several area divisions will probably be adopted. On the other hand, as foreign product diversification increases, the likelihood that product divisions will operate on a worldwide basis increases. In a company where there is both worldwide product diversity and large-

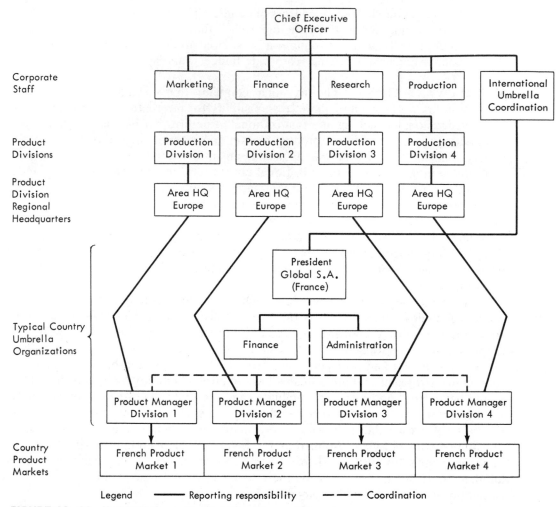

FIGURE 18–11 Umbrella Reporting Relationships and Structure

scale business abroad as a percentage of total business, foreign operation will tend to move toward the matrix structure. Companies with limited foreign product diversification (under 10 percent) and limited size as a percentage of total size will utilize the international structure. This formulation is summarized schematically in Figure 18–12.

Organization Structure and National Origin

Before 1960 the American multidivisional structure was rarely found outside the United States. This structure was introduced in the United States as early as 1921 by Alfred P. Sloan at General Motors. The multidivisional structure in the United

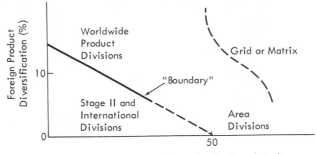

**FIGURE 18—12   The Relationships Among Structure, Foreign Product
Diversification, and Size Abroad (as a % of total size)**

Source: John M. Stopford and Louis T. Wells, Jr., *Managing the Multinational
Enterprise* (New York: Basic Books, 1972); adapted by author.

States had three distinctive characteristics. First, profit responsibility for operating
decisions was assigned to general managers of self-contained business units. Second,
there was a corporate headquarters that was concerned with strategic planning,
appraisal, and the allocation of resources among the business divisions. Third, executives at the corporate headquarters were separated from operations and were
psychologically committed to the whole organization rather than the individual businesses.[4]

During the 1960s European enterprises underwent a period of unprecedented
reorganization. Essentially they adopted the American divisional structure. Today
at the overall level there is little difference between European and American organizations. However, at the divisional level, a comparison of European and U.S.
multinational firms reveals that, in general, European firms typically give more responsibility to national organizations and typically give less attention to the home
market and more attention to international markets than does the average American
firm. These differences are really differences of focus and emphasis rather than
differences in structure and can be traced to the size of the domestic market and
the history of international growth. The initial geographic spread of U.S. firms was
from regional to national operations. When the U.S. firm expanded internationally,
the move was usually from its large U.S.-based position. For reasons discussed
earlier in this chapter, these circumstances favor the international division as a
structural device for concentrating limited knowledge, skills, and market positions
in the largest possible mass.

In his study of 56 subsidiaries of European companies in the United States,
Picard found seven basic "structures":

1. Direct reporting, with the chief executive officer of the subsidiary reporting directly to
   the president of the parent company (36 percent)

[4]Lawrence G. Franko, "The Move Toward a Multidivisional Structure in European Organizations," *Administrative Science Quarterly*, Vol. 19, no. 4 (December 1974), pp. 493–506.

2. President reporting to local board of directors (23 percent)
3. Chief executive officer of subsidiary also being chief executive officer of parent—no reporting is needed (7 percent)
4. Regional headquarters (7 percent)
5. Product division structure (7 percent)
6. International division structure (7 percent)
7. Holding company (7 percent)[5]

Getting off the Reorganizational Merry go Round

Bartlett studied 10 U.S. based MNCs that, according to the theory outlined above, should have moved from the international division to the worldwide product division, area, or matrix structure but did not.[6] He found that these successful companies avoided the myth of the ideal organization structure and instead concentrated on building and maintaining a complex decision-making, resource transfer, and information-sharing process. For example, Corning Glass Works's T.V. tube marketing strategy required local decision making for service and delivery and global decision making for pricing.

The successful companies, Bartlett found, developed in three stages. The first was to recognize the diversity of the world. In other words, the companies made the transition from ethnocentric and polycentric orientations to a geocentric orientation. The second stage involved the building of channels of communication between managers in various parts of the organization. An example of a communications channel building move might be a first time world meeting of executives at a conference center where, for the first time, executives in the companies businesses from all over the world get a chance to meet each other, and to learn about the business strategies of their counterparts in other countries and businesses.

In the third stage, the company develops norms and values within the organization to support shared decisions and corporate as opposed to country or product perspectives. The highest value is placed upon corporate goals and cooperative effort as opposed to parochial interests and adversarial relationships. Many Japanese companies fit this description perfectly, which is why they have been so successful. IBM probably fits this description better than any company in the world, and that is certainly why IBM is arguably the greatest of all the global strategy companies. It is interesting to note that IBM not only reflects this third stage of companies that have avoided the reorganization myth, it also is a company that is undergoing constant reorganization. IBM is clear proof that to reorganize or not to reorganize is not the question: structure (organization) should be a function of the company and its strategy. It is clear that corporate reorganizations are not a panacea nor are they

---

[5]Jacques Picard, "Organizational Structures and Integrative Devices in European Multinational Corporations," *Columbia Journal of World Business,* Spring 1980, pp. 30–35.

[6]This section draws heavily upon Christopher A. Bartlett, "MNCs: get off the reorganization merry-go-round," *Harvard Business Review,* March–April, 1983, pp. 138–146.

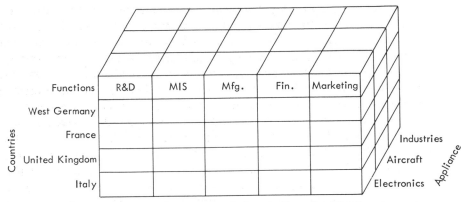

FIGURE 18–13   A One-Product Country, Industry, Function Matrix

even a necessary condition for success. On the other hand, it is also clear that there is no rule that says that reorganization is bad or that it must be avoided.

The important task of top management is to eliminate a one-dimensional approach to decisions and encourage the development of multiple management perspectives and an organization that will sense and respond to a complex and fast-changing world. By thinking in terms of changing behavior rather than changing structural design, companies can free themselves from the static nature and limitations of the structural diagram and instead can focus on achieving the best possible results with available resources.

A TYPICAL COMPANY EXPERIENCE[7]

The experience of Raychem Incorporated in Europe illustrates the enormous complexity of effectively structuring international marketing operations. Raychem has four product categories, each of which is part of a related line. These categories are wire and cable, heat-shrinkable materials, corrosion products utilizing heat-shrinkable materials, and machines and instruments to apply the company's heat-shrinkable products. These related products are sold to six major customer categories: aircraft, electronics, utilities, appliances, computers, and telecommunications. Raychem's European operations cover the entire continent of Europe, the United Kingdom, Israel, and South Africa. The European staff consists of a general manager, research and development, manufacturing, finance, MIS (management information systems), and marketing.

Figure 18–13 illustrates the complexity of functional, geographic, and consumer characteristics when they are viewed on a three-industry, four-country, five-function basis. In this matrix there are 60 combinations of industry, country, and function

[7]This section is based on interview notes and private communication with Robert J. Saldich, vice president, Raychem Corporation.

with which the organization must deal. For example, in the marketing of the company's products to the aircraft industry in West Germany, the need is to bring the company's competence in serving this industry to bear on customers located in West Germany. The challenge of assisting the country's sales and marketing team in this effort is considerable. If headquarters is to be of assistance to the West German management, it must have a knowledge of marketing and the aircraft industry and an interest in the unique characteristics of West German customers.

When Raychem first organized a regional marketing function, it followed the policy of appointing bright and talented young people to the regional headquarters position. This proved to be disastrous because these people were inexperienced in the actual selling task for the company's products in specific industries. Because of their inadequate knowledge, they were in constant conflict with the country sales representatives and were unable to contribute to effective marketing. Following this experience, the president of Raychem Europe decided to appoint marketing staff managers entirely from the ranks of successful country marketing and sales management. The specialist at European headquarters for the aircraft industry is now an experienced and extremely successful former West German sales manager for the company's activities directed toward this industry.

According to the president of Raychem Europe, the area staff must be so good at their jobs that the local managers, motivated from the point of view of their own self-interest, seek out their help. Intelligent local managers realize that when there is a competent staff person at the regional headquarters they can use this person as a sounding board and as a testing place for their own ideas and, in the process, more effectively perform their function.

To make this arrangement work, the European-area president must communicate to his general managers and their staffs in the different countries his commitment to the development of an effective headquarters staff. He must also communicate the rewards, which will accrue to managers and staffs who work effectively with the regional headquarters. On the other hand, he must communicate to the regional headquarters staff that their major function is to contribute toward the effectiveness of the individual country operations. They are aware that they, in general, are not in a position to direct action by country managers.

A second function of the headquarters staff is its role in advising the European manager on an overall European strategy for Raychem and also in assisting on a day-to-day basis the local managers in formulating their own strategic and operating plans.

The Raychem case illustrates the complexity of bringing a single related product group to market in a number of countries. When a company is involved in the marketing of unrelated products, a conceptual representation of its task requires the preparation of an industry, country, and function matrix for each related product group. Clearly, in these organizations there is pressure to rely on product divisions for the management of marketing efforts for the products concerned. The limiting factor is the size of each product division's business in each country.

During the next decade, Raychem Corporation continued to grow vigorously achieving *Fortune* 500 status in 1981. Growth was paced by activities outside the

United States until non-U.S. turnover represented 60–65 percent of total company sales.

The development of sales activities in a new country was typically delayed until a suitable local national was identified and trained in Raychem technology and Raychem culture. The use of local distributors and agents was discouraged as a result of company belief that a firm base could be built only with a professional Raychem team supporting and training its new customers.

Once installed, these young teams spent one to several years obtaining product approvals from local authorities, learning to operate in their country on behalf of Raychem, and teaching corporate management the intricacies of local operation.

Initially, the entire emphasis in each country was on getting approvals for and creating a demand for Raychem products. These products always represent new technology and replace long-established methods.

As time went on, pressures built up for local value added activities in many countries. These pressures stemmed from a variety of sources:

Local laws restricting imports
Prohibitive tariff barriers
Desire to reduce lead times
Desire to produce locally made or assembled goods
Desire to provide a large base on which to build a local management team
Need to be able to honor pressure to "buy locally"
Desire to avoid being blocked from market by competitive investments

As a result of these pressures and depending on the persuasiveness of the local manager, a series of local assembly and light manufacturing activities was developed. These were organizationally under the wing of the International Division—a sales-driven organization with no operations capability. This, in turn, led to coordination problems, confusion with regard to sourcing issues, and various levels of frustration throughout the organization.

Coincident with the development of sales, assembly, and light manufacturing activities in 35 countries, Raychem management decided to shift its focus to a marketing thrust—creating five major worldwide market-oriented divisions. These were

Electronics
Pipeline products
Telecommunications
Electrical power products
Process industries

Each division had responsibility for product development, marketing, sales, manufacturing, and business planning. In the smaller countries (excluding the United States, West Germany, France, and the United Kingdom), they sold through the International Division.

Corporate staff groups were developed to try to coordinate the activities of an increasingly complex matrix. These included legal, patent, finance, quality assurance, planning, and human relations. Their strength and influence depended largely on the clout and level of respect that the staff group manager developed.

As the leaders of a technically driven company, Raychem top management was concerned about the regeneration of its technologies. Consequently, the level of research and development emphasis was also increasing throughout this period. The president and founder pushed into new technologies while the executive vice president concentrated on operations.

Additionally, a new unit was created to explore totally new technologies and markets. All in all, the company was attempting simultaneously to concentrate its attack on a series of markets while strengthening its commitment to its own and to new technologies.

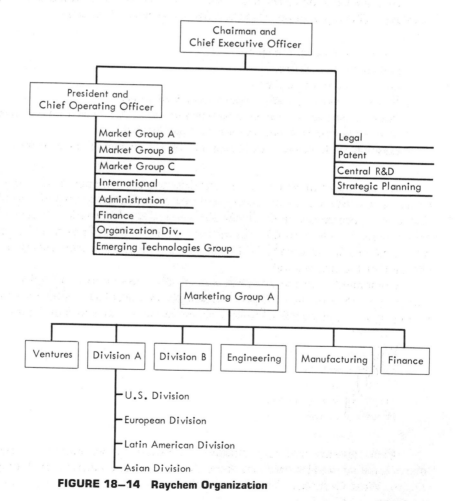

FIGURE 18–14 Raychem Organization

As a result, organizational complexity led to a variety of matrices—with the matrix occupants trying to cover all relevant colleagues who were properly concerned with the decisions being taken. For example, consider the cast of characters who "should" be included in a decision regarding product design and pricing strategy for a new product in a small country. The responsible group might be the Group for Emerging Technologies that would provide marketing and technical support for the project:

1. They would call on *technical expertise* from Central Technology.
2. They would rely on *end-market expertise* from the Market Division.
3. *Sales contacts* would be made by the local sales engineer and coordinated with his or her managers—the country manager and, if of sufficient importance, the intermediate managers up to and including the vice president of International.
4. If a *manufacturing issue* is potentially involved, the manufacturing manager of the affected division would become involved.
5. A *tariff question* would require corporate finance people.

And so on. The increasingly complex mix of product, market, geography, and technology had to be discussed and coordinated with a large number of people. The company's determination to push into new product and geographic markets made it necessary for management to become increasingly focused on making and implementing decisions.

In an effort to focus on the future and the present, a top-level change was made wherein the president became chairman and chief executive officer and the executive vice president became president and chief operating officer.

The new structure is illustrated in Figure 18–14.

BIBLIOGRAPHY

Books

HULBERT, JAMES M., AND WILLIAM E. BRANDT. *Managing the Multinational Subsidiary*. New York: Holt, Rinehart and Winston, 1980.

STOPFORD, JOHN, AND LOUIS T. WELLS, JR., *Managing the Multinational Enterprise*. New York: Basic Books, 1972.

Articles

BARTLETT, CHRISTOPHER A. "MNCs: Get Off the Reorganization Merry-go-round." *Harvard Business Review*, March-April 1983, pp. 138–146.

CLEE, GILBERT H., AND WILBER M. SACHTJEN. "Organizing a Worldwide Business." *Harvard Business Review*, November–December 1969, pp. 55–67.

DAVIS, STANLEY, M. "Trends in the Organization of Multinational Corporations." *Columbia Journal of World Business*, Vol. 11, no. 2 (Summer 1976).

DOZ, YVES. "Multinational Strategy and Structure in Government Controlled Business." *Columbia Journal of World Business*, Fall 1980, pp. 14–25.

FOURAKER, LAWRENCE E., AND JOHN M. STOPFORD. "Organizational Structure and the Multinational Strategy." *Administrative Science Quarterly,* June 1968, pp. 47–64.

FRANKO, LAWRENCE G. "The Move Toward a Multidivisional Structure in European Organizations," *Administrative Science Quarterly,* Vol. 19, no. 4 (December 1974).

GOGGIN, WILLIAM C. "How the Multidimensional Structure Works at Dow Corning." *Harvard Business Review,* January–February 1974, pp. 54–65.

"ORGANIZATION AND CONTROL OF INTERNATIONAL OPERATIONS," Conference Board Report No. 597. New York: The Conference Board, 1973.

PERLMUTTER, HOWARD V. "The Tortuous Evolution of the Multinational Corporation." *Columbia Journal of World Business,* January–February 1969, pp. 9–18.

PICARD, JACQUES. "Organizational Structures and Integrative Devices in European Multinational Corporations." *Columbia Journal of World Business,* Spring 1980, pp. 30–35.

PITTS, ROBERT A., AND JOHN D. DANIELS. "Aftermath of the Matrix Mania." *Columbia Journal of World Business,* Summer 1984, pp. 48–54.

RUEKERT, ROBERT W., ORVILLE C. WALKER, JR., AND KENNETH J. ROERING. "The Organization of Marketing Activities: A Contingency Theory of Structure and Performance." *Journal of Marketing,* Vol. 49, (Winter 1985), pp. 13–25.

BANCIL CORPORATION[1]

Struggling to clear his mind, Remy Gentile, marketing manager in France for the Toiletry Division of Bancil, stumbled to answer the ringing telephone.

"Allo?"
"Remy, Tom Wilson here. Sorry to bother you at this hour. Can you hear me?"
"Sacre Bleu! Do you know what time it is?"
"About 5:20 in Sunnyvale. I've been looking over the past quarter's results for our Peau Doux . . ."
"Tom, it's after 2 A.M. in Paris; hold the phone for a moment."

Remy was vexed with Tom Wilson, marketing vice president for the toiletry division and acting division marketing director for Europe, since they had discussed the Peau Doux situation via telex no more than a month

ago. When he returned to the phone, Remy spoke in a more controlled manner.

"You mentioned the Peau Doux line, Tom."
"Yes, Remy, the last quarter's results were very disappointing. Though we've increased advertising by 30 percent, sales were less than 1 percent higher. What is even more distressing, Remy, is that our competitor's sales have been growing at nearly 20 percent per year. Furthermore, our percentage cost of goods sold has not decreased. Has Pierre Chevalier bought the new equipment to streamline the factory's operation?"
"No, Pierre has not yet authorized the purchase of the machine, and there is little that can be done to rationalize operations in the antiquated Peau Doux plant. Also, we have not yet succeeded in securing another distributor for the line."
"What! But that was part of the strategy with our increased advertising. I thought we agreed to . . ."

Tom Wilson hesitated for a moment. His mind was racing as he attempted to recall the specifics of the proposed Toiletry Division

[1]This case was prepared by Lawrence D. Chrzanowski under the supervision of Ram Charan. Used with permission.

strategy for France. That strategy had guided his earlier recommendation to Gentile and Pierre Chevalier, the Bancil general manager in France, to increase advertising and to obtain a new distributor. Tom wanted to be forceful but tactful to ensure Gentile's commitment to the strategy.

"Remy, let's think about what we discussed on my last trip to Paris. Do you recall we agreed to propose to Chevalier a plan to revitalize Peau Doux's growth? If my memory serves me well, it was to increase advertising by 25 percent, groom a new national distributor, reduce manufacturing costs with new equipment, increase prices, and purchase the 'L'aube' product line to spread our marketing overhead."

"Oui, oui. We explored some ideas and I thought they needed more study."

"Remy, as you recall Peau Doux has a low margin. Cutting costs is imperative. We expected to decrease costs by 5 percent by investing $45,000 in new equipment. Our test for the new strategy next year was to increase advertising this quarter and next quarter while contracting for a new distributor. The advertising was for naught. What happened?"

"I really don't know. I guess Pierre has some second thoughts."

Tom spoke faster as he grew more impatient. Gentile's asking Tom to repeat what he had said made him angrier. Tom realized that he must visit Paris to salvage what he could from the current test program on Peau Doux. He knew that the recent results would not support the proposed Toiletry Division strategy.

"Remy, I need to see what's going on and then decide how I can best assist you and Chevalier. I should visit Paris soon. How about early next week, say, Monday and Tuesday?"

"Oui, that is fine."

"I'll fly in on Sunday morning. Do you think you can join me for dinner that evening at the Vietnamese restaurant we dined at last time?"

"Oui."

"Please make reservations only for two. I'm coming alone. Good night, Remy."

"Oui. Bon soir."

COMPANY BACKGROUND

Bancil Corporation of Sunnyvale, California, was founded in 1903 by pharmacist Dominic Bancil. During its first half-century, its products consisted primarily of analgesics (branded pain relievers like aspirin), an antiseptic mouthwash, and a first-aid cream. By 1974, some of the top-management positions were still held by members of the Bancil family, who typically had backgrounds as pharmacists or physicians. This tradition notwithstanding. John Stoopes, the present chief executive officer, was committed to developing a broad-based professional management team.

Bancil sales, amounting to $61 million in 1955, had grown to $380 million in 1970 and to $600 million in 1974. This sales growth had been aided by diversification and acquisition of allied businesses as well as by international expansion. Bancil's product line by 1970 included four major groups. (See Table 1). In 1974, Bancil's corporate organization was structured around these four product groups, which, in turn, were divided into two or three divisions. Thus, in 1973 the consumer products group had been divided into the Dominic Division, which handled Bancil's original product line, and the Toiletry Division, which was in charge of the newer product acquisitions. The objective of this separation was to direct greater attention to the toiletry products.

INTERNATIONAL OPERATIONS

International expansion had begun in the mid-1950s when Bancil exported through agents and distributors. Subsequently, marketing

TABLE 1 Bancil Sales, 1970 versus 1974 (in millions of dollars)

	SALES	
	1970	1974
Agricultural and animal health products (weedkillers, fertilizers, feed additives)	$ 52	$141
Consumer products (Bancil original line plus hand creams, shampoos, and baby accessories)	205	276
Pharmaceutical products (tranquilizers, oral contraceptives, hormonal drugs)	62	107
Professional products (diagnostic reagents, automated chemical analyzers, and surgical gloves and instruments)	60	76

subsidiaries, called national units (NUs), were created in Europe, Africa, Latin America, and Japan. All manufacturing took place in the United States. Virtually the entire export activity consisted of Bancil's analgesic, Domicil. An innovative packaging concept, large amounts of creative advertising, and considerable sales push made Domicil a common word in most of the free world, reaching even the most remote areas of Africa, Asia, and South America. A vice president of international operations exercised control at this time through letters and occasional overseas trips. By the mid-1960s, overseas marketing of pharmaceutical and professional products began, frequently through a joint venture with a local company. Increasing sales led to the construction of production facilities for many of Bancil's products in England, Kenya, Mexico, Brazil, and Japan.

Bancil's international expansion received a strong commitment from top management. John Stoopes was not only a successful business executive but also a widely read intellectual with an avid interest in South American and African cultures. This interest generated an extraordinary sense of responsibility to the developing nations and a conviction that the mature industrial societies had

an obligation to help in their development. He did not want Bancil to be viewed as a firm that drained resources and money from the developing world; rather, he desired to apply Bancil's resources to worldwide health and malnutrition problems. His personal commitment as an ardent humanist was a guideline for Bancil's international operations.

While Bancil had been successful during the 1960s in terms of both domestic diversification and international expansion, its efforts to achieve worldwide diversification had given rise to frustration. Even though the international division's specific purpose was to promote all Bancil products most advantageously throughout the world, the NUs had concentrated mainly on analgesics. As a result, the growth of the remaining products had been generally confined to the United States and thus these products were not realizing their fullest worldwide potential.

According to Bancil executives, these problems had their roots in the fact that the various product lines, though generically related, required different management strategies. For consumer products, advertising consumed 28 percent to 35 percent of sales; since production facilities did not require a large capital investment, considerable spare capacity was available to absorb impulses in demand created by advertising campaigns. For agricultural and animal health products, promotion was less than 1 percent of sales, but the capital-intensive production (a facility of minimum economic scale cost $18 million) required a marketing effort to stimulate demand consistently near full production capacity. Furthermore, the nature of the marketing activity for the professional and pharmaceutical products placed the burden on personal selling rather than on a mass-promotion effort.

In response to this situation, a reorganization in 1969 gave each product division worldwide responsibility for marketing its products. Regional marketing managers, reporting to the division's vice president of marketing, were given direct authority for most marketing decisions (e.g., advertising, pricing, distribution channels) of their division's products in their area. The manufacturing division, with headquarters in Sunnyvale, had worldwide responsibility for production and quality control. (See Figure 1 for the 1969 organization chart.)

Corporate management also identified a need in key countries for a single local executive to represent Bancil Corporation's interests in local banking and political circles. There was no single criterion for selecting, from the divisions' representatives in each

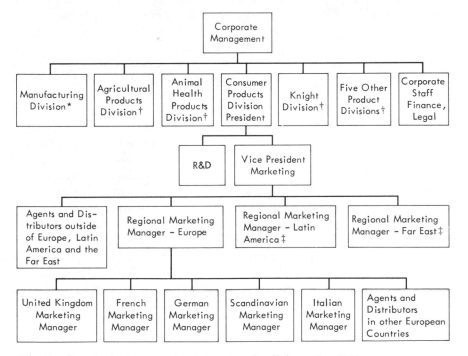

*The Manufacturing Division manufactured products for all the product divisions.
 Overseas manufacturing (not shown) reported to the manufacturing division in Sunnyvale.
†Organization similar to that of the consumer products division.
‡Organization similar to that for Europe.

FIGURE 1   1969 Organization Chart

Source: Company records.

country, the Bancil delegate, the title given to this position. A corporate officer remarked, ''We chose who we thought was the best business executive in each country. There was no emphasis on functional specialty or on selecting an individual from the division with the greatest volume. In one country, the major candidates were opinionated and strong-willed, and we therefore chose the individual who was the most controversial. The Bancil delegate generally had a marketing background if marketing was the primary Bancil activity in the country or a production background if Bancil had several manufacturing facilities in the country.''

While international sales had grown from $99 million in 1970 to $147 million in 1972, profit performance from 1971 to 1972 had been disappointing. A consultant's report stated,

There are excessive communications between the NUs and Sunnyvale. The marketing managers and all the agents are calling for product-line information from the divisional headquarters. Five individuals are calling three times per week on an average, and many more are calling only slightly less often.

It appeared that a great deal of management time was spent on telex and long-distance communications and travel. In response to these concerns, the divisions' staff increased in each country. Overhead nearly tripled, affecting the growth rate of profits from international operations.

With the exception of financial decisions, which were dictated by corporate headquarters, most decisions on inventories, pricing, new product offerings, and facility development were made by corporate headquarters in conjunction with the local people. Local people, however, felt that the key decisions were being postponed. Conflicting demands also were a problem as every division drew on the local resources for personnel,

inventories, receivables, and capital investment. These demands had been manageable, however, because even though profits were below target no cash shortages had developed.

Current Organization of International Operations

To improve the performance of its international operations, Bancil instituted a reorganization in mid-1973. The new organization was a matrix of NU general managers and area vice presidents, who were responsible for total resource allocation in their geographic area, and division presidents, who were responsible for their product lines worldwide. (See Figure 2 for a description of the matrix in 1975.)

The general manager was the chief executive in his country in charge of all Bancil products. He also was Bancil's representative on the board and executive committee of local joint ventures. The Bancil delegate usually had been chosen as the general manager. He was responsible for making the best use of financial, material, and personnel resources; pursuing approved strategies; searching for and identifying new business opportunities for Bancil in his NU; and developing Bancil's reputation as a responsible corporate citizen. The general manager was assisted by a financial manager, one or more plant managers, product line marketing managers, and other functional managers as required.

The divisions were responsible for operations in the United States and Canada and for worldwide expertise on their product lines. Divisions discharged the latter responsibility through local product line marketing managers who reported on a line basis to the NU general manager and on a functional basis to

Vice President
International Operations
Clark B. Tucker

Product Group Vice Presidents	Division Presidents	Europe Andre Dufour			Latin America Juan Vilas			Far East
Area Vice Presidents →	General Managers →	France P. Chevalier	West Germany D. Rogge	Four Other National Units	Argentina and Uruguay S. Portillo	Brazil E. Covelli	Two Other National Units	Four Other National Units
Agricultural and Animal Health (three divisions)	Rodgers Division							
	Division B							
	Division C							
Consumer Products (two divisions)	Dominic Division							
	Toiletry Division (Robert Vincent)							
Pharmaceuticals (two divisions)	Division A							
	Division B							
Professional (three divisions)	Knight Division							
	Division B							
	Division C							

FIGURE 2 Shared Responsibility Matrix

Source: Company records.

a division area marketing director. The latter, in turn, reported to the divisional marketing vice president. Where divisions were involved in other functional activities, the organizational structure was similar to that for marketing. The flow of product line expertise from the divisions to the NUs consisted of (1) operational inputs such as hiring/termination policies and the structure of merit programs and (2) technical/professional inputs to the NU marketing, production, and other staff functions on the conduct of the division's business within the NU.

Only the Dominic Division was represented in every NU. Some divisions lacked representation in several NUs, and in some cases a division did not have a marketing director in an area. For example, the Rodgers Division had area marketing directors in Europe, the Far East, and Latin America, all reporting to the divisional vice president of marketing to whom the division's U.S. marketing personnel also reported. However, the Knight Division, which had a structure similar to that of the Rodgers Division, could justify area marketing directors only in Europe and Latin America.

The new matrix organization established for each country a national unit review committee (NURC) with its membership consisting of the general manager (chairman), a financial manager, and a representative from each division with activities in the NU. Corporate executives viewed the NURC as the major mechanism for exercising shared profit responsibility. NURC met quarterly, or more frequently at the general manager's direction, to (1) review and approve divisional profit commitments generated by the general manager's staff; (2) ensure that these profit commitments, viewed as a whole, were compatible with and representative of the best use of the NU's resources; (3) monitor the NU's progress against the agreed plans; and (4) review and approve salary ranges for key NU personnel. When the division's representatives acted as members of the NURC, they were expected to view themselves as responsible executives of the NU.

Strategic Planning and Control

NURC was also the framework within which general managers and division representatives established the NU's annual strategic plan and profit commitment. Strategy meetings commenced in May, at which time the general manager presented a forecast of Bancil's business in his or her NU for the next five years and the strategies that would be pursued to exploit environmental opportunities. The general manager and the divisional representatives worked together between May and September to develop a mutually acceptable strategy and profit commitment. If genuine disagreement on principle arose during these deliberations, the issue could be resolved at the next level of responsibility. The profit commitment was reviewed at higher levels both within the area and within the product divisions, with the final approval coming from the corporate executive committee (CEC), which required compatible figures from the vice president of international operations and the product group executives. CEC, the major policy making forum at Bancil, consisting of the chief executive officer, the group vice presidents, the vice president of international operations, and the corporate secretary, met monthly to resolve policy issues and to review operating performance.

For each country, results were reported separately for the various divisions represented, which, in turn, were consolidated into

TABLE 2   1974 Division Profit Flow and National Unit Net Income, Argentine National Unit

	RODGERS DIVISION	DOMINIC DIVISION	TOILETRY DIVISION	NATIONAL UNIT
Division sales	$250,000	$800,000	$1,250,000	$2,300,000
Division expenses	160,000	650,000	970,000	1,780,000
Division profit flow	90,000	150,000	280,000	520,000
NU other expenses (general administrative, interest on loans, etc.)				350,000
NU income before taxes				170,000
Less: Taxes				80,000
NU net income				$ 90,000
Working capital	100,000	300,000	700,000	

a combined NU statement. The NU as well as the divisions were held accountable, though at different levels, according to their responsibilities. The division profit flow (DPF) and NU net income are shown in Table 2 for the Argentine national unit in 1974.

The product divisions were responsible for worldwide DPF defined as net sales less all direct expenses related to divisional activity, including marketing managers' salaries, sales force, and sales office expenses. The NU was responsible for net income after charging all local divisional expenses and all NU operating expenses such as general administration, taxes, and interest on borrowed funds. Because both the general managers and the divisions shared responsibility for profit in the international operations, the new structure was called a shared responsibility matrix (SRM). The vice president of

international operations and the division presidents continually monitored various performance ratios and figures (see Table 3). In 1975 international operations emphasized return on resources, cash generation, and cash remittance, while the division presidents emphasized product line return on resources, competitive market share, share of advertising, and dates of new product introductions.

The impact of the 1973 organization shift to the SRM had been greatest for the general managers. Previously, as Bancil delegates, they had not been measured on the basis of the NU's total performance for which they were now held responsible. Also, they now determined salary adjustments, hiring, dismissals, and appointments after consultations with the divisions. In addition, general managers continued to keep abreast of important political developments in their areas,

TABLE 3   Control Figures and Ratios

VICE PRESIDENT OF INTERNATIONAL OPERATIONS FOR NATIONAL UNIT		DIVISION PRESIDENT FOR PRODUCT LINE
X*	Sales	X
X	Operating income; % sales	X
X	General manager expense; % sales	
X	Selling expense; % sales	X
X	Nonproduction expense; % operating income	
X	Operating income per staff employee	
X	% staff turnover	
X	Accounts receivable (days)	X
X	Inventories (days)	X
X	Fixed assets	X
X	Resources employed	X
X	Return on resources	X
X	Cash generation	
X	Cash remittances	
X	Share of market and share of advertising	X
X	Rate of new product introduction	X

*X indicates figure or ratio on organization's (national unit or division) performance of interest to the vice president of international operations and the division presidents.

Source: Company records.

such as the appointment of a new finance minister, a general work strike, imposition of punitive taxes, and the outbreak of political strife, a not-infrequent occurrence in some countries.

Under the new organizational structure, the area marketing directors felt that their influence was waning. While they were responsible for DPF, they were not sure that they had "enough muscle" to effect appropriate allocation of resources for their products in each of the countries they served. This view was shared by Nicholas Rosati, Knight Division marketing manager in Italy, who commented on his job:

The European marketing director for the Knight Division keeps telling me to make more calls on hospitals and laboratories. But it is useless to make calls to solicit more orders. The general manager for Italy came from the Consumer Products Division. He will neither allocate additional personnel to service new accounts for the Knight Division nor will he purchase sufficient inventory of our products so I can promise reasonable delivery times for new accounts.

Divisions, nevertheless, were anxious to increase their market penetration outside the United States and Canada, seeing such a

strategy as their best avenue of growth. The recent increase in international sales and profits, which had by far exceeded that of domestic operations (see Table 4), seemed to confirm the soundness of this view. Not all NU general managers shared this approach, as exemplified by a statement from Edmundo Covelli, the general manager of Brazil:

The divisions are continually seeking to boost their sales and increase their DPF. They are not concerned with the working capital requirements to support the sales. With the inflation rate in Brazil, my interest rate of 40 percent on short-term loans has a significant effect on my profits.

The Peau Doux Issue

The telephone conversation described at the beginning of the case involved a disagreement between Tom Wilson, who was both marketing vice president for the Toiletry Division and acting division marketing director for Europe, and Pierre Chevalier, Bancil's general manager for France. It also involved Remy Gentile, who reported on a line basis to Chevalier and on a functional basis to Wilson.

TABLE 4   Sales and Profits for Bancil Corporation Domestic and International, Selected Years 1955–1974 (in millions of dollars)

Year	DOMESTIC		INTERNATIONAL		TOTAL	
	Sales	Profit	Sales	Profit	Sales	Profit
1955	$ 61	$ 5.5	—	—	$ 61	$ 5.5
1960	83	8.3	$ 6	$ .2	89	8.5
1965	121	13.5	23	1.3	144	14.8
1969	269	26.7	76	9.2	345	35.9
1970	280	27.1	99	12.3	379	39.4
1971	288	28.7	110	14.2	398	42.9
1972	313	32.5	147	15.8	460	48.3
1973	333	35.3	188	21.4	521	56.7
1974	358	36.7	242	30.9	600	67.6

Source: Company records.

Pierre Chevalier had been a general manager of France for 18 months after having been hired from a competitor in the consumer products business. Upon assuming the position, he identified several organizational and operational problems in France:

When I took this job, I had five marketing managers, a financial manager, a production manager, and a medical specialist reporting to me. After the consumer products division split, the new Toiletry Division wanted its own marketing manager. Nine people reporting to me was too many. I hired Remy for his administrative talents and had him assume responsibility for the Toiletry Division in addition to having the other marketing managers report to him. That gave me more time to work with our production people to get the cost of goods down.

In less than two years as general manager, Chevalier had reduced the cost of goods sold by more than 3 percent by investing in new equipment and had improved the net income for the French NU by discontinuing products that had little profit potential.

Remy Gentile had been the marketing manager for the Toiletry Division in France for the past year. In addition, five other marketing managers (one for each Bancil Corporation division operating in France) reported to him. During the previous six years Gentile had progressed from salesman to sale supervisor to marketing manager within the Knight Division in France. Although he had received mixed reviews from the Toiletry Division, particularly on his lack of mass-marketing experience, Chevalier had hired him because of his track record, his ability to learn fast, and his outstanding judgment.

The disagreement involved the Peau Doux line of hand creams that Bancil Corporation had purchased five years earlier to spread the general manager's overhead, especially in terms of marketing, over a broader product offering. Wilson's frustration resulted from Chevalier's ambivalence toward the division's strategy of increasing the marketing effort and cutting manufacturing costs on the Peau Doux line.

The total market in France for the Peau Doux product line was growing at an annual rate of 15–20 percent, according to both Wilson and Gentile. However, Peau Doux, an old, highly regarded hand cream, had been traditionally distributed through pharmacies, whereas recently introduced hand creams had been successfully sold through supermarkets. The original Peau Doux sales force was not equipped to distribute the product through other outlets. To support a second sales force for supermarket distribution, the Toiletry Division sought to acquire the L'aube shampoo and face cream line. When Gentile had informed Chevalier of this strategy, the latter had questioned the wisdom of the move. The current volume of the Peau Doux line was $800,000. Although less than 10 percent of Chevalier's total volume, it comprised the entire Toiletry Division volume in France.

Tom Wilson viewed the Peau Doux problems primarily in terms of an inadequate marketing effort. On three occasions within the past year, he or his media experts from Sunnyvale had gone to Paris to troubleshoot the Peau Doux problems. On the last trip, Robert Vincent, the Toiletry Division president, had joined them. On the return flight to Sunnyvale, Wilson remarked to Vincent,

I have the suspicion that Chevalier, in disregarding our expertise, is challenging our authority. It is apparent from his indifference to our concerns and his neglect in allocating capital for new machinery that he doesn't care about the Peau Doux line. Maybe he should be told what to do directly.

Vincent responded,

Those are very strong words, Tom. I suggest we hold tight and do a very thorough job of preparing for the budget session on our strategy in France. If Chevalier does not accept or fundamentally revises our budget, we may take appropriate measures to make corporate management aware of the existing insensitivity to the Toiletry Division in France. This seems to be a critical issue. If we lose now, we may never get back in the French market in the future.

After Wilson and Vincent had departed for Sunnyvale, Chevalier commented to Dufour, his area vice president,

I have the feeling that nothing we say will alter the thinking of Wilson and Vincent. They seem to be impervious to our arguments that mass advertising and merchandising in France do not fit the Peau Doux product concept.

André Dufour had been a practicing pharmacist for six years prior to joining Bancil Corporation as a sales supervisor in Paris in 1962. He had progressed to sales manager and marketing manager of the Consumer Products Division in France. After the untimely death of the existing Bancil delegate for France in 1970, he had been selected to fill that position. With the advent of SRM, he had become the general manager and had been promoted to vice president for Europe a year later. Dufour had a talent for identifying market needs and for thoroughly planning and deliberately executing strategies. He was also admired for his perseverance and dedication to established objectives. Clark B. Tucker, vice president of international operations and Dufour's immediate supervisor, commented,

When he was a pharmacist he developed an avocational interest in chess and desired to become proficient at the game. Within five years he successfully competed in several international tournaments and achieved the rank of International Grand Master.

In the fall of 1974, Dufour had become the acting vice president of international operations while his superior, Clark Tucker, was attending the 13-week advanced management program at the Harvard Business School. Although Dufour had considerable difficulty with the English language, he favorably impressed the corporate management at Sunnyvale with his ability of getting to the heart of business problems.

The Toiletry Division had only limited international activities. In addition to the Peau Doux line in France, it marketed Cascada shampoos and Tempestad fragrances in Argentina. The Cascada and Tempestad lines had been acquired in 1971.

Tom Wilson and Manual Ramirez, Toiletry Division marketing director for Latin America, were ecstatic over the consumer acceptance and division performance of Cascada and Tempestad in Argentina. Revenue and DPF had quintupled since the acquisition. In his dealings with Gentile, Wilson frequently referred to the Toiletry Division's success in Argentina. Given this sales performance and the division's clearly stated responsibility for worldwide marketing of toiletry products, Wilson felt that his position in proposing the new strategy for France was strong.

On the other hand, Sergio Portillo, general manager of Argentina and Uruguay, and Juan Vilas, vice president for Latin American operations, had become alarmed by the cash drain from marketing the Toiletry Division products in Argentina. The high interest charges on funds for inventories and receivables seemed to negate the margins touted by the division executives. In describing the Cascada and Tempestad operation to Vilas, Portillo commented,

I have roughly calculated our inventory turnover for the Toiletry Division products marketed in Argentina. Although my calculations are crude, the ratio based on gross sales is about 4, which is less than one-half the inventory turnover of the remainder of our products.

Neither Portillo nor Vilas shared the Toiletry Division's enthusiasm, and they suspected that Cascada and Tempestad were only slightly above break-even profitability. Chevalier and Dufour were aware of this concern with the toiletry products in Argentina.

As Chevalier contemplated the Toiletry Division strategy, he became convinced that more substantive arguments rather than just economic ones would support his position. In discussing his concerns with Dufour, Chevalier asked,

Are the Toiletry Division product lines really part of what John Stoopes and we want to be Bancil's business? Hand creams, shampoos, and fragrances belong to firms like Colgate-Palmolive, Procter & Gamble, and Revlon. What is Bancil contributing to the local people's welfare by producing and marketing toiletries? We have several potentially lucrative alternatives for our resources. The Rodgers Division's revenues have been increasing at 18 percent. We recently completed construction of a processing plant for Rodgers, and we must get sales up to our new capacity. The Knight Division is introducing an electronic blood analyzer that represents a technological breakthrough. We must expand and educate our sales force to take advantage of this opportunity.

Chevalier sensed that Gentile was becoming increasingly uneasy on this issue, and the feeling was contagious. They had never faced such a situation before. Under the previous organization, NUs had been required to comply, although sometimes reluctantly, with the decisions from Sunnyvale. However, SRM was not supposed to work this way. Chevalier and Gentile stood firmly behind their position, although they recognized the pressure on Tom Wilson and to a lesser degree on Vincent. They wondered what should be the next step and who should take it. Due to the strained relationship with Wilson, they did not rule out the possibility of Wilson and Vincent's taking the Peau Doux issue to the consumer products group vice president and having it resolved within the corporate executive committee.

QUESTIONS

1. What are the strategic business thrusts at Bancil? Which ones are the most critical for the future in the judgment of the corporate management?

2. Clearly identify the basic functioning of the new multiaxis structures implemented by the company. Where are the pressure points? Why was the structure changed? Will the new structure accomplish the purpose underlying the change? Under what conditions?

3. What are the opportunities and problems facing Chevalier, Dufour, and Vincent? Should the issue be resolved between Dufour and Vincent or by the corporate executive committee?

4. What should the president of the consumer products group do, if anything?

5. How would you determine the dimensions of the job for Dufour and Vincent?

APPENDIX: Organizing for International Marketing[1]

My intent today is to talk about a practitioner's view of international marketing and, in doing so, to expose a few of our paradigms.

Joel Barker, a futurist from Minnesota, has a wonderfully descriptive illustration of what a paradigm is. It goes like this!

Imagine a fine spring day. A man is driving cheerfully along a country road. Suddenly, from around the curve ahead, a car comes lurching towards him in *his* lane. He brakes hard, and as it swerves past, the woman driver screams at him, "Pig! Pig!" Furious, he shouts back at her, "Sow! Sow!" Pleased with himself, he drives around the curve and runs smack into a *pig*.

He was the victim of a paradigm, a habitual pattern of looking at things, of accepting certain information and rejecting what doesn't fit. What he mistook for an insult was in fact meant as a friendly warning.

Don't laugh it off. Each of us has his own paradigms, his own mindsets, his own set ways of seeing and interpreting. And the subject of this address—international marketing—is replete with them.

It is difficult, if not impossible, to talk about international marketing, because I assert categorically that much about what we have come to accept as international marketing isn't really international. I know—we have all read about it, heard about it, and even taken a course or two in it. Nevertheless, my own *practical* experience shows that the idea of taking a standardized product, developing a universal selling point for it and then marketing it all around the world is nothing but an illusion.

Besides offering a chance to expose a paradigm or two, which may be due for revision, marketing is my topic for yet another reason: It happens to be my field. I've spent more than a quarter of a century in marketing in all parts of the free world, from the Orient to Europe, from Africa to Australia, from Latin America to Canada and the U.S.A. My company brings you such brand names as Hellmann's, Best Foods, Knorr, Mazola, Skippy, Thomas' and others with which I hope you are familiar. Its name is CPC International.

And there is that word again! International!

Indeed, while a company *can* be international, I say that a product can*not*. At least not to anybody but a casual observer.

Although, for instance, our brands of mayonnaise are actively marketed to consumers in 28 countries, let me assure you they did *not* get there through international marketing, but quite a different route. How?

In the very same manner *any* product is sold. Every product everywhere is sold one at a time, bought by one person at a time. Each buyer is different from every other buyer. Different tastes, different prejudices. And no matter how wide-

---

[1]Eric D. Haueter, Vice President, CPC International Inc. Pace University, Lubin Lecture, used with permission.

spread your sales, you cannot lump these individuals into one international market or, *if* you do, you create nothing but mere statistics.

So, right here, let's puncture our first paradigm, one that has brought considerable woe to both businessmen and consumers alike. It is the misconception that: The more universal and massive the marketing approach, the more effective it will be.

It's called mass marketing! And its more widespread form—international marketing—simply carries the mis-concept one mis-step further!

I say it's the height of arrogance to assume you can standardize a product and sell it to people all around the world; to assume that if it works here it can be imposed there. That's what's often done in the name of international marketing, and I'll give you examples of how it generally fails to work. At best, it gets ignored; at worst, resented. It fails for two reasons, usually interrelated. One, a business reason, centered on what the product is—or is not; the other, for how it is presented to the potential buyer. Notice I said buy-*er*. Singular.

And, here goes another possible paradigm—that the word consumer is a collective noun! Because, as I said a moment ago, a product is sold one sale at a time, to one buyer at a time. That's the way it has always been. No seething mass of consumers stampeding into the supermarket to make a buy in unison. One at a time on the buyer's side—but somehow, some decades ago, came a significant change on the side of the seller. No more one-to-one relationship; the seller became remote, many layers removed, impersonal and unapproachable.

Gone was the face-to-face dealing of the ''butcher, baker, and candlestick-maker,'' who would chop or bake or dip to order, and who would be told the next day if their product failed to meet customer expectations. In came the era of remoteness, necessitated by mass production and mass distribution, and the resulting delusion of mass marketing.

Now, there's nothing wrong with mass production and mass distribution—if they make more things available to more people at less cost. My quarrel is with that canard called mass marketing—especially when you stretch it to international marketing. Nowhere does this come into sharper focus than in the marketing of processed foods. For instance: Both a famous American coffee and a favorite American soup made the dreadful mistake of trying to go abroad in their original form . . . after all, if it works here, it'll work there. But it didn't work. Taste, formula, price . . . they just didn't fit local expectations. They didn't even try to make it fit.

In France, a best-selling American soap, introduced without any adaptation, was rejected by French households because it smelled of carbolic acid, an odor not generally associated there with cleanliness, but rather—of all things—with houses of ill repute.

Instant tea, a staple in many American kitchens, was laughed out of England as offensive to both taste bud and custom.

What went wrong here in these cases? The seller, in his ignorance or arrogance, assumed that all buyers were alike, that his mass produced product, successful in its home country, could be mass marketed on an international scale.

The examples go on and on. You can read more in a book, newly published, called *Business Blunders* by David Ricks. You'd never believe the blunders committed in the name of international marketing, even to a product as simple, as basic as soup.

Everybody in the world eats soup. Just about. But the problem is: Not everybody eats the *same* soup. In fact, not everybody eats the same *tomato* soup. The English, for instance, want their tomato soup sweeter and redder than do the Americans. One American company sent its tomato soup unchanged to Britain and failed. Another tailored their formula to suit the English taste; they succeeded so mightily that today no British housewife would believe that the brand originated in "the colonies."

The Irishman wants cream in his tomato soup, as does the Italian. The German wants rice; and the Colombian, spice. That's a lot of talk about soup. But it points to a problem and to the popping of another paradigm.

You do not market a *product* . . . you market a *concept*. Business judgement leads you to the concept, and the consumer leads you to the product. A concept is applicable to a number of countries; a product usually to only one, or even to parts of one. Recognizing this, though still far removed from the approach prevailing in the era of the "butcher, baker, candlestickmaker," is an earnest step toward serving the needs of the individual. And doing what's best for the consumer, after all, is the only road to business success.

It follows therefore, that a particular kind of organization is called for. What *won't* work is a self-centered international corporation run from a distant headquarters. What *will* work is a careful balance between *corporate,* for *strategic* direction; and *local,* for *tactical* execution. What is required is a network of local units, operating on the spot, autonomously, independently, but under a common set of global guidelines, strategic, financial and ethical.

People in the local marketing unit must be steeped in the territory, participants in the culture, aware of the specific tastes and wants of their consumers: to be able to intelligently interpret and adapt concepts into specific products.

A simple premise! But *not* recognizing it or observing it, is what has gotten some of America's most successful marketers into big trouble, particularly when they ventured abroad. But this same error has also left enormous gaps in the geographical penetration of some leading brands right here at home. Because even the U.S.A. is truly a collection of many local markets, although they all happen to be surrounded by one common political border.

Economic constraints prevent us from achieving the one-to-one relationship of the good old days. But local marketing, or the local adaptation of general concepts, get us closer to this ideal by letting the consumer know that somebody cares to please him. And, as we observed earlier, pleasing the consumer is in the very best self-interest of business.

What is the business of business, really? It is to seek ever better ways to satisfy as many of the differing human needs as possible. And although there is a strong element of self-interest in this, it just so happens that the interests of consumers and marketers coalesce.

Each corporation seeks its own answers. In our case, in the case of CPC International, we have a different heritage from most other food companies based in the U.S.A. For several generations, we've been practicing what I am trying to preach here. Not necessarily because we are all that smart. Rather, we've had a global perspective and looked at the world as our market since we went abroad many generations ago, around the turn of the century.

Our unique structure, worldwide, grew as we set up to operate in countries, many much smaller and also poorer than the U.S.A. Within each border were different languages, cultures, politics—and, more significant to us, different tastes, habits and traditions.

We, in order to survive, much less prosper, had to study each separate market intensively, seek out specific differences to accommodate the *individual* consumer. No mass marketing here—nor any mass production. Within narrow national boundaries, we found success by producing a greater variety of products in smaller batches, and learned to minimize the effects of reduced scale economies by the application of new technologies. We determined that there are considerable business opportunities in even very small political entities—call them countries—if you search sensitively, then adapt and tailor your approach in many different ways.

So, it was at least partially the force of circumstances, and also the absence of parochial arrogance, which led CPC to adopt an attitude of tolerance to deviations from what others might have called the "norm." In fact, it led us to the realization that any sort of "norms" could at best apply to concepts, but never to their physical representations, the products.

Let's look at a real example, a quick case history: bouillons. You're familiar with the bouillon cube? It's not much of a product in the U.S., but in Mexico, for instance, the total market is more than 1 billion liters; that's about 100 servings for every man, woman and child per year.

Around the world, bouillon takes on many forms, shapes and flavors, and serves a large number of needs. Mostly as a flavor contributor, but also an appetizer, a pick-me-up, a general enhancer. It comes as a cube or as a powder. It comes in chicken or beef flavor, in the U.S.A., or Germany, or Switzerland. But in Mexico, in addition to these two flavors, you'd better have it also in tomato or shrimp variety. In Argentina, there you need a corn bouillon. In Kenya, a chili variety. In Ireland, mutton; and in Thailand, pork—all bouillons. Many products indeed, but all performing the one basic function of contributing flavor at a very nominal cost—truly one single concept!

Another case: bread spreads, or spreads for breads. You may know it as peanut butter. But the concept is much broader and simply offers a flavorful element to be conveniently spread on bread and eaten as a nutritious snack meal.

And what does this concept translate to in other parts of the world? Well, in many countries of Europe it is a paste made from chocolate and hazelnuts; in Latin America from milk and sugar; or from Guava. A far cry from peanut butter when you look at it through the narrow lens; but very much the same in conceptual terms.

Both bouillon and breadspreads demonstrate the success of our formula which combines *strategic concepts,* with *local implementation.* It has worked exceedingly well. So much so, in fact, that the thought occurred to us to extend this practice to units of our own making, not just to political entities. And, although we abhor fancy buzz words, for lack of a better term we began to refer to it as "modular marketing." That is marketing, module by module, bit by small bit, rather than trying to gobble the whole globe in a gulp. This is perhaps more reflective of an *attitude* than a scientific system. It stresses the need to flexibly meet specific demands in order to realize optimal opportunities.

But exactly what *is* a module? It can be a country, a target group or a product line. The one requirement for a "module" is that it must be small enough, and sharply enough defined to be the means by which a concept can be converted into a product which is seen by people as meeting their *individual* demands. That makes lots of buyers happy and thereby builds a business—yet maintains reasonable scale economies. And, we sincerely hope, it produces a profit.

A module may be geographic, or it may be demographic.

And here you might ask the question: How can a module be independent, free to answer the needs of its local consumer, yet at the same time, bound to its international headquarters, to answer to global guidelines? Who comes first, the consumer or the corporation? No conflict necessary. The corporation listens to the local people in matters of the consumer. For, without the consumer, there is no corporation.

However—the local manager makes an advantage of the guidelines, resources, stature and reputation of his corporation. Rather than being confined, he is reinforced by a huge pool of technologies and accumulated experience, the intelligence of all the modules combined. It prevents reinventing the wheel, as it shortens his path and increases his chances for success.

He is aided by corporate conceptual parameters which are sufficiently narrow to allow concentration of knowledge and the creation of critical mass, yet wide enough to encourage and accommodate specific opportunities in specific situations.

For instance, Knorr is just one of our many brands; but under Knorr alone we market more than 2,000 products in 36 countries, all of which are based on four fundamental concepts and guided by one global strategy. That's modular marketing!

Benign interaction between local and corporate, between the tactical and strategic levels, creates a synergism wherein the results are greater than the sum of the separate contributions. On one hand, the corporate level gives direction through strategic guidelines, counseling, support and coordination of strengths. On the other hand, the local unit is where all this focuses on the individual—the consumer, surely, but also all those who are members and partners in a business society, including potential buyers!

Modular marketing does come close to making the individual sale. The local manager is given heavy responsibility. He must be a commercial ambassador, with a social conscience and a keen economic sense. And a strong manager flourishes with such authority, with freedom to design his own success, to leave his footprints in the sand, as well as in the carpeting of the executive suite. And as he flourishes, so does the corporation, for it, too, is but the summation of successes of the individual modules.

What we've discussed here today about the business of marketing, and particularly the marketing of processed foods, applies, of course, to other industries where a number of paradigms seem so firmly entrenched. I imagine most of you read the article, "The Next American Frontier," by Robert Reich, which first appeared in the March issue of *Atlantic Monthly*.

Professor Reich, who teaches business and public policy at Harvard says—and I'm simplifying: What's killing American industry is American industry.

The problem, says Reich, comes from the very same preoccupation with standardized production that brought America such unparalleled wealth, starting some generations ago. In steel, autos, textiles, chemicals, machinery—the capital intensive, smokestack industries—heavy stuff produced and sold by what was called "scientific management."

But, in the 1970s, the era began to end, and with it the validity of the science. It was challenged by foreign industry, unhampered by paradigms, and aided by a global perception and novel technologies. While the foreign invaders were able to produce and offer the consumer exactly what he wanted in autos, T.V. sets, cameras, watches, and more, American industry was trapped in bureaucratic routine that resisted innovation, slowed down responses, and was thus unable to adapt to changes in consumer demand.

Reich goes on to say more, all rather gloomy. But I think it boils down to one essential problem: inflexibility.

I'm thankful that he did not have to talk about the food processing business, where flexibility has been, and is, our password into many different markets.

And yet, even in the food industry there were a majority of our competitors who steadfastly clung to fixed paradigms and refused to market flexibly, or modularly. How else can you explain that most leading brands in the U.S. produce but one formula of a given product—for all regions of the country, all ethnic groups, all walks of life? Habits, and traditions, just aren't all that uniform, not even here in the U.S.A.

At first glance, it might appear that the food business would be the most readily standardized. For thousands of years there has been little change in the fundamental way we feed ourselves, since the mastery of fire and the discovery of agriculture. But, today's consumer insists on more than fundamentals. Cultures, climates, traditions and habits have created basic demands which go way beyond basic needs. And he who ignores this changing perception is not likely to succeed in the long run!

To be sure, once upon a time, you could get away with being inflexible. Look, for example, at chocolate bars in this country. For generations, sales were confined to what we might call a "standard variety." But, as alternatives became widely available and people began to realize how chocolate can *really* taste, buying habits were changing.

Hark back further, to the early days of Henry Ford, when you could have your Model T in any color as long as it was black. Phenomenal as it was in its time, the Model T and subsequent variations became outmoded. Progress, and new technologies, made it possible to produce variety economically and thus satisfy more individual consumer demands in terms of color, size, shape, power, price, gadgetry—all within a few decades.

I wonder what our own era will look like several decades from now—or even a few years from now—with the speed at which we move today. I won't predict what might happen to our geography or demography, to our society or its politics. But, being an optimist, I predict that humanity will not only survive but flourish. The quality of life will be greatly improved, through many efforts, of which modulur marketing may be one.

In fact, you may recall that I have described modular marketing as more of an attitude than a system. And I believe it is this attitude, this sensitivity to specific conditions and demands which will be the driving force behind the development of new technologies which in turn permit tailor-making products at a profit.

It will bring us closer to the old-time kind of individual service, which the candlestickmaker was able to render his customer; it will lead us further and further away from the era of over-standardized disregard for specific wishes, the era of the black Model-T Ford.

In sum, I see a knowing consumer growing more sophisticated, more demanding. To pinpoint specific wants, business will have to hone its sensitivity, sharpen its perception. Brand new technologies will make it possible to localize the thrust and to produce specific goods—not necessarily new goods or exotic goods—but *good* goods, better goods, tailor-made for various needs of different consumers, while still achieving economies of a different scale. Already today, the trend is *away* from *mass* production, and *toward* a dispersion of production in smaller units—made possible by new technologies.

To succeed, all businesses will have to adapt and veer toward this new direction. Modular marketing, we think, is a step along the right path, toward the ultimate goal, the ultimate module: one person buying, one person selling. Is that so impossible—to be able to beam in one segment at a time—or one *individual* at a time? Not impossible at all, in my view. In this age of the robot and the computer, we shall soon reach the consumer on a one-to-one basis.

Is it *important* that we do so? And is it important that you, of the academic community, help us to do so? I believe it is you who can help us break free of our paradigms and away from the mis-concept of international marketing. You can help rewrite management theory and lead the way to a new era of management practices wherein we think *globally,* but act *locally;* to give the individual consumer *more* say-so in what *he* or *she* wants.

To what end? Is it primarily a matter of profit? I don't think so—not today, in these times of "business beware, consumer aware"! No! Your contribution, your helping us to develop into a coherent system the practices, the philosophies, the attitudes I have touched upon today—your contribution can help us to a far more significant result: an advance in human well-being, an improvement in the quality of life.

And that *is* important.

19

GLOBAL MARKETING MANAGEMENT CONTROL

We have decided to call the entire field of control and communication theory, whether in the machine or in the animal, by the name of cybernetics, which we form from the Greek for steersman.

Norbert Wiener, 1894–1964
Cybernetics, 1948

INTRODUCTION

Global marketing presents formidable problems to managers responsible for marketing control. Each national market is different from every other market. Distance and differences in language, custom, and practices create communications problems. In larger companies, the size of operations and number of country subsidiaries often result in the creation of an intermediate headquarters, which adds an organizational level to the control system. This chapter reviews global marketing control practices, compares these practices with domestic marketing control, and identifies the major factors that influence the design of a global control system.

CONTROL AND PLANNING

Every plan is conceived in the midst of uncertain internal and external forces that influence marketing success. Market growth, customer response to a new product, competitive moves, government regulations, and costs are just a few of the uncertain factors about which assumptions must be made to formulate a plan. Therefore, when a company plans, it must also make provisions to monitor the results of plan implementation programs and make adjustments to plans where necessary. Planning necessitates control.

In the managerial literature, *control* is defined as the process of assuring "that the results of operations conform to established goals" or as "the process by which managers assure that resources are obtained and used effectively and efficiently in the accomplishment of the organization's objectives."[1] Marketing literature parallels these definitions. A leading marketing textbook identifies four types of marketing control: annual plan, profitability, efficiency, and strategic control.[2]

Each of these definitions describes a process of activities and steps that are directed toward ensuring that planned organizational programs do in fact achieve desired objectives. Control activities are directed toward programs initiated by the planning process. In the ongoing enterprise, however, the data measures and evaluations generated by the control process are also a major input to the planning process. Thus planning and control are intertwined and interdependent. The planning process can be divided into two related phases: (1) Strategic planning is the selection of opportunities defined in terms of products and markets, and the commitment of resources, both human and financial, to achieve these objectives; and (2) operational planning is the process in which strategic product market objectives and resource commitments to these objectives are translated into specific projects and programs. The relationship among strategic planning, operational planning, and control is illustrated in Figure 19–1.

In domestic operations, marketing control has become increasingly important and challenging. Because enterprise is getting larger, the distance between top managers and marketing operations is growing. Top managers must take steps to ensure that they receive information that measures the operation's success. The growing size of enterprise makes the analysis of an operation an increasingly challenging task. The environment is also changing rapidly, making it essential that control systems generate data that will be timely enough to allow management to take steps to correct problems.

In global operations, marketing control presents additional challenges. The rate of environmental change in a global company is a dimension of each of the national markets in which the company operates, and the multiplicity of environments, each changing at a different rate and each exhibiting unique characteristics, adds to the complexity of this dimension. In addition, the multiplicity of national environments challenges the global marketing control system with much greater environmental heterogeneity and therefore greater complexity in its control. Finally, global marketing causes special communications problems associated with the great distance between markets and headquarters and differences among managers in languages, customs, and practices.

The need for control is underlined by the fact that when making marketing decisions, executives are right or substantially right only 58 percent of the time.

[1]Robert N. Anthony, *Planning and Control Systems: A Framework for Analysis* (Boston: Division of Research, Graduate School of Business Administration, Harvard University, 1965).

[2]Philip Kotler, *Marketing Management: Analysis Planning and Control,* 6th ed. (Englewood Cliffs, N.J.: Prentice-Hall, 1988), p. 746–752.

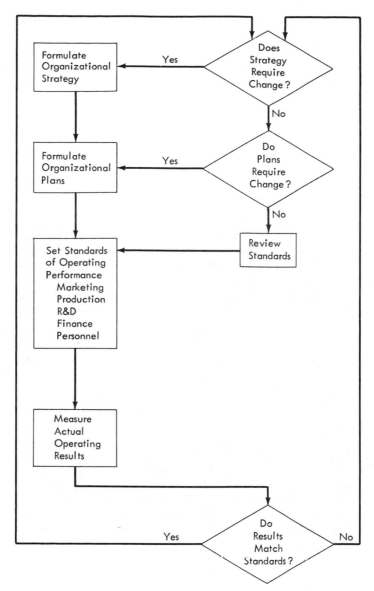

FIGURE 19–1   Relationship of Strategic Control and Planning

According to A. C. Nielsen, Jr.,[3] the 13 most common marketing errors in business today are:

1. *Failure to keep the product up-to-date.* If there is a product disadvantage at the start, success will be short-lived in spite of all the best sales and advertising efforts.

In general terms, in countries which are more developed from a marketing standpoint, any brand which fails to change its product after a competitor launches one which is preferred by the market, will find its potential sales reduced by at least 50 percent well within three years.

Timing is of vital importance. In many cases market leaders have lost the initiative because they were reluctant to change quickly after customers had clearly indicated a preference for another product.

2. *Failure to estimate the market potential accurately.* When entering a new market there is a natural tendency to overestimate the ultimate amount of business which can be achieved. Budgets must be drawn up based upon a sound estimate of the volume of business which can be expected.

If the production facilities are too large, overhead expenses can become burdensome and the resulting price of the finished product becomes too high.

Conversely, many managers assess their potential sales lower than they turn out to be. In such cases there is a real danger that the originator's market may be stolen by an aggressive competitor who correctly judges the potential market and makes his efforts on a larger scale.

3. *Failure to gauge the trend of the market.* Obviously, if the potential market is changing in size, many adjustments in the marketing program have to be made— either up or down.

4. *Failure to appreciate regional differences in market potential and in trend of market.* Most countries are complex in terms of ethnic, religious, or other traditional practices.

The variations between the patterns of circulation of advertising media, and demand for product, adds to the difficulty of achieving an optimum advertising allocation. Even when the facts are available, much detailed work is required to bring these two factors into balance. But it must be done if advertising money is to do its work effectively.

Likewise, getting the right number of salesmen in an area, achieving the proper number and frequency of sales calls throughout the year (as well as by size of account and size of city) also takes much detailed effort which must be accomplished if profitable results are to be obtained.

5. *Failure to appreciate seasonal differences in buyers' demand.* A good number of food and drug commodities have significant seasonal fluctuations. But, in many

[3]This section is condensed from an address given by A. C. Nielsen, Jr., to the first Argentine Marketing Forum.

cases, manufacturers concentrate their advertising and promotional efforts within the few months of the peak of the season (and withdraw it almost entirely during the so-called "off-seasons") ignoring the fact that "off-seasons" may represent between a quarter and a half of the total year's sales.

6. *Failure to establish the advertising budget by the job to be done.* Too many manufacturers appear to be using some historic formula for establishing their advertising budgets—such as a certain percent of sales. In our experience, any company which continues to set its advertising budget based upon sales performance alone, is asking for trouble.

7. *Failure to adhere to policies established in connection with long-range goals.* Once a goal has been set, there is a great temptation to shift policies whenever minor setbacks occur. Today's marketing executive must school himself in patience and allow ample time for a significant trend to develop. Often, it can be necessary to measure progress in terms of less than half a percentage point in a market.

8. *Failure to testmarket new ideas.* Experience is always helpful; but conditions change and what worked on one product, at one point in time, may not work on another product, a year or two later. Also, there is a big difference between what people say they will buy and what they actually buy.

9. *Failure to differentiate between short-term tactics and long-range strategy.* Special promotions will move a lot of merchandise, particularly out of the factory. But evidence would indicate that deals cannot be expected to change the long-term trends of well known brands. Successive and frequent use of deals generally produces smaller and smaller sales results, even temporarily.

Promotions can make it attractive for people to try a product once—but it is only through skillful and continuous merchandising that a brand can become a household name which can be relied upon year in and year out for profits for the shareholder.

10. *Failure to admit defeat.* None of us likes to see our creations classed as failures whether it be a product idea, a sales technique or a brilliant piece of copy. However, we should remind ourselves that we are dealing with human behaviour and that this is at best an inexact science.

11. *Failure to try new ideas while a brand is growing.* Understandably, there is a good deal of hesitancy to change a winner while it is still making progress. For this reason, many a good idea is ignored; and yet, a new package, a new design or a change in product formula might easily accelerate the progress of the brand. All too often, changes are made only after a competitor forces the change.

Don't let self-satisfaction get into your system. There is no room for complacency in selling.

12. *Failure to integrate all phases of the marketing operation into the over-all program.* No one phase of the marketing operation can be relied on for success. When moves like increasing advertising or changing the advertising theme are contemplated, big dividends can often be earned by giving consideration at the same

time to the many other phases of the marketing plan which will affect results; factors such as quality of the product, type of product, its packaging, distribution, and so on.

13. *Failure to appraise objectively your competitors' brands—as well as your own.* Underestimating the resources and ingenuity of your competitors, while at the same time overestimating the position or the reputation of your own brand, is the easiest thing in the world to do.

HOW HEADQUARTERS ACHIEVES CONTROL OF SUBSIDIARY OPERATIONS

When a company decides that it wants to develop a global strategy, it is essential that control of the subsidiary operations of the company shifts from the subsidiary to the headquarters. The subsidiary will continue to make vital inputs into the strategic planning process, but the control of the strategy must shift from subsidiary to headquarters. This involves a shift in the balance of power in the organization and may result in strong resistance to change.

In many companies there is a tradition of subsidiary autonomy and self-sufficiency that limits the influence of headquarters. To acquire control, there are three types of mechanisms: (1) data management mechanisms, (2) managers' management mechanisms that shift the perception of self-interest from subsidiary autonomy to global business performance, and (3) conflict resolution mechanisms that resolve conflicts triggered by necessary trade-offs. The major attributes of selected control mechanisms are shown in Table 19–1.[4]

FORMAL CONTROL METHODS

Planning and Budgeting

The basic formal marketing control technique used by companies is planning and budgeting. This practice is an extension of a basic technique used by companies in domestic marketing to global marketing. It involves expressing planned sales and profit objectives and expenditures on marketing programs in unit and money terms in a budget. The budget spells out the objectives and necessary expenditures to achieve these objectives. Control consists of measuring actual sales and expenditures. If there is no variance or favorable variance between actual and budget, no action is usually taken. If variance is unfavorable, this is a red flag that attracts the attention of line and staff executives at regional and international headquarters, and

---

[4] Yves L. Doz and C. K. Prahalad, "Headquarters Influence and Strategic Control in MNCs," *Sloan Management Review,* Fall 1981, pp. 15–29.

TABLE 19–1   Major Attributes of Selected Control Mechanisms

MECHANISMS	ORGANIZATIONAL ORIENTATIONS AFFECTED	STRENGTH AND SYMBOLIC VALUE OF MECHANISMS	SELECTIVITY	CONTINUITY	NEED FOR TOP MANAGEMENT'S ONGOING SUPPORT
Data Management					
1. Information systems	Cognitive, strategic, power	Variable*	High	Low	Low
2. Measurement systems					
Business performance	Cognitive	Medium	Medium	Medium	Low
Managers' performance	Power	High	Medium	Medium	Low
3. Resource allocation procedures					
Content	Strategic	Low	High	Low	Low
Impetus	Power	High	High	High	Medium
Approval	Administrative	High	High	Low	High
4. Strategic planning	Strategic	Variable*	Low	High	Medium
5. Budgeting process	Administrative	High	Low	Low	Low
Managers' Management					
1. Choice of key managers	Power	Strong	Low	High	Medium
2. Career paths	Power	Strong	Low	High	High
3. Reward and punishment systems	Power	Strong	Low	Medium	High
4. Management development	Strategic, cognitive	Variable*	High	Medium	Medium
5. Patterns of socialization	Cognitive	Low	Low	High	High
Conflict Resolution					
1. Decision responsibility assignments	Administrative	High	High	Medium	High
2. Integrators	Cognitive	Low	High	Low	High
3. Business teams	Cognitive	Low	Low	Medium	High
4. Coordination committees	Cognitive	Low	High	Low	High
5. Task forces	Strategic	Variable*	High	Low	High
6. Issue resolution processes	Strategic	Variable*	High	Low	High

*Variable means that the strength and symbolic value of the mechanism rest mainly on how the mechanism is set and managed.

Source: Yves Doz and C. K. Prahalad, "Headquarters Influence and Strategic Control in MNCs," *Sloan Management Review*, Fall 1981, p. 19.

they will investigate and attempt to determine the cause of the unfavorable variance and what might be done to improve performance.

Evaluating Performance

In evaluating performance, actual performance is compared with budgeted performance as described in the previous section. Thus the key question is, "How is the budget established? Most companies in both domestic and global operations place heavy reliance upon two standards—last year's actual performance and some kind of industry average or historical norm. A more normative approach is to develop at headquarters an estimate concerning the kind of growth that would be desirable and attainable in each national market. This estimate can be based upon exhaustive studies of national and industry growth patterns.

In larger companies there is enough business volume in a number of products to justify staff product specialists at corporate headquarters who follow the performance of products worldwide. They have staff responsibility for their product from its introduction to its withdrawal from the company's product line. Normally, a new product is first introduced in the largest and most sophisticated markets. It is subsequently introduced in smaller and less developed markets. As a result, the company's products are typically at different stages of the product life cycle in different markets. A major responsibility of staff specialists is to ensure that lessons learned in more advanced markets are applied to the management of their products in smaller less developed markets. Wherever possible they try to avoid making the same mistake twice, and they try to capitalize on what they have learned and apply it elsewhere. They also ensure that useful ideas from markets at similar stages of development are fully applied. Smaller companies focus on key products in key markets. Key products are those that are important to the company's sales, profit objectives, and competitive position. They are frequently new products that require close attention in their introductory stage in a market. If any budget variances develop with a key product, headquarters intervenes directly to learn about the nature of the problem and to assist local management in dealing with the problem.

In theory, if conditions in the subsidiary's business environment change during a planning period, the budget would be changed to reflect changes in underlying assumptions. In practice, budgets of the companies studied are not changed during an operating period. Companies recognize that refusing to change a budget can result in unfavorable variances that are not controllable by the subsidiary management, but the view of most companies is that it is better to allow these unfavorable variances to occur than it is to allow budget revision during an implementation period. When a company does not permit budget revision, it is emphasizing the importance of careful planning and of achieving plan objectives. If uncontrollable and unforeseeable changes do occur, these can be noted as mitigating reasons or even as a full explanation for failure to achieve budget.

Influences on Marketing Budgets

In preparing a budget or plan, the following factors are important:

MARKET POTENTIAL.   How large is the potential market for the product being planned? In every domestic market, management must address this question in formulating a product plan. An international company that introduces a product in more than one national market must answer this question for each market. In most cases new products are introduced on a serial rather than simultaneous basis and can be defined as new international products as opposed to new products per se. A new international product is analogous to a product that has been introduced in a test market. The major opportunity of a test market is the chance to project the experience in the test market to a national market, whereas its major pitfall is that the characteristics of the test market will be unlike those of the national market, thus invalidating the projections made. The same opportunities and pitfalls apply in an amplified way to new international products.

COMPETITION.   A marketing plan or budget must be prepared in light of the competitive level in the market. The more entrenched the competition, the more difficult it is to achieve market share and the more likely a competitive reaction will occur to any move that promises significant success in the target market. Competitive moves are particularly important as a variable in international market planning because many companies are moving from strong competitive positions in their base markets to foreign markets where they have a minor position and must compete against entrenched companies. Domestic market standards and expectations of marketing performance are based on experience in markets where the company has a major position. These standards and expectations are simply not relevant to a market where the company is in a minor position trying to break into the market.

IMPACT OF SUBSTITUTE PRODUCTS.   One of the sources of competition for a product in a market is the frequent existence of substitute products. As a product is moved into markets at different stages of development, improbable substitute products often emerge. For example, in Colombia a major source of competition for manufactured boxes and other packaging products is woven bags and wood boxes made in the handicraft sector of the economy. Marketing officials of multinational companies in the packaging industry report that the garage operator producing a handmade product is very difficult competition because of costs of materials and labor in Colombia.

PROCESS.   The manner in which targets are communicated to subsidiary management is as important as the way in which they are derived. One of the most sophisticated methods used today is the so-called "indicative planning method." Headquarters estimates of regional potential are disaggregated and communicated to subsidiary management as "guidance."[5] The subsidiaries are in no way bound by guidance. They are expected to produce their own plan, taking into account the headquarters guidance that is based on global data and their own data from the market, including a detailed review of customers, competitors, and other relevant market developments. This method produces excellent results because it combines a global perspective and estimate with specific country marketing plans that are developed from the objective to the program by the country management teams themselves. Headquarters, in providing "guidance," does not need to understand a market in depth. For example, it is not necessary that the headquarters of a manufacturer of electrical products know how to sell electric motors to a French consumer. What headquarters can do is gather data on the expected expansion in generating capacity in France and use experience tables drawn from world studies that indicate what each megawatt of additional generating capacity will mean in terms of the growth in demand in France for electrical motors. The estimate of total market potential together with information on the competitiveness of the French subsidiary can be the basis for a "guidance" in terms of expected sales and earnings in France. The guidance may not be accepted by the French subsidiary. If the indicative planning method is used properly, the subsidiary educates the headquarters if its guidance is unrealistic. If headquarters does a good job, it will select an attainable but ambitious target. If the subsidiary does not see how it can achieve the headquarters goal, discussion and headquarters involvement in the planning process will either lead to a plan that will achieve the guidance objective or it will result in a revision of the guidance by headquarters.

Many companies communicate sales and earnings expectations rather than guidance to subsidiaries. In one typical case these expectations were high and were based upon successful experience in the U.S. market. Subsidiaries accepted the expectations and budgeted programs to achieve them even though they did not have plans developed to achieve the budgeted goals. The problem in this company was the fear that subsidiaries had of challenging headquarters expectations. They felt it was better to fail to achieve headquarters expectations than to challenge them. The result in this case was an almost worldwide failure to achieve product plan objectives. If subsidiaries had taken headquarters initial goals for the product in question as guidance rather than as expectations, the result would have been a dialogue at the plan formulation stage between headquarters and subsidiaries that would have led to either the development of realistic plans to achieve headquarters guidance or the downward revision of the product's sales and earnings goals.

Other Measures of Performance

Another principal measure of marketing performance is share of market. In larger markets data are reported for subsidiaries and, where significant sales are involved,

---

[5]This term was coined by French planners in the 1950s to describe the function of the French National Planning Ministry in setting industry targets.

on a product-by-product basis. Share-of-market data in larger markets are often obtained from independent market audit groups. In smaller markets share-of-market data are often not available because the market is not large enough to justify the development of an independent commercial marketing audit service. Local managers or agents are asked to estimate their share-of-market position. In these smaller markets, it is possible for a country manager or agent to hide a deteriorating market position or share of market behind absolute gains in sales and earnings. This is a valuable measure because it provides a comparison of company performance with that of other competitors in the market. Companies that do not obtain this measure, even if it is an estimate, are flying blind.

It is important that this share of market be of the whole market, not just the import component. Until recently, one major U.S. corporation reported its business in foreign markets as a percentage of U.S. exports to each market. By this measure, in a period of declining U.S. export competitiveness in a number of markets, the company appeared to be doing very well when in fact its market position was rapidly deteriorating.

INFORMAL CONTROL METHODS

In addition to budgeting, informal control methods play an important role, particularly in multinational companies. The main informal control method is the transfer of people from one market to another. When people are transferred, they take with them their experience in previous markets, which will normally include some standards for marketing performance. When investigating a new market that has lower standards than a previous market, the investigation will lead to revised standards or to discovery of why there is a difference. Another valuable informal control device is face-to-face contact between subsidiary staff and headquarters staff as well as contact among subsidiary staff. These contacts provide an opportunity for an exchange of information and judgments that can be a valuable input to the planning and control process. Annual meetings that bring together staff from a region of the world often result in informal inputs to the process of setting standards.

VARIABLES INFLUENCING CONTROL

DOMESTIC PRACTICES AND THE VALUE OF STANDARDIZATION. One of the major assets of any organization is its operational and successful managerial practices. If a company has successfully developed and used a control system in its home or domestic operation, then this system is clearly a candidate for export because (1) it works, (2) there are people who understand it, and (3) these people can in most instances be persuaded to transfer their know-how to a foreign subsidiary. Today companies are using a standard reporting format for both domestic and foreign operations. The amount of detail and frequency of reports should be a function of the size of the foreign subsidiary. One sophisticated global marketer has designated 7 key markets and another 14 major markets in its 100-country multinational group. The amount and frequency of reporting is greatest for key markets.

The advantage of a standard system (adapted for market size differences) is that it allows comparisons to be made on a global basis, and it facilitates the easy transfer of people and ideas because all managers in the organization are working with the same system.

COMMUNICATIONS SYSTEM. A major development affecting control in international marketing operations is the communications infrastructure. A century ago international marketers had at their disposal various means of surface travel—horse, carriage, and train—as well as various means of water travel, such as sailboats and steamships. Electronic communications were limited to the telegraph. The business-person who wanted to control international operations had two choices: traveling by land, sea, or a combination of both or transmitting written messages either by post or by telegraph. Given the speed, cost, and comfort of the communications methods available a century ago, it is understandable that businesses operated on a highly decentralized basis. Operating policies consisted of sending out handpicked people with instructions as to their general areas of operations. These individuals were versed in the ways of the company, and therefore it was assumed that company policies and procedures would be implemented by them. They had total responsibility for carrying out the company's operations in their area. At the end of the designated operating period, which was typically a year, the results of operations would be reported. In those days, subsidiaries were controlled according to Saint Augustine's rule for Christian conduct: "Love God and do what you like!" The implication of this is that if you love God, then you will only ever want to do things that are acceptable to Him.[6] Men who were sent out to manage company affairs were expected to approach things in the approved manner.

Today the communications infrastructure is vastly enlarged. In addition to surface and sea travel, the airplane is now the major form of long-distance travel in the world. Face-to-face and written communications possibilities are vastly extended by high-speed jet aircraft. They allow managers to maintain regular direct contact with operating units all over the world. Given the importance of face-to-face communications in the information acquisition process, it seems reasonable to conclude that the jet aircraft has been a major tool in making it possible to manage a global enterprise. The very limited success of small businesses in international operations can be attributed to the reluctance or inability of the small business owner to invest money and time to travel to achieve instant familiarity with customers, agents, and distributors in foreign markets. The larger enterprise spends enormous sums to maintain contact with managers in foreign markets who are in direct contact with employees, customers, agents, and distributors in their markets.

In addition to the face-to-face communications possibilities, electronic com-

---

[6]Anthony Jay, *Management and Machiavelli* (New York: Holt, Rinehart and Winston, 1967).

munication is also vastly expanded. The teletype and telephone enable rapid, direct, high-speed voice and data communication to take place on a global basis. Increasingly, the communications systems of large corporations (large companies account for an estimated 80 percent of U.S. foreign direct investment) are being developed so that communication of voice and data will be available on a worldwide basis. In many large companies, internal communications systems allow direct dialing of any company telephone in the United States. And numerous companies are planning to expand their internal communications so that a company telephone anywhere in the world can be dialed direct.

DISTANCE. All other things being equal, the greater the distance between headquarters and an operating unit, the more autonomous the operating unit will be from headquarters. This relationship is due to physical and psychological differences. The physical distance imposes a time and cost barrier on communications because to travel to a distant point takes more time and therefore is more costly. To communicate by telephone, telex, or other telecommunications methods is also more costly and time consuming as distances increase. Thus, with less communication, particularly face-to-face communication, there is a greater delegation of responsibility as distances increase in international operations. Nevertheless, one of the major changes in the environment of international business is the development of communications technology, which has reduced the time and cost barriers of distance by increasing the speed, raising the quality, and covering the cost of voice, data, facsimile, telex, television, and air travel methods of communications.

THE PRODUCT. A major factor affecting the type of marketing control system developed for international operations is the product being controlled. A product that is technically sophisticated can be more extensively controlled because the product use is highly similar around the world. This similarity creates opportunities to apply standards of measurement and evaluation on an international basis. Computers, for example, are products that are applied today in the same manner in technologies wherever they are located in the world. The process control computer for the petrochemical industry is the same type of application in Rotterdam as it is in Baton Rouge, Louisiana. The technology for the application of microcircuitry is a universal technology that is applied in the same way in Japan as it is in the United States.

Environmental sensitivity is the relevant product dimension influencing the extent to which "international" control can be exercised. If a product is similar or identical in the way it is applied and used around the world, that is, if it is culturally insensitive, then international standards and measures of performance can be developed. Computers and many industrial products fit this category. If a product is sensitive to environmental differences, then it is more difficult to apply international standards. Drugs and packaged food are two examples of environmentally sensitive products that normally require adaptation to meet the preferences of different cultures and systems of medical practice.

ENVIRONMENTAL DIFFERENCES.   The greater the environmental difference, the greater the delegation of responsibility and the more limited the control of the operating unit. For example, most U.S. companies with operations in Canada apply their most extensive control of international operations to Canadian operations. Indeed, many U.S. companies with extensive international operations, some of which are semiautonomous with regard to U.S. headquarters, operate in Canada as if Canada were a part of the U.S. market. A major reason for this is that the Canadian market is perceived as being highly similar to the U.S. market. Therefore, the standards of measurement and evaluation applicable to the U.S. market are seen as being applicable and relevant to Canadian operations.

The development that has most accelerated the extension of control of international operations in regions that are highly different from the home country area is the regional headquarters. Regional headquarters copes with environmental difference by focusing on a group of countries that is formed to maximize within-group similarities and between-group differences.

ENVIRONMENTAL STABILITY.   The greater the degree of instability in a country, the less the relevance of external or planned standards and measures of performance. When a country moves into a period of sweeping political change, it is often impossible to predict environmental conditions. One company decided that whenever a subsidiary country went into a period of revolutionary change or turmoil it would scrap all plans and adopt a policy of simply delegating total on-the-spot discretion to local management to do whatever the managers thought best. Its experience had been that local management usually achieved much more than headquarters expected.

SUBSIDIARY PERFORMANCE.   A major variable influencing the kind of control exercised over international operations is the performance of subsidiary units. A subsidiary that is achieving budget is normally left alone. When a subsidiary fails to achieve budget, the variance between budgeted and actual performance is a sign that triggers intervention by headquarters. In addition, managers of successful profit centers have more leverage in holding off headquarters involvement in their operations. Subsidiaries reporting unfavorable variances find that headquarters is anxious to determine the cause of the problem, to correct the problem, and to maintain closer surveillance of operations to ensure that further difficulties do not emerge and develop undetected. Therefore a well-managed, successful subsidiary operation will be more loosely controlled than will an operation in difficulty. At the same time, the sophisticated multinational company headquarters wants to know how everybody, including successful units, is doing. It needs data on performance to help establish standards and comparisons to use in evaluating the performance of subsidiaries.

SIZE OF INTERNATIONAL OPERATIONS.   The larger the international operation in terms of sales and earnings, the greater is its ability to support its own headquarters staff specialists. The greater the specialization of a headquarters staff, the more extensive and penetrating is its control, or measurement and evaluation of performance. A large multinational company will have three or four levels of staff expertise focusing on operations in large country markets: country, region, and international and/or corporate. This fully developed staff organization is shown in Figure 19–2. A smaller company cannot afford to create a highly specialized multilevel staff and will therefore have less intensive control over its operations. A large multinational company assigns control responsibility to both line and staff executives. Normally, marketing control falls into the province of product group specialists and general managers. In smaller country markets, small staff organizations require a considerable simplification and abbreviation of the control process because the expertise and time required to generate and evaluate data are simply not available. One of the challenges to the large multinational company is the development of methods and procedures for the control of small subsidiaries that do not place an excessive data collection and reporting burden on the small subsidiary.

COMMUNICATIONS AND CONTROL IN THE GLOBAL ENTERPRISE

In their study of American, European, and Japanese subsidiaries in Brazil, Hulbert and Brandt found that subsidiary managers were unanimously of the opinion that the flow of communications between home office and Brazil had doubled or quadrupled in recent years.[7] Despite the increasing flow of communications aided by computers, satellites, telecommunications, and jet airplanes, there are significant problems in collecting relevant quality information, getting it to the right people, and actually making it useful for decision making and resource allocation. Additionally, few managers, particularly at headquarters, seem to be aware of the costs in time, effort, and direct expense linked to communications.

Types of Communications

Communications between home office and subsidiary in multinational companies can be divided into two broad categories: personal communication such as visits, meetings, and telephone conversations and impersonal communications such as regular or ad hoc reports and budget plans.

IMPERSONAL COMMUNICATIONS. Much information from subsidiaries to home office is reported on standardized forms that include statements of profit and loss, balance sheets, sales reports, sources and uses of funds, inventory positions, production schedules and output, production and marketing costs, and budgets and budget deviations.

[7]This section draws heavily upon James M. Hulbert and William K. Brandt, *Managing the Multinational Subsidiary* (New York: Holt, Rinehart and Winston, 1980).

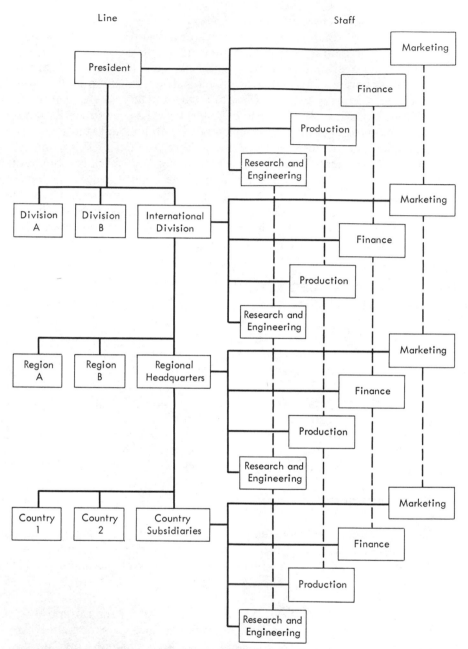

FIGURE 19–2 The Relationship of Staff and Line Profit Centers in a Large Multinational Company

American subsidiaries in Brazil report to their home offices in far greater detail and with greater frequency than do Japanese and European subsidiaries. Hulbert and Brandt found that managers in American firms complain bitterly about the burden of report requirements. Marketing managers in American companies estimated that they spent one day a week to "keep the home office happy." In contrast, their counterparts in European companies spent 10 percent of their time on such duties and in Japanese companies only 8 percent. American managers more frequently "touch base" to see whether the home office concurs with decisions or actions. In market contrast, European managers tend to be proud of the fact that they seldom call headquarters.

Corporations with many overseas subsidiaries seem to do a better job of evaluating reports from subsidiaries than do those with few subsidiaries. This is not surprising, since with more foreign subsidiaries and greater sales and earnings, the home office must respond by adding staff and procedures to review and evaluate the reports required by the system.

PERSONAL COMMUNICATIONS.   Managers of American companies in Brazil visited their home office an average of 2.4 times a year, as compared with 1.6 visits for European and 1.9 for the Japanese. Americans were visited far more often by executives responsible for Brazilian operations: home office personnel and the Brazilian chief executive met face to face 4.8 times a year on an average in American companies. In contrast, visits averaged 2.9 times a year for the European companies and 3.4 times a year for the Japanese companies.

Many European and American managers suffer from "overvisitation." It appears that at least for Brazil, there is a pattern of "vacation" visits that are perfunctory and are carried out simply because it is cold in New York.

Effects of Communications

Hulbert and Brandt concluded that the quantity of communications—number of reports, personal visits, or conferences—had no significant effect on perceived levels of understanding. The task of improving communications and control in multinational operations is to increase the quality and relevancy rather than quantity of information flows.

The need for improved communications in global operations is crucial. Many American companies are operating on the assumption that "more is better" and when in doubt send all information available. This burdens subsidiaries with the problem of sifting and sorting to find useful information and adds little to improving understanding in either home office or subsidiary. In contrast, some European companies use the opposite approach, which is to send nothing unless it is requested. This practice wastes time and also leads to decision making based on limited or inadequate information.

As companies develop standardized reporting formats, there is a pressing need for each subsidiary manager to sit down with headquarters and realistically assess the costs and benefits of providing the standardized information on the report form. Far too often a random request for specific data in one market gets locked into a worldwide reporting system, never again to be questioned as to why it is there and what purpose it serves.

For example, in one case a company president asked for market share data for a minor product in Finland. When he learned that no one at the home office knew the answer, he demanded that henceforth and forever more all overseas subsidiaries would report market share figures monthly, broken down by market segment for all products. While this is a valid and valuable exercise in the United States, it is a horrendous waste of time and money in many smaller overseas markets. Nonetheless, in this particular company the subsidiaries report market share data each month. Both the home office and the subsidiaries know that the data are garbage, but they continue to play the game and really do not want to know how much it is costing them each year to play this game.

CONTROL. Managers of European firms indicated much more freedom to make day-to-day decisions than did their American or Japanese counterparts. One concrete illustration of this was the much higher budgetary limit for chief executives of European firms than for those of Japanese or American firms. In European companies 23 percent had no effective limit, and 41 percent had a limit in the range of $50,000–500,000 dollars. In American companies 67 percent had a limit of less than $5,000.

When the plan represents a commitment rather than a coordinating device, as it often does in American companies as compared with other multinationals, the so-called "pressure-cooker syndrome" may develop. Budgets and plans can, instead of providing standards and benchmarks, be perverted to pressure devices if managers feel that they are caught in a "pressure cooker." When this happens, subsidiary managers respond predictably by doing everything possible to meet plan targets. In its most basic form this involves simple period-to-period manipulation of revenue and costs to make the bottom line, but more complex schemes might involve keeping a separate set of books or making major and undiscussed trade-offs in the short run to make the bottom line at the sacrifice of the longer-run profitability and health of the business.

Daley et al. compared American and Japanese attitudes toward control systems. They found that "relative to U.S. controllers, Japanese controllers were more concerned with controllability, autonomy in making purchases and having slack in budgets. They were also less concerned with participation in budget development, more concerned with evaluation using budgets, more concerned with using dollar values and more favorably disposed toward analytic approaches."[8]

[8]Lane Daley, James Jiambalvo, Gary L. Sundem, and Yasumasa Kondo, "Attitudes Toward Financial Control Systems in the United States and Japan," *Journal of International Business Studies,* Fall 1985, pp. 91–108.

Communications Guidelines

Effective communications requires both cooperation and adaptability on the part of home office and subsidiary executives. Each of these executives walks a thin line between chaos and rigidity. Systems are absolutely necessary to provide the possibility of integration and comparison across the international network. On the other hand, a rigid adherence to standardized systems results in garbage reports that provide the appearance of standardized and comparable information but actually are nothing of the sort.

All data reported by subsidiaries should meet the following test: Is this information necessary to help manage the subsidiary or the broader worldwide operation? Is the information worth the cost of collection? and What is the cost of collection? These are routine questions in a well-managed market research operation, particularly when the information is being purchased in an outside buy. Inevitably there is a tendency within a company to assume that management time is a free good. This of course is not true.

THE GLOBAL MARKETING AUDIT[9]

The global marketing audit is a tool for evaluating and improving a company's global marketing operations. The audit is an effort to assess effectiveness and efficiency of marketing strategies, practices, policies, and procedures vis-à-vis the firm's opportunities, objectives, and resources.

A full marketing audit has four basic characteristics. The first is that it is a broad rather than narrowly focused assessment. The use of this term should be reserved for a horizontal or comprehensive audit covering the company's marketing environment, competition, objectives, strategies, organization, and systems procedures and practices.

A second characteristic of a marketing audit is that it is conducted by someone who is independent of the operation being evaluated. There is loose talk about the so-called self audit and self evaluation. Experts agree that while a self audit may be quite valuable, it is not a bonafide audit because it lacks objectivity and independence. An objective, independent audit may be an inside audit conducted by a person or group inside a company but outside the operation being evaluated, or it may be an outside audit conducted by an outside, independent organization.

The third characteristic of a marketing audit is that it is systematic. Asking questions at random as they occur to the questioner may come up with useful insights, but this is not a marketing audit. The effectiveness of an audit normally increases

[9]This section draws heavily on Philip Kotler, William Gregor, and William Rodgers, "The Marketing Audit Comes of Age," *Sloan Management Review,* Winter 1977, pp. 25–43.

to the extent that it involves a sequence of orderly diagnostic steps as is the case in the conduct of a public accounting audit.

The final characteristic of a marketing audit is that it is conducted periodically. Most companies in trouble are well on their way to disaster before the trouble is fully apparent. It is therefore important that the audit be conducted periodically and that this should include even periods when there are apparent problems or difficulties inherent in the company's operations.

A global marketing audit can be defined as

> . . . a comprehensive, systematic, independent, and periodic examination of a company's—or business unit's—marketing environment, objectives, strategies, programs, policies and activities which is conducted with the objective of identifying existing and potential problems and opportunities and recommending a plan of action to improve a company's marketing performance.[10]

Setting Objectives and Scope of the Audit

The first step of an audit is a meeting between company executives and the auditor to agree on objectives, coverage, depth, data sources, report format, and time period for the audit.

GATHERING DATA.   One of the major tasks in conducting an audit is data collection. A detailed plan of interviews, secondary research, review of internal documents, and so forth is required. This effort usually involves an auditing team.

A basic rule in data collection is not to rely solely on the opinion of people being audited for data. In auditing a sales organization, it is absolutely essential to talk to field sales personnel as well as sales management, and of course, no audit is complete without direct contact with customers and suppliers.

Creative auditing techniques should be encouraged and explored by the auditing team. For example, if you are auditing an organization and you want to determine whether or not the chief executive or operating officer of the organization unit is really in touch with the organization and all of its activities, send an auditor into the mail room. Find out if the chief executive has ever visited the mail room. If he or she has never been there, it tells you volumes about the management style and the degree of hands-on management in the organization. If an organization has developed an elaborate marketing incentive program which is purported to generate results with customers, an audit should involve customer contact to find out if indeed the program is actually having any impact. For example, you can be certain that 99 percent of the material that is associated with frequent flier plans is never read or noted by fliers who have got better things to do with their time than read complicated rules and announcements.

[10]This definition is adapted from ibid.

PREPARING AND PRESENTING THE REPORT.   After data collection and analysis, the next step is the preparation and presentation of the audit report. This presentation should restate the objectives and scope of the audit, present the main findings, and present major recommendations and conclusions as well as major headings for further study and investigation.

COMPONENTS OF THE MARKETING AUDIT.   There are six major components of a full global marketing audit. They are:

> Marketing Environment Audit
> The Marketing Strategy Audit
> The Marketing Organization Audit
> The Marketing Systems Audit
> The Marketing Productivity Audit
> The Marketing Function Audit

Problems, Pitfalls, and Potential of the Global Marketing Audit

The marketing audit presents a number of problems and pitfalls. Setting objectives can be a pitfall, if indeed the objectives are blind to a major problem. It is important for the auditor to be open to expand or shift objectives and priorities while in the conduct of the audit itself.

Similarly, new data sources may appear during the course of an audit and the auditor should be open to such sources. The approach of the auditor should simultaneously be systematic, following a predetermined outline, and perceptive and open to new directions and sources that appear in the course of the audit investigation.

REPORT PRESENTATION.   One of the biggest problems in marketing auditing is that the executive who commissions the audit may have higher expectations about what the audit will do for the company than the actual results seem to offer. An audit is valuable even if it does not offer major new directions or panaceas. It is important for all concerned to recognize that improvements at the margin are what truly make a difference between success and mediocrity. In major league baseball, the difference between a batter with a .350 batting average ($3\frac{1}{2}$ hits out of 10 times at bat) and a .250 ($2\frac{1}{2}$ hits out of 10 times at bat) is the difference between a major league hitter and someone who is not even good enough for the minor leagues. Major league marketers understand this fact and recognize it in the audit. Don't look for dramatic revolutionary findings or panaceas. Accept and recognize that improvement at the margin is the winners's game in global marketing.

Global marketers, even more than their domestic counterparts, need marketing audits to assess far-flung efforts in highly diverse environments. The global marketing audit should be at the top of the list of programs for strategic excellence and implementation excellence for the winning global company.

SUMMARY

Lack of knowledge of basic market conditions is one of the major obstacles to the development of an effective control relationship between headquarters and subsidiary in international marketing. When headquarters commits itself to measure and evaluate subsidiary performance, the decision commits headquarters to participation in subsidiary planning. Measurement and evaluation of current performance are intrinsically involved in the cycle of planning for operations and programs in future time periods. To become effectively involved in this planning control cycle, headquarters must understand the basic characteristics and conditions of the subsidiary market. If there is inadequate understanding, headquarters may adversely or inadequately influence the design of the country marketing plan for future periods and may misunderstand the significance of operating results in current periods. The result of a headquarters misunderstanding can involve major failures when headquarters succeeds in imposing an inappropriate plan on subsidiaries or in influencing subsidiaries to accept inappropriate objectives. Perhaps even more dangerously, headquarters misunderstanding can result in a failure of subsidiaries to achieve their full potential in a market. If headquarters does not understand the basic characteristics of a market, it will not be able to pinpoint subsidiary underperformance. The problem in international operations is a counterpart of the problem of managing product divisions in a divisionalized company. To manage a product division, corporate management must understand the division's business. If it does not understand the business, divisional management virtually has free rein to develop its plan and explain its performance.

Companies expand headquarters' understanding of foreign markets in one important way: by being actively involved in the subsidiary planning process. This involvement ensures that headquarters executives learn about each subsidiary and region's market conditions. Sophisticated companies are developing career paths that give executives of different nationalities an opportunity to work in different countries and at different organization locations. An American bank might assign its U.S. executives to work in overseas branches and its non-U.S. executives to its U.S. headquarters. This mixture of people ensures that each organizational location has a mix of background and experience.

The three basic tools for controlling global marketing operations are the plan, the budget, and the global marketing audit. The budget is a key tool for controlling the implementation of the plan and the audit is an invaluable tool for evaluating the overall effectiveness of the marketing function in the company.

DISCUSSION QUESTIONS

1. What are the major variables influencing control in a global company?
2. What is the major complaint of managers in subsidiary companies about the control practices of headquarters?

3. What are the differences among control practices of U.S., European, and Japanese companies?
4. What is a global marketing audit?

BIBLIOGRAPHY

Books

ALSEGG, ROBERT J. *Control Relationships Between American Corporations and Their European Subsidiaries,* AMA Research Study 107. New York: American Management Association, 1971.

ANTHONY, ROBERT N. *Planning and Control Systems: A Framework for Analysis.* Boston: Division of Research, Graduate School of Business Administration, Harvard University, 1965.

BROOKE, MICHAEL Z., AND H. LEE REMMERS. *The Strategy of the Multinational Enterprise.* New York: American Elsevier, 1970.

Articles

AGGARWAL, RAJ, AND JAMES C. BAKER. "Using Foreign Subsidiary Accounting Data: A Dilemma for the Multinational Corporation." *Columbia Journal of World Business,* Vol. 10, no. 3 (Fall 1975), pp. 83–92.

AYDIN, NIZAM. "Marketing Know-how Transfers by Multinationals: A Case Study in Turkey." *Journal of International Business Studies,* Winter 1981, pp. 35–48.

AYLMER, R. J. "Who Makes Marketing Decisions in the Multinational Firm?" *Journal of Marketing,* Vol. 34 (October 1970), pp. 25–30.

BEHRMAN, JACK N., AND WILLIAM A. FISCHER. "Transnational Corporations: Market Orientations and R&D Abroad." *Columbia Journal of World Business,* Fall 1980, pp. 55–60.

DALEY, LANE, JAMES JIAMBALVO, GARY L. SUNDEM, AND YASUMASA KONDO. "Attitudes Toward Financial Control Systems in the United States and Japan." *Journal of International Business Studies,* Fall 1985, pp. 91–108.

DOZ, YVES, AND C. K. PRAHALAD. "Headquarters Influence and Strategic Control in MNCs." *Sloan Management Review,* Fall 1981.

FRANKO, LAWRENCE G. "Who Manages Multinational Enterprises?" *Columbia Journal of World Business,* Summer 1973.

GRAY, DANIEL H. "Uses and Misuses of Strategic Planning." *Harvard Business Review,* January–February 1986, pp. 89–97.

KEEGAN, WARREN J. "Multinational Marketing Management," working paper. Cambridge: Marketing Science Institute, January 1970.

———. "Multinational Marketing Planning: Headquarters Role." *Columbia Journal of World Business,* January–February 1971.

———. "Multinational Marketing Control." *Journal of International Business Studies.* Fall 1972.

KOTLER, PHILIP, WILLIAM GREGOR, AND WILLIAM RODGERS. "The Marketing Audit Comes of Age." *Sloan Management Review,* Winter 1977, pp. 25–43.

SORENSON, RALPH Z., AND ULRICH E. WEICHMANN. "How Multinationals View Marketing Standardization." *Harvard Business Review,* May–June 1975, pp. 38 ff.

WEICHMANN, ULRICH E., AND LEWIS G. PRINGLE. "Problems That Plague Multinational Marketers." *Harvard Business Review,* July–August 1979.

CLUB MED, INC.: THE SPECIAL CHALLENGE OF GROWTH[1]

INTRODUCTION

Gerald Martin, assistant vice president/ marketing, and Jean Prevert, vice president/ marketing,[2] had what each called a good working relationship as well as an understanding of each other's point of view. Martin, a native of New York City with extensive experience in the American leisure and lodging industry, had been lured to Club Med, Inc.[3] by Prevert, a Parisian whose 20 year affiliation with Club Med had been mostly spent with the parent firm, Club Mediterranee, S.A.

The two men had been wrestling with the issue of how to broaden Club Med's appeal to capture a bigger piece of the American market. Prevert, who had seen Club Med successfully market a basically standardized product offering on a global scale, felt that success depended on educating American consumers rather than tailoring the product to them. Once Americans understood what made Club Med a different and rewarding

experience, he reasoned, they would naturally choose to spend their hard-earned vacation time in one of his company's lovely villages. Martin saw things a little differently. While he agreed that educating the American consumer was important, he felt that certain concessions had to be made to American tastes as well. He believed that the Club Med product concept had global appeal, but he was more inclined to make adjustments to local market conditions than Prevert. Whatever their disagreements on methods, both agreed that the key to long-term success of Club Med, Inc. would lie in its ability to succeed in America.

THE STRATEGIC PROBLEM

After three decades of nearly unqualified success, Club Mediterranee, S.A. was at a crossroads. Both outside and internal research reports confirmed that its subsidiary, Club Med, Inc., had enormous and untapped growth potential. Part of Club Med, Inc.'s territory included North America, and a considerable effort was being made to expand its share of potential customers. The fundamental issue facing Gerald Martin and Jean Prevert was how to win the maximum share of the American market while at the same time retaining the identity and the formula that had always served Club Med so well.

THE CLUB MED CONCEPT

That Club Med would distinguish itself as a unique company should have been apparent from the start. How many successful com-

[1]This case was prepared by Charles Anderer, case writer and research associate, under the supervision of Warren J. Keegan, Professor of International Business and Marketing, as part of the Leading Edge Case Study Project, the Center for International Business Studies, Pace University. This project was funded in part by a grant from the United States Department of Education. Copyright © Pace University, 1987.

[2]These characters, as well as their discussions, are fictitious. Their purpose is to highlight some of the issues facing the company described herein.

[3]Club Med, Inc. is a Grand Cayman Island company, traded on the New York Stock Exchange; 73 percent of its shares outstanding are owned by its French parent, Club Mediterranee S.A. It has exclusive rights to the sale of Club Med packages and the operation of Club Med resorts in North and Central America and the Caribbean, the Pacific Basin, Oceania, Asia and the Indian Ocean (see Table 1).

TABLE 1   Club Med, Inc.

INCOME DATA (MILLION $)

Year Ended Oct. 31	Revs.	Oper. Inc.	% Oper. Inc. of Revs.	Net Bef. Taxes	Net Inc.	% Net Inc. of Revs.
1985	280	23.8	8.5%	16.8	14.2	5.1%
1984	235	21.2	9.0	13.4	12.0	5.1
1983	211	16.6	7.8	10.9	9.7	4.6
1982	207	13.3	6.4	9.0	7.1	3.5

BALANCE SHEET DATA (MILLION $)

Oct. 31	Cash	Current Assets	Current Liab.	Current Ratio	Total Assets	Ret. on Assets	Ret. on Equity
1985	47.5	78.4	46.5	1.7	269	5.9%	10.5%
1984	38.7	75.5	40.9	1.8	212	5.6	11.7
1983	27.3	47.1	40.9	1.2	158	7.1	19.8
1982	20.6	38.3	38.7	1.0	115	NA	NA

REVENUES (MILLION $)

Quarter	1985–6	1984–5	1983–4	1982–3
Jan.	85.4	71.9	62.1	—
Apr.	107.9	87.3	76.0	123.8*
Jul.		62.3	47.6	—
Oct.		58.2	49.6	87.7*

*Six months

Source: Standard NYSE Stock Reports.

panies, after all, are run by former journalists whose political inclinations are decidedly to the left, and the far left at that? Club Med's chairman, Gilbert Trigano, was a member of the French Resistance and, subsequently, a reporter for the Communist paper L'Humanite. Trigano joined Club Med as managing director in 1954 and founded the company's first "village" in Greece the following year. Under his leadership, Club Med became a veritable tourism empire composed of 104 villages (and three "auxiliary" ones), located in France and some 30 foreign countries or French overseas territories.

Central to Club Med's success is its concept of what vacationers need in order to truly feel removed from the everyday pressures they seek to escape. Villages are typically located in beautiful, warm-weather areas (see Table 2). Within each village, Club Med creates an environment that stresses the similarities between people. Its villages are closed societies where beads are used instead of money (everything is prepaid except for side trips and drinks, so the need for money is hardly acute), where there are no locks on doors, where the rooms are identical, where dining is done together at round tables and

TABLE 2 Club Med Inc.—Operations

Geographic Region	Villages	Number of Beds
North America/ Caribbean	Eleuthera-Bahamas	600
	Paradise Island-Bahamas	750
	Punta Cana-Dominican Republic	600
	Caravelle-Guadeloupe	600
	Fort Royal-Guadeloupe	304
	Magic Isle-Haiti	700
	Buccaneer's Creek-Martinique	750
	Cancun-Mexico	750
	Ixtapa-Mexico	750
	Playa Blanca-Mexico	580
	Sonora Bay-Mexico	750
	Copper Mountain-Colorado, USA	470
	Turkoise-Turks and Caicos	490
	St. George's Cove-Bermuda	680
	Five Archeological Inns-Mexico	400
Pacific Basin	Chateau Royal-New Caledonia	550
	Bora Bora-Tahiti	102
	Moorea-Tahiti	700
Indian Ocean	Pointe aux Canonniers-Mauritius	374
	Le Lagon-Reunion	120
Asia	Cherating-Malaysia	600
	Thulagiri-Maldives	60
	Farukolhufushi-Maldives	250
	Phuket-Thailand	600
	Bali-Indonesia	700

Source: Drexel Burnham Lambert.

where the style of dress, excepting the company's ski villages, is minimalist (some might call it skimpy.) Simply put, the spirit of competition in the outside world is replaced by a spirit of cooperation that evokes a simpler, less complicated way of life.

Nowhere is the spirit of cooperation more apparent than in the relationship between Club Med guests, who are called GMs (gentils membres—congenial members) and Club Med staff, who are known as GOs (gentils organisateurs—congenial organizers.) The GOs are the constant companions of the GMs.

They eat with the guests, their rooms are similar as is their style of dress. Each village has around 100 GOs. They work 14-hour days and serve as the guests' teachers, entertainers and friends.

The prepaid package that Club Med offers includes accomodations, all meals, sports and leisure activities, as well as air transportation, and land transfers (see Table 3). Unlike any number of "package deals" that are available to consumers, Club Med's offerings are decidedly upscale. The company only builds villages in exclusive coastal or moun-

**TABLE 3   The Price of a Club Med Vacation:
The Caribbean Example**

ONE WEEK STAYS (NOT INCLUDING AIRFARE)

Villages	Lowest Price (Early Nov.)	Highest Price (Early March)
Caribbean		
Buccaneer's Creek	$470	$ 980
Caravelle	600	980
Magic Isle	525	600
Punta Cana	450	660
St. Lucia	—	700
Turkoise	735	1,070

· ONE WEEK RATES WITH AIR & TRANSFERS

Villages	Lowest Price (Early Nov.)	Highest Price (Early March)
Caribbean		
Buccaneer's Creek	$ 879	$1,470
Caravelle	999	1,470
Magic Isle	824	925
Punta Cana	799	1,080
St. Lucia	—	1,090
Turkoise	1,049	1,425

Note: Rates are for the winter/spring 1986–87 season.
All rates are per person, double occupancy, and subject to Club
Med's terms and conditions.

Source: Company brochure.

tainside locations. The villages themselves are normally equipped with everything from tennis courts to discotheques and the food is reputed to be excellent.

1985—A WARNING AGAINST COMPLACENCY

Club Mediterranee, S.A. received a warning of sorts when its financial results for the year ended October 31, 1985 were reported. In a marked contrast to previous years, the company experienced a modest rise in net profit of 8.3 percent to FFr 266.6 million ($28.5 mil-

lion) on revenues that increased by 17.3 percent to FFr 6 billion. This represented an increase in earnings per share of only 0.8 percent in a year when consumer prices in France rose by 5 percent. This per share decline in real terms was all the more surprising in that the Paris stock market experienced a boom year in 1985. As a result of its lackluster performance, Club Med fell from its position of the 16th largest firm on the Paris exchange in terms of stock market capitalization to the 28th largest.

The parent company bounced back in the first six months of 1986 and realized a 22 percent increase in net profits. In fact, this figure would have been even greater had the dollar not weakened. This impressive first-half reinforced Club Med's overall image as a highly profitable, well-run company. Those who run the company had been at it for over three decades and had developed some fool-proof ways to generate revenues and cut costs.

Firstly, since all of its vacations are paid anywhere from three to eight weeks in advance, Club Med makes upwards of $3 million a year in annual interest income from this source alone. Furthermore, since it transports mosts of its guests in groups, Club Med can strike a hard bargain with airlines for bulk rates. The company makes a substantial amount of money ($17\frac{1}{2}$ percent of gross operating profits in 1983) buying air transport at wholesale prices and selling it to its vacationers at the going retail rate. While this policy often resulted in taxing the patience of its clientele (flights were often with "second-tier" airlines at odd hours of the day and rarely non-stop), the profits realized were too good to pass up. As for its villages, Club Med often builds at the request of host country governments in remote areas that would not otherwise be developed. The company can afford to do this because the success of its concept does not hinge on a specific locale or destination. By bringing business to distant areas, Club Med often gets the host country to put up much of the necessary capital (more than one-third of its $240 million North American/Asian expansion plan was being financed this way), while it takes a less than 10 percent ownership position in order to minimize tax liabilities (*The Economist*, 7/12/86.)

In spite of its strong financial condition, however, Club Med was not about to be lulled into a false sense of security. The company's product was at different levels of life cycle in each of its major markets. In France, for example, the product was fast reaching sat-uration. The United States and West Germany were still in the growth stage, and the product was still in the introductory phase in markets such as Japan and Brazil. Of all these markets, none carried the importance that the American market held. It was becoming more and more obvious that, in order for Club Med to realize its true growth potential, its American customer base had to be expanded.

SELLING CLUB MED TO AMERICA

Gerald Martin just knew he had the answers. When Jean Prevert asked him what he thought Club Med, Inc. needed to do in order to expand in America, he submitted the following:

1. The villages had to be internationalized. That is, English-speaking villages where the number of French GMs was necessarily limited needed to be created. Even more importantly, the number of American GO's needed to be substantially increased.

2. The popular perception of Club Med as a haven for young and virile singles had to be altered somewhat. The demographics of the travel industry and Club Med's clientele had changed. More mature customers, many of whom were married and had children, needed to feel that a Club Med village was an appropriate place for them to spend a vacation. American consumers, in short, needed to be better informed on the advantages that Club Med offered them.

3. Americans took less vacation time than almost any other country in the developed world. They were far more likely to take a long weekend than a week or two in the sunshine. It was therefore a considerable challenge for Club Med to

persuade them that it was beneficial for them to spend an important portion of the time they had away from their jobs in one of its villages.

4. Americans are very attached to convenience. While Club Med finds it lucrative to place many of its customers on flights that are marked by poor service and erratic scheduling, Martin felt that Club Med Inc.'s long-term interests would be better served by a more flexible approach to air travel. Martin also pushed for added amenities in the villages, such as telephones in the rooms.

THE NEED FOR MORE AMERICAN GOs

Martin considered GOs to be the key to the success of any American expansion. He felt that the same personnel policies used with French GOs could not work with American GOs because their expectations are different. French GOs had a significantly lower turnover rate than American GOs and it appeared that the major problem was money. Martin felt that it would be beneficial to the company to reward those American GOs who show promise or who are already good at what they do with good salaries. American GOs needed to feel that they were not making an unnecessary financial sacrifice by staying with Club Med (See *Appendix*). Presently, they had that feeling (they are paid $100 per week including room and board) and it showed in their turnover rate.

Prevert thought it would be destabilizing to pay American GOs more than the French GOs who worked alongside them. Of course, they could raise everybody's salary, but that would be too costly. Prevert also thought Martin was overestimating the importance of

American GOs to begin with. Club Med, Inc.'s French GOs were required to speak fluent English, so what was the big deal?

American GOs were important, Martin thought, because American GMs feel so much more comfortable around them than is the case with French GOs. Martin knew that the French GOs, whether deservedly or not, sometimes had a reputation among American GMs as being arrogant toward them. This could simply be a result of the misunderstanding that takes place between members of different cultures or the result of a popularly held perception amongst Americans who travel that the French are simply an arrogant group of people. Martin believed that many French were guilty until proven innocent when it came to the question of arrogance. However unfair this might be, it remained absolutely necessary, in Martin's view, that Club Med cultivate a solid group of American GOs.

THE FRENCH ACCENT: ASSET OR LIABILITY?

Even though the Club Med concept stresses the similarities between people, the villages themselves inevitably have a strong French feeling to them. The dominant language in the large majority of Club Med's enclosed villages is, quite naturally, French. While the French accent does lure Americans to underdeveloped countries that they would be otherwise hesitant to visit, it can be intimidating to non-French speakers. Many Americans have no doubt either heard the usual horror stories from friends about those legendary, ill-mannered Parisians or have themselves had humbling experiences during the course of their visit(s) to France. Some industry observers surmise that the company's strong French accent serves as a barrier to growth. For example, France's sometimes playfully antagonistic neighbor from across the Channel, the United Kingdom, accounted for only 10,800 GMs in 1985 (a 48 percent increase from the previous year) compared to the French total of 365,200. The British, it might be added, can also vacation at the villages of Club Mark Warner, an anglicized version of the Club Med concept.

Being French, Prevert was naturally sensitive about the charge of arrogance. Although he thought Americans such as Martin exaggerated the problem, he favored the development "international villages." At these villages, English is the dominant language spoken and the proportion of French GMs is limited to 25 percent. In Europe, 18 such villages were established in 1986 whereas another 14 were planned for the rest of the world. It remained to be seen, according to Martin, if "internationalizing" a mere one-third of its villages would be enough to enable Club Med

to substantially increase the number of American GMs.

JUGGLING THE IMAGE TO SATISFY THE MARKET

For years, the mere mention of the name "Club Med" evoked an alluring imagery of hedonism that only single people could enjoy in good conscience. In fairness to the company, Club Med had only passively cultivated this sort of image. Of course, the gates to its villages were not graced with signs reading "For Singles Only." On the other hand, once inside a Club Med village, one was far more likely to encounter single people than married couples. An example of how firmly entrenched this image was (and still is) in the minds of some was provided by members of Bermuda's political opposition in March of

TABLE 4   Club Mediterannee, SA and Club Med, Inc. Membership by Nationality (Percent of Total)

	1981	1982	1983	1984	1985E	1986E
Europe and Africa						
France	49.0	46.6	44.6	43.4	42.0	40.0
Italy	5.9	5.6	5.3	5.1	4.8	4.6
Belgium	5.2	5.1	4.8	4.7	4.5	4.4
W. Germany	4.5	4.4	3.8	4.5	4.4	4.4
Switzerland	2.9	2.7	2.6	2.5	2.3	2.2
Other	7.1	7.6	8.1	7.2	6.5	6.4
	74.6	72.0	69.2	67.4	64.5	62.0
North and Central America						
U.S./Canada	16.2	17.5	19.5	21.9	24.0	26.0
Other	1.5	2.1	2.3	1.7	2.0	2.0
	17.7	19.6	21.8	23.6	26.0	28.0
Asia, Indian Ocean and South Pacific						
Australia	2.7	2.6	2.2	1.7	1.8	2.0
Japan	0.9	1.2	1.5	1.5	1.5	1.7
Other	2.1	2.4	2.8	2.7	2.7	2.8
	5.7	6.2	6.5	5.9	6.0	6.5
South America	2.0	2.2	2.5	3.1	3.5	3.5
TOTAL	100.0	100.0	100.0	100.0	100.0	100.0

Source: Drexel Burnham Lambert.

1986 who called Club Med and its villages in the harbors of Castle and St. George immoral.

By 1984, Club Med would state in its annual report that significant changes in the makeup of its guest population had taken place. Nowhere was this change more apparent than among the American GMs. About half of them were married, the median age was said to be 37 years old, and more than half of them reported an annual income of at least $50,000. Club Med has catered to this demanding group of affluent baby boomers by offering more luxury, more options, special clubs for parents with children and a wider range of villages within reasonable travel time from the northeastern United States. American GMs are therefore steered to the village that best fits their personal tastes.

Even though Club Med's unstated goal was to portray itself as a provider of vacations for a maturing group of people, it initially found it difficult to resist the lure of selling the simple concept of sun and fun with beautiful people. A 1986 advertising campaign which revolved around the theme, "The perfect climate for body and soul," illustrates this point. Although the ads promoted such ideas as self-discovery, friendship, and improved communications between married couples, these messages were clearly marked by visuals of young, beautiful people flaunting toned-up physiques.

AMERICANS: ANYTHING BUT VACATION

As of 1986, in spite of some undeniable gains Club Med, Inc. still saw itself as underperforming with respect to the number of American guests it attracted per year. This view was no doubt reinforced by a 1985 study done by the investment bank Drexel Burnham Lambert (see Tables 4–7.) Drexel calculated that the French were over nine times more likely to be a Club Med GM than Americans. If the concept could only become half as popular in the United States as it is in France (meaning an increase in GM's per 1,000 peo-

TABLE 5 Selected Propensities to Visit Club Med

COUNTRY	APPROX. NO. OF NATIVE G.M.'s PER YEAR	% OF TOTAL G.M.'s	POP. (1980)	G.M.'s PER THOUSAND INHABIT.
Europe				
France	356,000	39.6%	53,580,000	6.6
Italy	106,000	11.8	57,080,000	1.9
Belgium	38,800	4.3	9,890,000	3.9
W. Germany	35,000	3.9	61,480,000	0.6
Switzerland	20,800	2.3	6,250,000	3.3
North America				
USA/Canada	179,800	20.0%	258,302,604	0.7
Asia, Indian Ocean and South Pacific				
Japan	12,000	1.3%	119,680,000	0.1
Australia	18,000	2.0	15,535,000	1.2

Source: Drexel Burnham Lambert.

TABLE 6   Estimated Potential Club Med Market

	CURRENT PROPENSITY TO VISIT CLUB MED (G.M.'s PER 1,000 POP.)	ESTIMATED POTENTIAL PROPENSITY (G.M.'s PER 1,000 POP.)	EXTRAPOLATED POTENTIAL NUMBER OF G.M.'s
Europe			
France	6.6	6.6	356,000
Italy	1.9	2.0	114,200
Belgium	3.9	4.0	39,600
W. Germany	0.6	3.5	215,250
Switzerland	3.3	4.0	25,200
North America			
Canada	0.7	2.5	62,750
U.S.A.	0.7	3.0	717,300
Asia, Indian Ocean and South Pacific			
Japan	0.1	2.5	299,250
Australia	1.2	2.5	38,750

Source: Drexel Burnham Lambert.

ple from 0.7 to 3.0), then North America alone could support 90 villages or six times the number of villages it had in 1985.

Drexel's optimistic numbers notwithstanding, Martin still saw a large problem. The group that was to fuel Club Med's ambitious growth plans, the Americans, took less vacation time than the French, the British or the Germans (see Table 8.) Europeans, who were responsible for Club Med's initial success, enjoy a decidedly more relaxed lifestyle than Americans. Vacations in Europe are traditionally taken in four to six week blocks in July or August.

Why is there such a big difference in vacation time between America and other developed countries? The reasons are mainly cultural in nature. American society is outwardly more competitive than those in Western Europe. The difference might be summed up by a commonly held notion among Europeans who have either worked in America or for American companies in Europe: Amer-

icans live to work and Europeans work to live. In any event, a typical American manager would be downright afraid to take that much time off in one stretch and most wouldn't even begin to contemplate the notion. In order to ease the guilt, Martin was able to convince Prevert, after some arm-twisting, to equip 7 villages with computer workshops.

TOYING WITH THE CONCEPT

Martin's controversial approach to the Club Med concept was largely based on his interpretation of Club Med's initial success with the French. At the heart of this success, he believed, was Club Med's ability to give people a home away from home. Martin believed very little in the notion of global Club Med villages where the peoples of the world comfortably coexist. He saw room for a little international flair, but he felt that Americans, in particular, did not want to spend their va-

TABLE 7 Current vs. Estimated Potential

	APPROX. CURRENT NO. OF GM's	ESTIMATED POTENTIAL	ESTIMATED % GROWTH POTENTIAL	APPROX. GROWTH POTENTIAL AS A % OF TOTAL GROWTH POTENTIAL
Europe				
France	356,000	356,000	0%	0.0%
Italy	106,000	114,000	8	0.6
Belgium	38,000	39,600	2	0.1
W. Germany	35,000	215,250	515	12.6
Switzerland	20,800	25,200	21	0.3
North America				
USA/Canada	179,800	780,050	334%	42.1%
Asia, Indian Ocean and South Pacific				
Japan	12,000	299,250	2,934%	20.1%
Australia	18,000	38,750	115	1.5

Source: Drexel Burnham Lambert.

cations in an environment basically alien to them and surrounded by GOs who do not speak their language.

On the other hand, Martin saw the Club Med concept as a natural for Americans because of their basic social instincts. There was no reason why the concept could not be successful here. The main problem, as Martin saw it, was management's ability to properly implement its growth strategy. One area where Martin was successful was in air travel. As stated above, the company buys air travel wholesale and sells it retail. Martin fought hard to ensure that the company would not

TABLE 8 Holidays With Pay (annual averages)

	STATUTORY	COLLECTIVE AGREEMENTS AND PRACTICE	PAID PUBLIC HOLIDAYS
Belgium	4 weeks	4 weeks	10 days
Canada	2 weeks	3 weeks	6–9 days
France	5 weeks	5 weeks	*
W. Germany	3 weeks	5–6 weeks	11–13 days
Italy	10 days	4 weeks	10 days
Japan	6 days	—	12 days
The Netherlands	3 weeks	4–4.5 weeks	8 days
Sweden	5 weeks	5 weeks	11 days
Switzerland	2–3 weeks	3–4 weeks	4–5 days
England	*	4 weeks	8 days
USA	*	1–2 weeks	*

*No generally applicable statutory provisions.

Source: International Labor Office.

risk losing customers for the sake of avoiding a decrease in interest income from the sale of airfare. As a result of his efforts, air travel for the American market was upgraded.

Martin was still worried by Prevert's reluctance to change the company's winning ways. An example was the horror with which Prevert greeted Martin's proposal to put telephones in guests' rooms. "A telephone is a direct link with the outside world and all of its miseries," sniffed Prevert, fully aware of the fact that his company had somehow managed to survive before Gerald Martin was hired. "Cut off the outside world, and you cut off the very anxieties that the guests are trying to escape. Computer workshops and better travel arrangements, yes. Telephones in the rooms, never."

Appendix: A Day in the Life of a Club Med GO[1]

What are the difficulties that Club Med faces in cultivating a solid group of American GOs? One problem is that, by American standards, the GOs actually are underpaid for the amount of work they do. One former American GO who lasted six months as a dance instructor at the Punta Cana resort in the Dominican Republic said that a major factor in her decision to leave was the rigorous schedule that she faced every day of the week:

7:30–10 a.m.	Breakfast duty. Greet and seat guests.
11–12	Teach dance class in the theater.
12–1:30 p.m.	Host luncheon buffet or perform mime skit with the animateur (club jester) in the dining room as guests eat lunch.
1:30–3 p.m.	Rehearsals in the theater.
3–6 p.m.	FREE! If I didn't have Arrivals and Departures, a GO meeting or a team meeting, or have to help prepare the set or costumes for the evening performance.
6–7 p.m.	Teach another dance class in the theater.
7–8 p.m.	Cocktail hour. Model a dress from the boutique and flirt with guests at the bar.
8–9:30 p.m.	SMILE! Host dinner or perform a mime skit.
9:30–10 p.m.	Change out of boutique dress or mime costume and gulp down dinner.
10–11 p.m.	Change into another costume and perform in show.
11–12 p.m.	Clean up backstage and mingle with guests at the bar.
12–1 a.m.	Midnight rehearsal if scheduled.
1–?	Disco. Lure shy guests onto the dance floor.

[1] *The Hartford Courant*, February 16, 1986.

20

THE FUTURE OF GLOBAL MARKETING

We should all be concerned about the future because we will have to spend the rest of our lives there.

Charles Franklin Kettering, 1876–1958
Seed for Thought, *1949*

INTRODUCTION

Anyone who maintains that he or she can predict the future is either a charlatan or a fool. Nevertheless, one of the more fascinating and valuable enterprises in human endeavor is the effort to forecast future developments on the basis of patterns, trends, and underlying factors that can be observed in the present situation. These forecasts are vitally important as an input to the strategic planning process for both domestic and international enterprises.

GLOBAL CORPORATIONS IN THE EVOLVING INTERNATIONAL ECONOMIC ORDER

Four major trends will undoubtedly affect the role and future of global corporations in the evolving international economic order. The first is the trend toward symmetry in the relative importance of global corporations based in different parts of the world. Only a decade ago, there was a fear of an American takeover of the world economy, and today there is a fear of a Japanese takeover. Tomorrow, there will no doubt be another region or country that is on the ascendent. What is clear is that no country or region has a monopoly on drive, creativity, and energy for commercial effort. Today, there are major new multinationals emerging in Third World countries. An increasing balance between U.S. and non-U.S. foreign direct investment and industrialized and less developed investment will create a common interest in the international economic order in preserving a framework for international investment and operations. In effect, each investor country will be a hostage to its own investment position in the rest of the world. A condition of mutual interdependence creates a fundamentally stable environment for continued growth and expansion of international business.

A second trend that is clearly observable is the emergence of an increasingly large number of world-scale industries. Today we are witnessing a shakeout of firms in industries ranging from electronics to automobiles that is analogous to the shakeout that occurred in the national economy of the United States between 1850 and 1950. The farm equipment industry provides an interesting illustrative example of this process. In 1850 there were hundreds of farm equipment manufacturers. Between 1850 and 1950, firms in this industry expanded their operations from local to regional to national scale. In the process of this expansion, many weaker firms were weeded out because of their higher operating costs and lower available operating margins. Since 1950 the shakeout has continued, but the arena has shifted from the national to the world frame. The emergence of world-scale industries is also apparent in more recently established technologies, such as integrated circuits and television receivers.

The implications of this trend are of enormous significance from both a private and a public policy perspective. From the point of view of the corporation, it is necessary to identify and recognize the world-scale trend if it applies to the company's product scope. Zenith, for example, made the mistake of assuming that it was number one in the color television market because of its leading position in the U.S. market. This proved to be a disastrous illusion, as Zenith found it increasingly difficult to compete with Japanese companies that were operating not only in the U.S. market but throughout the world. A more accurate description of Zenith's position is that of perhaps a fifth- or sixth-ranked world competitor as opposed to the illusionary perception of Zenith as number one in the United States. Companies that find themselves in world-scale industries must choose between going for positions as high-volume, low-cost producers for the volume markets of the world or carefully positioning themselves in niche markets where the value they create is based as much on knowing their customer as it is on being a low-cost producer. Each of these positions is a winning strategy. The losing strategy, which has been demonstrated by the now defunct British motorcycle industry, is to be a high-cost producer trying to compete in the volume market against a low-cost producer.

Swedish firms are an example of a national group of companies that has demonstrated a great deal of skill in treading the line between these strategy alternatives. Swedish companies are well represented as both low-cost, high-volume producers and as low-volume, premium-priced, niche marketers. The future will require even more attention to ensure that the strategic position of the enterprise is aligned with the competitive realities of the world market.

The public policy implications of this trend are especially important in the United States, which, until very recently, operated under antitrust laws that were based on the implicit assumption that the frame for determining the competitiveness of an industry is the national market. In the late nineteenth century, when these laws were formulated, this assumption was valid. In the 1980s it is sadly out of date. U.S. policymakers must recognize that U.S. companies will increasingly need to amalgamate so that they can form viable world-scale competitive enterprises if they are to operate without protection in the international economic order. The United States faces a choice: a continued commitment to an open competitive economy that will require a revision of the frame for evaluating industry competitiveness and that must necessarily allow the merger of independent organizations to form competitive, world-scale units, or, alternatively, an abandonment of the long-standing U.S. commitment to an open economy and the international economic order and the erection of barriers to protect U.S. companies that are unable to compete in the evolving world-scale industry.

A third trend is the steady shift toward a geocentric or world corporate orientation as opposed to an ethnocentric or home country orientation or, alternatively, a polycentric or host country orientation. A *geocentric* company is one that consciously recognizes that it is operating in the international economic order and that its stakeholders are customers, employees, and shareholders in every area of operation. In addition, a geocentric company is one that recognizes the possibility of creating a global strategic plan for each of its businesses in order to allocate and apply resources most effectively. An *ethnocentric* company is one that recognizes home country stakeholders as being preeminent in their rights to and claims on corporate resources and rewards. The operating style of the ethnocentric company is highly centralized. It seeks to impose a top-down approach to planning and operating programs and operates on the implicit assumption that the home country way is the best way. Many U.S. and Japanese-based multinationals have been highly ethnocentric in their orientation. A *polycentric* company is based on the assumption that the differences between countries are so great that the only effective way of managing a global company is to decentralize and locate virtually all decision responsibility for resource allocation in national organizations.

The geocentric company is based on the assumption that world markets consist of both similarities and differences and that the most effective strategies are those that reflect a full recognition of both similarities and differences. In marketing, this means that products will be adapted where necessary to conform to local market and competitive conditions, but there will also be an attempt to, wherever possible, standardize the product line and marketing procedures to minimize costs of research and development and manufacturing and to maximize the gains from scale and concentration of resources. This geocentric shift is evident in the creation of worldwide product divisions and the decision to locate strategic planning product market responsibility within these divisions. Another key measure of the extent to which a company is actually geocentric in its day-to-day operations is the extent to which men and women of many nationalities are promoted to positions of major product division and corporate responsibility. Whenever the corporate headquarters and product divisions are staffed with home country nationals, you can be sure that a basically ethnocentric orientation is present within the headquarters. This is often juxtaposed with a polycentric orientation in national organizations within the same enterprise. The mixing of nationalities in headquarters, product division, and national organizations is the surest way of breaking down the ethnocentric and polycentric attitudes that must give way before a company can operate geocentrically. As Laurence J. Farley, CEO of Black and Decker put it, "The goal is not to have a uniform product line worldwide. That would result in lowest common denominator products and wouldn't work very well in the marketplace. Rather the goal is to have a product line that is as standardized as possible, while recognizing that allowances for some local market conditions are both necessary and desirable." Black and Decker ". . . must operate as interdependent rather than independent units while recognizing that globalization is not a panacea."[1]

DECLINE OF THE UNITED STATES AND THE RISE OF THE PACIFIC BASIN

As James Fallows has observed,[2] for the past 40 years, the United States has tried to compete simultaneously with the Soviet Union and with Japan where "Japan" refers not to the specific country Japan but rather the technically advanced, globally oriented, fast growing, and ambitious market economies of the world. At the beginning of the period the United States effortlessly led in both races. For the past fifteen years America has found the effort increasingly onerous, and for the past five the United States staggered as the defense budget and the trade deficit have chased each other to record levels.

The declining relative role of the United States in the world economic order is more a reflection of the success of the world rather than a failure on the part of the United States. In 1946, the U.S. accounted for almost 50 percent of gross world product. This percentage has steadily declined and today stands between 20 and 25 percent, depending upon the exchange rate at the time of comparison. This shift has occurred because the rest of the world has been growing faster than the United States.

The declining relative size of the United States means that in an increasing number of industries, the United States is no longer the home of the largest and most powerful enterprises. Today the U.S. steel and automobile industries—once without peer in the world—have slipped to second place behind the Japanese. Tomorrow, the Japanese will be displaced by other countries. Increasingly, the U.S. company is faced by strong competitors with resources that are greater than its own.

A fourth important trend in multinational corporations is an expanding appreciation of the need for active participation of the corporate and product division

---

[1]Laurence J. Farley, "Going Global: Choices and Challenges," *Journal of Consumer Marketing,* Winter 1986, p. 68.

[2]James Fallows, "The Americans in Space," *The New York Review,* December 18, 1986, p. 34.

headquarters in business strategy formulation and implementation. The headquarters role, when expressed, is only effective when it fully incorporates responses to national conditions. Thus, strong, sensitive, and effective national organizations must be maintained as companies simultaneously develop the capability of active and constructive participation in the strategy formulation and implementation process.

Another aspect of the relative decline of the United States as a preeminent world market is the leveling of per capita incomes in the industrialized countries. Today the United States is no longer the richest market in the world as measured by national income on a per capita basis. This has important implications for product life-cycle patterns. In the past, new products or major innovations were almost always introduced in the United States and only later sold in foreign markets. This was because the United States, with the highest income per capita, presented the first opportunity for expensive and often untested or unproven product innovations. Today, with several countries having higher national incomes per capita, it is now possible to present new products first elsewhere in the world.

In short, the United States is still the world's largest national market, but its relative size and relative income advantage have declined substantially and will probably continue to decline. This means that U.S. companies are facing strong and established foreign competitors that will have opportunities to try out and establish product innovations outside of the United States before introducing them in the U.S. market. A major implication of these developments is that U.S. companies must increasingly monitor developments taking place in other parts of the world to stay abreast of the most advanced practices and the most important new product development and introduction activities. In the past, if one was informed about what was going on in the United States, one was informed about the frontiers of marketing practice. Today this is no longer the case. Marketing professionals who are committed to keeping up with the latest developments in the field must scan the world and not just the United States. In effect, there is no longer a separation between domestic and international marketing: they have become a part of a unified field.

The other side of the relative decline of the United States is the rapid rise of the countries of the Pacific Basin, especially Japan. The Pacific Basin countries have been growing faster than the world average: For marketers, this means that markets *and* competition in the Pacific Basin are growing and developing more rapidly than in other parts of the world. The Japanese market, for example, is today roughly one-half the size of the U.S. market.

The public is well aware of the competitive strength of Japanese and other Pacific Basin countries in highly visible consumer products industries such as home entertainment, automobiles, and motorcycles. What the public is not so well aware of is the competitive strength of these countries in industrial product sectors. The capacity of the Far Eastern recloseable plastic bag industry is probably four to five times greater than that of the United States. This capacity, combined with the fact that costs in the Far East are considerably lower (in 1987, wages in the Far East ranged from $0.40 per hour to $1.50 per hour as compared to $12.00 in the United States) than those in the United States, means that the Taiwan industry could wipe out the U.S. industry if U.S. firms were unable to obtain protection from the U.S. government.

These two developments—the relative decline of the United States and the rise of the Pacific Basin and of other developing countries—have contributed toward a more symmetrical world in which economic power and opportunity are more dispersed than they were two decades ago. This is a healthy trend that contributes toward the stability of the international economic order.

MARKETING: A GLOBAL PROFESSION

Type of Person Needed for Multinational Marketing[3]

There are certain *general* specifications that people should have if they are to do an outstanding job in multinational marketing. Before discussing the specific background a review of these *general* specifications is in order.

A WORLD-BEATER IN THE DOMESTIC ARENA (A).   If a candidate currently is working in Global Enterprise, he or she should be recognized as a "comer," as a well-rounded businessperson who has built a monument on each of his or her jobs; may have worked in more than one function and has shown expertise in each; is *bright, inquiring,* and *interested;* knows the Global Enterprise Company and how to use its strengths both domestically and offshore; is an authority on his or her product lines; is the kind of person who might conceivably develop into general managership, since he or she will be pioneering and establishing a new business in oftentimes an unfamiliar market area. This person must be a broad-gauge stemwinder, not the average performer who is ready to be "put out to pasture." (The promotability of this person is vital, so the knowledge gained in multinational marketing work may be further multiplied as Global Enterprise becomes a worldwide company.) This is such an outstanding person that, if career movement eventually took him or her to an offshore position, domestic departments would be interested in bringing the candidate back to the headquarters organization some day.

Since offshore marketing sometimes requires an adaptation of standard products or normal domestic marketing practices, the candidate must have, or be capable of establishing, excellent working relationships with associates, particularly in engineering, manufacturing, and finance, so as to gain their cooperation in design, production schedules, pricing, and shifting, speeded-up delivery dates. This person must get help and cooperation from many, many sources, so being able to integrate well is a requirement.

If the candidate being considered is not currently with Global Enterprise, he

---

[3]This job description was developed by an international marketing executive at Global Enterprise, a large U.S.-based global company that prefers to remain anonymous.

or she will need to bring to the job expertise about either a particular foreign country, or market, or market approach; also must have shown adaptable characteristics that will enable the candidate to learn in rapid fashion what is needed about Global Enterprise, its organization, nomenclature, policies, and strengths that can be used in the new assignment.

CAREER SHOWS A GLOBAL ORIENTATION (B). The candidate should have a genuine interest and desire to perform with distinction in multinational marketing work as one part of the career plan. He or she would be willing to parlay this particular experience to a challenging offshore job, should one develop. The candidate is *not* the international "thrill seeker"; is *not* the kind of person who is fascinated primarily with international travel; is not interested in this kind of work solely because it may be today's "popular trend" or because company top management currently is interested in international business. The candidate looks at an international assignment with the same interest as he or she would another challenging domestic assignment.

   The candidate needs to be broad-minded and have an international attitude with a minimum of racial, religious, and political prejudices; must have a normal interest in the history, culture, and mores of the countries with which he or she does business, without "going native"; must appreciate that the values placed on many things in personal and business life offshore are different from those in the United States; should have talents for understanding and be willing to invest the personal time and effort to understand the people and to learn their language. Must be sensitive immediately to the political scene offshore, have the interest and stick-to-it-iveness to wade through the morass of foreign government regulations and restrictions that may be vital to being able to do business in the country; should be a combination diplomat-judge-ward-alderman in each country in which he or she operates, recognizing that the political arena in one country may differ remarkably from that in the next.

COMPETENT PLANNER (C). Should be a strong business planner, must have a knowledge of where to get knowledge; will evaluate a confusing array of data— much of which is incomplete; separate the important from the unimportant; and develop a plan that fits the needs of the business and is responsive to the customer.

CUSTOMER ORIENTED (D). All good marketing people are *expected* to be customer oriented. But the international marketing person based in the United States must have an extra charge of this orientation. Different voltages, left-hand threads, strange mounting specifications, and other requirements (which to the modern, standards-conscious, American businessmanager may be quaint and curious) are customer needs offshore and must be satisfied.

PERSONAL QUALITIES. 1. *Self-sufficient*. Must be secure and be able to work on an independent schedule for an extended period of time; needs to be competent professionally in his or her field; self-confidence is a "must," for when traveling offshore the individual will not have immediate counsel of domestic counterparts; needs courage and willingness to make decisions, often with inadequate information and within a short period of time.

2. *Aggressive*. The doors to the customer do not open quite as easily internationally as they do domestically. So the marketer who tries to sell offshore needs a high degree of aggressiveness (in some foreign countries, such as Japan, *overt* aggressiveness may be fatal in marketing a product); must have persistence, perseverance, dedication, and drive and be willing to work.

3. *Adaptable*. Must be flexible and adapt quickly to new people and different surroundings and be prepared for the unexpected and the unusual experiences that cannot always be anticipated; will have demonstrated in previous work this flexibility (e.g., having supervised a widely dispersed sales force or sales territory in domestic work could be a plus toward a similar responsibility that involves regional differences, offshore). Also should be service oriented, sensitive, and observant.

4. *Creative*. Must have imagination to see new approaches or adopt new approaches to accomplishing mission; have an alert, open mind.

5. *Communicative*. Should have above-average ability to communicate and patience in achieving understanding through communication where English may not be the principal language and where only one-third of a conversation may be understood; listening skills must be turned to nuances, double-talk, or different word or phrase connotations; should have sufficient language aptitude to carry on a conversation in a foreign language after one hundred hours of training. (Global Enterprise's International Division's Employee Relations Operation has a Modern Language Aptitude Test, developed by the Psychological Corporation, that can help to determine a person's aptitude for learning a foreign language.)

6. *Patient*. Must have patience to put up with customer's delays (sometimes planned) in coming up with agreements; must expect to invest what will seem to be nonproductive hours in trying to see people on a scheduled basis.

7. *Travel Oriented*. Must be able to withstand the rigors of foreign travel; being away from home for weeks at a time; day and night work schedules and rapid changes of time zones; loss of sleep; irregular eating of widely varying food; different standards of cleanliness and sanitation; and many strange climates and customs.

If married, should have a spouse who understands the travel requirements of the job.

8. *Management Potential*. Even though his or her first work may be entirely a one-person operation, should have a potential to manage people and a larger operation, if it materializes; may have demonstrated these skills in a previous job.

JOB DESCRIPTIONS: U.S.A. WORLD TRADING COMPANY

The job descriptions that are reproduced below were developed by the vice president of marketing of a leading U.S. trading company. The regional managers are located in the United States at the company headquarters, and the regional directors are located in the overseas offices.

Position Specification: Regional Manager, Southeast Asia

CLIENT ORGANIZATION.   The firm is a major U.S. corporation engaged in a sweeping diversification program. Its newly established world trading company is projected to be a major growth area and will establish long-term relations with customers and suppliers to operate in the following modes worldwide:

1. Export sale and service of quality consumer and light industrial products
2. Importation and sale of quality consumer and light industrial products
3. Bilateral or third-country trade
4. Countertrade (swap, barter, etc.)
5. Sale of technology and management services

SUMMARY OF POSITION RESPONSIBILITIES

1. Originates, directs, and manages regional and product marketing programs, business plans, and strategies within assigned geographical market for the purpose of expanding profitable export and import sales, third-country trade, and countertrade.
2. Within established Trading Company business philosophies and principles, will define policies and priorities for assigned area; is directly responsible and accountable for the development and implementation of market plans and achievement of agreed-upon sales and profit goals.
3. Approves all contracts and business transactions originated by and *for* the region and approves all transactions originating *from* assigned respective regional offices.
4. Trains and manages a staff of marketing managers and assistant marketing managers in the definition of their priorities and the execution of their responsibilities; also supervises the allocation of marketing resources and administrative and operating budgets in the Southeast Asia business sector.
5. Develops and maintains an internal and external intelligence network, particularly with U.S. and foreign political commercial and financial entities, and utilizes this information to make rational market analyses and prudent business recommendations, judgments, and decisions.
6. Maintains effective relationships with supplier and customer senior managements in the development, establishment, and continuance of profitable, long-term business relationships; is directly responsible for all customer contact as "senior account executive" in matters relating to marketing and sales.
7. Maintains current knowledge on a wide spectrum of consumer products and their marketing techniques; is responsible for maintaining this knowledge and awareness through constant and effective communications with suppliers and customers, Trading Company senior marketing staff, product group staff, and regional directors. Supervises the development of sales presentation materials with distributors and buyers.
8. Provides appropriate direction to the Trading Company regional directors in the regions served in terms of new and ongoing contacts with customers and suppliers, routine

business matters, contract negotiations, and the establishment of distribution channels for products in foreign markets.

9. Recommends market research projects and uses results to initiate marketing programs.

RELATIONSHIPS

Reports to:	Director of Marketing/Trading
Manages:	Marketing managers and support functions
Coordinating Relationships:	Through the director of marketing/trading, with the respective regional directors in Hong Kong and Singapore and their staffs. Maintains liaison with other Trading Company offices and provides research and counsel on the opening of new offices or branches in Asia as the Trading Company becomes fully operative.

Maintains liaison with other regional directors and managers at headquarters and around the world.

Coordinates plans and activities closely with the director of product management, the staff, and product group managers based at corporate headquarters.

Will maintain normal communications and information exchanges, as needed, with the parent company staff, domestic and foreign.

Establishes and maintains relationships (through the group product staff) with outside product and service resources, manufacturers, and distributors and, as appropriate, their respective service arms—finance, insurance, research, advertising, packaging, warehousing, logistics, and so on—and "influence makers" and key sources of information in business, government, education, financial, and related sectors, both in the United States and the specific area assigned.

Candidate Specification: Senior Marketing Manager

KEY SELECTION CRITERIA

1. A broad knowledge of international consumer products marketing and its application in Southeast Asian markets
2. Knowledge and experience with proven skills in modern marketing techniques and methods
3. A person with exceptional communication and persuasion skills, both oral and written
4. An entrepreneurial self-starter who is oriented to sales and profit goals

IDEAL EXPERIENCE

1. Currently is in an international regional management or senior marketing position with substantial gross profit impact in a consumer or light industrial products company or possibly a trading company with extensive business relations throughout the designated Southeast Asia area.
2. Earlier positions should have included strategic market product planning, marketing research, sales, and sales management with broad exposure to distributors, agents, and others who sell products.

3. Has a proven track record of building, developing, and managing an international marketing organization, with personal involvement in having developed an effective distributor network.

4. Holds a management position with at least one North American multinational company in which there has been considerable interface with foreign government and commercial agencies and banks, requiring meaningful communications and negotiations between the regional offices and U.S. headquarters.

5. Has had broad exposure to a variety of business cultures and a successful record of negotiating and concluding agreements and contracts.

6. Has experience living in, or extended traveling within, foreign countries.

IDEAL PERSONAL PROFILE

1. A degree from a U.S. or other Western university is desirable, with an advanced degree an advantage.

2. A U.S. citizen is preferred, but candidate could be a resident alien. The candidate must speak English fluently and should have the ability to carry on business in at least one other language of the assigned market.

3. Company prefers a mature, stable executive of unquestioned integrity with a good image and presence who will represent the company effectively in dealing with others in business, government, financial, and social circles.

4. Candidate is a proven leader who will gain and hold the respect of associates throughout the world and the business communities with which the position interfaces.

5. Candidate is an innovative marketing executive, trader, and entrepreneur who understands risk-reward ratios; a decision maker who exercises good business judgment.

6. Candidate is a well-organized manager who can effectively handle stress, heavy travel, multiple organizational relationships, and complex communications requirements; is a person who can easily delegate and train his or her staff.

7. Company desires a strong person with enthusiasm for operating in a dynamic, rapidly evolving, and complex, unstructured environment with the ability to keep a multiplicity of projects moving forward at the same time to get desired results.

8. Candidate is a positive and cheerful individual who is persuasive, articulate, and a good communicator (which includes the ability to listen well)—one who can effectively prioritize.

Position Specification: Hong Kong Regional Director, Northern Asia, Singapore Regional Director, Southern Asia

CLIENT ORGANIZATION.   The firm is a major U.S. corporation engaged in a sweeping diversification program. The World Trading Company is projected to be a major growth area and will establish long-term relations with customers and suppliers to operate in the following modes:

1. Export sale and service of quality consumer and light industrial products
2. Importation and sale of quality consumer and light industrial products
3. Bilateral or third-country trade

4. Countertrade (swap, barter, etc.)
5. Sale of technology and management services

POSITION SUMMARY.   To establish and maintain productive long-term relations with selling outlets for U.S. products throughout the area and, at the same time, to seek high-quality products for sale and distribution in the United States and other countries. This will involve substantial interface with distributors, agents, and other sales outlets along with suppliers, government agencies, banks, and other financing institutions. The primary thrust of this office will be to *buy* products (profitably) that will be sold inside and outside the area and *sell* products sourced both in that region and in all other regions.

RELATIONSHIPS

Reports to: Vice President Marketing/Trading

Manages: All functions of the regional office, including marketing, sales, product management, finance, operations, and quality assurance

MAJOR RESPONSIBILITIES

1. Is responsible for attainment of sales and profit goals established for that region.
2. Provides input into development of the strategic plan and sales and profit objectives for that area.
3. Directs activities of regional marketing managers who will be servicing existing customers, identifying new customers, assisting in market research activities, and preparing marketing plans jointly with customers.
4. Directs activities of regional product managers who will be servicing outside suppliers and identifying new sources.
5. Directs activities of operational/logistical personnel to ensure that customers and suppliers are serviced adequately.
6. Maintains good relationships with key customers and suppliers, nurturing those contacts and frequently contacting their top-management personnel.
7. Maintains and builds excellent relationships with local and area government officials, banks, and other important outside agencies and organizations.
8. Maintains excellent relationships with key personnel in the Chicago office of the World Trading Company and the other components of the corporation. Provides for their proper treatment when they visit the area.
9. Reports directly to the vice president of marketing/trading and submits regular reports on the regional office's activities and programs.
10. Is responsible for the training, development, and compensation of people reporting to this position.
11. Maintains and develops local infrastructure required for effective operation of the office, such as (a) selection, training, and retention of good personnel; (b) good communications system; (c) good office equipment; (d) good housekeeping; and (e) effective filing system.
12. Travels throughout the region to maintain direct contact with key customers and suppliers.

13. Ensures that local product managers and marketing managers maintain proper contact with their counterparts in Chicago.
14. Maintains close working relationships with overseas buying offices, utilizing their services as required.

Candidate Specification

IDEAL EXPERIENCE

1. Is currently in a general/regional management or senior marketing position with profit and loss responsibility in a consumer or light industrial products company, or possibly a trading company with extensive business relations throughout the area.
2. Has a proven track record of building, developing, and managing a marketing organization while coordinating finance, sales, operations, and other functions normally under general management responsibility.
3. Earlier assignments could have included product planning, strategic and marketing planning, marketing research, and sales and sales management with extensive exposure to distributors, agents, and others who sell products.
4. Has a prior background in dealing with suppliers and/or distributors of consumer or light industrial products with heavy emphasis on negotiations for price, delivery, quality, documentation, shipping and receiving, and so on.
5. Has held at least one management position with an American multinational company in which there has been interface with governmental agencies and banks with the necessity for meaningful communications between the local area office and headquarters.
6. Has had a successful experience in negotiating and working in a variety of business cultures.

IDEAL PERSONAL PROFILE

1. A college degree is desirable with an M.B.A. an advantage.
2. Some U.S. or other Western education would be a plus.
3. Nationality is open, but the individual must speak English fluently and preferably have the ability to use Mandarin and possibly other dialects of the Chinese language for business conversations.
4. A mature, stable executive of unquestioned integrity with a good image and presence is required who will represent the company effectively in dealing with others in business, government, financial, and social circles.
5. The candidate is a proven leader who will gain and hold the respect of others inside the company and out—ambitious with high potential for promotion.
6. The company desires a strong person who is comfortable and productive operating in a changing, unstructured environment and has the ability to keep a multiplicity of projects moving forward simultaneously to get desired results.
7. The company requires a persuasive, articulate communicator who also listens well and who uses good judgment about what information to communicate to headquarters.
8. The candidate must be an innovative, entrepreneurial deal maker who understands risk-reward ratios and uses good business judgment in making decisions.
9. The candidate must be a well-organized manager who can handle stress and heavy travel in an organization with growing pains and all of this with a sense of humor.

SUMMARY

The opportunities in global marketing have never been greater than they are today. The companies that seize these opportunities will offer the best combination of product, price, promotion, and place. This is as it always was, is, and always will be. In addition, over the long term, successful companies will also be sensitive to the aspirations and needs not only of the individual customers in each national market but also the collective aspirations. This point was made very well by Reginald H. Jones, former chairman and chief executive officer of General Electric Company:

> We have found over many years that the key to business success in any country is to consult with the people who are there, both the officials in charge of economic policy and the private sector people who have a sense of the people's wants and needs. Find out what they are trying to do—their priorities, their plans for the nation, their most urgent needs, their rules for participation in the local economy. Then figure out the best way to make your capabilities and products and services fit their needs and regulations. If a company takes the trouble to do this ground work, then the odds are in favor of business success because both parties—the company and the host country—want the venture to succeed.[4]

BIBLIOGRAPHY

Books

OHMAE, KENICHI. *Triad Power: The Coming Shape of Global Competition*. New York: The Free Press, 1985.

PORTER, MICHAEL E. *Competition in Global Industries*. Boston, Mass.: Harvard Business School Press, 1986.

TOFFLER, ALVIN. *The Third Wave*. New York: Bantam Books, 1981.

Articles

CAVUSGIL, S. TAMER, AND JOHN R. NEVIN. "State-of-the-Art in International Marketing: An Assessment." In *Review of Marketing 1981* by Ben M. Enis and Kenneth J. Roering, pp. 195–216. Chicago: American Marketing Association, 1981.

FARLEY, LAURENCE J. "Going Global: Choices and Challenges." *The Journal of Consumer Marketing*, Vol. 3, no. 1 (Winter 1986), pp. 67–70.

HENZLER, HERBERT, AND WILHELM RALL. "Facing up to the Globalization Challenge." *The McKinsey Quarterly*, Winter 1986, pp. 52–68.

MURRAY, F. T., AND ALICE HALLER MURRAY. "SMR Forum: Global Managers for Global Businesses." *Sloan Management Review*, Winter 1986, pp. 75–80.

ONDRACK, DANIEL. "International Transfers of Managers in North American and European MNEs." *Journal Of International Business Studies*, Fall 1985, pp. 1–18.

---

[4]Reginald H. Jones, "The Basic Formula for Business Success," *Harvard Business Review*, November–December 1980, p. 155.

WIND, YORAM, AND HOWARD PERLMUTTER. "On the Identification of Frontier Issues in Multinational Marketing." *Columbia Journal of World Business,* Winter, 1984, pp. 17–26.

WINRAM, STEVE. "The Opportunity for World Brands." *International Journal of Advertising,* Vol. 3, pp. 17–26.

Appendix: Global Business: Strategic Issues and Career Implications[1]

I've been asked to talk a bit today about international business management which is my area of responsibility at General Foods.

You may remember a remark several years ago by that great philosopher of the human condition. Yogi Berra. Told that the people of Dublin, Ireland, had elected a Jewish mayor. Yogi shook his head and said, "Only in America!"

Well, my job is basically everything *not* in America at General Foods. General Foods International is the sector of our company that encompasses almost all GF businesses outside the United States. We have major operations in more than 20 countries—in Canada, Latin America, Europe and the Asia-Pacific area.

Last fiscal year, we accounted for roughly $1.7 billion in net sales, or about 20 percent of the total worldwide General Foods Corporation. Roughly 20,000 people work for GF International, about a third of the corporate total.

Our businesses vary from country to country. They're a mixture of adaptations of General Foods' U.S. products—particularly coffee and powered beverages—and strong national franchises. For example, we are leaders in snack foods in Canada, decaffeinated coffee in Germany, ice cream in Brazil, canned meats in Italy, desserts in Great Britain, and chewing gum in France.

As for my own background, I've spent most of my career in the U.S. I've learned a great deal about international business management in my present job. And I got first-hand experience previously when I was stationed in Brussels, as president of General Foods Europe.

Today, I want to cover three topics. One is, what are the similarities to and differences from U.S. business management? Second, what are the key strategic issues facing the international manager? And the third is, what are the implications of international management for personal career directions?

To start off, then, what are the similarities and differences between U.S. and international managers? The similarities are the fundamentals of strategy. The way

---

[1] Ervin R. Shames, executive vice president, General Foods, Inc., Lubin Lecture, Pace University, November 2, 1984.

you think about strategy and the considerations of developing a strategy are the same in international business as in domestic.

For instance, you've got to evaluate the external environment. You've got to do a competitive assessment. You've got to look at your own strengths and weaknesses. And you've got to attempt to find the sustainable competitive advantage.

All of these basic concepts are the same, wherever you do business.

Likewise the basics of the business functions. For instance, the fundamentals in marketing and finance are the same. So if you understand the fundamentals of marketing in the U.S., you're going to understand them in Germany or France.

Obviously, various cultures are different, so you have to factor them in. Consumer orientation is the same, but consumers themselves often are different from country to country.

The third similarity is the principles of management. The lessons learned from books like *In Pursuit of Excellence* or *The Art of Japanese Management* are applicable virtually everywhere.

So the fundamentals of strategy, the basics of the functions, the fundamentals of managing are all the same.

And crucially, motivating people is basically similar. People strive for similar rewards in their personal lives. They want recognition, they want advancement. Those are basic human needs, no matter what the country.

Having noted the similarities, the differences are major. It's like comparing space travel to airplane travel. The aeronautical principles may be the same. But they are two very different experiences. And piloting a space ship certainly requires a different set of skills than piloting an airplane.

There are four major forces that create these differences. The first is the external environment and its impacts. Many political and social influences overseas are far stronger than they are here. For instance, in the U.S., if you decide you have too many employees, you work to reduce that number in a humane way.

It's not so simple abroad—particularly in European countries. General Foods owned a business in Holland which, despite our best efforts, was not successful. But we were unable to reduce the number of employees. The restrictions on doing it and the cost were so onerous that it was less costly to simply give the company way.

Price controls are another example of a differing external environment. They are used far more widely overseas, again particularly Europe.

In Sweden in 1976, there were newspaper reports that coffee prices were about to come down. So the government ordered us to lower our prices, even though our costs had not come down yet. They hadn't considered the length of time it takes for our actual inventory costs to drop. It cost us millions of dollars because of government fiat. But that's just a fact of doing business in Europe.

Just a couple of years ago, the French government deregulated the price of bread for the first time in 300 years. But they couldn't keep their hands off. It stayed deregulated for only about a year.

Another difference is advertising access. We here in America are used to a free marketplace. That's just not true in most of the rest of the world. The government controls where and when you advertise. And there are very few free commercial broadcast stations.

An international manager has to learn to do business with these kinds of constraints. And managing them is a measure of your effectiveness as an international manager.

Another difference is in the economic area. For instance, the volatility of some foreign economies. Volatility in the U.S. means going from a growth rate of 4.5 to 2.5 or maybe plus 1.

Compare that to Mexico or Brazil, where you deal with a 200 percent inflation rate. You can see economic growth change by 10 to 20 points. And we literally have seen consumer markets go from plus 10s to minus 20s inside of a year!

Volatility also is a problem in exchange rates and currency in management—something else you don't worry about as a domestic manager, except if you're in the export business. For the bulk of American managers, it's immaterial. But you sure worry if you're an international manager!

And in recent months, it's been crazy. The exchange markets move more now in a day than they used to move in a month.

The third external force with major impact is that the retail and wholesale trade is far more concentrated and powerful overseas. One major customer of ours in Europe accounted for about 30 percent of our product line in that country.

One time, they called in our salesmen and made demands for discounts and allowances that were very high. While our people were arguing that it was totally unreasonable, their buyer reached under his desk and took out a metronome. He put it on his desk and activated it. And he said, "O.K. Let me make sure you understand. When this thing stops ticking, either you've agreed to my terms or every one of your products is out of my store. Period."

We did come to an agreement. But the point is, that kind of naked force is just not something we're used to here in the U.S.

Another factor abroad is labor. In Germany, we manage our company through a supervisory board that has six labor and six management members. We discuss with them all major moves of the company.

That's totally different than in the U.S. It creates different lead time issues about getting things done.

Another difference is how politicized labor can be abroad. Two years ago we had a strike at one of our French plants. It really had nothing to do with us. It was right before Mitterand took office. And the Communist-controlled labor union wanted to send a message to the French government.

The last major difference concerns competition. Here, the mentality is different. We are used to a mentality of competition in the U.S.—Adam Smith's free market.

But the competitive mentalities in other parts of the world are far different. For instance, the central Europeans are much more interested in alliances and balances of power. They love to discuss what their various competitors are up to, and try to join with one against another. It's a whole different way of competing than what we're used to, where you don't talk to your competition and you just don't think about power alliances against another competitor.

Another competitive mentality is that of the Far East. The Japanese often use a book called the *Sun Tzu,* which is the art of war. It was written in the third century. And it's literally the principles of warfare. How to mass your forces against someone else, and how to apply force and persistence. You can learn a lot about competition in the Far East if you read that book.

A caveat here. Obviously, in discussing these characteristics of business overseas, and in some of the points that follow, I have to generalize. Of course, there are exceptions to the rule, just as there are here in America. But generally, what I'm saying holds true in most cases.

It reminds me of someone's explanation of the difference between heaven and hell. In heaven, the British are the cops, the French are the chefs. The Swiss are the organizers, and the Italians are the lovers. In Hell, the British are the chefs, the French are the cops, the Swiss are the lovers, and the Italians are the organizers!

Anyway, granting that there are exceptions, let me move to the second major area of differences I want to cover—which deals with culture.

One such difference is in business priorities. In Europe, the major business priority is preservation. What much of the European business community really wants—and the government wants from them—is preservation of jobs, preservation of the status quo. So when a maverick like Freddie Laker comes along, they really get quite upset about it.

In contrast, in Latin America, the concern is much more local impact. They don't care as much what you do in the grand scheme. Their concern is what you are going to do for this city or that particular area.

And in the Far East, they care a great deal more about growth. How much you're going to help us grow in employment. How much you can contribute to make our economy boom.

These are all perfectly legitimate. But they *are* different!

And you've got to understand these priorities if you want to get something done in one of these societies.

Still another difference is in business customs. Here, I compare the directions of the Germans with the indirectness of the French. You work with a German, and he comes right to the point. And that's it. Here is what I am—bam, bam! In contrast, I asked a French advertising man what makes French advertising unique. And he said, in the rest of the world you *sell*. In France, we *seduce*.

Well, again, that may be a bit overdrawn. But it *is* true that their approach to business relationships is more indirect that ours. They like to surround an argument and then come in, as opposed to coming head-on into it.

If you tried the head-on approach that works in Germany, the French would dismiss it as very bad manners. On the other hand, if you used the round-about approach with the Germans, you'd be out of there with no business.

And in Japan, patience is required. Quite often, the first meeting is limited to formalities—an exchange of business cards, a cup of tea and so forth. Nothing of substance gets done until at least the second meeting.

Another very obvious cultural difference is language. It's a fact of life that enormously complicates doing business.

And then there are a myriad of other differences from country to country, over which you might have no control. In some countries, business people still have a hard time dealing with Americans who are too young-looking. And in some, women are still not fully accepted.

The third major difference between domestic and international management is distance. Managing a far-flung international business reduces the frequency of contact between a boss and subordinate—particularly in the Pacific. This puts a premium on clear communication and the ability of a manager to give direction without being too detailed.

When your subordinates are sitting in the office next to you, you see them eyeball to eyeball. You can sense whether they're understanding you or not. And if things get a little off track, you'll know it pretty quickly.

But if you're dealing with your managers 3,000 miles away, you can't do that. So both of you have to be clear enough to make sure you understanding each other. But you can't be too specific, because you really don't know all the details of the local situation. You've got to leave them some latitude.

That's a whole different situation than you encounter as a domestic manager. But there's a beneficial aspect—this creates autonomy for managers. An international manager has more autonomy than a domestic manager every time.

The fourth major difference from domestic management is the area of internal relationships. Unfortunately, most *Fortune* 500 companies view the international area as of less corporate importance that they do their domestic business.

Again, there are exceptions. But I think it is inescapable due to distance, cultural differences and so forth.

The result is that the home office usually is not able to help you with the same involvement as in the domestic area. Because they just aren't close to the business.

But—a major plus—they don't mess with you as much either. It cuts both ways.

So those are the similarities and differences with working in a domestic business.

Now, what are the key strategic issues facing an international manager? The first one is strengthening company product portfolios. That's because of those environmental factors I talked about earlier. They demand strength. You've got to have a strong product portfolio. You've got to have strong share positions because the international business environment punishes weakness.

That's much more so than it is in this country. And I think it's going to be even truer in the future, because of the phenomenon that I call "competitive confluence." That means that all your competitors can see the same opportunities. And they're all heading toward those same opportunities.

Unless your portfolio is stronger than theirs in the areas where you chose to compete, it's not going to be very profitable for you.

A General Foods example: We used to have a small instant coffee business in Spain. We were a weak second, with less than 10 percent of the market, far behind Nestlé. Then, about two years ago, the government legalized the sale of ground roast coffee.

We saw an opportunity. But instead of going it alone. We set up a joint venture with an established Spanish roaster. We moved into the market with some horsepower behind us. Today, we've got ___ per cent of the Spanish roast and ground market.

We knew that it wasn't enough to be a small player. We either had to make a big commitment, or get out.

It takes more than money alone to strengthen a portfolio. It requires betting right on which business to invest in, and then establishing clear competitive advantages.

Bruce Henderson, one of the founders of BCG, says the "strategy is causing your competitors to *disinvest* from areas of *your* interest."

That requires carefully defining markets, skillfully segmenting those markets, understanding the fundamentals of the business, and establishing sustainable competitive advantages. Those are crucial manager challenges anywhere. But it is particularly true in international because the environment is unforgiving.

If the first key issue facing the international manager is building a strong portfolio, the second is deciding which countries you want to invest in and how heavily you want to invest. Speaking personally from a consumer goods industry viewpoint. There are few countries that are clear standout. And very, very few that surpass the U.S. in terms of attractiveness.

All things considered, the U.S. is the most attractive investment area in the world today. So if you're going to do business internationally, you've got a challenge.

For instance, Europe is suffering from stagnation and still has a lot of anti-business attitudes.

The Far East—Japan is a dynamic country but it's nearly close to foreign investment.

Other areas of the Far East that are attractive present significant ethical challenges in terms of the way we want to do business versus the way they are used to doing business.

Latin America has a fragile economy and difficult business practices.

So you sort through country by country and area by area. And it's difficult to find a place. And the net is, you have to decide what are acceptable places to invest in, and under what conditions and to what extent. You have to keep your eyes open for specific opportunities—such as bringing GF's strengths in coffee to Spain, or building on the growing taste for coffee in the U.K. and Japan—where the traditional drink is tea.

The third strategic challenge is the balance of centralized direction versus giving each country autonomy. To what extent do you want to try to manage globally, and to what extent do you want local management? Centralization brings the efficiencies of scale.

I don't buy all of what Harvard's Ted Levitt says in his essay on global marketing. But there is a lot of truth in what he says about the growth of uniformity due to the forces of economics and changes in consumer receptivity to similar products throughout the world.

They are clear forces pushing toward more centralized direction of the business.

On the other hand, the pull for country autonomy comes from the desire of the managers of a country to exercise control over their own businesses, and the strong case for local effectiveness.

I don't think there is any one right answer. But my bias for a consumer goods operation is toward localized autonomy. In our business, satisfying the consumer must be paramount. And strong local preferences have to be taken into consideration. But there still can be a balance with global strategies and economies of scale.

What are the implications of all this on the career of an international manager? Well, for one thing, they mean that there are certain characteristics an international manager must have.

He or she has got to have breadth. He or she must be interested in other cultures, with an ability to understand them. A person who goes to Paris and eats at MacDonald's is probably not a good candidate for an international manager. That person probably doesn't have the interest and curiosity about other cultures that one needs in international business.

An international manager has to have the ability to operate independently. Dave Hurwitt, our former general manager in France, came back to his office in Paris one day, to find that the local labor union had occupied it.

They were having a local dispute and decided to do a sit-in in the office of the general manager. David had to decide right then what to do. You can't pick up the phone and call New York and say, "O.K. What do I do now?"

David avoided the confrontation, which was the wise thing to do, I think. And eventually they left his office with no long-term damage done to our labor relations there. But he had to think fast. He could have made the situation a lot worse had he been clumsy or inept.

An international manager also has to be experienced in his or her function. International business is no place for rookies. Don't send me somebody who is just getting started. Send me somebody who knows the ropes.

That's because of this need to operate autonomously. An international manager needs judgment, self-confidence. You want to know that the person is going to act with seasoned judgment when facing those unpredictable situations alone, far from the home office.

The last thing I would note is that it really takes physical stamina and emotional stability to be an international manager. A lot of traveling demands physical strength. And you need emotional stability because you keep getting those surprises. You simply cannot control everything, and if you can't live with that, you're going to be a basket case.

A piece of that emotional stability is a very sound family life. A person can be single and deal with it that way. But to a married person, an international career or an international assignment is a family affair. Families also have to be able to handle the travel, and the relocations from time to time.

Finally, what's the impact of international management on a business career? I believe that it is helpful to some people's careers. The world is turning more toward a global approach to business. The auto industry shows that.

People who know how to deal with that situation are going to be better equipped to face the 1990s than people who have managed solely domestically. Also, they'll have been more autonomous and therefore will have more ability to operation their own. With that comes a self-confidence that you don't get when you manage in a setting where your boss is close by.

They also are going to become more experienced because of the faster pace of international business and the wider range of challenges—such as the volatility of currency I mentioned earlier—that an international manager faces.

There are some risks, however. As I said, international business is less important to most companies than domestic businesses. People in international business are usually remote from the power center of the company. Out of sight, out of mind is a risk one runs.

Caesar used to send his troublesome generals to the provinces for a good reason. A few of them would come back, but many of them were never heard of again!

Another risk is that you have less control over events than you do in a domestic business. Go back to all of those environmental forces that I cited. Any one of them could lead to a disastrous situation.

But quite frankly, if you are not willing to take some prudent risks, to try something different and challenge yourself in new ways, you're probably not going to be successful in *any* kind of business—domestic or international. The business world is too tough and too competitive today.

So all in all, I believe that some international experience is good for a business career.

And even if it were not, it still would be worthwhile because of what it does for a person. Clearly, the ability to experience other cultures, to live overseas, is a very valuable personal experience.

While most of my career has been spent in the states, I think I have learned more—and certainly had more fun—in my assignments with GF International. And I know that my family is immeasurably richer for it.

So, as they used to say in the commercials, you only go 'round once. Why not at least try for some of that time to live in a country other than this one, and experience a culture other than this one? It will make you a better, broader and, I believe, happier person.

That has been my own personal experience. And I hope that it is yours as well, in the years to come.

THE NEWS CORPORATION LTD. (A)
RUPERT MURDOCH'S GLOBAL VILLAGE:
IMPOSSIBLE DREAM OR TOMORROW'S REALITY?[1]

INTRODUCTION

A man who started out with a small Australian newspaper now possesses one of the most impressive communications companies on earth. Rupert K. Murdoch made his name in the print industry but, in 1985, he made a strong move into American television when he acquired seven stations from the Metromedia Broadcasting Corporation (now known as the Fox Broadcasting Corporation) for US$ 1.65 billion. Murdoch had a reputation as a shrewd businessman who bought floundering or undervalued properties and made them successful. He was also known as a visionary who "saw around corners" and defied the odds as he set out to establish his personal global communications empire.

Murdoch didn't see himself as owning an empire merely for the prestige. All of his important holdings generated revenue by selling advertising space (in the case of newspapers) or time (in the case of television). By positioning himself globally, Murdoch saw himself as riding the crest of the new global marketing wave. Central to his strategy was the idea of a global village, where electroni-

cally shared ideas and information were reducing cultural and geographical boundaries between nations. It is therefore appropriate that the story of Rupert Murdock begins with a discussion of what is actually meant by the term "global village."

THE DREAM OF THE GLOBAL VILLAGE

The idea of the global electronic village where artificial national barriers are easily crossed with the aid of satellites has been around for several decades. An early exponent was Marshall McLuhan, a professor at the University of Toronto who is best known for the phrase "the medium is the message." Writing in the 1960s, McLuhan proclaimed that as technology progressed, the effect on the world would be to make it a smaller place, "a global village of ever contracting size." (Marshall McLuhan. *Counter Blast*. Harcourt, Brace & World Inc., 1969). McLuhan's vision was that of an information society where experiences and ideas would be shared instantaneously.

In the field of marketing, one might say that McLuhan's intellectual blood brother is Theodore Levitt. Levitt, perhaps the best known exponent of global marketing, wrote in his celebrated *Harvard Business Review* article of a "new commercial reality—the emergence of global markets for standardized consumer products on a previously unimagined scale." According to Levitt, "A powerful force drives the world toward a con-

[1]This case was prepared by Charles Anderer, case writer and research associate, under the supervision of Warren J. Keegan, professor of International Business and Marketing. The case was developed with the support provided by the Leading Edge Case Study Project of the Center for International Business, Pace University. The project was funded by a grant from the United States Department of Education. Copyright © 1986, Pace University.

verging commonality, and that force is technology. It has proletarianized communication, transport, and travel. It has made isolated places and impoverished peoples eager for modernity's allurements. Almost everyone, everywhere wants all the things they've heard about, seen, or experienced via the new technologies." (*The Harvard Business Review,* May–June 1983)

For many, the problem with the concept of the global village was that nations continued to operate on their own in the field of communications. Networks rarely extend their work beyond their respective national frontiers and, when they do, it is for domestic not international consumption. Many nations also maintain strict regulations regarding the scope and nature of television transmissions. This is especially true in Europe, where most networks are tightly controlled by sovereign governments. What the global village has lacked is not technological capability but a unifying force capable of orchestrating communications technology on a global scale. Furthermore, advertisers continued to market their goods differently from country to country although this is a trend that appeared to be changing. In fact, in view of the rash of worldwide advertising agency mergers in the early part of 1986, most advertising executives believed that the industry would soon be consolidated until there were only six to ten "mega-agencies." Part of the rationale behind the agency mergers was that only those agencies capable of servicing clients on a global scale would be able to thrive on a long-term basis.

RUPERT MURDOCH'S GLOBAL COMMUNICATIONS STRATEGY

Enter Rupert Murdoch. In 1985, Murdoch's Australian-based News Corporation set out to expand on its three-nation media empire. Having decided in the early seventies that a global media company required a presence in the United States, Murdoch acquired properties ranging from trade magazines to television stations. When he had finished, Murdoch increased News Corporation's asset base from A\$2.099 billion to A\$3.463 billion and, in the process, saddled himself with an enormous amount of debt. In its quest to create a fourth television network in the United States, News Corporation borrowed some US\$ 2.6 billion. Never mind that the interest charges on this debt will cost some \$300 million per year (at 1986 interest rates), Murdoch has a vision. The underlying strategy of News Corporation is to provide global marketers with advertising media the world over, thereby enabling it to get in on the ground floor of the budding global advertising market:

I do believe we're going to see a lot more global marketing all the way from IBM to McDonald's. The advertising agencies have become global. A company that can offer media all over the world is going to have an advantage. I don't necessarily mean a tie-up or an exclusive thing, but you're going to have an in. (*Ad Age,* 9/16/85)

The list of Murdoch's holdings is indeed impressive. News Corporation consists of television stations, newspapers and magazines, film companies, and book publishers in Australia, the United States, and the United Kingdom:

Australia:

Newspapers: 45, including *The Daily Telegraph, Daily Mirror,* and *Daily Sun*
Magazines: *New Idea* and *TV Week*
Television: Channels Ten-10, ATV-10
Publishing: Bay Books, Angus and Robertson Publishers.

Films and Records: Associated R&R Films, Festival Records

United States:

Newspapers: *New York Post, Boston Herald,* and others

Magazines: *Star, New York, New Woman,* 12 trade publications, *Elle,* a joint venture with Hachette

Television: Seven Metromedia stations and Metromedia Producers Corp.

Film: Twentieth Century Fox

United Kingdom:

Newspapers: Includes *The Times, The Sun, News of the World,* plus *The Times'* weekly literary

Television: Sky Channel (reaches nine countries)

Publishing: Times books, William Collins & Sons

(See Table 1 for a breakdown of revenues by industry and geographical area.)

THE ACQUISITIONS OF 1985

Prior to 1985, The News Corporation Ltd. was considered a major player in the international communications market. The 1985 acquisitions advanced The News Corporation from its position as a major player to a new position as the most extensive global communications company in the world. Over a 14 month period, News Corporation bought 14 magazines for $350 million, Twentieth Century Fox for $575 million and the six television stations which comprise the Fox Broadcasting Corporation for $1.65 billion. The resulting $2.6 billion in debt created problems that will be examined in further detail below. The logic behind Murdoch's shopping spree is that, in addition to possessing the global capability he has always dreamed of, his company sorely needed these acquisitions in order to survive in an ever changing advertising market. By focusing on magazines and television, Murdoch gave every indication that the future of The News Corporation Ltd. lay more and more in these two areas:

Classified advertising is under threat from specialized publications . . . National advertising has been rushing into TV. Department stores are going into catalog printing as their main thrust. So where's the growth in newspapers? (*Ad Age,* 9/16/85)

Statistics do support Murdoch's reasoning. Any media company has basically two types of customers: The consumer who either reads publications, listens to the radio, or watches television, and advertisers, who select the best medium for their products. The principal behind Murdoch's move into television is simple; consumers are watching more television than ever and advertisers are spending more money on television than ever. Television as well as radio advertising expenditures have increased dramatically since 1970 (See Figure 1) while newspaper advertising revenues have increased at a much slower rate. The obvious step for a man of Murdoch's ambition was to establish himself in the United States, the commercial television capital of the world.

A detailed description of The News Corporation Ltd.:

TABLE 1 Notes on Financial Statements—Notes to and forming part of the accounts for the year ended June 30, 1985

16 DIRECTORS' EMOLUMENTS

The total of the emoluments received, or due and receivable (whether from the Company of from a related corporation) by:

a. Directors of the Company engaged in the full-time employment of the Company and its related corporations (excluding payments by way of fixed salaries) were $Nil (1984 $Nil).

b. Other Directors of the Company were $155,000 (1984 $133,000).

No commission for subscribing for, or agreement to procure subscriptions for, any shares in or debentures of the Company or any related corporations, were received or are due and receivable by any Director.

17 ASSOCIATED COMPANIES

	Principal Activities	Ownership Interest %
Adelaide Art Engravers Pty. Limited	Photo engraving	50.0
Advertiser-News Weekend Publishing Company Pty. Limited	Newspaper publishing	50.0
Ansett Transport Industries Limited	Airline passenger and freight services	49.9
Associated R and R Films Pty. Limited	Production, sale and distribution of motion picture films	50.0
Ayr Newspapers Pty. Limited	Newspaper publishing	44.2
*William Collins plc	Book publishing	19.4
Computer Power Group Holdings Pty. Limited	Computer software development and sales	50.0
Independent Newspapers Limited	Newspaper publishing	21.6
Lotto Management Services Pty. Limited	Lotto promotion and operation	33.3
**News Offset Limited	Investment	87.5
Nordstress Limited	Airline operation	50.0
TCF Holdings Inc.	Production, sale and distribution of television series and motion picture films	50.0

18 INDUSTRY AND GEOGRAPHIC SEGMENT DATA

	1985 $'000 Consolidated	1984 $'000 Consolidated
By Industry		
Revenues		
Newspapers	1,600,126	1,253,431
Magazines	339,953	225,735
Television	193,531	135,210
Commercial Printing	120,706	112,832
Other	192,768	138,428
	$2,447,084	$1,865,636
Operating Income		
Newspapers	79,551	75,645
Magazines	54,728	39,771
Television	8,920	8,298
Commercial Printing	6,985	5,779
Other	14,055	24,648
Consolidated Operating Income	164,239	154,141
Investment Income	61,741	45,848
Interest Expense	(73,706)	(66,315)
Income before Taxes, Minority Interest and Extraordinary Items	$152,274	$133,674
Identifiable Assets		
Newspapers	1,326,639	963,624
Magazines	866,332	205,602
Television	258,538	262,809
Commercial Printing	68,831	43,043
Other	361,968	228,941
Corporate Assets and Investments	580,699	395,331
	$3,463,007	$2,099,350

TABLE 1 (cont.)

18 INDUSTRY AND GEOGRAPHIC SEGMENT DATA (continued)

	1985 $'000 Consolidated	1984 $'000 Consolidated
By Industry (continued)		
Depreciation and Amortisation		
Newspapers	27,232	19,136
Magazines	4,434	2,521
Television	3,735	3,256
Commercial Printing	2,173	1,517
Other	5,031	3,434
	$42,605	$29,864
Capital Expenditures		
Newspapers	110,518	32,152
Magazines	15,292	4,673
Television	6,466	2,126
Commercial Printing	9,963	6,474
Other	13,134	8,879
	$155,373	$54,304
By Geographic Area		
Revenues		
Australia	827,503	658,529
United Kingdom	790,909	695,387
United States	828,672	511,720
	$2,447,084	$1,865,636
Operating Income		
Australia	62,859	63,673
United Kingdom	75,536	63,104
United States	25,844	27,364
Consolidated Operating Income	164,239	154,141
Investment Income	61,741	45,848
Interest Expense	(73,706)	(66,315)
Income before Taxes, Minority Interest and Extraordinary Items	$152,274	$133,674
Identifiable Assets		
Australia	750,717	733,922
United Kingdom	854,690	539,872
United States	1,276,901	430,225
Corporate Assets and Investments	580,699	395,331
	$3,463,007	$2,099,350
Depreciation and Amortisation		
Australia	14,222	10,245
United Kingdom	9,995	8,556
United States	18,388	11,063
	$42,605	$29,864
Capital Expenditures		
Australia	39,759	30,258
United Kingdom	91,583	14,031
United States	24,031	10,015
	$155,373	$54,304

* Although the equity interest is less than 20%, the Company also holds shares carrying 41.7% of the voting power.

** Acquired June 28, 1985—50% held directly and 37.5% indirectly. The company is not a subsidiary for purpsoes of the Companies Code.

There was no material intersegment sales and no transfers within geographic areas. Investment income consists principally of the equity earnings of associated companies.

Source: Annual Report.

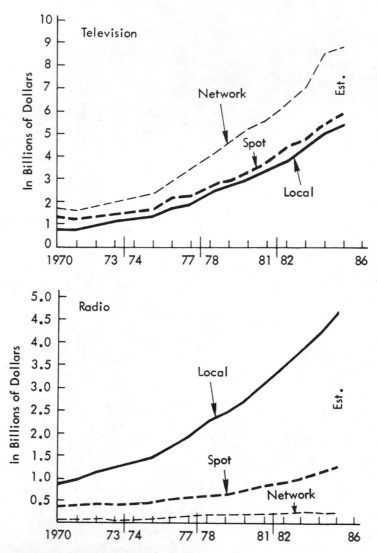

FIGURE 1 Breakdown of Television and Radio Advertising Expenditures (In Billions of Dollars)

Sources: McCann-Erickson; Television Advertising Bureau; Estimates by S&P

Fox Broadcasting Company (FBC)

FBC owns and operates four very high frequency (VHF) and three ultra high frequency (UHF) television stations in the United States. Fox's television stations include one network-affiliated and six independent stations in seven of the country's ten largest media markets. Its seven television stations have the largest potential audience coverage of any commonly owned and operated television station group, reaching 23.9 percent of U.S.

homes. The television advertising revenues of the seven media markets in which its television stations are located account for approximately 25 percent of the total television advertising revenues in the United States (see Tables 2–4.)

Fox Television was incorporated in May 1985 to purchase the above stations from Metromedia Broadcasting Corporation (MBC). Fox Television's business consists of the ownership and operation of these stations. The company is a wholly-owned subsidiary of Twentieth Century Fox (TCF), which was

TABLE 2   Top 20 TV Markets*

| | ADI TV HOUSEHOLDS[1] | | |
Market	Number of television homes	Percent of total (U.S.)	Number of[2] TV stations
New York	6,565,700	7.72	20
Los Angeles	4,365,800	5.13	21
Chicago	3,015,600	3.55	18
Philadelphia	2,582,600	2.97	18
San Francisco	2,054,300	2.42	20
Boston	1,943,300	2.28	19
Detroit	1,650,800	1.94	9
Dallas/Ft. Worth	1,506,600	1.77	13
Washington, D.C.	1,490,000	1.75	11
Cleveland/Akron	1,436,800	1.69	9
Houston	1,395,100	1.64	15
Pittsburgh	1,229,000	1.44	9
Minn./St. Paul	1,155,900	1.36	11
Miami/Ft. Lauderdale	1,154,600	1.36	14
Atlanta	1,135,900	1.34	10
Seattle/Tacoma	1,133,700	1.33	13
St. Louis	1,041,000	1.22	8
Tampa/St. Pete./Saras.	1,013,000	1.19	9
Denver	977,600	1.15	11
Sacramento/Stockton	903,700	1.06	9

*Based on television household and population estimates for the 1984–1985 season.

[1]ADI-Area of Dominant Influence, a geographic market design that defines each television market exclusive of the others, based on measurable viewing patterns.

[2]Includes non-commercial stations.

Source: *Broadcasting/Cablecasting Yearbook,* 1985.

TABLE 3   Fox Television Stations

STATION, LOCATION AND YEAR COMMERCIAL OPERATIONS COMMENCED	NATIONAL RANKING OF MARKET SERVED
WNEW-TV (changed to WNYW) New York, N.Y., 1944	1
KTTV Los Angeles, Calif., 1949	2
WFLD-TV Chicago, Illinois, 1966	3
WCVB-TV (An ABC Affiliate) Boston, Mass., 1957	6
KRLD-TV (changed to KDAF) Dallas/Ft. Worth, Texas, 1980	8
WTTG Washington, D.C., 1947	9
KRIV-TV Houston, Texas, 1971	10

also incorporated in May 1985. Murdoch's goal is to establish Fox Television as America's fourth network in the not so distant future.

Revenues.   Fox derives television broadcasting revenues from network, national spot, and local advertising. Only WCVB-TV, an affiliate of the ABC Television network, receives significant revenues from network advertising. A substantial percentage of Fox's television broadcast revenues is derived from national spot advertising, which consists principally of short announcements and sponsored programs on behalf of national and regional advertisers. Local advertising consists of short announcements and sponsored programs on behalf of advertisers in the immediate area served by the station. Most national spot sales and local advertising contracts are short term, usually only running for several weeks (contrasted with network

TABLE 4   Television's New Top 20*

COMPANIES	TOTAL % U.S. PENETRATION	COMPANIES	TOTAL % U.S. PENETRATION
1. Capcities/ABC	24.40	11. Scripps Howard	9.01
2. CBS	20.59	12. Cox	8.10
3. NBC	19.79	13. Spanish International	7.64
4. Tribune	18.60	14. Gaylord	7.11
5. News Corp.	18.11	15. Hearst	6.92
6. KKR	13.71	16. Gannett	6.63
7. RKO	13.5	17. Belo Broadcasting	5.65
8. Taft	11.12	18. Outlet/Rockefeller	5.00
9. Chris Craft Industries	10.35	19. Post-Newsweek Stations	4.70
10. Group W	10.12	20. Times Mirror	4.69

*These will be the 20 at the top in TV group ownership (ranked by their penetration of the total U.S., including UHF discounts) should all proposed sales take place. The Capcities/ABC listing anticipates permission to keep WPVI-TV Philadelphia. (If disallowed, it would retain WXYZ-TV Detroit and would have a total of 23.37%.) The chart also presupposes the final purchase of Storer Communications by KKR (Kohlberg, Kravis, Roberts & Co.), the sale of KTLA (TV) Los Angeles to Tribune, the sale of Gulf Broadcasting to Taft, the sale of Metromedia's stations to Rupert Murdoch's News Corp. and the subsequent spinoff of WCVB-TV Boston by News Corp. to Hearst.

Source: *Broadcasting* magazine.

advertising contracts, which are typically longer term). National spot and local advertising have tended to be more volatile and more susceptible to fluctuation in the economy than network advertising revenues.

Programming.   Fox's independent stations and WCVB-TV (with respect to that part of its broadcast time not used or made available by ABC), depend heavily on independent third parties as a source of programming. Programs obtained principally from independent sources consist mainly of syndicated television programs, many of which have previously aired on network television, and feature movies licensed for television use, many of which have been shown previously in theaters or on network or cable television. (Syndicated programs are programs that are licensed to individual stations for one or more showings in a particular market as contrasted with programs licensed for national, generally first-run, distribution through one of the three networks.)

Fox estimates that more than 85 percent of the television programming aired on its stations is currently provided or licensed to it by independent third parties. The remaining portion of Fox's programming consists principally of local programs, such as news and public affairs programs, produced by the individual television stations and a limited number of original programs produced by MBC and by Fox Producers Corporation (FPC). FPC, a production and distribution subsidiary of FBC, which acquires, finances, produces, and syndicates television programs will offer its programming to Fox's television stations as well as to other television stations domestically and internationally.

MBC's cost of syndicated programming increased significantly during the period 1982–84. At the beginning of 1986, programming costs represented about 50 percent of Fox's operating costs. These costs are expected to continue to rise in the years ahead because of increased competitive demand from independent stations and network affiliates and because of higher production costs and the limited supply of suitable programming. Increased programming costs, together with increased purchases of programming inventory for future use, accounted for significant increases in the cost of MBC's inventory of film and videotape rights, as indicated by the financial statements for the years 1982–84:

Programming Cost Increases, 1982–84

End of Year	
1984	$231,581,000
1983	192,370,000
1982	155,891,000

An important part of Fox's strategy in television broadcasting and the control of programming costs in the future will be to become increasingly involved in the financing, production, and distribution of television programming for its own television stations. Fox believes it will be able to attract leading television producers with new programming projects to work with it to generate programming because the programs can be aired in up to seven of the top ten television markets, reaching approximately 24 percent of all U.S. television households. This level of immediate coverage is important for a production's success because it facilitates efforts to secure financing and the necessary national advertiser support. The benefits of producing programming independently are threefold:

1. The stations get to quality programming.
2. The stations are provided an alternative

to the increasingly expensive syndicated programming which is first aired on networks.

3. The cost of this alternative programming is fixed so that the stations are not exposed to large future price increases should a program or series generate strong ratings.

By increasing its involvement in acquiring, financing, and producing programming rather than remaining dependent on syndicated programming, Fox hopes to be able to exercise more control over the availability, quality, and cost of the programming which it must acquire for its stations.

Competition. After ABC, CBS, and NBC, Fox is one of the largest broadcast organizations in the U.S. in terms of broadcast revenue. Nonetheless, each of Fox's stations faces competition from other television stations in its market area. Moreover, Fox's six independent television stations may be at a disadvantage in competing with network affiliated stations in their respective markets. For example, programming costs of an independent station are considerably higher than the programming costs of a network-affiliated station. Furthermore, network programs generally achieve higher ratings than programs shown by independent stations.

Fox's television stations compete for

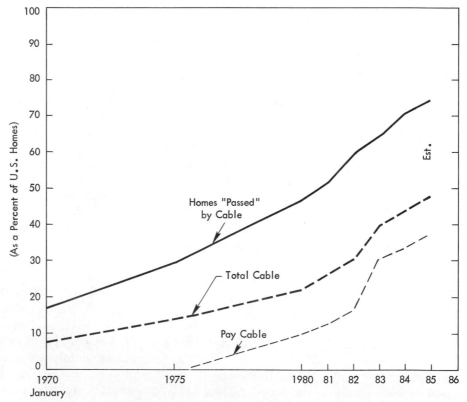

FIGURE 2   Cable Television Penetration (As a Percent of U.S. Homes)

Sources: Paul Kagan Associates, 1985.

revenues with other television stations in their respective markets, as well as with other advertising media such as newspapers, magazines, outdoor advertising, transit advertising, and direct mail.

There are sources of television other than conventional television stations, the most common being cable television ("CATV"), which can increase competition for a broadcasting station by bringing into its market distant broadcasting signals not otherwise available to the station's audience and also serving as a distribution system for programming originated on the cable system. Programming is now being distributed to CATV by both terrestrial microwave systems and by satellite. All of Fox's television stations are car-

ried by cable television systems both within and without their respective market areas.

The Federal Communications Commission (FCC) has also authorized intermediate carriers to pick up the signals of so-called "superstations" and to deliver them to CATV via satellite, including CATV systems in markets where Fox's television stations are located. It should be added that cable television enjoyed phenomenal growth in terms of homes reached and advertising revenue during the first half of the 1980s (see Figures 2 and 3.) Other sources of competition include subscription television (STV), pay cable, multipoint distribution systems, satellite-fed master antenna systems, and home entertainment systems (including television game devices,

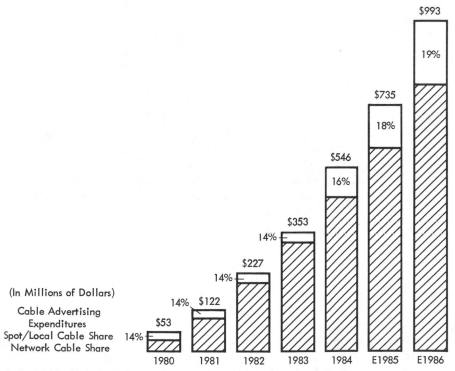

FIGURE 3   Cable TV Advertising Revenues (In Millions of Dollars)
Source: Paul Kagan Associates, 1985.

video cassette recorder and playback systems and video discs). In the future, Fox's television stations may also face competition from direct broadcast satellites (DBS). Clearly, there is no shortage of competition in the television industry.

News America Holdings Incorporated

News America is a wholly owned subsidiary of The News Corporation Ltd. News America, through its subsidiaries, is principally engaged in the publishing of newspapers and magazines and the production, financing, acquisition, and distribution of motion pictures and television programs and film processing.

News America's principal newspapers are the *New York Post*, the *Boston Herald*, and the *San-Antonio Express-News*. Under present FCC regulations, Murdoch had to sell both the Chicago *Sun-Times*, and the *New York Post* because of his purchase of television stations in each of these markets. (In the summer of 1986, the *Sun-Times* was indeed sold.) Under FCC regulations, no license for television stations is granted or assigned to any party which, directly or indirectly, owns, operates, or controls a daily newspaper in the same community. Although Murdoch applied for, and was granted, a two-year waiver to permit the orderly disposition of conflicting newspaper properties, some observers believe he was preparing to eventually challenge the FCC's regulation. Other observers believe that Murdoch wants to wait until the value of these properties appreciates before he must sell them in order to meet his considerable debt obligations.

News America publishes 18 magazines, of which 14 are business magazines and 4 are consumer magazines. News America's business magazines are all related to the aviation and travel industries, and include *Hotel and Travel Index* and *Business and Commercial Aviation*. News America's consumer publications consist of the *Star*, a mass-market general interest weekly magazine, *New York*, a weekly metropolitan feature magazine, *New Woman*, a monthly women's magazine, and *Elle*, a monthly women's magazine published by a joint venture in which News America is a 50% participant.

News America also owns TCF Holdings, the sole shareholder of Fox Film. The principal businesses of Fox Film are the production, financing, acquisition, and distribution of motion pictures and television programs and film processing. Fox Films is also in two partnerships; one that is constructing an office building adjacent to the Fox Film studios in Los Angeles and another that produces and distributes prerecorded video cassettes.

During its fiscal year ended June 30, 1985, News America operated in three industry segments: (a) newspaper publishing; (b) magazine publishing; and (c) other operations. Following the increase in its interest in TCF Holdings to 100 percent in December, 1985, News America has been engaged in a fourth industry segment, filmed entertainment operations.

Newspapers. News America presently publishes the above three daily newspapers (two of which have Sunday editions) as well as the Houston Community newspapers, a group of eight weekly suburban newspapers. All three daily newspapers are mass circulation, metropolitan newspapers with broadly based readerships. In 1985, News America's newspapers accounted for 71 percent of its consolidated revenues. Based on data published by an independent circulation audit service, the combined average daily paid circulation of News America's three daily newspapers for the six-month period ended September 1985, was approximately 1,148,000. As of the six-month period ended march 1985, News America's combined daily newspapers ranked seventh in daily and tenth in Sunday circulation among the major newspaper groups in the U.S. The newspapers which had the highest daily circulation are the *New York Post* and the now departed Chicago *Sun-Times*. Each of News America's daily newspapers and the Houston Community Newspapers contributed the following percentages of the company's total newspaper publishing revenues for 1985: Chicago *Sun-Times*—43.9 percent; *New York Post*—26.1 percent; *San-Antonio Express News*—15 percent; *Boston Herald*—12.6 percent; and Houston Community Newspapers—2.4 percent.

News America's daily newspapers and the Houston Community Newspapers compete for readership and advertising with other local and national newspapers and with television, radio, and other communications media. Competition for newspaper circulation is based on the news and editorial content of the newspaper, cover price, and, from time to time, various promotions. Competition for advertising among newspapers is based upon circulation levels, reader demographics, advertising rates, and advertiser results. The success of News America's newspapers in competing with other media for advertising depends on advertisers' judgements as to the most effective use of their advertising budgets.

Magazines.   In 1985, News America's 18 magazines accounted for 28% of its consolidated revenues. The frequency of publication of News America's business magazines ranges from each business day (*Aerospace Daily* and *Aviation Daily*) to annually (*World Travel Directory*), while the frequency of publication of its consumer magazines is either weekly (the *Star* and *New York*) or monthly (*New Woman* and *Elle*). The average circulation of News America's magazines during 1985 ranged from fewer than 3,000 copies for certain specialized aviation magazines, such as *Aviation Weekly*, to approximately 3,250,000 copies for the *Star*.

For the twelve-month period ended June 30, 1985, News America's consumer magazines (other than *The Village Voice* which was sold in June 1985 and *Elle* which it co-publishes with Hatchette) contributed the following percentages of total consumer magazine publishing revenues: the *Star*—56 percent; *New York*—31.3 percent; and *New Woman*—12.7 percent. From the date of their acquisition on January 4, 1985 through June 30, 1985, the revenues of News America's business magazines constituted 22.6% of its total magazine publishing revenues.

Each of News America's consumer and business magazines competes on basically the same terms as the newspapers outlined above (i.e., editorial content, price, circulation levels, reader demographics, advertising rates, and advertiser results.)

Filmed Entertainment Operations

In addition to its newspaper and magazine publishing operations, News America is engaged, through Fox Film, in producing, acquiring, and distributing theatrical motion pictures and television series and films, and in certain other film-related activities. Motion picture revenues are derived by Fox Film from four basic sources: (a) theatrical (and non-theatrical) exhibition, (b) licensing for exhibition on commercial television networks and stations, (c) licensing to pay cable and other pay television systems, and (d) the duplication and distribution of video cassettes and motion pictures.

In the past few years, Fox Film has emphasized the acquisition of motion pictures from independent producers, although its stated intention is to reverse this trend by increasing the number of pictures it produces directly in the future. Theatrical exhibition of motion pictures contributed 33 percent of Fox Film's total revenues in its 1985 fiscal year, 39 percent in 1984, and 53 percent in 1985. In addition to theatrical exhibitions, Fox Film licenses motion pictures to airlines, educational institutions, government departments, and certain other organizations for what is referred to as "non-theatrical exhibition." License fees received from non-theatrical exhibition do not represent substantial sources of income to Fox Film.

The year 1985 was a success for Fox Film in both a critical and a financial sense. The company placed in general release 17 motion pictures for theatrical exhibition including "Cocoon," "The Man With One Red Shoe," "The Flamingo Kid," and "Prizzi's Honor." Of these films, six were produced by Fox Film, ten (including "The Flamingo Kid" and "Prizzi's Honor") were produced by others and one ("Return of the Jedi") was a re-release of a film produced by another organization. All 17 of these motion pictures was released in the United States and 9 were released in foreign markets. Since the end of its 1985 fiscal year, Fox Film has released "Command," which it produced, and "Plenty" and "The Jewel of the Nile," which it did not.

The other major money-earner for Fox is the production, co-production, and acquisition of filmed or videotaped series for television presentations over an extended period of weeks. Fox Film also produces, alone or in association with others, filmed or videotaped feature length motion pictures and miniseries whose initial U.S. release is on network or pay television. Although revenues from foreign television exhibition can occa-

sionally be significant with respect to a particular series, the primary market for Fox Film's television programming consists of the three major U.S. television networks and independent television stations operating in the U.S. New programming, for both prime time licensing to networks and for syndication, is constantly under development.

Television programs contributed 31 percent of Fox Film's total revenues in its 1985 fiscal year, 31 percent in 1984, and 23 percent in 1983.

News Limited

News Limited is a diversified international communications company principally engaged, through subsidiaries, in the publishing of newspapers and magazines in Australia, the United Kingdom, and the United States. News Limited also has substantial financial interests in two television stations in Australia and Sky Channel, a television broadcasting system in England that is transmitted via satellite to nine other European countries. Other interests include paper manufacturing, storage and transport; air transport; livestock farming; and computer software development and distribution.

Newpapers: Australia. News Limited presently owns and publishes 8 daily and 26 weekly, bi-weekly, and tri-weekly newspapers in Australia and owns a 50 percent interest in another Australian weekly newspaper. Except for *The Australian*, which is distributed nationwide, each of these newspapers is published and distributed regionally. News Limited publishes newspapers in four of Australia's six State capitals as well as the capital of the Northern Territory of Australia. In addition to its Australian newspaper interests, News Limited owns a 22 percent equity interest in Independent Newspapers Limited which publishes 20 weekly and bi-weekly newspapers in New Zealand.

During the fiscal year ended June 30, 1985, the following publications accounted for the indicated percentages of News Limited's total revenues from its newspapers published in Australia: *The Daily Telegraph*—13 percent, *Daily Mirror*—12 percent, *The Australian*—10 percent, and *The Sunday Telegraph*—10 percent.

United Kingdom. News Limited publishes two daily and two Sunday newspapers in the United Kingdom. These newspapers are published in London and distributed nationwide.

The following table sets forth the name, circulation, and frequency of each of the newspapers published in the United Kingdom by News Limited:

Name	Circulation	Frequency
The Times	480,000	Daily, Morning
The Sunday Times	1,258,000	Weekly
The Sun	4,066,000	Daily, Morning
News of the World	4,787,000	Weekly

The Times and *The Sunday Times* are the oldest and most respected daily and Sunday newspapers published in the United Kingdom. Both are directed towards college-educated readers engaged in business or professional activity. Since 1981, the daily paid circulation of *The Times* has increased from 285,000 copies to 480,000 copies. These increases have continued despite a 15 percent increase in its cover price in February 1985. Advertising revenues of *The Times* increased approximately 32 percent in the fiscal year ended June 30, 1985 as compared to the previous fiscal year. *The Sunday Times* has en-

joyed similar good fortune under Murdoch. In 1985, its advertising market share exceeded that of its principal competitors, *The Observer* and *The Sunday Telegraph*.

The Sun and *The News of the World* are both popular, mass market newspapers. Each paper boasts the largest daily and Sunday circulations, respectively, in the English-speaking world. *The Sun* is the largest contributor to News Limited's revenues, providing approximately 11% of the company's total revenues in fiscal 1985.

Magazines: Australia. Of the five leading Australian magazines in terms of circulation and advertising revenues, two are published by News Limited: *New Idea*, a weekly with predominantly female readership, and *TV Week*, a weekly television magazine whose readership is neither predominantly male nor female. The other three leading Austrailian news magazines are *Austrailian Women's Weekly* (AWW), *Woman's Day*, and *Family Circle*, all of which have predominantly female readerships. All five magazines are distributed nationwide in Australia.

New Idea's principal competitors for circulation and advertising are *AWW* and *Woman's Day*. Based upon data published by an independent circulation audit service for the six-month period ended September 1985, the average weekly paid circulation of *New Idea* exceeded that of *Woman's Day*. Further data indicate that, during the six-month period ended December 1985, *New Idea's* advertising revenues exceeded those of each of its principal competitors, accounting for approximately one-third of all advertising revenues for the five leading Australian magazines.

TV Week is the only nationally distributed Australian television magazine containing comprehensive television listings. It competes for circulation and advertising sales directly with several regional television magazines and one nationally-distributed specialized publication named *T.V. Soap*, and indirectly with daily and Sunday newspapers which carry extensive television coverage including listings. As of December 1985, *TV Week* ranked fourth out of the five leading Australian magazines already referred to.

United Kingdom. News Limited publishes three weekly news magazines in the United Kingdom, The *Times Literary Supplement, The Times Educational Supplement,* and *The Times Higher Education Supplement*. These magazines, published in London and distributed throughout the United Kingdom, were acquired together with *The Times* and *The Sunday Times* newspapers in 1981. In November of 1985, a joint venture in which News Limited is a 50% participant began monthly publication of a United Kingdom edition of the women's magazine *Elle*. News Limited's co-venturer is Hatchette, which independently publishes the original *Elle* magazine in France. The previous month, News America began its publication of a U.S. monthly edition of *Elle* as a 50 percent joint venture participant with Hatchette.

Television and Radio Broadcasting: Australia. News Limited has substantial interests in two television stations in Australia, Channel TEN-10 (TEN-10) located in Sydney and Channel ATV-10 (ATV-10) located in Melbourne. News Limited acquired TEN-10 in 1979 and it acquired its initial interest in ATV-10 in the same year as a result of its acquisition of an approximately 50 percent interest in Ansett (a company described below.) News Limited acquired 100 percent of ATV-10 from Ansett in 1983. News Limited also owns and operates a small commercial AM radio station in North Queensland, and held a 20 percent interest in a company which owns and operates a larger commercial FM station in Melbourne.

TEN-10 and ATV-10 are VHF television stations which broadcast commercial television programming throughout the metropolitain areas of Sydney and Mebourne, respectively. Sydney and Melbourne are the two largest cities in Australia, the populations of which account for approximately 40 percent of the total population of Australia. Approximately 42 percent of all Australian television homes are within the geographical area served by TEN-10 and ATV-10. The Sydney and Melbourne metropolitain areas are major industrial and commercial urban centers. TEN-10 and ATV-10 each derive over 90 percent of their revenues from the broadcast of advertising.

Both stations participate with two television stations in Brisbane and Adelaide (the third and fifth largest cities in Australia, respectively) in an informal arrangement known as network 10, for the sharing of costs of producing and acquiring television programming. The television stations in Brisbane and Adelaide which participate in Network 10 are owned by independent third parties. Network 10, like Networks 7 and 9 which link other television stations in principal cities in Australia, is principally a mechanism by which separately-owned television stations combine their financial resources to produce or acquire television programming that would be too costly to produce or acquire alone. Network 10 is not a "network" in the same sense as are the three principal U.S. television networks, nor is the term "network" defined by Australian statutes of regulations. *United Kingdom.* In 1983, New Corporation purchased a 68.6 percent interest in Satellite Television P.L.C. known as "Sky Channel"; this interest has since been increased to 81 percent. Sky Channel uses the European Communications Satellite (ECS-1) which enables its London-based broadcasts to reach

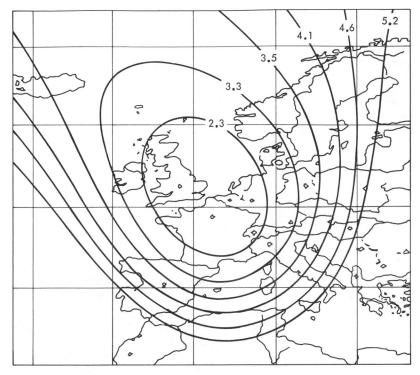

FIGURE 4   Coverage of the ECS-1 satellite footprint with major towns marked
+. The next few years will see the launch of the next generation
of medium- and high-density, high-powered satellites which will extend the present market.

Source: J.B. Were & Son.

cable viewers across the continent (see Figure 4.) Sky Channel presently broadcasts 18
hours a day of music and entertainment shows
and reaches over 5 million homes in 14 European countries including the United Kingdom, France, West Germany, Holland, Belgium, and Sweden. Sky Channel has been a
money loser to date (estimated losses as of
May 1986 were approximately $35 million),
but it has increased its number of viewers
threefold since its inception and appears to
be on the road to profitability. Its client list
of advertisers consists of more than 400 companies, including such multinationals as Philips, Benetton and Mars Cadbury-Schweppes.
(*Marketing and Media Decisions*, May 1986)

Appendix: Financial Ratios of Selected Competitors

CBS Summary

CBS operates one of the 3 nationwide TV networks, operates 2 radio networks, and owns 5 TV and 18 radio stations in major U.S. cities. It is also the world's largest producer of recorded music and is a leading publisher of consumer magazines. The company's debt was increased considerably by the August 1985 buyback of 21 percent of its outstanding common shares for nearly $955 million. Loews Corp., which had owned 17 percent of the common, raised its stake to 25 percent in the buyback.

	1981	1982	1983	1984	1985
Current	1.9	1.7	1.6	1.8	1.2
LTD/Capital	14.3%	14.4%	13.3%	18.4%	53.5%
ROS	4.7%	3.7%	4.2%	5.1%	N/A
ROI	8.1%	5.9%	6.6%	7.8%	N/A
ROE	15.6%	11.6%	13.5%	16.4%	22.4%
EPS	6.82	5.35	6.31	8.24	7.27
P–E Ratio	9	13	13	11	17

Capital Cities/ABC Summary

Capital Cities/ABC was formed by the January 1986 merger of American Broadcasting companies into Capital Cities Communications in a transaction valued at about $3.5 billion. The combined company operates one of the three national TV networks and seven radio networks, owns TV and radio stations in major U.S. markets, is a major publisher of magazines and newspapers, and provides cable TV programming. Earnings for 1986 will be impacted by losses at the ABC TV network.

	1981	1982	1983	1984	1985
Current	1.0	1.1	2.9	2.5	5.7
LTD/Capital	15.7%	5.1%	23.8%	21.7%	43.2%
ROS	6.0%	6.1%	5.4%	5.3%	N/A
ROI	9.8%	9.1%	8.0%	8.8%	N/A
ROE	15.9%	15.4%	13.8%	15.2%	17.4%
EPS	6.12	7.25	8.53	10.40	10.87
P–E Ratio	13	19	18	17	21

Gannett Co. Summary

This leading newspaper publisher (91 daily and 40 nondaily newspapers) owns USA Today, and has interests in broadcasting (8 television stations and 15 radio stations) and outdoor advertising. Gannett completed a number of significant acquisitions in 1985, and in February, 1986, it acquired The Evening News Association, including 11 newspapers, 5 TV stations and 2 radio stations, for about $717 million. In May 1986, Gannett agreed to acquire 2 Louisville stations from the Bingham family for about $300 million.

	1981	1982	1983	1984	1985
Current	1.1	1.3	1.4	1.3	1.6
LTD/Capital	19.7%	21.7%	20.8%	13.0%	25.5%
ROS	12.6%	11.9%	11.3%	11.4%	N/A
ROI	13.0%	11.9%	11.7%	12.8%	N/A
ROE	21.5%	20.4%	19.6%	20.7%	20.9%
EPS	2.11	2.26	2.40	2.80	3.16
P—E Ratio	15	19	20	18	21

Time Inc. Summary

This company, the nation's leading magazine publisher, circulates such well-known magazines as *Time, Sports Illustrated, Fortune,* and *People.* It is also a major book publisher, operates the second largest group of cable television stations in the U.S., and owns the largest pay cable TV programming service, Home Box Office. The company recently announced its intention to sell up to 20 percent of its cable system operation in a public offering. Time and four other firms agreed in December 1985 to acquire Group W Cable for $1.6 billion plus the assumption of over $400 million in liabilities.

	1981	1982	1983	1984	1985
Current	1.9	1.6	1.8	1.6	1.4
LTD/Capital	24.2%	21.9%	27.7%	24.0%	24.2%
ROS	5.6%	4.4%	5.3%	7.1%	N/A
ROI	7.2%	5.5%	5.5%	8.9%	N/A
ROE	18.5%	12.9%	12.9%	22.7%	17.5%
EPS	3.02	2.50	2.25	3.37	3.15
P—E Ratio	14	21	35	19	21

Comparative Stock Analysis (c. 9/20/86)

CBS Inc.

Price	Range (1986)	P–E Ratio	Dividend	Yield	EPS (e)
126	152–107	37	3.00	2.4%	$8.30

Capital Cities/ABC

Price	Range (1986)	P–E Ratio	Dividend	Yield	EPS (e)
254	272–183	26	.20	0.1%	$7.50

Gannett Co.

Price	Range (1986)	P–E Ratio	Dividend	Yield	EPS (e)
68	87–53	21	1.68	2.5%	$3.55

Time Inc.

Price	Range (1986)	P–E Ratio	Dividend	Yield	EPS (e)
73	91–52	22	1.00	1.4%	$3.70

News Corp.

Price	Range (1986)	P–E Ratio (e)	Dividend (e)	Yield (e)	EPS (e)
33	35–23	28	0.106	0.4%	A$1.92

(See Figures 5–7 for an analysis of the News Corporation Ltd. stock.)

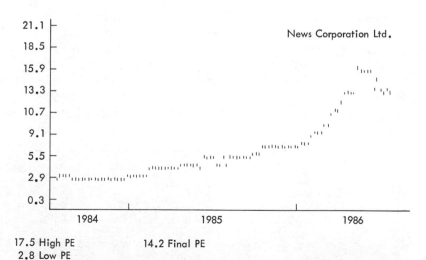

17.5 High PE   14.2 Final PE
2.8 Low PE

FIGURE 5   **Graph of the Price/Earnings ratio of The News Corporation Ltd. common stock over the period of July 1984 to July 1986.**

Source: J.B. Were & Son.

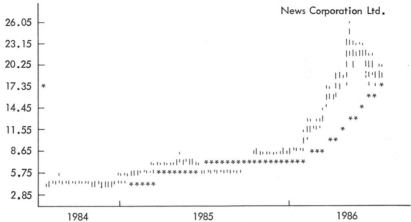

FIGURE 6   Graph of the five-day moving average of the share price of The News Corporation Ltd., over the period of July 1984 to July 1986. The graph presents price both exponentially and arithmetically smoothed. The asterisks (*) indicate a smoothing of the data; the vertical lines indicate price.

Source: J.B. Were & Son.

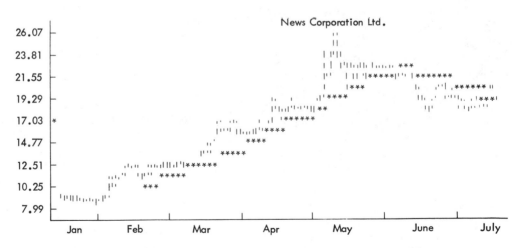

FIGURE 7   Graph of the five-day moving average of the share price of The News Corporation Ltd., from January 1986 to July 1986. The graph presents price both exponentially and arithmetically smoothed. The asterisks (*) indicate a smoothing of the data; the vertical lines indicate price.

Source: J.B. Were & Son.

DISCUSSION QUESTIONS

a.   What is Rupert Murdoch's strategy?
b.   Give Murdoch a grade on his strategy and explain why you assigned your grade.
c.   What would you recommend regarding The News Corporation Ltd. to ABC's clients: Buy? Hold? Sell? Why?

THE NEWS CORPORATION LTD. (B)
THE FINANCIAL SIDE OF RUPERT MURDOCH'S STRATEGY: TO INVEST OR NOT TO INVEST

INTRODUCTION

Tom Raines, media analyst for Aston Baker & Chen (ABC),[1] faced one of the more difficult decisions in his career. Because of his expertise in analyzing media stocks, Tom had been asked to make a recommendation on The News Corporation Ltd. After studying the company in depth, Tom felt one thing for sure: Murdoch was either going to wind up a huge success or fall flat on his face. The same might be said for Tom himself.

Murdoch's record up to the Fox acquisition was one of almost unqualified success. Most every property he managed appreciated considerably in value—he bought low, created value, and either held the property or sold high. In 1985, he spent some US$ 2.6 billion, most of it on seven television stations and Twentieth Century Fox. The acquisitions left Murdoch with annual interest and dividend payments of US$ 300 million, which substantially exceeded the amount of cash that these properties generated in 1985. Yes,

[1]This individual, the company, and the situation are fictional. Its purpose is to highlight the issues facing the company described herein.

Murdoch did have other properties that could pick up the slack, but not all of it. In the year ended June 30, 1985, The News Corporation Ltd.'s entire cash flow was far less than the required amount:

Sources and Application of Funds

	1985	1984
Funds from Operations:	A$'000	A$'000
Inflows	2,446,486	1,865,388
Outflows	2,296,328	1,732,815
	A$150,158	A$132,573

Note: A$1 = US$.6288

(See Tables 1–4 for more financial data.)

Tom walked down the hall for a drink of water. On his way he passed colleagues who analyze utilities, others who specialize in insurance companies. He privately wondered when was the last time they had to figure out a guy like Murdoch. Who are the high rollers in the insurance business anyway? Well, forget the comparisons. Once back in his office, Tom decided to take a closer look at the risks that Murdoch was running by shooting at such lofty goals.

TABLE 1 Financial Highlights

Year Ended June 30:	1985	1984	1983
	(in Thousands)	(in Thousands)	(in Thousands)
Group Turnover (excluding Associated Companies)	$2,447,084	$1,865,636	$1,503,326
Profit on Trading before Interest Expense	164,239	154,141	131,303
Profit on Trading Operations	90,533	87,826	74,226
Profit (Equity Share) before Tax of Associated Companies and Other Dividends	61,741	45,848	31,480
Profit before Income Tax and Extraordinary Items	152,274	133,674	105,706
Profit after Income Tax and before Extraordinary Items	96,086	95,874	86,918
Profit per ordinary and special dividend share after Income Tax and before Extraordinary Items (Adjusted for bonus issue)	$0.71	$0.71	$0.61
Profit and Extraordinary Items	$147,308	$35,450	$44,353
Dividend distributions to Public Shareholders			
On ordinary shares of The News Corporation Limited:			
Ordinary dividend (Adjusted for bonus issue)	$11,353	$8,199	$6,938
Cents per share	9c	6½c	5½c
Special bonus dividend	$946	—	—
Cents per share paid in:			
Shares of subsidiary company	½c	—	—
Cash	¼c	—	—
On special dividend shares of News International plc:	$805	$653	$970
Cents per share	18½c	13c	11c
Equivalent pence per share	10.5920p	8.4358p	6.7113p
Total Assets	$3,463,007	$2,099,350	$1,166,218
Total Capital and Reserves	$1,358,560	$986,272	$405,882
Operations by country (excluding Associated Companies)			
Turnover:			
Australia	$827,503	$658,529	$515,819
United Kingdom	790,909	695,387	648,233
United States	828,672	511,720	339,274
	$2,447,084	$1,865,636	$1,503,326
Profit on Trading before Interest Expense:			
Australia	$62,859	$63,673	$43,176
United Kingdom	75,536	63,104	67,648
United States	25,844	27,364	20,479
	$164,239	$154,141	$131,303

Note: Tables 1 through 4 are taken from the 1985 Annual Report of The News Corporation Ltd. All figures are therefore in A$ which may be converted at the (10/86) rate of A$1 = US$.6288

TABLE 2   Consolidated Balance Sheet—The News Corporation Limited and Subsidiary Companies as at June 30, 1985

	Notes	1985 $'000	1985 $'000	1984 $'000
Authorised Capital	2		$200,000	$100,000
Issued Capital	2		63,072	31,536
Reserves and Retained Profits	3		1,122,068	958,590
Less Goodwill on Consolidation			—	(73,003)
			1,185,140	917,123
Interest of Outside Shareholders				
In Special Dividend Shares and Preference Shares of News International plc		5,620		4,521
In Preference and Ordinary Capital, Reserves and Retained Profits of other Subsidiary Companies		167,800	173,420	64,628
Total Capital and Reserves			$1,358,560	$986,272
Fixed Assets				
Land and Buildings	4	297,607		217,214
Plant and Motor Vehicles	5	292,141		196,277
Publishing Rights, Titles and Television Licenses	6	1,301,955	1,891,703	679,560
Investments	7			
Shares in Other Corporations		495,645		301,543
Equity in Post — Acquisition Retained Profits and Reserves of Associated Companies	8	69,414		82,696
Other Investments		15,640	580,699	11,093
Non-Current Assets				
Amounts Receivable				
Trade Debts		5,210		7,772
Other Debts	9	48,318		21,365
Prepayments		10,787	64,315	5,132
Future Income Tax Benefit	10		20,268	21,790
Current Assets				
Inventories	11	245,954		220,602
Amounts Receivable				
Trade Debts	9	375,315		269,285
Other Debts		115,142		25,285
Cash at Bank and in Hand		143,814		19,989
Prepayments		25,797	906,022	19,747
Total Assets			3,463,007	2,099,350
Non-Current Liabilities and Provisions				
Loans (Secured $3,864,000; 1984 $3,382,000)		267,215		152,347
Bank Loans (Secured $277,000; 1984 $233,000)		904,511		256,448
Registered Unsecured Notes		—		3,142
Mortgage Debenture Stock		2,229		2,432
Trade Creditors		77,402		53,951
Provisions — Income Tax		24,356		8,202
— Long Service Leave and Pensions		5,329		6,796
— Sundry		4,752	1,285,794	2,530
Deferred Income Tax	10		64,870	19,730
Current Liabilities and Provisions				
Loans (Secured $1,234,000; 1984 $850,000)		15,964		24,945
Bank Loans (Secured $29,000; 1984 $26,000)		29		20,826
Registered Unsecured Notes		—		4,341
Trade Creditors		669,855		481,741
Other Creditors		17,656		9,781
Provisions — Income Tax		24,812		45,510
— Dividends		7,760		5,110
— Long Service Leave and Pensions		13,905		9,692
— Sundry		3,802	753,783	5,554
Total Liabilities			2,104,447	1,113,078
Net Assets			$1,358,560	$986,272
Contingent Liabilities	12			
Contracts and Commitments	13			

TABLE 3   Consolidated Profit and Loss Statement—The News Corporation Limited and Subsidiary Companies for the year ended June 30, 1985

	Notes	$'000	1985 $'000	1984 $'000
Profit on Trading Operations	14		90,533	87,826
Equity in Pre-Tax Profits of Associated Companies	8		56,534	36,067
Dividends from Other Corporations			5,207	9,781
Profit before Income Tax Expense and Extraordinary Items			152,274	133,674
Income Tax Expense				
The News Corporation Limited and Subsidiary Companies	10	34,004		29,476
Associated Companies Equity	8	21,284	55,288	8,322
			96,986	95,876
Minority Interest in Subsidiary Companies			900	2
Profit before Extraordinary Items			96,086	95,874
Extraordinary Items				
The News Corporation Limited and Subsidiary Companies	15	46,945		(109,428)
Associated Companies Equity	8	4,277	51,222	49,004
Profit and Extraordinary Items			147,308	35,450
Appropriations Made:				
By Holding Company				
Payment and Provisions for Dividends:				
Ordinary Shares 9 cents per share after one for one bonus issue (1984 13 cents per share)		11,353		8,199
Special Bonus Dividend:				
To be satisfied by the distribution of preference shares in a subsidiary company equivalent to 0.5 cents per share ($631,000) and the payment of 0.25 cents per share ($315,000)		946		—
By News International plc				
Payment and Provision for Dividends:				
Special Dividend Shares		805	13,104	653
Added to Reserves and Retained Profits			$134,204	$26,598
Statement of Reserves and Retained Profits				
Balances brought forward			958,590	387,082
Added as above			134,204	26,598
Other Movements in Reserve	3		29,274	544,910
			$1,122,068	$958,590
Consisting of:				
Parent Company			24,686	60,112
Subsidiary Companies			1,027,968	815,782
			1,052,654	875,894
Associated Companies Equity			69,414	82,696
			$1,122,068	$958,590

TABLE 4 Consolidated Statement of Source and Application of Funds—The News Corporation Limited and Subsidiary Companies for the year ended June 30 1985

SOURCE OF FUNDS:

	1985	1985	1984
	$'000	$'000	$'000
Funds from Operations:			
Inflows of Funds from Operations		2,446,486	1,865,388
Outflows of Funds from Operations		2,296,328	1,732,815
		150,158	132,573
Dividends Received:			
Associated Companies	54,214		78,328
Other Companies	5,207	59,421	9,781
Non-Trading Items:			
Proceeds from Sale of Non-Current Assets		228,959	126,989
Issue of Redeemable Preference Capital by Subsidiary Companies		146,731	—
Share Issue of a Subsidiary		2,941	2,433
Increase in Current Liabilities		60,655	151,503
Increase in Non-Current Liabilities		698,735	192,693
		$1,347,600	$694,300

APPLICATION OF FUNDS:

	1985	1985	1984
	$'000	$'000	$'000
Outlay for Plant, Machinery and Property		153,665	130,122
Capital Expenditure on Mining		685	14,562
Launch Costs of New Publications		—	21,692
Purchase of Investments		246,028	151,929
Income Tax paid		48,581	6,114
Long Service Leave paid		9,738	6,898
Sundry Provisions paid		6,690	2,322
Dividends paid to:			
— The News Corporation Limited Shareholders	9,776		6,938
— Special Dividend Shareholders	678		545
— Outside Shareholders of Subsidiaries	5,145	15,599	3,355
Realised Exchange Loss		14,898	126,694
Redemption of Preference Capital of a Subsidiary		40,800	1,000
Increase in Goodwill on acquisition of Subsidiaries		—	4,679
Goodwill on acquisition during period written-off		3,206	—
Acquisition of minority interest in Subsidiary Company		—	16,363
Increase in Current Assets		276,749	122,847
Increase in Non-Current Assets		24,936	18,887
Increase in Publishing Rights and Titles		506,025	59,353
		$1,347,600	$694,300

WHAT ARE THE RISKS?

The key to Murdoch's strategy is the establishment of Fox Broadcasting Company (FBC) as the fourth American television network. The seven Metromedia stations presently reach 24 percent of American homes. In order to be classified as a "network," by Murdoch's own estimations, these owned stations and affiliates would have to reach 80 percent of American homes. Combined with his other television properties, Murdoch has at his disposal the makings of a true global television network, which would fit nicely the aspirations of global marketers who, through Murdoch, would have access to much of the English speaking world, and to Europe and the United States, two legs of the so-called triad markets—the U.S., Europe, and Japan. According to *Business Week,* the global network could take on the form shown in Table 5.

The Fourth Network Concept: The Mount Everest of Would-Be Challengers

Making FBC into a fourth network was far from a sure thing. Others have tried to po-sition themselves in order to gain network status without success. There were several syndication companies already using the term "network" in their names. LBS Communications was syndicating Inday, the "independent daytime network." There is the MGM/UA Premiere network of movies. Tribune Co. had the Independent Network News. Embassy Telecommunications and Paramount Television have also tried to establish themselves as networks. Still others claim to be providing a "networking service." None of these efforts have resulted in something that might be compared to the Big Three American networks.

What made Murdoch believe that he could succeed where others have failed? First, Murdoch made a major financial commitment to make Fox into a network, having publicly stated that he will spend more than $100 million if necessary. Murdoch's first move was to get himself qualified personnel. In what was generally acknowledged to be a wise decision, he hired former Paramount CEO Barry Diller as Fox Television CEO. In Diller's first year, overheads were slashed by 30%, and

TABLE 5   How a Fourth TV Network Might Operate 20th Century Fox

Theaters	Production and Distribution of Movies Film Library Television Programming		
SATELLITE TV		*AUSTRALIAN TV*	*NEW U.S. TV CO.*
Holland	Norway	TEN 10 Sydney	WNEW New York
Switzerland	W. Germany	ATV 10 Melbourne	KTTV Los Angeles
Finland	Britain	*2 million homes*	KRLD Dallas
France	Austria		WTTG Wash., D.C.
Belgium	Sweden		KRIV Houston
5 million homes			*15.4 million homes*
			INDEPENDENT UHF STATIONS
			INDEPENDENT VHF STATIONS

Fox's distribution, marketing, and production divisions were reorganized.

FBC's first direct confrontation with the networks will be from 11 P.M.–12 midnight in the fall of 1986 when Joan Rivers will begin hosting "The Late Show Starring Joan Rivers." Ms. Rivers' $10 million deal with Fox led many *Boston Herald* employees, miffed at the slight pay raises accorded them in June of 1986, to don T-shirts that said: "Joan Rivers got my raise." In any event, the choice of this time segment is a gamble because many memorable (and not so memorable) names have failed to overcome Johnny Carson, long a fixture in the late night time slot. The fact that the show airs one-half hour before "The Tonight Show" is perhaps testimony to Carson's strength. The Carson Show is aired on some 200 stations as opposed to the six independents that will automatically carry the Rivers show. Fox's goal is to erode Carson's share of the late night segment by signing up stations that have carried his show for years and years. Carson's network, NBC, has vowed to do all in its power to keep "The Tonight Show" atop the late night ratings. Any spending war with a prominent network such as NBC will most certainly prove costly to Murdoch.

In addition to the Joan Rivers show, Fox had plans to begin beaming via satellite to interested stations a two-hour block on Saturday nights and a three-hour block of programming on Sundays. This programming would be the first genuine indication of Fox's ability to compete with the networks, since it would run during the prime time hours of 8 P.M.–11 P.M.

Whatever the fate of Fox Broadcasting might be, it is important that it quickly demonstrate its ability to seriously challenge the networks. According to J. B. Were & Son, an Australian brokerage house, one major source of risk is that the Fox television stations do not grow as quickly as anticipated:

"It is difficult to assess the time it will take to improve ratings and draw more advertising revenue. Our predictions for success are based on the belief that The News Corporation Ltd.'s ability to put in place the formula that has boosted the circulation of its newspapers worldwide, improved the ratings of its Australian television stations, and is proving successful for Sky Channel, will once again be demonstrated by its management and strategy for U.S. television."

Those who have been associated with previous attempts to create a fourth network believe that while Murdoch has his work cut out for him, his willingness to spend money just might get him over the hump. Says Bob Bennet, former president of MBC: "It's very, very difficult. The good independents will be hard to get. They [Fox] may have to make compromises but I'm pulling for them. I wouldn't bet against Rupert Murdoch. He looks around corners. And they will lose money to succeed." (*Ad Age*, 5/5/86)

None of the Big Three networks were visibly concerned with Murdoch's initial programming announcements or his stated intention to spend $100 million if necessary. A CBS spokesman said that the three networks spend about $1 billion a year on programming and that each spends about $50 million a year on program development "for stuff that might never get on the air." As for NBC, it too downplayed the importance of Fox Television. "They just don't have a full-service network. . . . They also don't have a lot of programming and programming is what makes a network." (*The Village Voice*, 5/20/86)

FINANCIAL RISKS

In order for Murdoch to survive, several things must happen. First of all, he needs relatively stable interest rates—plus or minus one or two percentage points—in the United States. In the United Kingdom, where a large part of the cash flow is, the pound must stay at or near its present level in relation to the Australian dollar. He also needs low newsprint costs for his London newspapers, especially *The Times,* which, after becoming profitable in 1984 for the first time in years, lost $7 million in 1985.

Having to juggle the uncertainties of three economies presents Murdoch with more than a few imponderables. News Corp. is both very highly leveraged and vulnerable to sudden shifts in any of these three economies. J.B. Were & Son calculates that interest rate and currency volatility would have the effects on earnings per share shown in Table 6. (See Table 7 for a review of recent US/A currency relationships.)

There still remains the possibility that Murdoch may have gotten in over his head.

A June 1985 *Business Week* story included among its "seven deadly sins in mergers and acquisitions" two warnings that could apply to Murdoch: Paying too much and assuming that a boom market won't crash. The Fox properties were priced based on multiples of 1984 cash flow and estimates of 1985 cash flow. The year 1984, however, was an unusually good one, and prospects for 1985 and 1986 were better at the time of Fox's purchase than they are presently. Furthermore, although Murdoch can ease his debt burden by selling off current or acquired assets, he still remains vulnerable to economic downturns or a significant rise in interest rates. Any economic setback could tempt Murdoch to cut back spending for new programming and scare advertisers away. In short, a shift of the economic winds could quickly devour the $100 million that Rupert Murdoch says he is willing to spend.

TABLE 6 Interest Rate Volatility (U.S.)

	UNDER CURRENT RATE: E.P.S. $	A 1% INCREASE E.P.S. $	A 1% DECREASE E.P.S. $
1985/86	.951	.874	1.027
1986/87	1.041	.946	1.135
1987/88	1.291	1.204	1.380

Currency Volatility

	1985/86	1986/87	1987/88
E.P.S. Est. $ @A$ = $US 0.70	.951	1.041	1.291
A$ Appreciates			
1. 5% A$ = $US 0.735	.906	.984	1.268
2. 10% A$ = $US 0.77	.865	.932	1.248
A$ Depreciates			
1. 5% A$ = $US 0.665	1.001	1.104	1.315
2. 10% A$ = $US 0.63	1.057	1.155	1.342

TABLE 7 US/A Exchange Rates*

MONTH END	EXCHANGE RATE IN $US PER A$
September 1983	0.8971
December 1983	0.8965
March 1984	0.9362
June 1984	0.8615
September 1984	0.8290
December 1984	0.8250
March 1985	0.7000
June 1985	0.6685
September 1985	0.7020
December 1985	0.6818
March 1986	0.7116
June 1986	0.6931
September 1986	0.6288

*Australian dollars are fully exchangeable into U.S. dollars without legal restriction and have traded on a floating exchange basis since December 12, 1983.

TOM RAINES' DILEMMA

Raines felt as if he was between a rock and a hard place. On the one hand, he saw the trend of the world toward the global vision espoused by McLuhan, Levitt et al. He was especially interested in the impact that a concentration of global advertising agencies would have on the ability for corporations to implement global marketing strategies. In a way, he shared the vision of Murdoch. Furthermore, he certainly respected the man's ability to get things done and the vigor with which he undertook to establish Fox Television as a major network.

One thing had been eating at Raines since the start—the frailty of it all. Even if Murdoch was on the right track, one sudden shift of the economic wind and he could be ruined. Another possible scenario that repeated itself inside Raines' mind was that the numbers were against Murdoch. The fourth network would have to get its feet off the ground rather fast. Should it turn into a money loser, even Murdoch might not be able to afford to carry on. The TV graveyard was full of failed challenges to The Big Three.

Worst of all, Raines knew that no amount of rational analysis would enable him to come up with a risk-free recommendation. For the first time in his career he was stumped. A sober analysis of the facts would have to be combined with his intuition and judgement this time. One thing was certain: He had to make a decision. What should he recommend: Buy, sell, or wait and see? He had the facts. Now he had to face the inevitable truth: There are no easy answers—no certain bets.

APPENDICES

APPENDIX I: SECONDARY RESEARCH FOR GLOBAL MARKETS[1]

Secondary research skills are an important tool for global marketers. The analysis of available published data on a given topic proves to be a time- and cost-effective method of examining foreign markets. Through secondary research, an abundance of pertinent information can be found to serve as a foundation for marketing decisions. Although use of this research method does not always supply all the necessary information to complete a project, an analysis of the data collected often provides insight into the "information gaps" that must be closed through primary research efforts.

Considering the expense associated with conducting primary research overseas, it is logical first to develop an awareness of the information available from secondary sources. The researcher will find that sources are available on a wide range of topics relevant to examining the marketing environment of a particular country or region. These sources provide information and/or statistical data on subjects such as economic, financial, political and social conditions, population, labor conditions, levels of technology, legal requirements, business practices, and cultural characteristics.

[1] Prepared by Strategic Information Services, Inc., 4450 Hansen Drive, Columbus, Ohio 43220.

A number of indexes, bibliographies, directories, and computer data bases are available to assist in locating the specific information sources.

The task of researching international markets can be simplified recognizing that some seemingly basic sources offer a wide variety of information and statistics on foreign markets. For example, the U.S. government, primarily through the International Trade Administration of the Department of Commerce, offers publications and services that assist in identifying markets, researching market characteristics, and obtaining information on potential agents, distributors, representatives, and joint venture partners. Other U.S. government bodies, such as the Department of State or the Department of Agriculture, can provide businesses with foreign market information.

Most national governments are sources of market information and the information necessary for operating in the particular country. Statistical abstracts are published for each country and include information on data similar to that appearing in the U.S. government's annual Statistical Abstract of the United States. Also, a country's central bank may provide reports detailing its monetary and economic situation. Additional information on trade often can be located through a country's embassy.

International organizations such as the United Nations, the Organization for Economic Cooperation and Development, the World Bank, and various regional organizations also publish statistical and other country information.

Private information sources in the United States also provide published data and/or special services for international business. For example, Business International publishes a variety of reference materials for clients; Strategic Information Services provides custom-designed research studies that assist clients in strategic decision making for international markets; and major international banks can be sources of international market information and international marketing assistance.

Global Market Research

The conceptual framework for conducting secondary research for global markets (see Figure A.1) outlines five steps inherent in the research process. However, the steps taken by the researcher and the order in which they are taken should be determined by the nature of the particular project. Moreover, the research necessary for the project may be complete after any one particular step in the process.

The obvious starting point for any research project is to determine whether a similar study already exists. (See step 1, Figure A.1.) If such a study is identified, the decision must be made as to whether it is more cost effective to purchase the report or to conduct the research independently. Assuming that a similar study is procured, the researcher then ascertains what, if any, additional information is necessary for the project.

The search for new information begins with the identification of general, overview sources. (See step 2, Figure A.1.) The purpose of using these overview sources is to gain assistance in locating the specific information sources relevant to the

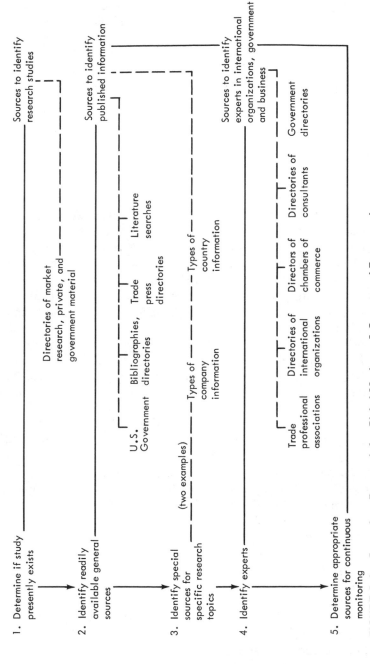

FIGURE A.1. Secondary Research for Global Markets: A Conceptual Framework

757

project. The researcher saves time and effort by quickly determining where to look for the appropriate information. Also, the general sources of published information will aid in the identification of experts, a step occurring later in the research process.

A number of sources of published information—bibliographies, directories, abstracts, indexes, and computer data bases—are available to assist in locating information on a given topic. These sources may focus on such subjects as geographic areas, business topics, or statistical data. The use of computer literature searches often provides a fast method of identifying specific sources. If access to a computer data base is not available, much of the same source identification can be accomplished via manual indexes.

Information from the sources identified in step 1 is then gathered and reviewed by the researcher. (See step 2, Figure A.1.) Recognize that the information itself will provide leads to additional sources relevant to the project. Presumably, at this point in the process, the information "gap" has narrowed in scope to one or more specific topics. Thus, the research efforts are focused on these selected subjects.

Gathering and analyzing data on two specific topics—companies and countries and regions—is a challenge commonly faced by international researchers. Consequently, examples of the types of information available on these topics are given in the source list that appears later in this section. Numerous sources of information are available on international corporations as well as on companies in other nations. Directories, lists of major corporations, indexes, bibliographies, and computer data bases are examples of such sources.

Information on U.S. public companies that have international operations can be found in annual reports, Securities and Exchange Commission 10-K and 10-Q reports, proxy statements, prospectuses, and listing applications. Also, information on public companies in some countries may be available in publications such as *The Japan Company Handbook*.

Information on countries and/or regions is published on a wide range of subjects important in marketing research. Statistical data primarily are published by international organizations such as the United Nations and the Organization for Economic Cooperation and Development. However, data can be obtained through various private sources. It is important to note that the amount of data and the type of data available for a particular country most likely will differ considerably from that which is available for the United States.

Country profiles, publications that address one or more subjects in a number of countries, are also published by public and private sources. Examples of topics addressed in such profiles include economic and financial conditions, political conditions, legal requirements, historical data, and marketing information.

Published information does not always provide all that is required for a research project. In this case, seeking experts (or external contracts) in the field is the next step in the research process. (See step 4, Figure A.1.) Often, some of the experts are identified through researching the published information gathered in previous steps. Likewise, experts can provide leads to additional sources of published information. Contact with experts, therefore, is important in the research process.

In identifying experts for international market research, the principal sources include trade and professional associations, international organizations, chambers of commerce, U.S. and foreign governments, international businesses, and consulting firms. Also, a number of committees, business councils, and so on have been formed to address trade with a given geographical area. These organizations often provide assistance to companies. Some examples are U.S.-German Democratic Republic Trade and Economic Council, Committee for the Caribbean, and ASEAN-U.S. Business Council.

Important sources of information for business are the commercial attachés at embassies around the world. Because they are located in-country, they may be able to provide information or a source for information that possibly cannot be found at home.

The following pages of this appendix include a case study in which the steps in the international secondary research process just outlined are applied to a hypothetical research project. Subsequently, a source list is provided that can aid the researcher in completing each step of the process.

Although the U.S. government appears as a principal source in each research step (see Figure A.1), the great quantity and variety of sources in the U.S. government can best be outlined in a separate source category. Therefore, the majority of U.S. government sources appear in the final pages of the source list.

Project Example: Global Secondary Research

The following example of global secondary research, based on the conceptual framework outlined in Figure A.1, illustrates the research process and the type of information sources that can be found for each of the five steps. The example clearly illustrates the interrelationship among the various steps.

RESEARCH REQUIREMENT. A U.S. retail conglomerate is looking into overseas acquisitions of supermarkets and other large-sized retailing firms. The company is examining prospects in the United Kingdom.

EXAMPLES OF THE TYPE OF INFORMATION TO BE FOUND. Structure of retailing; financial performance of the industry; characteristics, trends, and so on of the consumer markets; largest retail companies/groups; financial and other pertinent information on those companies; and legal requirements for doing business in the United Kingdom.

STEP 1. The first step is to locate a source that will assist the researcher in identifying an existing study (or studies) on supermarkets and/or retailing in the United Kingdom.

Source Example: Findex—The Directory of Market Research Reports, Studies, and Surveys. From this source, the following studies are identified:

> *Supermarkets*—Key Note Publications Ltd. Report analyzes multiple grocers, super-markets, and retail outlets in the United Kingdom.
>
> *Supermarkets*—I.C.C. Business Ratios. Report analyzes the financial and managerial performance of the leading U.K. companies in this industry sector.

STEP 2. Assuming that the company determines that it is more cost effective to conduct the research independently than to purchase it or that the reports do not provide all the required information for the project, the search for new or additional information begins. In this step, general sources are sought that will identify published information relevant to the research topic.

Source Example: Directory of European Business Information. The following information sources found in this directory include specific published information sources (step 3), sources for experts (step 4), and periodicals that may be used as continuous monitoring sources (step 5):

> *Retail Business*—Economist Intelligence Unit Ltd. London. Monthly publication.
>
> *A Guide to Key British Enterprises*—Dun & Bradstreet Ltd.
>
> *Retail and Distribution Management*—Newman Publishing Ltd. Bi-monthly publication.
>
> *Index to Special Reports in U.K. Newspapers and Certain Periodicals*—Association of British Chambers of Commerce.
>
> *Jordans Company Information* (London)—An information service on British and overseas companies. (This directory also provides a section on finding information about companies in the United Kingdom.)

Source Example: Statistics Europe—Sources For Social, Economic, and Market Research. The following sources were identified from this index:

> *Retail Trade in the United Kingdom*—Euromonitor Publications Ltd.
>
> *Business Monitor: Services and Distributive Series* (retailing)—Business Statistics Office. (Additional *Business Monitor* abstracts that pertain to retailing were identified.)
>
> *Food Industry Statistics Digest. Volume I*—Institute of Grocery Distribution.
>
> *Annual Abstract of Statistics*—Central Statistical Office, London.

STEP 3. In step 3, the information sources identified in step 2 are gathered and reviewed. While the information provides much of what is required to complete the project, the researcher determines that more in-depth material focusing on retail industry growth and trends is needed. By following leads to further sources that are contained in the information reviewed to this point, additional specific sources are identified.

Source Example—The Retail World, The Concepts. For the United Kingdom, this source provides information on the factors that affect the future of retailing, the characteristics of retailing (food, clothing, and footwear), variety stores, department stores, and so on. The source also provides company information (including financial data).

STEP 4. For this particular project, the researcher determines that trade interviews with experts in the field of retailing in the United Kingdom are important to the study. The experts contacted may provide additional insights on the subject and either confirm or refute information obtained in previous steps. Step 4 entails the identification of these experts. A number of sources can be consulted to locate these experts; however, experts are generally identified during the research process itself. For example, the following experts (or sources of experts) have been identified in steps 2 and 3 of this project:

Gerald Horner, *The Retail World, The Concepts*
The Institute of Grocery Distribution
International Association of Department Stores

STEP 5. The project is complete and a presentation is made to the principals of the corporation. The researcher is asked to continue monitoring retail trends in the United Kingdom and report any changes in the business environment to management. Thus, step 5 is the identification of sources for continuous monitoring. Through the research process, a number of periodicals provided relevant information for the project. Therefore, subscriptions to these periodicals are obtained for the continuous monitoring effort:

Retail Business—Monthly publication.
Retail and Distribution Management—Bimonthly publication.
Retail Newsletter—A newsletter published by the International Association of Department Stores.

APPENDIX II: GROSS NATIONAL PRODUCT[1]

The World Bank uses estimates of GNP as the main yardstick of economic activity in a country.

GNP does not measure items important to welfare in most societies, such as employment status, the distribution of income and wealth, the quality of the environment, the availability of health and education services, and job security and the opportunities for advancement. The complexity of incorporating these conditions in a comprehensive indicator of welfare leads economists to settle for such measures as GNP—which covers most of the goods and services available for consumption and investment.

GNP data need, therefore, to be complemented by other indicators, particularly those that relate more directly to the quality of life, such as social data.

How GNP is Estimated

GNP estimates comprise estimates of gross domestic product (GDP) and net factor income from abroad. GDP measures the value of final goods and services produced by a country's domestic economy. To obtain GNP, which is the output claimed by residents of the country, GDP must be adjusted by the net factor income from abroad.

Production		Income		Expenditure
Net output of:		Wages and salaries of employees		Private consumption
Agriculture				
+ Mining and manufacturing		+ Profit and income from self-employment		+ General government consumption
+ Construction				+ Investment
+ Utilities		+ Rent and interest		
+ Trade and transport	=	+ Depreciation	=	+ Exports of goods and nonfactor services
+ Government services				− Imports of goods and nonfactor services
+ Other private services		+ Net indirect taxes		
= Gdp at market prices		= Gdp at market prices		= Gdp at market prices
+ Net factor income from abroad		+ Net factor income from abroad		+ Net factor income from abroad
= Gnp at market prices		= Gnp at market prices		= Gnp at market prices

FIGURE A.2. Summary of the three ways of estimating GNP at market prices

Source: *The World Book Atlas, 1986*, p. 10. Used with permission.

[1]Gross National Product is the market value of the final output of goods and services claimed by the residents of a country in a year.

That income comprises the income residents receive from abroad for factor services (labor, investment, and interest) less similar payments made to nonresidents who contributed to the domestic economy.

There are three ways of estimating GDP (see Fig. A.2). The *production* method focuses on the net output of an economy's various sectors (that is, on the value of the gross output of goods and services produced, less the value of goods and services used as inputs in the production process). The *income* method focuses on the income that goes to the various factors of production (labor, capital, and land). The *expenditure* method focuses on the final expenditure on consumption, investment, and exports (less imports, which are subtracted because imported goods and services are included in consumption and investment). Since some goods and services are not exchanged for money but are produced for own use or barter, the value of many such goods and services is imputed and included in the GDP estimates.

APPENDIX III: STATISTICS ON 184 COUNTRIES AND TERRITORIES

COUNTRY OR TERRITORY	GNP AT MARKET PRICES			POPULATION		
	MILLIONS OF CURRENT U.S. DOLLARS		REAL GROWTH RATE (PERCENT)	THOUSANDS		GROWTH RATE (PERCENT)
	1983	1984p	1973–83	1983	1984p	1973–83
Afghanistan	n.a.	n.a.	n.a.	n.a.	n.a.	n.a.
Albania	n.a.	n.a.	n.a.	2,841	2,900	2.1
Algeria	47,720	50,680	5.8	20,577	21,265	3.1
American Samoa[a]	150	160	0.4	34	35	1.8
Angola	n.a.	n.a.	n.a.	8,202	8,420	2.6
Antigua and Barbuda	130	150	3.6	78	79	1.2
Argentina	74,340	67,150	−0.2	29,627	30,104	1.6
Australia	176,170	184,980	2.3	15,369	15,562	1.3
Austria	69,660	68,800	2.6	7,549	7,527	0.0
Bahamas[a]	900	960	2.0	222	226	2.1
Bahrain[a]	4,100	4,260	6.4[b]	391	407	4.7
Bangladesh	12,400	12,360	5.5	95,497	98,012	2.4
Barbados	1,010	1,100	2.4	253	255	0.3
Belgium	89,970	83,070	1.6	9,856	9,856	0.1
Belize	170	180	5.6	153	156	1.9
Benin	1,110	1,060	5.3	3,801	3,921	2.8
Bermuda[a]	780	920	4.5	58	58	0.2
Bhutan	n.a.	n.a.	n.a.	1,187	1,213	1.9
Bolivia	2,890	2,560	0.3	6,034	6,198	2.6
Botswana	910	940	10.5	998	1,031	4.5
Brazil	241,910	227,280	4.4	129,662	132,582	2.3
Brunei[a,c]	4,270	n.a.	3.5	208	216	3.6
Bulgaria	n.a.	n.a.	n.a.	8,939	8,960	0.3
Burkina Faso	1,170	1,040	3.7	6,457	6,559	1.9
Burma	6,460	6,620	5.9	35,492	36,212	2.0
Burundi	1,050	1,010	3.9	4,465	4,587	2.2
Cameroon	7,840	8,000	6.8	9,562	9,868	3.1
Canada	305,940	330,870	2.1	24,907	25,183	1.2
Cape Verde	100	100	6.9	315	321	1.5
Central African Rep.	700	680	0.6	2,470	2,534	2.3
Chad	n.a.	n.a.	n.a.	4,789	4,900	2.1
Channel Islands[a]	1,440	1,340	0.8	130	130	0.5
Chile	22,080	20,340	2.2	11,682	11,880	1.7
China	306,060	318,310	6.1	1,019,102	1,030,150	1.5
Colombia	38,740	38,410	4.1	27,515	28,076	1.9
Comoros	n.a.	n.a.	n.a.	368	381	2.5
Congo, People's Rep.	2,170	2,060	7.6	1,777	1,838	3.1
Costa Rica	2,540	2,930	2.4	2,379	2,435	2.4
Cuba	n.a.	n.a.	n.a.	9,782	9,782	0.8
Cyprus	2,400	2,390	n.a.	655	665	0.7

| GNP PER CAPITA | | | | LIFE EXPECTANCY AT BIRTH (YEARS) | | INFANT MORTALITY RATE (AGED UNDER 1) | | PRIMARY SCHOOL ENROLLMENT (PERCENT) | |
| CURRENT U.S. DOLLARS | | REAL GROWTH RATE (PERCENT) | | | | | | | |
1983	1984p	1973–83	1983–84p	1970	1983	1970	1983	1970	1983
n.a.	n.a.	n.a.	n.a.	n.a.	n.a.	n.a.	n.a.	n.a.	n.a.
n.a.	n.a.	n.a.	n.a.	67	71	n.a.	42	92	102
2,320	2,380	2.6	2.8	52	57	144	107	76	93
4,500	4,690	− 1.4	0.4	n.a.	n.a.	27	17	n.a.	n.a.
n.a.	n.a.	n.a.	n.a.	37	43	n.a.	148	39	n.a.
1,690	1,830	2.3	5.1	n.a.	72	21	32	n.a.	80
2,510	2,230	− 1.8	0.4	67	70	53	36	106	119
11,460	11,890	1.0	4.9	71	74	18	10	115	108
9,230	9,140	2.5	2.6	70	73	26	12	104	99
4,050	4,260	− 0.1	1.1	63	69	36	33	78	99
10,480	10,480	1.8[b]	0.0	62	68	74	36	102	101
130	130	2.9	0.6	45	50	150	132	52	60
3,990	4,340	2.0	2.2	68	72	40	23	108	110
9,130	8,430	1.5	1.7	71	73	21	11	n.a.	98
1,130	1,150	3.6	0.3	60	66	51	30	110	85
290	270	2.4	− 1.5	44	48	180	148	36	65
13,540	15,810	4.3	0.1	n.a.	n.a.	15	15	n.a.	n.a.
n.a.	n.a.	n.a.	n.a.	34	43	173	162	7	23
480	410	− 2.2	− 4.3	46	51	154	123	76	86
880	910	5.7	10.4	58	61	100	74	69	102
1,870	1,710	2.0	2.2	59	64	96	70	84	96
20,520	n.a.	− 0.1	n.a.	n.a.	74	34	17	n.a.	n.a.
n.a.	n.a.	n.a.	n.a.	70	70	27	17	101	100
180	160	1.8	− 5.9	43	45	180	148	12	28
180	180	3.8	2.5	49	55	128	93	87	84
240	220	1.7	− 6.7	45	47	162	123	29	33
820	810	3.6	3.8	48	54	143	116	91	107
12,280	13,140	0.9	2.6	73	75	18	9	101	104
320	320	5.3	− 1.6	56	64	98	76	n.a.	n.a.
280	270	− 1.7	0.2	42	48	172	142	64	70
n.a.	n.a.	n.a.	n.a.	40	43	172	142	35	35
11,070	10,300	0.3	0.8	72	75	18	11	n.a.	n.a.
1,890	1,710	0.5	5.9	62	70	82	40	107	112
300	310	4.6	12.7	61	67	69	38	110	110
1,410	1,370	2.1	0.0	59	64	70	53	108	130
n.a.	n.a.	n.a.	n.a.	47	48	110	91	34	103
1,220	1,120	4.3	− 0.3	58	63	106	82	n.a.	n.a.
1,070	1,210	− 0.1	4.3	67	74	58	20	110	106
n.a.	n.a.	n.a.	n.a.	70	75	41	20	121	109
3,670	3,590	n.a.	n.a.	71	74	28	17	88	84

COUNTRY OR TERRITORY	GNP AT MARKET PRICES			POPULATION		
	MILLIONS OF CURRENT U.S. DOLLARS		REAL GROWTH RATE (PERCENT)	THOUSANDS		GROWTH RATE (PERCENT)
	1983	1984p	1973–83	1983	1984p	1973–83
Czechoslovakia	n.a.	n.a.	n.a.	15,415	15,464	0.6
Denmark	59,020	57,700	1.5	5,114	5,110	0.2
Djibouti	n.a.	n.a.	n.a.	345	358	6.5
Dominica	70	80	1.0	74	72	1.1
Dominican Rep.	6,910	6,040	3.5	5,961	6,102	2.4
Ecuador	11,670	10,340	5.0	8,216	8,451	2.6
Egypt, Arab Rep.	31,320	33,340	9.1	45,169	46,172	2.5
El Salvador	3,550	3,820	−0.2	5,232	5,386	3.0
Equatorial Guinea	n.a.	n.a.	n.a.	359	366	1.7
Ethiopia	4,840	4,780	2.7	40,900	42,019	2.7
Faeroe Islands[a]	500	500	4.5	45	45	1.3
Fiji	1,190	1,250	3.0	670	677	1.9
Finland	52,090	53,090	2.6	4,863	4,902	0.4
France	572,610	542,960	2.4	54,652	55,089	0.4
French Guiana	n.a.	n.a.	n.a.	77	80	3.9
French Polynesia[a,c]	1,280	1,300	5.4	156	159	2.1
Gabon	2,740	2,830	−3.4	797	812	1.4
Gambia, The	200	180	2.3	697	712	3.6
German Dem. Rep.	n.a.	n.a.	n.a.	16,699	16,701	−0.1
Germany, Fed. Rep.	700,450	678,880	2.1	61,421	61,205	−0.1
Ghana	4,080	4,730	−1.5	12,818	13,372	3.1
Gibraltar[a]	140	130	1.2	30	30	0.2
Greece	38,490	36,940	2.9	9,840	9,888	1.1
Greenland[a]	400	380	1.7[d]	52	53	0.6
Grenada	80	80	2.6	91	92	n.a.
Guadeloupe	n.a.	n.a.	n.a.	318	318	−0.3
Guam[a]	730	760	−0.8	113	115	0.9
Guatemala	8,790	9,110	3.7	7,932	8,167	3.1
Guinea	1,720	1,810	2.2	5,830	5,948	2.0
Guinea-Bissau	160	160	2.1	863	877	4.3
Guyana	450	470	−1.0	802	806	0.7
Haiti	1,560	1,710	3.0	5,300	5,401	1.8
Honduras	2,760	2,980	3.9	4,093	4,234	3.5
Hong Kong[c]	32,240	33,970	9.3	5,313	5,394	2.5
Hungary	22,960	21,950	5.3	10,699	10,692	0.3
Iceland	2,430	2,250	2.1	237	240	1.1
India	192,940	197,210	4.2	733,248	749,880	2.3
Indonesia	86,900	85,400	6.8	155,669	158,907	2.3
Iran, Islamic Rep.	n.a.	n.a.	n.a.	42,503	43,815	3.1
Iraq	n.a.	n.a.	n.a.	14,654	15,164	3.6

| GNP PER CAPITA | | | | LIFE EXPECTANCY AT BIRTH (YEARS) | | INFANT MORTALITY RATE (AGED UNDER 1) | | PRIMARY SCHOOL ENROLLMENT (PERCENT) | |
| CURRENT U.S. DOLLARS | | REAL GROWTH RATE (PERCENT) | | | | | | | |
1983	1984p	1973–83	1983–84p	1970	1983	1970	1983	1970	1983
n.a.	n.a.	n.a.	n.a.	70	72	22	16	98	89
11,540	11,290	1.3	3.8	73	74	14	8	98	98
n.a.	n.a.	n.a.	n.a.	n.a.	50	33	30	n.a.	n.a.
970	1,080	−0.1	7.2	n.a.	74	58	20	123	n.a.
1,160	990	1.0	−1.7	57	63	91	63	95	103
1,420	1,220	2.3	−0.6	56	63	108	76	97	114
690	720	6.4	2.8	50	58	117	102	72	78
680	710	−3.0	−1.4	58	64	106	70	85	61
n.a.	n.a.	n.a.	n.a.	37	43	167	136	75	n.a.
120	110	0.0	−5.0	47	42	158	142	16	46
11,220	11,030	3.2	2.8	n.a.	n.a.	18	8	n.a.	n.a.
1,780	1,840	1.1	5.2	61	68	50	28	101	110
10,710	10,830	2.2	3.4	70	73	13	7	82	98
10,480	9,860	2.0	0.9	72	75	18	9	n.a.	113
n.a.	n.a.	n.a.	n.a.	n.a.	n.a.	44	28	n.a.	n.a.
8,210	8,190	3.2	3.4	n.a.	63	n.a.	n.a.	n.a.	n.a.
3,430	3,480	−4.7	3.1	45	50	137	111	n.a.	n.a.
290	260	−1.3	−2.1	32	36	216	191	24	56
n.a.	n.a.	n.a.	n.a.	71	71	18	11	93	94
11,400	11,090	2.1	2.9	70	75	23	11	n.a.	100
320	350	−4.5	−1.2	53	59	122	97	64	76
4,630	4,240	1.0	0.9	n.a.	n.a.	9	10	n.a.	n.a.
3,910	3,740	1.8	1.3	72	75	30	15	107	106
7,640	7,190	0.3d	−3.0	n.a.	n.a.	46	32	n.a.	n.a.
830	880	n.a.	0.4	67	69	33	39	90	109
n.a.	n.a.	n.a.	n.a.	68	73	46	18	151	164
6,490	6,580	−1.7	−0.5	n.a.	71	22	26	n.a.	n.a.
1,110	1,120	0.7	−3.3	53	60	96	67	57	73
300	300	0.2	0.7	35	38	186	158	33	33
190	180	−2.1	8.4	35	38	186	158	45	88
560	580	−1.7	5.8	63	68	56	36	99	96
290	320	1.2	0.8	49	54	142	107	53	64
670	700	0.4	−1.0	53	60	118	81	87	99
6,070	6,300	6.6	7.9	71	76	20	10	117	105
2,150	2,050	5.1	2.5	70	70	36	19	97	100
10,240	9,380	1.1	−2.5	74	77	13	9	104	97
260	260	1.9	2.1	47	55	139	93	73	79
560	540	4.4	2.9	47	54	121	101	77	100
n.a.	n.a.	n.a.	n.a.	55	60	136	100	73	97
n.a.	n.a.	n.a.	n.a.	55	59	104	71	69	109

APPENDIX III: STATISTICS ON 184 COUNTRIES AND TERRITORIES (continued)

COUNTRY OR TERRITORY	GNP AT MARKET PRICES			POPULATION		
	MILLIONS OF CURRENT U.S. DOLLARS		REAL GROWTH RATE (PERCENT)	THOUSANDS		GROWTH RATE (PERCENT)
	1983	1984p	1973–83	1983	1984p	1973–83
Ireland	17,490	17,500	2.2	3,508	3,533	1.3
Isle of Man[a]	410	390	0.9	68	69	1.6
Israel	21,580	21,290	3.1	4,097	4,172	2.3
Italy	363,100	367,040	2.1	56,836	57,033	0.3
Ivory Coast	6,700	6,030	4.5	9,472	9,876	4.6
Jamaica	2,860	2,480	−2.3	2,258	2,289	1.3
Japan	1,204,330	1,248,090	4.2	119,259	120,075	0.9
Jordan[e]	4,220	4,340	10.9	3,247	3,372	2.7
Kampuchea, Dem.	n.a.	n.a.	n.a.	n.a.	n.a.	n.a.
Kenya	6,430	5,950	4.7	18,902	19,723	4.0
Kiribati[a,c]	30	30	−11.2	60	61	1.6
Korea, Dem. People's Rep.	n.a.	n.a.	n.a.	19,185	19,633	2.5
Korea, Rep. of	80,280	84,860	7.0	39,951	40,576	1.6
Kuwait	27,080	27,570	8.4	1,672	1,790	6.4
Lao PDR	n.a.	n.a.	n.a.	3,657	3,738	2.2
Lebanon	n.a.	n.a.	n.a.	n.a.	n.a.	n.a.
Lesotho[a]	810	790	6.4	1,451	1,490	2.5
Liberia	990	990	2.0	2,057	2,122	3.3
Libya	29,170	29,790	3.6	3,447	3,620	4.3
Luxembourg	5,330	4,980	3.5	365	365	0.3
Macao	n.a.	n.a.	n.a	304	310	1.9
Madagascar	2,930	2,600	0.0	9,452	9,712	2.6
Malawi	1,390	1,430	4.1	6,626	6,831	3.0
Malaysia	27,720	30,280	7.2	14,863	15,206	2.4
Maldives	n.a.	n.a.	n.a.	168	173	3.0
Mali	1,110	1,060	4.3	7,175	7,341	2.5
Malta	1,250	1,210	9.7	360	360	1.4
Martinique	1,320	n.a.	n.a.	311	311	−0.5
Mauritania	780	750	2.4	1,629	1,664	2.2
Mauritius	1,150	1,100	3.6	993	1,003	1.4
Mexico	163,510	158,310	5.0	75,011	76,949	2.9
Mongolia	n.a.	n.a.	n.a.	1,803	1,852	2.8
Montserrat	30	30	5.1	13	14	0.4
Morocco	15,750	14,340	4.5	20,801	21,347	2.6
Mozambique	n.a.	n.a.	n.a.	13,083	13,427	2.6
Namibia[a]	1,820	1,660	4.1	1,089	1,128	2.8
Nepal	2,480	2,630	3.1	15,738	16,054	2.6
Netherlands	141,730	135,830	1.4	14,362	14,411	0.7
Netherlands Antilles	n.a.	n.a.	n.a.	256	259	1.1
New Caledonia[a,c]	960	920	0.1	145	147	1.2

| GNP PER CAPITA | | | | LIFE EXPECTANCY AT BIRTH (YEARS) | | INFANT MORTALITY RATE (AGED UNDER 1) | | PRIMARY SCHOOL ENROLLMENT (PERCENT) | |
| CURRENT U.S. DOLLARS | | REAL GROWTH RATE (PERCENT) | | | | | | | |
1983	1984p	1973–83	1983–84p	1970	1983	1970	1983	1970	1983
4,990	4,950	0.8	2.5	71	73	20	11	106	100
5,980	5,600	−0.8	1.8	n.a.	n.a.	n.a.	10	n.a.	n.a.
5,270	5,100	0.9	−2.3	71	74	24	14	96	95
6,390	6,440	1.8	2.6	72	76	30	12	110	101
710	610	0.0	−9.3	46	52	148	121	63	76
1,270	1,080	−3.6	−6.2	67	71	44	28	119	99
10,100	10,390	3.3	5.0	72	77	15	7	99	100
1,720	1,710	6.6	0.0	54	64	98	62	72	103
n.a.	n.a.	n.a.	n.a.	n.a.	n.a.	n.a.	n.a.	30	n.a.
340	300	0.6	−5.4	52	57	112	81	61	104
460	460	−12.6	2.6	n.a.	52	49	n.a.	n.a.	n.a.
n.a.	n.a.	n.a.	n.a.	59	65	50	32	n.a.	n.a.
2,010	2,090	5.4	5.9	59	68	50	29	103	100
16,200	15,410	1.8	−3.2	66	71	49	29	89	91
n.a.	n.a.	n.a.	n.a.	40	44	186	159	54	97
n.a.	n.a.	n.a.	n.a.	n.a.	n.a.	n.a.	n.a.	n.a.	n.a.
560	530	3.8	0.0	49	53	131	109	90	112
480	470	−1.3	−3.8	43	49	138	111	50	66
8,460	8,230	−0.8	−4.7	52	58	128	91	78	94
14,620	13,650	3.2	0.9	70	73	25	20	116	94
n.a.	n.a.	n.a.	n.a.	60	68	36	38	n.a.	n.a.
310	270	−2.5	−7.3	45	50	89	66	88	100
210	210	1.0	4.2	40	44	194	164	36	62
1,870	1,990	4.6	3.6	61	67	46	29	87	92
n.a.	n.a.	n.a.	n.a.	47	47	n.a.	88	n.a.	61
150	140	1.7	−1.0	40	45	174	148	23	27
3,480	3,370	8.1	2.1	70	73	28	21	113	106
4,260	n.a.	n.a.	n.a.	67	75	34	14	152	150
480	450	0.3	−1.9	42	46	162	136	14	33
1,160	1,100	2.2	1.8	62	67	61	32	97	106
2,180	2,060	2.0	2.2	61	66	74	52	104	121
n.a.	n.a.	n.a.	n.a.	59	65	74	49	113	106
2,420	2,360	4.2	n.a.	n.a.	63	n.a.	57	n.a.	n.a.
760	670	1.9	−0.2	51	52	136	98	52	80
n.a.	n.a.	n.a.	n.a.	40	46	136	106	47	104
1,670	1,470	1.3	−3.5	52	58	137	114	n.a.	n.a.
160	160	0.4	4.8	41	46	172	143	26	73
9,870	9,430	0.7	0.9	74	76	13	8	102	98
n.a.	n.a.	n.a.	n.a.	n.a.	71	n.a.	25	n.a.	n.a.
6,600	6,240	−1.1	1.6	61	66	41	42	n.a.	n.a.

COUNTRY OR TERRITORY	GNP AT MARKET PRICES			POPULATION		
	MILLIONS OF CURRENT U.S. DOLLARS		REAL GROWTH RATE (PERCENT)	THOUSANDS		GROWTH RATE (PERCENT)
	1983	1984p	1973–83	1983	1984p	1973–83
New Zealand	24,690	23,530	0.6	3,203	3,249	0.6
Nicaragua	2,630	2,700	−1.3	2,999	3,116	3.9
Niger	1,460	1,190	5.3	6,062	6,252	3.0
Nigeria	71,710	74,120	1.5	93,642	96,816	2.7
Norway	57,820	57,080	3.4	4,133	4,151	0.4
Oman	7,050	7,380	9.4	1,131	1,186	4.8
Pacific Islands, Trust Terr.[a]	150	160	1.1	141	143	2.2
Pakistan	34,710	35,420	6.2	89,729	92,411	3.0
Panama	4,140	4,210	4.8	1,964	2,009	2.3
Papua New Guinea	2,430	2,480	1.3	3,190	3,253	2.1
Paraguay	4,250	4,120	8.5	3,211	3,291	2.5
Peru	18,590	17,960	1.3	17,877	18,297	2.4
Philippines	39,270	35,040	5.3	52,055	53,404	2.7
Poland	n.a.	n.a.	n.a.	36,571	36,918	0.9
Portugal	22,490	20,050	2.6	10,099	10,202	1.1
Puerto Rico	12,530	14,000	1.2	3,295	3,331	1.4
Qatar[a]	5,950	6,020	−3.1	281	292	7.0
Reunion[a]	2,050	1,950	1.7	523	529	1.1
Romania	n.a.	n.a.	n.a.	22,553	22,628	0.8
Rwanda	1,550	1,610	5.7	5,674	5,864	3.4
Saint Christopher & Nevis	60	60	1.3	45	46	0.2
Saint Lucia	140	150	5.3	131	134	1.6
Saint Vincent	90	100	4.0	107	109	1.2
Sao Tome and Principe	40	30	2.3	103	106	2.1
Saudi Arabia	127,330	116,380	9.2	10,421	10,833	4.7
Senegal	2,730	2,440	2.4	6,211	6,393	2.8
Seychelles	160	n.a.	4.3	64	64	1.2
Sierra Leone	1,180	1,120	1.7	3,588	3,668	2.1
Singapore	16,650	18,390	8.0	2,502	2,533	1.3
Solomon Islands	n.a.	n.a.	n.a.	254	263	3.5
Somalia	1,270	1,360	2.5	5,086	5,231	2.8
South Africa	73,160	73,970	2.8	31,551	32,722	2.8
Spain	182,350	172,360	1.7	38,228	38,523	1.0
Sri Lanka	5,130	5,660	5.2	15,416	15,646	1.7
Sudan	8,250	7,360	5.8	20,807	21,467	3.2
Suriname	1,270	1,350	3.8	374	384	−0.3
Swaziland[a]	610	590	3.2	705	730	3.4
Sweden	103,640	99,060	1.0	8,331	8,337	0.2
Switzerland	105,300	105,060	0.8	6,482	6,572	0.0
Syrian Arab Rep.	17,190	18,540	8.0	9,606	9,927	3.3

| GNP PER CAPITA | | | | LIFE EXPECTANCY AT BIRTH (YEARS) | | INFANT MORTALITY RATE (AGED UNDER 1) | | PRIMARY SCHOOL ENROLLMENT (PERCENT) | |
| CURRENT U.S. DOLLARS | | REAL GROWTH RATE (PERCENT) | | | | | | | |
1983	1984p	1973–83	1983–84p	1970	1983	1970	1983	1970	1983
7,710	7,240	0.0	1.1	71	73	17	13	110	101
880	870	−5.0	−2.8	53	58	116	84	83	104
240	190	2.2	−14.5	41	45	171	139	14	23
770	770	−1.1	−3.9	43	49	140	113	37	98
13,990	13,750	3.0	2.8	74	77	13	8	89	99
6,230	6,230	4.4	−1.7	44	53	158	121	3	74
1,080	1,100	−1.1	−0.4	n.a.	71	30	31	n.a.	n.a.
390	380	3.1	2.1	56	50	143	119	40	44
2,110	2,100	2.5	−2.2	65	71	49	26	106	110
760	760	−0.8	2.4	46	53	133	97	52	65
1,320	1,250	5.8	2.0	61	65	60	45	109	103
1,040	980	−1.1	0.0	54	59	118	98	105	114
750	660	2.5	−7.9	59	65	75	49	108	106
n.a.	n.a.	n.a.	n.a.	70	71	33	19	101	100
2,230	1,970	1.5	−4.4	67	71	58	25	98	103
3,800	4,200	−0.1	6.4	72	74	29	16	117	82
21,160	20,600	−9.4	−6.3	65	72	76	36	102	116
3,920	3,690	0.6	3.7	62	67	55	19	151	140
n.a.	n.a.	n.a.	n.a.	69	71	40	28	112	100
270	270	2.3	−3.2	48	46	150	125	74	70
1,320	1,390	1.1	2.3	n.a.	63	48	56	n.a.	n.a.
1,050	1,130	3.6	5.7	n.a.	69	60	30	n.a.	95
840	900	2.8	3.3	n.a.	70	56	45	97	90
340	320	0.2	−6.0	n.a.	63	70	62	n.a.	n.a.
12,220	10,740	4.2	−2.9	49	56	146	101	45	67
440	380	−0.4	−7.0	42	46	164	140	38	48
2,430	n.a.	3.1	n.a.	66	70	40	27	n.a.	95
330	300	−0.4	−1.7	34	38	228	198	33	40
6,660	7,260	6.6	7.1	68	72	22	11	106	108
n.a.	n.a.	n.a.	n.a.	51	57	52	52	61	60
250	260	−0.3	−1.1	37	44	158	142	11	30
2,240	2,260	0.0	1.0	58	64	114	91	99	n.a.
4,770	4,470	0.7	1.7	72	75	28	10	123	110
330	360	3.4	3.9	64	69	59	37	99	103
400	340	2.5	−5.4	42	48	150	117	38	52
3,390	3,520	4.2	−1.0	64	65	51	31	131	103
870	800	−0.2	0.2	47	55	145	128	89	111
12,440	11,880	0.8	3.2	74	78	11	8	94	99
16,250	15,990	0.8	1.1	73	79	15	8	78	100
1,790	1,870	4.6	−0.4	57	67	96	56	78	101

APPENDIX III: STATISTICS ON 184 COUNTRIES AND TERRITORIES (continued)

COUNTRY OR TERRITORY	GNP AT MARKET PRICES			POPULATION		
	MILLIONS OF CURRENT U.S. DOLLARS		REAL GROWTH RATE (PERCENT)	THOUSANDS		GROWTH RATE (PERCENT)
	1983	1984p	1973–83	1983	1984p	1973–83
Tanzania[f]	4,900	4,460	2.6	20,771	21,489	3.3
Thailand	40,380	42,760	6.3	49,169	50,109	2.3
Togo	790	730	2.2	2,836	2,928	2.6
Tonga	n.a.	n.a.	n.a.	104	106	1.6
Trinidad and Tobago	7,850	8,350	5.1	1,149	1,170	0.6
Tunisia	8,920	8,840	5.9	6,886	7,068	2.5
Turkey	58,860	57,810	3.5	47,279	48,266	2.2
U.S.S.R.	n.a.	n.a.	n.a.	272,500	275,029	0.9
Uganda[a]	3,050	3,290	−2.1	13,881	14,325	2.8
United Arab Emirates	28,660	28,480	11.6	1,206	1,277	11.3
United Kingdom	517,110	480,680	1.0	56,334	56,327	0.0
United States	3,300,560	3,670,490	2.4	234,496	236,961	1.0
Uruguay	7,340	5,900	2.5	2,969	2,990	0.5
Vanuatu	n.a.	n.a.	n.a.	127	131	2.9
Venezuela	66,020	57,360	2.4	17,257	17,829	3.5
Viet Nam	n.a.	n.a.	n.a.	58,538	60,069	2.7
Virgin Islands (U.S.)[a]	850	900	1.9	101	102	1.6
Western Samoa	n.a.	n.a.	n.a.	161	163	0.7
Yemen Arab Rep.	4,170	3,940	7.4	7,595	7,790	2.9
Yemen, PDR	1,020	1,130	7.4[g]	1,974	2,021	2.2
Yugoslavia	56,820	48,690	4.4	22,800	22,955	0.8
Zaire	5,040	4,220	−0.6	29,671	30,583	2.5
Zambia	3,620	3,020	0.6	6,259	6,477	3.2
Zimbabwe	5,800	6,040	3.5	7,856	8,173	3.2

p: preliminary.

n.a.: not available.

[a] Estimates of GNP, GNP per capita, and their growth rates are tentative.

[b] Refers to 1977–83.

[c] Estimates of GNP, GNP per capita, and their growth rates refer to gross domestic product.

[d] Refers to 1979–83.

[e] Figures for GNP, GNP per capita, and their growth rates are for the East Bank only.

[f] Figures for GNP, GNP per capita, and their growth rates are for mainland Tanzania only.

[g] Refers to 1975–83.

Source: *The World Bank Atlas, 1986.* Used with permission.

| GNP PER CAPITA | | | | LIFE EXPECTANCY AT BIRTH (YEARS) | | INFANT MORTALITY RATE (AGED UNDER 1) | | PRIMARY SCHOOL ENROLLMENT (PERCENT) | |
| CURRENT U.S. DOLLARS | | REAL GROWTH RATE (PERCENT) | | | | | | | |
1983	1984p	1973–83	1983–84p	1970	1983	1970	1983	1970	1983
240	210	−0.7	−2.8	45	51	125	97	36	98
820	850	4.0	5.1	58	63	74	50	83	96
280	250	−0.4	−1.2	44	49	140	112	69	106
n.a.	n.a.	n.a.	n.a.	n.a.	63	n.a.	26	n.a.	n.a.
6,830	7,140	4.5	−2.2	66	69	42	28	107	99
1,290	1,250	3.3	2.3	54	62	131	83	101	111
1,250	1,200	1.3	3.8	56	63	136	82	110	102
n.a.	n.a.	n.a.	n.a.	70	69	24	n.a.	104	106
220	230	−4.7	1.4	50	49	113	109	39	60
23,770	22,300	0.2	−4.4	65	71	76	44	98	132
9,180	8,530	1.0	2.0	72	74	18	10	104	102
14,080	15,490	1.3	5.6	71	75	21	11	109	100
2,470	1,970	1.9	−2.7	69	73	46	38	113	122
n.a.	n.a.	n.a.	n.a.	n.a.	55	n.a.	n.a.	n.a.	n.a.
3,830	3,220	−1.1	−5.0	63	68	58	38	94	105
n.a.	n.a.	n.a.	n.a.	55	64	79	53	n.a.	113
8,460	8,800	0.3	−0.1	n.a.	69	25	23	n.a.	n.a.
n.a.	n.a.	n.a.	n.a.	61	65	48	51	91	n.a.
550	510	4.4	−7.0	39	44	188	152	12	59
520	560	5.0g	−0.4	40	46	177	137	57	64
2,490	2,120	3.5	1.4	68	69	56	32	106	101
170	140	−3.0	−0.2	45	51	132	106	88	90
580	470	−2.5	−6.8	46	51	125	100	89	96
740	740	0.3	4.6	54	56	95	69	74	130

NAME INDEX

SUBJECT INDEX